Lecture Notes in Computer Science   13323

More information about this series at https://link.springer.com/bookseries/558

Marcelo M. Soares · Elizabeth Rosenzweig ·
Aaron Marcus (Eds.)

Design, User Experience, and Usability

Design Thinking and Practice in Contemporary and Emerging Technologies

11th International Conference, DUXU 2022
Held as Part of the 24th HCI International Conference, HCII 2022
Virtual Event, June 26 – July 1, 2022
Proceedings, Part III

 Springer

Editors
Marcelo M. Soares
Southern University of Science
and Technology – SUSTech
Shenzhen, China

Elizabeth Rosenzweig
World Usability Day and Bubble Mountain
Consulting
Newton Center, MA, USA

Aaron Marcus
Aaron Marcus and Associates
Berkeley, CA, USA

ISSN 0302-9743   ISSN 1611-3349 (electronic)
Lecture Notes in Computer Science
ISBN 978-3-031-05905-6   ISBN 978-3-031-05906-3 (eBook)
https://doi.org/10.1007/978-3-031-05906-3

This Springer imprint is published by the registered company Springer Nature Switzerland AG
The registered company address is: Gewerbestrasse 11, 6330 Cham, Switzerland

Foreword

Human-computer interaction (HCI) is acquiring an ever-increasing scientific and industrial importance, as well as having more impact on people's everyday life, as an ever-growing number of human activities are progressively moving from the physical to the digital world. This process, which has been ongoing for some time now, has been dramatically accelerated by the COVID-19 pandemic. The HCI International (HCII) conference series, held yearly, aims to respond to the compelling need to advance the exchange of knowledge and research and development efforts on the human aspects of design and use of computing systems.

The 24th International Conference on Human-Computer Interaction, HCI International 2022 (HCII 2022), was planned to be held at the Gothia Towers Hotel and Swedish Exhibition & Congress Centre, Göteborg, Sweden, during June 26 to July 1, 2022. Due to the COVID-19 pandemic and with everyone's health and safety in mind, HCII 2022 was organized and run as a virtual conference. It incorporated the 21 thematic areas and affiliated conferences listed on the following page.

A total of 5583 individuals from academia, research institutes, industry, and governmental agencies from 88 countries submitted contributions, and 1276 papers and 275 posters were included in the proceedings to appear just before the start of the conference. The contributions thoroughly cover the entire field of human-computer interaction, addressing major advances in knowledge and effective use of computers in a variety of application areas. These papers provide academics, researchers, engineers, scientists, practitioners, and students with state-of-the-art information on the most recent advances in HCI. The volumes constituting the set of proceedings to appear before the start of the conference are listed in the following pages.

The HCI International (HCII) conference also offers the option of 'Late Breaking Work' which applies both for papers and posters, and the corresponding volume(s) of the proceedings will appear after the conference. Full papers will be included in the 'HCII 2022 - Late Breaking Papers' volumes of the proceedings to be published in the Springer LNCS series, while 'Poster Extended Abstracts' will be included as short research papers in the 'HCII 2022 - Late Breaking Posters' volumes to be published in the Springer CCIS series.

I would like to thank the Program Board Chairs and the members of the Program Boards of all thematic areas and affiliated conferences for their contribution and support towards the highest scientific quality and overall success of the HCI International 2022 conference; they have helped in so many ways, including session organization, paper reviewing (single-blind review process, with a minimum of two reviews per submission) and, more generally, acting as goodwill ambassadors for the HCII conference.

This conference would not have been possible without the continuous and unwavering support and advice of Gavriel Salvendy, founder, General Chair Emeritus, and Scientific Advisor. For his outstanding efforts, I would like to express my appreciation to Abbas Moallem, Communications Chair and Editor of HCI International News.

June 2022   Constantine Stephanidis

HCI International 2022 Thematic Areas and Affiliated Conferences

Thematic Areas

- HCI: Human-Computer Interaction
- HIMI: Human Interface and the Management of Information

Affiliated Conferences

- EPCE: 19th International Conference on Engineering Psychology and Cognitive Ergonomics
- AC: 16th International Conference on Augmented Cognition
- UAHCI: 16th International Conference on Universal Access in Human-Computer Interaction
- CCD: 14th International Conference on Cross-Cultural Design
- SCSM: 14th International Conference on Social Computing and Social Media
- VAMR: 14th International Conference on Virtual, Augmented and Mixed Reality
- DHM: 13th International Conference on Digital Human Modeling and Applications in Health, Safety, Ergonomics and Risk Management
- DUXU: 11th International Conference on Design, User Experience and Usability
- C&C: 10th International Conference on Culture and Computing
- DAPI: 10th International Conference on Distributed, Ambient and Pervasive Interactions
- HCIBGO: 9th International Conference on HCI in Business, Government and Organizations
- LCT: 9th International Conference on Learning and Collaboration Technologies
- ITAP: 8th International Conference on Human Aspects of IT for the Aged Population
- AIS: 4th International Conference on Adaptive Instructional Systems
- HCI-CPT: 4th International Conference on HCI for Cybersecurity, Privacy and Trust
- HCI-Games: 4th International Conference on HCI in Games
- MobiTAS: 4th International Conference on HCI in Mobility, Transport and Automotive Systems
- AI-HCI: 3rd International Conference on Artificial Intelligence in HCI
- MOBILE: 3rd International Conference on Design, Operation and Evaluation of Mobile Communications

List of Conference Proceedings Volumes Appearing Before the Conference

1. LNCS 13302, Human-Computer Interaction: Theoretical Approaches and Design Methods (Part I), edited by Masaaki Kurosu
2. LNCS 13303, Human-Computer Interaction: Technological Innovation (Part II), edited by Masaaki Kurosu
3. LNCS 13304, Human-Computer Interaction: User Experience and Behavior (Part III), edited by Masaaki Kurosu
4. LNCS 13305, Human Interface and the Management of Information: Visual and Information Design (Part I), edited by Sakae Yamamoto and Hirohiko Mori
5. LNCS 13306, Human Interface and the Management of Information: Applications in Complex Technological Environments (Part II), edited by Sakae Yamamoto and Hirohiko Mori
6. LNAI 13307, Engineering Psychology and Cognitive Ergonomics, edited by Don Harris and Wen-Chin Li
7. LNCS 13308, Universal Access in Human-Computer Interaction: Novel Design Approaches and Technologies (Part I), edited by Margherita Antona and Constantine Stephanidis
8. LNCS 13309, Universal Access in Human-Computer Interaction: User and Context Diversity (Part II), edited by Margherita Antona and Constantine Stephanidis
9. LNAI 13310, Augmented Cognition, edited by Dylan D. Schmorrow and Cali M. Fidopiastis
10. LNCS 13311, Cross-Cultural Design: Interaction Design Across Cultures (Part I), edited by Pei-Luen Patrick Rau
11. LNCS 13312, Cross-Cultural Design: Applications in Learning, Arts, Cultural Heritage, Creative Industries, and Virtual Reality (Part II), edited by Pei-Luen Patrick Rau
12. LNCS 13313, Cross-Cultural Design: Applications in Business, Communication, Health, Well-being, and Inclusiveness (Part III), edited by Pei-Luen Patrick Rau
13. LNCS 13314, Cross-Cultural Design: Product and Service Design, Mobility and Automotive Design, Cities, Urban Areas, and Intelligent Environments Design (Part IV), edited by Pei-Luen Patrick Rau
14. LNCS 13315, Social Computing and Social Media: Design, User Experience and Impact (Part I), edited by Gabriele Meiselwitz
15. LNCS 13316, Social Computing and Social Media: Applications in Education and Commerce (Part II), edited by Gabriele Meiselwitz
16. LNCS 13317, Virtual, Augmented and Mixed Reality: Design and Development (Part I), edited by Jessie Y. C. Chen and Gino Fragomeni
17. LNCS 13318, Virtual, Augmented and Mixed Reality: Applications in Education, Aviation and Industry (Part II), edited by Jessie Y. C. Chen and Gino Fragomeni

39. CCIS 1582, HCI International 2022 Posters - Part III, edited by Constantine Stephanidis, Margherita Antona and Stavroula Ntoa
40. CCIS 1583, HCI International 2022 Posters - Part IV, edited by Constantine Stephanidis, Margherita Antona and Stavroula Ntoa

http://2022.hci.international/proceedings

Preface

User experience (UX) refers to a person's thoughts, feelings, and behavior when using interactive systems. UX design becomes fundamentally important for new and emerging mobile, ubiquitous, and omnipresent computer-based contexts. The scope of design, user experience and usability (DUXU) extends to all aspects of the user's interaction with a product or service, how it is perceived, learned, and used. DUXU also addresses design knowledge, methods and practices, with a focus on deeply human-centered processes. Usability, usefulness, and appeal are fundamental requirements for effective user-experience design.

The 11th Design, User Experience, and Usability (DUXU) Conference 2022, an affiliated conference of the HCI International Conference, encouraged papers from professionals, academics, and researchers that report results and cover a broad range of research and development activities on a variety of related topics. Professionals include designers, software engineers, scientists, marketers, business leaders, and practitioners infields such as AI, architecture, financial and wealth management, game design, graphic design, finance, healthcare, industrial design, mobile, psychology, travel, and vehicles.

This year's submissions covered a wide range of content across the spectrum of design, user-experience, and usability. The latest trends and technologies are represented, as well as contributions from professionals, academics, and researchers across the globe. The breadth of their work is indicated in the following topics covered in the proceedings.

Three volumes of the HCII 2022 proceedings are dedicated to this year's edition of the DUXU Conference:

- Design, User Experience, and Usability: UX Research, Design, and Assessment (Part I), which addresses topics related to processes, methods, and tools for UX design and evaluation; user requirements, preferences and UX influential factors; as well as usability, acceptance, and user experience assessment.
- Design, User Experience, and Usability: Design for Emotion, Well-being and Health, Learning, and Culture (Part II), which addresses topics related to emotion, motivation, and persuasion design; design for well-being and health; learning experience-design; as well as globalization, localization, and culture issues.
- Design, User Experience, and Usability: Design Thinking and Practice in Contemporary and Emerging Technologies (Part III), which addresses topics related to design thinking and philosophy, analysis of case studies, as well as design and user experience in emerging technologies.

Papers of these volumes are included for publication after a minimum of two single–blind reviews from the members of the DUXU Program Board or, in some cases, from members of the Program Boards of other affiliated conferences. We would like to thank all of them for their invaluable contribution, support, and efforts.

June 2022   Marcelo M. Soares
                                                  Elizabeth Rosenzweig
                                                       Aaron Marcus

11th International Conference on Design, User Experience and Usability (DUXU 2022)

Program Board Chairs: **Marcelo M. Soares**, Southern University of Science and Technology – SUSTech, China, **Elizabeth Rosenzweig**, World Usability Day and Bubble Mountain Consulting, USA, and **Aaron Marcus**, Aaron Marcus and Associates, USA

- Sisira Adikari, University of Canberra, Australia
- Ahmad Alhuwwari, Orange Jordan, Jordan
- Claire Ancient, University of Winchester, UK
- Roger Ball, Georgia Institute of Technology, USA
- Eric Brangier, Université de Lorraine, France
- Tian Cao, Nanjing University of Science & Technology, China
- Silvia De los Rios, Indra, Spain
- Romi Dey, Solved By Design, India
- Marc Fabri, Leeds Beckett University, UK
- Wei Liu, Beijing Normal University, China
- Zhen Liu, South China University of Technology, China
- Martin Maguire, Loughborough University, UK
- Judith Moldenhauer, Wayne State University, USA
- Gunther Paul, James Cook University, Australia
- Francisco Rebelo, University of Lisbon, Portugal
- Christine Riedmann-Streitz, MarkenFactory GmbH, Germany
- Patricia Search, Rensselaer Polytechnic Institute, USA
- Dorothy Shamonsky, Brandeis University, USA
- David Sless, Communication Research Institute, Australia
- Elisangela Vilar, Universidade de Lisboa, Portugal
- Wei Wang, Hunan University, China
- Haining Wang, Hunan University, China

The full list with the Program Board Chairs and the members of the Program Boards of all thematic areas and affiliated conferences is available online at

http://www.hci.international/board-members-2022.php

HCI International 2023

The 25th International Conference on Human-Computer Interaction, HCI International 2023, will be held jointly with the affiliated conferences at the AC Bella Sky Hotel and Bella Center, Copenhagen, Denmark, 23–28 July 2023. It will cover a broad spectrum of themes related to human-computer interaction, including theoretical issues, methods, tools, processes, and case studies in HCI design, as well as novel interaction techniques, interfaces, and applications. The proceedings will be published by Springer. More information will be available on the conference website: http://2023.hci.international/.

General Chair
Constantine Stephanidis
University of Crete and ICS-FORTH
Heraklion, Crete, Greece
Email: general_chair@hcii2023.org

http://2023.hci.international/

Contents – Part III

Design and User Experience in Emerging Technologies

Design Thinking and Philosophy

How Related Are Designers to the Personas They Create?

Guy-Serge Emmanuel ⓘ and Francesca Polito⁽✉⁾ ⓘ

Iowa State University, Ames, IA 50011, USA
franpolito2020@gmail.com

Abstract. In the world of User Experience (UX), personas are tools that represent what designers learn during research into potential customers and a population that might use a product, website, service, or represent a brand. They also serve to help designers and engineering teams focus on user values, as well as understand possible user constraints and limitations [1]. This study asks the question "how related are designers to the personas they create?" UX designers create for an ever-changing world and increasingly diverse audiences. It is important to ensure that their personas reflect evolving consumer base demographics.

Our hypothesis grew out of studies discussing implications of innate human stereotyping behavior on the creation of personas [2]. However, to our knowledge, no previous studies directly examined how related UX design practitioners and the personas they create are. Turner and Turner [2] suggest, in their article "Is stereotyping inevitable when designing with personas?", that we tend to display our biases in the form of stereotypes. Without examining these biases, designers may fail to create representative personas that demonstrate empathy for the user's specific needs, values, and constraints, instead creating products around their own needs and vision [3].

Analyzing the data, we found most UX designers created personas that were closely related to themselves, with very little deviation from this norm. The sole exception was Black designers, who tended to produce a wider array of more diverse personas.

Keywords: HCI · UX design · Personas · Bias · Stereotypes

1 Introduction

Designing a fictional character representation, or persona, whose needs speak for a larger group of researched users, is an important part of the modern User Experience [UX] and product design process. However, a question arises as to how often these personas are influenced by bias. A persona is defined as a representation of a user segment by a fictional character described with attributes in profile form [4]. Personas are used in design to represent a population that might use a product, website, service, or represent a brand. In theory, personas allow design teams to gain a better understanding of their users' needs, experiences, and goals as well as build empathy with users they are designing for. They also serve to help designers focus on user values, as well as understand possible user constraints and limitations [1].

In the world of UX, personas are a tool widely used across many industries to represent what designers learned in their research. In healthcare, for example, personas are used to create a representation of the diversity of a population. While they may have benefits when used correctly, research into personas indicates that they are often misused in numerous ways. The hypothetical nature of the persona leaves its content dependent on what the designer of the persona chooses to highlight as well as the archetype the designer wishes to portray. Designers may create a persona description that "leaves room for user-data interpretation" where "the missing data is elicited from the design professionals' own experiences and perceptions of reality, not from user data" [5]. Additionally, design teams tend to modify personas to fit their needs. Although this is common practice with many design tools, changes to the methodology of persona design can significantly impact the usability and validity of the persona, thus greatly affecting the product design [6]. It is important to make sure personas reflect evolving demographics. As the world becomes more globalized, societies are becoming similarly increasingly diverse. The days of designing products only for the "western, educated, industrialized, rich, and democratic" [5] fringe population of the world must become a thing of the past if personas are to remain useful. UX designers' products are reaching many, yet only serving the few. It is important to update persona design processes to address this issue.

So, personas should depict a segment of the population they want to serve, but how much does designer bias affect them? Just how closely related are personas to the designers that create them? In order to investigate the relationship between designer demographics and persona design, we gathered and analyzed over 250 individual personas created by over 70 designers and collected designer demographic information. We assessed how much, if at all, designers' genders and ethnicities relate to their generated personas' genders and ethnicities using a two-way factorial ANOVA.

1.1 Literature Review

In his book, *Inmates Are Running the Asylum: Why High-Tech Products Drive Us Crazy and How to Restore the Sanity*, Alan Cooper was the first to introduce personas. The persona is meant to be representative of an actual user [7]. Cooper wanted personas to be utilized by individuals who were not trained in design [7]. An image, an age, and an occupation would suffice. While working for Microsoft, Pruitt and Grudin expanded on Cooper's work on personas by making sure they are grounded in ethnography and qualitative inquiry [7]. Personas have also been used extensively in engineering efforts for several decades; "usability methods, have, from the beginning of time, that is to say the early 80s, always included users to varying degrees" [8]. These personas have typically been used as reference points to help focus the team and develop the product for a specific user or target audience. In the Human Factors and Ergonomics fields, personas can be used to understand use requirements and inform inclusive design [1]. According to Wu and Lu [9], in product design, personas are a "design tool of product concepts analysis used to identify user-roles features in his specific social context including user's social statistical characteristics, such as age, height, income, and so on, especially product related characteristics".

UX designers have used personas as valuable communication tools especially with other product group members and stakeholders who are often not positioned to see the user's needs and concerns [6]. In their research, *How do designers and user experience professionals actually perceive and use personas?*, Matthews et al. concluded that personas are difficult to design because they are equally as creative as they are factual. Because of this, verifying if the data contained in a persona is accurate can be challenging and problematic. They noted that the "personification" process of designing personas often misleads and distracts the designer from design constraints that matter; particularly when the personifying details have been poorly selected [7].

The intent of a persona is to create an example of a typical user to help focus the product on meeting the needs of the end user while implying empathy to their specific needs. Unfortunately, it is easy to introduce bias as designers tend to focus the persona on their own personal background and situations. Freiss [3] found that designers may resist using personas for various reasons, including the fact that it may be difficult or impossible to verify their accuracy and because their hypothetical nature "leads to a false sense of understanding." These situations may lead designers to design products around their idea of what products should be, instead of designing based on the user's needs, values, or constraints. In another study, Turner and Turner [2] ask the question, "is stereotyping inevitable when designing with personas?" The authors note that we tend to display our biases in the form of stereotypes. These stereotypes are, in a sense, a psychological shorthand that becomes intertwined with personas and undermine their purpose, which is to create a detailed representation of users.

To ensure the accuracy of design, persona creation needs to be based on interviews, research, and data collection. The strength of the data supplied from these research methods is highly dependent on severable variables, namely the number of interviews; interviewing subjects must also be representative of the product's real user groups. Similar to scientific research, there needs to be rigor in the selection of participants interviewed as well as the sample size. Small participant pools of interviewees as well as interviews with individuals who do not accurately reflect product users or represent the diversity of the population lead to poor design [10].

We collected self-described demographic data from designer portfolio websites, as well as descriptions of the personas they created, including characteristics such as age, profession, salary, gender, and race. Our interest in personas lies in the context of UX. Hassenzahl and Tractinsky [11] defined UX as the combination of three dimensions: the user's internal state, the design of the system itself, and the context of where, when, and how the interaction takes place. There have been studies done that discuss the implications of innate human stereotyping behavior on the creation of personas [12], which led us to our hypothesis. Although personas may not have an impact on some UX and product designers, they are often the spark needed to inspire the creation of new products [13]. To our knowledge there is a lack of research on the true impact of personas on UX and product designers when it comes to how related designers are with the personas they create.

2   Method

To test our hypothesis, we gathered and analyzed 73 designer portfolios by examining their website, their LinkedIn, or a combination of both. Each profile was individually combed through in a snapshot manner; we navigated their profiles, searched for relevant demographic information of both the designer and the personas they created, and collected the data within the spreadsheet. All profiles were subject to the same conditions, as standard for within-subjects grouping. We chose to conduct a correlational study to investigate whether there was any relationship between a designer's gender and ethnicity and their personas' gender and ethnicity. Because of this, we cannot make any causal inferences about these relationships. However, our findings are an important addition to the ongoing discussion about personas, stereotypes, and bias.

2.1   Sample

We initially began our search by looking for websites of UX designers who had attended DesignLab or General Assembly UX Design Academies, as one of their graduation requirements was to include UX case studies in their online portfolios. We also chose random UX designers that had links to online portfolios containing UX case studies via LinkedIn. In the second stage of participant selection, we looked for designers that had case studies on their websites showing how they generate personas as part of their design process. All designer website links were logged into a Google sheet; a total of 127 UX designer profiles were generated by the selection process. Participants' online professional portfolios were additionally used to generate eight objective, quantitative measures. Designers' areas of expertise, gender, ethnicity, and race, as well as persona age, ethnicity, race, and occupation were all considered. In order to organize our results, we defined gender as the socially constructed roles and qualities that are associated with being a man, woman, or other gendered category [12] and ethnicities were coded with the knowledge that "common racial categories in the contemporary United States are Asian, Black or African American, Hispanic or Latinx, Native American, Pacific Islander, and White, but these categories are neither fixed nor exhaustive" [14].

The goal of this study was to understand if the race, gender, and occupation of designers created bias in their design of personas. Designers' gender and ethnicity were established by reference to their profile pictures. If the ethnicity and/or gender were inconclusive, we labeled the participant from the data set unknown and/or non-binary. Designers lacking case studies containing personas were removed from the data set. In some instances, personas were represented by illustrations instead of photographs that did not clearly describe the gender and ethnicity of the persona. In those cases, the personas were removed from the data set. The results of our analysis of the data can be seen in Fig. 1. The selection refinement resulted in a total of 73 designer profiles, 37 of which were female, 27 of which were male, and the remaining designers were designated as unknown. This procedure yielded 250 personas, of which 149 were female, 98 were male, 1 was a family, 1 was a couple, and 1 was either male or female. From our collection of designers and personas, we then researched the correlation between the designer and the personas they created for their projects.

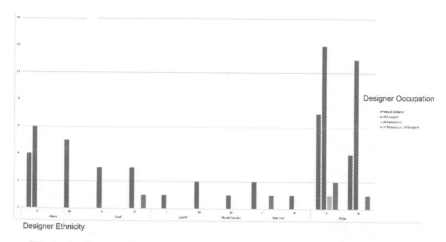

Fig. 1. Designer demographics, including gender, ethnicity, and occupation title.

Quota sampling was used to find participants from the target population. People between the ages of 20 and 60 were selected, with a total number of 73 participants, most between the ages of 20 and 35, and all of whom were below the age of 50. The effect size for our analysis would ideally include the entire UX designer community in order to be representative. Our sample size included roughly 250 randomly gathered UX personas from 73 designers across the country. The current UX designer community consists of roughly 10,178 people in the United States as of 2021 [15]. However, utilizing a smaller sample size of the UX designer community, we feel, provided enough insight to help us validate our hypothesis or null hypothesis. We set the significance of the statistical test at 5%, with a desired power of 80%, according to typical standards, in order to attain validity.

2.2 Materials

73 UX designer profiles were gathered and placed into a spreadsheet matrix, which included portfolio site links, LinkedIn profile links, as well as designer name, background, gender, ethnicity, project type, and persona gender, age, ethnicity, occupation, and salary. Any personal characteristics that might have aided us in understanding the personas' use of the product being built, such as pain points or frustrations, product utilization goals, lifestyle, and so forth, were also included.

The matrix was then populated for further analysis of the comparison between designer and persona to help us better answer our research question. The spreadsheet was broken down into columns for each designer/persona as well as persona gender, age, race, occupation, salary, and any personal attributes for data collection that could help us determine, based on our sample group, if our hypothesis that personas are representative of their populations was correct or validate our null hypothesis that personas typically include bias based on the UX designer's background.

2.3 Procedure

We were given the designer's name, portfolio link, and in some instances their LinkedIn profile. Most of our participants had their LinkedIn profile on hand; we were able to search for the rest. If a participants' LinkedIn profile was not found, we discarded that participant. Once we found their profile, we confirmed their ethnicity, gender, and specialization. Gender and race were established using their pictures, while specializations were clearly listed on their LinkedIn profiles. If the race or gender were inconclusive, we discarded the participant. Gender was divided by male or female. Race was divided into Black, Asian, Pacific Asian, Latinx, and White. Areas of specialization were divided into UX designer or product designer.

We then examined the participant's website. A designer website often includes the projects they have worked on. Most UX and product designers' projects often include personas as a way to describe the target audience for whom they are creating an app, product, or website. If the participant's projects did not include a persona, the project was discarded from our study. Under each designer, we listed all projects which had personas. Projects were divided into three categories: web responsive website, app development, and product designs. For each persona, we listed the race, age, gender, and profession. Where personas were represented by illustrations, which did not clearly describe the persona's gender or race, we removed them from the study. We used the remaining designers and personas to conduct our analysis.

3 Analysis

As hypothesized, we found correlations between designers' personal characteristics and the personas they designed. Female designers created more female personas while male designers created more male personas. Our findings also showed a correlation between the ethnicity of the designer and persona. White designers created white personas more than any other ethnic group and Asian designers created more Asian personas than any other ethnic group. Black designers, however, created personas with a more diverse mix of ethnicities. We also found a correlation between the occupation of the designer and that of the persona. The majority of the designers held the position of UX designer or product manager. We found that most designers created personas with occupations in the high tech and creative fields, with marketing professionals being the most favored profession, followed by student nurses, teachers, software engineers, and graphic designers. Finally, we found a correlation between the number of years of experience of the designer and the age of the personas they created. Our findings, as pictured in Fig. 2, show that designers who had very few years of experience created personas under 32 years of age with the majority of personas being 27 years old, followed by 30, 28, 31, and 32.

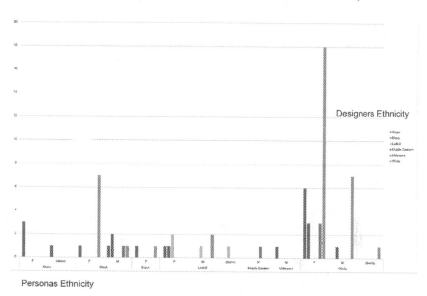

Personas Ethnicity

Fig. 2. Designer and persona demographics, including gender and ethnicity.

4 Discussion

4.1 Analysis

Our goal was to analyze existing personas created by UX designers to assess if correlations existed between the demographic characteristics of the persona and the demographic characteristics of the designer. We aimed to cast a wide net when selecting our
sample through the inclusion of varied races, ethnicities, genders, and age groups. Our
main goal was to see how the independent variables of ethnicity, gender, experience,
and background affected the dependent variable of inclusive persona building. After
reviewing the data, we discovered that most UX designers generated personas that were
quite similar to themselves, with little variation from this norm. There was, however, one
notable exception: Black UX designers did not adhere to this convention as strictly as
others, and tended to offer, overall, personas with a more inclusive range of demographic
characteristics.

4.2 The Meaning of Our Findings

When we set out to begin this study, we realized that if our research uncovered a substantial association between designers and their personas, it might imply that bias existed
within the persona construction process. This could imply that many, if not most, of their
final products were biased and designers therefore must reconsider their existing design
techniques. This could also imply that their products were less effective or ethical for
their customers, who would suffer as a result. It is possible that designers construct their
personas based on user data and personas are created merely as justifications, but this
is not frequently the case. We must also examine the possibility that we arrived at this

conclusion incorrectly, due to the nature and design of our study, and we must continue to challenge our findings.

It is important for UX designers to understand that both they and users are culturally situated [16]. UX designers must comprehend that technology and design add to the delivery of cultural values, logics, and perspectives [17]. When looking at how this research can educate designers on persona creation and bias, we must first understand the limited exposure that UX design students and practitioners have toward race. Looking at UX design programs at Google UX Design, and many other bootcamps in the country, courses on race, technology, and design are rarely offered. Students coming from bootcamps have little to no exposure to race and its impact on design during their training. This outline of suggested Race and UX design modules follows a similar module built on Gender and HCI. Race and racism have played a role in UX design, so there must be a move toward educating design students and professionals on the impact of race on UX design. We must establish effective methods, share vocabularies, and normalize ethical practices around the incorporation of personas in UX design [18]. Our suggested outlines provide two core topics on bringing awareness to race in UX design: the social construct of race and ethnicity and *intersectional perspective on race and ethnicity* [16], as well as race and knowledge in UX design.

Students will be introduced to the fact that race is a social construct. Race is not a biological reality, but a social, cultural, and political reality [17]. A man could be considered Black in the United States, White in Brazil, and multi-racial in another part of the world. By introducing the vocabulary, definitions, and theories relating to race and ethnicities and their significance in relation to understanding and designing technologies [12], UX designers will become more aware when creating their personas and products. In forthcoming research, more detail will be given on how students will learn the difference between race and ethnicity, as well as how these differences relate to UX design [12].

Race and knowledge in UX design will be our second core topic. It will follow the foundation set in the social construction of race and ethnicity and we will attempt to survey it from an intersectional perspective. However, the focus will be a critical exploration of UX design practices and methodologies in relation to the significance of race [12]. As students in schools, UX designers should be introduced to "critiques and scientific objectivity developed in science and technology studies and race technology studies" [12]. Finally, UX designers will investigate how race relates to "defining users, knowledge, and expertise, and how these things relate to different design, text, and development practices" [12].

While these cores are still being researched and written, in order to allow UX designers to create personas more inclusively, existing guidelines by professional organizers already exist, such as the User Experience Professionals Association (UXPA) and the Association for Computing Machinery (ACM). However, it is possible that practicing UX designers, educators, and students are unaware of these professional organizations. UXPA has listed among their ethical guidelines, that UX practitioners should "act in the best interests of everyone", "be honest with everyone", "do no harm and if possible, provide benefits", and "avoid conflicts of interest" [17]. In order to ensure that future designers will incorporate this information into their design process, it will be crucial for design educators to share this information with them. Finally, a future paper will detail the proposal of alternative processes for UX designers and highlight educational needs for the development of more inclusive personas.

While this study focuses on persona creation for UX designers, we can also briefly elaborate on how the presented work can be extended to designers and programmers of algorithms. The Nielsen Group, led by Jakon Nielsen and Don Norman, the leaders of persona creation and design, established three persona types: Light, Qualitative, and Quantitative [19]. While our research can help reshape the proto persona, or ad-hoc personas put together with no current research, and qualitative personas which are currently considered the best approach for creating personas, it sadly cannot solve the issues of quantitative persona creation. However, designers and programmers of algorithms can be trained and educated with the same models as UX designers. Algorithms can be programmed in such a way that the social construct of race is addressed. No modules can compete with quantitative personas created by social media users [20]. Artificial Intelligence (AI) and Machine Learning (ML) algorithms are technologies that have increasingly come under scrutiny in recent years due to biases they present in gender, race, ethnicity, and age. ML algorithms, in particular, are rapidly encoding human qualities and defaults into the datasets used to train algorithms, the tasks the algorithms are programmed to do, and the infrastructure of the algorithms themselves [21]. Their constructs are flawed due to how identity is represented in infrastructure and which sorts of identities are privileged, while others are omitted ignored, and deleted. It is crucial to take a closer look at who is writing those algorithms; are they representative of our diverse society? Or are they a duplication of the UX design practitioner world, which is 75% white [15].

4.3 Limitations

There are limitations in our study design which can be improved upon in subsequent research. First, only 73 UX designers were selected for this study. Participants were selected from only two UX Bootcamp academies within the United States. Beside getting more participants from a wider variety of academies, our goal would be to find participants from UX programs in higher education, both at the undergraduate and graduate levels. This would not only increase our participant pool overall, but also would give us an opportunity to investigate whether a difference in the portrayal of personas exists between UX Bootcamp academies and UX programs in higher education.

Analyzing how demographic information is related across designers and personas does not give us sufficient evidence to articulate a causal relationship between these variables, however it does offer us insight into a correlative relationship between designers' characteristics and the personas they created. In order to better understand these relationships, we would need to gather further insight from our participants via qualitative study.

4.4 Future Research

Further studies might explore the persona creation process from practitioners in different sectors of design including engineering, agency, technology, healthcare, as well as service, urban, and educational design, to see how personas compare across industries, in order to determine how their designs possibly change in practice versus when developed in educational settings. Involving participants in a future study in a more active may give users additional valuable insights into the designers' thought processes around designing personas as well as representing themselves in their work. It would also be possible to learn more about how their education and careers impact their design and perception of users and personas. Participant consent and involvement would also allow researchers to obtain more reliable demographic information which might further clarify data analysis and correlational opportunities.

Three of the identified correlations between designers and the personas they design, (gender, race, and years of experience), can also aid with the generation of propositions for further research. The impact of gender and race on persona design can be explored further, as can designers' cultural backgrounds, to better understand how their relationships, biases, and personal experiences factor into the creation process, part of which includes the designer's articulation and illustration of the users through the persona. Therefore, prevention of self-referential design is critical for the persona's ability to serve as a tool to establish a customer-centered design as well as challenge designers' personal assumptions. Further research into how gender, race, and culture inform the creation of both qualitative and quantitative values would help designers and researchers better understand the role they might play in addressing biases that creep into persona creation.

Finally, marginalized user groups are often hard to gain access to during initial user research. Studies on methods used by designers to compensate for lack of user-based research on these marginalized groups is needed in order to better understand their accuracy, authenticity, and true value in the design process.

References

1. Vincent, C., Blandford, A.: The challenges of delivering validated personas for medical equipment design. Appl. Ergon. **45**, 1097–1105 (2014). https://doi.org/10.1016/j.apergo.2014.01.010
2. Turner, P., Turner, S.: Is stereotyping inevitable when designing with personas? Des. Stud. **32**(1), 30–44 (2011). https://doi.org/10.1016/j.destud.2010.06.002
3. Freiss, E.: Personas and decision making in the design process: an ethnographic case study. In: Proceedings of the Conference on Human Factors in Computing Systems, pp. 1209–1218 (2012). https://doi.org/10.1145/220676.2208572
4. Nielsen, L.: Personas – User Focused Design Human–Computer Interaction Series HI. S, Springer, London (2019). https://doi.org/10.1007/978-1-4471-7427-1
5. Cabrero, D.G.: Participatory design of persona artefacts for user experience in non-WEIRD cultures. ACM Int. Conf. Proc. Ser. **2**, 247–250 (2014). https://doi.org/10.1145/2662155.2662246
6. Floyd, I., Jones, M., Twidale, M.: Resolving incommensurable debates: a preliminary identifications of persona kinds, attributes, and characteristics. Artifact **2** (2008). https://doi.org/10.1080/17493460802276836

7. Matthews, T., Judge, T.K., Whittaker, S.: How do designers and user experience professionals actually perceive and use personas?. In: Proceedings from the Conference on Human Factors in Computing Systems, pp. 1219–1228 (April 2012). https://doi.org/10.1145/2207676.2208573

8. Blomquist, A., Arvola, M.: Personas in action: ethnography in an interaction design team. In: Proceedings of NordicCHI, pp. 197–200 (2002). https://doi.org/10.1145/572020.572044

9. Wu, K., Lu, C.: Integrating the personas technique into the product configuration. Proc. Int. Conf. Manage. Serv. Sci. MASS **2009**, 1–6 (2009). https://doi.org/10.1109/ICMSS.2009.5301420

10. Salminen, J., et al.: Persona perception scale: developing and validating an instrument for human-like representations of data. In: Extended Abstracts of the 2018 CHI Conference, pp. 1–6 (2018). https://doi.org/10.1145/3170427.3188461

11. Hassenzahl, M., Tractinsky, N.: User–experience – a research agenda. Behav. Inf. Technol. **25**(2), 91–97 (2006). https://doi.org/10.1080/01449290500330331

12. Breslin, S., Wadhwa, B.: Towards a gender HCI curriculum. Proc. Conf. Hum. Factors Comput. Syst. **18**, 1091–1096 (2015). https://doi.org/10.1145/2702613.2732923

13. Pruitt, J., Grudin, J.: Personas: practice and theory. In: Proceedings of the 2003 Conference on Designing for User Experiences, pp. 1–15 (2003). https://doi.org/10.1145/997078.997089

14. Ogbonnaya-Ogburu, I.F., Smith, A.D.R., To, A., Toyama, K.: Critical race theory for HCI. In: Proceedings from the Conference on Human Factors in Computing Systems, pp. 1–16 (2020). https://doi.org/10.1145/3313831.3376392

15. USER EXPERIENCE DESIGNER: Demographics and Statistics in the US, Zippia. https://www.zippia.com/user-experience-designer-jobs/demographics/ (14 December 2019)

16. Valdez, Z., Golash-Boza, T.: Towards an intersectionality of race and ethnicity. Ethn. Racial Stud. **40**(13), 2256–2261 (2017). https://doi.org/10.1080/01419870.2017.1344277

17. Sano-Franchini, J.: What can Asian eyelids teach us about user experience design? A culturally Reflective framework for UX/I design. Rhetoric Prof. Commun. Global. **10**(1), 27–53 (2017)

18. Race in HCI Collective, et al.: Keepin' it real about race in HCI. Interactions **28**(5), 28–33 (2021). https://doi.org/10.1145/3477097

19. Laubheimer, P.: 3 Persona Types: Lightweight, Qualitative, and Statistical. Nielsen Norman Group. https://www.nngroup.com/articles/persona-types (21 June 2020)

20. Spiliotopoulos, D., Margaris, D., Vassilakis, C.: Data-assisted persona construction using social media data. Big Data Cogn. Comput. **4**(3), 1–14 (2020). https://doi.org/10.3390/bdcc4030021

21. Scheuerman, M.K., Paul, J.M., Brubaker, J.R.: How computers see gender: an evaluation of gender classification in commercial facial analysis and image labeling services. In: Proceedings of the ACM on Human-Computer Interaction, vol. 3, pp. 1–33. CSCW (2019). https://doi.org/10.1145/3359246

Meta-usability: Understanding the Relationship Between Information Technology and Well-Being

Ian Michael Hosking(⊠) ⓘ and Kate Livingstone ⓘ

University of Cambridge, Cambridge CB2 1PZ, UK
{imh29,kl491}@cam.ac.uk

Abstract. Information and communication technology (ICT) plays a critical role in the modern workplace. Yet it is a double-edged sword consisting of a set of resources that can help improve our lives while at the same time placing demands on us that can have a profound negative impact on our well-being. This action research study explores the relationship between usability and well-being in the IT function of a large UK University. It considers four key models: (1) Usability Socio-Technical Model; (2) Technology Acceptance Model; (3) Information Overload Framework; and (4) ICT Demand-Resource Framework. From these four different complementary models, a fifth is derived that describes the concept of meta-usability. Collectively the models help explain the relationship between ICT and well-being more fully than just by considering the user's interaction with it. Importantly they show that well-being is influenced by a complex range of socio-technical factors that influence the user's experience. This represents a basis for devising practical interventions at a technological and organizational level to further enhance the actual and perceived user experience to help ensure ICT empowers staff in the workplace.

Keywords: Usability · Meta-usability · Well-being

1 Introduction

ICT (information and communication technology) plays a critical role in the modern workplace and has a profound impact on employee well-being, both positively and negatively. ICT can place distinct demands on employees compared to other stressors which can lead to burnout, absenteeism, and poor sleep [1–4]. This work is driven from within the ICT operation at a large university concerned with understanding the relationship between usability and well-being and how this can be improved as part of a major digital transformation programme. This leads to two key overarching research questions which are:

1. What is the relationship between usability and well-being?
2. How can systems be designed to increase usability and in turn improve well-being?

© The Author(s), under exclusive license to Springer Nature Switzerland AG 2022
M. M. Soares et al. (Eds.): HCII 2022, LNCS 13323, pp. 14–32, 2022.
https://doi.org/10.1007/978-3-031-05906-3_2

The research found that traditional approaches to usability do not directly address all the underlying factors relevant to answering these questions. This paper describes the findings of this work. Although undertaken in an operational function, as opposed to an academic department, it has used an academic mindset and approach to develop a deeper conceptual understanding of the issues.

The Cambridge Dictionary defines ICT [5] as "information and communication technology: the use of computers and other electronic equipment and systems to collect, store, use, and send data electronically". Although a useful starting point, it is a somewhat narrow description. Here we are considering a wider socio-technical systems view bringing in organizational and human elements [6].

This extended view is warranted to consider the relationship to well-being, which can be characterized as a complex, multi-dimensional concept with a range of underlying theories for it. It is the subject of ongoing development in its understanding and measurement bringing increasing scientific rigour [7–9].

The World Health Organization [7] defines positive mental health as "a state of well-being in which the individual realizes his or her abilities, can cope with the normal stresses of life, can work productively and fruitfully, and can make a contribution to his or her community". Well-being goes beyond mental health and just an absence of ill-health. It encompasses both 'feeling good' and 'functioning well' and contributes to the development of potential where someone has a level of control of their life and sense of purpose within it. It is a sustainable condition that allows individuals and the population more generally to develop and thrive. It is linked to success at both a personal and professional level where greater productivity is exhibited in the workplace as well as more effective learning and enhanced creativity. It has also been associated with improved economic performance at a national level [8].

1.1   A Gap in Understanding

Although usability is centered in a social-technical context [10, 11], it has historically focused on task-level, application-specific, interactions [12–14]. Usability can be confused as an attribute of a system, but it is an outcome of using that system [10, 11]. It is defined in the ISO 9241 standard as the "extent to which a system, product or service can be used by specified users to achieve specified goals with effectiveness, efficiency and satisfaction in a specified context of use" [15]. The three core attributes of effectiveness, efficiency and satisfaction have been extended by others [16–18]. However, except for satisfaction, the measures typically relate to the time taken to complete tasks and any associated errors that may occur. Satisfaction has often been addressed narrowly through questionnaires such as the System Usability Scale (10 items) [19] and the more comprehensive Questionnaire for User Interaction Satisfaction (34 items in version 7.0) [20, 21]. The view of usability has expanded to put a greater emphasis on experience and there has been a shift to using the expression 'user experience' or 'UX' [22, 23]. Even with this development, it remains about user experience not job experience, task performance and not job performance, satisfaction and not well-being. Therefore, this focus is often on the use of single applications or services and how to improve them. Although appropriate for this purpose it does not easily address the more complex issues of people's well-being across the entirety of their role within an organization where they are likely to use a multitude of applications and services. This is a starting point and driver for looking at other models to gain a better understanding of the relationship between usability and well-being.

2 Method

The research context is an operational function within an academic institution. The decision to apply an academic 'lens' to the work was operationally driven in that it was deemed it would produce a better operational outcome. It fits within an action research methodology where "it brings together action and reflection, theory and practice, in the pursuit of practical solutions to issues of pressing concern". The research is targeted at developing a deeper conceptual understanding of the impact of usability on well-being. As such, at this stage, it does not represent a full action research cycle that includes action and evaluation. However, the researchers were 'embedded', the research is very much 'with' and not 'for', focused on "the here and now with reflection on past issues to influence future designs" [24]. This represents the 'conceptualisation' part of the cycle [25]. The research approach was an open, inductive one [26] and more specifically the orientation was that of 'grounded theory' [27] letting the context and associated findings 'speak' to the key driving question, "what is happening here?" [28, 29]. The approach aligns with Charmaz's view [29] that the researcher is not a 'tabula rasa' (blank slate) and as such bring their knowledge, experiences, and interests to the enquiry. It was a process of continual reflection [26, 30] but ultimately 'reflexive' in that it involves "all aspects of ourselves and our contexts" and therefore influences "the way we research" [31]. As Reason and Bradbury [32] stress, action research is "not so much a methodology as an orientation to inquiry" bringing the "qualities of engagement, curiosity and question posing" to "significant practical issues". Understanding usability and its relationship to well-being is not only a practical issue but a profound one as we seek to address people's quality of life in the workplace.

The orientation of action research manifested itself in the following key elements and centred around a mindset of reflection. These are shown in Fig. 1. The key activities where issues would be 'observable' were regular project meetings of around an hour in length. In addition, there were workshops targeted at progressing issues with a range of stakeholders. These would be half to a full day in duration and occasionally over multiple days. Related to these activities would be technical documents that would either be directly authored for, or in response to, these activities or other relevant documents referenced from related work. A more strategic view was documented and discussed in the form of 'positioning' papers and presentations that would often address higher-level organizational goals or issues and draw several related areas together. Staff would make use of grey literature [33], typically in the form of vendor technical documentation and web-based 'opinion' articles from relevant practitioners. These elements described so far represent a business-as-usual operation. The key additional elements that bring the academic mindset to the process are the use of academic literature and the exploration of models from this literature (described in Sect. 2.2). The models were used to reflect on the 'real-world' examples (described in Sect. 2.3), which showed their value in explaining what was being observed and experienced in them. This typically happened in weekly meetings between the authors where they would 'step back' and reflect and refine the understanding of what was happening.

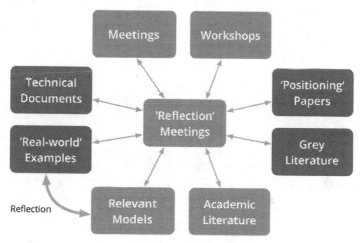

Fig. 1. Key elements of the research approach centered on reflection. The green elements represent business as usual activities and the blue ones associated documentation. The orange items are specific academic-oriented activities.

2.1 Real-World Examples

Table 1 highlights the key 'real-world' examples, drawn from different projects within the transformation programme. They are referred to in Fig. 1 and were used to reflect on the models from the literature as well as wider project related discussions.

2.2 Models

The search for relevant models made use of academic search engines with a diverse range of keywords to uncover literature across different domains. Searching included bi-directional citation (earlier and later related citations). The bidirectional citation searches were seeded with seminal or key papers which Hinde and Spackman [34] describe as "initial pearls". These formed the basis for "snowballing" to uncover related literature. This helps overcome the weaknesses of relying on narrow keyword searches and in this case the models uncovered were not found within the HCI domain so widening keywords to include 'stress' and 'ICT' uncovered related work from several research domains. The following models, in Table 2, were chosen based on a holistic judgment of how they explain different factors that relate usability to well-being, as well as how they potentially address the examples highlighted in Table 1.

Usability Socio-technical Model. The work of Bevan, Kirakowski, and Maissel [10] describes human-computer interaction in a socio-technical context. A useful graphical representation of this is provided by Bevan [11] and extended further by Hosking [35] and replicated below in Fig. 2.

Table 1. 'Real-world' examples and the impact on usability

Technology/system	Impact on usability
Single sign-on	Not having to remember multiple usernames and passwords across different systems
Site-wide search	The ability to find the required content quickly without being overloaded with apparently spurious search results
APIs	Enabling more seamless inter-operation across different applications which, for example, reduces 'manual' copying of data across applications
Design system	Creating a consistent user interface in terms of 'look & feel' across multiple applications helps increase user confidence and reduces training and support demands
Document management	Ensuring the users can find and securely access documents with clear and consistent control of the associated workflow
Flexible access to tools	Allows users to adapt their working patterns and locations to better fit their needs and context
Information architecture	Ensuring that information of different types and formats can be accessed in a secure and timely manner by the right users
Reporting and monitoring	Enabling access to key operational data in a succinct form that enables staff to have an up-to-date understanding of operational performance
Communication	Ensuring that staff can communicate effectively and efficiently without being overloaded with information
Training and support	Helping users have the skills and confidence to use systems so that they can get the most out of their functionality in performing their job

Table 2. Relevant models for understanding the relationship between usability and well-being

Model	Focus
Usability socio-technical model	Application interaction
Technology acceptance model	Adoption behaviour
Information overload framework	Information load
ICT demand-resource framework	Job stress

Figure 2 includes the organizational and technical environments and explicitly mentions satisfaction and workload. However, the focus is heavily on the interaction. With regards to satisfaction, as already mentioned, this is often addressed through questionnaires. Workload can be assessed with the NASA TLX [36] which is also a questionnaire. All are appropriate when concerned with the efficacy of the interaction but limited when

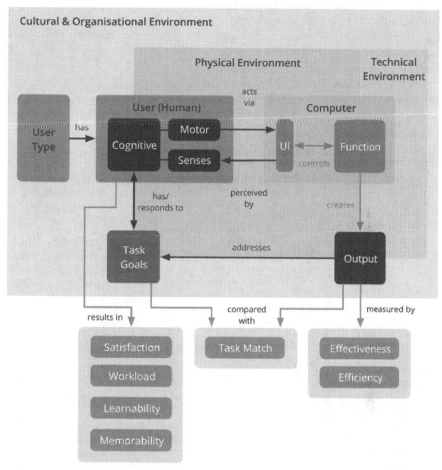

Fig. 2. A model of usability in a socio-technical context (reproduced from [35] with permission)

considering the wider impact of ICT across a person's job role. Although the technical and organizational environments are included in the model, the impact on usability is not explicit and these gaps in understanding became a key theme early in this work.

Technology Acceptance Model. The Technology Acceptance Model (TAM) [37] is an adaption of the well-established Theory of Reasoned Action (TRA) [38] to specifically address technology acceptance. The importance of a user's self-beliefs in driving use is consistent with the theory of self-efficacy [37, 39]. Self-efficacy is an individual's beliefs about what they think they can do and this has a profound impact on what they do in practice. The TAM has two multi-item scales for assessing a user's 'perception' of 'usefulness' and 'ease of use'. Work on the TAM has been updated through TAM 2 [40] that extends the model further. Firstly, in terms of the impact of 'social influence processes', such as the impact of colleagues' views ('subjective norm'), and how its impact is moderated by the degree to which system use is mandatory ('voluntariness'). Secondly, concerning how users make judgements when "assessing the match between important work goals and the consequences of performing the act of using a system". The later extension includes the determinants of 'job relevance', 'output quality', and 'result demonstrability'. 'Job relevance' concerns how a user perceives the applicability of the system to their job. 'Output quality' considers how well the system performs these tasks relevant to the job. Linked to this is 'result demonstrability' which considers how 'tangible' the results are from system use. TAM is well established with improvements such as TAM2 aimed at addressing weaknesses, albeit with the value of these being disputed [41].

TAM and related work lead us to the reality that a well-designed user interface, on its own, is not enough to ensure effective uptake in the context of a job role. It is not just about 'ease of use' but 'perceived ease of use' too. Therefore, understanding and helping build appropriate perceptions of a system's usefulness (utility) and ease of use (usability) are also critical.

This broadens out the characterization of the user in the interaction and factors impacting technology adoption. It provides an instrument to assess this and is a useful extension to the basic model of the user shown in Fig. 2, adding valuable understanding to the impact of the 'cultural and organizational' environment as well as expanding the issues surrounding 'task match' in the model.

Information Overload Framework. At the core of information overload is the potential negative impact of increasing information load on decision-making performance. This can result in "the feelings of stress, confusion, pressure, anxiety, and low motivation" that are "crucial factors that signal the occurrence of information overload". Eppler and Mengis [42] have developed a conceptual framework to explore the phenomenon which contains the following five causes of information overload:

1. Personal factors
2. Information characteristics (including quantity, frequency, intensity, quality)
3. Task and process parameters
4. Organizational design
5. Information technology

The framework has a cycle of 'causes' leading to 'symptoms' that can be addressed by 'countermeasures'. Their work, underpinned by a systematic literature review, helpfully provides comprehensive tables of symptoms and countermeasures. The literature review searches across the four domains of accounting, marketing, management information systems, and organization science. A notable exclusion is the domain of Human-Computer Interaction which might explain the absence of a detailed view of usability in the analysis.

Despite the understandable narrow focus on information and the relatively limited view of usability the framework does systematically address the wider context of ICT operation and provides, in part, the ability to understand the aggregate impact of multiple system use and its impact on job performance and well-being. It also provides a strong practical dimension through the inclusion of countermeasures to information overload.

ICT Demand-Resource Framework. Day, Scott and Kelloway's [43] framework is based around the premise that ICT is a "double-edged sword" that can have a positive or negative impact on employees. It is based on two key models. The first is the Job Demands-Resources Model (JD-R) [44] where job demands are any aspects of the job such as the workload, time pressure, difficult social interactions or even acoustic noise that result in increased physical or psychological cost. The other edge of the sword, so to speak, are aspects that help in the completion of work and therefore reduce the burden, leading to improved productivity and well-being. This double-edged nature was particularly pertinent during the COVID-19 (SARS-CoV-2) pandemic where there was an increased reliance on ICT [45, 46]. Day, Scott and Kelloway [43] provide a comparison of how five key areas can be a *'demand'* or *'resource'*.

1. **Employee availability:** modern ICT provides an unprecedented 'always on' connectedness whatever the location. This can put undue 'demand' on an employee beyond the traditional working day. However, as a 'resource' it can provide great flexibility to work at convenient times and locations.
2. **Information access:** the proliferation of information can create a 'demand' leading to information overload. Conversely, as a 'resource' it can improve decision making and task efficiency.
3. **Communication:** a myriad of communication platforms and channels can lead to a 'demanding' communications environment, potentially leading to poor or miscommunication. At its worst, it can enable cyber aggression. On the other hand, the diversity of communication options is a valuable 'resource' to help meet the needs of different contexts and personal preferences. Synchronous options such as video-based meetings are complemented by asynchronous options such as messaging applications, allowing richer communication. Some platforms allow these to be seamlessly integrated.
4. **Electronic performance monitoring:** performance monitoring can take different forms such as building access control systems, security cameras and direct monitoring of task performance. In addition, the 'always connected' nature of ICT means there is the potential for more indirect monitoring. Even if this is not happening it may be implied by the feeling of being 'online' at work. It is not surprising that the 'demands' of monitoring can increase employees stress levels and lead to a variety of negative health outcomes as well as reducing trust. Yet used appropriately monitoring is a 'resource' that enables positive feedback and indeed may lead to encouraging staff to work less.
5. **Job control:** where ICT places 'demands', particularly time-critical ones, it can lead to actual or perceived lack of control with the consequential impact on increased stress and strain. From a 'resource' perspective ICT can result in greater control and associated flexibility that can lead to a better work-life balance and well-being.

The second model is the transactional theory of stress and coping (TTSC) [47] which conceives stress as a 'transaction' between the person and their complex environment. The model is useful as it explicitly addresses individual variability and the different perceptions people have of how demanding an ICT system will be on them. The model also covers how these individual and other external factors impact the transaction positively or negatively.

Figure 3 shows the combination of the JD-R and the moderating individual and organizational factors from the TTSC. The combined model has been simplified to show the outcomes in terms of well-being and performance.

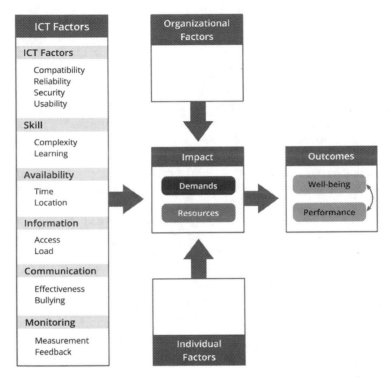

Fig. 3. A simplified version of the ICT demand-resource framework

It is noteworthy that perceptions of ICT in this model are like the TAM and the relevance of self-efficacy [39] is also mentioned. However, the researchers deliberately exclude the TAM as a relevant input as they consider it to cover the antecedents of employee use as opposed to the outcome of use. It should be noted that when discussing the exclusion, they do reference another chapter in the same book that covers it, but all the same further exploration of the relationship to the TAM would potentially be illuminating for both models.

Information overload is also mentioned as one factor, but no reference is made to the body of work explicitly addressing this. Similarly, usability is discussed as a stressor, but no link is made to the wider work such as that outlined in the first model. Despite these points, it does represent the most complete model for relating usability to well-being. It also identifies four specific "hassles" for employees that can impact well-being. 'Hassles' are defined as "critical and regular demands placed on the individual" [43].

1. **Malfunctions:** this is a broader view than just faults, covering what it describes as "user-friendliness" and problems completing tasks. The stress caused by malfunctions can even lead to employees hitting or throwing ICT equipment. The paper cites a survey that reported that 83% of corporate ICT managers has witnessed such behaviour [43].
2. **Incompatible technologies:** this refers to the adaptions required to make ICT fit the task in specific workplaces. Such adaptions may not be that effective and introduce additional problems.
3. **Security demands:** growing issues and risks with security have resulted in a proliferation of passwords and associated systems such as multi-factor authentication. Managing this complexity and the associated anxiety around security, particularly when dealing with sensitive and confidential information, can increase stress.
4. **Expectations for continuous learning:** in addition to the problems outlined above, is the rapid pace of change meaning that staff must continuously learn updated or new ICT.

These 'hassles' and the model as a whole resonate strongly with the experiences across the examples outlined in Sect. 2.1 and more widely within the work. As mentioned, the model is comprehensive and provides a rich framework for exploring the impact of usability on well-being.

Analysis. Despite a degree of overlap, the specific focus of each of the four models provides a distinctive and useful insight into the link between usability and well-being. The models that do not directly focus on usability help provide a broader socio-technical context to the traditional interaction focus of usability. They help unpack the technical and organizational contexts outlined in the first model. They raise the importance of how the perception of usability impacts use and how this in turn is influenced by the organizational context and more specifically the influence of peer groups. Indeed, it shows that there is something over and above usability. This led to exploring the concept of 'meta-usability' to understand the usability and well-being relationship more fully and how it can proactively be addressed. This term has already been used by Li and Nielsen [48]. They are specifically addressing the issue of how many large ICT systems are generic and must be customized to work in a local context. Therefore, they argue that such systems not only have to be 'designed for use' but also 'designed for design'. In other words, to design the systems to enable effective customization in what they call 'implementation-level design'. This directly addresses the 'hassle' of 'incompatible technologies' discussed earlier [43]. Their use of 'meta-usability' addresses how usable the design system is in developing a well-designed user interface during implementation-level design. They describe two types of meta-usability the first being how usable the software is regarding customization for local practice or 'design-usability'. The second concerns the support resources for the process of implementation-level design, which they describe as 'method-usability'.

This is still largely an application-centric perspective and extending this further to a social-technical one leads to arguing for widening the concept of meta-usability. This means including a wider range of technological and organizational factors that impact usability and users' perceptions of usability. This led to conducting a comparison between usability and the proposed wider perspective of meta-usability informed by the examples outlined in Table 1.

2.3 Comparing Usability to Meta-usability

The comparison between usability and meta-usability was undertaken to help determine if it is a sufficiently distinct concept. The result of this is shown in Table 3 as follows:

Table 3. A comparison of usability versus meta-usability

Usability	Meta-usability
Application	System
ICT device	Technical infrastructure
User interface	Architecture
Interaction	Interoperation
Individual	Organization
Procedure	Policy
Task	Role
Performance	Perception
Satisfaction	Well-being
Direct use	Indirect use
Visible	Invisible

The comparison highlights something that extends or at least clarifies the field and fits the Oxford English Dictionary definition of 'meta-' as a prefix that denotes something that is "beyond", "above" and at a "higher level". It fits well with the definition of a prefix "to the name of a subject or discipline to denote another which deals with ulterior issues in the same field, or which raises questions about the nature of the original discipline and its methods, procedures, and assumptions" [49]. Having established the potential of this extended concept of meta-usability the impact on the socio-technical model of usability was considered to see if it could be usefully extended to cover these wider issues.

2.4 A Framework for Meta-usability

The model shown in Fig. 2 was taken as the starting point. This was reduced to the core elements relevant to show the position and role of meta-usability. The influence of the organization on the users' 'perception' of usability is emphasized as it is a key factor from the TAM model, self-efficacy more broadly and also features in the ICT Demand-Resource Framework. Regarding the technological environment, the impact of system-wide considerations is focused on enhanced functionality. The diagram uses

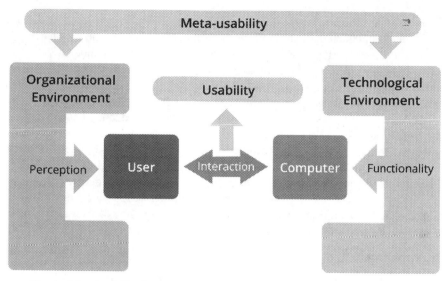

Fig. 4. Meta-usability framework based on the socio-technical model of usability

arrows to show a broad cycle of meta-usability decisions and design within organizational and technology environments that lead to improvements in usability.

Looking back to Fig. 2 it is possible to develop a more elaborate framework with more entities and to express more factors in a similar way to the ICT Demand-Resource Framework. However, the aim here is to express the basic positioning and role of meta-usability and also to focus it on being a complement to the other models rather than trying to replace them. This framework represents a graphical description that helps inform a textual definition.

2.5 An Extended Definition of Meta-usability

The aim of developing a textual definition is not simply for academic purposes but as a practical way of introducing the concept to colleagues and in turn, opening up a wider discussion. The challenge is to develop something short, memorable yet sufficiently descriptive. The following is the current working definition:

Meta-usability concerns technological and organizational system-wide, cross-application factors that impact the perception and actual usability of applications

Combining this definition with the framework in Fig. 4 and the comparison between usability and meta-usability as shown in Table 3 represents a core set for characterising what meta-usability is. In conjunction with the 4 models explored it represents a basis for exploring practical changes to improve usability within the context of well-being.

2.6 Towards Practical Changes

The ongoing reflection on the examples in Table 1 and the four models led to the following proposed 'meta-usability interventions' aimed at being applied in future work. One intervention was identified in each of the areas of organization and technology as follows.

Organizational: Results Demonstrability. The impact of the organization and groups within it on an individual's perception of usability stood out and resonated with the experience of the authors. This manifests itself in different ways that include how different groups and individuals can have a preference, indeed a very strong one, for a particular vendor's solution. For example, basic cloud-based services such as file storage and office applications. At times it can seem as if there is a 'tribal-like' allegiance to a particular vendor. Understanding 'social influence processes' when introducing a new solution is important and addressing these perspectives is seen to be key to encouraging uptake and in turn, the formation of positive views shared amongst peers. One factor that stands out is 'results demonstrability' from the TAM2 [40]. A reflection on this highlighted the opportunity to proactively demonstrate or explain the results. In particular, a number of high impact but 'low tangibility' solutions were identified. A simple example of this is multi-factor authentication [50] which provides a more secure way of accessing services. One method of doing this is a smartphone app that generates a frequently changing code to use for authentication in addition to something like a user password. The question is what does this mean to a range of users including ones who are not technical? It is techno-jargon, with a new app and additional steps. Therefore, on the surface, it is a 'demand' and not an obvious 'resource'. It needs explanation, to understand the weakness of security without it, the risks this brings and therefore the relative convenience of a smartphone app to bring this higher level of security. This explanation and ideally complemented with a demonstration, needs to be different for different groups to build up peer support within them.

Technological: Enabling Infrastructure. The preceding organizational example concerns improving the 'perception' of usability whereas the technological example focuses on using cross-application infrastructure to improve application functionality and the 'actual' user experience. The often-hidden nature of infrastructure is typified by the problem that most users are unaware of it until it goes wrong. The key in this work is to elevate the status of such infrastructure for its importance, and significant potential, in improving usability. The different technological systems that were repeatedly highlighted in the transformation programme with regards to improving usability are:

- **Application Programming Interface (API):** API's are a way of enabling cross-application integration and interoperation as well as helping automation. For example, by avoiding having to search for and copy information from another application. An API can allow direct access to this data from within an application.
- **Identity and access management:** Identity and access management is the key to accessing multiple services across a job role. The aim is to make this access seamless and secure, avoiding having to have multiple accounts with different log-in credentials. Good access management can also allow convenient and precise control of information access based on clearly defined roles.
- **Metadata:** At a basic level metadata is 'data about data' but in practice takes different forms and performs many key roles [51]. Notable amongst these include ensuring that, in conjunction with identity and access management, the right people get the right information when they need it with the minimum of effort. Metadata also enables the filtering of information so that people only see what is relevant to them, helping

significantly in controlling information overload. Metadata is also important in driving effective search, underpinning document management and the ability to systematically audit a range of different content.

- **Document management:** document management draws on identity and access management and metadata. Effective document management helps eliminate the unnecessary duplication of documents creating a single source of truth and not a myriad of often unsynchronized copies. It allows robust and convenient workflows to be created that ensure good control of a document through its life cycle. Good document management can change the use of digital documents from being a 'demand' to a strong 'resource'.
- **Design System:** The web browser is becoming the dominant interface for accessing content and services. Ensuring a consistent and well-designed web-based interface is facilitated by a design system that enables a common 'look and feel' in web-based content and applications. It relates most strongly to Li and Nielsen's [48] definition of meta-usability as it is something that is 'designed for design'.

The elements outlined above do not work in isolation this means that a well-designed technical systems architecture also plays a key role in meta-usability and downstream usability from this. Therefore, the impact on usability needs to be a core consideration in systems architecture design.

3   Discussion

3.1   The Relationship Between Usability and Well-Being

Returning to the two initial research questions:

1. What is the relationship between usability and well-being?

By looking beyond the field of HCI it has been possible to better characterize the relationship between usability and well-being and also show its importance in the workplace. It has also highlighted a gap that has led to the proposed extended concept of meta-usability to better understand the link between technological and organizational environments in influencing this. Three key things have been developed to explain this which are, (1) a definition, (2) a framework and (3) a comparison between usability and meta-usability. This helps frame and understand how things can be improved.

2. How can systems be designed to increase usability and in turn improve well-being?

Two key areas have been explored. The first concerns the organizational environment and how it can be used to positively drive the perception of usability amongst users which has a strong influence on technology adoption. A key approach in this is to demonstrate the value of new technologies, and indeed existing ones to users in a way that is optimized for different user types and groups. The second is the technological environment and cross-application technologies that have consistently been raised in projects with regards to their potential to enhance usability through improving access to services, increasing the levels of automation, and reducing information overload.

This represents the early stages of exploring the potential of this thinking, but it is already starting to become a more normal part of the discussion in service development projects.

3.2 The Case for a New Term

At an academic and practical level, it is important to step back and consider the justification for another concept and term i.e. meta-usability to explain the relationship between ICT and well-being. This leads to three logical positions which are addressed as follows:

1. **Usability is enough as it is:** we have argued, through four different models and associated studies, that there is a range of related factors beyond the interaction level of ICT use that impact well-being. Therefore, an interaction-only perspective as characterized by usability is not enough to fully represent the role of these factors.
2. **Usability can be extended to consider the wider factors:** We have already mentioned that the socio-technical aspects are part of the context of usability. However, we argued that their relationship to and impact on usability are not described in the detailed way that the other models do. Table 2 shows the significant contrast between usability and meta-usability and that it stands as a distinctive concept that complements the interaction focus of usability. Further to this Fig. 4 positions meta-usability, to an extent, as an input to the design and operation of systems whereas usability is an outcome.
3. **A new concept and term are justified:** The arguments presented above, against the first two options, come from a stance developed in this work that is in favor of a new concept. However, in practical terms, the case for something new is empirically driven as to whether there is real-world value in using meta-usability as a term and framework for driving change. Indeed, this is likely to vary in different organizations and different contexts. This is an action research study currently confined to a single institution. How it generalizes to other organizations remains an open question. However, the use of well-established models and associated evidence suggests strongly that it could.

3.3 Limitations

As mentioned above this work is limited to a single organization albeit based on substantial bodies of work that relate it to other organizations. It is also focused on the workplace and clearly, ICT has a big role outside of the workplace and plays a major role in people's personal lives. Finally, as a piece of action research, it is at a relatively early stage and largely qualitative in nature. Understanding these limitations helps inform the direction of future work.

3.4 Future Work

The next steps are to firstly, try out the practical approaches outlined in Sect. 2.6. These are a focus on 'perceived usability' through 'result demonstrability' and highlighting the role of technological systems and the associated architecture in driving functionality pertinent to usability. Secondly, to explore the models further to generate a deeper understanding of the organizational factors beyond just 'result demonstrability'. Thirdly, to interact further with colleagues to constructively debate the concept of meta-usability to understand its value and refine its definition.

Beyond the boundary of this work, the extended concept of meta-usability outlined here needs to be tested in other organizations and contexts to see if it provides insight and informs action to help ensure that ICT has a positive impact on well-being and its negative demands are minimised.

4 Conclusion

ICT is a double-edged sword. It represents a set of resources that can help improve our lives while at the same time placing demands on us that can have a profound negative impact on our well-being. Ensuring that it is mostly the former and not the latter is critical in delivering effective ICT provision. The role of a well-designed user interface in driving usability is central in achieving this, but on its own is not enough. We have made the case, that to fully explain the impact of ICT on well-being and control it, a wider perspective using the concept of meta-usability is required. This brings in other key factors to enable a more complete understanding of the technological and social drivers behind 'ease of use' and critically 'perceived ease of use' that in turn have an impact on well-being.

This work has brought together four different complementary models from different fields and used them to derive a fifth that describes an extended concept of meta-usability. Collectively they help explain the relationship between ICT and well-being which is often mediated by the user interface but influenced by a range of socio-technical factors. They represent a basis for devising practical interventions at technological and organizational levels to further enhance the actual and perceived user experience to help ensure ICT empowers staff in the workplace.

Acknowledgements. The authors would like to thank their colleagues and the end-users whom we work with and develop services for. In particular, we would like to thank Prof. Ian Leslie whose questioning around the relationship between usability and well-being was the spark that set the work in motion and David Marshall for his constructive comments.

Conflicts of Interest. This work was an internally funded project at the University of Cambridge as part of a digital transformation programme. The authors declare they have no competing interests in the dissemination of this work. While the authors receive funding in an operational capacity, this work is free from any interests and has no direct link to work that would influence any outputs or conclusions.

References

1. Sparks, K., Faragher, B., Cooper, C.L.: Well-being and occupational health in the 21st century workplace. J. Occup. Organ. Psych. **74**, 489–509 (2010). https://doi.org/10.1348/096317901 167497

2. Kowalski, T.H.P., Loretto, W.: Well-being and HRM in the changing workplace. Int. J. Hum. Resour. Manage. **28**, 2229–2255 (2017). https://doi.org/10.1080/09585192.2017.1345205

3. Day, A., Barber, L.K., Tonet, J.: Information communication technology and employee well-being: understanding the "iParadox triad" at work. In: The Cambridge Handbook of Technology and Employee Behavior, pp. 580–607 (2019). https://doi.org/10.1017/9781108649636.022

4. Biggs, A., Brough, P., Drummond, S.: Lazarus and Folkman's psychological stress and coping theory. In: Cooper, C.L., Quick, J.C. (eds.) The Handbook of Stress and Health: A Guide to Research and Practice. John Wiley & Sons (2017)

5. ICT: https://dictionary.cambridge.org/dictionary/english/ict (2022)

6. Winter, S., Berente, N., Howison, J., Butler, B.: Beyond the organizational 'container': conceptualizing 21st century sociotechnical work. Inform. Organ-UK **24**, 250–269 (2014). https://doi.org/10.1016/j.infoandorg.2014.10.003

7. World Health Organization: Promoting Mental Health. World Health Organization. https://apps.who.int/iris/handle/10665/42940 (2004)

8. Ruggeri, K., Garcia-Garzon, E., Maguire, Á., Matz, S., Huppert, F.A.: Well-being is more than happiness and life satisfaction: a multidimensional analysis of 21 countries. Health Qual. Life Out. **18**, 192 (2020). https://doi.org/10.1186/s12955-020-01423-y

9. Crisp, R.: Well-Being. The Stanford Encyclopedia of Philosophy, Winter 2021 edn. https://plato.stanford.edu/archives/win2021/entries/well-being (2021)

10. Bevan, N., Kirakowski, J., Maissel, J.: What is Usability? Presented at the September (1991)

11. Bevan, N.: Measuring usability as quality of use. Software Qual. J. **4**, 115–130 (1995). https://doi.org/10.1007/bf00402715

12. Licklider, J.C.R.: Man-Computer Symbiosis. IRE Transactions on Human Factors in Electronics, HFE-1, pp. 4–11 (1960). https://doi.org/10.1109/thfe2.1960.4503259

13. Hutchins, E., Hollan, J., Norman, D.: Direct manipulation interfaces. Hum.-Comput. Int. **1**, 311–338 (1985). https://doi.org/10.1207/s15327051hci0104_2

14. Myers, B.A.: A brief history of human-computer interaction technology. ACM Interact. **5**, 44–54 (1998). https://doi.org/10.1145/274430.274436

15. Standardization, E.C. for: Ergonomics of human-system interaction – Part 11: Usability: Definitions and Concepts. European Committee for Standardization (2018)

16. Shneiderman, B.: Human factors of interactive software. In: Blaser, A., Zoeppritz, M. (eds.) IBM 1983. LNCS, vol. 150, pp. 9–29. Springer, Heidelberg (1983). https://doi.org/10.1007/3-540-12273-7_16

17. Nielsen, J.: Usability Engineering. Morgan Kaufmann (1993)

18. Seffah, A., Donyaee, M., Kline, R.B., Padda, H.K.: Usability measurement and metrics: a consolidated model. Software Qual. J. **14**, 159–178 (2006). https://doi.org/10.1007/s11219-006-7600-8

19. Brooke, J.: System Usability Scale (SUS): A Quick-and-Dirty Method of System Evaluation User Information. Digital Equipment Co. Ltd., Reading (1986)

20. Chin, J.P., Diehl, V.A., Norman, K.L.: Development of an Instrument Measuring User Satisfaction of the Human-Computer Interface. ACM (1988)

21. Norman, K.L., Shneiderman, B., Harper, B., Slaughter, L.: Questionnaire for User Interface Satisfaction (2007)

22. Scapin, D., Senach, B., Trousse, B., Pallot, M.: User experience: buzzword or new paradigm? In: ACHI 2012, The Fifth International Conference on Advances in Computer-Human Interactions. https://hal.inria.fr/hal-00769619 (2012)

23. Berni, A., Borgianni, Y.: From the definition of user experience to a framework to classify its applications in design. Proc. Des. Soc. **1**, 1627–1636 (2021). https://doi.org/10.1017/pds.2021.424

24. Bradbury, H. (ed.): The SAGE Handbook of Action Research. Sage Publications (2015). https://doi.org/10.4135/9781473921290
25. Moghaddam, A.: Action research: a spiral inquiry for valid and useful knowledge. Alta. J. Educ. Res. **53**, 228–239 (2007)
26. Creswell, J.W.: Research Design. SAGE (2009)
27. Glaser, B.G., Strauss, A.L.: The Discovery of Grounded Theory: Strategies for Qualitative Research. Aldine (1967)
28. Glaser, B.G.: Theoretical Sensitivity. Sociology Press (1978)
29. Charmaz, K.: Qualitative interviewing and grounded theory analysis. In: Gubrium, J.F., Holstein, J.A. (eds.) Handbook of Interview Research, pp. 675–694 (2011). https://doi.org/10.4135/9781412973588
30. Schön, D.A.: The reflective practitioner (1991). https://doi.org/10.4324/9781315237473
31. Fook, J.: In: Lishman, J. (ed.) Reflective Practice and Critical Reflection, pp. 440–454. Jessica Kingsley (2015)
32. Reason, P., Bradbury, H. (eds.): The SAGE Handbook of Action Research Participative Inquiry and Practice. Sage Publications (2008)
33. Farace, D., Schöpfel, J. (eds.): Grey Literature in Library and Information Studies. De Gruyter Saur (2010). https://doi.org/10.1515/9783598441493
34. Hinde, S., Spackman, E.: Bidirectional citation searching to completion: an exploration of literature searching methods. Pharmacoeconomics **33**(1), 5–11 (2015). https://doi.org/10.1007/s40273-014-0205-3
35. Hosking, I.M.: Understanding and Evaluating User Interface Visibility (2021). https://doi.org/10.17863/CAM.62228
36. Hart, S.G., Staveland, L.E.: Development of NASA-TLX (Task Load Index): Results of Empirical and Theoretical Research. Elsevier (1988). https://doi.org/10.1016/S0166-4115(08)62386-9
37. Davis, F.D.: Perceived usefulness, perceived ease of use, and user acceptance of information technology. MIS Quart. **13**, 319–340 (1989). https://doi.org/10.2307/249008
38. Bagozzi, R.P., Davis, F.D., Warshaw, P.R.: Development and test of a theory of technological learning and usage. Hum. Relat. **45**, 659–686 (1992). https://doi.org/10.1177/001872679204500702
39. Bandura, A.: Self-efficacy mechanism in human agency. Am. Psychol. **37**, 122–147 (1982). https://doi.org/10.1037/0003-066x.37.2.122
40. Venkatesh, V., Davis, F.D.: A theoretical extension of the technology acceptance model: four longitudinal field studies. Manage. Sci. **46**, 186–204 (2000). https://doi.org/10.1287/mnsc.46.2.186.11926
41. Bagozzi, R.: The legacy of the technology acceptance model and a proposal for a paradigm shift. J. Assoc. Inf. Syst. **8**, 244–254 (2007). https://doi.org/10.17705/1jais.00122
42. Eppler, M.J., Mengis, J.: The concept of information overload: a review of literature from organization science, accounting, marketing, MIS, and related disciplines. Inform. Soc. **20**, 325–344 (2004). https://doi.org/10.1080/01972240490507974
43. Day, A., Scott, N., Kelloway, E.K.: Information and communication technology: implications for job stress and employee well-being. In: New Developments in Theoretical and Conceptual Approaches to Job Stress, pp. 317–350 (2010). https://doi.org/10.1108/s1479-3555(2010)0000008011
44. Bakker, A.B., Demerouti, E.: The job demands-resources model: state of the art. J. Manage. Psychol. **22**, 309–328 (2007). https://doi.org/10.1108/02683940710733115
45. Lee, Y.-C., Malcein, L.A., Kim, S.C.: Information and communications technology (ICT) usage during COVID-19: motivating factors and implications. Int. J. Environ. Res. Public **18**, 3571 (2021). https://doi.org/10.3390/ijerph18073571

46. Hasan, N., Bao, Y.: Impact of "e-Learning crack-up" perception on psychological distress among college students during COVID-19 pandemic: a mediating role of "fear of academic year loss". Child. Youth Serv. Rev. **118**, 105355 (2020). https://doi.org/10.1016/j.childyouth.2020.105355
47. Lazarus, R.S., Folkman, S.: Stress Appraisal and Coping. Springer, New York (1984)
48. Li, M., Nielsen, P.: Making usable generic software. A matter of global or local design? In: 10th Scandinavian Conference on Information Systems (2019). https://aisel.aisnct.org/scis2019/8
49. meta-, prefix: www.oed.com/view/Entry/117150 (2021)
50. Ometov, A., Bezzateev, S., Mäkitalo, N., Andreev, S., Mikkonen, T., Koucheryavy, Y.: Multi-factor authentication: a survey. Cryptography **2**, 1 (2018). https://doi.org/10.3390/cryptography2010001
51. Riley, J.: Understanding Metadata: What is Metadata, and What is it For? National Information Standards Organization (2017). http://www.niso.org/publications/understanding-metadata-2017

The Dialectic Between System Space and Design Space

A Systems Thinking Approach to Addressing Complexity in the Design Process

Bertil Lindenfalk[1]([⊠]) [iD] and Andrea Resmini[1,2] [iD]

[1] Jönköping Academy for the Improvement of Health
and Welfare, School of Health and Welfare, Jönköping University, Jönköping, Sweden
`bertil.lindenfalk@ju.se, andrea.resmini@hh.se`
[2] Department of Intelligent Systems and Digital Design, School of Information Technology,
Halmstad University, Halmstad, Sweden

Abstract. System space is introduced as a conceptual design space and as a distinct space from that traditionally addressed by most design processes. The paper intends to address the increasing complexity deriving from the ongoing blend of physical and digital in a postdigital culture and contribute to the current understanding of the effect of "systemic" ways of thinking in design disciplines. We argue that a systemic perspective cannot simply be "added" to the design process and that addressing postdigital complexity, that is, producing solutions to contemporary design problems, requires instead its own conceptualization, in its own space, to be acknowledged, practiced, and formalized as a different way of thinking. We propose that system space lives in a dialectical relationship with design space within the space of the experience and that it provides a way to escape the cognitive traps in design space. We posit that the relationships between system space and design space can be apprehended by means of an exo-process adapted from systems thinking, and that the exo-process provides a supporting structure for the intentional and necessary movement between the different spaces, scales, and modes of thinking required by contemporary design work. We then illustrate such a dialectical relationship through the analysis of three different cases and draw final considerations.

Keywords: System space · Design space · Systems thinking · Complexity · Dialectics

1 Introduction

This paper introduces "system space" as a conceptual design space and as a distinct space from that traditionally addressed by most design processes. Design processes often describe design activities as happening in a problem space, requiring reflection, and in a solution space, requiring action (Design Council 2007). A number of models incorporate variations of these to account for the opening, exploring, and closing activities typical of design (Gray et al. 2010) and to better identify and specify the convergent and divergent moments happening in the solution space (Curedale 2019).

In recent years, the increasing complexity deriving from the ongoing blending of digital and physical (Institute for the Future 2009) and the emergence of a postdigital culture (Kirby 2009; Resmini and Lindenfalk 2021) have challenged the current procedural relationship between problem and solution as the preferred approach to solve complex problems, spurring a resurgence of interest in systems thinking and of its role in design theory and practice. This renewed interest has manifested itself in approaches focusing on the dynamic commingling of digital and physical (Benyon 2014), entirely novel perspectives such as systemic design (Jones 2014) and transition design (Irwin 2015), led to new methodologies such as giga-mapping (Sevaldson 2011) and to the conceptual reframing of existing fields to address said complexity (Resmini 2014).

It has been argued that the problem space, as defined and bounded in the practice by an organizational need and made explicit in a design brief, should no longer be accepted as-is by designers as the single originating point of a design process (Irwin 2015; Tonkinwise 2015; Resmini and Lacerda 2016; Resmini and Lindenfalk 2021). Designers should instead first and foremost acknowledge and assess the complexity embedded within and expressed by the context in which the organizational need originates (Lindenfalk and Resmini 2016; 2019).

This is akin to the cognitive trap presented by the 9-dot puzzle variously described in design literature (Akin and Akin 1996; Lawson 2005, p. 222): most of those who engage with the solution space introduce self-imposed rules or constraints that are never specified in the problem space, simply requiring one to connect all nine dots with four lines without lifting one's pen from the paper. As Lawson points out, people treat the problem space as an over-rigid structure and considerably reduce their chances of solving the puzzle. In current design practice, any number of such traps are created by anchoring one's process to design space only, since elements of the design space engage in relationships with elements outside of it (Resmini and Lindenfalk 2021), factually preventing or seriously hindering the possibility of a successful resolution (Fig. 1).

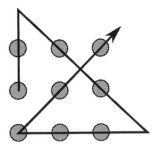

Fig. 1. The 9-dot puzzle can only be solved by exiting dot space

To this extent, we propose the introduction of an exo-process, external to the design process as defined in traditional design theory, that focuses on the systemic acts of searching, mapping, and telling the story (Gharajedaghi 2011). These steps in the exo-process are intended to acknowledge how the current "socio-technic development is itself an important influence on both the design process and the role of the designer in society" (Lawson 2005, p. 116) and account for the novel opportunities and challenges introduced by the postdigital condition (Resmini and Lindenfalk 2021). They: help understand the assumptions and conditions that are "responsible for repeatedly regenerating the problematic pattern" captured in the organizational need or design brief (searching); identify and formalize "why the system behaves the way it does" (mapping); and "generate a shared understanding about the nature of the current reality among the major actors" (telling the story).

The exo-process should, on one hand, help remove obstacles by "minimiz(ing) the resistance to change" and "maximiz(ing) the courage to act"; and, on the other hand, address the right problem by "identify(ing) the areas of greatest leverage, vulnerability, and/or possible seeds of the system's destruction" (Gharajedaghi 2011, p. 159). In this sense, the exo-process allows to better specify the ongoing shift from the problem space being an organization-space problem to it being primarily an actor-space problem as a consequence of the postdigital condition, in that "instead of focusing on what individual touchpoints in a specific sequence a generic 'consumer' interacts with", it concerns itself with the broader context of the experience, "the semantic and spatial relationships of its components, their interplay, and the resulting mess" (Resmini and Lindenfalk 2021).

To this extent, the paper introduces the concept of system space; provides a theoretical framing for the adoption of a dialectical approach; examines the ambiguous nature of design problems in design literature; discusses the relevance of dialectics in design disciplines; details an exo-process for the exploration of the dialectic relationship between system space and design space; derived from systems thinking; illustrates said dialectic relationship through the analysis of three design projects.

The first case illustrates the dialectic through a design of a ubiquitous smart home monitoring service with the intention to detect the early onset of disease. The second case illustrates the dialectic through the analysis of a public transportation system where the travel experience was to be improved. Finally, the third case illustrates the dialectic through the redesign of a museal experience. Together, the three cases document the relationship between system space and design space in different domains, how the introduction of system space allows designers to avoid the cognitive trap of self-imposed constraints and overcome the bounded, point-to-point, reductionist approach that characterizes design space in traditional design processes.

2 The System Space of Design

The introduction of an exo-process implies the existence of a process space outside of design space: we suggest that this space, that we call system space, engages in a dialectical relationship with traditional design space.

Design theory has long embraced processes that configure "an iterative interplay" to 'fix' a problem from the problem space and to 'search' plausible solutions from the corresponding solution space" (Maher et al. 1996). In such processes, "designers gain new insights into the problem (and the solution) which ultimately result in the formation of a new view" in which both "the problem and the solution are redefined" (Logan and Smithers 1993). This approach posits that design processes are conversational in nature and do not configure "a linear logical progression" but rather "a circular process of discursive exchange" in which "the pursuit of the design problem coincides with the discovery of its solution" (Beckett 2017). This means that, within design space, the problem space and the solution space also engage in a dialectical relationship of complementarity.

An important theoretical contribution to the concept of a dialectic relationship between a system space and the design space is the one provided by Jones (1992, p. xxvi) with his formalization of the design "process", concerned with thinking and making, and the "procedure", concerned with the paperwork and with milestones, as two distinct activities obeying very different logics: a free-form, creative movement the former, and a rigid, orderly and timely directed flow the latter. Another important contribution comes from systems thinking and the conceptual framing it offers for dealing with complex, non-linear, ill-determined problems as webs of relationships. More specifically, with the problems of assessing boundaries (Meadows 2008) and of handling multiple scales and perspectives (Armson 2011).

Similarly, design practice has repeatedly demonstrated how design problems are not properly determined until a solution is determined (Beckett 2017). Tentatives to formulate such a proposition in logical terms in design theory encounter formal obstacles, since solutions are deduced by establishing a problem first, and temporal obstacles, since the "design solution appears to determine the premises from which it is deduced" (Beckett 2017).

The use of a dialectical approach allows to resolve these temporal and formal paradoxes that currently frame design conceptualizations and "helps explain the underlying logical passage from problem to solution by presenting both as moments of the same concept" (Beckett 2017). This resonates with Jones' own dialectic description of "process" and "procedure", since "movement from moment to moment ought not be considered a temporal succession", but rather a possibility to "jump around in any sequence" (Jones 1992, p. xxvi).

Even more importantly, from a systemic perspective, the "process", requiring thinking and making, is not "self-propelled": concepts do not think themselves, artifact do not make themselves, but are rather "the result of the active involvement of a thinking subject", which in turn illuminates the "nature and extent of the designer's subjective intervention into the design scenario" (Beckett 2017) and how this effectively reconfigures the design problem. This in contrast with "procedure" as formalized by Jones and characterized by simple progression through time happening constantly and independently of action or thought.

A dialectical relationship is characterized by contradiction, the "dynamic interplay between unified opposites" that represent these different "moments of the same concept" rather than two entirely different concepts. These unified opposites are interdependent, as each one defines the other, and while "one may predominate at any particular point in time or space" both are "simultaneously present and functioning" (Montgomery 1993). Central to this notion of unified opposition is mutual negation, by means of which the opposites are generated (Lee 1947).

When applied to the design process, this interactive whole (Altman et al. 1981) configures opposition as complementarity, in the sense that the two opposites, the system space and design space pair but also problem space and solution space as specifications of design space itself, dynamically regulate and modulate connection and autonomy. Without a connection, "relationships have no identity and so cannot exist": without autonomy, opposites "have no identity and so cannot exist in a relationship" (Montgomery 1993).

   System space and design space can then be represented as "two portions of a more extended space" whose discontinuity also implies a "notion of contact between them" (Denis 2018, p. 25) that is expressed by means of a dialectical relationship. This "more extended space" is the space where the experience of actors unfolds (Benyon and Resmini 2017) and whose information architecture constitutes the second-order machine that design interventions have to challenge to produce change (Fig. 2).

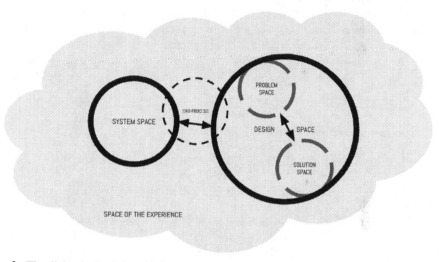

Fig. 2. The dialectical relationship between system space and design space within the space of the experience

3   Theoretical Foundations

The concept of a system space builds on Jones' (1992) differentiation between process and procedure in design work and on the parallel idea that different scales, or orders of magnitude, reveal different structures (Eames and Eames 1977; Armson 2011; Spool 2018). It also draws from the information architecture approach to "dissolving the second-order machine" that is responsible for "generating undesirable patterns of behavior" that maintain and recreate the current homeostasis described in Resmini and Lindenfalk (2021) and based on Gharajedaghi (2011).

   Jones argues that "procedure" focuses on keeping track of what designers are doing in respect to a formal project's timeline, and that "process" is instead centered on the act of designing itself (Jones 1992, p. xxvi). We posit that system space is a necessary conceptual part of "process" in the postdigital condition as design space imposes arbitrary, organization-centric boundaries and limitations that do not account for the lived experience of the actors at play (Resmini and Lindenfalk 2021). These boundaries and limitations act as invisible cognitive traps (Lawson 2005) that prevent designers from identifying those vital relationships that connect design space to what exists outside of it.

In system space, designers move from a deictic, designer- and organization-centered view typical of design space, with its cognitive and procedural traps, to an allocentric, bird's eye view that allows to capture the individual choreographies of actors and the relationships between the various elements that exist within the larger context in which the design space resides.

Systemically, this broader view acquired with the formalization of system space introduces variations in scale or granularity in the level of inquiry that provide insights that cannot be obtained within the boundaries of problem space. The intentional dialectical movement forces designers to alternatively "focus on detail or (…) the context" (Armson 2011, p. 36), zooming out and in as "process" suggests, in order to uncover the systemic behavior embedded in the second-order machine hidden in system space (Gharajedaghi 2011), thus decisively contributing to the exploration of the problems that exist in design space.

3.1 Problems in Design Disciplines

Simon (1996) stipulated that design problems are essentially well-defined and should be derived through the act of omitting irrelevant features and only including relevant ones in order to build a problem space and hence an understanding of how to solve the problem.

Building on Rittel and Webber (1973), who claim design problems to be "wicked" in nature and embedded in a web of complexity that makes its formulation in simple terms impossible, Buchanan (1992) rather sees proposing a solution to a problem as an act through which the designer "must discover or invent a particular subject out of the problems and issues of specific circumstances", therefore making "any solution proposed (…) as much an argument for its own applicability as it is a logical solution to the problem, implying a rhetorical rather than a logical relation" (Beckett 2017).

Krippendorff expands on this notion, noting that "artifacts are not necessarily good for everyone, and aid not just individuals but influence also how they live together" (2005, p. 25). This implies more than just avoiding impairing someone else's life and, for larger communal problems, poses a problem of consensus (Agre 2000). Design then should produce improvements that "must be understandable and decidable by those affected, not imposed by lone designers or authorities who are not acknowledged by the community in question", because "artifacts must make sense to most, ideally to all of those who have a stake in them" (Krippendorff, 2005, p. 26).

Drawing on Ryle (1949), Lawson advances a definition of design as a polymorphous activity (Lawson 2005, p. 130). Lawson contends that design is a complex and specialized form of thinking, not merely "a" way of thinking but "several", whose general characteristic is that of generating a matching problem-solution pairing in which the problem is as designed as the solution is (Lawson 2005).

Cross (1990; 2006) and Dorst (2010) have also argued that the relationship between design problem and design solution cannot be understood without considering that design professions think in a radically different way from professions purely based on analysis and problem-solving. The problematic situation is co-evolved along with the solution using methods and processes that "have been professionalized in the design disciplines" (Dorst 2010) and that rely on abductive reasoning, implying that reasonable assumptions are used to advance from one to the other, evaluate and refine until a satisfactory novel form is produced that also reframes the original problem.

More recent theories based on problem-solving approaches have also abandoned any notion of problem and solution as discrete phases of a linear process and instead posit a model of design as "an iterative interplay to 'fix' a problem from the problem space and to 'search' plausible solutions from the corresponding solution space" (Beckett 2017). Examples of such logic include, but are not limited to, the double diamond (Design Council 2007) or the "pencil" model (Gray et al. 2010).

These views all lead to a human-centered concept of design that radically departs from Simon's seminal and influential definition and that does not shy away from ill-defined, ill-determined, ethically ambiguous questions, opening the door to generally framing postdigital design questions as systemic messes.

3.2 Dialectics in Design Disciplines

Dialectic relationships between opposites are at the heart of design discourse. "Form" and "function" (Sullivan 1896) or "less" and "more" (Filler 2007, p. 50) are probably two of those that have acquired a degree of recognition outside of design conversations, but the tension between what presently is and what ought to be, inherent in having to create something new by observing what already exists, and the fact that "designers are not just dependent on the future, they also help to create it" (Lawson 2005, p. 116), has resulted in a vast collection of reciprocally validating pairs. After all, "the very concept of the situation as problematic could not exist if it were not placed in contradiction to another situation deemed preferable" (Beckett 2017).

Their opposition clearly configures contradiction through negation in a dialectical sense (Beckett 2017): the elements in these pairs remain part of the same concept and cannot be separated and still be understood. When Mies van der Rohe stipulates that "less is more", none of these two opposites can be properly understood, in design terms, outside of the validation they reciprocally provide to each other. They are a single concept engaged in a dialectical relationship.

Norman posits similar oppositions by framing design as a craft and practice on one side, and as a mode of thinking where cognitive processes are imbued with emotional responses and intuitions on the other (2016). In addition, Norman and Ortony (2003) place emphasis on the dialectic between the designer's perspective on what is being designed and the user's perspective on what is being designed. It is through the interactions between the designer and the user that the problem space is explored.

Rittel and Webber (1984) introduce a conception of design that accommodates for indeterminacy and the participation of multiple actors in the design process. Working with planners of large social systems, Rittel and Weber recognized that Simon-like problem-solving could not provide guidance where individuals, organizations, and communities are involved, because "the information needed to understand (an ill-defined) problem depends upon one's idea for solving it" (1984, p. 136). In doing so, they not only pointed out the specific nature of problems in the social realm, which are only temporarily resolved through consensus only to resurface later on as different conflicts that call for further resolution (Rittel and Webber 1984), but dialectically engaged so-called "tame" problems with wicked problems.

This conversational nature of the design process, that requires some degree of consensus, requires discursive exchanges evolving non-linearly and "usually held via a medium such (as) paper and pencil, with an other (either an 'actual' other or oneself acting as an other) as the conversational partner" (Glanville 1999). It also means a movement from implicit to explicit, something Schön (1992) connected to what he called the reflexive aspects of design, and configuring yet another dialectic relationship.

Wurman (2017) highlights a similar juxtaposition between what we know and what we don't know, stipulating that we can only understand something new in comparison to something we already understand. "Understanding" is central to Wurman's focus on "making the complex clear", and clearly establishing another dialectic relationship between known and unknown as elements of the design process, since "determining the situation as it ought to be necessarily determines the situation as it is, as no ought can be determined without positing a difference in the is" (Beckett 2017). Armson (2011) maintains a similar position affirming that any and all interactions between an agent and a system influence both the system and the agent, constantly introducing change that represents both a consequence of previous behavior and a disruptive element that requires system-wide adjustments.

The dialectic between system space and design space can then be formulated as an intentional movement of inquiry between the two spaces, at varying levels of detail and abstraction, with the intention to structure the relationships that shape the space of the experience and acquire a richer understanding of both system and design space. This can be accomplished by means of the exo-process.

3.3   The Exo-Process and System Space

According to Gharajedaghi, "the obstructions that prevent a system from facing its current reality are self-imposed". This resonates with the cognitive traps of design space: these obstructions are hidden and "reside at the core of our perceptions and find expression in mental models, assumptions, and images" that "set us up, shape our world, and chart our future. They are responsible for preserving the system as it is and frustrate its efforts to become what it can be". (Gharajedaghi 2011, p. 159).

This formulation of the mess, that is capturing the "dynamic behavior of a system" (Gharajedaghi 2011, p. 159), happens in system space, is cognate of what Ackoff called "idealized design" (Ackoff 1993), and is identified by Resmini and Lindenfalk as the overlap of the prescriptive, organization-constrained vision of the initial problem space, and the emergent, actor-driven actualization of the multiple ecosystems of which the problem space is one of the constituents (2021).

To formulate the mess first and to resolve the mess second, we adapt as a foundational part of the exo-process Gharajedaghi's three-part systemic inquiry centered on searching, mapping, and telling the story in order to "capture the iterative nature of the multiple feedback loops by demonstrating the nature of interdependencies in the system" and how its "future (is) implicit in the present behavior" (Gharajedaghi 2011, p. 159).

Searching is meant to produce knowledge about the system, its environment, and "why it does what it does". It formally consists of three steps: systems analysis, obstruction analysis, and systems dynamics. These respectively produce a snapshot describing the "structural, functional, and behavioral aspects" of the system, identify where and how the system malfunctions, and illuminate not only "what is wrong but also about how we got there".

Elements identified during the obstruction analysis represent first-degree obstacles whose reinforcing interactions "produce second-order obstructions" that negatively impact the information architecture of the system and prevent change, contributing to "'generating undesirable patterns of behavior' that maintain and recreate the current homeostasis" (Resmini and Lindenfalk 2021).

Mapping produces a synthesis of the elements, issues, obstructions, and drivers identified during searching. Categories are created and a structure imposed on the mess, so that relationships can be examined and understood. Visual representations of these relationships among the elements constituting the system are necessary to capture their interdependence.

Telling the story means "formulating and disseminating the mess", and it is "a significant step toward solving it". The production of knowledge about and of the mess is a necessary moment in dissolving it: "a believable and compelling story (…) reveals the undesirable future implicit in the current state" laying the foundations for "a desire for change" (Gharajedaghi 2011, p. 166).

More pragmatically, if we consider system space as the allocentric space for those systemic explorations that are necessary to instantiate a dialectic relationship with design space, the exo-process acts as a conduit for the identification and formalization of said relationship and the assessment of the overall architecture of the experience across system space and design space. By means of the exo-process, designers can identify its ontology, or possibly its multiple ontologies, its topology (Benyon 2014), and the way actors perform their personal choreographies in pursuit of a desired future state (Resmini and Lindenfalk 2021).

4 Dialectics: Three Cases

The three cases briefly discussed hereafter exemplify aspects of the dialectic relationship between system space and design space. The cases span design research and practice across different industries and will not be examined in detail: after providing a necessary but synthetic overview, focus will be on the analysis of those elements that pertain to discussing the conceptual framing proposed in this paper. For a more in-depth account of their individual instances, we defer to the original sources (Hobbs 2013; Lindenfalk and Vimarlund 2017; Lindenfalk and Imre 2019; Lindenfalk and Resmini 2019; Resmini et al. 2021).

4.1 Healthcare

The Healthy Life support through Comprehensive Tracking of individual and Environmental Behaviours (HELICOPTER) was a project in the Fifth Call in the Ambient

Assisted Living Programme funded by the European Union. The call addressed ICT-based solutions for the (self-)management of daily life activities of older adults at home. Within this space, HELICOPTER aimed at inferring end-users' healthiness simply and unobtrusively, through the monitoring of daily life behaviors, and at supporting end-users and their caregivers with feedback, advice, and motivation in pursuing a healthy and safe lifestyle. The project addressed people over 65 that did not suffer from major chronic diseases or severe disabilities, yet could possibly be affected by (or be at risk of) metabolic or circulatory malfunctioning such as hypertension or mild diabetes, or by mild cognitive deficits.

The project brief required the design of a ubiquitous smart service that could constantly monitor and measure a person's activity in order to detect the early onset of disease, and provide a direct connection to healthcare institutions and professionals in case of need. Besides technical challenges connected to managing the data flows, the design team's primary goal was to seamlessly and unobtrusively integrate the service with the everyday life routines of the elderly.

A first dialectic relationship between the structuring and presentation of the data collected from the sensors and its connection to the self-image of the person being monitored, affecting motivation (to change or persevere), became apparent during the exploration of the problem space. Their contradiction led the designer to realize that the "problem" was much more complex than what it initially appeared to be: any "solution" to the structuring and presentation of data would have repercussions on how the person reading the data would act or react.

A second dialectic relationship existed between establishing what should be monitored and processed for the service to successfully deliver its value proposition and a user's personal social sphere, affecting both their intentions of use and their usage patterns. The prototyping phase showed that social relationships and their associated spatial patterns (such as eating out, spending time outside, or living elsewhere for part of the year) profoundly affected service use.

A third dialectic relationship existed between designing for a current state and designing for a future, unknown state. The service was meant to monitor healthy individuals and detect early onsets of disease, notifying the person and the appropriate healthcare institution in such a case. However, the service was supposed to keep monitoring the person after onset to report any improvements or deteriorations: this meant that, contrary to what the brief stated, the service was supposed to cater to the needs and wants of both healthy elderly individuals and chronically ill elderly individuals.

All of these dialectic relationships pointed at the necessity to break free of the constraints of design space to embrace a systemic approach centered on how data could motivate a person to act healthier and make healthier choices in their day-to-day life, and that such a goal cannot be achieved via the initial reductionistic framing in which "data" excluded the ill-defined social and personal daily routines of individual users. While a specific solution was explored in design space, additional factors pointed at larger, unexplored systemic relationships that greatly influenced the ability of the service to deliver value, requiring a thorough exploration of system space to shed light on the inner workings of the second-order machine structuring the user's experience in their using the service to live a healthier life.

4.2 Mobility

The second case concerns the public transport system in Augsburg, Germany and addresses the restructuring and redesign of co-modal mobility with a focus on sustainability and the traveler's experience. Augsburg is a university city of 300.000 inhabitants in the southwest of Germany. Stadtwerke Augsburg (swa) runs a number of public transportation and shared mobility services, including bike-sharing and car-sharing. Stadtwerke Augsburg decided to develop a shared mobility service with the aim to create a tightly connected chain in which all modes of mobility offered come from the same provider. Access was provided through a subscription model called Mobil-Flat. When services from different providers are bundled together as part of a shared mobility system (see e.g. Whim!), the individual providers are reluctant to renounce their brand name: the city of Augsburg however branded the entire Mobil-Flat offer as a swa Augsburg initiative.

Mobil-Flat was launched in 2019 as a city-wide flat rate that could be used across all of swa's mobility services for a fixed monthly fee. On 1 January 2020, the City Zone was applied in Augsburg city center. This model, now suspended, which made using all local public transport free of charge in a certain area of the city, was at the time unique in Germany. The city of Augsburg and Stadtwerke Augsburg, which were jointly responsible for the introduction of the City Zone, hoped that the policy would result in a number of well-being- and sustainability-related positive effects, such as improving the air quality in the city center by reducing motorized private transport (Resmini et al. 2021).

A first dialectic relationship existed between improving the public transportation system, populated by multiple actors pursuing their own different goals and visions, and reinforcing any of these individual actors' dominance within the mobility space. Although the aim of swa was to unite all mobility services in Augsburg under one single umbrella, each individual part of the Mobil Flat transportation system (car-sharing, bike-sharing, tram and busses) was still designed in partial isolation and within the boundaries of the respective, organization-determined, design spaces.

An example of these boundaries can be appreciated in the difference between the bike-sharing branch and the car-sharing branch of the service. swa was the original driver behind the creation and development of the latter: they created and directly controlled the booking and locking systems, the fleet, and the mobile app. Based on then current contractual agreements with the provider, swa had no insight into the bike-sharing app (use, diffusion, data), fleet status, and booking system, factually finding themselves in the position of being a customer rather than a provider to the bike-sharing branch. This severely constrained any possibility to create a seamless and unified user experience and deeply constrained any systemic improvement to the overall customer experience of the swa service.

A second dialectic relationship existed between the desire to improve individual elements within the mobility system and the lack of acknowledgment of their mutual relationships. Interviews conducted with people traveling using Mobil Flat showed that this unexplored contradiction caused them to develop ad hoc coping mechanisms, from avoiding certain co-modal combinations to downloading multiple independent mobile apps in an effort to fill user experience gaps or simply be able to use the service (Resmini et al. 2021).

The case in Augsburg, Germany sheds light on the constraints imposed on the design process by the social and economic constructs embedded in the system and how a design process conforming to the boundaries of the design space neglects to see the connections between various actors and modalities and how they, in turn, affect the experience by hampering changes to its second-order machine.

4.3   Culture

In 2012 and 2013, a locally coordinated international and multidisciplinary team comprising designers, researchers, marketing firms, architectural firms, gallery administrators and staff, and students from the Faculty of Arts, Design, and Architecture at the University of Johannesburg, was engaged in a redesign project for the Johannesburg Art Gallery (JAG) in Johannesburg, South Africa.

The JAG is home to one of the largest art collections on the continent, with paintings and sculptures bridging 19th and 20th century Europe and modern-day Africa. It is located in downtown Johannesburg, in what was at the time of the project a particularly troubled and unsafe neighborhood close to the railway lines and on the edge of Joubert Park. The gallery had long suffered from access and visibility issues, and these in turn had resulted in a systemic shortage of attention, visitors, funding, and resources.

The project design brief included the task of providing solutions that could minimize or resolve the problems of visibility and access of the gallery and make it into a viable proposition that could engage local, national, and international support: the research team framed the problem space as part of the larger wicked problems grounded in the social reality of Johannesburg.

Particular attention was devoted to producing milestone results that could be scientifically communicated and disseminated, and to research, document, and demonstrate how local, point-to-point interventions meant to resolve individual issues as they emerged were steadily weakening any chance of producing positive, long-term change (Hobbs 2013). There was a need to redefine the problem to define its solution, asking different questions so that different boundaries could be drawn (Meadows 2008).

A major dialectic relationship emerged as the design team progressively gained an understanding of the key civic and ethical values at play, including for example those related to the economic and cultural position of black culture in post-apartheid South Africa, that could not be conflated with the simple production and delivery of a measurable business outcome to a few stakeholders. As the project progressed, the team moved away from considering the information architecture that was taking shape a design space solution that should, necessarily and immediately, be turned into actionable design deliverables for a new set of point-to-point interventions, and "fought the idea that (it) would be a website, or a mobile app, or an addition to the gallery (…) (T)he design solution is the resolution of the problem. The design artifacts can be either a website or a new room" (Hobbs 2013).

The Johannesburg case illustrates the dialectical opposition between social change and long-standing cultural structures that emerged through the information architecture that structurally tried to describe the underlying systemic behavior, outlining the tension emerging between system space insights and design space, organizationally-centered goals pointing instead at a rapid identification of point-to-point interventions in the absence of the explicit movement between the two enabled by the exo-process.

5 Discussion and Final Considerations

This paper contributes to the current understanding in design disciplines of the effect of "systemic" ways of thinking on the design process (Jones 2014; Irwin 2015; Tonkinwise 2015; Sevaldson 2011) from a design theory point of view. We argue that a systemic perspective cannot simply be "added" to the design process and that addressing postdigital complexity, producing solutions to contemporary design problems, requires its own explicit process, its own space, to be acknowledged, practiced, and formalized just like the design process has been acknowledged, practiced, and formalized as its own mode of thinking (Cross 1990, 2006; Dorst 2010; Norman 2016).

Therefore, the paper explores the existence of system space as a dialectical opposite of design space, to which it provides a way to escape its cognitive traps (Lawson 2005), and stipulates that their relationship can be apprehended by means of an exo-process adapted from systems thinking (Gharajedaghi 2011).

The paper builds on the notion that the ongoing blending of digital and physical (Institute for the Future 2009) and the emergence of a postdigital culture (Kirby 2009; Resmini and Lindenfalk 2021) have challenged the current procedural (Jones 1992) relationship between problem and solution as the preferred approach to solve complex problems. In the paper, we define the dialectic relationship between system space and design space as an intentional movement of inquiry between the two spaces, at varying levels of detail and abstraction, with the intention to structure the relationships that shape the space of the experience (Benyon 2014) and acquire a richer understanding of both system and design space.

The concept of dialectic relationship builds on Beckett (2017). Concepts in a dialectic relationship are said to be in an opposition that configures contradiction through negation, meaning that they mutually validate each other's identity while remaining part of the same concept (Beckett 2017). As much as we understand something in relation to something else, concepts in dialectic relationships cannot be separated and still be understood. A dialectic relationship exists between problem space and solution space, as one implies the other. But the very existence of design space, traditionally intended as the sum of the problem and solution spaces, also implies the existence of another space, that we identify as system space, and that engages in a dialectic relationship with it.

Once dialectically established, system space can be formalized and integrated into design practice more explicitly to overcome the limitations embedded within traditional approaches to design space. The three cases dealing with healthcare, mobility, and culture, provide insights into contradictions and opposition pairs (Montgomery 1993) embedded in the design process, and specifically residing in design space, that illuminate the existence, and necessity, of system space.

For example, the physical, environmental and social contradictions weighing on motivational aspects (healthcare case); the lack of acknowledgment of the relationships existing between individual elements from an information and an activity point of view (mobility case); and the opposition between social change and long-standing cultural structures (culture case).

System space is closely related to the second-order machine structuring the space of experience (Benyon 2014; Resmini and Lindenfalk 2021) and the systems thinking acts of searching, mapping and telling the story (Gharajedaghi 2011), that the paper adapts under the concept of the exo-process. The dialectic relationships identified in the cases hint at the existence of elements of problem space or solution space that escape the boundaries of design space and that cannot be understood, explained, or resolved from within it: the extension of the design process to system space and the adoption of the exo-process allow designers to unveil system behaviors, identify the structure of the second-order machine, and help them situate design as a systemic activity in its own right.

The dialectical relationships identified in the cases do not only hint at the existence of a system space for design, but also provide further evidence that new media design practices are ill-equipped for an easy transition towards systemic ways of doing. Organizational structures, legacy methods, and processes that reinforce linearity and reductionism variously constrain, hinder or dissuade from systemic approaches in all of the cases, often reproducing product design logic in their address of the object of design as finite, finished, and artificially constrained within organizational boundaries (Lindenfalk and Resmini 2016) that are made to coincide with design space.

The existence, usefulness, and necessity of system space may not be self-evident to designers residing in design space unless they either consciously reflect upon and affirm their influence on its formulation (Beckett 2017) or they introduce changes into the system, for example by prototyping and testing a possible solution, that unbalance design space so that the existence of system-wide, non-linear connections or loops are brought to their attention. We submit that the intentional inclusion of the exo-process as part of the free-form activities constituting "process" according to Jones (1992) helps avoid the cognitive traps (Lawson 2005) inherent within design space as traditionally framed and clarify the existence, and necessity, of system space.

References

Ackoff, R.: Idealized design: creative corporate visioning. Omega **21**(4), 401–410 (1993). https://doi.org/10.1016/0305-0483(93)90073-t

Agre, P.E.: Notes on the New Design Space. http://polaris.gseis.ucla.edu/pagre/ (2000)

Akin, Ö., Akin, C.: Frames of reference in architectural design: analysing the hyperacclamation (A-h-a-!). Des. Issues **17**(4) (1996)

Altman, I, Vinsel, A., Brown, B.: Dialectic conceptions in social psychology: an application to social penetration and privacy regulation. In: Berkovitz, L. (ed.) Advances in Experimental Social Psychology, vol. 14. Academic Press (1981)

Armson, R.: Growing Wings on the Way: Systems Thinking for Messy Situations. Triarchy Press Limited (2011)

Beckett, S.J.: The logic of the design problem: a dialectical approach. Des. Issues **33**(4) (2017). https://doi.org/10.1162/DESI_a_00470

Benyon, D.: Spaces of Interaction, Places for Experience. Morgan and Claypool (2014)

Benyon, D., Resmini, A.: User experience in cross-channel ecosystems. In: Proceedings of the British HCI Conference 2017, Sunderland (2017)

Buchanan, R.: Wicked problems in design thinking. Des. Issues **8**(2) (1992)

Cross, N.: The nature and nurture of design ability. Des. Stud. **11**(3), 127–140 (1990). https://doi.org/10.1016/0142-694x(90)90002-t

Cross, N.: Designerly Ways of Knowing. Springer (2006)

Curedale, R.: Design Thinking: Process and Methods, 5th edn. Design Community College (2019)

Denis, M.: Space and Spatial Cognition. Routledge (2018)

Design Council: A Study of the Design Process. https://www.designcouncil.org.uk/sites/default/files/asset/document/ElevenLessons_Design_Council%20(2).pdf (2007)

Dorst, K.: The nature of design thinking. In: Proceedings of DTRS8, 8th Design Thinking Research Symposium, pp. 131–139 (2010)

Eames, C., Eames, R.: Powers of Ten. YouTube. https://www.youtube.com/watch?v=0fKBhvDjuy0 (1977)

Filler, M.: Makers of modern architecture. The New York Review of Books (2007)

Gharajedaghi, J.: Systems Thinking: Managing Chaos and Complexity: A Platform for Designing Business Architecture. Morgan Kaufmann (2011)

Glanville, R.: Researching design and designing research. Des. Issues **15**(2) (1999)

Gray, D., Brown, S., Macalufo, J.: Gamestorming: A Playbook for Innovators, Rulebreakers, and Changemakers. O'Reilly (2010)

Jones, J.C.: Design Methods. Van Nostrand Reinhold (1992)

Jones, P.H.: Systemic design principles for complex social systems. In: Metcalf, G.S. (ed.) Social Systems and Design. TSS, vol. 1, pp. 91–128. Springer, Tokyo (2014). https://doi.org/10.1007/978-4-431-54478-4_4

Hobbs, J.: Research Summary and Strategic Recommendations for the Johannesburg Art Gallery. Johannesburg Art Gallery Internal Report (2013)

Institute for the Future: Blended Reality. https://www.iftf.org/uploads/media/SR-122~2.PDF (2009)

Irwin, T.: Transition design: a proposal for a new area of design practice, study, and research. Des. Cult. **7**(2), 229–246 (2015). https://doi.org/10.1080/17547075.2015.1051829

Kirby, A.: Digimodernism. Continuum (2009)

Krippendorff, K.: The Semantic Turn. CRC Press (2005)

Lawson, B.: How Designers Think, 4th edn. Routledge (2005)

Lee, O.: Dialectic and negation. Rev. Metaphys. **1**(1), 3–23. http://www.jstor.org/stable/20123087 (1947)

Lindenfalk, B., Imre, Ö.: Narratives of value co-creation: elderly's understanding of their own role in the value creation process. In: Proceedings of the 27th European Conference on Information Systems (ECIS), Stockholm, Uppsala. https://aisel.aisnet.org/ecis2019_rp/133 (2019)

Lindenfalk, B., Resmini, A.: Blended spaces, cross-channel ecosystems, and the myth that is services. In: Proceedings of ServDes 2016. Aalborg University (2016)

Lindenfalk, B., Resmini, A.: Mapping an ambient assisted living service as a seamful cross-channel ecosystem. In: Pfannstiel, M., Rasche, M. (eds.) Service Design and Service Thinking in Healthcare and Hospital Management: Theory, Concepts, Practice, pp. 289–314. Springer, New York (2019). https://doi.org/10.1007/978-3-030-00749-2_17

Lindenfalk, B., Vimarlund, V.: Guidance through use: value as a pathfinder in e-health services implementation. In: 16th World Congress of Medical and Health Informatics: Precision Healthcare through Informatics (MedInfo 2017). Hangzhou (CN) (2017)

Logan, B., Smithers, T.: Creativity and design as exploration. In: Gero, J.S., Maher, M.L. (eds.) Modelling Creativity and Knowledge-Based Creative Design. Lawrence Erlbaum (1993)

Maher, M.L., Poon, J., Boulanger, S.: Formalising design exploration as co-evolution. In: Gero, J.S., Sudweeks, F. (eds.) Advances in Formal Design Methods for CAD. ITIFIP, pp. 3–30. Springer, Boston, MA (1996). https://doi.org/10.1007/978-0-387-34925-1_1

Meadows, D.H.: Thinking in Systems: A Primer. Chelsea Green Publishing (2008)

Montgomery, B.M.: Relationship maintenance versus relationship change: a dialectical dilemma. J. Soc. Pers. Relat. **10**(2), 205–223 (1993). https://doi.org/10.1177/026540759301000203

Norman, D.A.: The Future of Design: When you come to a fork in the road, take it. Design X – Dieci anni di design a San Marino con uno sguardo ai prossimi cento, pp. 194–207. Quodlibet (2016)

Norman, D.A., Ortony, A.: Designers and users: two perspectives on emotion and design. In: Symposium on Foundations of Interaction Design, pp. 1–13 (2003)

Resmini, A. (ed.): Reframing Information Architecture. HIS, Springer, Cham (2014). https://doi.org/10.1007/978-3-319-06492-5

Resmini, A., Lindenfalk, B.: Mapping experience ecosystems as emergent actor-created spaces. In: Hameurlain, A., Tjoa, A.M., Chbeir, R. (eds.) Transactions on Large-Scale Data- and Knowledge-Centered Systems XLVII. LNCS, vol. 12630, pp. 1–28. Springer, Heidelberg (2021). https://doi.org/10.1007/978-3-662-62919-2_1

Resmini, A., Lindenfalk, B., Simeone, L., Drabble, D.: Using PLR syntax to map experience-based digital/physical ecosystems for strategic systemic change. In: Proceedings of the 23rd HCI International Conference (HCII 2021), Part III (2021)

Resmini, A., Lacerda, F.: The architecture of cross-channel ecosystems: from convergence to experience. In Proceedings of the 8th International Conference on Management of Digital Ecosystems (MEDES16). Hendaye (FR) (2016)

Rittel, H.W.J., Webber, M.M.: Dilemmas in a general theory of planning. Policy Sci. **4**, 155–169 (1973)

Rittel, H.W.J., Webber, M.M.: Planning problems are wicked problems. In: Cross, N. (ed.) Developments in Design Methodology, pp. 135–144. John Wiley & Sons (1984)

Ryle, G.: The Concept of Mind. Hutchinson (1949)

Schön, D.A.: Designing as reflective conversation with the materials of a design situation. Knowl.-Based Syst. **5**(1), 3–14 (1992). https://doi.org/10.1016/0950-7051(92)90020-g

Sevaldson, B.: Giga-mapping: visualisation for complexity and systems thinking in design. In: NORDES, Nordic Design Research Conference 2011, Helsinki (2011)

Simon, H.A.: The Sciences of the Artificial. The MIT Press (1996)

Spool, J.: The Evolution of a New UX Resolution. UI23. https://asset.uie.com/ui23/transcripts/the-evolution-of-a-new-ux-design-resolution.pdf (2018)

Sullivan, L.H.: The Tall Office Building Artistically Considered. Lippincott's Magazine. March. https://archive.org/details/tallofficebuildi00sull (1896)

Tonkinwise, C.: Design for transitions-from and to what? Des. Philos. Pap. **13**(1), 85–92 (2015)

Wurman, R.S.: UnderstandingUnderstanding. RSW & JL Publication (2017)

On Regulation of Over-Registration of Copyright

Jia Liu[1(✉)] [iD] and Sixuan Zheng[2] [iD]

[1] Jiangsu Copyright Research Center, Nanjing University of Science and Technology
School of Intellectual Property, Nanjing 210094, Jiangsu, China
lyuuka@aliyun.com
[2] Jiangsu Copyright Protection Center, Nanjing 210094, Jiangsu, China

Abstract. China enforces a system of voluntary copyright registration, and only carries out formal examination of works. Now in China, over-registration of copyright is very common. Through empirical research, it can be divided into two types of over-registration of the copyright of other' works and over-registration of the copyright of his own works. Over-registration of copyright not only destroys the demonstration effect of copyright registration, but also reduces the public credibility of copyright registration institutions and the evidence effect of copyright registration. Therefore, it should be regulated by a series of measures. Through theoretical and empirical analysis, it is suggested to regulate over-registration of copyright by improving the registration clause of *Copyright Law*, formulating supporting registration measures and unifying registration review standards.

Keywords: Copyright registration · Over-registration · Revision of *Copyright Law* · System improvement

1 Introduction

Most countries in the world have established the system of voluntary registration of copyright, but the effect of copyright registration differs from each other. For example, copyright registration in the USA is a precondition for copyright infringement prosecution while the effect of copyright registration in China is to initially determine the copyright ownership of works [1].

According to laws and regulations about copyright registration, China's copyright registration, in a broad sense, mainly includes the following three types: The first is registration of works, which can be divided into voluntary registration [2] of ordinary works and registration of computer software according to China's regulations about registration of works. The second is copyright transfer registration, which involves a dispute between registration antagonism and registration element essentialism [3]. The third is copyright mortgage registration, which mainly regulates registration of copyright pledge. In order to increase the strictness and pertinence of the research, copyright registration discussed in this paper is only restricted to voluntary registration of ordinary works.

© The Author(s), under exclusive license to Springer Nature Switzerland AG 2022
M. M. Soares et al. (Eds.): HCII 2022, LNCS 13323, pp. 49–56, 2022.
https://doi.org/10.1007/978-3-031-05906-3_4

In China, the copyright automatic acquisition principle makes it difficult to affirm the right ownership of the copyright subject of works. In addition, preliminary evidence effect of copyright registration stimulates different subjects to make copyright registration of works, even causing a large amount of over-registration of copyright in practice. It not only makes it more difficult to affirm the right of copyright subjects of works but also disturbs the copyright registration system and copyright management order. In order to solve the problem, this paper focuses on the research of over-registration of copyright in China and explores a feasible path to regulate over-registration of copyright.

2   Status Quo of Over-Registration of Copyright in China

According to the materials and data about registration and over-registration of copyright obtained through practice, the status quo of over-registration of copyright in China is induced and analyzed as follows.

2.1   Background for Over-Registration of Copyright in China

According to the statistics of National Copyright Administration of China, the total copyright registration in China for 2020 exceeded 5.00 million, with an increase rate of 20.37% as compared with that for 2019. Of it, the total copyright registration of ordinary works (not including software copyright) reached 3.30 million [4]. The total copyright registration for 2019 had an increase rate of 21.09% as compared with that for 2018. Of it, the total copyright registration of ordinary works (not including software copyright) reached 2.70 million [5]. For consecutive two years of 2019 and 2020, Beijing, Shanghai, Copyright Protection Center of China and Jiangsu ranked the top four places respectively in terms of copyright registration increase of China. In recent years, China's copyright registration is keeping on increasing. In 2017 and 2020, photography works had the largest copyright registration. In 2018 and 2019, fine art works had the largest copyright registration (Please see Fig. 1).

On the one hand, China enforces the copyright automatic acquisition principle, which deems the nature of copyright registration as confirmation of the ownership of works rather than administrative authorization. Therefore, the registration authority can only make a formal examination of the copyright registration of ordinary works. Photography and fine art works have the largest registration in China, but these two types are quite controversial in confirmation of creativity and aesthetic artistry. Considering that only formal examination is enforced for copyright registration, over-registration of same or substantially similar works tends to occur for the above two types. On the other hand, China has established a copyright registration management system with national and local copyright bureaus as responsibility subjects and with Copyright Protection Center of China and local copyright protection centers as execution subjects. Copyright Protection Center of China and local copyright protection centers are public institutions or social organizations approved to be established by national or local copyright bureaus, mainly executing registration of works. If necessary, each local copyright bureau can set primary-level organizations for executing detailed registration work. For example, in Jiangsu Province, copyright workstations are set in each city/district and county. National

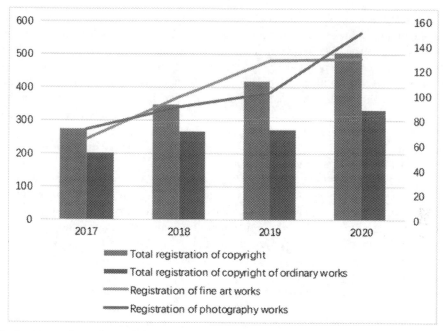

Fig. 1. Comparison of copyright r egistration in China for 2017–2020 (Unit: ten thousand pieces)

and local copyright bureaus are responsible for audit of copyright registration, award-ing of certificates and filing of copyright contracts. Copyright registration certificates awarded by national and each local copyright registration authority have completely the same effect, so there is over-registration of the same works in different registration authorities.

2.2 Main Circumstances of Over-Registration of Copyright in China

Based on the above analysis of China's existing copyright registration management system and copyright registration in national and local copyright registration author-ities, over-registration of copyright in China can be divided into the following two circumstances.

Over-registration of the copyright of other' works. According to investigations, it can be divided into two cases. One is over-registration of others' influential works. Specifically, some registrants or copyright registration agencies will apply for registration of works with a certain influence or economic value for gaining illegitimate benefits. For example, after the American marvel movie Spider-Man was shown in China, someone applied for registration of fine art works containing Spider-Man the next day. However, Spider-Man had been registered for copyright in America and its copyright should be protected in China because both China and America are member countries of Berne Convention. The other case is unintentional registration of others' works. It can be divided into the following two circumstances. The first is that the works independently created by an author happen to be others' works already registered. In this circumstance, according to the principle that works registered first will gain evidence effect first, the author applying for registration later cannot be registered but still hold the copyright. The second is over-registration caused by copyright ownership disputes, that is, the registrant himself thinks that the works have copyright but in fact, the copyright belongs to others. For example, when an author transfers the copyright of his works several times, different transferees will think that they have the copyright and apply for registration. In this circumstance, there are different rules for affirming and handling copyright ownership. However, in China, a contract must be signed for ownership transfer, so in juridical practice, the rule that "the earlier transferee will gain the right" in applicable sales contracts will be followed in general.

Over-registration of the copyright of his own works. According to investigations, it mainly includes over-registration before obtaining the certificate for registration of works and over-registration after obtaining the certificate for registration of works. The first means that after submitting a registration application to a registration authority, the registrant submits another copyright registration application to other registration authorities before obtaining the registration certificate. Due to auditing cycle of registration, different registration authorities receiving registration application will award registration certificates independently due to a time gap of audit and different registration standards. The second means that after obtaining the certificate for registration of works, the registrant makes over-registration of his same works in other copyright registration authorities. In practice, in order to obtain a registration agency expense, some copyright registration agencies lie to the right holder that copyright registration certificates awarded by national and local copyright bureaus have different effects, seducing the right holder to make over-registration of his registered works in different places. In ordinary cases, a registration authority will claim in the registration announcement and Q&A that registration is for free and that all certificates for copyright registration have the same effect. However, some copyright registration agencies will claim the locality of registration certificates in order to gain a high commission fee for registration of works.

3 Necessity for Regulating Over-Registration of Copyright

Copyright registration is not a precondition for gaining copyright; however, if not infringing priority right, over-registration of copyright will not affect the obtainment copyright of ordinary works. Therefore, the large quantity of over-registration of copyright in practice has not aroused enough concern in practice and theoretical circles. However, copyright registration is not only an important path for publicizing copyright ownership of works but also a core content of public service function about copyright performed by copyright administrations at all levels. It is very necessary to regulate over-registration of copyright.

3.1 To Regulate Over-Registration of Copyright Is a Preconditioned Element for Promoting the Development of the Copyright Industry

Under the condition of market economy, to affirm property ownership is a precondition for fair transaction of properties. Property transaction is the foundation for realizing property value, which is a basic element for formation and benign development of an industry. Therefore, in the copyright transaction market, the more definite the copyright ownership is, the lower the risk of copyright transaction, the more flourishing the copyright industry.

As compared with other types of intellectual property, copyright ownership is the hardest to be affirmed. In the present copyright transaction market, the copyright ownership is mainly affirmed by certificate for copyright registration or presumption of copyright subject. In view of the evidence effect of copyright registration, the right holder recorded in the certificate for copyright registration is deemed as the copyright subject. When there is no certificate for copyright registration, the copyright subject will be presumed according to the signature of works or other ownership proofs. However, over-registration of copyright produces two or more certificates for copyright registration and arouses a dispute about copyright ownership. Therefore, only to regulate over-registration of copyright can we lower the risk of copyright transaction and maintain the order of the copyright transaction market.

3.2 To Regulate Over-Registration of Copyright Is Beneficial to Maintaining Public Credibility and Stability of the Right

From the perspective of international comparison, the copyright registration in Germany, having the same effect as that in China, also serves as a preliminary evidence for affirming copyright ownership. It can be said that the copyright systems of both countries have a common source. The copyright law regulation of Germany serves as a model for formulating the copyright law of China. Germany's copyright theory, especially the theory on right of personality of copyright profoundly influenced the establishment of China's copyright theory system. According to Germany's copyright law theory, copyright is deemed as a right for protecting the communication between human beings meeting specific conditions [7]. In the era of market economy, "human beings meeting specific conditions" should be broadly understood as people contributing to the realization of work values, specifically including a person contributing to the generation of works, or the author; a person contributing to the dissemination of works, or the owner of neighboring rights; and a person contributing to the realization of work values, or the copyright operator. This expansion of copyright protection scope can also be applied to China. The copyright law has identified the protection of authors and owners of neighboring rights, while in the copyright transaction market, copyright registration is ownership proof and right guarantee for copyright operators.

Over-registration of copyright not only destroys the demonstration effect of copyright registration but also reduces the public credibility of copyright registration institutions. It makes copyright ownership in an unstable state, hampers copyright holders from claiming and exercising their rights legitimately and harms the reliance interest of relevant subjects of copyright interest and the public. Only to regulate over-registration of copyright can we maintain the right stability of copyright holders and the public credibility of copyright registration institutions.

4   Suggestions on Feasible Paths for Regulating Over-Registration of Copyright

4.1   Improve *Copyright Law* by Setting Special Clauses About Copyright Registration

The new *Copyright Law* formally enforced from Jun. 1ˢᵗ, 2021 has added "Authors and other copyright holders can apply to a registration institution designated by national copyright competent departments for registration of works" to Article 12, and adjusted the clause about copyright pledge registration from the original Article 26 to Article 28. Except for the above, there is no regulation about other copyright registration. The main basis for registration of ordinary works is *Proposed Regulation on Voluntary Registration of Works* promulgated by National Copyright Administration of China in 1994, which identifies the initial proving effect of registration of works and specially stresses that whether a work is registered or not will not affect the automatic acquisition of copyright. Therefore, whether from the perspective of legal hierarchy and systematization of legal norms, or from the perspective of stimulating copyright holders to make a registration, legal norms should be established for copyright registration in *Copyright Law* since the initial proving effect of copyright registration has been identified. To be specific, it can be designed and improved through the following ways.

According to the existing types of copyright registration, make a clear distinction between "copyright registration", "copyright pledge registration" and "copyright transfer registration" in *Copyright Law*. "Copyright registration" should be restricted to "registration of ordinary works". This definition method conforms more to the habit of formulating legal norms about intellectual property. For example, patent or trademark involves transfer and pledge, but "application for patent" in *Patent Law* and "registration of trademark" in *Trademark Law* refer in particular to the right affirmation of that category of intellectual property.

Set several detailed copyright registration clauses respectively. Add Article 3 about "Copyright Registration Effect" to *Copyright Law*, i.e. "Copyright registration is an initial copyright proof and does not affect the obtainment of copyright." At the same time, in order to maintain and follow the existing copyright system, stipulate "copyright transfer registration" and "copyright pledge registration" in Chapter III of *Copyright Law*.

4.2   Promulgate Supporting Methods for Copyright Registration to Regulate Over-Registration

National Copyright Administration of China is suggested to optimize the copyright registration procedure and improve the registration efficiency by promulgating supporting methods for copyright registration as a support and engagement for setting copyright registration clauses in *Copyright Law*. The following settings can be used for regulating over-registration of copyright.

Refine the regulation about cancellation of over-registration. According to Article 5 and Article 6 of *Proposed Regulation on Voluntary Registration of Works* "If the work registration authority finds over-registration, the registration shall be canceled", the copyright registration authority shall have the right to cancel over-registration. Practice has proved that when over-registration of copyright is found, to cancel over-registration of copyright is the most direct and effective remedy. The relevant methods can be refined based on original regulations, identifying that cancellation of over-registration can be made according to the application of the right holder, or actively performed by the copyright registration authority according to its function. The essence of over-registration cancellation is error correction. If over-registration is caused by an audit error of the copyright registration authority, to cancel over-registration is to rectify wrong authorization of copyright; if over-registration is caused by deliberate over-registration application of the right holder, to cancel over-registration is to wipe out the right improperly gained.

Set punitive measures for serious over-registration. The relevant methods should identify the scope of punished objects of over-registration, i.e. behaviors of an individual or organization repeatedly registering his own or others' works for gaining illegitimate benefits, especially "over-registration of works several times" or "registration of others' influential works". The detailed punitive measures are as follows: The first is to establish the "objection against right" mechanism so that the right holder can report the behavior of over-registration to relevant copyright registration authorities. Once the behavior is verified, the registration right of the over-registration subject will be frozen within a definite period. The second is to establish the "integrity registration list" mechanism and to identify and put on file a "blacklist". Among others, individuals or organizations of "over-registration several times" or "registration of others' influential works" should be put on the "blacklist". An object on the "blacklist" should be excluded from registration within a definite period or be reviewed strictly for registration.

4.3 Unify Copyright Registration Review Standards and Promote the Dovetailing of Different Copyright Databases

Disunity of registration standards of copyright registration authorities is an important reason for severe over-registration of copyright. The registration review standards of some registration authorities are very loose while the registration review standards of others are relatively strict. Many registrants will make over-registration in different registration authorities. The essence of the problem concerns the basis for copyright registration. According to traditional theories, copyright registration has no basis because copyright registration does not affect automatic acquisition of copyright. Therefore, registration authorities cannot make a substantive examination of works. However, what the opinion neglects is that copyright should be obtained on the precondition of not infringing others' priority right. Therefore, the standards for formal registration of copyright can be relatively loose but the review standards for copyright ownership proof should be raised and unified. *Notification on Further Standardizing the Procedure of Registration of Works* promulgated by National Copyright Administration in 2011 mentions especially that "The registration authority should improve the information statistics and submission system for registration of works and establish a database for registration of works." For copyright registration review, different registration databases should be compared with each other. At present, copyright database systems have been established in Shanghai,

Tianjinand Jiangsubut the registration data are not interconnected. To promote the dovetailing of copyright databases and unify review standards for copyright registration can reduce over-registration of copyright from the origin.

Acknowledgement. The paper is a research achievement of Youth Project of Humanity and Social Science of Ministry of Education "Study on Copyright Authorization Mechanism toward Digital Publishing" (18YJCZH099), Youth Project of the National Philosophy and Social Science Fund of China "Study on Copyright Authorization Mode in the Era of Omnimedia" (19CXW040) and the "Experienced Teacher Assisting New Teacher" Project for Colleges and Universities of Jiangsu Province (Su Jiao Shi [2021] No. **11**).

References

1. Suo, L.: Introduction to Copyright Registration System. The People's Court Press, Beijing (2015)
2. Yuan, X., Song, L., Zheng, S.: Research on the achievements and problems of registration of works in China. J. Nanjing Univ. Sci. Technol. (Social Sci. Ed.) (10), 12–15+51 (2017)
3. For relevant disputes, please refer to: Bao, H.: Defense and Improvement of Copyright Transfer Registration Antagonism – Comment on Article 59 of *Draft of Amendment to Copyright Law (for Review)*. Sci. Technol. Law (3), 27–33+65 (2019); Xu, X.: Inspection of Copyright Transfer and "Registration Antagonism" – On "Double Selling of Copyright". Graduate Law Rev. (6), 155–156 (2016)
4. National Copyright Administration.: Homepage, http://www.ncac.gov.cn/chinacopyright/contents/12228/353816.shtml. Last accessed 2 Feb 2022
5. Xinhuanet.: The Total National Copyright Registration for 2019 Exceeding 4.18 million. China Intellectual Property News, 27 Mar 2020
6. Suo, L.: Introduction to Copyright Registration System. People's Court Press (2015)
7. Lettl, T.: Copyright Law of Germany, 2nd edn. Translated by Zhang Hailing & Wu Yiyue. Beijing: China Renmin University Press (2019)

The City as a Product of Digital Communication Design

Luís Moreira Pinto[1]([⊠]) [iD] and Emilian Gwiaździński[2] [iD]

[1] CITAD Research Center, from Lusiada University of Lisbon, and UBI University, Covilhã, Portugal
lmoreirapinto.arq@gmail.com

[2] Department of Marketing, Faculty of Management, University of Lodz, Lodz, Poland

Abstract. When we think about the meaning of a city, we all somehow have an idea of what it means, but we can't have a clear image about the city. For that reason, we have to look for some references about those cities that we have seen, in order to be able to build a closer image of reality.

In other words, to be recognised, a city needs to have references that are well known by everyone. For example, how can we talk about Paris without remembering the famous Eiffel Tower? How can we talk about London without linking it to the image of the Big Ben?

Through this article, we aim to describe how cities are recognised nowadays. What icons are associated with them, what monuments or works of art make them highlight and differentiate one from the other, promoting the local linked with the capacity to develop the place.

We know that the use of the internet and the online uploading of images and photos, which have been taken by several persons, are now available on the internet and in platforms such as Instagram. These images are taken by people who somehow want to show a little bit of themselves and of moments which they perceive as being special. For this reason, photos with urban spaces of cities, streets, monuments and works of art are currently one of the great scenarios chosen for the famous selfies or photographs in the form of digital albums, which are saved in the profiles of each person in the social networks.

The cities strongly take advantage of this free publicity to attract more and more visitors and tourists, social networks are now, more than ever, a platform for communication and dissemination of images, of cities and of moments or events, which are based at the city [7].

The urban scenario becomes evident across a large number of personal profiles existing in Instagram and other online platforms. People choose certain places because they know they are easily recognised by everyone, and thus somehow end up being able to tell others that they are in those cities through the photos they post through Instagram.

But in this increasingly global and digital world, there are, besides images, some key words that connect all the people who have common interests or are looking for something in special. These words are here called hashtags. It is these hashtags that organise the search and promote, in a freeway, cities, places or simply some special moments.

M. M. Soares et al. (Eds.): HCII 2022, LNCS 13323, pp. 57–68, 2022.
https://doi.org/10.1007/978-3-031-05906-3_5

Research was carried out to identify which were the cities that are most represented by hashtags containing their names and which are the main monuments that pop up in the search engines linked to those cities.

As a conclusion, we intend to show that the idea we have about a city is directly influenced by its features, monuments, works of art or events, which are "communicated" through the internet and spread all over the world. Cities end up fighting among themselves, through digital platforms, creating events, performances, or specific spots, which they know will attract visitors to shoot those spots and post them on social media.

In this way, cities become a brand and a product, where design and communication are directly associated with marketing that turns them into a desirable product that attracts more and more visitors.

The number of visitors becomes essential, as consumption and the appearance of new ways of doing business appear as an opportunity that is almost always picked up by the most creative people. Social media has radically changed the way how people travel, and how people organize them holidays [10].

The city is thought of as a product of design, where its places and monuments have become products that sell a specific image, associated with good taste, happiness or culture in general. The modern city has been transformed into places with urban atmospheres designed to create emotions among visitors. The colours and shapes of city icons are exploited to their fullest extent and can be found in a variety of souvenirs or in objects with a good design that range from fashion to decoration. That is why those symbols can act as a vehicle for the development of an identity [36].

The digital media, associated with the design of communication, are now the mirror of the cities, since we can visit them physically or through specific platforms. Images posted on the web affect the way people see, experience and remember destinations [35].

Social networks and their hashtags have helped to boost the knowledge that we have about cities, but also to transform them into a product.

We hope that this article will contribute to the understanding of the importance of social media as a way of spreading the name of cities and thus making them better known in order to attract more visitors, which will help to develop the local economy as well.

Keywords: Marketing communication · Brand · City · Instagram · Hashtag

1   Literature Review

Why does a state government leader, or a specific city, reach the conclusion that they need to turn that place into a brand? The most common argument is that the city's image is obsolete and no longer fits to support its economic, political, or institutional objectives. When the region is simply unknown to its target market, it must be addressed, focusing on the sectors in which it can provide successfully, economically, and sustainably [24]. "The brand images of places are usually communicated through a complex mixture of their tourism offerings and promotions, their products or other business activities, their cultural, social and political scene as reflected in the media ..." [3].

The literature defines the importance of Branding as a crucial component of every marketing plan. Even for a product to be successful, it must first develop strong brand perceptions. Organizations use branding to attract and retain customers by promoting value, image, status, or a lifestyle [37]. That's why the authors linked the branding concept of a city with the Instagram and those images about the city that are published online in the social network.

Cities and city tourism, according to the Report "Destination 2030: Global Cities' Readiness For Tourism Growth" play a vital role in both national and sector growth. Cities are global centres that stimulate business globally, innovation, and employment growth [8]. That is why the authors believe that cities are now like brandings in the global world. The purpose of the city branding methods is to generate a visual idea of a city and then transmit that image both locally and globally, to attract more visitors [33]. In other words, city tourism is linked to city branding, which is also the process of promoting a city's identity in order to attract tourists and consumers [26].

In Instagram the use of hashtags is linked with the idea that we have about a visual content [16] or like a key word about feelings, ideas and beliefs [34]. According to a survey from MarTech, done by Amy Gesenhues on March 27, 2013, "70 percent of the hashtag users are doing so from their mobile device (…) hashtags are being used primarily to communicate personal ideas and feelings. The second most popular reason for using hashtags was to search or follow categories and brands of personal interest" [15]. After consulting several articles and literature, it became obvious and clear that the use of social media has become extremely valuable for business and for promoting brands and products, besides being a mirror of the society and the people who upload pictures there every day.

Travelers used to explore through postcards and visit the physical offices of travel agencies for inspiration for their next vacation trip, according to the website Statista, today, however, potential travellers, use social media to arrange their next vacation, the "instagrammability" of a destination is the most essential criterion for digital natives when planning a holiday [11]. Sarah Feldman also wrote in her article that three main countries dominate the top ten Instagram places of the world: the United States, the United Kingdom, and France.

Instagram Stories are like a window into what's going on around a subject and, they can help people to find or discover new places or what people are thinking about a specific subject. Instagram became to be a powerful skill, and cities know that, because using this social network, people will notice and discover the city and will get more virtual and real followers. Only content tagged with a location sticker and hashtag sticker, will appear in the associated Stories, and that is the way how Instagrammers do to promote or to check about a place, for example.

The cultural economy literature [38] shows a strong connection between location and the industries that produce cultural products. One of those industries are Tourism and the way how tourists fell attracted by a city to visit and explore.

Instagram, among other social networks, requires special attention in this context since its contents allow for the exchange of both personal and shared representations and meanings [27]. Instagram posts do indeed emphasis on how people feel about a location. And that is why some other people will choose those cities do visit. "A growing body of research is showing that Instagram now plays a considerable role in influencing where people decide to go in the world. A Facebook study has found that: 70% of "travel enthusiasts" (people using travel-oriented hashtags) share their travel plans on Instagram; 67% of them use Instagram to find inspiration for where to go next" [20].

2   How Cities Are Recognised Nowadays?

Kevin Lynch published in 1960 the image of the city, and all of his research was about the way how we understand and represent a city. One of the main ways to understand what we perceive about a city is by the imageability, 'that quality in an object which gives it a high probability of evoking a strong image in' the observer' [29]. In somehow, today, people upload pictures about specific places in and out of a city, and those pictures will help to show the city to the world. Those pictures help to develop an image about a specific city or place, by the use of the imageability.

One of the main roles that a city has to play, nowadays, is to encourage a route towards the construction of a more dynamic and modern society based on a progressive social inclusion. Cities are increasingly using new technologies and the internet to develop strategies that regulate and standardise the way of living and inhabiting within the urban spaces.

Thanks to the concentration of a high number of people, cities end up leading in a world where innovation is almost always present to solve global and structural problems. Innovation has become part of the solution [9].

We can foresee those cities, in the near future, will organise their public spaces in such a way that their inhabitants will be more satisfied. In other words, the occupation of streets and squares with restaurants and outdoor terraces, turning the city centre back to its people and removing car traffic from these places. The regeneration and requalification of old city spaces offers opportunities to (re)create and (re)invent, transforming urban spaces into cultural and leisure spaces. These places end up becoming real hotspots of the cities [12].

The appearance of highly sophisticated and evolved chips and sensors has opened the door to a technological evolution that can be seen in most of our cities nowadays. These chips, together with a faster internet and mobile phone applications, help to implement the inclusion and movement of people within cities, with access to detailed information about all imaginable things, from technical to cultural issues.

People who live in a city or town tend to feel more comfortable using the internet with its associated technology through mobile applications than people who live in smaller towns. Technological advances and the use of some digital tools benefit some people but can also negatively affect others. We have as an example, the real estate market, and short-term rental platforms, which have developed this market, boosting it and at the same time promoting tourism, but on the other hand, property prices have risen, and become insupportable for the common citizens, in addition to the decharacterisation of typical areas of cities, which end up pushing away their local inhabitants in favour of a high number of tourists who increasingly seek those areas of the cities.

The cities that use technology have the notion of its importance in becoming an example for other cities, and at the same time to attract more people and visitors. The future will be different for each city, since it depends directly on their society, their culture and their memories, but one thing is certain, the use of new technologies, associated with the internet, is here to stay.

The cities that work in a network, inside and outside their limits, end up being better known, and with this, their development will be greater. It is because of this reason that the idea we have about a city is no longer only a set of buildings and companies where we live and work, but it will also be associated with the idea of technological comfort and its respective comforts. That is why cities have surrendered to technological innovation and, as a result, have attracted more people to live in, and benefiting the local economy.

The networks between cities contribute to stimulate the economy, because the services are linked to each other, providing greater comfort to their inhabitants [31]. But cities also need to create strategies to become better known and attract tourists and provide new touristic offers.

To understand and know the place, people use images that are stored in their minds. Afterwards, they act according to how such images influenced their decisions. That is why social networks play a very important role in the dissemination of images over the internet [25].

One of the strategies that some cities are using is to use social media, such as Instagram, to spread the city name as well as to show iconic places through the number of posts that people upload to their social networks. Its people generate data in their day-to-day activities, by holding smartphones in their hands. This data is mostly focused on the Instagram platform and can be used by the cities to promote themselves [4].

The images posted online are usually associated with hashtags with key words, which usually include the name of the place or the name of the city or words about emotions. Through hashtags, the cities end up benefiting from this dissemination, in a freeway and therefore, the more hashtags are published with reference to a specific city, the more known it becomes, because through social networks, this information travels around the world.

The cities are recognised both by their places and icons, and also by the images that are circulating through the social networks, showing both historically iconic places and hotspots that have been discovered by several visitors and that have caught the attention of others who have subsequently felt attracted to visit that city and those places. Instagram and virtual technology used in social network often interact in a powerful way to influence and shape public opinion [18].

The modern city interacts very well with new technologies, with the internet and with tourists, because cities know that tourism provides richness. Tourism takes advantage of these iconic places and turns them into images that will later become a powerful attraction for visitors to enjoy the place [22].

Cities are increasingly linked to digital communication and marketing strategies that turn them into brands, as if they were a product that is the city itself.

In the beginning of 2015, it was reported that there were more than 200 million users The world uses the service to share 70 million images every day, and marketing knows about that and use it as a skill to promote the city [32].

Isabela Frikkee explains her views on how Instagram has promoted certain popular places. Today, citizens and tourists are noticed for wanting to get a picture in a specific place and tag that place. This is how Instagram users behave, they just react or act like other users and because these specific places have been flagged by other people, these places become trendier and attract other people to visit and take new pictures and use the same hashtag about that place [14].

Those Instagram posts, liked with hashtags, helps to improve the number of visitors to a specific place of the city, that specific place it turns like a hotspot, and very soon it will be a new icon of the city, because so many people will visit that place, and will promote it even more, taking new pictures and uploading them to the Instagram. Those icons are often used to represent a community in a way that unites its people. That's why cities are investing in what we call public art, or in specifics hotspots, that they are not so expensive to do, but they give a good way to catch the curiosity of people to take selfies [17].

This is a new season a new paradigm, where digital marketing is linked with design in the point of view of communication, and by this way the city turns to be more well known around the world.

3   Cities Become a Brand and a Product – Case Studies

Brand connections can help consumers develop, cultivate, and express their identities in addition to processing, organizing, and retrieving information in memory [1]. Many cities use the brand concept as a way to promote the city by images and pictures. That is why, cities are creating cultural and artistic hotspots, who will offer an opportunity to attract Instagrammeres to take selfies, and by that way, they are also, promoting the city in the social medias.

The popularity of social media, which serves a variety of roles such as mass communication, individual activity posting, and photo sharing, has opened up new avenues for tracking ideas, narratives, and impressions [6]. City branding, as a subgenre of destination branding, has its theoretical roots in the branding concepts developed for products by conventional product marketing [40].

In The Guardian Journal, Elle Hunt, wrote in 2018, and article about the city of Atlanta, with the title: "#weloveatl: how Instagram fell in love with Atlanta – in pictures", She refers to a hashtag (#weloveatl) that was invented by 3 local photographers in 2012 in order to publicise pictures of the city and later be included in an exhibition. Thanks to this hashtag, they received over 5000 submissions from over 100 local photographers. Subsequently, this hashtag was posted on Instagram for more than 1 million posts and had about 69 000 followers.

The city of Atlanta took advantage of this case, and continued to spread its brand on Instagram, and seeks to promote the city's hotspots [19]. Like this example, there are many others around the world, for example, the Algarve Tourism Region, in the South of Portugal, uses Instagram as a tool for dissemination through the profile @AlgarveTourism, by the use of the main hashtag #algarve, and according an article with the title "Instagram as a Co-Creation Space for Tourist Destination Image-Building: Algarve and Costa del Sol Case Studies", @AlgarveTourism, got 61400 followers during the Summer of 2019 and 110,798 likes. According to this article, Algarve Region made it a priority for their followers to be encouraged to have their own experiences at their respective destination, enjoying attractive beaches or rocky cliffs [21]. Algarve is a very well-known Portuguese tourist place, but more then ever, now it is also a brand, and that brand is also promoted on social media, and of course in Instagram.

Another example about the importance that Instagram plays in the dissemination of the image that we have about a city and the way in which this same city uses this platform to promote itself, is described in an article entitled "An Instagram Content Analysis for City Branding in London and Florence" here the authors describe In the case of London and its hashtag #London, most of the images, from a total of 600, are related to panoramic views of the city (13.64%), or to historical buildings (12.07%). most posts published belong to individuals (87.6%), whilst the rest principally belong to brands (12.42%). This reveals the importance of this city as an important tourist destination since most of the posts are from visitors. In Florence, according to this research, the use of the hashtag #Florence, most pictures are related to historic buildings and heritage (28.65%) and scenic view of the city (24.54%), but in a higher percentage, and only 10% are posts from brands. Anyway, it means that this city, is also and important touristic place, and those iconic buildings or places, make part of the memory and of the image that we have about those 2 cities. Also, those images are icons from those brands, that are London and Florence [2].

There are all over internet many examples of how internet and Instagram improves tourism and the number of visits to a city. One other example that we found during our research is about Iceland. According to Iceland's official tourism board, many individuals first learn about the country as a destination through social media, with Instagram playing a large role. Nomadic suggests creating "special backdrops, art installations, or photobooth style setups" that can help to brand the city, also linked with posts tagged with a location, they get 79% more engagement than those without [20]. (And that it is what most of the cities are doing nowadays. Iceland use the hashtag #icelandic_explorer, and by it, people who wants to find inspiration for them next travel, they will follow this hashtag and will see many pictures of beautiful paces inside Iceland, and those places are like postcards from the country and also the promote the country.

We may conclude that step by step, cities are constructing a brand with them names and also they promote that brand by the use of Instagram and hashtags. We chose as an example, some less obvious places, to be able to confirm our suspicions, that Instagram, among other social networks, besides being one of the most used networks, is also a working tool for cities and for city marketing managers. It is through the hashtags, that the city promotes itself, mostly in a freeway, but which is also influenced by some local hotspots or through urban art which cities promote themselves, since people are drawn to visit these places and take more and more photos.

4   Identify Which Were the Cities that Are Most Represented by Hashtags

Given the purpose of this study, the authors decided to focus on Instagram as a way to disseminate the city name across the global world, by the use of images, pictures and hashtags. In 2018, a survey done carried out by "socialmedia18" research group in December 3 from the year 2018, concluded that Snapchat and Instagram were the main social network in use by young people, 45.8% to Snapchat and 30.8% to Instagram. In 2020, were 467,759,338 Instagram posts with the hashtag #travel and thousands more secondary travel-related hashtags as of this writing [20].

City Stakeholders knows that tourists can express their perspectives and thoughts, plan common actions for personal and community development, exchange assistance and resources, and observe local social interactions by visiting these locations [13].

First of all, we must try to find a meaning for the word "hashtag". For any brand, and in our research case, the brand refers to a city, to ensure a constant presence in a digital network becomes very important. In order to achieve this, the city, in a general context, must implement measures that will enhance its identity in the world of social media keywords. Those keywords are the hashtags who serves as indexes for their functions and meanings, they also help us to reach our target audience [28].

According to the American CNN travel channel [5], the top "instagrammable" cities in 2020 and 2021 are: New York City is No. 1, London is No. 2, Paris is No. 3, Dubai is No. 4, and Los Angeles is No. 5. 6. Istanbul, 7. Miami, 8. Las Vegas, 9. Barcelona, and 10. Moscow round out the top ten. However, if we take a look on a European channel, we found it, as an example, a list of the Top 10 Instagram Cities which have been published in the Cosmopolitan online [30]. And here we can find a list, which is more European in character: 1. London (119.9 million hashtags), 2. Paris (100.8 million hashtags), 3. Barcelona (47.4 million hashtags), 4. Rome (44.8 million hashtags), 5. Berlin (36.1 m hashtags), 6. Madrid (31.2 m hashtags), 7. Amsterdam (26.7 m hashtags), 8. Lisbon (17.7 m hashtags), 9. Hamburg (15.3 m hashtags), 10. Valencia (14.1 m hashtags).

There are several reports about the number of visitors that cities have seen over the last few years. However, for this article, the authors decided to consider only the year 2019, not including the subsequent years, since it was considered that they are very atypical due to the recent pandemic situation that we are currently going through and therefore they could suggest results that are not consistent with the reality that was being experienced and that we hope to experience in the near future. So, we have collected results from various surveys, from the website "Statista" we found an article about the Leading European city tourism destinations in 2019 and 2020, and we collected the information about bed nights during 2019 [39]. Also we collect information from the Portuguese "Jornal de Negocios" [23] that it is a Journal about Business and Economic, where we found information from the European Union (EU) statistical office about the top city destinations in 2019, and reached the following conclusion about the number of visitors in from the TOP 10 cities must hashtaged: 1. London (85.1 million), 2. Paris (52.45 million), 3. Barcelona (19.85 million), 4. Rome (29.07 million), 5. Berlin (34.12 million), 6. Madrid (20.68 million), 7. Amsterdam (18.38 million), 8. Lisbon (10.5 millions), 9. Hamburg (15.43 million), 10. Valencia (4.5 million).

In summary, we compared the number of visitors who slept in each of those cities with the number of pictures posted from the same cities, linked with hashtags with their names:

1. London (85.1 million), (119.9 million hashtags),
2. Paris (52.45 million), (100.8 million hashtags)
3. Barcelona (19.85 million), (47.4 million hashtags)
4. Rome (29.07 million), (44.8 million hashtags)

5. Berlin (34.12 million), (36.1 million hashtags)
6. Madrid (20.68 million), (31.2 million hashtags)
7. Amsterdam (18.38 million), (26.7 million hashtags)
8. Lisbon (10.5 million), (17.7 million hashtags)
9. Hamburg (15.43 million), (15.3 million hashtags)
10. Valencia (4.5 million), (14.1 million hashtags)

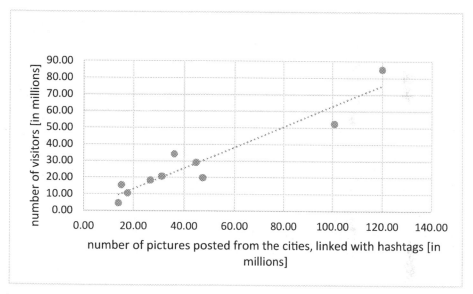

Fig. 1. Relationship between number of visitors [in millions] and number of pictures posted from the cities. Linked with hashtags [in millions] (n = 10). Source: Elaborated on the basis of [5, 30].

When we compare the number of visitors with the number of hashtag published in Instagram (see Fig. 1.), we can note that there is a linear positive relationship between these variables (R-square = 0.903) with high strength r = 0.950, p < 0.001. This means that the increase in the variable number of photos posted from cities, linked by hashtags [in millions] is accompanied by the increase in the variable number of visitors [in millions]. The most visited cities can achieve more photos on the social network Instagram, thus promoting themselves online and achieving greater visibility around the world.

5 Conclusion

Tourism must be beneficial to both visitors and citizens, and its expansion must be well-organized and coordinated. City Tourism or visitors has a good social impact by contributing to public investment, because they invest money in a travel and spent money in the city. Later that town or city becomes a brand and people also see it like a brand. That's why some cities are liked to fashion or fashionable places. Visitors do not mind to spent money to go there and take a few pictures to upload in social networks and also promote themselves.

Our research contributes to the literature in two ways. We advance the literature on City Brand by adding a social media information, in this case by Instagram, as a way for evaluation of the city importance. While this raises some methodological concerns, it does allow us to see how Instagram influences city images. Secondly, this methodology allows us to directly use Instagram as a research gate, and a place to collect information about many subjects, but in our case, about city and "city mood".

This paper empirically explores and discovers the relevance of hashtags in social media, specifically in Instagram, to promote the city name and to improve the city to be recognized as a Brand.

We conclude that Instagram and other social networks, play an important role in the world of marketing and communication. Instagram is a powerful platform, in wish we can find and construct, by the use of pictures, images about some cities or other specific places. We also can feel attracted to visit or explore those places. It means that users and scholars should start looking to the social networks in general and to Instagram in particular, in a way to see them not just like a simple digital platform where we can enjoy and have some fun, but also as a communication tool.

We also find that there is a relationship between the number of visitors to a city and the number of posts linked to hashtags with the city name.

Acknowledgement. This work is financed by National Funds through FCT – Fundação para a Ciência e a Tecnologia, I.P., within the scope of Project "UIDB/04026/2020" of CITAD – Research Centre in Territory, Architecture and Design, and the Lusíada University of Lisbon, Portugal.

References

1. Aaker, D.A.: Managing Brand Equity: Capitalizing on the Value of a Brand Name. Free Press, New York, NY (1991)
2. Acuti, D., Mazzoli, V., Donvito, R., Chan, P.: An instagram content analysis for city branding in London and Florence, online publishing from University of Portsmouth, https://pure.port.ac.uk/ws/portalfiles/portal/15970961 (2019)
3. Anholt, S.: Why Brand? Some Practical Considerations for Place Branding, Place Branding and Public Diplomacy, vol. 2, issue 2, pp. 97–107. Palgrave Macmillan Ltd. https://www.academia.edu/40069380/2_2_Anholt_Editorial_Why_Brand_Some_Practical_Considerations_for_Place_Branding?auto=citations&from=cover_page (2006). Consulted 15 Dec 2021
4. Boy, J., Uitermark, J.: How to study the city on Instagram. PLoS ONE (2016). https://doi.org/10.1371/journal.pone.0158161
5. Carrington, D.: CNN updated 27th June 2016 Instagram travels: these cities get you most 'likes'. https://edition.cnn.com/travel/article/travel-vacation-instagram/index.html (2016). Consulted 20 Dec 2021
6. Casadei, P., Lee, N.: Global cities, creative industries and their representation on social media: a micro-data analysis of Twitter data on the fashion industry. SAGE J. **52**(6), 1195–1220 (2020). https://doi.org/10.1177/0308518X20901585

7. Deffner. A., Liouris. C.: "City marketing: a significant planning tool for urban development in a globalised economy". 45th Congress of the European Regional Science Association, 23–27 Aug. vrije universiteit Amsterdam. https://www.econstor.eu/handle/10419/117606 (2005)
8. Destination 2030.: Global cities' readiness for tourism growth, JLL and World Travel &Tourism Council. https://wttc.org/Portals/0/Documents/Reports/2019/Global%20Cities%20Readiness%20For%20Tourism%20Growth-Jun%202019.pdf?ver=2021-02-25-182751-627 (2019). Consulted 12 Jan 2022
9. European Commission, Joint Research Centre.: The future of cities: opportunities, challenges and the way forward, (J,Aurambout,editor,I,Vandecasteele,editor,C,Baranzelli,editor,A,Siragusa,editor) Publications Office. https://data.europa.eu/doi/10.2760/364135 (2019)
10. Fatanti, M.N., Suyadnya, I.W.: Beyond user gaze: how Instagram creates tourism destination brand? Procedia Soc. Behav. Sci. **211**, 1089–1095 (2015). https://doi.org/10.1016/j.sbspro.2015.11.145
11. Feldman, S.: Around the world in 10 Hashtags, Sep 27, 2018 Statista.com. https://www.statista.com/chart/15613/around-the-world-in-10-hashtags/ (2018). Consulted Jan 2022
12. Florida, R., Adler, P., Mellander, C.: The city as innovation machine. Reg. Stud. **51**(1), 86–96 (2017). https://doi.org/10.1080/00343404.2016.1255324
13. Francis, J., Giles-Corti, B., Wood, L., Knuiman, M.: Creating sense of community: the role of public space. J. Environ. Psychol. 32(4), 401–409 (2014). https://doi.org/10.1016/j.jenvp.2012.07.002
14. Frikkee, I.: The increasing influence of Instagram at city marketing. https://medium.com/@isabel.frikkee/the-increasing-influence-of-instagram-at-city-marketing-e97fd401c3d4 (2019). Consulted Aug 2019
15. Gesenhues, A.: MarTech, March 27, survey: 71% of hashtag users are using hashtags from their mobile device. https://martech.org/mobile-hashtag-survey-finds-users-more-likely-to-explore-content-using-hashtags-if-offered-discounts/ (2013). Consulted 12 Jan 2022
16. Giannoulakis, S., Tsapatsoulis, N.: Evaluating the descriptive power of Instagram hashtags. J. Innov. Digit. Ecosyst. **3**(2), 114–129 (2016). https://doi.org/10.1016/j.jides.2016.10.001
17. Ginty, R.M.: The political use of symbols of accord and discord: northern Ireland and South Africa. Civil Wars **4**(1), 1–21 (2001). https://doi.org/10.1080/13698240108402461
18. Green, D.M., Strange, D., Lindsay, D.S., Takarangi, M.K.T.: Trauma-related versus positive involuntary thoughts with and withoutmeta-awareness. Conscious. Cogn. **46**, 163–172 (2016). https://doi.org/10.1016/j.concog.2016.09.019
19. Hunt, E.: #weloveatl: how Instagram fell in love with Atlanta – in pictures, The Guardian, online Wed 24 Oct 2018, 15.00. https://www.theguardian.com/cities/2018/oct/24/weloveatl-how-instagram-fell-in-love-with-atlanta-in-pictures. Consulted 10 Jan 2021
20. ICEFGmbH.: Instagram's profound effect on travel destination choice. https://monitor.icef.com/2020/01/instagrams-profound-effect-on-travel-destination-choice/ (2020) Consulted 10 Jan 2022
21. Iglesias-Sánchez, P.P., Correia, M.B., Jambrino-Maldonado, C., de las Heras-Pedrosa, C.: Instagram as a co-creation space for tourist destination image-building: Algarve and Costa del Sol case studies. Sustainability **12**(7), 2793 (2020). https://doi.org/10.3390/su12072793
22. Jenkins, O.H.: Photography and travel brochures: the circle of representation. Tour Geog. **5**(3), 305–328 (2003). https://doi.org/10.1080/14616680309715
23. Jornal de Negócios.: "Lisboa foi a 4.ª cidade mais procurada e Portugal o 5.º país nas plataformas de reserva turística em 2019" https://www.jornaldenegocios.pt/empresas/turismo---lazer/detalhe/lisboa-foi-a-4-cidade-mais-procurada-e-portugal-o-5-pais-nas-plataformas-de-reserva-turistica-em-2019 (2021). Consulted 14 Dec 2021

24. Kemp, E., Childers, C.Y., Williams, K.H.: Place branding: creating self-brand connections and brand advocacy. J. Prod. Brand Manag. **21**(7), 508–515 (2012). https://doi.org/10.1108/10610421211276259
25. Kotler, P.: Marketing management: Analysis, Planning, Implementation and Control, pp. 1–107. Prentice Hall, Upper Saddle River, New Jersey, 7458 (1997)
26. Lazzeretti, L., Capone, F., Casadei, P.: The role of fashion for tourism: an analysis of Florence as a manufacturing fashion city and beyond. In: Bellini, N., Pasquinelli, C. (eds.) Tourism in the City, pp. 207–220. Springer, Cham (2017). https://doi.org/10.1007/978-3-319-26877-4_14
27. Lee, E., Lee, J.A., Moon, J.H., Sung, Y.: Pictures speak louder than words: motivations for using Instagram. Cyberpsychol. Behav. Soc. Netw. **18**(9), 552–556 (2017)
28. Liu, A.: Digital humanities and academic change. Eng. Lang. Notes **47**, 17–35 (2009). https://doi.org/10.1215/00138282-47.1.17
29. Lynch, K.: The Image of the City. MIT press (1964)
30. Malbon, A.: The most Instagrammed cities in Europe have been revealed. Cosmopolitan, https://www.cosmPlitviceLakesopolitan.com/uk/entertainment/travel/a26781939/most-instagrammed-cities-europe/. https://doi.org/10.1089/cyber.2015.0157 (2019). Consulted Aug 2021
31. Marres, N.: Digital sociology: the reinvention of social research. Polity Press. https://doi.org/10.1080/17530350.2013.772070 (2017)
32. McCracken, H.: Instagram's all-new search & explore features will change how you use Instagram. Fast Company. Available: http://www.fastcompany.com/3047726/tech-forecast/with-new-searchexplore-features-instagram-is-changing-how-youll-use-instagram (2015)
33. Merrilees, B., Miller, D., Herington, C.: Antecedents of residents' city brand attitudes. J. Business Res. **62**(3), 362–367 (2009). https://doi.org/10.1016/j.jbusres.2008.05.011
34. Paparachissi, Z.: Affective Publics: Sentiment, Technology, and Politics. Oxford University Press (2015)
35. Pocock, N., Zahra, A., McIntosh, A.: Proposing video diaries as an innovative methodology in tourist experience research. Tour. Hosp. Plan. Dev. **6**, 109–119 (2009). https://doi.org/10.1080/14790530902981480
36. Resane, K.T.: Statues, symbols and signages: monuments towards socio-political divisions, dominance and patriotism? HTS Theological Stud. **74**(4), 1–8 (2018). https://doi.org/10.4102/hts.v74i4.4895
37. Rooney, J.: Branding: a trend for today and tomorrow. J. Prod. Brand Manag. **4**(4), 48–55 (1995)
38. Scott, A.J.: The cultural economy of cities. Int. J. Urban Reg. Res. **21**, 323–339 (1997). https://doi.org/10.1111/1468-2427.00075
39. Statista.: Leading European city tourism destinations in 2019 and 2020. https://www.statista.com/statistics/314340/leading-european-city-tourism-destinations-by-number-of-bednights/ (2021). Consulted 10 Dec 2021
40. Yoo, B., Donthu, N., Lee, S.: An examination of selected marketing mix elements and brand equity. J. Acad. Mark. Sci. **28**(2), 195–211 (2000). https://doi.org/10.1177/0092070300282002

Bio-Centred Interaction Design: A New Paradigm for Human-System Interaction

Sónia Rafael[1]([✉]) [iD], Eunice Santiago[2], Francisco Rebelo[3] [iD], Paulo Noriega[3] [iD], and Elisângela Vilar[3] [iD]

[1] ITI – Interactive Technologies Institute/LARSyS, Universidade de Lisboa, Faculdade de Belas-ArtesLargo da Academia Nacional de Belas Artes, 1249-058 Lisboa, Portugal
srafael@campus.ul.pt

[2] Lisbon School of Architecture, University of Lisbon, Rua Sá Nogueira, Pólo Universitário, Alto da Ajuda, 1349-055 Lisbon, Portugal

[3] CIAUD – Research Center for Architecture, Urbanism and Design and ITI – Interactive Technologies Institute/LARSyS, University of Lisbon, Lisbon School of Architecture, University of Lisbon, Rua Sá Nogueira, Pólo Universitário, Alto da Ajuda, 1349-055 Lisbon, Portugal
frebelo@fa.ulisboa.pt, {pnoriega,ebpvilar}@edu.ulisboa.pt

Abstract. Biodiversity loss has been an issue mentioned for many years, but now, more than at any other time in history, action is needed.

In terms of sustainability, design has long integrated several aspects that concern themselves with biodiversity, such as eco-design, bio-design, and sustainable design. But it is necessary to develop tools that designers can include in the creative processes and thus provide an adequate response to the needs of creating sustainable products, systems, or services.

In this context, and beyond the anthropocentrism that places the human being at the centre of the universe, we propose a biocentrism that states that all life forms are important and that the other species do not exist to simply serve humans. On the other hand, in the context of interaction design, Human-Centred Design (HCD) is an ISO (International Organization for Standardization) standardized concept. In Standard Ergonomics of Human-System Interaction – Part 210: Human-Centred Design for Interactive Systems (ISO 9241-210), there is no description about environmental concerns.

The concept proposed in this article is Bio-Centred Design, which integrates a third pillar – environmental sustainability – in addition to those already approved by the standard – the economic and social pillars. We propose this to be a fundamental pillar for the future of the planet and development of sustainable products, systems, and services.

Keywords: Human-centred design · Bio-centred interaction design · Sustainable design

1 Introduction

In the last century, human beings have witnessed the consequences of the degradation of the balance of the planet's biodiversity. The overexploitation of resources and the production of waste began to have a direct, rapid, and negative impact on life on earth.

© The Author(s), under exclusive license to Springer Nature Switzerland AG 2022
M. M. Soares et al. (Eds.): HCII 2022, LNCS 13323, pp. 69–79, 2022.
https://doi.org/10.1007/978-3-031-05906-3_6

As Dam and Siang point out our consumption has transformed global warming from a growing issue to a looming crisis that threatens to change the way we live (and even survive) [1]. This condition has a philosophical foundation in the dawn of the Humanist tradition and the Modern project that conceived the human species and Nature as opposing poles.

Humanism has always been associated with an idea of transcendence of the human condition based on scientific (rational) knowledge, technological progress, and the separation of humanity from the laws of nature. Maia shares the same point of view – with humanism the theocentric conception was replaced by an anthropocentric conception. A whole movement took place in the West, and particularly in Europe, that sought the rational explanation for man's actions in society [2]. This anthropocentric condition distanced the human being from the theocentric matrix (God, Nature) and caused the belief in the existence of an antagonistic relationship – an almost state of war, between the two.

The man of humanism, reinforces Renaut, is the one who no longer conceives of receiving norms and laws either from the nature of things or from God, but who intends to find them himself, based on his reason and his will [3].

Heidegger, in 1946, writes his Letter on Humanism where he rescued a meaning for Humanism in Hellenic-Roman culture, in Roman civics, in the cult of the humanities (art, philosophy, wisdom), which was opposed to barbarism [4]. There the philosopher finds essential elements to think about what he calls supreme humanism.

The Industrial Revolution effectively established the imbalance between humans and nature. So did the social transformations carried out by capitalism, which established relations of subalternity in relation to women, the "savage", and nature. These transformations have led to dichotomies such as nature/culture, traditional/modern, wild/civilized [5], so that there can be no harmony, connection, and respect between different perspectives.

Design was mainly considered a humanist and anthropocentrist discipline, focused on the human being, on his needs and at the service of capitalism [36, 37]. It is difficult to dissociate the decisive role of complicity it has played in this process. As a discipline it has gradually moved away from this prism to integrate perspectives closer to cultural, social, and political values and with humanitarian and environmental concerns. We are now led to question what the role of design is and how it can contribute to help restore the balance of the planet. Through its praxis.

The environmental dimension is already present and solidified in some areas of design, such as fashion design, interior design, product design since the results are physical objects. For this reason, it is possible to intervene in the choice of materials for their manufacture.

This study focuses on the urgency of incorporating environmental concerns into the development of Interaction Design products, services, and systems.

To this end, we will convene John Elkington's framework, which he called the Triple Bottom Line (TBL framework) [6], which frames the concept of sustainability on three pillars – economic, social and the environmental/ecological. We will also analyse the possibility of introducing the third pillar of sustainability – the environmental one, through the perspective of Bio-Centred Interaction Design.

2   In the Human-Centred Design Matrix

2.1   User vs Human-Centred Design

Human-Centred Design (HCD) is a concept standardized by International Organization for Standardization (ISO) [7]. Focusing on the norms referring to this concept with a focus on interactive systems, we proceed to an analysis from a critical point of view and from a sustainable perspective.

The publication of the standards ISO 13407:1999 (1999): Human-Centred Design processes for interactive systems [8] and the associated ISO TR 18529:2000 (2000): Human-Centred Lifecycle process descriptions, represents a maturing of the discipline of User-Centred Design. The term User-Centred Design (UCD) was proposed by Norman in the 1980's and has been widely used since the publication of the book "User Centred System Design: New Perspectives on Human-Computer Interaction", co-authored with Draper. They defined User Centred-Design as a broad term to describe design processes in which end-users influence how a design takes shape. It is both a broad philosophy and variety of methods [9].

In 1999, the ISO 13407 standard considered the concept of Human-Centred Design as "an approach to interactive system development that focuses specifically on making systems usable. It is a multi-disciplinary activity which incorporates human factors and ergonomics knowledge and techniques" [10]. On User-Centred Design, Verganti clarifies that it favours the growth of the economy, but not the increase of sustainability [11].

2.2   Human-Centred in Design

In 2010, the standard was updated and renamed ISO 9241-210:2010 Ergonomics of Human-System Interaction – Part 210: Human-Centred Design for Interactive Systems [12]. In 2019, it underwent a new update – ISO 9241-210:2019.

The concept of Human-Centred Design is described by the ISO 9241-210:2010 standard as "an approach to interactive systems development that aims to make systems usable and useful by focusing on the users, their needs and requirements, and by applying human factors/ergonomics, and usability knowledge and techniques. This approach enhances effectiveness and efficiency, improves human well-being, user satisfaction, accessibility and sustainability; and counteracts possible adverse effects of use on human health, safety and performance" [12].

In the transition from ISO 13407 to ISO 9241-210, the change to be highlighted focused on the term User-Centred Design, which became Human-Centred Design, due to a greater understanding of the various stakeholders that are involved in the creation and process of development of a product, abandoning the exclusive reference to the user. We can measure it in the following sentence "NOTE 1 The term "human-centred design" is used rather than "user-centred design" to emphasize that this part of ISO 9241 also addresses impacts on a number of stakeholders, not just those typically considered as user" [12]. This is a relevant point because there was a need for an update of the user designation for all possible users/stakeholders.

It is in this standard that the concern with sustainability appears for the first time: "Systems designed using human centred methods improve quality, for example, by: a) increasing the productivity of users and the operational efficiency of organizations; b) being easier to understand and use, thus reducing training and support costs; c) increasing usability for people with a wider range of capabilities and thus increasing accessibility; d) improving user experience; e) reducing discomfort and stress; f) providing a competitive advantage, for example by improving brand image; g) contributing towards sustainability objectives" [12].

However, there are no guidelines on what sustainable goals are and how to achieve them. The standard states that now only the impact of the product's life cycle is considered. It is, however, unclear whether such an impact has a strictly economic meaning – "the complete benefits of human centred design can be determined by taking into account the total life cycle costs of the product, system or service, including conception, design, implementation, support, use, maintenance and, finally, disposal" [12]. At the end of the text, the standard reinforces the two pillars that govern Human-Centred Design: the economic and the social. One of the pillars of the TBL framework [6] is excluded – the environmental (or ecological).

In general, the standard is governed by economic and social sustainability. Not effectively considering environmental sustainability. The concern with the impact of the product's life cycle should clearly refer to the environmental impact caused.

About Human-Centred Design, Crul and Diehl state that "the idea is still to meet the consumer's requirements, but in a more sustainable way" [13].

In this sense, it is necessary to act to change mentalities since it is not possible to "buy" another planet. A 21st century product that is not created from a sustainable perspective is a failed product.

We defend that the planet should also be considered a stakeholder, since the consequences and impacts of the creation of all products developed directly fall upon it.

Methodologies such as Human-Centred Design should focus on user requirements, but with sustainable principles as a starting point [14]. The entire product development cycle should be designed with sustainability in mind.

Thus, Brown reinforces that "the goal is not to replace users as the focus of the design process, the objective is to elevate the importance of sustainability to the same level as user focus" [15].

An environmental crisis is also a design crisis, because until now design has not considered the effects that products have on biological systems, thinking exclusively about the needs of human beings [16]. But the quality of human life largely depends on the "well-being" of the planet.

In the IDEO.org perspective "Human-Centred Design is uniquely situated to arrive at solutions that are desirable, feasible, and viable. By starting with humans, their hopes, fears, and needs, we quickly uncover what's most desirable" [17]. They then explain that this is just a lens through which we look at our solutions. Once we have determined a variety of solutions that might appeal to the community we wish to serve, we begin to focus on what is technically feasible to implement and how to make the solution financially viable.

They add, finally, that "it's a balancing act, but one that's absolutely crucial to designing solutions that are successful and sustainable" [17]. In this model proposed

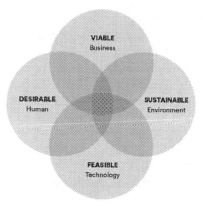

Fig. 1. Adaptation of the diagram of components of a product, system, or service (Source: IDEO.org)

by IDEO.org, sustainability is also a residual topic. But sustainability needs a more comprehensive and complex solution by building a good system with norms and rules towards the same goal – a sustainable planet and the maintenance of biodiversity. For this reason, we propose to add the Sustainability component to the IDEO.org model (Fig. 1).

2.3   Bringing Human-Centred Design Closer to Design Perspective

Several designers and researchers have been using Human-Centred Design over the years making their own modifications or considerations.

A relevant contribution in this regard is that of Giacomin, who began by investigating the meaning of the word "design" to explain what HCD is. The author used other authors to describe the original meaning of the word and some of its early meanings. "In this usage 'design' can signify the shaping power described in philosophical analysis by terms such as 'thought processing' (Heim 1993) and 'instrumental realism' (Ihde 1991; Ihde 1998) or in applied linguistics by terms such as 'professional vision' (Goodwin 1994)" [18].

For this reason, the evolution of design practice beyond ergonomics and human factors, suggests the need to identify stakeholders and contexts of use, and to apply creative processes [19].

HCD methodologies have guided design practice by seeking a focus on the human to probe, classify, and describe the interactions that occur between people and their environments. The use of personas and scenarios has provided a basis for describing people and contexts. In addition, the recent trend to focus on emotional involvement during the design process has also distanced design practice from the systems engineering approach [18].

One of the HCD tools is to collect data about users (such as anthropometric, biomechanical, cognitive, emotional, psychophysical, psychological, and sociological data and models). Such information, whether treated as ergonomics or human factors issues, provides basic factual statements about the abilities and limitations of human beings. But, according to Giacomin, these tools that define the boundaries within which to operate generally act more to inform the human-centred design process than to drive it. [18].

It also clarifies that the definition to which he refers in his research places at the centre of the designer's activity the meaning that the product or system must offer to people.

It validates the point of view of a multidisciplinary activity, whose ultimate objective is to clarify purpose and meaning, and is therefore fully consistent with the claim that design itself is a pragmatic and empirical approach, which aims to make sense of the world that surrounds us.

A growing set of Human-Centred Design tools have emerged over time that stimulate reflection and discussion. We emphasize the Speculative Critical Design (SCD) of Dunne and Raby [24], used to imagine possible future scenarios within a project context and a design perspective in relation to interactions, behaviours and objects that integrate a given situation. Other methodologies such as design criticism, design case studies and reflective practice, such as Cross [20], Fallman [34], and Schön [35].

2.4 In the Utopia of Design and Outside the HCD Matrix

In the 1960's, when people were trying to "scientify" design, Cross highlighted Fuller who called for a "scientific revolution in design", that is, a revolution based on science, technology, and rationalism, to overcome the problems of the environment, environment that he believed could not be resolved by politics and economics [20].

At that time, people were already looking for a design that integrated values with more humanity, and that with it found solutions to problems in various areas and in a real context, which were not only conditioned to economic or political issues.

Several designers had concerns about sustainability, such as Papanek (1923–1998) who defends the designer's responsibility in creating methodologies, processes and social and ecological projects; Manzini (1945-) designer and academic, author known for his work on design for social innovation and sustainability; Blevis (1959-) known for his studies in the area of sustainable interaction design, and currently also known for the fusion of design with HCI and a defender of transdisciplinary; and Mau (1959-) designer who followed the Eco-Environmental aspect of design.

Papanek wrote, in 1971, the book "Design for the Real World" where he defends the integration of social and ecological concerns in the entire design process and not only in the result, referring that "in an age of mass production when everything must be planned and designed, design has become the most powerful tool with which man shapes his tools and environments (and, by extension, society and himself)" [21].

The designer, for Papanek, has the role of focusing on the needs of the world as a unit, a whole, believing that Design is the conscious effort to impose meaning full order [21], the order that the human being himself undid by separating himself from nature in favour of reason.

In addition to Papanek, Manzini has also worked on sustainable design. Wrote about building scenarios for solutions that encompass environmental and social quality; innovative processes in the production and consumption system; and the relationship between product strategies and environmental policies from the perspective of sustainable development.

He made it clear that if designers understand the new role they must play, they will transform new business models and position themselves as catalysts for change. Understanding the new designer role: designers as connectors and facilitators, as quality producers, as visualisers and visionaries, as future builders (or co-producers) [29].

Another designer who also stands out for his ecological thinking is Mau, author of the books "Massive Change, Lifestyle" and "S, M, L, XL". Mau makes it clear that the "idea that we are above nature – that we have dominion over it, and that it is endlessly abundant – is a dangerous relic of an age of arrogance and ignorance. We are part of nature; we depend on ecological systems to sustain us. Our approach to everything we do, design, and produce must be informed by this knowledge" [23].

Over the years we have seen how new tools and methodologies oriented towards the environment have appeared. For this, as mentioned by Vallet, studies and evaluations were carried out both creative design process, as well as of the various stages of it [26].

Already identified by Holt and Cameron, there is a trend towards the expansion of new cultural directions through the design [27], of new products, whether objects, services, or systems, which breathe the correct message throughout their process and implementation and environmental concerns needed at this time. The designer can and must contribute to the development of a sustainable society and in this context, Stegall states that "is not simply to create 'sustainable products,' but rather to envision products, processes, and services that encourage widespread sustainable behaviour" [25].

3   Bio-Centred IxDesign (BCIxD)

3.1   Biocentrism

On biocentrism, Junges says that nature is subject to rights. And that starts from the "scientific knowledge of ecology, the recognition of nature as an interdependent set and the place of human beings in this set to arrive at norms in relation to the environment" [5]. Thus, there are also several aspects within biocentrist ethics itself, making it clear that "environmental ethics is not human creation, but systematization of norms inscribed in nature. The task of human beings is to become aware of these norms and adapt their behaviour to the homeostatic balances and energy flows of the ecosphere" [5]. The ecological crisis does not only mean the emergence of environmental problems demanding a response, but the emergence of the need for a new paradigm of perception of the world and nature. Hence it follows that nature deserves "moral consideration not only insofar as it serves human interests, but in itself as the matrix of life" [5]. From biocentrism we must gather the thought that the world is an ecosystem and therefore it is composed of a greater diversity of elements besides the human being, and that he could not live without these others. For all the elements together bring balance to the planet.

3.2   In the Case of Sustainable Interaction Design (SID)

One of the pioneers and researchers of Sustainable Interaction Design was Blevis. To the author sustainability can and should be a central focus of Interaction Design [14] having created the concept of Sustainable Interaction Design (SID), in which it defines the concept of Design in relation to sustainability as "an act of choosing among or informing choices of future ways of being. This perspective of sustainability is presented in terms of design values, methods, and reasoning" [14].

SID aims to embed sustainability in Interaction Design research and practice. It states that the focus should be on environmental sustainability and the link between interactive technologies and the use of resources to create sustainable behaviours. In summary SID operates as a "critical lens to the design of interactive systems" [14] changing the values, methods, and reasoning of the elaboration of products, systems, and services to promote sustainable behaviours. The sustainable practices in Design enunciated by Blevis are "disposal, salvage, recycling, remanufacturing for reuse, reuse as is, achieving longevity of use, sharing for maximal use, achieving heirloom status, finding wholesome alternatives to use, and active repair of misuse" [14].

In recent years, researchers such as Roshko [30], Van Der Ryn and Cowan [31], Brown [15], Findeli [31], Cooke [32] or Pazmino [33] have proposed new aspects of sustainable design such as Bio-design, Eco-design, or Green Design.

3.3 Bio-Centred Interaction Design (BCIxD)

The perspective we share is that the duality between human beings and nature must end and it is necessary to invest in the harmony between them.

We can learn, as Brown suggests, by imitating nature – in its elegance, economy, and efficiency remembering that "as citizens and consumers we too can learn to respect the fragile environment that surrounds and sustains us" [15].

Designers have a fundamental role to play in putting the focus on concerns regarding the defence of the environment and the obligation to be proactive in solving this problem.

Solutions should be sought together with specialists from other areas so that the development processes of products, services and systems can be more complete, and to cover all stages of development until market introduction.

This thinking must be part of the entire process – from concept, from idea to practice so that products, systems, or services have an intrinsic meaning with biocentrist values. As mentioned, the SID concept is a key pillar for this proposal. It defends a perspective where sustainability is the focus of Interaction Design. It sets out fundamental principles for products, systems, or services to promote sustainable behaviours and serve as a critical lens for them. Maguire's article is also relevant since he enunciates the Methods to support human-centred design [19]. It will be necessary to integrate, in each of the stages that it states, concerns with sustainability from the conception to the implementation of products, services or systems.

The concept, Bio-Centred Interaction Design (BCIxD) continues, like Human-Centred Design, to focus on human needs while incorporating environmental concerns.

The definition of BCIxD would be: "an approach to interactive systems development that aims to make systems usable and useful; sustainable from an ecological, social and economic point of view; focusing on users and their particularities, applying human factors/ergonomics; usability knowledge; accessibility and inclusion values".

Finally, the structure of this new concept will be the same as that of the HCD but reinforcing that all stages of development of a product, service or system must include sustainable values.

As already referenced in ISO 9241-210 "Human-Centred Design shall be planned and integrated into all phases of the product life cycle, i.e., conception, analysis, design, implementation, testing and maintenance" [10].

If we consider this principle in the BCIxD of designing for the environment, and if this is the norm and not an exception in all phases of the product life cycle, we would find the solution to the planet's environmental problems. An objective of the BCIxD is to suggest ways in which sustainability concerns can be integrated into existing design methods so that Interaction Design is considered a sustainable practice.

We propose that BCIxD is an informed fusion from the sustainable lens in ISO 9241-210:2019, along with Blevis's SID concept [14] and Maguire's Methods to support HCD [19]. This framework offers the Interaction designer the necessary tools to respond to the challenges that contemporaneity imposes on him in terms of sustainable creations from an ecological point of view.

4 Conclusion

The new concept we are proposing in this article – Bio-Centred IxDesign – is based on Human-Centred Design. But we believe that the term "human" is not very inclusive and suffers from an anthropocentric perspective – nature, animals, human beings with certain gender, class and race profiles that are outside the convention, individuals with reduced accessibility, etc., are not covered.

This is a critical moment in the practice of design and in the accession to its "critical" future, both in the sense of an imperative to deal with the social and environmental crisis, and in a reflexivity on the foundations and definitions of its field of study.

After surveying the strands of thought in relation to the positioning of human beings on the planet; aspects of design with concerns about sustainability; and the need to update methodologies in Interaction Design to create sustainable products, services, and systems from an ecological point of view, the need to propose a new standard arose. One should speak of a sustainable society and a sustainable planet as indispensable preconditions for truly integral development. It does not mean going back to the past but offering a new approach to the common future. It is not simply a matter of not consuming, but of consuming responsibly. The designer also plays an important role in these solutions.

The proposal is therefore to give the same importance to sustainability as the user is at the centre of the design process.

We need a new standard that allows us to develop sustainable products, systems, and services. Will you join us?

Acknowledgements. Research funded by ITI -LARSyS-FCT Pluriannual funding's 2020–2023 (UIDB/50009/2020) and CIAUD Project UID/EAT/4008/2020.

References

1. Dam, R., Siang, T.: Design Thinking: Getting Started with Empathy. Interaction Design Foundation (2020), https://www.interaction-design.org/literature/article/design-thin-king-get ting-started-with-empathy. Last accessed 16 Jan 2022

2. Maia, J.J.M.: Transumanismo e pós-humanismo: descodificação política de uma problemática contemporânea. PhD Thesis (2018) http://hdl.handle.net/10316/80671. Last accessed 1 Feb 2022
3. Renaut, A.: O indivíduo. Reflexão acerca da filosofia do sujeito. Difel, Rio de Janeiro (2004)
4. Heidegger, M.: Letter on Humanism. In: Krell, D.F. (ed.) Basic Writings. Harper Collins Publishers Inc, New York (2008)
5. Junges, J.R.: Ética Ecológica: Antropocentrismo ou Biocentrismo? Perspectiva Teológica, **33**(89) (2001). https://doi.org/10.20911/21768757v33n89p33/2001. http://www.faje.edu.br/periodicos/index.php/perspectiva/article/view/801. Last accessed 20 Jan 2022
6. Elkington, J.: Towards the sustainable corporation: win-win-win business strategies for sustainable development. California Manage. Rev. **36**, 90–100 (1994). https://doi.org/10.2307/41165746
7. ISO – International Organization for Standardization. https://www.iso.org
8. Earthy, J., Jones, B., Bevan, N.: The improvement of human-centred processes – facing the challenge and reaping the benefit of ISO 13407. Int. J. Human-Computer Stud. **55**, 553–585 (2001). https://doi.org/10.1006/ijhc.2001.0493
9. Norman, D.A., Draper, S.: User Centered System Design: New Perspectives on Human-Computer Interaction. Lawrence Erlbaum Associates, New Jersey (1986)
10. ISO 13407:1999 Human-Centred Design Processes for Interactive Systems. https://www.iso.org/standard/21197.html. Last accessed 15 Jan 2022
11. Verganti, R.: User-centered innovation is not sustainable. Harvard Business Review. (2010). https://hbr.org/2010/03/user-centered-innovation-is-no. Last accessed 21 Jan 2022
12. ISO 9241-210:2010 Ergonomics of Human-System Interaction – Part 210: Human-Centred Design for Interactive Systems. https://www.iso.org/standard/52075.html. Last accessed 28 Jan 2022
13. Cruhl, M., Diehl, J.: Design for sustainability, a step-by-step approach. UNEP, United Nations Publications. D4S publication (2009). https://wedocs.unep.org/handle/20.500.11822/8742. Last accessed 18 Jan 2022
14. Blevis, E.: Sustainable interaction design: invention & disposal, renewal & reuse. In: CHI '07: Proceedings of the SIGCHI Conference on Human Factors in Computing Systems, pp. 503–512. Association for Computing Machinery, NY (2007). https://doi.org/10.1145/1240624.1240705
15. Brown, A.S.: A Model to Integrate Sustainability into The User-centered Design Process. Electronic Theses and Dissertations, 1830 (2011). https://stars.library.ucf.edu/etd/1830. Last accessed 19 Jan 2022
16. Van Der Ryn, S., Cowan, S.: Ecological Design: 10th Anniversary Edition. Island Press, Washington D. C (1996)
17. IDEO.org: The Field Guide to Human-Centered Design. Design Kit (2015). https://www.designkit.org. Last accessed 29 Dec 2021
18. Giacomin, J.: What is human centred design? Des. J. **17**(4), 606–623 (2014). https://doi.org/10.2752/175630614X14056185480186
19. Maguire, M.: Methods to support human-centred design. Int. J. Human-Computer Stud. **55**(4), 587–634 (2001). https://doi.org/10.1006/ijhc.2001.0503
20. Cross, N.: Designerly ways of knowing: design discipline versus design science. Des. Issues **17**(3), 49–55 (2001). https://doi.org/10.1162/074793601750357196
21. Papanek, V.: Design for the Real World, 3rd edn. Thames & Hudson Ltd, London (2019)
22. Fry, T.: The scenario of design. Des. Philos. Pap. **3**(1), 19–27 (2005). https://doi.org/10.2752/144871305X13966254124158
23. Mau, B.: Massive Change a Manifesto for The Future Global Design Culture. Phaidon Press Ltd, New York (2006)

24. Dunne, A., Raby, F.: Speculative Everything: Design, Fiction, and Social Dreaming. The MIT Press, Massachusetts (2013)
25. Stegall, N.: Designing for sustainability: a philosophy for ecologically intentional design. Des. Issues **22**(2), 56–63 (2006)
26. Vallet, F., Eynard, B., Millet, D., Mahut, S.G., Tyl, B., Bertoluci, G.: Using eco-design tools: an overview of experts' practices. Des. Stud. **34**(3), 345–377 (2013). https://doi.org/10.1016/j.destud.2012.10.001
27. Holt, D., Cameron, D.: Cultural Strategy: Using Innovative Ideologies to Build Breakthrough Brands. Oxford University Press, UK (2010)
28. Brown, T.: Change by Desing: How Design Thinking Transforms Organisations and Inspires Innovation. HarperCollins, New York (2009)
29. Manzini, E.: New design knowledge. Des. Stud. **30**(1), 4–12 (2009)
30. Roshko, T.: The pedagogy of bio-design: methodology development. WIT Trans. Ecol. Environ. **135**, 545–558 (2010). https://doi.org/10.2495/DN100491
31. Findeli, A.: Rethinking design education for the 21st century: theoretical, methodological, and ethical discussion. Des. Issues **17**, 5–17 (2001). https://doi.org/10.1162/074793601521 03796
32. Cooke, P.: Green design aesthetics: ten principles. City Cult. Soc. **3**(4), 293–302 (2012)
33. Pazmino, A.V.: Uma reflexão sobre Design Social, Eco Design, e Design Sustentável. International Symposium on Sustainable Design (2007)
34. Fallman, D.: The interaction design research triangle of design practice, design studies, and design exploration. Des. Issues **24**(3), 4–18 (2008). https://doi.org/10.1162/desi.2008.24.3.4
35. Schon, D.: The Reflective Practitioner: How Professionals Think in Action. Basic Books, New York (1983)
36. Forlano, L.: Posthumanism and design. She Ji: J. Des. Econ. Innov. **3**(1), 16–29 (2017)
37. Braidotti, R.: The Posthuman. Polity Press, Berlin (2013)

The False Dichotomy of Usability and Aesthetics in the Field of HCI Design

Dorothy Shamonsky(✉) (iD)

Brandeis University, 415 South St, Waltham, MA 02453, USA
dshamonsky@ics.com

Abstract. The profession of Human-Computer Interface (HCI) Design has a history of considering usability and aesthetics as separate aspects of a design. The dichotomy has perpetuated a common split in the profession between the subspecialities of Interaction Design and Visual Design, or a split between who designs the logic and who designs the look. This split creates more opportunity for diminished synergy between the logic and the visual design. The concept of "wrapping wireframes in a visual design" reflects a narrow view of aesthetics as focused on branding, style, and visual appeal [1]. Aesthetics plays a role in everything we experience, including usability, and this broad view is more in line with designing a whole user experience [2–4]. What is ignored by not considering usability and aesthetics as fundamentally integrated might be the deep harmony of logical order, the simple elegance of minimal options, or the perfect marriage of shape and behavior. Three reasons for the dichotomy of usability and aesthetics in the HCI profession might be: 1.) Using computers is much more complicated than using non-computer products. 2.) The HCI field has been historically filled with people from mostly science-based backgrounds that don't value aesthetics. 3.) HCI designers lack the power to assert aesthetic priorities in the way that designers can in Architecture or Industrial Design due to business and engineering priorities. Now that computation is escaping the limitations of the GUI, gaining varied physical embodiments, mobility, intelligence, even personalities, it is time embrace a broad view of aesthetics.

Keywords: Aesthetics · Form follows function · UX design

1 Introduction

1.1 The Disconnect of Logic and Look

The profession of Human-Computer Interface (HCI) Design has a history of considering usability and aesthetics as separate aspects of the design. "Don't let the aesthetics diminish the usability," has been a common rule of thumb in the profession. Belief in the dichotomy has perpetuated a common split in the profession between the subspecialities of Interaction Design and Visual Design, or a split between who designs the logic and who designs the look. This split creates more opportunity for disconnection and diminished synergy between the logic and the visual design. The concept of "wrapping wireframes

M. M. Soares et al. (Eds.): HCII 2022, LNCS 13323, pp. 80–89, 2022.
https://doi.org/10.1007/978-3-031-05906-3_7

in a visual design" reflects a narrow view of aesthetics as focused on branding, style, and visual appeal [1]. Aesthetics plays a role in everything we experience, including usability, and this broad view is more in line with designing a user experience [2–4]. What is ignored by not considering usability and aesthetics as fundamentally integrated might be the deep harmony of logical order, the simple elegance of minimal options, or the perfect marriage of shape and behavior. *Good usability depends on aesthetics.* The goal of this paper is to elucidate how the profession of HCI has developed a narrow view of interface aesthetics and how it might move beyond it.

1.2 Why "Aesthetics"

I use the term aesthetics rather than beauty or appeal because it implies a direct connection with the senses. Aesthetics can be defined as, "How things are known via the senses" [1]. The term aesthetics has its roots in a Greek word which means "pertaining to sense perception." Compare it to the term anesthesia which means the opposite, a general loss of the senses of perception [5]. The comparison brings home the meaning more clearly; to experience aesthetics is to be alive, to be aware, to be taking in information with our senses.

Thus, in using the term aesthetics, I am not referring to its definition as a branch of philosophy or as it applies to the making of art. I am referring to aesthetics related to design fields which is often referred to as "applied aesthetics." Applied aesthetics is defined as the application of aesthetics to cultural constructs such as human-created artifacts. These artifacts can be either physical or virtual and have both functionality and beauty. "At best, the two needs are synergistic, in which 'beauty' makes an artifact work better, or in which more functional artifacts are appreciated as aesthetically pleasing. This achievement of form and function, of art and science, of beauty and usefulness, is the primary goal of design, in all of its domains" [6]. Or stated more concisely, a thing's function is integral to its aesthetic character [7].

1.3 Form Follows Function

Other product design professions such as Architecture or Industrial Design do not struggle with the integration of form and function, or at least not to the extent that the HCI profession does. In 1896 architect Louis Sullivan coined the expression, "form follows function" [8]. In user experience terms that might mean, "Good usability is more beautiful than bad usability" [1]. Frank Lloyd Wright, Sullivan's mentee, later modified the expression to be, "Form and function should be one, joined in a spiritual union." By that he meant, "to create spaces that function well intuitively while at the same time possess a timeless beauty…" [9]. The field of HCI should be able to go even deeper into the synergy of form and function because form can direct behavior or interaction. Form informs about function. I am not suggesting that it is an easy addition to an HCI practice. Good design is difficult and interactive digital artifacts are complicated. However, I am suggesting that as HCI designers, we should take the challenge to fully integrate form and function to our best ability.

1.4   The Experience of Beauty

Key here is the idea that applied aesthetics is concerned with the experience of beauty rather than the concept of beauty. Humans experience beauty, or the opposite, at every level of existence, and it influences our emotions and behaviors. Consider this perspective by computer scientist Terry Winograd: "The experience of a person who is interacting with a computer system is not limited to the cognitive aspects that have been explored in the mainstream literature on human-computer interaction. As humans, we experience the world in aesthetic, affective, and emotional terms as well. Because computing evolved initially for use in the laboratory and the office, noncognitive aspects have been largely ignored, except by creators of games. Yet, whenever people experience a piece of software – whether it be a spreadsheet or a physics simulation – they have natural human responses. They experience beauty, satisfaction, and fun, or the corresponding opposites [10].

Also consider this perspective by computer scientist, David Gelernter: "The sense of beauty is a tuning fork in the brain that hums when we stumble on something beautiful. We enjoy the resonant hum and seek it out. And when we return numb and weary from a round of shoveling the grim gray snow of life, beauty is the hearth, beauty's the fire, beauty's the cup of coffee (the fragrance, the saucer's clink, the curl of the cream) that makes it all worthwhile." Gelernter goes on to say, "Strangely enough, beauty is also the truth-and-rightness meter, and science and technology could not exist without it. Its tuning-fork hum guides scientists toward truth and technologists toward stronger and more useful machines" [11].

But ironically one can argue that it is the need for deep engineering involvement in computers that maintains a focus on function over aesthetics. It is about software budgets and lack of time to polish interface design implementation or prioritizing more features over more polish. Engineers have "owned" computers from their beginnings and HCI professionals have yet to fully drive the design implementation in the way that architects drive the construction process to adhere to their designs. The fear of code not working keeps engineers in the driver's seat. Also, HCI Design began as a field of scientists and engineers. "The field of usability design takes root in cognitive science – a combination of cognitive psychology, computer science, and engineering…" [12].

1.5   Broad View and Narrow View

I consider Winograd's and Gelernter's perspective on beauty as a broad view where humans perceive all their activities through the filter of aesthetics. In contrast HCI Design has historically taken a narrow view of aesthetics, where it is isolated to the visual design of the graphical user interface (GUI) rather than about the whole experience of using a computer. I include the synergistic integration of form and function in this broad view. What is groundbreaking in HCI Design and contrasts with other design professions is a focus on users and the practice of well-developed user centered design (UCD) methodologies. One might assume aesthetics would be a part of UCD but Norman himself, a strong proponent of UCD practices, admits to not paying emotions and aesthetics their due in his early work. "In the 1980s, in writing The Design of Everyday Things, I didn't take emotions into account. I addressed utility and usability, function and form, all in a logical, dispassionate way… But I've changed. Why? In part because of new scientific advances in our understanding of the brain and how emotions and cognition are thoroughly intertwined… Along with emotions, there is one other point as well: aesthetics, attractiveness and beauty" [12].

Norman is referring to recent advancements in understanding how the brain works, and recent research into Evolutionary Aesthetics that suggest that we are adapted for certain aesthetic preferences because they contribute to our survival as a species. He is also referencing numerous studies that have been done on the relationship of usability and aesthetics. For example, one of the first was performed in the early 1990s by Kurosu and Kashimura using ATM machines. They tested two ATMs that were identical in function but one was more attractively designed. The more attractive one was perceived as having higher usability. [13] Numerous subsequent research projects that tested for similar factors validated the findings: beautiful things appear to work better. But it appears to take more than a some research projects and books to alter longstanding practices.

1.6   Three Reasons for the Narrow View

I propose three possible reasons for the longstanding dichotomy of usability and aesthetics in the HCI profession: 1.) Using computers is much more complicated than using non-computer products and even compared to other advanced machinery, computers are complicated and require a large amount of attention to usability. 2.) The HCI field has been historically filled with people from a variety of backgrounds, such as engineering, cognitive science, psychology, and human factors, and in the mix of specialties, mostly science-based, aesthetics is perceived as having low value. 3.) HCI designers lack the power to assert aesthetic priorities in the way that designers can in Architecture or Industrial Design due to the business of software and the engineering priorities.

Can the HCI profession get past the narrow view of aesthetics? Can it grow and change at the speed of science research breakthroughs and advances in emerging tech such as robotics, both which challenge the narrow view of aesthetics?

2   Background – A Very Brief History of HCI Aesthetics

2.1   Machines and Interaction

Early computers were the sole domain of scientists and engineers whose priorities were the workability of them, using mechanical switches, punch cards, and command line interfaces [14]. But in the broad view of aesthetics, it shouldn't preclude aesthetics consideration. Gelernter expresses it this way: "Beauty is important in engineering terms because software is so complicated. Complexity makes programs hard to build and potentially hard to use; beauty is the ultimate defense against complexity" [11]. But if this kind of thinking was present among early computer science engineers, it was likely not in the foreground where concerns about advancing the technology were the priority.

2.2 GUI and Visual Language

The invention of the mouse and the GUI were pivotal in creating a visual/spatial language that users could learn and use to interact with a computer. The evolution of the GUI into the desktop/document metaphor connected directly into 2-D and 3-D design disciplines such as Graphic Design. One of the first steps soon after the development of the GUI was to take visual design principles familiar to paper-based designers and apply them to digital screen design. Designers such as Aaron Marcus recognized a need for graphic design to be applied to GUIs, even while screen resolutions were still low. The goal was to bring the "clear, distinct, consistent visible language" of graphic design to the practice of HCI design [15].

The GUI required a visual pattern language of interactive controls as well as a system of layout, use of templates and design systems, skill with font readability, iconography, information design, animation, and 3-D design. Usability was greatly improved as interaction went from typed text to visual/spatial representations. Interacting with a computer went from very complex to less complex and heavily cognitive to somewhat intuitive.

2.3 WWW and Multimedia

Color GUIs and the World Wide Web opened the floodgates of visual design in interfaces. Applications aren't only tools, but games, entertainment, and means of communication. It was difficult for interface designers to resist the enthusiasm for multimedia and interfaces became graphic-heavy, super colorful, and animated. Companies hired visual designers to create these highly graphical interface elements and websites with a strong emphasis on style rather than usability. Computers become tools for creating art, design, movie effects, animation. Maximalism as a style in interface design graphics becomes common.

2.4 Apple and Style

Maximalism became too inefficient; users wanted better performance. Apple creates the iPod, iPad and iPhone and establishes a design culture of easy-to-use, simplicity, and minimalism. Apple took the computer from a weird and cool technology to a sleek computer product. They transformed the profession to some extent by showing that it can prioritize aesthetics and be highly successful with users, but Apple's success draws attention to style as much as usability.

2.5 Last Decade

Usability best practices have matured and at the same time the expansion of the HCI field, particularly with many visual designers entering the field creates confusion with usability vs visual style. Figuring out how to explain the success of visual design aesthetics was taken on by some longstanding experts in the field. In 2004 Norman found his breakthrough when he declared, "Beautiful things work better." Based on research that showed that a more attractive interface worked better for the users, he explained that aesthetically pleasing interfaces work better because, "Emotions, we now know, change the way the human mind solves problems – the emotional system changes how the cognitive system operates. So, if aesthetics would change our emotional state, that would explain the mystery… attractive things make people feel good, which in turn makes them thing more creatively. How does that make something easier to use? Simple, by making it easier for people to find solutions to the problems they encounter" [12].

However, Norman was not saying aesthetics and usability are wholly integrated. Instead, he was suggesting that beauty is a component of a design that changes a user's emotions which then affects their thinking to be more flexible in problem solving like using a computer interface. Although very significant, it isn't the same thing as full integration of form and function. That would occur, for instance, if a design can convey the available interaction. Take the simple example of a button that is a flat rectangle compared to a button that is slightly raised, as a physical button is. "Perceived affordances" communicate how the user can interact with the computer. Another example would be using color, such as red, to bring attention to an error. These fall into my definition of the narrow view of aesthetics, but they are powerful integrators of aesthetics and usability. [1] Form follows function is illustrated by these examples.

3 Why Did Interface Aesthetics End up Here? Three Proposed Reasons

3.1 #1. Using Computers Is Much More Complicated Than Using Non-computer Products

It's hard to argue with the fact that computers simply have so much capability that to utilize them we need interfaces beyond what existed previously to interact with machines – buttons, dials, and switches. Comparing the design of a computer interface to an industrial design product like a can opener or even a car (prior to computation in cars) may be like comparing apples and oranges. Computers simply will require years of evolving design practices to both achieve excellent usability and incorporate aesthetics in a truly integrated manner.

3.2 #2. The HCI Field Has Been Historically Filled with People from a Variety of Backgrounds, Mostly Science and Engineering

Computer Science Engineers and Human Factors Engineers, with Cognitive Scientists, and Psychologists populated the early interface design labs [12]. Related to reason #1, the challenge of inventing and developing early interface technology precluded any consideration of aesthetics. Although any of the subspecialties of HCI design can bring attention to aesthetics, if you take the broad view, are HCI professionals their own worst enemy and maintain skepticism about the value of aesthetics? Also, the profession of HCI has grown exponentially in the last decade and although no data is available about this, perceptually the bar has been lowered for designers working on user experience and they appear to be collectively less skilled in usability design than prior decades, which can lead to holding less power in an organization, which ties into reason #3.

3.3 #3. HCI Designers Lack the Power to Assert Aesthetic Priorities in the Way that Designers Do in Architecture or Industrial Design

Even though Architecture and Industrial Design work with building and fabrication technologies, they may be overall less difficult or complicated technologies than computation, or they are simply more mature and have better-established processes for implementation. The complicated nature of writing software wins again, and computer science engineers hold the make-or-break skills for product delivery. Also, aesthetics is perceived as having more value in the business of Architecture and Industrial Design; the software business doesn't value aesthetics to the same degree [16].

4   What's Next – Can HCI Professionals Embrace a Broad View of Aesthetics?

4.1 The Narrow View

If you consider the design disciplines typically employed in a GUI visual design – the narrow view of aesthetics – it will be:

- Graphic Design
- Information Design
- Animation
- 3-D Design
- It could also encompass, particularly for a mobile device:
- Industrial Design
- Ergonomics

The elements of a design include:

- Composition/Layout
- Iconography
- Fonts
- Colors

The immediate goal is to achieve a simple, elegant, organized, frictionless flow of interaction, on the screen with good readability and clarity of meaning [17].

4.2 The Broad View

To expand an interface design into a broader view of aesthetics, one would look for deeper and more subtle ways that aesthetics and usability can be integrated. This obviously can encompass an infinite range of possibilities. Here are some examples:
    Is the workflow organization simple, elegant, and apparent to the user?

- Do the elements in the interface appropriately grab attention to direct attention or the progress of a workflow?

- Do animations inform possible behaviors and interactions rather than just entertain or worse, distract?
- Does the shape of elements let you know how you can interact with them; are affordances represented clearly and accurately?
- Does the computer have an appropriate demeanor; does it have manners and responsiveness?
- Is the meaning that one makes from the shapes and colors in the interface appropriate to the interaction and the design as a whole?
- Does visceral appeal direct attention appropriately and stimulate appropriate interaction?
- Is intuition employed to make understanding of the interface easier?
- Is instinct employed to make using the interface faster and more frictionless?
- Does the design have a wholeness or gestalt?
- Is the design highly accessible to all appropriate users?
- Does the design adhere to the common definition of a good design: Every aspect of the design serves a purpose; nothing is superfluous?
- Does the form of the content and the interaction with that content harmonize?

This quote from designers Gillian Crampton Smith and Philip Tabor describes the relationship of content and form through a broad view of aesthetics: "There is a commonly held assumption that content is somehow separate from form… We think that this assumption is mistaken. Content cannot be perceived without form, and the form of a message affects the content… the form of a design (almost any design or any kind, we claim) is inseparable from the content. How a design conveys a message is an important part of the message itself. Moreover, every piece of design carries an aesthetic charge, whether or not it has been consciously attended to; even inattention will be interpreted by the audience as meaningful… The fulfillment of function inevitably generates, and is generated by, an aesthetic. Yet closely related to the notion that content and form are separable is the myth that function and aesthetics are divisible. This idea has several lamentable aspects. One is that it usually comes bundled with the puritan assumption that function takes precedence over aesthetics… Another is that this precedence tends to be temporal; that is, artist-designers are invited to only the final stages of a design's development, to apply a final coat of spray-on aesthetics… Aesthetics, moreover, are concerned with more than visual appearance. There is a delight in a program that is rigorously consistent, elegantly clear and lean, where sound and vision are perfectly at one, or where the representation chosen neatly fits the ways that users think about what they are doing" [10].

5   Conclusion

The HCI practice grew out of a science mindset. Science continues to study human behavior, psychology, and physiology more deeply. Emerging fields such as Evolutionary Aesthetics have proposed theories that connect aesthetics and instinctual behaviors. Theories such as, we have evolved to be attracted to fitness because it supports survival of our species relates directly to, the notion that we find beauty in good usability. A deeper understanding of how instinct influences our perception and preferences is valuable knowledge for designing effortless, easy-to-use interfaces [2–4].

Human behavior in relationship to design has never been so well understood. When the field of HCI is positioned considering recent research into the science of the human body, mind, and emotions, a deeper understanding of usability is possible, which is coincidentally necessary to the address the complicated usability needs of emerging technologies such as AI, AR/VR and robotics.

Now that computation is escaping the limitations of the GUI, gaining varied physical embodiments, mobility, intelligence, even personalities, the field of HCI is poised for transformation and expansion. Digital tech bridges machine design, physical design and virtual design. Creative possibilities are huge, and aesthetics will play a large part in the design of near-future systems. Imagine a smart car, which are soon to be ubiquitous. New automobiles combine the disciplines of Industrial Design, Ergonomics, and Human Factors with HCI. The automobile is a thing of beauty and elegance.

Considering the larger picture of quickly advancing computing technology becoming more and more embedded in everyday life coupled with an expanding understanding of human behavior, it is the time to put that narrow view of aesthetics aside and embrace a broad view of aesthetics in what might be considered a more mature design perspective – the synergistic integration of form and function.

"Great technology is beautiful technology… good technology is terribly important to our modern economy and living standards and comfort levels…" [11].

References

1. Anderson, S.P.: Seductive Interaction Design: Creating Playful, Fun, and Effective User Experiences, pp. 16, 19. New Riders, Berkeley, CA (2011)
2. Chatterjee, A.: The Aesthetic Brain: How We Evolved to Desire Beauty and Enjoy Art. Oxford University Press, Oxford (2014)
3. Dissanayake, E.: Homo Aestheticus: Where Art Comes From and Why. University of Washington Press, Seattle (1995)
4. Starr, G.G.: Feeling Beauty: The Neuroscience of Aesthetic Experience. MIT Press, Cambridge, MA (2013)
5. Dictionary.com: https://www.dictionary.com/browse/aesthetic
6. Wikipedia: Applied Aesthetics. https://en.wikipedia.org/wiki/Applied_aesthetics
7. Parsons, G., Carlson, A.: Functional Beauty, p. 2. Oxford University Press, Oxford (2008)
8. Wikipedia: Form Follows Function. https://en.wikipedia.org/wiki/Form_follows_function
9. Handcrafted Movement: https://handcraftedmovement.com/blog/2017/3/7/formfunction
10. Smith, G.C., Tabor, P.: The role of the artist-designer. In: Winograd, T. (ed.) Bringing Design to Software, pp. 43–46. Addison Wesley, Reading, MA (1996) (Chapter 3)
11. Gelernter, D.: Machine Beauty: Elegance and the Heart of Technology, pp. 1, 22, 129. Basic Books, New York (1998)
12. Norman, D.: Emotional Design: Why We Love (or Hate) Everyday Things, pp. 8, 17–18. Basic Books, New York (2004)
13. Kurosu, M., Kashimura, K.: Apparent usability vs. inherent usability: experimental analysis on the determination of the apparent usability. In: Conference Companion on Human Factors in Computing Systems, Denver CO, 7–11 May 1995, pp. 292–293
14. Campbell-Kelly, M., Aspray, W.: Computer: A History of the Information Machine, pp. 207–229. Basic Books, New York (1996)

15. Marcus, A.: Graphic Design for Electronic Documents and User Interfaces, p. 2. ACM Press, New York (1992)
16. Bennett, A.M., A.I.A.: Interview about architectural best practices and business practices (21 Nov 2021)
17. Cooper, A., Reimann, R., Cronin, D.: About Face 3: The Essentials of Interaction Design, pp. 287–320. Wiley Publishing Inc., Indianapolis (2007)

DUXU Case Studies

A Case Study—Applying a Design Thinking Process and User Experience Goals in Developing Solutions for a Smart Construction Site

Susanna Aromaa[1]([⊠]), Inka Lappalainen[1], Eija Kaasinen[1], and Janne Öfversten[2]

[1] VTT Technical Research Centre of Finland Ltd., P.O. Box 1000, 02044 VTT, Finland
{susanna.aromaa,inka.lappalainen,eija.kaasinen}@vtt.fi
[2] KONE Oyj, Keilasatama 3, P.O. Box 7, 02150 Espoo, Finland
janne.ofversten@kone.com

Abstract. Digitalization is increasing in the construction industry. However, there are still challenges that may delay its progress, such as the heterogeneity in construction sites, complexity in its environment and the uniqueness of each construction project. To smoothen this progress, it is important to apply human-centric approaches when designing digitalization. The goal of this study was to understand how user experience (UX) goals could be utilized during the design thinking (DT) process when developing digital solutions to be used in a construction site. A case study approach was applied in studying this phenomenon. Based on the case study, it was seen that DT supports co-innovation in complex development projects. However, DT is not always one iterative process but can be more complex and include many parallel DT processes. The integration of UX goals to the DT process could provide a more systematic view to the development process and help to avoid a disconnection of parallel DT processes. The findings of this study can be used as guidance when applying UX goals during the DT process in complex project contexts.

Keywords: User experience goals · Design thinking · Construction

1 Introduction

The use of digital tools is increasing in construction industry and as a result, construction sites are becoming smarter [1, 2]. Possible technologies that could be utilized in smart construction site are numerous, such as smart sensors, the internet of things (IoT), 5G networks, digital twins, and virtual reality technologies. However, the utilization of digital tools to support the construction work can be challenging due to the incomplete and continuously evolving physical environment and the various stakeholders involved in the work.

Due to the complexity of the construction processes, it is important to choose appropriate human-centric approaches when designing new digital solutions to support construction work. Design Thinking (DT) [3] is a good approach to understand what kinds

© The Author(s), under exclusive license to Springer Nature Switzerland AG 2022
M. M. Soares et al. (Eds.): HCII 2022, LNCS 13323, pp. 93–105, 2022.
https://doi.org/10.1007/978-3-031-05906-3_8

of needs different stakeholders working at the construction site have and how digital solutions should be designed to support their work. According to Dunne and Martin [4], design thinking is a way designers think and apply their mental processes in order to address problems creatively and understand users. Efeoglu et al. [5] have listed character-istics of the design thinker (empathic, observational, and curious, knowledgeable, holistic and integrative thinking, tolerant, pragmatic and experimentalistic, and optimistic) and the DT method (human-centricity, collaboration and teamwork, interdisciplinary teams, ideation and experimentation, and timeboxing). There are many variations of the DT process models available with a different number of phases [e.g., 3, 6, 7]. Institute of Design at Stanford [7] has described DT as a process that has five phases: empathize, define, ideate, prototype, and test. The process is iterative: the phases do not follow any specific order and can occur in parallel.

Another promising approach is user experience (UX) goals, which in experience design concretize the intended experiences for the users and then guide the design toward them [8]. According to Hassenzahl [9], key UX elements for the user are the product's apparent characteristics (pragmatic and hedonic attributes) and consequences (such as the product's appeal, emotional consequences, and behavioral consequences). On the construction site, different stakeholders both experience smart construction site solutions and contribute to other stakeholders' experiences. Holistic experience and the entire context of use are important, as people are not only using the smart construction site solutions, but they are working at the site and the solutions should support that smoothly. Technology should be viewed in its context of use and as part of social and symbolic wellbeing [10].

There are not many studies that investigate the practical application of UX goals integrated with the DT process. However, there are some studies related to the integration of user-centric methods and the DT process [11, 12] that can be also complemented with other design approaches such as agile design [13]. Park and McKilligan [6] made a review of human-computer interaction and DT process integration. They discovered that both approaches are similar but could still learn from each other, e.g., human-computer interaction is a systematic approach and DT highlights building empathy to understand users. It can be said that the integration of user-centric methods and DT could be beneficial because they complement each other [6, 11–13]. However, their practical use should be studied further [11].

The aim of this study was to understand how UX goals could be utilized during the DT process when developing digital solutions for a construction site. A case study approach [14] was selected for use in studying the phenomenon, because it enables observation of the DT process and the use of UX goals in a real-life project context. Section 2 describes the case study. Then the findings are discussed in Sect. 3 and finally, the main conclusions are drawn in Sect. 4.

2   A Case Study: Proof-of-Concepts for a Construction Site

2.1   Background

The case study has been conducted in the KEKO Blossoming Building Ecosystem project [15], in which industrial and research partners in Finland came together to research and develop a platform-based ecosystem in the smart building context in 2019–2021. The project covered the whole life cycle of smart buildings, but this case study focuses especially on the construction phase.

The design thinking process and its five phases (empathize, define, ideate, prototype, and test) were iteratively applied during the KEKO project to engage project partners to work together in the development of new digital solutions (proof-of-concepts, or POCs). The DT approach was used to integrate the viewpoints of human users (desirability), technology (feasibility), and business (viability) in the creative design process. The project included various interactive, engaging, and empathizing activities in which project partners participated. The aim was to facilitate co-innovation between project partners and stakeholders of different building life cycle phases throughout the design process. User experience goals were used to keep users' views in mind throughout the DT process (Fig. 1).

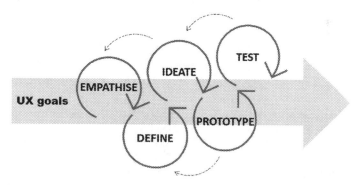

Fig. 1. User experience goals integrated with the design thinking process.

2.2   User Experience Goals Definition

To get an overview of the different stakeholders and their needs, two building ecosystems were studied in detail in the empathize phase at the beginning of the KEKO project. One of these was a building that was in the planning phase and the other was a recently renovated business building. The study started with two building ecosystem-specific focus group meetings to identify key stakeholder groups and to see how they were connected. Then user expectations and current challenges were identified based on observations, design probes, and interviews. The aim was to identify the different stakeholders' needs but also to have more holistic view of it by considering the whole building ecosystem and the social dynamics within it. In total there were 79 participants in the two workshops, 25 stakeholders were interviewed, and of the interviewees, 18 also completed the preceding design probe.

During the define phase, the data from the user studies was synthesized to identify user expectations and current challenges. In order to also focus on future possibilities, two other viewpoints were introduced: possibilities offered by smart building technologies and new business scenarios. Utilizing these three viewpoints in a workshop with project partners, concrete UX goals and a further UX vision were formulated. The UX goals were defined separately for stakeholders at different life cycle phases (plan, construct, renovate, operate, and use) and for each phase there was its own UX vision. Once the UX goals were defined, they were presented in an online collaboration tool (Howspace) and project partners and other stakeholders were invited to discuss and comment on the UX goals. The UX goals were refined accordingly. Thirty-eight project partners participated in the UX goal setting workshop and 10 partners further commented on the UX goals.

After defining the UX goals and the vision at the project level, smaller working groups that focused on certain smart building life cycle phases (e.g., in this case for a construction phase) were formed. In the construction phase working group, there were further user studies with the actual stakeholders from the construction site. In this case study, the construction site included an eight-story residential building that was used as a testbed for developing digital solutions. Based on these further studies it was seen that the UX vision should be updated. The interviewed stakeholders stressed the importance of sensing smooth progress of work at the construction site. Therefore, the UX vision was changed from the initially suggested "I feel proud being part of constructing sustainable and smart buildings" to "A feeling of smooth and successful progress in constructing sustainable and smart buildings." The six initial UX goals were still relevant and were used as such: (1) well informed and situationally aware; (2)

Table 1. User experience goals

User experience goal	Definition
UX-G1: well informed and situationally aware	Mutual understanding and transparent access to site status and special requirements. Real-time personalized and contextual access to relevant information and intuitive guidance to perform successfully
UX-G2: sense of coordinated progress	Experiencing own work as part of a complex construction project that progresses in a safe, efficient, sustainable, and planned manner
UX-G3: resilient	Being confident that relevant risks are anticipated and considered. Feeling capable to adapt to deviations and changes during construction project
UX-G4: collaboration for common success	Inspired of shared goals. Processes and tools support effective involvement, communication, and collaboration among multiple stakeholders
UX-G5: motivated to share life cycle data	Being motivated and capable of contributing to effective data sharing (e.g., via shared BIM models) throughout the building life cycle
UX-G6: feeling of presence	Experiencing common space, even if working remotely

sense of coordinated progress; (3) resilient; (4) collaboration for common success; (5) motivated to share life cycle data; and (6) feeling of presence (Table 1).

2.3 Proof-of-Concept Ideation and Development

As mentioned above, the KEKO project had many partners and therefore, a smaller working group was established for the construction phase of the smart building life cycle. The working group included project partners (e.g., developers, researchers) and stakeholders from the construction site [16]. To support the design of digital solutions different activities were started: there were weekly meetings with the working group, construction site visit(s), and an interview round. These were used to understand the construction site context, challenges in construction, potential business concepts, and stakeholder expectations toward new digital technologies. The interview round included 10 interviews and one group interview (N = 4) with the following stakeholders: builders (N = 6), key logistics solution providers (N = 2), private network providers (N = 2), technology providers (N = 2), a technology integrator (N = 1), and an equipment and tool rental provider (N = 1). Interview participants signed a consent form. Empathize, define and ideate phases from the DT process were iteratively applied at this time.

Based on the interviews, discussions in weekly meetings, and visits to the construction site, seven digital solution ideas were proposed for implementation as proof-of-concepts (POCs). POCs were designed for a construction site of the eight-story residential building. The implementation of POCs focused on the interior finishing phase where projects have the largest number of people working on-site and the most material items being delivered to the site. Therefore, the impact of the use of new digital solutions could be high in terms of productivity and schedule. POCs are described briefly in the following list:

- **Digital infrastructure for construction site**: The first POC was the enabler for all other POCs that built the digital infrastructure on-site. An internet of things mesh network was installed on the site to enable data gathering for sensors and the indoor positioning of wearable tags. Radio frequency identification readers (RFIDs) were installed in building entrances and the elevator to enable material flow tracking. An edge computing server "KEKO box" was installed for local data collection and processing, and internet connectivity. It provided application programming interfaces (APIs) that enabled developers to build POCs and ideate new solutions. The server was installed in the elevator shaft where it is protected and does not take up any space from the site.
- **Equipment tracking**: The second POC utilized the digital infrastructure to reduce time searching for tools on-site and monitoring the tool usage rate in the back office. Selected tools were tagged so that their location could be monitored and shown to site personnel on a user interface. The usage rate was calculated from the time the tool was in motion.
- **Dust monitoring**: The third POC built a set of sensors to measure particle levels on-site. The focus was on the particle sizes that are most harmful for people and that cause occupational diseases in construction work. Data from particle sensors were shown to end users and site managers in weekly reports and real-time heat maps.

– **Situational awareness and analytics**: The fourth POC utilized the material and people flow data provided by KEKO APIs to produce a situational picture of the construction site. Progress on tasks and potential issues on-site can be shared digitally in real time to all project stakeholders to improve communication. Several key performance indicators (KPIs) were defined and calculated to measure progress and productivity.

– **Building digitalization and data visualization**: The fifth POC used 360-degree imaging and laser scanning equipment to build a digital model of the site. This enabled virtual remote visits to the site, reducing the need to travel. The virtual model was augmented with data measured from the site, such as temperature, humidity, and particle levels, that would not have been seen on physical visits. The model also enabled the comparison of measurements with the original building information model (BIM) to check that the building was constructed according to plans.

– **Private cellular network**: The sixth POC was built on-site to improve public network coverage. This solves a typical pain point on construction sites in that cell phones do not work well, because the network coverage is not there yet. The private network also enabled new high bandwidth and low latency use cases such as BIM model viewing and video communication between site personnel.

– **Smart elevator for construction**: The building's elevator was installed early and used during construction time to improve people and material flow on-site. The seventh POC utilized data gathered from the site to optimize elevator control and improve transport capacity. Elevator usage data was shared to other stakeholders and could be utilized, for example, in productivity analysis and the situational picture. The user interface was developed for end users to prioritize and monitor elevator use.

The POCs were developed at a different pace. For example, the development of the equipment tracking POC started at the beginning while other ideas were still emerging and were implemented later in the project. Therefore, it was possible that some of the POCs were still in the ideation phase when others were already implemented and tested at the construction site. In addition, there were many different approaches during the prototype and test phases; for example, some of the POCs were evaluated based on their technical feasibility and some were tested using a small user group.

2.4   Achievement of User Experience Goals

After testing the POCs, the achievement of UX goals was assessed. Twelve participants from the KEKO project completed an online questionnaire and afterwards they were interviewed to further explain their selections. Five of the twelve interviewees were actively working in the construction working group, four occasionally worked there, and three did not take part in the construction phase but were otherwise involved in the project. The questionnaire briefly introduced the developed digital solutions and asked respondents to state how the "previously described KEKO smart infra with its solutions and services could…" support achieving each UX goal using a five-point Likert scale (5 = strongly agree, 1 = strongly disagree). Those participants who were not familiar with the actual POCs evaluated statements based on their previous experience of similar technologies. In total, there were eight statements: one on the UX vision and seven on UX goals. One of the UX goals (Motivated to share life cycle data) was divided into two sub-goals—one addressing generally motivation (UX-G5.1 Motivated to share data) and one life cycle aspect (UX-G5.2 Motivated to share life cycle data).

Based on the assessment, it can be said that most of the UX goals could have been achieved by using this set of developed solutions: mean values between 3.3 and 4.6 (Fig. 2). Participants agreed that the developed solutions would improve situation awareness and coordination on construction sites. In addition, it was felt that these solutions could be useful and provide real-time information, especially for those who are not working on the site. Despite the positive comments, there were also concerns that as such these solutions do not support the actual work on-site. POCs were evaluated as a whole and therefore, one POC does not address all UX goals.

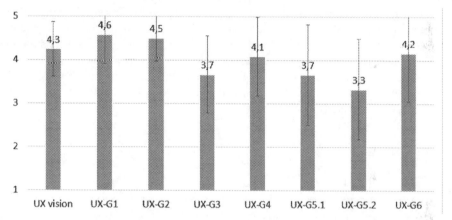

Fig. 2. Mean values for user experience vision and goals (N = 12). (Scale from 1 = strongly disagree to 5 = strongly agree with the statement)

After completing the questionnaire, all participants commented on their questionnaire answers. For the UX vision, the participants agreed that it was achieved quite well with this set of digital solutions (M = 4.3). The participants state that the solutions could support proactive, efficient, and remote ways of working, and therefore support the vision of "Feeling of smooth and successful progress in constructing sustainable and smart buildings".

The participants also commented on the UX goals. The participants agreed that situation awareness (UX-G1, M = 4.6) could be increased by using the solutions due to the fact that it would be easy to follow materials, equipment, people, and working conditions. The participants said that the sense of progress (UX-G2, M = 4.5) would improve, especially among those people who are not always present at the construction site. The resilience goal (UX-G3, M = 3.7) received positive comments (e.g., "the solutions could tackle issues related to information logistics"), but some challenges were also identified. For example, it can be a more resilient and efficient way to solve problems by being physically present at a construction site rather than using only data gathered from the site. It was also noted that it is important to have knowledge about a company's culture and processes because they need to change when implementing new solutions. Most of the comments related to "Collaboration for common success"

(UX-G4, M = 4.1) were positive. The participants agreed that collaboration would be increased due to the availability of information regardless of the company (builder vs. subcontractor) and nationality (language). However, one participant commented that the solutions would not support efficient collaboration in terms of how they currently are (maturity/technology). It was discussed that the motivation to share data (UX-G5.1, M = 3.7) comes from the usefulness of the solution and what kind of value it provides for the worker rather than from the technology itself. There were also concerns that it is possible that companies do not want to share data because they only target their own success. When thinking about data sharing throughout the building life cycle (UX-G5.2, M = 3.3), it was seen that the data collected with these solutions could be used when planning new construction sites and projects. However, to be able to use these solutions first in the building phase and then in the usage phase, more long-lasting solutions should be applied (e.g., battery life). It was seen that these solutions could increase the feeling of presence (UX-G6, M = 4.2) of office workers who are not present at the construction site. In addition, it could be useful for teams and subcontractors to know when to come to the construction site. However, some participants commented that these solutions do not necessary support the feeling of presence and cannot substitute the value of being physically present at the construction site.

3 Discussion

The purpose of this study was to understand how to use UX goals during the DT process. Based on the case study, it was seen that the process was not so straightforward as illustrated in Fig. 1 due to the large project group and how the project proceeded. In the end, the use of UX goals during the DT process looked more like the figure below (Fig. 3). There were parallel iterative DT processes with different focus levels and working groups. Some people took part in all the groups and some joined only for one group. These parallel DT processes were iterative in themselves, but also the connection with each other, such as the findings from the POC development being distributed to the whole KEKO project group. The user experience goals followed through these three different levels. In the beginning, the research question was how to use UX goals during the DT process. During the case study, another question emerged with the concern related to how DT processes form and should be managed in a large research project. Based on the case study, this section initially discusses the complexity of the DT process in large research projects and secondly UX goals in the DT process.

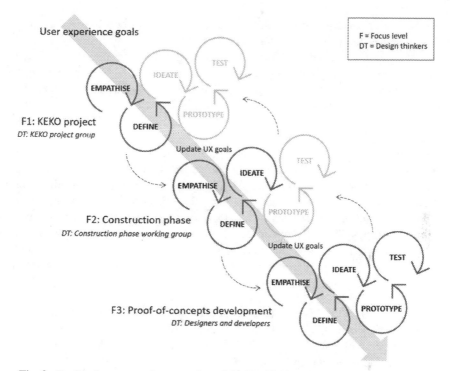

Fig. 3. Realized user experience goals and design thinking process in this case study.

3.1 Design Thinking in the Proof-of-Concept Development

Based on this study, it was seen that *the use of the DT process supports collaboration and teamwork in a research project*. In the KEKO project, DT was used as a way to guide collaborative exploration on value creation and to provide an empathically charged shared object for the development work [17]. This was achieved by using human-centric methods, especially in the empathize phase, integrating three topics (human, business, and technology) throughout the project and using interdisciplinary teams. The knowledge-sharing and mutual support was appreciated in the construction working group [16].

It was seen that *utilizing DT as a process in a complex research project is not straightforward*. The use of the DT process was active, especially at the beginning of the project, but when progressing the usage of its phases was not systematic and clear. Some of the DT approach's typical characteristics [5] were still applied because they were established effectively at the beginning of the project, e.g., cooperative heterogenous working groups. However, the use of the DT process was not systematic and visible for all people. It may have even seemed to be "chaotic" as Braun [3] says—the DT process sometimes appears thus to those who are experiencing it for the first time. This lack of systematic implementation may have occurred due to solving several challenges with multiple solutions in the construction working group. It led to a situation where seven different kinds of POCs were developed in parallel. In addition, a discussion can be had in terms of whether DT is a process that the research project work follows or if it is more the way designers and developers think in a project [4].

Another reason why the DT process was not straightforward in this case study was that there were many stakeholders involved. At the project level, there were many partners from which few led the use DT in the project. In the beginning, empathizing with the whole project group was useful and easy to apply. In the next phase, project partners formed smaller working groups related to their interests, such as developing solutions for the smart building construction phase. In this group, there were stakeholders from the construction phase—some of them were part of the empathize phase at the beginning of the project and some of them only joined this group. At this point, it was not clearly stated how to proceed with the DT approach in these smaller working groups. However, these working groups included three viewpoints that were considered: user experience, technology, and business, and therefore the user-centric view was part of the process. During the development, sub-contractors were also used, such as a user interface designer. This was the third "design thinker" group in the project, in addition to KEKO project level and construction phase working group. This third group joined the work later in the project and therefore they did not have experience of the first whole project empathize phase. In that sense, they did not feel that they were iteratively getting back to the empathize phase that was performed in the beginning of the project—instead, they felt that they had their own DT process that they were following. Due to the fact that there can be multiple "design thinkers" in a project who have different focal points and that they might join the project in different phases, it is suggested that *within large and complex projects it could be useful to have one person or a few people who are responsible for the overall DT view and that the DT process is applied systematically throughout the project by various design thinkers.*

In addition to multiple stakeholders, there were different focus levels. In the beginning, the whole project group empathized in the context of the smart building life cycle. The view was broad, and the purpose was to get familiar with the smart building industry context. The second level was the working groups. These were focused on developing POCs in a certain smart building life cycle (e.g., usage phase, construction phase). Again, it was important to empathize here with the actual construction experts on what the needs and challenges on construction site are in general. The third detail level was to design POCs and their user interfaces. Here, it was important to understand the POCs' users and the tasks in which they are used. According to Braun [3], the design thinking process is iterative. However, there can be different "design thinkers" with different roles/participation in the project who focus on a different level of details (challenges that are solved). It can be questioned whether the process in this case is iterative or rather are there several different iterative, detail-leveled DT processes that progress in parallel (Fig. 3). *It is important to understand that at different detail levels of design there are different problems that are solved and therefore, there can be many parallel iterative DT processes.*

3.2   User Experience Goals and Design Thinking Process

Based on this case study, it can be said that the proposed UX goals guided the design process, especially in the beginning. The stakeholder survey and interviews revealed that most of the UX goals were addressed well in the developed POCs. However, it was seen that the UX goals should have been more actively and iteratively updated during the process and promoted more in the project because some partners joined later. In this case study, only the UX vision was updated in the construction phase, but *it could have been beneficial to update goals and create new ones, especially when moving toward the detailed design.*

One reason for not actively updating UX goals could have been that the DT process was not comprehensively adopted by the key stakeholders as a guiding approach to coordinate multi-level, iterative, and dynamic co-development processes, which included many changing stakeholders and various challenges to be solved. In addition, there seemed to be some confusion among key partners in the construction working group about who should be responsible for ensuring that both the DT process and UX goals are applied throughout the multi-level co-development processes. As a critical reflection, the use of the DT process in the KEKO project should have been elaborated in more detail at the beginning of the project. It was agreed that DT is used as a co-innovation approach but how to actually utilize it with UX goals throughout the whole project and its sub-tasks (e.g., in the construction working group) was not verbalized. With a more systematic utilization plan there would have been nominated responsible people in the project who could have had an active role in highlighting the UX goals and DT process approaches during the co-development processes. *When using multiple user-centric approaches in the development, it should be considered how they are integrated together, which kinds of process they form and who are the responsible stakeholders.*

When the project is large and complex, there is a risk that multiple DT processes become separate from each other. *The UX goals could be one solution to ensure that the parallel DT processes follow the same goals.* For example, when a user interface designer joins the project it is easy to show the targeted UX goals to them and possibly create new, more detailed ones together to guide the designers' own DT processes. Kaasinen et al. [8] agree that concrete and shared UX goals help to keep users in focus throughout the complex product development processes. In addition, Park and McKilligan [6] say that the DT process could benefit from a more systematic approach that is often used in human-centered design processes.

In general, it was seen that *the UX goals and the DT process complement each other* because they both promote a user-centric approach throughout the development process. However, the integration of these two approaches could have been easier if there had been a better understanding of the multi-leveled DT process in this project. Park and McKilligan [6] agree that the DT process could benefit from considering the user requirements and guidelines defined in human-centered design processes.

3.3 Study Limitations

The study had limitations that may have affected the validity of the results. When collecting feedback for the achievement of the UX goals, interviewees had different degrees of familiarity with the developed POCs. This may have influenced their answers. In addition, only one case study was researched that may have influenced the validity of the results.

4 Conclusions

The purpose of this study was to understand how UX goals could be utilized during the DT process when developing digital solutions for a smart building construction site. A case study approach was used to understand the phenomenon in a real-life project context.

In terms of main conclusions, it can be said that the use of the DT process supports co-innovation and teamwork in research projects. However, careful planning of the use of the DT approach and, where necessary, applying several (possibly parallel) DT processes that focus on different detail levels are recommended in order to fully acknowledge all stakeholders' needs. In addition, a systematic way of using and updating UX goals in complex projects is recommended since general UX goals may work well in high level design but they do not necessary reflect the needs of the actual users of the solutions. When using both DT and UX goal approaches, it was seen that UX goals could decrease the risk of complex projects with multi-level DT processes becoming disconnected. User experience goals could help to avoid disconnection by communicating a shared experience vision for the design, and support ensuring that the project is heading toward common human-centric goals.

The findings of this study can be used as guidance when applying UX goals during the DT process in complex project contexts, such as different life cycle phases of smart buildings. For research communities, the paper highlights the multi-level DT approach and how to apply UX goals in DT. For the validation of the approach, further empirical research is needed.

Acknowledgments. The work was carried out in the KEKO project, funded by Business Finland and the project partners KONE, Nokia, YIT, Caverion, Halton, Netox, and VTT Technical Research Centre of Finland Ltd. The authors would like to thank the interviewees for participating in the study and the whole project group.

References

1. Liu, H., Song, J., Wang, G.: A scientometric review of smart construction site in construction engineering and management: analysis and visualization. Sustainability **13**(16) (2021)
2. Edirisinghe, R.: Digital skin of the construction site: smart sensor technologies towards the future smart construction site. Eng. Construct. Architect. Manage. (2019)
3. Brown, T.: Design thinking. Harv. Bus. Rev. **86**(6), 84 (2008)
4. Dunne, D., Martin, R.: Design thinking and how it will change management education: an interview and discussion. Acad. Manage. Learn. Educ. **5**(4), 512–523 (2006)
5. Efeoglu, A., Møller, C., Sérié, M., Boer, H.: Design thinking: characteristics and promises. In: Proceedings 14th International CINet Conference on Business Development and Co-creation, pp. 241–256. Continuous Innovation Network (2013)
6. Park, H., McKilligan, S.: A Systematic Literature Review for Human-Computer Interaction and Design Thinking Process Integration. In: Marcus, A., Wang, W. (eds.) DUXU 2018. LNCS, vol. 10918, pp. 725–740. Springer, Cham (2018). https://doi.org/10.1007/978-3-319-91797-9_50

7. Institute of Design at Stanford Webpage: An Introduction to Design Thinking: Process Guide. https://web.stanford.edu/~mshanks/MichaelShanks/files/509554.pdf. Last accessed 12 Jan 2021
8. Kaasinen, E., et al.: Defining user experience goals to guide the design of industrial systems. Behav. Inform. Technol. **34**(10), 976–991 (2015)
9. Hassenzahl, M.: The thing and I: understanding the relationship between user and product. In: Funology, vol. 2, pp. 301–313. Springer, Cham (2018)
10. Shove, E.: Users, technologies and expectations of comfort, cleanliness and convenience. Innov.: Eur. J. Soc. Sci. Res. **16**(2), 193–206 (2003)
11. Fauquex, M., Goyal, S., Evequoz, F., Bocchi, Y.: Creating people-aware IoT applications by combining design thinking and user-centered design methods. In: IEEE 2nd World Forum on Internet of Things (WF-IoT), pp. 57–62. IEEE (2015)
12. de Paula, D.F., Menezes, B.H., Araújo, C.C.: Building a quality mobile application: a user-centered study focusing on design thinking, user experience and usability. In: International Conference of Design, User Experience, and Usability, pp. 313–322. Springer, Cham (2014)
13. Adikari, S., McDonald, C., Campbell, J.: Reframed contexts: design thinking for agile user experience design. In: International Conference of Design, User Experience, and Usability, pp. 3–12. Springer, Berlin, Heidelberg (2013)
14. Yin, R.K.: Case Study Research: Design and Methods, 5th edn. Sage Publications (2013)
15. KEKO Blossoming Building Ecosystem Project: https://kekoecosystem.com/. Last accessed 11 Jan 2021
16. Lappalainen, I., Aromaa, S.: The emergence of a platform innovation ecosystem in smart construction. In: ISPIM Connects Valencia – Reconnect, Rediscover, Reimagine. Proceedings, p. 110. LUT Scientific and Expertise Publications (2021)
17. Nuutinen, M., Lappalainen, I., Halttunen, M., Turtiainen, R., Kaasinen, E., Hyvärinen, J.: Tensions as drivers for co-innovating towards new digital business ecosystem. In: 21st International CINet Conference: Practising Continuous Innovation in Digital Ecosystems (2020)

A Systematic Review of User-Centered Design Framework Applied to the Redesign of Purchase Order Modules

Alexis Avelino[✉] [iD], Rony Cueva[iD], and Freddy Paz[iD]

Pontificia Universidad Católica del Perú, Lima 32, San Miguel, Perú
{avelino.johan,cueva.r}@pucp.edu.pe, fpaz@pucp.pe

Abstract. Usability is a quality attribute that concerns all professionals involved in the software development process. For this reason, several methods have been established to determine if a software product is easy to use, intuitive, understandable, and attractive to users. However, despite the relevance of this software quality attribute, there are still applications with a low level of usability. Enterprise Resource Planning (ERP) software products still provide graphical interfaces that do not consider the context, the conditions of use, and the final objectives of the user. There is evidence that many of these applications, which are widely used in the market, especially the purchase order generation modules, have been designed without following a user-centered design process and without going through an evaluation process. This fact leads many companies to redesign the graphical interfaces that allow user interaction with ERPs. This study reports the results obtained from a systematic literature review (SLR) that aims to identify case studies on which redesign of purchase order modules are reported. The purpose was to identify and analyze the methodologies, tools, and methods most used in the redesign of this type of software application as well as the reasons that lead companies to modify the interfaces. A total of 159 studies were identified, of which 22 were selected as relevant to this review. According to the analysis, frustration and little comfort lead companies to use a User-Centered Design (UCD) framework to redesign the graphical interfaces.

Keywords: Human-computer interaction · Usability and user experience · Systematic literature review · Human-centered design

1 Introduction

Software development professionals are concerned with ensuring that their technology products are usable [1]. That a software application is easy to use, understandable, intuitive and allows the achievement of the user's objectives makes it successful in a currently highly competitive market. However, even though usability is highly relevant and there are methods to design usable interfaces, many systems are still difficult and complex to use [2]. Enterprise Resource Planning (ERP) are systems that integrate and support multiple business models associated with its production operations and

© The Author(s), under exclusive license to Springer Nature Switzerland AG 2022
M. M. Soares et al. (Eds.): HCII 2022, LNCS 13323, pp. 106–123, 2022.
https://doi.org/10.1007/978-3-031-05906-3_9

the distribution aspects. However, since these computer products cover many scenarios and possibilities, their graphical interfaces are extensively saturated with components, making the system difficult to use and poorly understood [3]. The low level of usability can be evidenced specifically in the purchase order modules of the ERP systems. These software components offer a minimum level of user experience because they have been developed without following a user-centered methodology [4].

The current modules for generating purchase orders, in general, are developed without considering the context and conditions of use, which implies little understanding of the user needs [5]. For this reason, the tasks that the user performs during their experience are not entirely appropriate since users usually visualize contradictory and irrelevant information. Similarly, purchasing systems have been implemented without considering the final objectives of the users, which harms their degree of interaction with the system since it is difficult for them to complete the tasks proposed. Likewise, by not meeting the user's final goals, the design can generate frustration and hinder the successful completion of tasks, which leads to an increase in the cost of product development due to the need to provide intensive training courses for users [6]. These reasons lead companies to redesign or create graphical interfaces that allow users to interact with the purchase order generation modules. However, the most appropriate methodologies, tools, methods, and the specific reasons that lead to redesign are still unknown. In this study, we present the results of a systematic review of the literature that aims to analyze all the research that reports the redesign of purchase order modules that are part of ERP systems. From the analysis of this information, it has been possible to determine the usability problems presented by the current design proposals of the purchasing systems and the tools and design methods used to solve them. This study intends to serve as a guide to carry out redesigns of this type of software application and can be used both in academia and in the industry by professionals immersed in the area of Software Engineering and Human-Computer Interaction.

2 Conceptual Framework

2.1 User-Centered Design

User-centered design, better known by its acronym UCD, is an iterative design process framework that incorporates user-centered validations in each of the phases of its development. This process is carried out under constant interaction with users [7].

The interactions allow a deep understanding of the user and how they will ultimately interact with each part of the product to be developed. According to ISO 9241–210 [8], this framework consists of 4 steps which are detailed below:

- Identify user needs according to the context
- Specify the requirements for both the user and the company
- Solution Design
- Design evaluation

2.2 Usability

According to Nielsen [9], usability is a quality attribute that defines how easy interfaces are to use. Usability is a measurable factor directly involved in the experience perceived by the users. Applied in this context, it allows the achievement of user goals more easily.

Niclsen classifies usability on the following attributes:

- Learnability: How easy it is for users to accomplish basic tasks on the first encounter with the design.
- Efficiency: Once users know the interface, how fast can they accomplish their tasks
- Memorization: How easy it is for users to recover their learning after spending a long time without interacting with the interface.
- Errors: How many errors users make, how severe the errors are, and how easy it is for the user to recover from them.
- Satisfaction: How pleasant it is for the user to interact with the design.

2.3 User Experience

The two letters "UX" are the popular acronym for User Experience. UX refers to all the sensations perceived by the user before, during, and after interacting with a product or system [10].

The first requirement for an exemplary user experience is to meet the exact needs of the customer, without fuss or bother. Next comes simplicity and elegance that produce products that are a joy to own, a joy to use. True user experience goes far beyond giving customers what they say they want or providing checklist features [11].

2.4 Purchase Order

They are the actual order documents that are sent to specific suppliers either through a request for a quotation or when the company knows from which supplier, they want to order a set of certain goods that will help them continue their business operations [12].

2.5 Human-Computer Interaction

Human-Computer Interaction (HCI) is the technological science that investigates communication between humans and computers through understanding and exchange, achieving management, service, and information processing functions to achieve maximum operability [13].

Likewise, it makes the computer become a fundamental assistant in the different tasks of people. The HCI process is an input/output process.

2.6 User Interface

It is the medium in which users interact with computers. In addition, the areas of Human-Computer Interaction (HCI) and Software Engineering processes are linked. That is, it is the basis of all interactions between users and applications [14].

2.7   User Interface Design

User Interface Design is concerned with "facilitating clear and accurate information exchanges, efficient transactions, and high-quality collaborative work." Likewise, it is a fundamental concern for the usability of a software product [14].

2.8   User Interface Prototype

The graphical user interface prototype is the result of a development used for the planning and design of software development projects for experimentation purposes [15].

A prototype benefits software development projects by allowing potential problems to be identified in areas of design quality and user engagement. Likewise, it helps to evaluate the quality of a solution in the early stages of development.

3   Systematic Review

A systematic review can be defined as clear and structured summaries of available information aimed at answering one or more questions focused on a research topic. Since it is made up of multiple articles and sources of information, they represent the highest level within the hierarchy of evidence [16].

For this chapter, the guidelines proposed by Kitchenham and Charter were applied [17].

It should be noted that the systematic review is applied in this study as it seeks to find evidence of tools, techniques, and methodologies whose results, when applied, allow carrying out the redesign process of modules that generate purchase orders.

3.1   Research Questions

According to Kitchenham [17], the specification of review questions is an important part of a systematic review.

The review questions fully manage the methodology of the systematic review and consider the following criteria:

- The search process should identify primary studies that address the questions.
- The data extraction must extract elements necessary to answer the questions.
- The data analysis process must synthesize the data so that the questions are answered.

Petticrew and Roberts suggest using the PICOC (Population, Intervention, Comparison, Outputs, and Context) criteria to frame research questions [18].

- Population
- Intervention
- Comparison
- Outcomes
- Context

It should be noted that the comparison criterion was not applied, since everything starts from a search for methodologies, tools, or techniques in the elaboration of a redesign of a purchase order module and will not be compared with other concepts.

In addition, in the population criterion, the term redesign will be considered mainly because it corresponds to the topic of the current thesis project.

Next, we can observe the elements of PICOC (Population, Intervention, Comparison, Outputs, and Context) contained in Table 1.

Table 1. PICOC criterions

Criterion	Description
Population	Redesign of graphical user interfaces in purchase order generation software systems
Intervention	UX methodologies, techniques, and tools
Comparison	Does not apply
Outcomes	Literature that describes the results and impact of using the various techniques, tools, and methodologies associated with usability and User Experience (UX) in the redesign of the generation of purchase orders As well as the reasons or motives that justify the use of the various redesign tools, methodologies, and techniques
Context	Academic, industrial, commercial, and business

Likewise, by the protocol proposed by Kitchenham and based on the PICOC criteria, after having identified the review objectives, the following research questions are established.

- RQ1: What are the difficulties for which the redesign of purchase order generation modules is proposed and what do they mainly deal with?
- RQ2: What methodologies, techniques, or tools are used and how are they applied in the redesign of purchase order generation modules?
- RQ3: What results are obtained when using the various methodologies, techniques, and tools in the redesign of purchase order modules?

3.2 Search Strategy

Once the review questions have been raised, a search strategy is used to, in this way, be able to find relevant information that will allow us to answer the questions raised.

The results obtained from the search must be presented accurately. The search must be carried out in electronic databases [16].

In this section, the various search engines, relevant in the area of computing, are detailed, which will be used to obtain information to find documents and academic resources that allow us to answer the questions posed in Sect. 3.1.

The search for information on this project was carried out in three search engines are presented below:

- SCOPUS (https://www.scopus.com/)
- IEEE Digital Library (https://ieeexplore.ieee.org/Xplore/home.jsp)
- ISI Web of Science (https://webofknowledge.com

Next, Table 2 is presented in which we can observe the choice of synonyms and keywords within each relevant concept whose origin is based on the elements of Table 1.

Table 2. Keywords related to PICOC criterions

Concept	PICOC criterion	Keywords
Redesign	Population	Redesign, design, build, develop, reorganization
Purchase order	Population	Purchase order, procurement system, purchase system, POS system, point of sale, point-of-sale, Supplier Relationship Management, supply management, supply chain management, SAP
Methodology	Intervention	Methodology, approach
Tool	Intervention	Tool, software tool, instrument
Technique	Intervention	Technique, method
User experience	Intervention	UCD, User-Centered Design, Usability, User-centered, UX, User Experience, UI, User Interface, HCI, Human-Computer Interaction, User Interface Design
Result	Outcome	Result, outcome, answer
Impact	Outcome	Impact, consequence, advantage, disadvantage, influence
Reason	Outcome	Reason, barrier, challenge, difficulty, impediment, attempt, obstacle

Once the keywords presented in Table 2 have been obtained, it is possible to propose the following search strings for the engines mentioned in the previous point of this document.

- SCOPUS
TITLE-ABS-KEY (("redesig*" OR "design*" OR "build*" OR "develop*" OR "re-organiz*") AND (("purchas* order" OR "procur* system" OR "purchas* system*" OR "Point Of Sale" OR "Point-Of-Sale" OR "POS System" OR "suppl* relationship management" OR "supply management" OR "supply chain manage*" OR "SAP")) AND (("methodolog*" OR "approach*") OR ("techniqu*" OR "method*") OR ("tool*" OR "software tool*" OR "instrument*")) AND (("UCD" OR "User Centered Design" OR "User-Centered Design" OR "usability" OR "User centered" OR "UX" OR "User Experience" OR "human computer interaction" OR "HCI" OR "user interface")) AND (("result*" OR "outcome*" OR "answer*") OR ("impact*" OR

"consequence*" OR "advantag*" OR "disadvantage*" OR "influence*") OR ("reason*" OR "barrier*" OR "challenge*" OR "difficult*" OR "impediment*" OR "attemp*" OR "obstacle*"))) AND NOT TITLE-ABS-KEY("Mobile" OR "Hardware" OR "Hardware Redesign" OR "supply chain process" OR "vendor").

- IEEE Digital Library
  ("redesig*" OR "design*" OR "build*" OR "develop*" OR "reorganiz*") AND (("purchas* order" OR "Procur* system" OR "purchas* system*" OR "Point of sale" OR "point-of-sale" OR "POS System" OR "suppl* relationship management" OR "supply management" OR "supply chain manage*" OR "SAP")) AND (("methodolog*" OR "approach*") OR ("techniqu*" OR "method*") OR ("tool*" OR "software tool*" OR "instrument*")) AND (("UCD" OR "User Centered Design" OR "User-Centered Design" OR "usability" OR "User centered" OR "UX" OR "User Experience" OR "human computer interaction" OR "HCI" OR "USER INTERFACE")) AND (("result*" OR "outcome*" OR "answer*") OR ("impact*" OR "consequence*" OR "advantag*" OR "disadvantage*" OR "influence*") OR ("reason*" OR "barrier*" OR "challenge*" OR "difficult*" OR "impediment*" OR "attemp*" OR "obstacle*")) NOT ("Mobile" OR "Hardware" OR "Hardware Redesign" OR "supply chain process" OR "vendor").

- ISI Web of Science
  TOPIC:("redesig*" OR "design*" OR "build*" OR "develop*" OR "reOrganiz*") AND TOPIC:("purchas* order" OR "Procur* system" OR "purchas* system*" OR "Point of sale" OR "point-of-sale" OR "POS System" OR "suppl* relationship management" OR "supply management" OR "supply chain manage*" OR "SAP") AND TOPIC: ("methodolog*" OR "approach*" OR "techniqu*" OR "method*" OR "tool*" OR "software tool*" OR "instrument*") AND TOPIC: ("UCD" OR "User Centered Design" OR "User-Centered Design" OR "usability" OR "User centered" OR "UX" OR "User Experience" OR "human computer interaction" OR "HCI" OR "user interface") AND TOPIC: ("result*" OR "outcome*" OR "answer*" OR "impact*" OR "consequence*" OR "advantag*" OR "disadvantage*" OR "influence*" OR "reason*" OR "barrier*" OR "challenge*" OR "difficult*" OR "impediment*" OR "attemp*" OR "obstacle*") NOT TOPIC: ("mobile" OR "hardware" OR "hardware redesign" OR "supply chain process" OR "vendor").

3.3 Study Selection

Below is a list of both inclusion and exclusion criteria, in order to consider only documentation that is relevant to answering the review questions posed in Sect. 3.1 of this document.

Inclusion Criteria. The articles that fulfilled at least one of the following criteria were selected:

- The study describes the use of tools, techniques, or methodologies that are used for the elaboration of a design related to a purchasing system.
- The study describes the importance of usability in interfaces or the application of the User-Centered Design framework.

- The study describes the impact of using the User-Centered Design framework in the redesign of graphical interfaces of purchasing systems.
- The study describes an analysis of interaction problems that users often have with purchasing systems.
- The study describes motives or reasons to elaborate a redesign of a purchasing system.

Exclusion Criteria

- The study describes an organizational redesign of a company and does not focus on the redesign of graphical interfaces.
- The study describes an app redesign for mobile devices.
- The study describes a redesign related to the hardware architecture of a system.
- The study describes usability concepts in another field than computer science.
- The study focuses on the structure and construction of information systems.
- The study focuses on a topic unrelated to the redesign of a purchasing system.
- The study focuses on the concept of graphical objects in an interface.
- The study focuses on the redesign of an organization's database architecture.
- The study does not focus on usability or the User-Centered Design framework in user interfaces.
- The study could not be located for reading.
- The study is in a language other than Spanish or English.
- The study is older than 30 years.

3.4 Search Results

The number of scientific articles returned by each of the databases, when searching with the respective strings, in addition, to duplicate and relevant articles can be seen in Table 3. It should be noted that the search for results was carried out in April 2021.

Table 3. Number of articles for each database

Source	N° Articles	Duplicated articles	Selected articles
SCOPUS	105	3	9
IEEE Digital Library	33	4	9
ISI Web of Science	21	13	4
Total	159	20	22

3.5 Selected Results

At the end of the search process, a total of 22 research articles relevant to this project were obtained. Table 4 details the articles obtained.

Table 4. List of articles selected based on the acceptance criteria

Article ID	Authors	Year	Extraction database
A1 [19]	Bhargava H. K., Sridhar S., Herrick, C	1999	ISI Web of Science
A2 [6]	Tseng, K. C., Abdalla, H	2006	SCOPUS
A3 [5]	Engelmann C., Ametowobla D	2017	ISI Web of Science
A4 [20]	M. Aly, A. Charfi, M. Mezini	2013	IEEE Digital Library
A5 [21]	Röhrig R., Beuteführ H., Hartmann B. A., Niczko E., Quinzio B., Junger A., Hempelmann G	2007	SCOPUS
A6 [22]	Bastholm S. M., Munksgaard, K. B	2020	ISI Web of Science
A7 [23]	Kull T. J., Boyer K., Calantone R	2007	ISI Web of Science
A8 [24]	A. Namoun, T. Nestler, A. De Angeli	2010	IEEE Digital Library
A9 [25]	F. Redzuan, N. Hassim	2013	IEEE Digital Library
A10 [26]	Sroczynski, Z	2017	SCOPUS
A11 [27]	M. Rauschenberger, S. Olschner, M. P. Cota, M. Schrepp, J. Thomaschewski	2012	IEEE Digital Library
A12 [28]	Uflacker Matthias, Busse Daniela	2007	SCOPUS
A13 [29]	G. Meszaros, J. Aston	2007	IEEE Digital Library
A14 [30]	W. Cadek	2002	IEEE Digital Library
A15 [31]	R. Dividino, V. Bicer, K. Voigt, J. Cardoso	2009	IEEE Digital Library
A16 [32]	A. Valerian, H. B. Santoso, M. Schrepp,G. Guarddin	2018	IEEE Digital Library
A17 [33]	Brandon-Jones A., Kauppi K	2018	SCOPUS
A18 [34]	Rankl F., Magyar C., Halasz J., Orosz T	2018	SCOPUS
A19 [35]	Liu J., Hwang S., Yund W., Neidig J. D., Hartford S. M., Boyle L. N., Banerjee A. G	2020	SCOPUS
A20 [36]	Xu W., Furie D., Mahabhaleshwar M., Suresh B., Chouhan H	2019	SCOPUS
A21 [37]	Rachmaniah M., Rafdi R., Miftah M. R. A., Yanuar A	2019	SCOPUS
A22 [38]	Ibem E. O., Aduwo E. B., Afolabi A. O., Oluwunmi A. O., Tunji-Olayeni P. F., Ayo-Vaughan E. A., Uwakonye U. O	2020	SCOPUS

3.6 Results Analysis

In this section we present the results for each question, we will give some details explaining all the concepts which we found on the systematic review:

RQ1. What are the main reasons why the redesign of purchase order generation modules is proposed and what are they mainly about?

For the answer, the reasons oriented to the need that exists to apply a redesign were grouped, the grouping is presented in Table 5.

Table 5. Main reasons that lead to a redesign

Reason	Study case	Quantity
The feeling of frustration and little comfort in the user	A02, A10, A12, A17, A18, A22	6
Inflexible, unintuitive design that lacks ergonomics	A01, A07, A08, A20	4
Lack of interoperability	A06, A09	2
Poor fault tolerance	A05	1
Contradictory and irrelevant information	A03	1

Based on the results obtained, it can be seen that the majority of the reasons that lead to the need for a redesign is the difficulty of interacting with the system, these are mainly due to:

- **Feeling of frustration and little comfort** (A02, A10, A12, A17, A18, A22).
  This reason leads to a redesign because poor usability generates a negative impact on the user that affects the performance of the operations performed. If this feeling is continuous, another consequence is that the user begins to feel little reliability in the system. Ultimately, there is a profound effect on an employee's workflow and productivity.
- **Inflexible, unintuitive design that lacks ergonomics** (A01, A07, A08, A20).
  This reason leads to a redesign since it generates a substantial barrier in new users who "face" very complex interfaces. In this way, performance-related issues can be caused since the user spends a lot of time on tasks due to the unintuitive design. Causing delays in processes that, being automated, should respond quickly and efficiently. In addition, additional costs can be generated in training to familiarize the user with the system.
- **Absence of Interoperability: it is associated with functionalities of other processes** (A06, A09). This reason leads to a redesign, because, punctually, in the purchasing module the search for solutions and the resolution of problems, with other internal and external functions, are involved, and there is a simultaneous interaction between other functions (not necessarily including the purchase), so sometimes difficulty in this interoperability and connection with other tasks leads to a redesign and is necessary for its optimization.

In addition to the reasons presented, other relevant reasons in common can be observed, such as low fault tolerance and contradictory and irrelevant information.

Regarding the first reason (fault tolerance, A05), it was found in a study of interfaces related to SAP 3 that the evaluated software did not have enough tolerance to error prevention and correction; that is, the confirmation and error messages were not clear to the user. However, errors made by the user were easily correctable and verified before the data is permanently deleted. Even though, the software does not warn when it is used incorrectly and entries made are not checked for correctness before being processed.

Therefore, it is necessary to improve fault tolerance. These types of warnings for traceability in the processes for the user are necessary and lead to a redesign in systems lacking these functionalities, generating a loss related to time and cost.

About the second reason (contradictory and irrelevant information, A03), according to the information collected, in a health system regarding the electronic form "Request for operation" (which constitutes the beginning of a reservation process) and the Central "planning view" of the program (which is the main result), surgical planners said that 36 $\pm$ 26% of the screen area seemed irrelevant to all stakeholders in the OR, as it contained specific aspects of billing and programming, as well as empty fields.

Therefore, a design with a structure without organizing the information to be displayed can confuse the user and generate erroneous reservations, requests, among others.

In conclusion, to the proposed answer, various reasons can be obtained for which a redesign is proposed in systems that are under interaction with the user. Among the most recurrent is the impact it generates on the end-user and how it affects the performance of their activities, followed by the aesthetic part of the unintuitive interfaces and the lack of simplicity in the user experience, generating costs to the company by employing extra training to understand the views of a system. These negative consequences in companies force them to carry out a redesign, following new frameworks or methodologies such as DCU, to guarantee that user-friendly interfaces are obtained that meet the expectations of users and stakeholders.

RQ2. What methodologies, techniques, or tools are used and how are they applied in the redesign of purchase order generation modules?

For the answer, the various methodologies, tools, and techniques oriented to redesign were grouped, the grouping is presented in Table 6.

Table 6. Methodologies, techniques, or tools that precede or guide the redesign

Methodology, technique, or tool	Study case	Quantity
Surveys focused on usability evaluation	A03, A04, A05, A11, A16, A17, A19	7
User-Centered Design	A02, A10	2
Heuristic evaluation and software guides	A09, A14	2
Layered Modeling	A15	1
Progressive Information	A12	1
Lean UX	A21	1

Based on the results obtained, it can be seen that most articles mention the application of surveys in various companies to carry out multiple evaluations in versions of the products. In addition, it can be mentioned that there are variants in the types of survey that are applied, for example:

- Simple surveys (A03, A04, A17), whose application has the purpose of evaluating the conditions of usability perceived by users.
- Surveys using IsoMetric (A05), which evaluates the software from an ergonomic point of view, the surveys go on 5 scales, from 1 which is "totally disagree" to 5 which is "totally agree".
- User Experience Surveys (UEQ) (A11, A16), various frameworks use UEQ, mainly because they offer a group of advantages; for example, they allow quick metrics on user experiences (A16). In addition, it is efficient and inexpensive, which is why it is widely used for the construction of various questionnaires (A11).

The second-largest number of incidents corresponds to the User-Centered Design (UCD) framework (A02, A10), the general philosophy behind the User-Centered Design framework is to involve the participation of users within the design process, the Users can present intense participation through each stage of development as partners.

The practicality of the present design framework is the subject of many research projects, both theoretical and formal, including real-life examples. In general, the evaluation of satisfaction and experience, concerning objective characteristics, confirm the usefulness of the User-Centered Design framework.

The third-largest number of incidents corresponds to heuristic evaluation (HE), which allows evaluators to find the probable usability problems in applications or products. HE is applied in various fields such as:

- Usability Engineering
- Visual Design
- Graphic Design
- Information Architecture

In the fourth-largest number of incidents, we can find the application of Lean UX (A21), this method consists of four stages:

- State assumptions

  - State the problem
  - Prioritize assumptions
  - Pose hypotheses
  - Define Proto-Person

- Create a minimum viable product (MVP)

  - Create a medium-fidelity design using a functional sketch

- Run an experiment

- – Make a functional demo in addition to a preview
- – Internal tests

- Feedback and Research

  - – Uses the cognitive walkthrough technique
  - – Employs usability metrics regarding efficiency and effectiveness

In the investigations found, it was possible to obtain that an interface under the Lean UX methodology gives Micro, Small, Medium-sized Enterprises (MSMEs) a realistic feeling when using a computer-based system and provides a continuous flow of valuable information. In addition to that, the Lean UX method captured deficiencies in terms of interface design and flow and other features that may not be realized during application construction. Finally, the results obtained, through the Lean UX method, in the PayPOS system proposed in the research, consisted of 26 tasks, 24 of which were successful and two of them were completed outside the standard time limit. The overall success rate was 100% and the efficiency value was 92%

The fifth highest incidence corresponds to the principle of interface design methodologies called modeling in layers (A15), consists in the separation of the approach concerning the modeling of the structure, behavior, and presentation aspects in user interfaces, with the main idea of fully describing the set of flaws and considerations involved in interfaces with high complexity. The usefulness of using this methodology lies in the independence of models that allow the explicit relationship between business processes and UI models.

The sixth-highest incidence corresponds to the progressive information technique (A12), it is defined in this way to how the information is displayed, for correct execution of the progressive information the user receives only the information he needs, that is, no receive all the information in a single moment. It is useful for users with little experience in the system because it provides only the required information, however, it may result in an increase in the number of interactions to acquire certain information and, therefore, be uncomfortable or even inefficient for expert users.

To conclude with the answer, we can observe that most of the documentation found focuses on surveys, this is due to the ease of carrying them out and how cheap they are concerning the others, even methods can be applied to focus on certain aspects of what one seeks to evaluate. It should be noted that each evaluation or application of any methodology, tool, or technique must be focused on the needs of the company. Incurring in the application of methodologies, tools, or techniques without prior analysis of the context will only lead designers and evaluators to unnecessary expense, considering both time and economic resources.

RQ3. What results are obtained when using the various methodologies, techniques, and tools in the redesign of purchase order modules?

For the answer, the results obtained after applying various methodologies, techniques, and tools aimed at redesign were grouped, the grouping is presented in Table 7.

Based on the results obtained, it can be seen that most research documents find user learning to be a highly important factor when interacting with the various systems. Ease

Table 7. Results and conclusions of applying methodologies, tools, and techniques.

Result	Study cases	Quantity
The high importance of user learning	A07, A12, A16, A19	4
The User Experience (UX) is fundamental and must be found in every development process	A08, A09, A21	3
The barriers between humans and computer systems have been eliminated	A02, A15	2
The redesign of interfaces can bring implications	A06, A14	2
Employing DCU is important	A10	1
Using questionnaires offers the possibility of finding important long-term answers	A11	1

of learning is one of the important concepts within usability, which in turn encompasses terms like "memorization" and "satisfaction", which need to be examined before the effects on learning rates can be fully understood.

Regarding the second result obtained, the User Experience (UX) is fundamental and must be found in every development process, by studying the user experience and its impact on usability, the end-user manages to obtain more confidence when developing complex tasks in a time. less efficiently. Likewise, usability is not only a vital component to consider, but must be present throughout the development process. This is because, in the different stages of development, factors that contribute to usability can be obtained; for example, in the analysis stage. Finally, in the investigations found, when carrying out a comparative study and applying usability techniques, an improvement of 12% was obtained about interaction, this was done based on the ease that users reported using the system prototype.

The third result obtained explains the barriers or limitations that were eliminated thanks to the application of the various usability-oriented methodologies, tools, or techniques. That conclusion is reached after carrying out a series of tests on the system (A02), with results that reveal that development time and costs were reduced. Thus, in this way an efficient product is generated. In addition, it is mentioned that under the need to model human needs within the processes, tools can be combined (A15) to achieve a certain goal, for example, they mention the application of the standard modeling process language tool (BPMN) and DIAMOND, proposed notation for interface component abstraction (A15), to model the structure and behavior of User Interfaces (UI).

The fourth result obtained concludes that the redesign of interfaces can have implications, this occurs when a change of resources is made in the purchase task interfaces. These changes occur due to three factors: the purchasing tasks are defined interactively, the existence of a division and alignment of tasks in intra- and inter-organizational networks, and the performance of performing the tasks. Therefore, the implications that these changes can generate are a relearning of the tasks that involve the interfaces that were redesigned and a non-immediate performance while learning is carried out. On the other hand, practical experience shows that complex relationships cannot be simplified without losing information, and most functionalities cannot be simplified, however, they can be made easier to reproduce and redesign.

The fifth result obtained deals with the importance of applying the User-Centered Design (UCD) framework. According to document A10, the importance of applying DCU lies in how useful it can be when designing an interface that is pleasing to users, that adjusts to their needs and that is not very complex. In this way, the quality perceived by the user increases with each new version of the software, a version that is evaluated and improved under the criteria of the User-Centered Design framework. In general, the evaluation of satisfaction, aligned with the company's objectives, confirms the usefulness of the DCU methodology.

The sixth result obtained concerns the long-term usefulness of applying questionnaires since they offer the possibility of answering very important questions that arise as the design process develops (A11). In this context, surveys and questionnaires should be used in conjunction with other usability-oriented methodologies, tools, or techniques.

From what was obtained, it can be concluded from the investigations that the ease of learning that the client can perceive is an important factor in all development, it could even mark if a user wishes to continue using the system or if he comes to consider it very complex. It can also be mentioned that if a company focuses more on visualization than the easy learning of its environment, then it is not making a good investment. The UX is also a factor to take into account, they mention the research that should always be considered in all development, due to the great impact it has on a final product. Finally, it can be seen that many barriers between man and machine have been disappearing thanks to technological progress, many physical elements are digitized and the various design frameworks can contribute a lot to products from their development and later development.

4   Conclusions and Future Works

It can be concluded that the search for methods and procedures stems from the need to have a product that provides the best possible experience to the user during the development of their activities. This search allows us to focus on the development of the interfaces of a purchase order generator module based on the User-Centered Design framework, which, having various phases, provides the possibility of developing the process in an orderly, incremental and iterative manner. In this way, in each of the DCU phases, various tools and techniques can be applied, even making use of a combination of several of them to obtain a greater degree of user understanding. Likewise, after applying the methods and procedures, it is finally possible to obtain and know the degree of benefit and usefulness of the application of each one of them related to the system in which the development of the complete framework was applied.

As future work, we will carry out the redesign process following the phases of the user-centered design framework. To apply the tools, techniques, and methodologies obtained in the research and focus on the main problem raised in this article based on the results explained.

Acknowledgment. This study is highly supported by the Section of Informatics Engineering of the Pontifical Catholic University of Peru (PUCP) – Peru, and the "HCI, Design, User Experience,

Accessibility & Innovation Technologies" Research Group (HCI-DUXAIT). HCI-DUXAIT is a research group of PUCP.

References

1. Wallace, S., Reid, A., Clinciu, D., Kang, J.-S.: Culture and the importance of usability attributes. Info. Technol. People **26**, (2013). https://doi.org/10.1108/09593841311307150
2. Paz, F., Paz, F.A., Pow-Sang, J.A.: Comparing the effectiveness and accuracy of new usability heuristics. In: Nunes, I.L. (ed.) Advances in Human Factors and System Interactions, pp. 163–175. Springer International Publishing, Cham (2017). https://doi.org/10.1007/978-3-319-41956-5_16
3. Parks, N.E.: Testing & quantifying ERP usability. In: Proceedings of the 1st Annual Conference on Research in information technology, pp. 31–36. Association for Computing Machinery, New York, NY, USA (2012). https://doi.org/10.1145/2380790.2380799
4. Topi, H., Lucas, W., Babaian, T.: Identifying Usability Issues with an ERP Implementation. Presented at the January 1 (2005)
5. Engelmann, C., Ametowobla, D.: Advancing the integration of hospital IT: pitfalls and perspectives when replacing specialized software for high-risk environments with enterprise system extensions. Appl. Clin. Inform. **8**, 515–528 (2017). https://doi.org/10.4338/ACI-2016-06-RA-0100
6. Tseng, K.C., Abdalla, H.: A novel approach to collaborative product design and development environment. Proc. Ins. Mechan. Eng. Part B: J. Eng. Manuf. **220**, 1997–2020 (2006). https://doi.org/10.1243/09544054JEM485
7. User-centered design: Definition, examples, and tips I Inside Design Blog. https://www.invisionapp.com/inside-design/user-centered-design-definition-examples-and-tips/. last accessed 08 Feb 2022
8. ISO 9241–210:2010. https://www.iso.org/cms/render/live/en/sites/isoorg/contents/data/standard/05/20/52075.html. last accessed 09 Feb 2022
9. Nielsen, J.: Usability 101: Introduction to Usability. https://www.nngroup.com/articles/usability-101-introduction-to-usability/. last accessed 09 Feb 2022
10. Hartson, R., Pyla, P.S.: The UX Book: Agile UX Design for a Quality User Experience. Elsevier Science (2018)
11. Norman, D., Nielsen, J.: The Definition of User Experience (UX). https://www.nngroup.com/articles/definition-user-experience/. last accessed 09 Feb 2022
12. Firdaus, S.K., Puspitasari, W., Lubis, M.: Enterprise resource planning system implementation with purchase management module in lembaga amil zakat nasional. In: 2019 Fourth International Conference on Informatics and Computing (ICIC), pp. 1–7 (2019). https://doi.org/10.1109/ICIC47613.2019.8985878
13. Bian, P., Jin, Y., Zhang, N.: Research on human-computer interaction design for distance education websites. In: 2010 5th International Conference on Computer Science Education, pp. 716–719 (2010). https://doi.org/10.1109/ICCSE.2010.5593511
14. Feizi, A., Wong, C.Y.: Usability of user interface styles for learning a graphical software application. In: 2012 International Conference on Computer Information Science (ICCIS), pp. 1089–1094 (2012). https://doi.org/10.1109/ICCISci.2012.6297188
15. Baumer, D., Bischofberger, W., Lichter, H., Zullighoven, H.: User interface prototyping-concepts, tools, and experience. In: Proceedings of IEEE 18th International Conference on Software Engineering, pp. 532–541 (1996). https://doi.org/10.1109/ICSE.1996.493447

16. Moreno, B., et al.: Revisiones sistemáticas: definición y nociones básicas. Revista clínica de periodoncia, implantología y rehabilitación oral. **11**, 184–186 (2018). https://doi.org/10.4067/S0719-01072018000300184

17. Kitchenham, B., Charters, S.: Guidelines for performing Systematic Literature Reviews in Software Engineering (2007)

18. Petticrew, M., Roberts, H.: Systematic Reviews in the Social Sciences: A Practical Guide. Blackwell Pub. (2006)

19. Bhargava, H.K., Sridhar, S., Herrick, C.: Beyond spreadsheets: tools for building decision support systems. Computer **32**, 31–39 (1999). https://doi.org/10.1109/2.751326

20. Aly, M., Charfi, A., Mezini, M.: Building extensions for applications: towards the understanding of extension possibilities. In: 2013 21st International Conference on Program Comprehension (ICPC), pp. 182–191 (2013). https://doi.org/10.1109/ICPC.2013.6613846

21. Röhrig, R., et al.: Summative software evaluation of a therapeutic guideline assistance system for empiric antimicrobial therapy in ICU. J Clin Monit Comput. **21**, 203–210 (2007). https://doi.org/10.1007/s10877-007-9073-0

22. Bastholm, S.M., Munksgaard, K.B.: Purchasing's tasks at the interface between internal and external networks. J. Bus. Indu. Mark. **35**, 159–171 (2019). https://doi.org/10.1108/JBIM-12-2018-0393

23. Kull, T., Boyer, K., Calantone, R.: Last-mile supply chain efficiency: an analysis of learning curves in online ordering. Int. J. Oper. Prod. Manage. **27**, (2007). https://doi.org/10.1108/01443570710736985

24. Namoun, A., Nestler, T., De Angeli, A.: Service composition for non-programmers: prospects, problems, and design recommendations. In: 2010 Eighth IEEE European Conference on Web Services, pp. 123–130 (2010). https://doi.org/10.1109/ECOWS.2010.17

25. Redzuan, F., Hassim, N.: Usability study on integrated computer management system for royal malaysian air force (RMAF). In: 2013 IEEE Conference on e-Learning, e-Management and e-Services, pp. 93–99 (2013). https://doi.org/10.1109/IC3e.2013.6735973

26. Sroczyński, Z.: User-centered design case study: ribbon interface development for point of sale software. In: 2017 Federated Conference on Computer Science and Information Systems (FedCSIS), pp. 1257–1262 (2017). https://doi.org/10.15439/2017F273

27. Rauschenberger, M., Olschner, S., Cota, M.P., Schrepp, M., Thomaschewski, J.: Measurement of user experience: a spanish language version of the user experience questionnaire (UEQ). In: 7th Iberian Conference on Information Systems and Technologies (CISTI 2012), pp. 1–6 (2012)

28. Uflacker, M., Busse, D.: Complexity in enterprise applications vs. simplicity in user experience. In: Proceedings of the 12th international conference on Human-computer interaction: applications and services, pp. 778–787. Springer-Verlag, Berlin, Heidelberg (2007)

29. Meszaros, G., Aston, J.: Agile ERP: "You don't know what you've got 'till it's gone!" In: Agile 2007 (AGILE 2007). pp. 143–149 (2007). https://doi.org/10.1109/AGILE.2007.9

30. Cadek, W.: Fuzzy technologies and their advantages in commercial advanced planning systems (APS). In: Proceedings 2002 IEEE International Conference on Artificial Intelligence Systems (ICAIS 2002), pp. 56–61 (2002). https://doi.org/10.1109/ICAIS.2002.1048052

31. Dividino, R., Bicer, V., Voigt, K., Cardoso, J.: Integrating business process and user interface models using a model-driven approach. In: 2009 24th International Symposium on Computer and Information Sciences, pp. 492–497 (2009). https://doi.org/10.1109/ISCIS.2009.5291872

32. Valerian, A., Santoso, H.B., Schrepp, M., Guarddin, G.: Usability evaluation and development of a university staff website. In: 2018 Third International Conference on Informatics and Computing (ICIC), pp. 1–6 (2018). https://doi.org/10.1109/IAC.2018.8780456

33. Brandon-Jones, A., Kauppi, K.: Examining the antecedents of the technology acceptance model within e-procurement. Int. J. Oper. Prod. Manag. **38**, 22–42 (2018). https://doi.org/10.1108/IJOPM-06-2015-0346

34. Rankl, F., Magyar, C., Halasz, J., Orosz, T.: SAP screen personas applications for post-implementation business requirements. In: 2018 19th International Carpathian Control Conference (ICCC), pp. 451–455 (2018). https://doi.org/10.1109/CarpathianCC.2018.839 9672

35. Liu, J., et al.: A predictive analytics tool to provide visibility into completion of work orders in supply chain systems. J. Comput. Inf. Sci. Eng. **20**, 1–12 (2020). https://doi.org/10.1115/1.4046135

36. Xu, W., Furie, D., Mahabhaleshwar, M., Suresh, B., Chouhan, H.: Applications of an interaction, process, integration and intelligence (IPII) design approach for ergonomics solutions. Ergonomics **62**, 954–980 (2019). https://doi.org/10.1080/00140139.2019.1588996

37. Rachmaniah, M., Rafdi, Miftah, M.R.A., Yanuar, A.: PayPOS user experience improved small and medium-sized micro business existence in the disruptive era. In: IOP Conference Series: Earth and Environmental Science, p. 012070 (2019). https://doi.org/10.1088/1755-1315/299/1/012070

38. Ibem, E.O., et al.: Electronic (e-) procurement adoption and users' experience in the nigerian construction sector. Int. J. Constr. Educ. Res. **17**, 258–276 (2021). https://doi.org/10.1080/15578771.2020.1730527

Research About Strategy-Tactic-Method Framework of Catering Brand Construction Based on Service Design Thinking

Xiong Ding[✉], Zhe Zhu, and Ying Zhao

Guangzhou Academy of Fine Arts, Guangzhou 510006, China
dingxiong@gzarts.edu.cn, 499283982@qq.com

Abstract. In the context of fierce competition and service design thinking, this paper discusses the strategy and framework of catering brand construction. Through the analysis and integration of marketing, management and design theories, combined with the interpretation of many well-known brand cases, this paper puts forward the Strategy-Tactic-Method Framework of catering brand construction from three aspects: service brand based on SWOT, service marketing integrated with 7Ps and service design centered on multi role stakeholders. The framework is a top-down and executable model and paradigm, which provides effective and accurate guidance for brand planning, user definition, product & service positioning and touch point design of catering enterprises from three dimensions of strategy, tactic and method.

Keywords: Catering · Brand strategy · Marketing tactic · Service design · Framework

1 Introduction

As the consumption level is upgrading in the Chinese market, consumers are increasingly having higher demands towards catering brands and dining experience, leading to fiercer competition. Therefore, the catering service industry has begun to think about how to upgrade and transform their business. To begin with, how to create distinctive services and make the brand stand out from many other competitors are important issues that must be considered. Service design is a cross-disciplinary research characterized by strategy and system. Re-planning and organizing resources with users and customers as the center can effectively help catering brands to sort out their own businesses and reflect on their operations and management methods. This paper cuts in from the perspective of service design, and provides more systematic theoretical guidance for the construction and building of catering brands, so as to achieve service design empowerment.

2 Catering Brand Building as the "Strategy"

The strategy was originally a military term, referring specifically to the tactics which a general uses to direct his troops in a battle. In the modern context, countries, enterprises and universities all have their own development strategies. The brand strategy discussed in this paper is the highest-level decision of how an enterprise makes use of its own resources and strength to choose suitable fields and products, so as to form core competitiveness and obtain competitive advantages. It is a series of comprehensive and coordinated agreements and actions.

2.1 The Concept of Brand

Brand, is derived from the Gustandevinaya word "Brandr" meaning "to burn", as ancient people would demonstrate their ownership by burning the steel to stamp a logo on their products [1]. At present, brand is no longer a symbol of private property but also a symbol of design, business or even politics with broader meaning. Brand, as a symbol, is to better distinguish, intuitively express their own characteristics and convey information to consumers. For catering industry, brand is a centralized demonstration to maintain its independence and competitiveness, which can be used as a strategy to enhance the competitiveness, establish a relationship with consumers, influence consumers' psychological preferences and consumption decisions, so as to improve consumers' loyalty to catering enterprises.

2.2 SWOT Model and Brand Construction

SWOT model is one of the tools to analyze the advantages and disadvantages of brands and assist in developing corporate strategies [2]. It was first proposed in the 1970s by Heinz Weihrich, a professor of management at the University of San Francisco. It is composed of two dimensions: one is to find the advantages and disadvantages of a brand from its own perspective; The second is to find out the opportunities and threats facing the brand by analyzing the external environment of the brand. On this basis, different quadrants can be combined to help brands minimize disadvantages and capture as well as utilize opportunities.

Relatively speaking, the catering industry is an industry with a low threshold but fierce competition. As consumers have more diversified needs, traditional catering brands also need to keep pace with the changes in the internal and external environment. SWOT model analysis can be regarded as an effective method to help catering enterprises formulate the right brand strategy so as to win some advantages in the competition. To be specific: a) Strengths analysis can help brands find out the advantages of their own products or services compared with other competitors in the market and find the right direction for development. For example, by building an exclusive culture of catering brands, providing quality service and improving dining experience, brands can increase their own advantages and attract more consumers. b) Weakness analysis can enable brands to find out their own weaknesses and shortages. For example, products fail to meet the market and consumer needs, catering enterprises lack of brand marketing awareness, the service quality is unstable, online exposure is not adequate, companies do not have a perfect rewarding and punishment and management system leading to the loss of talents, etc. c) Opportunities analysis is for an external development environment which can be exemplified by predicting the development opportunities of brands. For example, in the context of the rapid development of mobile Internet, the "Internet plus" model, namely the combination of online food delivery platforms such as Meituan and Ele as well as the offline physical restaurants, has provided new opportunities and momentum for the development of catering industry. On the other hand, the younger generation of consumers is gradually becoming the main targeted consumers, indicting that the younger version of catering brands is one of the future trends and opportunities. d) Threats analysis is about formulating and developing differentiated competition strategy aiming at existing competitive brands. For example, to build an exclusive and unique image, operation mode, featured products and catering services that are different from other catering brands.

3   Catering Service Marketing as the "Tactic"

Strategies also refer to tactics, but they focus more on specific, achievable plans and action plans. From a strategic perspective, what consumers can feel the most intuitively is not the abstract brand strategy or brand concept, but the specific product and service that a brand can provide.

3.1   Service and Service Marketing

Services have specific connotations and characteristics. The International Organization for Standardization (ISO) believes that service is the result of the contact between the service provider and the customer, as well as the internal activities of service providers. It aims to meet the needs and expectations of the customer [3]. Christine Grolus also defined service in the book "Service Management and Marketing": it consists of a series of intangible activities, usually it is about the interaction between customers and service providers as well as tangible resources (commodities or systems). It is a solution provided to customers based on their needs and demands [4]. Scholars and professors represented by Besant have defined the basic characteristics of services, including intangibility, difference, synchronization, non-storability, and non-transferability. The simultaneous carry out of services production and service consumption is one of the main characteristics that distinguish services from other commodities [5]. The key and focus of service marketing are to think about how to combine the process of service production and service consumption, and how to create and deliver better service value, so that consumers can feel high-quality services so that they are willing to establish a long-term cooperative relationship with enterprises [6]. Therefore, service marketing is about the specific action path of the corporate brand strategy at the strategic level.

3.2   7Ps Service Marketing Tactic

The 7Ps service marketing theory was put forward by an American marketing expert Neil Boden in the 1950s at the Marketing Institute. He believed that market demands would be affected by certain factors. Thus, the effective combination of these factors can help companies achieve marketing goals [7]. In his book Basic Marketing, Jerome McCarthy summarized these factors into four categories: Product, Price, Place, Promotion, or 4P. In the 1980s, American scholars Booms and Bitner added three new dimensions on the basis of the 4Ps theory, namely People, Process and Physical Evidence, thus forming a more complete structure of service marketing theory.

Take the catering industry as an example: a) Products are the premise of marketing strategies for catering industry, which can be divided into core products and additional products. The core products can be special dishes, brand image, physical environment, etc., and the additional products can be the service form and service content. b) Prices will directly affect the sales and profits of products. Catering companies should analyze the advantages and disadvantages of their products in market competition, and set appropriate prices to attract customers based on the income level of the target group. c) The selection of restaurant location is an important work. A good store location can bring a good sales channel, which is particularly critical for the operation of a restaurant. It should be comprehensively considered by factors such as target customer consumption power, regional type, surrounding traffic, transportation facilities, rent level, and competition density. d) Catering companies can attract customers through certain promotional activities to achieve the goal of increasing sales and profits. For example, the promotion plan can be formulated on the basis of holiday pace, and special menus can be launched for different holidays. What's more, discount combinations can be made for different dishes, and so on. e) People is an important factor in terms of the provision and quality of catering services, and all service processes rely heavily on service personnel and customers. Therefore, on the one hand, it is necessary to strengthen skill training, improve the overall quality of service personnel, and establish a reasonable incentive mechanism, so as to facilitate the mutual development of catering companies and employees; on the other hand, it is necessary to have a relatively accurate understanding and analysis of the types, preferences, habits, etc. of target customers, so as to improve the quality of service by providing appropriate and personalized as well as tailored services. f) The catering service process is related to the service provided by the restaurant's assistants and the dining experience of the customer. Standardizing and improving service content and service methods at different stages, gaining trust through interaction with customers, and satisfying the special needs of different customer groups, all of these changes and improvements can increase customers' favorability and loyalty to catering brands. g) Since the service process is intangible and imperceptible, it needs to be presented through specific touch points or specific media. Tangible display is the most intuitive and effective way for catering companies to convey their products or services to customers, which is embodied in service products and service scenarios, such as the restaurant's brand image, food display, and physical environment style.

It can be seen that catering service marketing requires companies to formulate a variety of tactics, integrate all sorts of advantageous resources inside and outside the brand, meet customer needs, create business opportunities, optimize customer resources, and maximize profits [8]. The 7Ps service marketing theory can be used as a tactic to help catering operators comprehensively and systematically analyze their products, improve service quality, enhance core competitiveness and improve dining experience from multiple dimensions of product, price, promotion, place, service personnel, physical & tangible evidence, and service process.

4 Catering Service Design as the "Method"

The previous parts have discussed service brand strategy and service marketing strategy respectively. How do they guide the development of specific service activities? Can these specific actions or activities be designed? This requires us to discuss the design of catering services on a "method" level. In 1982, G. Lynn Shostak first proposed that services need to be designed from the perspective of service management and marketing [9]. In the field of design, Bill Hollins formally proposed the concept of service design in 1991 [10]. In 2008, the International Design Research Association further defined service design that it is about designing the function and form of the service from the perspective of the customers and clients, and the service interface provided to the service recipient is useful, available, and desired. What's more, the service provider believes that the services are supposed to be effective, efficient and recognizable [11]. In 2018, the definition given by the Ministry of Commerce of China emphasized that service design is a design activity that enhances service experience, efficiency, and value through innovation in service content, processes, and touch points [12].

Based on the above definition and combined with years of industry observation as well as practical experience, the author believes that service design is a thinking and method with users, system and stakeholders as the center [13]. Its uniqueness lies in the overall thinking and innovative design of the "intangible" service "journey" and "experience", meaning that it must be relied on are the "tangible" "scenario" and "touch points" design capabilities. For catering brands, service design thinking can be used as a methodology to improve the catering service experience, enhance the brand's core competitiveness, and thereby increase user satisfaction and loyalty.

4.1 Service Collaborative Innovation

Co-design or co-innovation, with the user as the center, is to involve service providers, service recipients and other stakeholders in design activities, to discuss the content of the service together, and to find and identify new design opportunities. Co-creation workshops are considered as an important method of collaborative innovation. Especially when a service designer enters a new field, it can help the designer directly obtain the most candid views and suggestions from practitioners in a certain field, quickly understand user needs, gain insight into design opportunities, and generate multiple design ideas. It is worth noting that the co-creation workshop is not a "joint decision" made between designers and stakeholders. Instead, it involves the guidance from service designers, the carry out of creative output by co-creators [14] and the deepening and improvement on the concept of workshop introduced by service designers. Only in this way, it can be developed into a service process and touch points design strategy in the new stage.

Kai Ba, a sober bar in Shanghai that specializes in craft beer. It is not only selected as one of the most popular restaurants in Shanghai, but also acquired by AB InBev at a premium price. It is a successful business practice of Huang Wei, the founder of CBI (China Bridge, a service design donsulting institution). At the beginning of the project, Kai Ba focused on three types of typical users under the concept of "user-centered": beer lovers, food lovers, and atmosphere enjoyers [15], and then invited key opinion leaders, foodies, suppliers, consumers and other stakeholders with different interests to brainstorm and participate in the innovation of Kai Ba's experience process. It is expected that people with different occupations, from multiple backgrounds, and with diversified thinking modes can explore new design schemes. For example, they have redesigned the platter that combined with craft beer and more easy-to-access food are provided. They co-designed and co-created cross-boundary activities with customers and clients have been developed, such as the Crayfish Festival, the Kai Ba Music Festival, the designer night, and entrepreneurial sharing. Kai Ba uses service design thinking and methods to build its own beer culture through "co-creation", and finally creates an "open cultural platform" that integrates drinking, food and social networking (Fig. 1).

Fig. 1. Co-design workshop and themed activity poster of Kai Ba

4.2 Service Journey Optimization

The service journey is the service process, which refers to the process in which the designer designs the various experience links of the service in advance, and then delivers the service to a customer. The purpose is to ensure that the customer can have a good service experience in the entire service process. In the service design, designers often use user journey maps to optimize the entire service experience process. The service process is divided into three different stages, namely "before the service", "during the service" and "after the service" from a comprehensive perspective. And the entire customer journey is described and displayed by finding and identifying the contact points, behavioral processes, pain points or opportunities, and user emotions of the interaction between users and services. This can help service providers clarify user pain points and their needs, so that they can define opportunities for products or services [16]. The service providers in the catering industry relies on a large number of personnel and equipment resources. Whether the service process is reasonable or not directly determines the operating efficiency and effectiveness of the restaurant, which plays an important role in the improvement of service quality and buildup of reputation. The process optimization of catering services can be divided into multiple stages, which need to be specifically analyzed and optimized in different stages [17].

Haidilao is a Sichuan-style hot pot catering company, which is quite renowned around China for its service. Adhering to the business philosophy of "service first, customer first" is the most effective means to maintain its core competitiveness. Haidilao has developed a complete and meticulous service that runs through the entire experience process [18].

Fig. 2. Meticulous service experience of Haidilao Hotpot

a) In the "before-service" stage, when customers arrive at the offline store to pick up the number and wait, the merchant provides free snacks, fruits, drinks, board games, nail caring and other services to alleviate the anxiety of customers of waiting for a long period of time. b) In the "during-service" stage, the attendants will carefully hang up the clothes for the customers, provide the ladies with hair bands, and send the glasses cloth to the customers who wear glasses after the customers are seated; what's more, during the whole process of dinning, the attendants will actively put hot towels and take the initiative to cook food that needs precise time control for customers. If they happened to serve a birthday customer, the servants will also enthusiastically give birthday cakes and sing birthday songs, which is kind of a birthday party. c) In the "after-service" stage, the servants will give customers candies, snacks and coupons, and say goodbye to customers while smiling and waving their hands (Fig. 2). It is not difficult to find out that Haidilao has provided customers with the services they want in advance through the innovation and optimization of service processes and content. The "sincere" and "thoughtful" services have enabled Haidilao to build up their reputation, increase customer's satisfaction and improve the repurchase rate.

4.3 Service Touchpoint Setting

Service touch points run through the whole service process, which is the contact points during the interaction between service recipients and service providers. It can help the service provider directly deliver the service to the recipient, or indirectly interact with the service recipient [19]. Service touch points can reflect all details of the service process. Thus, it is an important perspective for design. Designers analyze and upgrade service touch points by observing the existing service process, and provide new ideas for the innovation and setting of new service touch points [20]. Service touch points can be intangible or tangible, and can be roughly divided into physical touch points, information touch points, and interpersonal ones [21]. Such kind of classification can also be applied into the catering industry. Among them, physical touch points include those tangible display elements such as the restaurant's environment, dishes, and menus; information touch points include promotion and interaction on online social media platforms, and ordering systems; interpersonal touchpoints refer to the direct relationship and interaction that have been built between service providers and recipients, such as pouring water, serving dishes, placing orders manually, etc. These three types of touch points connect the entire catering service journey, and none is indispensable. Each touch point interacts and influences each other. The good or bad design of one or several key touch points that can bring peak experience to the entire journey basically determines the success or failure of the service.

Tai Er is a sub-brand founded by Jiumaojiu Group in 2015 to target young consumers. It is positioned as a restaurant located in first- and second-tier cities. There have been hundreds of chain stores, and the annual turnover has exceeded 100 million yuan within just a few years. a) In terms of the physical touchpoints, a black and white visual image combining prints and comics was designed; publicity posters, vouchers, menus are using the same visual language, and personalized copywriting, indicting the spirit of funny and free can be seen everywhere in the store. Such kind of design can not only indict the brand tonality, but also caters to the aesthetics of young consumers. b) In terms of interpersonal contacts, the service process and the input from service personnel have been simplified, and customers are encouraged to use self-service such as self-service ordering, self-service tea drinking, etc. Frankly speaking, this is in line with the consumption habits of young users. What's more, they also formulate a light-social networking catering strategy for less than four customers to increase the turnover rate. c) In the design of digital or information touch points, customers can directly make online appointments and order by themselves through mini programs; at the same time, they actively carry out online marketing and promotion activities, establish online interactive WeChat communities so as to connect and gather more potential users, and convert them successfully into new consumers. The elaborate design of a series of tangible and intangible touch points (as shown in Fig. 3) has successfully shaped "Tai Er" into a young, energetic and unique restaurant brand with great influence on the Internet, which has won the recognition of the market and consumers.

Fig. 3. A series of touch points design of Tai Er

4.4 Service Scene Creation

Because the service process has intangible attributes in its nature, it is often difficult for consumers to perceive and evaluate a service directly and effectively, and the building of service scenarios can provide consumers with tangible support. The concept of service scenario was first proposed by Bitner in 1992. It refers to various physical environmental factors designed and controlled after careful consideration during the service process [22]. Specifically speaking, it includes spatial layout and function; symbols, signs and decorations; atmospheric environment. In the catering industry, building and developing a good and enabling service scenario can not only increase customers' willingness to eat, but also improve customers' perception and favorability of catering services.

Take the food and beverage brand Super Wenheyou as an example. It comes from Changsha City, Hunan Province. It has a large space with an area of more than 5,000 square meters. Through nostalgic, retro and market-like characteristic scenario design, it tries to restore the old-fashioned feelings and setting of real roads in the 80s and 90s of 20th century. Nostalgic objects such as cement walls, mosaic tiles, retro light box signs, old posters, vintage bicycles can be seen everywhere, and cross-border scenarios such as game halls, video halls, hardware stores, beauty salons, ice rinks, community art galleries, etc. are integrated. This can not only provide users with a full-scene and immersive dining experience, but also evokes people's memories of the past era (Fig. 4). Whether it's for food or taking photos, Super Wenheyou uses "scenario" to provide consumers with sufficient reasons to come and eat.

Fig. 4. Nostalgic scenes of Super Wenheyou in Changsha

5 Strategic-Tactic-Method Framework of Catering Brands Under the Service Design Thinking

Based on the above theoretical combing and case analysis, it is clear to see that from service branding, service marketing to service design, it is more like a top-down linear model, a way of thinking from macro to micro, and it is a kind of theoretical framework and paradigm to build catering brand. When having the strategic thinking based on a brand, it is necessary to formulate a clear marketing strategy. The strategy serves the brand and depends on the design method to be concretely presented.

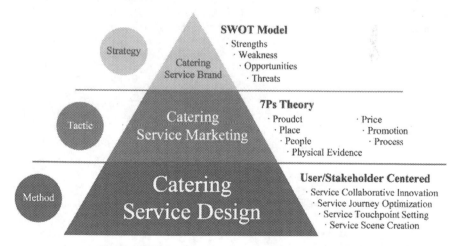

Fig. 5. STM framework of catering brand construction

This theoretical framework is divided into three levels (Fig. 5): a) The strategic level, that is, the service brand strategy. The SWOT model is used to analyze the advantages and disadvantages of the catering brand and the external market environment so as to determine the top-level strategy suitable for brand development; b) The tactic level, that is the service marketing tactics. To find out the core competitiveness of the catering brand based on the multiple dimensions of the 7Ps theory, and formulate corresponding marketing tactics; c) The method level, which is centering on users and multi-role stakeholders, using service design methods, including service collaborative innovation, service journey optimization, service touch point setting and service scenario creation, to guide the establishment of catering brand and the implementation of service strategies implement.

6 Conclusion

In the context of service design thinking, the catering service design framework constructed by combining marketing and management can provide effective, accurate and efficient guidance for catering companies' brand positioning, target users, product and service positioning, and touch point design. It can also provide a reference for the transformation of traditional catering enterprises. However, it is still in the preliminary exploration stage. Catering companies in different types and with different positions need to be analyzed specifically according to their own situations, formulate appropriate strategies or tactics, and use appropriate design methods to achieve optimization for specific problems. The catering industry is an industry that keeps pace with the times and is constantly changing. The subsequent operation and execution of catering brands still requires the collaborative innovation and joint efforts of multi-role stakeholders such as enterprises, supply chains, service personnel, and designers.

Acknowledgment. This paper is supported by the Graduate Innovation and Entrepreneurship Training Program of Guangzhou Academy of Fine Arts, which is "Catering Brand Construction based on STM Framework: Taking Secret Travel as an Example (604012021CXCY06)".

References

1. Kevin, L.K.: Strategic Brand Management (The third edition). LU Taihong, WU Shuilong (Translation). China Renmin University Press, Beijing (2009)
2. Weihrich, H.: The TOWS matrix: a tool for situational analysis. Long Range Plan. **15**, 54–66 (1982)
3. Zhou, M..: Influencing Factors of Hotel Service Interaction Quality Research. Zhejiang University, Hangzhou (2008)
4. Gronroos, C.: Service Management and Marketing. Publishing House of Electronics Industry, Beijing (2009)
5. Bateson, J.E.G., Douglas Holfman, K.: Managing Service Marketing, 4th edn. China Citic Press, Beijing (2004)
6. Liu, D., Chen, A., Huang, K.: A review of service marketing research. Inner Mongolia Sci. Technol. Econo. **9**, 36–38 (2006)
7. Bian, L.: A comparative study of 4P marketing mix and 7P marketing mix. Market Modernization (35), 85 (2007)
8. Liu, Y.: Service marketing and service innovation of catering industry in China. Market Weekly **11**, 32–33 (2010)
9. Shostack, G.L.: How to design a service. Eur. J. Mark. **16**(1), 49–63 (1982)
10. Bill, H.: Total Design: Integrated Methods for Successful Product Engineering. Europe: Pitman, United Kingdom (1991)

11. Duckett, B.: Design dictionary: perspectives on design terminology. Ref. Rev. **22**(8), 46–47 (2008)
12. Ministry of Commerce of the People's Republic of China: Directory of Guidance on key Development Areas of Service Outsourcing Industry (2018 edition). Ministry of Commerce,Ministry of Finance and General Administration of Customs of the People's Republic of China, Beijing (2018)
13. Ding, X., Du, J.: The primary principle of service design: from user-centered to stakeholder-centered. Zhuangshi **3**, 62–65 (2020)
14. Ding, X.: Service co-creation: co-creation in service design and its mechanism. Zhuangshi **10**, 116–119 (2019)
15. Huang, W.: Revolution Driven by Service Design: The secret that Causes Users to Follow. China Machine Press, Beijing (2019)
16. Ding, X., Zhu, Z.: Analysis about the application of service design tools from the perspective of psychology. Design **33**(13), 66–69 (2020)
17. Gao, G.: The Optimization Design for A-Catering Company's Service Process. Beijing Jiaotong University, Beijing (2015)
18. Zhang, M.: Haidilao: well-known for its service. Modern Enter. Cul. (8), 80–81 (2018)
19. Miriam, F.: Service Encounters in Tourism. Events and Hospitality. Channel View Publications, United Kingdom (2020)
20. Deng, C.: Touch the service touchpoints. Zhuangshi **6**, 13–17 (2010)
21. Cheng, X.: Narrative research in the service design. Chinese Art **4**, 90–97 (2020)
22. Bitner, M.J.: Servicescapes: the impact of physical surroundings on customers and employees. J. Mark. **56**(2), 57–71 (1992)

Furniture Design Identity: Discover the Identity of Design Through User Semantics

João Fidalgo[1](✉) and Ernesto Filgueiras[1,2] (iD)

[1] University of Beira Interior, Covilhã, Portugal
j2fidalgo@gmail.com

[2] CIAUD – Research Centre for Architecture, Urbanism and Design, Lisbon, Portugal

Abstract. The presence or absence of characteristics is what will allow us to establish an identity for Portuguese furniture products. Studies carried out by followers of Darwinism point out that what works best tends to survive and become dominant. In humans, the more intense a feeling is, the more it becomes dominant. In this way, our emotional mind tends to prevail over our rational mind. This domination appears to result from the evolutionary benefit of allowing emotions to be the engine of the vast majority of our decision-making and actions. This study proposes, through the application of the Kansei Method and using this engineering of the senses in a non-traditional way, to try to determine, not the characteristics of a product under development, but a possible identity of existing products. In our case, Portuguese furniture. Ours goals with our study is to expose Portuguese furniture design products, to the scrutiny of the user's senses and subsequently to measure the senses and sensations. We used to carry out the present Kansei engineering application study involved: (1) A selection of antonym words (twenty six pairs of semantic descriptors) that best characterize the furniture design produced in Portugal. In the comparative study we will find the similarities and distortions between products that resulted from the sensory impressions of the respondents. This comparative analysis of the sensorial qualities between products is determinant for the assumption of the similarity of the Portuguese furniture design and also its comparison with the international one. This final analysis will allow us to know if there is a Portuguese identity or a link to one or several international design trends. The results obtained by the selected Portuguese furniture products point to higher results than the international ones, which indicates the strong possibility of the existence of a Portuguese identity.

Keywords: Furniture design · Semantic analysis · Kansei methodology · Portuguese design

M. M. Soares et al. (Eds.): HCII 2022, LNCS 13323, pp. 136–156, 2022.
https://doi.org/10.1007/978-3-031-05906-3_11

1   Introduction

"Today, Identity seems so obvious that not having it, or not knowing anything about it, just seems like something from a fool or a wind-head."

Marcel Detienne

Following the normal use of the Kansei engineering method, whose word is divided into (kan) sensitivity and (sei) sensitivity, we seek measuring the sensations and feelings of potential consumers, showing their relationship with environments, situations, products or certain product properties. Users' senses, such as smell, taste, touch, hearing, vision and even synesthesia are used to collect data on what they are given to observe. Subsequently, the results of this analysis of feelings are translated into the characteristics of the environments, situations or products to be developed.

By the Kansei method, designers and others responsible for products propose to measure the user's feelings and emotions of an object or its properties, thus being able to work towards obtaining a final product that reflects the consumers feeling. This emotional connection will contribute to consumer satisfaction, the products success and their durability. But instead of transposing them to the characteristics of the products, we will check whether one or more defined characteristics, identified by semantic descriptors, is present or not in the furniture product.

The collection was carried out according to the techniques of Osgood's (1957) semantic differential scaling technique, which uses a series of bipolar adjectives to measure people's judgments toward a range of stimuli, offers a simple and accurate means of data collection. Investigators interested in studying attitudes would be wise to consider employing semantic differential scales in their research (Rosenberg, 2017). (2) Choice of images of national furniture on which feelings will be expressed by the selected observers, (3) Evaluation of the samples of chosen furniture using a semantic scale questionnaire, (4) Statistical analysis of the evaluation data collected.

For many, the main responsibility for the globalization that we are witnessing today lies with the Portuguese, who, in the 15th century, began their great feat of discovery. It was with the action of the Portuguese people and the example followed by the Spanish, English, French and Dutch that the economic, religious, political and cultural frontiers of the World that was being discovered were extended. If our main objective was the search for cereals, gold, slaves and spices, we also took much of what was produced in Portugal to the places where we established trading posts.

As a result of the launching of the caravels built by the Portuguese, nothing would ever be the same again, myths and barriers would be broken down. The Portuguese gave the world new worlds, but they too were at the mercy of all kinds of new things that had remained undiscovered until then. Everything began to intersect in the direction of the four corners of the globe. In addition to raw materials and transformed goods, all kinds of plants, animals, people, customs and ideas began to be exported and imported to and from all corners of the globe. It globalized the production and consumption of a wide variety of spices such as pepper and cinnamon, products such as coffee, tea, chocolate and tobacco or manufactured goods such as textiles, ceramics, porcelain and even weaponry. Along with the panoply of products and people that travelled on the caravels, also travelled wars, the domination of developed countries, the acculturation of some societies and the overlapping and loss of identity of peoples.

If with the Portuguese the steps towards globalization were taken unconsciously, but with a predetermined objective, from the fourth quarter of the twentieth century and throughout the twenty-first century we have witnessed a deliberate form of globalizing domination by the developed nations in relation to all the others. Here economic globalization gains prominence and takes precedence over all the others.

Globalization has brought with it the standardization and massification of products, the control of markets and the creation of a common identity that is indistinguishable from any other part of the so-called "global village" in which we live, with the consequent loss of national identity and individual identity. Our choices of the products we consume are an emotional response, which our self gives, to the stimuli that brands and producers present to us. Brands do not limit themselves to working on the functionality of products, but also how best to arouse the emotions of consumers with a view to their acquisition, by identifying with objects leading us to become imbued with a common destiny with other human beings. Thus, globalization and the sense of global belonging is not limited to the economic domain, enhanced by technology and the media, but is involved by multiple factors resulting from the domination of markets over human beings.

2 Literature Review

2.1 Emotional Factors in Connections with Objects

Identification with an object is the original and emotional way in which we connect with this object (Freud, 1949), just as the recognition of an emotion in someone else facilitates the creation of empathy and the incorporation of the same emotion. Emotions can be induced in the individual, automatically obtaining responses from the brain to a certain emotion. These responses can also be induced by the choice of emotions that we reveal. Human beings are driven by empathy and easily reproduce in themselves an emotion that they observe in other human beings or objects (Romão, 2015). Emotions work by contagion, provoking identical emotional and bodily reactions in different individuals.

The way in which we process information varies according to the different emotional states in which the individual finds him/herself. Happy states are conducive to highly creative brain activity, launching large amounts of new and bolder ideas. We are tempted to push our boundaries and feelings like fear and security take a back seat. We connect with others and create empathy with objects more easily. If the emotional state reflects sadness, everything flows more slowly and thoughtfully, less empathy, more delay in decision making, more concentration in the search for solutions and negative burden on choices (Romão, 2015).

Different emotions give rise to different ways of processing information. When we are happy our brain is more predisposed to creative tasks in which we have to think intuitively or more expansively in order to have new ideas and broaden perspectives. The moods associated with sadness, on the other hand, lead to slower processing of information, in which problem solving takes longer, but also induce us to be more focused, to pay more attention to details and to be more thoughtful when elaborating strategies. Emotions and their study have proven to be an increasingly important field of study for designers, especially when in the acquisition of products these overcome the rational side in terms of choices.

Kansei engineering uses the study of consumers' emotions and their psychological states to better design and develop new products (Nagamavhi, 2002). This emotional identification with products allows their classification and determination of an identitarian, between consumers and products. Our identity is also an emotional state, resulting from the recognition of a common language, a history, our space as a country, a nation, an individual identity marked by belonging to a national collective, a family with which we acquire the first identification, the first emotions and experiences in the most diverse domains (Sobral, 2012).

2.2 To Kansei Measure

Kansei is individual. It must be able to be grasped and transformed, together with other individual kansei, into valid information for product development. Kansei is a manifestation of an internal sensation, but for the time being, it can only be measured using methods based on external sensations. To measure Kansei, a set of standardized measurement methods have been worked out and developed, as Nagamachi (2002) points out, can be used: People's behaviours and actions; Words (spoken language); The facial and body expressions; The physiological responses (such as heart rate). It is mainly used as the main input to define much of the quality of products, allowing the configuration of detailed design specifications (Lokman, 2010).

Osgood (1957) is behind a method called the semantic differential scale. This method is used by Kansei Engineering, with the objective of measuring the reaction of people selected and exposed to words and concepts by means of scales of two opposite poles, being composed by pairs of antonymous adjectives. This technique allows recording, quantifying and comparing the attributes belonging to one or more concepts under assessment (Neto, 2014).

As is implied, the Kansei process cannot be directly measured. What can be observed are actually not Kansei, but the causes and consequences of the Kansei process (Nagasawa 2004). Therefore, Kansei can be measured only indirectly and partially by measuring sensory activities, internal factors and psychophysiological and behavioral responses (Harada 1998; Nagamachi, 2003; Ishihara et al., 2005; Lévy et al., 2007). In the intent of Kansei studies, sensory activities are measured by assessing the impact of a specific sensory stimulus on brain activity. Physiological measures are performed by assessing responses to specific external stimuli. The responses can be physiological or behavioral (measured by electromyography, heart rate, electroencephalography, event-related potentials, functional magnetic resonance imaging or expressive (by body or facial expression). Psychological measurements can be performed by personality tests (Eysenck, 1964), semantic differential scales method (Osgood et al., 1957) or other questionnaires (Nagamachi, 2003; Ishihara et al., 2005; Lévy et al., 2007). In Kansei Engineering, there is a method in which people are asked to express their Kansei in words when viewing products or products they wish to buy in the future. These types of words are called "Kansei words" (Nagamachi, 2003; Ishihara et al., 2005). Kansei researchers need to think about what input is appropriate to achieve human Kansei and how to measure the expression or expressions that translate it. Kansei input is not always just one input, but may be a combination of several inputs.

2.3 Kansei Engineering Using Images

The shift from analogue photography to digital technology and the development of the Internet along with multimedia tools have given a further boost to the value of images and the information they carry. Kansei image research and creation has been made easier with the Internet, as has the dissemination and management of network questionnaires, so that researchers can more easily perform Kansei image research, analyse representative samples, trace Kansei image semantics, classify Kansei images and obtain analysis results. The chosen images should be matched with appropriate adjectives to describe Kansei images, a well-organized Kansei space with various adjectives is needed.

In this method, an analysis of the object or what we want to measure is done visually. Cumulatively if a person sees something interesting, they will want to not only look at it, but also touch, smell, and even taste the object. It may also arouse feelings and emotions that can be representative of the product design. The involvement of the sensory organs is high, and they have a strong effect on Kansei. Overall it can be said that the more affective signals are given, the more clearly the message can be understood. For Kansei Engineering a higher number of senses involved, results in a better mental image and Kansei of higher intensity (Balduíno, 2012).

2.4 Design Factors v.s Comsumer Factors

The aim of this study was to find traces of a Portuguese DNA in furniture design produced in Portugal. Traces of a national identity that differentiates us. An identity that puts us on the same level as other societies, which much earlier recognized and adhered to design as a philosophy of being in the world and contributing to its improvement. To search for an identity in furniture design produced in Portugal. What kind of design do we do? There will be a common thread that is based on our national identity, on being Portuguese or on the Portuguese way of solving problems. If in the beginning we only produced tools to get food and to protect ourselves from the aggressions of other animals or bad weather conditions, with our brain development this changed and we started to produce many more objects and we had to supply new needs. One of those needs was the interior comfort of the spaces destined to shelter human beings, which resulted in the production of the first furniture. In a natural way, our biological cycle and the efforts of individuals in performing their daily tasks made it mandatory to rest the body. The first furniture produced by human beings would have rudimentary and practical shapes, resorting to what nature made available to them. Stretching out on the ground or sitting on a rock or fallen trunks (Martins, 2016).

2.5 Semantic Differential Method

The use of the Kansei Engineering methodology, by companies and designers forces there is the application of some unusual processes. In its initial phase, the responses of are obtained and quantified in terms of the evaluation of the sensory attributes of the product (Balduíno, 2012). The technique used as general practice to measure product user perception in Kansei Engineering is the so-called "semantic differential", proposed by Osgood (Linare and Page, 2011). Osgood (1969) developed a method designed to make the measurement of emotional content through words. It became known as the "semantic differential technique", which became one of the foundations of Kansei Engineering (Balduíno, 2012). To study the perceptive dimension of user preferences, the semantic differential, this method has often been used for visual evaluation of products. As an example, in furniture design, the designer has always dealt with diffuse information in the production of the piece with specific needs and requirements. The use of Kansei in this specific evaluation will better insight the subjects' satisfaction in design. It is quantitative treatment of how people feel about the materials and furniture pieces. It aims to identify the exact Kansei desired in the products. SD is used to find out consumers' feelings about the product as an ergonomic and psychological evaluation. It is used for measuring the meaning of things and concepts. Semantic differential questions serve to measure people's attitudes towards words, objects and stimulus concepts. This type of differential consists of a series of contrasting adjective pairs (e.g. good-bad, female-male, massive-hard) listed at opposite ends of a bipolar scale (Shaari, 2016).

We begin the first phase of applying the Kansei methodology by searching for a set of autonomous concepts (semantic axes or semantic space) that the user employs to describe their sensations regarding the product. This semantic space constitutes an important tool for measuring a product or comparing different products from the perspective of their symbolic attributes (Linares and Page, 2008).

In this technique, the preference matrix is resolved into a defined orthogonal preference dimension representing samples and users. Respondents show the position of their attitude towards the object of research against a five-point scale. This scale is revealing the strength and direction of the attitude. The ends are anchored by a pair of polarized adjectives or adjectival statements, with the alternative 'neutral' in the center. Each pair of adjectives measures a different dimension of the concept. By choosing one of the five points on the scale you reflect what is closest to your feeling. In DS we can also use a graph to demonstrate comparisons of groups or objects by plotting the observed means (Wrenn et al., 2007). In Kansei engineering studies, this technique is one of the most used methods in order to evaluate the perception of the product under analysis. The use of SD has already been referenced and there are studies in several areas, ranging from architecture to environmental design, from ergonomics to product design and in product engineering with a focus on the emotional importance of products and the responses given by users (Mordagrón et al., 2005).

2.6 Emotional Semantic Selection

Corresponding to the list of antonym words of emotional nature, images were chosen, whose signifier was close to the word that was at the basis of its choice and which are the composition of the database of the study. If for each adjective its antonym was collected, the same was done in the case of the images. For example, for the adjective "Natural" there is an image of a countryside area with grass and trees, and for its antonym "Synthetic" there is an image of a sports field with synthetic grass. Another example would be the case of the adjective "fun" to which corresponds an image of a smiling face and to its antonym "serious" corresponds an image of a serious face. It was tried for the study, although it was not at all possible, to avoid images referring to furniture, so as not to condition the choices or direct results, since the study intends to classify furniture.

In order to obtain validation of the images corresponding to the antonyms we were going to use, a group of selected participants was asked to indicate what they identified each of the images with and so we proceeded to their indexation. After collecting the evaluations, a comparison was made to determine whether the responses obtained according to the emotions of the participants before the images corresponded to what would be expected. With this action we proceeded to refine the images, using only those that allowed us to be more objective in the answers. The final result was 26 pairs of images.

1-	Functional	Decorative
2-	Robust	Fragile
3-	Simple	Complex
4-	Familiar	Weird
5-	Elegant	Unelegant
6-	Usable	Useless
7-	Industrialized	Handcrafted
8-	Funny	Serious
9-	Ellitist	Popular
10-	Concrete	Abstract
11-	Comfortable	Uncomfortable
12-	Light	Dark
13-	Creative	Common
14-	Lasting	Disposable

15-	Modern	Old Fashioned	
16-	Natural	Artificial	
17-	Original	Copy	
18-	Imaginative	Disimaginative	
19-	Detailed	Coarse	
20-	Hot	Cold	
21-	Regular	Irregular	
22-	Clean	Dirty	
23-	Modular	Single	
24-	Sustainable	Pollutant	
25-	Sober	Excessive	
26-	Light	Heavy	

2.7 Furniture Samples

The furniture chosen as a sample is intended to be a portion of what we considered most representative for our study. We tried to make them as comprehensive as possible in terms of time periods, different types of use and, of course, some of the characteristics expressed by the emotional descriptors. In selecting the images, we were careful not to fall into the temptation of choosing only chairs. These are pieces of furniture that are also part of the study, but the choice was also divided among benches, sideboards, desks and tables. This is despite the predominance of the chair in the furniture or the fact that it is pointed out by critics and design historians such as Santos (2003), who has written: "...the most iconic piece of furniture that exists. It is a very sensitive piece of furniture. Of all the pieces of furniture, it is the one that best portrays a country. The chair is a barometer of who produces it: it reflects power, social practices, culture, technology, innovation and, of course, Design." (Fig. 1)

Fig. 1. Furniture selected to semantic analysis.

3 Materials, Methods and Results

The practical part of this study was carried out during the master studies of the Industrial Design Course, at the University of Beira Interior during a period of twelve months.

Our object of study is the Portuguese furniture design. This choice was due to the need to find an identity categorization for the furniture design produced in national territory. To achieve our objectives, in addition to a research that took us from the beginnings of modern furniture design to our days. We used for the determination of the identity, the method of Kansei engineering, of Japanese origin. The material was collected throughout the study, and initially large volumes of written and visual material were collected, which were subsequently refined until only those which we considered relevant to our study remained.

The QuestionPro online platform (https://www.questionpro.com/) was used to carry out the surveys and obtain data. The data obtained were processed using the Online QuestionPro platform. This platform allowed us to make a dynamic and extensive statistical data analysis of the variables we belonged to study in order to reach a conclusion about the existence or not of a national identity in Portuguese furniture.

3.1 Questionnaire Design

The questionnaire design and development was based on the Kansei engineering methods. This technique allows the elaboration of questionnaires to assess the feelings of the consumers towards the products and in our case, it will be used to determine the identity of the national furniture product.

The type of questionnaire chosen, with the necessary adaptations, was the "Visual Selection" (Visual Preferences/Photo Questionnaires). This type of opinion gathering is based on techniques that rely on the exploration of the visual attributes of the images, which were considered representative of the products previously selected for the study. This type of method proposes the participation of the users of the products in the design process. It seeks the identification of visual qualities in the products of industrial production, architectural design, interior design or other project typologies. We used the Question Pro platform (https://www.questionpro.com/pt-br/?) for the execution of the questionnaire, as well as for obtaining the data and their primary processing (Fig. 2).

3.2 Process for Obtaining the Emotional Calculation

At the beginning of the questionnaire a summary presentation is made of what is proposed to those who will answer the surveys, followed by two examples of the type of answers that are expected from the respondents.

After comprehension of what is asked and positive answer to the examples previously presented, 15 images of furniture pieces are sequentially shown, each one immediately followed by the twenty-six pairs of descriptors.

The Semantic Differential method was used, represented with a five-point scale composed of twenty-six pairs of antonymous images in the opposite polarities.

The antonymous image pairs were placed in opposite polarities on the semantic scale in order to stimulate the emotion of the observer. The image on the left represents one meaning and the one on the left its opposite. The emotion is measured by one of the five points of the scale, in which it will be shown that the feeling was related to one of the polarization points or both, "extreme", "strong", "neutral", "extreme" and "strong".

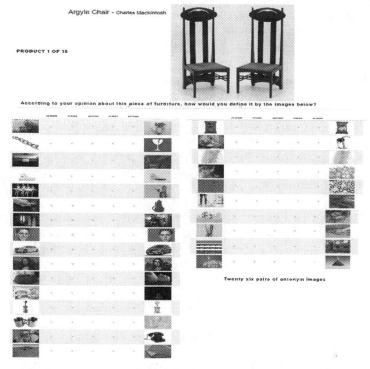

Fig. 2. Example of the survey. (https://www.questionpro.com/pt-br/?)

Neutral indicates situations where there was no definition greater than fifty percent for any of the images.

After answering the questions about the fifteen furniture products, a series of questions about the interviewees followed. The data collected may lead to further in-depth studies in the future.

In order to obtain answers, survey questionnaires were sent via email or presented in digital format to people of both genders, of the most diverse professions and ages.

We will use descriptive statistics to summarize the data collected in our research, organizing them in percentage numbers and tables. This will result in reports containing information about central trends or the dispersion of the data. These trends will be analyzed in a simple way and from a qualitative perspective.

Qualitative data will be those that represent all the information that recognizes a quality, characteristic or category, which may not be able to be measured, but rather classified. This is the case of our semantic descriptors. To summarize qualitative data in numerical form, percentages, rates, proportions and counts can be used.

The data we will work with is the final result of our survey. So that there are no distortions in the results, we can base all the data obtained on only the data relevant to the objectives of the study or on exponents relevant to the study. In our case we will focus on the results above fifty percent. This percentage is indicative that the characteristic in question resides in the product and will have a strong presence. Results higher than eighty percent undoubtedly indicate the alignment of the product and that the presence of the descriptor in question is extreme.

Whenever the values fall below the minimum established for the presence of the descriptor to be considered as determining the characteristics of the product, we will consider that there is neutrality between the opposing semantic criteria. Thus, there is no semantic definition.

After answering the questions about the fifteen furniture products, a series of questions about the interviewees followed the data collected may lead to further in-depth studies in the future.

4   Final Results

The comparative study in its generality allowed us to find the similarities and distortions between products resulting from the respondents' sensory impressions. In our study we were looking for in the emotional responses of the respondents, similarities and distortions in the semantics represented by the images presented in relation to furniture products, which would allow us to establish the existence or not of a strong correspondence between national and international furniture products.

4.1   Emotional Calculation Results of the Portuguese Furniture

The Caravela is semantically classified as a concrete, highly comfortable, creative and durable product. However, the weight of the years is evident in the design and most consider it old-fashioned, while retaining the originality, detail and imagination that José Espinho imprinted on it, such as regularity and cleanliness. It was also considered a warm piece, endowed with the semantic criterion of sobriety, where natural materials and sustainability prevail. Its compact design and shapes lead it to be considered heavy. Even allowing for several choices in its constitution, modularity was discarded, as was its opposite (single). It was considered equally undefined/neutral in the semantic criteria light/dark, elitist/popular and fun/serious.

Caravela - José Espinho

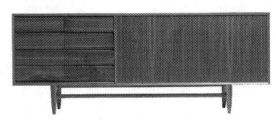

Sideboard Carvela - José Espinho

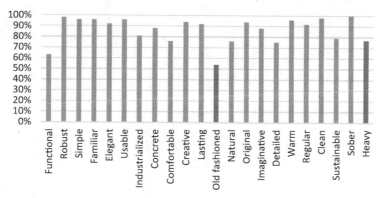

The Roots chair is a very Portuguese piece of furniture, both in shape and materials, it is considered by most respondents as a functional product, extremely usable, robust, simple, elegant and industrial. Its design is easily recognized and is therefore strong in the familiar semantic criterion. Roots is also recognized as fun, elitist, concrete and comfortable. The creative criteria, durable, natural, detailed, warm, regular and clean get extreme recognition from the viewers. Even though it is a reinterpretation, Alexandre Caldas' chair is identified as original, imaginative and modern. It is also considered to be free of excesses and therefore sober. Its construction materials are also considered to have the semantic criterion of sustainable. For the pairs of semantic criteria light/dark, model/unique and light/heavy, the respondents did not answer so that a semantic definition could be attributed.

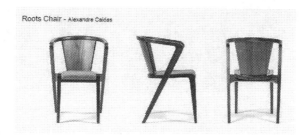

Roots Chair - Alexandre Caldas

Roots Chair - Alexandre Caldas

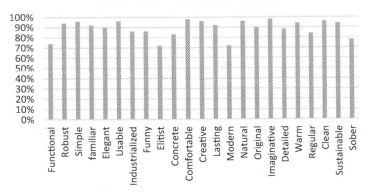

Our consumers have analyzed and considered the Troia chest of drawers by Eduardo Afonso Dias to be a functional piece of furniture, totally robust, long-lasting, and endowed with simplicity, with an extremely familiar and elegant appearance. Troia is also seen as an industrially produced, usable product, with a fun connotation, but transmitting an image of an elitist, concrete and comfortable product. It also collected the opinion that it is an original piece of furniture, full of imagination and creativity. Recognized as a natural and sustainable product, but with a heavy configuration. It was also considered fully aligned with the semantic criteria detailed, warm, regular, clean and sober. Regarding the semantic criterion pairs model/unique and light/dark, the respondents did not answer so that we could get a clear and objective definition. Thus they showed that there was no semantic definition, for any of these criteria.

Tróia ~ Eduardo Afonso Dias

CôModa Troia - Eduardo Afonso Dias

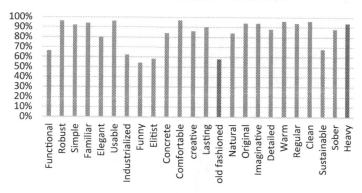

When we exposed the Vinco chair to the scrutiny of our respondents, the piece of furniture by Toni Grilo was considered to be functional, markedly robust, as in the durable and one hundred per cent simple criteria. Its design was considered to be totally familiar, usable, fun, concrete and comfortable. The general opinion is that it is an industrial and elitist product, in line with cork-based products, which, contrary to the installed idea of a cheap product, are products of high economic value. Its dominant colors are the silver and beige of the cork agglomerate and in line with this it was considered to be light and warm, with extreme creativity, imagination and originality. All those polled considered Vinco to be modern and detailed, with a regular design and a clean product. The fact that it uses cork in its design led to very strong results in the semantic criterion of sustainable, despite the fact that the hull and feet are made of polished steel. It also achieves results that lead it to be considered sober and light by the respondents. Only in one semantic pair, out of the twenty-six existing in the questionnaire, was there no definition for one of the criteria, and that was the case of the model/unique pair.

Vinco - Toni Grilo

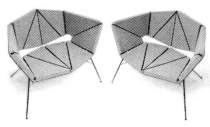

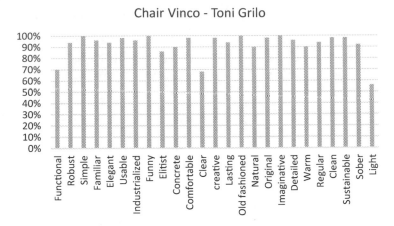

The Cortez Line desk is assumed to be fully functional. As it is a work piece its robust and durable appearance is also clearly identified by the wearers as being familiar. The familiarity of the objects, according to Daciano, is what elevates them to good objects. The horizontal and vertical lines of its design make it considered concrete, sober, simple and elegant. That same design has ergonomic features, which allows it to be classified as usable and comfortable. Produced mechanically, by Metalúrgica Longra, largely by the technique of bending the metal, giving it extreme weight in the industrialized criteria. The respondents consider this piece of the Cortez Line, a detailed furniture product, creative, with originality, but where the weight of time is felt and therefore was connoted with the old-fashioned criterion. Other semantic criteria that were recognized by the viewers were clean, warm, regular and heavy. Time sometimes determines a way and the sixties, as well as the national state in Portugal, may have contributed to the non-definition of the criteria fun/serious, elitist/popular, light/dark. The materials are at the base of the lack of definition in the natural/artificial and sustainable/polluting criteria. In the pair model/unique as opposed to the modularity of the equipment that Daciano da Costa gave him, since the Cortez desk could be sold without drawer modules, with just one or with both modules. This modularity was not recognized and resulted as undefined for this semantic pair.

Linha Cortez - Daciano da Costa

Linha Cortez - Daciano da Costa

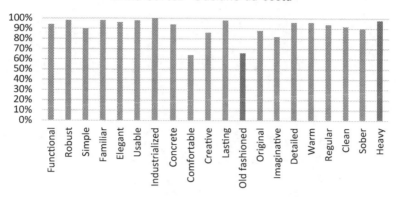

The sofa of the DAM duo, only does not reach definition in four pairs of semantic criteria natural/artificial, sustainable/polluting, model/unique and light/heavy. In the remaining twenty-three pairs of semantic criteria it is a well-defined piece of furniture, The Valentine sofa is considered strongly functional and usable, although it is identified as robust and durable, it is nonetheless considered elegant, simple, of concrete design, but fun and elaborate within familiar shapes. Although the surveyors connote it as an industrial product, they also consider it comfortable. The wood tones and the light blue upholstery lead it to be considered light, clean and regular in an extreme way. For the wearers it is almost perfectly aligned with the semantic criteria original, sober, detailed and imaginative, the last of which is fully aligned.

Valentim - Joana Santos & Hugo Silva

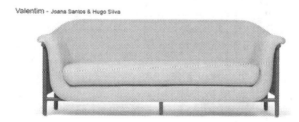

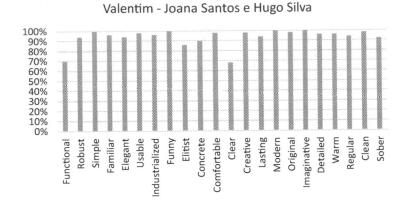

Valentim - Joana Santos e Hugo Silva

5 Conclusion

The comparative study in its generality allowed us to find the similarities and distortions between products resulting from the sensorial impressions of the respondents. This comparative analysis of the sensorial qualities between products, transmitted by the consumers was determinant for the assumption of similarity in the Portuguese furniture design pieces and later in their comparison with the international ones. This analysis allowed us to assess that the semantic descriptors are present in a strong and extreme way in the six Portuguese furniture pieces. From the data obtained and according to the answers of the consumers, we can generally consider that the Portuguese furniture is considered as functional, markedly robust, of durable and simple character. Its design is familiar, usable, fun, concrete and comfortable. The general view is that they are products of industrial origin, with an elitist connotation and consequently products of high economic value. The dominant shades and materials lead them to be considered light and warm. The respondents extremely recognize their creativity, imaginative semantic criteria and originality. The Caravela sideboard, the Troia chest of drawers and the Cortez line desk have a design marked by time and do not hide the sixties of the 20th Century, but the modern style is also evident in the Roots, Vinco and Valentim sofa. The detailed semantic criterion, the regular design and the clean criterion were extremely common for all the pieces. Sustainability was only not recognized in the desk of the Cortez line. Sobriety is a semantic criterion common to all, which may indicate that the national furniture is devoid of excesses. In general, they are considered heavy, with the exception of Vinco, which was considered light.

Only in the semantic pair modular/unique there was a vagueness for all the national pieces, even in those that had modular component, like the desk of the Cortez line or those that are part of collections like the sideboard Caravela and the chest of drawers Troia.

The total alignment of answers between national and international furniture, only proved to coincide in the descriptors Creative, Durable, Original, Imaginative, Detailed and Clean. Which accommodates twenty-four percent of the sample with exact matches.

Descriptors such as Elegant, Wearable, Elitist, Comfortable and Regular, twenty percent of the sample, the alignment is very strong and can also be considered coincident, as the deviation is only one or two responses and of neutral tendency. There were no opposite emotional responses to these descriptors. This reinforces the very strong alignment between the furniture products.

In the semantic descriptors Functional, Robust, Simple, Familiar, Industrial, Fun, Concrete, Warm, Sober and Heavy which represent thirty eight percent of the sample, the alignment between national and international furniture is above fifty percent, which allows us to conclude that in these descriptors the alignment is quite strong. Only in the Functional/Decorative descriptor pair, was there a greater split. This tendency in this pair of descriptors can be explained by the fact that a furniture product has in itself a decorative component. It is even used in decorative compositions or locations, intended to create environments of pleasant use for users. The profusion of colors and less conventional shapes may also be responsible for a certain vagueness in some products.

For the descriptor pairs Light/Dark, Modern/Old Fashioned, Natural/Artificial, Modular/Single and Sustainable/Polluting, which represent eighteen per cent of the sample, there is a tendency towards neutrality in both national and international products. Although these are pairs of descriptors that denote objectivity and that at first sight would leave no room for doubt. Here the tendency towards neutrality is identical for both domestic and international furniture. This shows that even when tending towards neutrality, there is also correspondence here.

Compared to the international furniture, the viewers recognize the existence of common points in all semantic criteria, but this coincidence is higher in the most recent international furniture products or in the case of the classics that are better known by the public. In general, the two types of furniture under analysis are very much in line with each other. This is not surprising, considering the late birth of the design discipline in Portugal. The learning that the pioneers of Portuguese design did abroad and the need for recognition in foreign markets.

References

Balduino, M.A.: Aplicação da Metodologia de Engenharia Kansei na Análise de Consumo de Chás. Faculdade Ciências da Universidade do Porto (2012)

Dahlgaard, J., Schutte, S., Ayas, E.: Kansei/affective engineering design. A methodology for profound affection and attractive quality creation. TQM J. (2008)

Detienne, M.: A Identidade Nacional, Um Enigma. Autêntica Editora (2013)

Harada, A.: On the definition of Kansei. In: Modeling the Evaluation Structure of Kansei Conference, vol. 2 (1998)

Ishihara, S., Ishihara, K., Nagamachi, M., Matsubara, Y.: An automatic builder for a Kansei engineering expert system using self-organizing neural networks. Int. J. Ind. Ergon. **15**(1), 13–24 (1995). https://doi.org/10.1016/0169-8141(94)15053-8

Ishihara, I., Nishino, T., Matsubara, Y., Tsuchiya, T., Kanda, F., Inoue, K.: In: Nagamachi, M. (ed.) Kansei and Product Development (In Japanese), vol. 1. Kaibundo, Tokyo (2005)

Lee, S., Harada, A., Stappers, P.J.: Desing based in kansei. In: Green, W.S., Jordan, P.W. (eds.) Pleasures with products: Beyond usability. Taylor & Francis, London (2002)

Lévy, P., Lee, S.H., Yamanaka, T.: On Kansei and Kansei design: a description of a Japanese design approach. In: Proceeding of the International Association of Societies of Design Research Conference, Hong-Kong (2007)

Lineares, C., Pages, A.: Kano's model in Kansei engineering to evaluate subjective real estate consumer preferences. Int. J. Ind. Ergon. (2011)

Linares, C. e Pages, A. (2008). Differential semantics as a Kansei Engineering tool for analysing the emotional impressions which determine the choice of neighbourhood: the case of Valencia, Spain. Landsc. Urban Plan.

Mondragon, S., Company, P., Vergara, M.: Semantic differential applied to the evaluation of machine tool design. Int. J. Ind. Ergon. (2005)

Nagamachi, M.: Kansei engineering as a powerful consumer-oriented technology for product development. Appl. Ergon. (2002)

Nagamachi, M.: Image technology based knowledge engineering and its application to design consultation. Ergon. Int. (1988)

Nagamachi, M.: Kansei engineering and comfort. Int. J. Ind. Ergon. (1997)

Nagamachi, M.: Introduction of Kansei Engineering. Japan Standard Association, Tokyo (1996)

Nagamachi, M.: Kansei engineering: a new ergonomic consumer-oriented technology for product development. Int. J. Ind. Ergon. (1995)

Nagamachi, M.: Kansei Engineering. Kaibundo Publishing, Tokyo (1989)

Nagamachi, M.: The Story of Kansei Engineering (in Japanese), vol. 6. Japanese Standards Association, Tokyo (2003)

Nagamachi, M.: Framework and Economical Power of Kansei Engineering. Kansei Engineering Seminar, Hong Kong (2004)

Nagasawa, S.Y.: Kansei and business. Int. J. Kansei Eng. 3, 2–12 (2002)

Nagasawa, S.: Present State of Kansei Engineering in Japan. IEEE (2004)

Osgood, C.E., Suci, G.J., Tannenbaum, P.H.: The Measurement of Meaning. University of Illinois Press, Illinois (1957)

Osgood, C.E.: The nature and measurement of meaning, in C.E. Osgood and (1969)

Snider, J.G., (ed.) Semantic Differential Technique– A Source Book. Aldine Publishing Company, Chicago

Rosenberg, B., Navarro, M.: Semantic differential scaling. Edit by: Bruce B. Frey Print ISBN: 9781506326153 (2017)

Schutte, S., Eklund, K.: Design of rocker switches for work-vehicles—an application of Kansei engineering. Appl. Ergon. (2005)

Schütte, S.: Designing feelings into products. integrating Kansei Engineering methodology in product development. Thesis. Linköping Studies in Science and Technology. Linköpings University (2002)

Sobral, J.M.: Portugal Portugueses: Uma Identidade Nacional. edit by: Fundação Francisco Manuel dos Santos, isbn: 9789898424655 (2012)

A Web-Based Application for TWS Earphone Design and Fit Evaluation

Kexiang Liu, Haining Wang$^{(\boxtimes)}$, Qianling Liu, and Qi Chen

School of Design, Hunan University, Changsha 410082, China
Haining1872@qq.com

Abstract. As one of the most frequently used wearable devices, the demand for True Wireless Stereo (TWS) earphones is quite substantial. Fit performance is a major factor that influences customer satisfaction, which contributes greatly to the success of wearable products. Ergonomics is a crucial approach to design well-fitting products. Nevertheless, there's no existing tools or platforms aiding TWS earphone design from a perspective of ergonomics. In this paper, an interactive and web-based application was developed. It integrates up-to-date Chinese 3D ear anthropometric database and an online deviation analysis algorithm to (1) provide ear anthropometric information as design reference, and (2) evaluate the fit between TWS earphones and human ear. A user-centered contextual inquiry was performed to identify user requirements. As a result, an initial prototype was accordingly created, including the interface and interactive design. The interactive and user-centered online application can efficiently facilitate the ergonomic design of TWS earphones in both design and evaluation phase, and thus help improve the customer satisfaction.

Keywords: TWS earphone design · Ergonomics · Fit evaluation · Chinese external ear · User-centered design

1 Introduction

Strong consumer demands have driven true wireless stereo (TWS) devices to become the most dominant category of product shipments in the past few years [1]. The global TWS earphones market size was valued at USD 25.32 billion in 2020 and is expected to grow at a compound annual growth rate of 36.1% from 2021 to 2028 [2]. TWS earphones are popular for pairing with smart watches, phones, and laptops in various scenes of our daily lives due to the true wireless, intelligence, diversified interaction methods and active noise reduction (ANC) technology [3]. Good fit with the human body is a critical factor to ensure the success of wearable products [4]. Ear-related products fitting poorly with the external ear shape may lead to discomfort by local pressure and are easy to slip off [5, 6]. To create well-fitting TWS earphones, it's essential to attach great importance to ergonomic design.

Anthropometry is considered the very ergonomic core of any attempt to resolve the dilemma of fitting the tasks to the human [7]. The advancement of three-dimensional

© The Author(s), under exclusive license to Springer Nature Switzerland AG 2022
M. M. Soares et al. (Eds.): HCII 2022, LNCS 13323, pp. 157–167, 2022.
https://doi.org/10.1007/978-3-031-05906-3_12

(3D) laser scanning technique has been utilized to collect more accurate anthropometric data effectively [8]. However, most of the previous studies of ear anthropometry focused merely on the 3D data acquisition, preprocessing and statistical analysis [9–11]. Little research and design have been reported concerning the use of this wealth of 3D data for improving customer products [12]. Fan, H. et al. proposed a categorization mode of ear-worn wearables based on the results of principal component analysis of measurements and human physical characteristics, which simplified the process of data matching for different types of products [13]. Stavrakos, S.-K. et al. discussed various applications of 3D data set of human ears achieving a more accurate benchmarking of ear dimensions against ear-related product data for physical comfort [4]. Lee, W. et al. collected the 3D scan images of whole outer-ear including auricle, concha and ear canal, and applied 3D ear scans to design more proper size and shape of earphones based on virtual fit analysis [14]. However, the conclusions in these studies are rather obscure and hard to use directly for earphone designers.

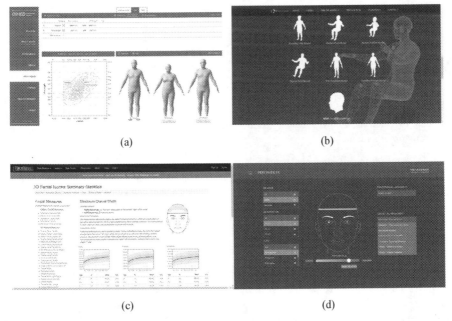

(a)   (b)

(c)   (d)

Fig. 1. User interfaces of wearables aided design application, (a) DINED anthropometric database, (b) BIOHUMAN, (c) FaceBase, (d) Chinese Headbase.

Over the last decades, several applications have been established to assist the design of wearable products. DINED is an online platform aims to help designers create better products by providing information on using anthropometric data in design and set of free tools makes it easy to explore, compare and utilize anthropometric data (refer to Fig. 1a) [15]. BioHuman framework aims for intuitive yet accurate 3D manikin generation from a minimal set of parameters, which are based on statistical analyses of high-resolution laser scans and anthropometric measurement data of men, women, and children with a wide range of age, stature, and body weight (refer to Fig. 1b) [16]. The 3D Facial Norms Database is a web-based and interactive craniofacial normative database, which provide access to the large-scale high-quality head and facial anthropometric normative data (refer to Fig. 1c) [17]. Chinese Headbase is a responsive Html5-based database based on a full-scale Chinese head and facial 3D anthropometry which allows access to both summary-level statistics and individual-level data (refer to Fig. 1d) [12]. However, the existing ear anthropometric databases open to the public, such as Open Hear Database [18] and SYMARE database [19], (1) cannot represent the specific population with insufficient samples according to ISO 15535 [20], (2) cannot provide accurate references for TWS earphone design with low-resolution 3D scans, and (3) cannot assist designers directly with deliverables of 3D scan files and summary-level statistic document. More importantly, no Chinese ear anthropometric database has ever been established whose ear anthropometric information was validated significantly different from that of western population in the former studies [9, 21]. Thus, there's a crucial demand for an auxiliary tool or platform for TWS earphone design to provide well-fitting products for Chinese customers.

In this paper, we developed an interactive and user-centered web-based tool to facilitate the ergonomic design of TWS earphones, and thus help to improve the satisfaction of Chinese customers by providing well-fitting TWS earphones. This online application will assist earphone designers by integrating up-to-date Chinese ear anthropometry information, and providing an online deviation analysis algorithm for evaluating the fit of earphones.

2   Methods

2.1   Data Sources

Wang, H. et al. established Chinese Headbase using 3D scanning technology in 2018 [22]. This 3D digital anthropometric survey on Chinese head and face was enriched to the sample size of 3400 in 2020 from which the anthropometric ear data integrated in this application were extracted. The high-resolution bilateral external scans were collected using Artec Spider (Artec 3D, Luxembourg) 3D scanner and 3Shape Phoenix (3Shape, Denmark) in-ear scanner.

36 landmarks defined according to previous studies were extracted from the high-resolution ear models (as shown in Fig. 2). 47 measurements relevant to ear-worn products were calculated based landmark coordinates, which consist of 35 linear measurements, 10 angular measurements, and 2 circumferences. Next, statistical analysis of the measurements was performed using IBM SPSS Statistics 24.0 (IBM Inc., USA).

2.2   Correspondence Analysis

To improve the utilization of the anthropometric characteristics, research on the correspondence between external ear and TWS earphones is necessary. TWS earphones in the market can be categorized into two types according to the part that contact with the external ear. In-ear TWS earphones such as Airpods Pro are designed specifically to slide past the concha and extend into the ear canal with a silicone tip, while most half-in-ear TWS earphones such as Airpods are shaped to fit the concha and lie outside of the canal. As a result, the correspondence of these two types with external is different. 3D coordinate planes of TWS earphone key features are defined through analysis of real wearing condition (refer to Fig. 3), by which the design parameters of TWS earphones are discussed.

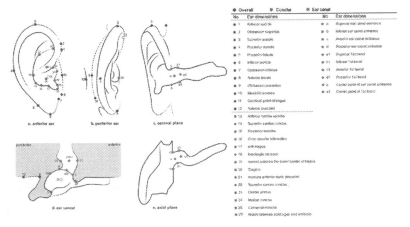

Fig. 2. 36 landmarks of external ear.

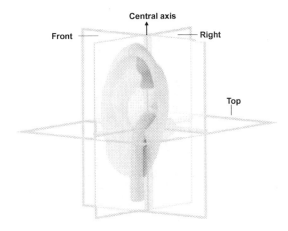

Fig. 3. 3D coordinate planes of half-in-ear TWS earphone.

2.3   User Requirements

Compared to public websites or software, this web-based aided application is precisely aimed for the designers with their specific context's experiences, whose requirements should be taken into consideration as a priority. Therefore, we performed a user-centered and contextual inquiry to explore and refine the user requirements [22]. A group of experts is selected based on their experience in the ergonomic design, including two earphone designers, two industrial designers and one expert of human factors (see Table 1). The purpose of this contextual inquiry is to understand (1) the present process of earphone design and common problems they might encounter; (2) their experience of earphone fitting evaluation; (3) the specific expectations for this auxiliary tool.

Table 1. Demographics of interview participants.

ID	Gender	Age	Education level	Occupation	Years of experience
01	Female	24	Master	Industrial designer	6 years
02	Female	35	Bachelor	Earphone designer	15 years
03	Female	26	Doctor	Human factor expert	8 years
04	Male	29	Master	Industrial designer	10 years
05	Male	34	Bachelor	Earphone designer	12 years

The interviews reflected two drawbacks of the earphone ergonomic design: (1) in the sketch and modelling phase, designers have no access to the anthropometric information of Chinese external ears. Besides, the correspondence between the complex ear shape and earphone design is complicated. Therefore, designer's experience instead of scientific information was used as reference; and (2) in the evaluation and iteration phase, the conventional methods to evaluate the fitting of wearable products are highly professional and time-consuming. Thus, most designers adjust the shape and size of TWS earphones based on their observations, lacking scientific evidence. Accordingly, this user-centered application will assist the ergonomic design of TWS earphones in the above two phases.

3   TWS Earphone Design Aided Application

3.1   Website Structure

The TWS earphone design and fit evaluation application website (Earphone Design Aided System) comprises two modules: (1) design reference, and (2) fit evaluation. The structure of this website is shown in Fig. 4.

Home. In the right side of the home page, a 3D model of external ear with key landmarks is rendering in-real-time, and two core modules are located in the middle, with navigation bar fixed at the top (seen in Fig. 5 below).

Design Reference. This module provides design reference from two perspectives of ear anthropometric information and TWS earphone products respectively, which can be indicated by the second level tab bar navigation on the left side of the webpage.

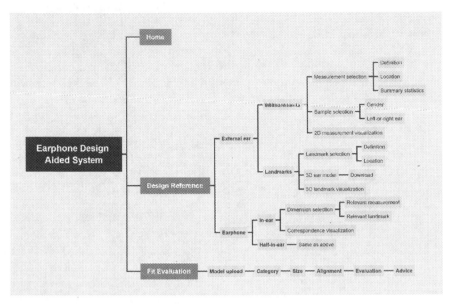

Fig. 4. The structure of the earphone design aided system website

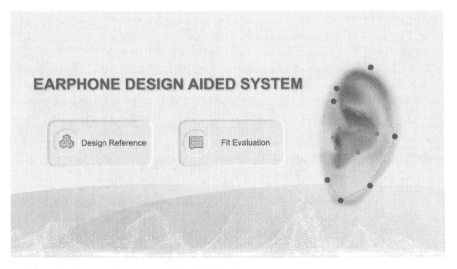

Fig. 5. The home page.

The 3D ear landmarks and measurements are categorized into three groups for better presentation and selection, which are auricle, concha, and ear canal according to anatomy. Apart from the measurement definition and location, summary statistics including percentiles (5th, 10th, 25th, 50th, 75th, 90th and 95th), mean, median, variance, SD, maximum, minimum, skewness and kurtosis of each measurement are also presented, which could be customized by gender, left and right ear. Besides, the specific location

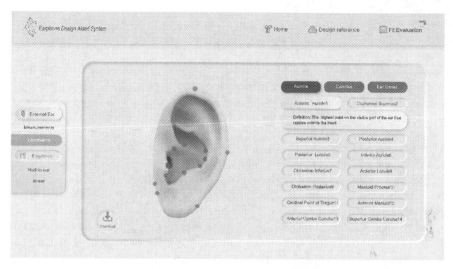

Fig. 6. The design reference page with 3D landmarks.

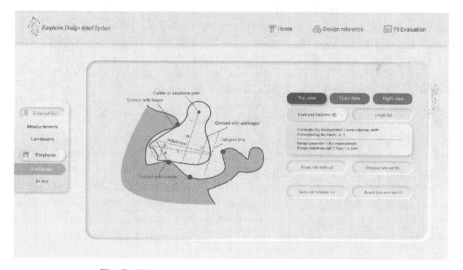

Fig. 7. The design reference with half-in-ear earphone.

of landmarks is showing on the 3D ear model in real time according to the landmark the users choose (refer to Fig. 6). Users could not only quickly understand the external ear shape in the form of text descriptions, pictures and 3D models, but also obtain summary-level statistics documents in this module.

TWS earphones are split into two categories named in-ear and half-in-ear according to whether they go deeper into the ear canal. Thus, the size range of TWS earphones is also suggested as well as the correspondence with external ear based on different earphone types. When designing TWS earphones, a more intuitive size recommendation of earphone's critical parts and planes is available in this module so that designers can effectively adjust the surface of earphone models (seen in Fig. 7).

Fit Evaluation. This is a module for evaluating the fitting of earphones by computing the distances between the built-in representative ear models and TWS earphone model that users upload. On this website, users need six steps to obtain the deviation analysis results and recommendations for optimizing design parameters of earphone models.

The first step is to upload the earphone model of STL format that needs to be optimized. Next, the earphone category is chosen by users. Third, users are required to select the key points on the uploaded model following the instruction so that the key dimensions could be identified by the system (as shown in Fig. 8). Next, these two models are aligned automatically before computing the deviation analysis, which can be manually adjusted by the users based on prompts. By conducting these procedures sequentially, the deviation analysis is then performed. The result is shown in a form of visualization image, together with gradient bar and summary statistics of deviation including Pos Max Dev, Neg Max Dev, Mean Dev, Std Dev, Pos Mean Dev, and Neg Mean Dev (refer to Fig. 9). The negative value and blue color mean interference between the earphone and adjacent area of external ear. The smaller negative value with the bluer bar means more interference, which indicates the corresponding area of external ear will suffer more pressure in a real wearing scenario. On the contrary, the positive value and red color mean gap between these two models. Improper gap may induce the stability of earphones. Finally, the advice of modification according to the deviation analysis result is presented, by which users are able to optimize the design.

It is worth noting that the external ear is divided into eight regions in this module according to anatomy and previous ear anthropometry studies to produce precise local deviations. These are ear canal, anterior notch, tragus, helix crus, antihelix, antitragus, concha, and intertragic notch. The helix or other parts of auricle are excluded from the deviation analysis since they have no contact with TWS earphones. As shown in Fig. 9, the max gap is around the intertragic notch region, while the concha interferes significantly with the earphone model. The global and local deviations show the dissimilarities of fit performance throughout the whole external ear, which can ensure the appropriate adjustment and optimization of earphones.

3.2 Deviation Analysis Algorithm

One crucial function of this application is the fit assessment of TWS earphones, which is fairly beneficial of optimizing the model into a well-fitting one. The deviation analysis is achieved by computing the distance between the built-in representative external ear models and TWS earphone model uploaded by the user. The embedded online deviation analysis algorithm consists of five steps: (1) the built-in representative human ear is identified as reference model while the earphone is target model, and all the point coordinates of two models are obtained; (2) duplicate points of the target model are removed to reduce computation; (3) all the point-to-point Euclidean distances between the two models are calculated, of which the minimum distances for each point of the target model are obtained; (4) minimum distances of target points detected inside of

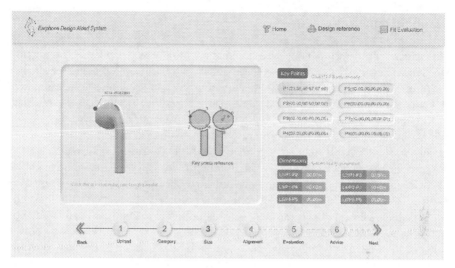

Fig. 8. The fit evaluation page with key points selection.

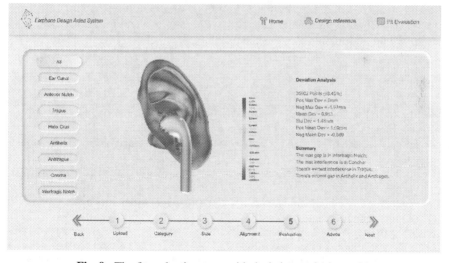

Fig. 9. The fit evaluation page with deviation analysis results.

the reference model are assigned as negative values indicating the interference between the two models, otherwise they are positive values meaning the gap; (5) the statistical analysis are performed on the values and visualization image is produced accordingly. Furthermore, similar analyses are conducted on the other eight local regions to produce local deviation results.

4   Conclusion

In this paper, a user-centered and web-based application was developed by integrating up-to-date Chinese 3D ear anthropometric database and an online deviation analysis algorithm. Firstly, on this website, both summary-level anthropometric measurements and individual-level 3D models of external ear are accessible, by which users could have a comprehensive understanding of the complex ear shape. Besides, the size range of TWS earphones is suggested as well as the correspondence with external ears. These functions are beneficial to the involvement of ergonomics in the TWS earphone design phase. Secondly, the embedded deviation analysis algorithm provides an easy and intuitive method to evaluate the TWS earphone fitting performance. Designers are able to adjust and optimize the size and shape of TWS earphones according to the generated interference and gap values with reference ear models. This online algorithm facilitates the application of ergonomics in the TWS earphone evaluation phase. Thirdly, the functions of this application were determined in accordance with the user requirements concluded from the experts, which ensures the practicability of this application. In conclusion, this website is the first web-based tool to provide design reference and evaluation method for TWS earphone designers. It will increase the utilization of ergonomics in both design and evaluation phase of TWS earphones, thus improve the fitting performance of TWS earphones and Chinese customer satisfaction. The interface and interactive design will be optimized in the future to improve the usability.

References

1. APEI Events Page: https://audioproducteducationinstitute.org/modeling-and-measurement-of-true-wireless-stereo-wearables/. Last accessed 10 Feb 2022
2. Grand View Research: https://www.grandviewresearch.com/industry-analysis/true-wireless-stereo-earbuds-market-report. Last accessed 10 Feb 2022
3. Device Next: https://devicenext.com/smartwatch-tws-will-drive-the-accessories-market/. Last accessed 10 Feb 2022
4. Stavrakos, S.-K., Ahmed-Kristensen, S.: Methods of 3D data applications to inform design decisions for physical comfort. Work **55**(2), 321–334 (2016)
5. Song, H., Shin, G.W., Yoon, Y., Bahn, S.: The effects of ear dimensions and product attributes on the wearing comfort of wireless earphones. Appl. Sci. **10**(24), 8890 (2020)
6. Liu, B.S.: Incorporating anthropometry into design of ear-related products. Appl. Ergon. **39**(1), 115–121 (2008)
7. Sanders, M.S., McCormick, E.J.: Human Factors in Engineering and Design, 7th edn. Mcgraw-Hill Book Company, New York, NY, England (1993)
8. Lu, J.-M., Wang, M.-J.J.: The evaluation of scan-derived anthropometric measurements. IEEE Trans. Instrum. Meas. **59**(8), 2048–2054 (2010)
9. Lu, P., Tsao, L., Yu, C., Ma, L.: Survey of ear anthropometry for young college students in China and its implications for ear-related product design. Hum. Factor Ergon. Manuf. **31**(1), 86–97 (2021)
10. Yu, J.F., et al.: Anthropometry of external auditory canal by non-contactable measurement. Appl. Ergon. **50**, 50–55 (2015)
11. Wang, B., Dong, Y., Zhao, Y., Bai, S., Wu, G.: Computed tomography measurement of the auricle in Han population of north China. J. Plast Reconstr. Aesth. **64**(1), 34–40 (2011)

12. Wang, H., Yu, Y., Chen, W., Yang, W., Ball, R.: Responsive web design for Chinese head and facial database. In: Rau, P.-L. (ed.) CCD 2018. LNCS, vol. 10911, pp. 216–231. Springer, Cham (2018). https://doi.org/10.1007/978-3-319-92141-9_17
13. Fan, H., et al.: Anthropometric characteristics and product categorization of Chinese auricles for ergonomic design. Int. J. Ind. Ergon. **69**, 118–141 (2019). https://doi.org/10.1016/j.ergon.2018.11.002
14. Lee, W., et al.: Measurement and application of 3D ear images for earphone design. In: Proceedings of the Human Factors and Ergonomics Society Annual Meeting, pp. 1053–1057 (2016)
15. DINED: https://dined.io.tudelft.nl/en/about. Last accessed 10 Feb 2022
16. BIOHUMAN: http://humanshape.org/. Last accessed 10 Feb 2022
17. FaceBase: https://www.facebase.org/. Last accessed 10 Feb 2022
18. OpenHear: http://www2.imm.dtu.dk/projects/OpenHear/. Last accessed 10 Feb 2022
19. SYMARE: http://www.ee.usyd.edu.au/carlab/symare.html
20. ISO, I. 15535: General requirements for establishing anthropometric databases. https://www.iso.org/standard/57179.html. Last accessed 10 Feb 2022
21. Fu, F., Luximon, Y., Shah, P.: A systematic review on ear anthropometry and its industrial design applications. Hum. Factor Ergon. Manuf. **30**(3), 176–194 (2020)
22. Wang, H., Yang, W., Yu, Y., Chen, W., Ball, R.: 3D digital anthropometric study on Chinese head and face. In: Proceedings of 3DBODY. TECH 2018–9th Int. Conference and Exhibition on 3D Body Scanning and Processing Technologies, pp. 287–295 (2018)
23. Holtzblatt, K., Wendell, J. B., Wood, S.: Rapid Contextual Design: A How-To Guide to Key Techniques for User-Centered Design. Elsevier (2004)

Inclusive Design: Furniture Design for Autism Parents Support

Inês Lopes[1]([⊠]) [iD], Ernesto Filgueiras[1,2] [iD], Alexandre Guerreiro[1] [iD],
and João Monteiro[1,3] [iD]

[1] Universidade da Beira Interior, Convento de Sto. António, Covilhã, Portugal
{ines.pereira.lopes,evf,monteiro}@ubi.pt
[2] CIAUD - Research Centre for Architecture, Urbanism and Design, University of Beira
Interior, Convento de Sto. António, Covilhã, Portugal
mafaldacasais.ciaud@fa.ulisboa.pt
[3] CISE - Electromechatronic Systems Research Centre, University of Beira Interior, Convento
de Sto. António, Covilhã, Portugal
cise@ubi.pt

Abstract. Autism Spectrum Disorder (ASD) is a neurological disorder that affects the functioning of the brain and is frequently associated with problems related to feelings, thoughts, language, as well as difficulties in social interactions. The goal of this project is to develop therapeutic home furniture, focused on children with ASD in the age group of 2 to 6 years old, the one with the highest prevalence of diagnostics and where the best results are likely to be achieved if therapy is started early. Five product proposals have been developed: bed, sensory pouf, tent, ball pool and swivel chair. The products were designed following interviews and questionnaires with occupational therapists and parents/caregivers, with a key characteristic targeted being the fostering of the child's interactivity with other persons. Each product has the possibility of applying sensory maps as well as extra textures and shapes, with neutral and calm colors being used in accordance with the research done. A natural fabric called Burel was abundantly used in the products due to its many advantageous properties that can be used to bring benefits in the sensory and cognitive development of children with ASD. Applying the fabric beyond the usual, for tactile and kinesthetic properties.

Keywords: Inclusive design · Autism spectrum disorder · Children's · Therapy · Burel

1 Introduction

1.1 Presentation of the Problematic

The COVID-19 pandemic has brought significant impact to all people, but it has been particularly challenging for individuals with special needs, such as of children with Autism Spectrum Disorders (ASD), worsening their symptomatology. Social communication became almost impossible beyond the family circle, which has led to an even

M. M. Soares et al. (Eds.): HCII 2022, LNCS 13323, pp. 168–186, 2022.
https://doi.org/10.1007/978-3-031-05906-3_13

greater difficulty in improving this crucial skill. Sensory input has been reduced with isolation, and children with this deficit will require further reintegration into society to adapt to normal life outside the home environment, with the use of masks being particularly problematic for children with ASD problems [1]. Analyzing the current market of children's furniture, it is possible to see that the products are focused at neurotypical children, putting parents of atypical children in a difficult position when trying to find products that are suitable. Children with ASD need daily therapy to promote their development, and some of it can be induced by everyday products, leading the child to perform the therapy without realizing it, in a form of play. Many assistive products and equipment for children with special needs are designed with the intention of easing their limitations. However, a larger percentage of them do not encompass a design input, and consequently, many products prescribed by professionals, such as Occupational Therapists, are rejected for being stigmatizing [2].

This project is aimed to design a set of furniture, targeted at children with Autism Spectrum Disorder (ASD). According to the APA (American Psychiatric Association), ASD is a neurological disorder that affects the functioning of the brain, and, for this reason, it can cause problems related to feelings, thoughts, language, as well as difficulties in social interactions. It is a disorder that is diagnosed in childhood, and, over the years, the number of autistic children has been increasing [3] being estimated that worldwide about 1 in 160 children have ASD [4]. Although there is no cure, with some therapies, children can successfully develop a range of domains. Unfortunately, many of these children do not have the help they need, and their development is thus compromised. The earlier therapy is started, the more positive developments are possible. Autism symptoms can be present early on in a children's development but are often only remarked when certain skills, such as language, do not develop at the expected time. More obvious abnormal behaviors are observed between the ages of 2 and 5, thus making diagnostic easier. The focus of the current work was the age group from 2 to 6 years old, as it the one with the highest prevalence of diagnosis and where the best results are likely to be obtained if early therapy is started [5].

The pandemic also caused limitations in medical appointments, and many children in need were left without therapy. Delayed pediatric appointments can cause delayed diagnosis, a situation in which worse cognitive and behavioral outcomes have been demonstrated [1]. It is thus extremely important for children with ASD to have therapeutic products at home to mitigate their pathologies, which became even more pronounced with the pandemic, leading children to not progress but also sometimes even regress, losing skills already developed and creating new barriers.

It was recognized that the therapeutic products, available on the market, have evolved technologically, but also that the problem of acceptance remains [2]. Many of the children undergo therapy only at a medical center and sometimes only once a week. Needy families typically enjoy therapy at zero cost for a few months, but then proceed without therapy, or have therapy only once a week at a medical facility. These situations, unfortunately frequent, lead to children not having the necessary support as there is no daily home therapy due to lack of means and products that are only directed to therapy in a hospital setting. Many of the existing products are not targeted to ASD children, leading them to reject the product if, for example, they have sensory processing dysregulation, such as being unable to tolerate intense lights or sounds and/or textures.

Inclusive Design and Universal Design is a logical response to a changing social reality, putting the user at the heart of the design process. Universal Design does not usually focus on very particular needs, this exclusion happening because there is neglect, ignorance, and lack of information [2]. All people are different, and even if it is not apparent that there is a functional difference, some people may have limitations beyond the physical ones, such as differences in behavior, or in the way they deal with others and/or with themselves. When it will be considered normal for a human being to have limitations and strong variations, differences will start to be seen as natural. It is thus necessary to know that limitations exist, but it is also necessary to understand that limitations do not set absolute limits. The focus should be on the abilities of the human being and their limitations. A project designed with the focus on Universal Design is designed for everyone, i.e., the project aimed at children with ASD can also be used by children without this disorder. The absence of Inclusive Design is a reality in many countries, and therefore there is an absence of inclusive products in many markets. Most design courses do not foster inclusive products, albeit sometimes there is limited theoretical teaching [6].

1.2 Symptoms and Behaviors

Autism Spectrum Disorder (ASD) is a disorder encompassing autistic disorder (autism), Asperger's disorder, childhood disintegrative disorder, Rett's disorder, and pervasive developmental disorder [7]. According to DSM-V (2012), ASD is characterized by deficits in two core domains: a) deficits in social communication and social interaction in multiple contexts, and b) repetitive patterns of behavior, interests, and activities, manifesting in at least two of them (Table 1).

Table 1 Diagnostic criteria of autism spectrum disorder (DSM-V, 2012)

a) Deficits in social communication and social interaction in multiple contexts:	b) Repetitive patterns of behavior, interests, and activities', manifesting in at least two:
1. Deficits in social emotional reciprocity, ranging, for example, from abnormal social approach and difficulty in establishing a normal conversation to reduced sharing of interests of interests, emotions, or affect, to difficulty initiating or responding to social interactions.	1. Stereotyped or repetitive motor movements, use of objects, or speech (e.g., simple motor stereotyping, lining up toys or spinning objects, echolalia, idiosyncratic phrases).

(*continued*)

Table 1 (*continued*)

2. Deficits in nonverbal communicative behaviors used for social interaction, ranging, for example, from poorly integrated verbal and nonverbal communication to abnormal eye contact and body language or deficits in understanding and using gestures, to complete absence of facial expressions and nonverbal communication.	2. Insistence on the same things, inflexible adherence to routines or ritualized patterns of verbal or nonverbal behavior (e.g., extreme distress over small changes, difficulty with transitions, rigid thought patterns, greeting rituals, need to take the same route or eat the same foods daily).
3. Deficits in developing, maintaining, and understanding relationships, ranging, for example, from difficulty adjusting behavior to fit diverse social contexts to difficulty sharing imaginative play or making friends, to absence of interest in peers.	3. Fixed and highly restricted interests that are abnormal in intensity or focus (e.g., strong attachment to or preoccupation with unusual objects, overly circumscribed or perseverative interests).

According to the FPDA (Portuguese Federation of Autism), between ages 2 and 5, ASD tends to become more obvious. The child typically does not speak or, when speaking, uses echolalia (repetition of words, phrases, or expressions), which is an idiosyncratic language that has no communicative function and can be immediate (repeated immediately) or deferred (repeated hours, days, or weeks after being heard). Isolated words thus emerge that are verbalized unconsciously [8]. There are children who speak correctly but do not use language in its communicative function, continuing to show problems in social interaction and interests. Some of the behavioral characteristics of ASD that become more evident in early childhood, besides delayed language development, is lack of interest in social interactions (e.g., pulling people by the hand without any attempt to look at them), odd patterns of play (e.g., carrying toys but never playing with them), and unusual patterns of communication (e.g., knowing the alphabet but not responding to one's own name) [7]. The child not smiling in response to the parent's smile, not looking in the same direction, not following the parent's gaze, not pointing, and not seeking social sharing, are early signs of disturbed social interaction and joint attention. Joint attention is the ability to share attention with others about an object or event, translating in looking alternately at the object and the other person [8]. Another name for joint attention is "triadic attention", referring to the 3 points of the attention triangle: the child, the reader, and the child's focus of attention [9]. In a child, this skill is naturally acquired in the first few months of life, while a child with ASD has usually a great difficulty learning and establishing joint attention. Not responding to name is a skill that emerges at 8/10 months but children with ASD have a very difficult time learning it [8]. Another limitation that children with ASD have, is related to the difficulty in understanding the perspective of others, that is, the "Theory of Mind" [8]. The term "Theory of Mind" first appeared in 1978 in the seminal article, "Does the chimpanzee have a theory of mind"? [10]. This theory refers to the ability to understand that other people have thoughts and feelings independent of our own, thus allowing to infer the other's mental state based on his/her external behavior, a skill that children with ASD have great difficulty to acquire [8], making social interactions unrewarding and very difficult [11].

An atypical gait, lack of coordination, and other abnormal motor signs are often present in ASD children [7], that usually have deficits in fine and gross motor skills. Fine motor skills are precision movements, with arms, hands, and fingers, requiring greater coordination and dexterity (handling zippers, buttons, pencils). Gross motor skills are related to posture, static and dynamic balance, and displacement [8].

Many of the children with ASD may exhibit hyporeactivity or hyperreactivity to sensations (sight, hearing, smell, taste, and touch) [12] with sensory processing dysfunction being divided into sensory hyperreactivity, sensory hyporeactivity, and sensory seeking. Sensory hyperreactivity can be characterized by an exaggerated, disproportionate reaction to sensory stimuli, the person thus having a low sensory threshold. This problem relates to the tactile, vestibular, proprioceptive, visual, olfactory, gustatory, and/or auditory senses, and may affect any or all of them. There may be an overreaction in normal everyday situations such as to loud sounds, strong textures, and abrupt movements/activities [13]. It is common to find children with ASD that show discomfort to just a light touch, or smooth textures in clothing. They may experience pain with sounds, such as thunderstorms or the sound of the vacuum cleaner, and the reaction of screaming and covering their ears is frequent [12]. Sensory hyporeactivity can be characterized by a too high threshold of sensation to sensory inputs, with a lack of ability to register the sensation. An example is that of a child does not respond when called, with intense, fast, or bright inputs needed to get their attention. Another example is the lack of response to pain or cold [13]. A child with sensory seeking behavior is characterized by excessive impulses to seek sensory experiences a behavior that can be dangerous [13].

Sensory integration theory was developed by Jean Ayres in 1972 and is identified as the neurological process that enables us to make sense of our world by receiving, registering, modulating, and interpreting information that comes to our brains from our senses. Ayres Integration Therapy primarily addresses disorders in sensory processing [14].

Sensory processing is the ability work with the information received through the senses (touch, smell, taste, sight, hearing, and movement), organize it and subsequently interpret it to decide the course of action. This process is automatic for most people, but those with Sensory Processing Dysregulation are affected by how the brain interprets the information and how it corresponds at the motor and emotional levels and other reactions [15] with the process divided in the following steps: sensory registration; orientation; interpretation; response organization and execution of a response [16]. For better understanding the example of receiving a splash of water on the face will be given. Registration occurs when we become aware of the sensation (when we feel the splash). Orientation is when we pay attention to the stimulus. Interpretation is when we assign it a meaning (when we identify what touches us, what we hear, what we see, and verify if it's dangerous or not, "It's a splash of water, it's not dangerous". Response organization is when we determine a cognitive, affective, or motor response, when we decide what to do "Let's clean up the splash immediately". Finally, the execution of a response is the last step, which consists in the execution of the previously elaborated response, in this case the cleaning of the splash. We can only observe the response, but we know that previously it was necessary to register, orient, interpret and organize all the information, so that the response is appropriate and adapted to the situation. The child learns about his body, the objects, the environment and to regulate his emotions and behavior through sensory information [16]. For example, some children with ASD feel that they are constantly being bombarded with sensory information because their brain responds differently [15]. The brain's ability to form the concept of the whole, is only possible because it has been able to give meaning to all the sensations experienced by the sense [16]. With Sensory Integration Therapy the goal is for the child to progressively reduce their reaction to their sensory inputs, with an improvement in concentration and behavior. The therapy is composed of specific sensory activities to help the child react appropriately to light, sound, touch, smell, among others [15]. Intervening in sensory processing dysfunctions, allows barriers to be removed to make the child calmer and more focused, developing skills for a better learning. An occupational therapist usually designs a sensory diet/lifestyle for a child, keeping in mind his/her unique sensory needs [17]. A large percentage, 60% to 70%, of children with ASD have some type of sensory processing dysfunction [16]. Children who start therapy early increase the likelihood of developing skills and abilities, and of doing well in school while avoiding secondary problems such as low self-esteem, anxiety, social and behavioral difficulties [16]. Studies show that people with ASD take longer to interpret the inputs received through their senses, lacking "filters" that eliminate information that is not needed, justifying why they are prone to "collapse." Sensory overload can be presented in many ways, such as a child entering school, trying to process the noise heard in the school's hallway, while trying to cope with the inputs from classmates and the teacher. "Crashes" can lead to challenging behaviors, withdrawal from activity, or complete shutdown [17]. Sensory dysregulation can thus be very disabling, as it interferes with daily life, such as the inability to cope with the noise of the washing machine, or the need to self-inflict pain to be aware of his/her own body [15].

1.3 Burel

Burel is a 100% wool fabric, which results from a sequence of operations in the manufacturing process. The wool, after being sheared, washed, spun, warped on the organ, and woven on the loom, is stepped on a machine called pisa, which beats and scales the wool transforming the fabric (Xerga) into Burel, making it tighter, more resistant, and waterproof. Its characteristics are versatility, high resistance, and robustness. These characteristics lead to a high resistance to traction, rupture, pressure, a great opacity, and the ability to support intensive use without altering its color and shape. Other characteristics are a high fire resistance; a high degree of impermeability; a good thermal and acoustic hygroscopic; a good abrasion resistance, flexibility, and the fact that it does not create pilling. The wool fiber is composed of keratin, which is a protein rich in sulfur, an element that is not found in any other fiber [18].

One of the most sensorial materials used in the design is burel. With this test it was possible to evaluate how a single material can be transformed into various textures and shapes, analyzing that a natural material, can be used in a way that serves as a sensory stimulator and integrator. Considering the unique properties of burel, and how they can be used to advantage, tests were created to see how a single material could be converted into various textures. The first group of samples was made with 4 raw burel disks, of different weights, (790 g, 800 g, 1100 g and 1400 g) and 1 disk with xerga, Fig. 1.

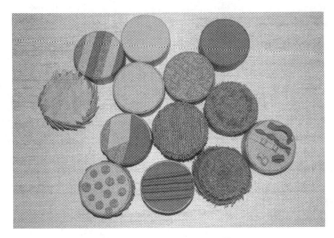

Fig. 1. Burel textures studies

1.4 Project Phase

This project aimed to design a furniture line for children with ASD, to promote their development and well-being. It is intended to give children a safe and therapeutic place in their family, so that they can have therapy while playing and enjoy a space where they feel safe. In addition, the therapeutic furniture is supposed be integrated into the home environment (i.e., child's bedroom), and not deconstruct it with its presence. This equipment should be seen by the child as a toy and not as a therapeutic tool, with negative connections to a medical environment. A sample collection was conducted in which questionnaires were addressed to parents, caregivers, relatives, educators, and people with proximity to children with ASD. The questionnaire was structured in closed questions, and a total of 94 responses were obtained. There was only one open-ended question in the questionnaire, which was aimed at providing data on what products the parents did not purchase but would like to get. The obtained results are summarized in Fig. 2.

There were 12 answers in which the responders said they did not know what they would like to get, or that they already had the products they thought they needed. Looking at the products deemed important, the swing was the one that got more responses. In fact, the respondents considered the swing to be the product they would like most to purchase, since it provides regulation for the child in the form of energy discharge. However, some said that it would not be possible to purchase the swing because it is not compatible with the structure of the house. Others mentioned that it would be important because of the constant need for the sensation of movement that calms the child. Next, with the highest number of positive answers, were the educational toys, some of which were described as painting material, books, and computers. The trampoline got some comments like there

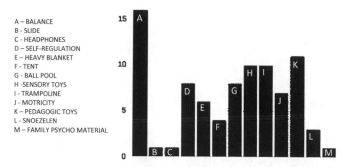

A – BALANCE
B - SLIDE
C - HEADPHONES
D – SELF-REGULATION
E – HEAVY BLANKET
F - TENT
G - BALL POOL
H -SENSORY TOYS
I - TRAMPOLINE
J - MOTRICITY
K – PEDAGOGIC TOYS
L - SNOEZELEN
M – FAMILY PSYCHO MATERIAL

Fig. 2. ASD therapeutic home furniture proprieties (n. 94 therapeutic responses)

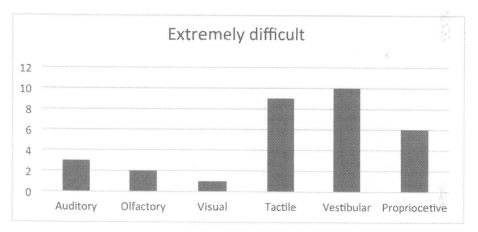

Fig. 3. Graph of responses of sensory processing dysfunction rated as extremely dificult

was no space to put it, or it had a high cost, some of the answers mentioning that they would like to get it for the energy discharge it provides to the child. Possible sensory toys were described as quiet lights, sounds and sensory mats. Self-regulation products were described as products that would help the regulation of the child, such as lycra or restraint products. The ball pool got the same number of responses as the self-regulation products but did not get any comments added to the responses.

The inquiries' response on sensory processing dysfunction rated as extremely difficult to the child are presented in Fig. 3, with vestibular and then tactile deficits being the ones that received the highest scores.

When grading the dysfunctions with a level considered difficult, the highest number of responses related to vestibular, proprioceptive, and tactile problems, Fig. 4.

Interviews were carried out with three Occupational Therapists. They were asked which equipment they usually use directed to the problems they intend to work with the child, which ones they considered to obtain the best results, which ones could be improved, which ones are problematic and which objects, not being directly linked to therapy, could be used for this purpose. The traditional ball pool and swing were the two products that the Occupational Therapists considered could bring most advantages. The

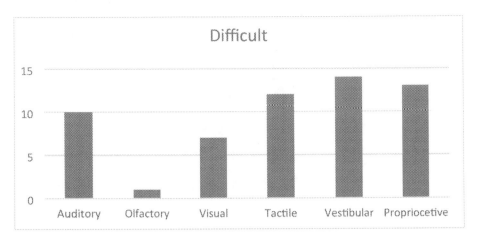

Fig. 4. Graph of responses of sensory processing dysfunction rated as dificult

ball pool providing tactile and proprioceptive input, and the swing providing vestibular input. Nevertheless, there are associated difficulties with the traditional therapeutic ball pool (high cost and large size) and with the traditional swing (need for supervision and necessary surrounding space) as most commercially available products are not designed for home use.

After the preliminary research was completed, and the data from the questionnaires and interviews analyzed, the following set of equipment was designed: ball pool, bed tent, sensory pouf, and a swivel chair.

1.5 Ball Pool

The decision to design a ball pool came from the fact that it was one of the most liked products in the questionnaires, deemed to offer excellent proprioceptive and tactile inputs. Initially several shapes were designed, such as the traditional round pool, with the shape of a cone trunk being finally chosen by transmitting the shape of a "nest" with safety and comfort, Fig. 5.

An important particularity of the pool is that the balls are covered with Burel fabric, with several different types of textures and different colors, with their interior made of cherry pit. Initially sand was thought of to fill the balls, however it was dismissed as it could give a too heavy feeling, and the child could suffer or cause physical harm to himself or his surroundings by not handling the product properly, such as throwing the ball at something or someone. The pool's interior would coat with cotton cloth and its exterior in Burel.

The cherry pit is sustainable, environmentally friendly and is considered therapeutic.) The ball with cherry pits can be warmed up by the child's parents and given to the child to stimulate the tactile sensation of heat, The balls are 7 cm in diameter (so that the child cannot put the ball in his mouth) and weight approximately 100 g. Heated balls and being able to knead them could also provide therapeutic advantages in terms of relaxation. The deep pressure felt by the child when in the pool and under the balls is also considered therapeutic.

The pool contains a side storage along the entire upper diameter, where 48 balls can be stored, arranged by color. The storage is divided into 12 tabs, and each tab will contain a circle of one color, corresponding to the placement of the ball to be stored, depicted by detail B in Fig. 5. This storage can be useful in the simulation of daily activities, stimulating the child to put objects in the correct place. There will be a total of 200 balls, but only the 48 balls that can be stored will have cherry pits inside, so that there is not too much weight on the child. The remaining balls will be filled with cotton.

If the child wants to use the space just for comfort, the balls can be placed in the storage bag that will come with the set, detail C in Fig. 5. The storage space also allows hypersensitive children to gradually try out the balls and adapt to the different textures, without having to deal with all the balls already in place. This product aims to provide daily therapy at home for sensory processing dysfunctions and can be used spontaneously and individually by the child or with the help of the parents, thus fostering parent/child interaction.

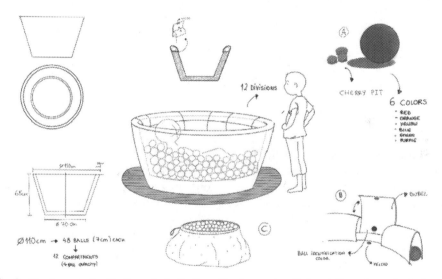

Fig. 5. Final concept of ball pool. A: Balls with cherry pits; B: burel flap where the balls are placed; C: storage bag balls

The ball pool aims to give hypersensitive children sensory integration at the tactile level, so that they can gradually adapt to textures thus gaining tolerance to them. On the other hand, it will give hyposensitive children the sensory stimulation they need. At the level of the proprioceptive system, besides the fact that the balls can be kneaded and heated, they aim to give proprioceptive input to children who avoid touch and have some motor incoordination, while allowing energy discharge to children who seek proprioceptive stimulation. The ball pool also gives the opportunity for parents to interact with the child and train divided attention and eye contact, teaching the child to play with other persons, using the balls in a way that increases social interaction.

Based on research related to color perception in interior spaces aimed at people with autism, the following colors should be used: neutral colors (ivory, beige, light mocha, muted teal, and soft gray); tranquil tones such as light blue, soft green, and muted purple. The primary blue color, it should be kept in mind that some people cannot distinguish it. The colors that should be avoided are white; bright, saturated colors, which can cause glare and unpleasant eye sensation; red and yellow (warm saturated colors) should also be avoided [19]. The color of the ball pool will be beige, a friendly neutral color well suited to a home environment. The colors of the balls will be six (red, yellow, blue, green, purple, and orange, always with low saturation).

Figure 6 depicts a graph rating from 0 to 5 the perceived benefits of the ball pool.

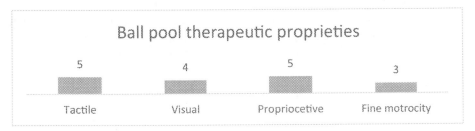

Fig. 6. Ball pool benefits graph

1.6   Bed

The bed is estimated to be a shelter and a cozy space for any child and is one of the products that parents considered a very difficult element to adapt to children with ASD. It is considered by many parents that there is a difficulty with hypersensitivity to sounds and lights, which makes it very difficult for the child to fall asleep and then stay asleep. Initially, beds of different shapes were de-signed, always thinking about two points of connection to support the hammock bed and how it could serve as a shelter for the child. There are blinds or curtains on the sides so that it can be completely closed to provide the child with a safe space. After several approaches on how these blinds would work, it was chosen to be supported on both sides for ease of use. Initially it was thought in the form of a roll, in which it could unroll up to the mattress, but it was dismissed as it could cause constraints when rolling up again. The simplified shape of the structure of the bed was based on the archetype of a house, transmitting security to the child, giving the feeling of shelter, all corners are rounded to avoid sharp edges, Fig. 7.

The bed has an incorporated hammock that the child can use therapeutically for self-regulation or play, to give vestibular and proprioceptive input, detail A in Fig. 7. The size of the bed was thought of to give the parents the opportunity to lie with the child, being designed around a mattress of 190 cm × 90 cm, thus also giving the opportunity to serve for the future, not being necessary to buy another bed when the child grows up. The bed will have a circular opening, reminiscent of a tunnel, offering fun for the child, and allowing the parents see the child when sleeping if the cover is closed, details B in Fig. 7. The light blue color was chosen, being a color that conveys calm [19]. In Fig. 8 the estimated benefits of the bed are rated from 0 to 5.

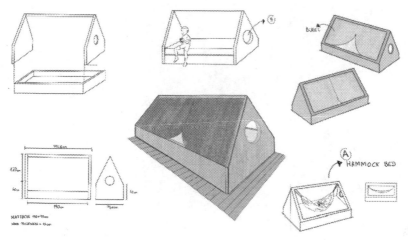

Fig. 7. Final concept of bed. A: Hammock bed; B: circular entrance referring to a tunnel

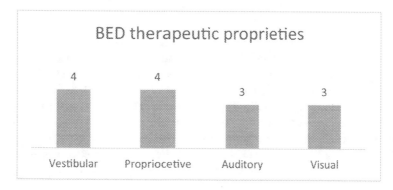

Fig. 8. Bed benefits graph

1.7 Tent

Analyzing the questionnaire's responses of the parents, a pattern can be observed in the perceived need by the children for isolation and sensory discharge, thus leading to the design of a "shelter". After some initial concepts were considered, the option of a folding tent that turned into a couch was chosen. After some exploratory concepts were tried the selected concept was arrived at and is depicted in Fig. 9. The tent is designed to serve as a shelter but also as a means of sensory discharge. Being composed of five "petals", the tent aims to lead the children to be stimulated in terms of gross motor skills, by pulling, pushing, and throwing the "petals", in a way that also promotes energy discharge.

The "petals" can also be pulled down, creating tunnels, where the child can play, promoting a proprioceptive input for energy discharge and for better body and space awareness, detail A in Fig. 9. By pulling the "petals" up and creating a safe space, the tent can serve as a shelter and quiet space for the child to concentrate on a task, or just for isolation when needed, such as in moments of sensory overload, detail B in Fig. 9.

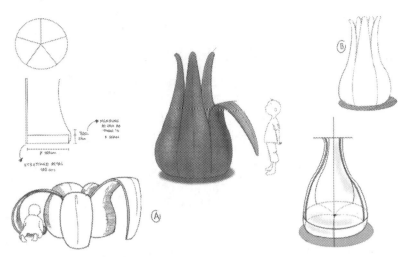

Fig. 9. Final concept of tent. A: petals downward creating tunnels; B: petals upward creating a tent

The representative form of a flower refers to nature, thus seeking to transmit calm. Its exterior is covered with Burel and seeks to take advantage of its properties previously mentioned, such as its acoustic, thermal, and visual insulation. When playing in the tunnels, touch stimulation is expected. The interior of the tent will made in cotton cloth with beige color, matching the rest of the furniture set. This choice results from the need of a neutral color, so that there are no strong stimuli inside the tent when it is used for isolation or concentration. The exterior color will be light blue, to provide calm and security [19]. In Fig. 10 the expected benefits of the tent are depicted in a scale from 0 to 5.

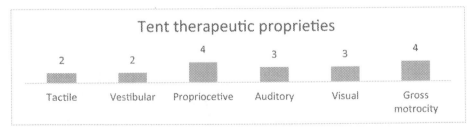

Fig. 10. Tent benefits graph

1.8 Sensory Pouf

The sensory pouf was designed thinking beyond its basic function as a seat, therefore aiming to become a therapeutic play object. The sensory pouf consists of two flaps on its top and, when opened, there will be a game/exercise for the child on each flap. The pouf's exterior will be in beige Burel, as it is a neutral color. Figure 11 depicts the final concept of the sensory pouf.

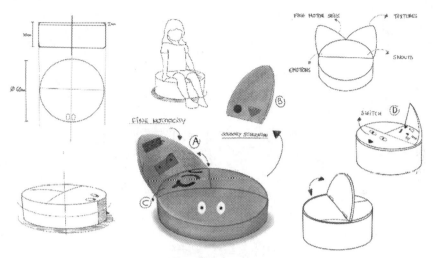

Fig. 11. Final concept of sensory pouf. A: flap with fine motor exercises; B: flap with tactile sensory stimulation; C: emotions; D: animal snouts

One of the flaps contains fine motor skills exercises, detail A in Fig. 11, and the other contains various textures for sensory stimulation and integration, detail B in Fig. 11. The flaps can be opened and closed using Velcro. When the flaps are lifted, several "mouths" and eyes can be found, referring to different emotions (sadness, joy, laughter, anger, etc.), detail C in Fig. 11. These emotion objects will have Velcro on their backside, so that the child can place and remove the desired emotion on the poof. This way the child can be stimulated to understand and identify emotions and they can even be used by the child to transmit feelings to the parents. At the base of the other flap there will be several animal "snout" shapes, leading the child to the symbolic game of transforming the poof into an "animal", thus stimulating the child's verbal and non-verbal communication, detail D in Fig. 11. For example, "Make the elephant", "Point out which elephant", are among possible forms of interaction between parents and child, aiming to the stimulation of symbolic play, a feature many times lacking or non-existent in children with ASD. The pouf is designed in a way that it could be used to promote divided attention and social interaction. The sensory pouf will have a storage space that can be accessed by lifting the part of the top apart the flaps, thus serving as a trunk, or toy storage space, for example for the pool balls, with the two products working as a set. In Fig. 12 the perceived benefits of the sensory pouf are presented in a scale from 0 to 5.

1.9 Swivel Chair

In the interviews with the Occupational Therapists, the swing was considered one of the objects with more potential. However, its indoor use was considered problematic as it

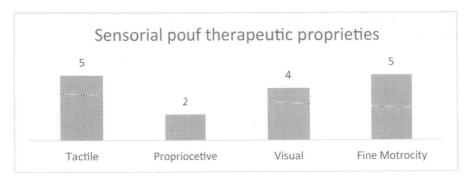

Fig. 12. Sensory pouf benefits graph

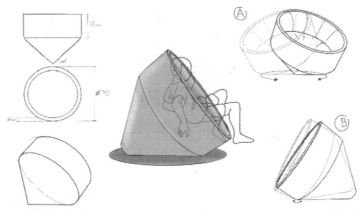

Fig. 13. Final concepts of the swivel chair. A: whirling movement; B: back and forth movement

typically needs to be hung from the ceiling and demands a large space to be operated. In the survey analysis, it was found that the swing is the main piece of equipment that parents have not purchased but would like to have, mentioning that it could have a calming effect on children. A non-conventional swing-like apparatus, a swivel chair, was thus designed and is presented in Fig. 13. In this device, besides whirling, detail A in Fig. 13, the child can just swing back and forth, detail B, promoting his/her self-regulation and relaxation, as well as offering proprioceptive and vestibular therapy.

It is expected that the swivel chair can be used with or without parental support and that can serve as integration therapy for children with poor coordination and fear of stairs, swings, and movement, in which parental interaction would be required for integration. It could also serve for children who can't stop still and in which there is a need to be in constant movement. The expected benefits of the swivel chair are depicted in Fig. 14 in a scale from 0 to 5.

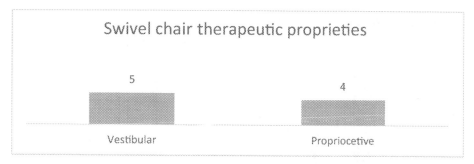

Fig. 14. Swivel chair benefits graph

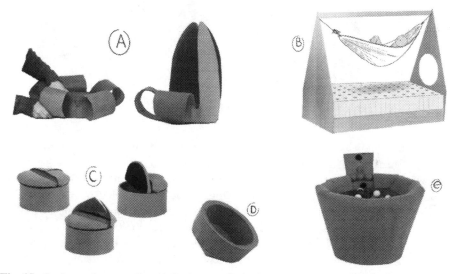

Fig. 15. Scale mockups studies (1:5). A: tent; B: bed; C: sensory pouf; D: swivel chair; E: ball pool

1.10 Study Mockups

Mockups of the designed therapeutic furniture were made at a 1:5 scale, to better perceive its tridimensional character and as a help to understand how their functionalities would work. The mockups are presented in Fig. 15.

1.11 Shapes and Textures

Fig. 16. Illustrative drawings of possible texture shapes

The set aggregates a series of textures and shapes in Burel, with velcro on the backside. The set is designed so that the child can insert them into any of the products previously described, giving the child freedom of exploration alone or with the parents. For example, the parents could put a fluffy texture on the bed curtain to help the child fall asleep, or use it to explore symbolic or cognitive games, such as ordering from smallest to smallest, creating stories, stimulating the child's communication and so on. The textures depicted in Fig. 16 are merely illustrative, so that one can visualize the diversity of shapes that could be created to stimulate the child. They will have an average height of 15 cm so that they impossible to be swallowed by the children.

2 Conclusion

Given the data collected through the research process, an attempt was made to design objects that could provide therapeutic benefits in children with Autism Spectrum Deficit (ASD). The designed products consist of a ball pool, a bed, a tent a sensory pouf, and a swivel chair, complemented with a set of textures that can be applied to any of these devices. It is expected that the products are not perceived by the children as a therapy, but instead fit into their daily lives in an almost unnoticeable way, bringing, besides therapy, moments of relaxation and fun. The products were designed to be used indoors, thus allowing the opportunity, almost unheard of in today's market, to be able to take therapy home. All the decisions in the design process were made so that all products fit the home environment, making them more appealing not only for the children, but for the parents as well. This project was designed in such a way that the conceived furniture could also be enjoyed by neuro-typical children. Preliminary research into the medical aspects of the ASD pathology was fundamental to obtain the necessary knowledge to be able to ask pertinent questions to parents, family members, and medical assistants, indispensable for the prosecution of the project. The methodology carried out allowed us to get to know the real needs of the children with ASD and the difficulties experienced by their parents, as well as the therapeutic products that could help their development. The tests performed with the Burel material allowed the understanding of how this material could be transformed into different shapes and textures, thus using it for a purpose totally different from the original one.

This project is currently under development and its next steps are to create full scale working prototypes of the designed therapeutic furniture, so that real life feedback on it is obtained, including an analysis by specialized medical doctors. After the real-life study is completed, the details of each product will be reviewed, analyzing whether improvements are needed. It is expected that the designed products will address the lack of domestic therapeutic devices adapted for children with ASD and will encourage designers to give extra attention to the inclusive side of design, with the heart of the project centered on the user, independently of the very special needs targeted.

Acknowledgements. This project is the product of the contribution of many people, who throughout the whole process showed their support and generosity. In addition to the literary research carried out, which was fundamental, the great-test source of knowledge was the contribution made by parents, family members, educators, and therapists, who shared their reality with us and let us understand their real needs, allowing us to see the perspective of the people who go through the care and evolution of children with ASD. An acknowledgement to all the people who contributed their experience and knowledge.

References

1. Bellomo, T., Prasad, S., Munzer, T., Laventhal, N.: The impact of the COVID-19 pandemic on children with autism spectrum disorders. J. Pediatr. Rehabil. Med. **13**(3), 349–354 (2020)
2. Coleman, R., Clarkson, J., Dong, H., Cassim, J.: Design for Inclusivity: A Practical Guide to Accessible, Innovative and User-Centred Design. Gower Publishing Limited (2007)
3. American Psychological Association: https://www.apa.org/. Accessed 12 Nov 2021
4. Elsabbagh, M., et al.: Global prevalence of autism and other pervasive developmental disorders. Autism Res **5**, 160–179 (2012)
5. Federação Portuguesa do Autismo: https://www.fpda.pt/. Accessed 18 Dec 2021
6. Gomes, D., Quaresma, M.: Introdução do Design Inclusivo, 1st edn. Appris, Brasil (2018)
7. American Psychiatric Association: Diagnostic and Statistical Manual of Mental Disorders, 5th edn. American Psychiatric Publishing, London (2013)
8. Lima, C.: As Perturbações do Espectro do Autismo, 2nd edn. Lidel – Edições Técnicas Lda, Portugal (2012)
9. Rogers, S., Dawson, G., Vismara, L.: Autismo: Compreender e agir em família, 1st edn. Lidel – Edições Técnicas Lda, Portugal (2015)
10. Premack, D., Woodruff, G.: Does the chimpanzee have a theory of mind? Behav. Brain Sci. **1**(4), 515–526 (1978)
11. Filipe, C.: Autismo: Conceitos, Mitos e Preconceitos, 1st edn. Babel Lda, Portugal (2012)
12. National Institute of Mental Health: https://www.nimh.nih.gov/. Accessed 10 Nov 2021
13. Michelle, A., Suarez, M.: Sensory Processing in Children with Autism Spectrum Disorders and Impact on Functioning, pp. 2–10. Elsevier Inc., USA (2012)

14. Ayres, J.: Sensory Integration and Learning Disorders, 1st edn. Western Psychological Services, Los Angeles (1972)
15. Thye, M.D., Bednarz, H.M., Herringshaw, A.J., Sartin, E.B., Kana, R.K.: The impact of atypical sensory processing on social impairments in autism spectrum disorder. Dev. Cogn. Neurosci. **29**, 151–167 (2018)
16. Serrano, P.: A integração sensorial no desenvolvimento e aprendizagem da criança, 3rd edn. Papa-Letras Lda, Portugal (2018)
17. Adamson, A., O'Hare, A., Graham, C.: Impairments in sensory modulation in children with autistic spectrum disorder. Br. J. Occup. Ther. **69**(8), 357–364 (2006)
18. Burel Factory: https://www.burelfactory.com. Accessed 02 Jan 2022
19. Shareef, S.S., Farivarsadri, G.: The impact of colour and light on children with autism in interior spaces from an architectural point of view. Int. J. Arts Technol. **11**(2), 153 (2019)

A Design Method of Knee Pad Based on User Data

Kaice Man[✉], Fei Yue, and Wenda Tian

Tsinghua University, Beijing, People's Republic of China
mkc18@tsinghua.org.cn

Abstract. Lattice structures are designed structures with excellent mechanical properties. Because of the continuous development of parametric design and additive manufacturing, lattice structures can be more easily applied to products design. Therefore, we explore how to combine different lattice structures through the parametric design of a knee pad. Our research shows the possibility of creating customized knee pads using lattice structures. The research can be divided into three parts: the understanding of lattice structures, the acquisition of user data, and the use of user data. In the first part, the mechanical properties of various lattice structures are compared to provide the selection basis of lattices in knee pads design. In the second part, the user's knee pressure data are collected and analyzed with the self-made wearable pressure detection device. In the third part, through the generative design program developed for our research, the designs of customized knee pads are completed. Finally, we select one design solution for the 3D-printed prototype and conduct the user test.

Keywords: Lattice structure · Knee pad · Parametric design · Digital manufacturing

1 Introduction

Lattice structures are topologically ordered, three-dimensional structures composed of repeating unit cells [1], having many excellent properties such as lightweight, energy absorption, high strength, and high stiffness. The mechanical properties of lattice structures are highly dependent upon the type of the building unit cells [2]. Based on their mechanical response, lattice structures can generally be classified as either bending-dominated or buckling-dominant. Habib et al. [3] show that the lattice structures with bending-dominated deformation provide good energy absorption performance but have low stiffness and strength. The buckling-dominated lattice structures are stiffer and stronger but have low energy absorption capability. For our research, understanding the mechanical behavior of lattice structures is the foundation.

The knee is under strain in daily life and during sporting activities [4]. 20–25% of all knee injuries occur during exercise [5]. In some sports, the usage of knee pads is mandatory. Knee pads can reduce the impact forces acting on the knee by temporarily storing energy. The use of knee pads reduces knee injures by 56% [6]. However, in

M. M. Soares et al. (Eds.): HCII 2022, LNCS 13323, pp. 187–199, 2022.
https://doi.org/10.1007/978-3-031-05906-3_14

non-competitive and social sports activities, the infrequent use of personal protective equipment (PPE) is a rising challenge. The reason for this appears to be discomfort due to an ill-fitting fit, which generally results in constrained body movements and a feeling of bulkiness. An ill-fitting pad also causes increased pad displacement upon impact, negatively affecting its protective function [7]. Therefore, it is essential to study the customized design of knee pads.

Research on the use of lattice structures in 3D printed protective gears has increased significantly. The 3D printed protective gears, which consist of lattice structures, can achieve customized protection and are also conducive to the heat dissipation and perspiration of the human body. Inspired by the above, we developed a knee pad design workflow. By discussing our design process, we illustrate how to analyze the mechanical behavior of lattice structures, obtain the knee pressure data, and complete the creations of customized knee pads.

2   Design Process

In the following section, we discuss how we explored the mechanical lattice structures concept of programming and how user data influenced the creation of the knee pad designs. Our design approach consists of five phases:

1. Understanding the mechanical behavior of lattice structures by performing FEA of a collection of lattice structures;
2. Analyzing data from one user's knee pressure, as well as its pressure maps;
3. Building the program to generate knee pad designs, which key is to map various lattice structures to the different positions of a knee pad according to a pressure map;
4. Prototyping through 3D printing.

3   Understanding Lattice Structures

By comparing the mechanical properties of 10 lattice structures, we could provide the selection basis of lattices in knee pads design. Figure 1 shows the computer-aided design models of 10 lattice structures. Ten lattice structures are designed based on different unit cells, and the software used was Rhino (RH). The dimension of each lattice structure is $5 \times 5 \times 5$ cm^3. Each lattice structure consists of $3 \times 3 \times 3$ unit cells by duplicating cells in the three directions. Each lattice structure is designed to have a constant relative density of 12%.

Ansys Workbench was applied to simulate the mechanical behavior of lattice structures under quasi-static uniaxial loading. The material parameters were defined according to the properties of PA12, including density (1020 kg/m^3), Young's modulus (1800 MPa), and Poisson's ratio (0.3). Fixed support was added to the bottom surface of each lattice structure model, and a 50 N uniform load down the Z-axis was added to the top surface of each lattice structure model. The way to generate meshes of lattice structures was the autonomic division method, and other parameters were the default settings in Ansys. We performed FEA of 10 lattice structures and exported the analysis results, including total

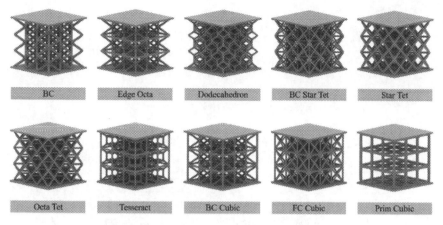

Fig. 1. The CAD models of 10 lattice structures

deformation, equivalent stress, and strain energy. Taking the Star Tet as an example, its load and constraint setting and the analysis result are shown in Fig. 2.

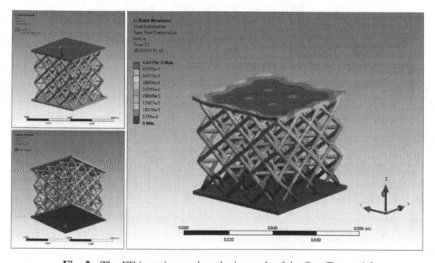

Fig. 2. The FEA setting and analysis result of the Star Tet model

The data are summarized in Table 1. The FEA data show that the three lattices which deform by bending, such as BC, Edge Octa, Dodecahedron, have greater equivalent stress and strain energy than the other lattices. It indicates that the three lattice structures have good energy absorption capacity. The three lattices that deform by buckling, such as Prim Cubic, FC Cubic, BC Cubic, have smaller total deformation than the others. It indicates that the three lattice structures have good load-bearing capacity. Understanding the mechanical behavior of lattice structures plays an essential role in guiding the knee pads design in the sixth phase.

Table 1. The FEA data of 10 lattice structures

	BC	Edge Octa	Dodecahedron	BC Star Tet
Total deformation [m]	5.55e−005	4.60e−005	4.16e−005	2.86e−005
Equivalent stress [Pa]	5.98e+005	5.59e+005	5.79e+005	4.59e+005
Strain energy [J]	2.81e−003	2.33e−003	2.03e−003	1.46e−003
Star tet	Octa Tet	Tesseract	BC Cubic	FC Cubic	Prim Cubic
1.99e−005	1.93e−005	1.64e−005	1.44e−005	1.26e−005	9.45e−006
3.85e+005	4.26e+005	3.27e+005	2.90e+005	3.04e+005	2.15e+005
1.03e−003	9.66e−004	8.67e−004	7.71e−004	6.82e−004	5.24e−004

4 Designing a Wearable for Knee Pressure Detection

We applied FSR pressure sensors to detect the pressure values between the human knee and the ground and then used the data for the parametric design of lattice-structural knee pads. First, we considered how to use the pressure sensors and Arduino toolkits. In our study, we wanted to detect knee pressure in different body positions to obtain average pressure values. It would facilitate the rational arrangement of varying lattice structures in a knee pad.

Therefore, we designed a wearable device for knee pressure detection. It is modified from a cloth dance knee pad, as seen in Fig. 3. When creating the detection device, the core factor we considered was correctly arranging the pressure sensors. The knee is straightforward to damage the patella and meniscus when squeezed or hit by external forces. The pressure values of these two parts are essential references for knee pads design. Therefore, we connected 5 pressure sensors to 5 positions on the dance knee pad, corresponding to the meniscus (A1, A5), the patella (A3), and the upper part of the patella (A2, A4).

As a wearable pressure detection device, its lightweight and comfort are essential. We applied the thin-film pressure sensor. This sensor is light and thin, making it suitable for non-invasive measurements. But it cannot directly detect a pressure value. When pressed, its resistance changes and an analog output value (AO value) is output. The heavier the applied load, the larger the output AO value. In Arduino, we wrote a program that can convert AO values to the corresponding pressure values.

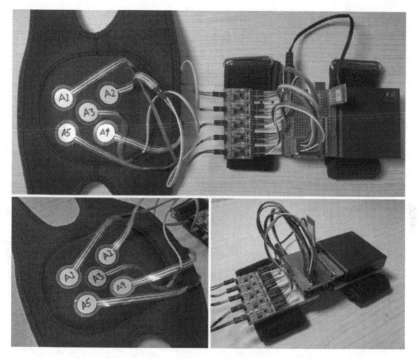

Fig. 3. The wearable pressure detection device

Since the Arduino Uno has no data storage function, it must transmit data to the computer in real-time. We applied the way of wireless transmission of data. As seen in Fig. 4, these are the data transmission modules matched with the pressure detection device. The wireless transmission modules are two HC-05 Bluetooth, which can realize real-time mutual transmission of data within a range of 10 m.

Fig. 4. The wireless transmission modules

5   Collecting and Analyzing User's Data

After getting the wearable pressure detection device, the following phase was to collect the user's data. We recruited a male participant for the experiment and completed the knee pad design based on his data. Our experimental scheme was to record pressure values on his right knee in contact with the ground while the participant made different body movements. He needed to complete the body movements: 1. Kneeling on one knee and kneeling on both knees; 2. kneeling on one knee, leaning left, right, front, and back; 3. kneeling on both knees, leaning left, right, front, and back. Therefore, we asked the participant wear a left knee pad to prevent injury. According to the scheme above, we perform the knee pressure detection experiment and record the whole process through video, as seen in Fig. 5.

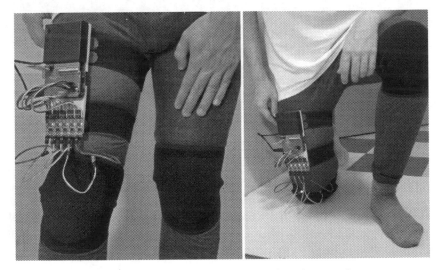

Fig. 5. The process of the knee pressure detection experiment

By using the Firefly Uno component, the real-time pressure values were shown in Grasshopper. The participant performed different kneeling positions, and we recorded pressure values when there were no significant fluctuations in pressure values.

As seen in Table 2, the result shows that the patella (A3) has a greater pressure value than the other four parts in the first kneeling position. There are similar situations in the other kneeling positions, such as the third, fifth, and eighth. These indicate that the patella is typically the maximum stress part in the several kneeling positions. In addition, the pressure values of the medial (A1) and lateral (A5) meniscus positions are generally very similar while the participant kneels on one knee. While he kneels on both knees, pressure values are generally higher on the medial meniscus (A1) than on the lateral (A5).

On this base, it was also essential to understand the pressure changes on the knee. It required two data elements for the participant's knee.

Table 2. The knee pressure values in different kneeling positions

Kneeling on one knee	1. No leaning	2. Leaning left	3. Leaning right	4. Leaning forth	5. Leaning back
A1 [N]	84.8	61.0	114.2	79.8	86.4
A2 [N]	37.5	67.7	44.6	38.7	8.5
A3 [N]	162.3	97.4	127.0	79.9	192.6
A4 [N]	36.4	9.4	45.7	39.0	16.4
A5 [N]	72.1	28.5	118.6	66.5	68.0
Kneel on both knees	6. No leaning	7. Leaning left	8. Leaning right	9. Leaning forth	10. Leaning back
A1 [N]	109.8	79.9	143.7	48.6	80.8
A2 [N]	36.0	66.4	31.5	43.4	21.8
A3 [N]	73.1	43.7	159.0	127.0	80.8
A4 [N]	39.9	8.7	17.4	63.3	14.5
A5 [N]	74.3	26.3	40.5	21.8	47.1

First, obtain a 3D digital model of the participant's knee. We took multi-angle photographs of his right knee for modeling reference. Because of the complex shape of the knee, we used the Sub D component in RH for modeling. It is an efficient modeling tool, especially for modeling irregular shapes. Second, provide visual feedback of changes in knee pressure. We built a related program in GH to output knee pressure maps in gradient colormaps. The redder the color, the higher the pressure value. The greener the color, the lower the pressure value. We re-topologized the design model of the knee, i.e., creating a denser mesh: the denser the model mesh, the more accurate the pressure analysis results. We analyzed changes in the force on the right knee when he kneeled.

As seen in Fig. 6, in the two kneeling positions, the patella and meniscus are the first parts of the knee to be stressed. After that, the pressure gradually spread to all areas of the patella and meniscus. The most stressed areas are the center of the patella and the medial meniscus.

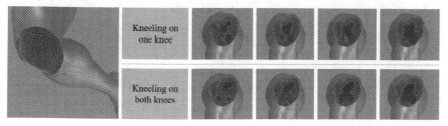

Fig. 6. The pressure changes on the right knee

In the next phase, we algorithmically manipulated the arrangement of lattice structures in a knee pad. With the data above, the program can arrange the energy-absorbing lattice structures to the most stressed parts of the knee and arrange the load-bearing lattice structures to the other stressed parts of the knee.

6   Generating the Designs

Additive manufacturing allows producing complex 3D shapes. It means that different components, which have different capabilities, can be fabricated together in one piece with the same features [8]. We used Grasshopper (GH) to build the generative design program for creating knee pads. The program allows generating the design model of a knee pad, which consists of different lattice structures. It needs three requirements as input: the mid-surface of a knee pad geometry, the pressure map of the knee, and a library of various lattice structures. To illustrate how a knee pad is generated, we briefly explain the key points of this program:

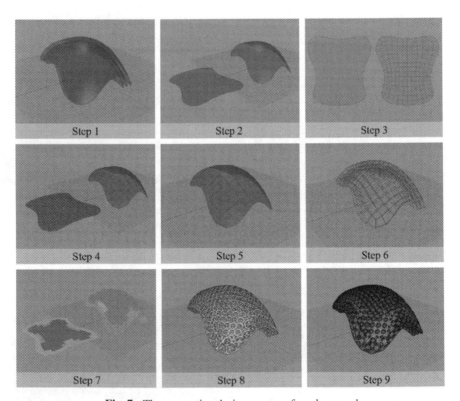

Fig. 7. The generative design process for a knee pad

1. One surface was created in RH representing the middle of the knee pad's 3D shape, i.e., the mid-surface. With the Offset Surface component, the inner and outer surfaces

of the knee pad were obtained from the mid-surface. These three surfaces serve as the reference for the generative design program to fill the spaces between the surfaces with lattice structures.

2. Our approach was first to unfold the mid-surface and then mesh on the unfolded mid-surface. Meshing tools included Mesh Brep and Quad Remesh, transforming the unfolded mid-surface into uniform meshes. After obtaining the meshes, they needed to be mapped to the mid-surface. To create meshes on the mid-surface, we applied the ShapeMap, a GH plug-in. It allows uniformly mapping meshes to a curved surface. In addition, the operation of mapping meshes is not constrained by the UV lines on the surface. Figure 7 Step 4 shows these are the meshes mapped on the mid-surface. However, due to the local deformation of the mapped meshes, it was necessary to optimize their shapes appropriately. We applied the Kangaroo, a GH plug-in. It allows enabling geometric forms to be shaped by applied forces and interacted with in real-time [9]. With the components such as Equal Angle, Equal Length, and Edge Length, the shape-optimized meshes are generated, as seen in Fig. 7 Step 5.

3. The sixth step addresses creating the voxels. In our research, voxels are cubic spaces that fill lattice structures, and there is only one lattice structure in each voxel. Using the Twisted Box component allows generating voxels between meshes from the faces. Therefore, the meshes on the knee pad's inner and outer surfaces also were generated.

4. In the second phase, we had analyzed the mechanical behavior of 10 lattice structures. According to our understanding of these lattice structures, we created a subprogram to position different lattice structures to the specific voxels. The subprogram can read the RGB values from a knee pressure map and facilitate the use of the read result to group voxels. Each voxel is preset with various selected colors in GH before performing the grouping operation. The subprogram matches a selected color for each voxel based on the RGB values obtained, as seen in Fig. 7 Step 7. These colored voxels are used as anchors to guide the positioning of the lattice structures. Voxels of the same color can be assigned to one type of lattice structure. The lattices in the red voxels are energy-absorbing lattice structures such as BC or Dodecahedron, which help protect the most stressed parts of the knee. The lattices in the green voxels are load-bearing lattice structures such as Prim Cubic or FC Cubic, which contribute to the structural rigidity of a knee pad.

5. The final step addresses creating the thickness of the lattice structures and exporting the model to an STL format for 3D printing. We applied the MultiPipe component, which can create a branched pipe around a network of lines/curves. With this component, the program generated the geometry of the knee pad. In order to facilitate the 3D printing of the model, it was necessary to improve the smoothness of the model's surfaces. Finally, the model's surfaces were subdivided with the Weaverbird's Subdivision component. As seen in Fig. 8, these are the final design models of different lattice-structural knee pads.

Fig. 8. The digital models of different knee pads

7 Manufacturing and Testing

Rapid prototyping of flexible TPU materials can be achieved through the 3D printing process of MJF (Multi Jet Fusion). The 3D printer used for our prototyping was an HP 3D Jet Fusion 4200. The material chosen was ESTANE® 3D TPU M95A as it presents notable properties such as flexibility, good shock absorption, and high wear. Figure 9 shows the 3D printed knee pads with complete structures and smooth surfaces.

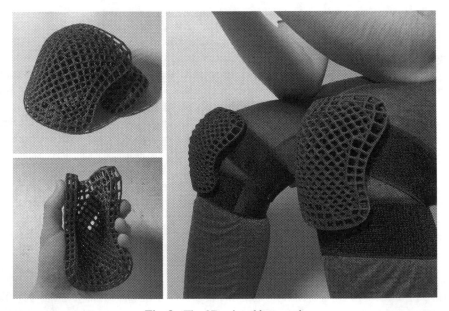

Fig. 9. The 3D printed knee pads

Finally, we conducted the usability evaluation with the participant. This experiment was the same as the previous knee pressure detection experiment in terms of the method used. We glued the pressure sensors to the inner surface of the 3D printed knee pad. The participant was on one knee while wearing the knee pad, and we recorded the images of knee pressure maps. Compared to the knee pressure maps from the previous experiment, the new pressure maps show an even stress distribution, as seen in Fig. 10. This knee pad, composed of lattice structures, plays an effective protective role.

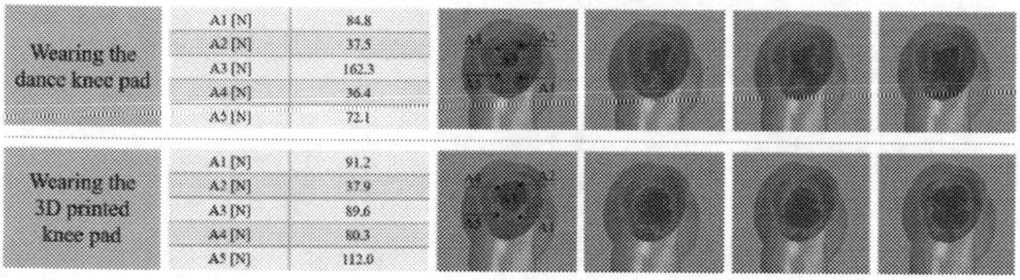

Wearing the dance knee pad	A1 [N]	84.8
	A2 [N]	37.5
	A3 [N]	162.3
	A4 [N]	36.4
	A5 [N]	72.1
Wearing the 3D printed knee pad	A1 [N]	91.2
	A2 [N]	37.9
	A3 [N]	89.6
	A4 [N]	80.3
	A5 [N]	112.0

Fig. 10. The comparison between the previous pressure maps and the new pressure maps

8 Conclusion

In this paper, we proposed a design method for customized knee pads. This method can be divided into three parts: the understanding of lattice structures, the acquisition of user data, and the use of user data. In the first part, we analyzed the mechanical behavior of 10 lattice structures. In the second part, we collected and analyzed the participant's knee pressure data. In the third part, we used the pressure data to complete the designs of knee pads. We briefly summarize the key points in these three parts:

1. In the first part, we analyzed the mechanical properties of 10 lattice structures to provide the selection basis of lattices in knee pads design. Rhino and Grasshopper were used to create lattice structures, and Ansys Workbench was used to simulate the mechanical behavior of the lattice structures. The FEA data show that the lattices which deform by bending under the compression loading, such as BC, Edge Octa, Dodecahedron, have good energy absorption capacity. The lattices that deform by buckling, such as Prim Cubic, FC Cubic, BC Cubic, are stiffer and stronger. Understanding the mechanical behavior of lattice structures plays an essential role in guiding knee pads design.
2. In the second part, we collected the knee pressure data from the participant in different body positions and analyzed these data to output knee pressure maps. In the data collection, we first designed and fabricated a wearable pressure detection device equipped with 5 thin-film pressure sensors to detect the pressure values of different parts on the knee. We then recruited a male participant for knee pressure detection experiment. He wore this device and completed the body movements as kneeling on one knee and both knees, and we recorded the pressure values generated. In the data analysis, we built a program that can output the knee pressure map by a color gradient image. The participant's knee pressure maps show that his patella and meniscus are the most stressed areas on the knee.
3. In the third part, we built the generative design program in GH for creating knee pads. The program created for our study allows positioning different lattice structures to

the specific areas of a knee pad by a knee pressure map. It can arrange the energy-absorbing lattice structures to the most stressed parts of the knee and arrange the load-bearing lattice structures to the other stressed parts of the knee. With this program, we completed the designs of customized knee pads and exported the final model for 3D printing.

Support Information

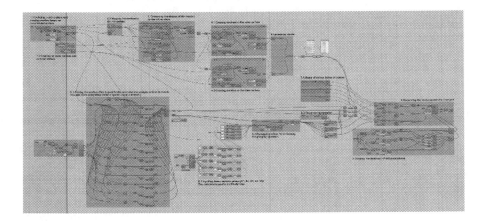

The program for generating the design of a knee pad

References

1. Maconachie, T., et al.: SLM lattice structures: properties, performance, applications and challenges. Mater. Des. **183**, 108137 (2019)
2. Habib, F.N., et al.: Fabrication of polymeric lattice structures for optimum energy absorption using multi jet fusion technology. Mater. Des. **155**, 86–98 (2018)
3. Ahmadi, S.M., et al.: Additively manufactured open-cell porous biomaterials made from six different space-filling unit cells: the mechanical and morphological properties. Materials **8**(4), 1871–1896 (2015)
4. Majewski, M., Susanne, H., Klaus, S.: Epidemiology of athletic knee injuries: a 10-year study. Knee **13**(3), 184–188 (2006)
5. Schäfer, F.K., et al.: Sport injuries of the extensor mechanism of the knee. Radiologe **42**(10), 799–810 (2002)
6. Schwarze, M., Hurschler, C., Welke, B.: Force, impulse and energy during falling with and without knee protection: an in-vitro study. Sci. Rep. **9**(1), 1–6 (2019)
7. Kajtaz, M., Subic, A., Brandt, M., Leary, M.: Three-dimensional printing of sports equipment. In: Materials in Sports Equipment, pp. 161–198. Woodhead Publishing (2019). https://doi.org/10.1016/B978-0-08-102582-6.00005-8

8. Pelanconi, M., Ortona, A.: Review on the design approaches of cellular architectures produced by additive manufacturing. In: Meboldt, Mirko, Klahn, Christoph (eds.) Industrializing Additive Manufacturing: Proceedings of AMPA2020, pp. 52–64. Springer International Publishing, Cham (2021). https://doi.org/10.1007/978-3-030-54334-1_5
9. Piker, D.: Kangaroo: form finding with computational physics. Archit. Des. **83**(2), 136–137 (2013)

Research on the Design of Handheld Gimbals Based on KANO Model

Yuanyuan Meng[✉]

East China University of Science and Technology, Shanghai, China
Myyywork@163.com

Abstract. In view of the serious homogenization of handheld gimbal products in the market nowadays and the lesser number of products suitable for mass consumers, the kano model is used to analyze the functional demand attributes of users for handheld gimbal and the influence of related functions on user satisfaction, so as to carry out the innovative design of handheld gimbal. This research collected user feedback through desktop research and user interviews to refine users' functional requirements for handheld gimbals. Then, the kano questionnaire was prepared and distributed according to the functional requirements, and the functional attributes were categorized using the kano evaluation results. Finally, a scatter plot was constructed by calculating the Better-Worse coefficient to determine the priority of functional requirements. The results accurately position the design elements of the handheld gimbal in terms of shape, function and interaction, and use them to create innovative designs that improve user satisfaction and experience. By using the kano model, this research shows the degree of the target users' needs for each function of the handheld gimbal from the user's perspective, and provides a guiding direction for the innovative design of the handheld gimbal.

Keywords: The Kano model · User needs · Hand-held head · Functional design · User satisfaction

1 Introduction

Handheld gimbal is a portable photographic equipment developed from drone technology, the core function is anti-shake and anti-shock, specifically to assist in filming, playing an important role in the process of filming movies, TV series, etc. In recent years, the short video and live industry continues to become popular, the tendency of video logging is also gradually emerging, handheld gimbal is no longer exclusive to professional videographers, and gradually penetrate to the mass consumers. However, although the handheld gimbal is developing rapidly in the global market, but the market size is still relatively small, and the product homogenization is serious, mainly designed for professionals rather than mass consumers, there is still more room for development.

In this paper, we take users as the center, refine users' functional requirements for handheld gimbal through qualitative analysis, adopt Kano model to guide the design of quantitative questionnaire, and categorize the functional demand attributes of handheld gimbal according to the results of questionnaire feedback. Using the Better-Worse coefficient to measure user satisfaction on this basis, we obtain the priority ranking of functional requirements, so as to get the innovative design direction of the handheld gimbal.

2   Materials and Method

2.1   Handheld Gimbals

Handheld gimbal, also known as handheld stabilizer, is a derivative development product of the drone industry, transferring the technology of automatic stabilization and coordination system used on drones to cell phone (or camera) shooting applications, is a high-tech portable mobile photography equipment [1]. As shown in Fig. 1, the handheld gimbal is divided into two main modules, the gimbal module and the grip module. The upper gimbal module can fix the cell phone or camera and other shooting equipment, and use the three-axis motor to enable it to rotate in any direction. The three-axis motor will compensate for jitter in time when it occurs during the shooting process, so as to ensure the stability of the picture. The lower grip module mainly plays the role of support and can be held, the user can hold for shooting. At the same time, the function area is set above the handheld lever and follows the principle of one-handed control, allowing manual focus, auto fill light, shooting mode selection and other functions.

There are many kinds of handheld gimbals. According to the load of the gimbal, it can be divided into low load gimbal and high load gimbal. According to whether it can be put into other equipment, it can be divided into airborne and conventional handheld gimbal. According to the equipment and professional degree of operation, it can be divided into professional grade and non-professional grade handheld gimbal, which is also the most common way of classification [2]. Professional level handheld gimbal is usually equipped with micro SLR, DSLR or video camera, with a larger load range, suitable for professional shooting scenes, such as program follow-up, news interview, film and television shooting, etc. Non-professional handheld gimbal is usually equipped with cell phone, sports camera, lighter quality mini SLR camera, etc. The load range is smaller, and it suitable for life shooting scenarios, such as vlog shooting, sports selfie,

Fig. 1. Handheld gimbals (image from the web, https://www.dji.com/cn)

live shooting, etc. The research in this paper is mainly about non-professional handheld gimbal for mass consumers.

According to the research, there are mainly two types of non-professional grade handheld gimbals on the market. One is a handheld gimbal that can be put into a cell phone or camera, and the other is a pocket camera that combines the camera and gimbal into one, which is more lightweight and compact.

2.2 Kano Model Overview

Kano model, proposed by Noriaki Kano, a professor at Tokyo Institute of Technology, Japan, is a set of questionnaire analysis methods developed based on the principle of user needs segmentation. It mainly conducts research through standardized structured questionnaires, analyzes the impact of different user needs on user satisfaction, and classifies and prioritizes user needs according to the research results to address the positioning of product attributes and improve user satisfaction, reflecting the non-linear relationship between product performance and user satisfaction [3]. In the kano model, user needs are classified into five categories based on the relationship between the type of user needs and user satisfaction [4], as shown in Fig. 2.

1 Must-be Quality: The demand element that users think the product must have. When the product provides this requirement, user satisfaction will not increase, but if it does not, satisfaction will decrease significantly.

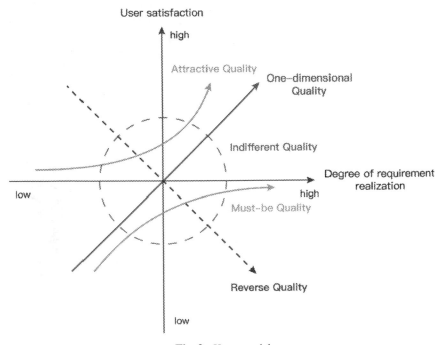

Fig. 2. Kano model

2 One-dimensional Quality: What users expect. When the product provides this requirement, user satisfaction will increase, and when it does not, user satisfaction will decrease.

3 Attractive Quality: A need that users can't imagine. When this requirement is provided, user satisfaction increases dramatically, but does not decrease when it is not provided.

4 Indifferent Quality: Whether the product provides or does not provide this demand, the user does not care and the satisfaction will not change.

5 Reverse Quality: A requirement that will make users dissatisfied. When this requirement is provided, user satisfaction decreases, and when it is not provided, user satisfaction increases.

2.3 Research Process

Identify User Needs Hierarchy. The functional design of the product needs to meet the needs of users at different levels, understand the attitude of target users towards the design needs of handheld gimbals, and use the kano model to analyze the attribute attribution of product functions. First, we need to collect numerous requirements or functions from users and compile the kano questionnaire. Each requirement or feature in the questionnaire has two questions, positive and negative. The positive question measures the user's satisfaction when a function is available, and the negative question measures the user's satisfaction when a function is not available. The answers to the questionnaire used the five-pole option. The satisfaction levels from high to low are like (I like this feature very much, having it would make me happy and satisfied), must-be (it is a must-have function and should be available), neutral (it does not matter whether it is available or not), live with (it is possible to have it, but it is better without it), and dislike (this feature makes me feel very dissatisfied), as shown in Table 1. Before the user answers, the meaning of each level is explained to the user to prevent misunderstanding. Secondly, the collected kano questionnaire data need to be cleaned, analyzed, and the obviously illogical and invalid data eliminated. Then the user functional requirements are categorized according to the kano evaluation result classification comparison table, as shown in Table 2.

Table 1. Questionnaire topic setting mode

How do you feel about a particular function?					
	Like	Must-be	Neutral	Live with	Dislike
Functional	○	○	○	○	○
Dysfunctional	○	○	○	○	○

Table 2. Kano evaluation results classification comparison table

		Dysfunctional				
		Like	Must-be	Neutral	Live with	Dislike
Functional	Like	Q	A	A	A	O
	Must-be	R	I	I	I	M
	Neutral	R	I	I	I	M
	Live with	R	I	I	I	M
	Dislike	R	R	R	R	Q

A = attractive; O = One-dimensional; M = Must-be; I = Indifferent; R = Reverse; Q = Questionable.

Analyze User Satisfaction Using the Better-Worse Coefficient. In addition to functional attribute attribution using the Kano model, the Better-Worse coefficient can also be calculated from the percentage of functional attribute attribution, indicating the degree to which a feature can increase satisfaction or eliminate the impact of very dislike. The calculation formula are as follows.

$$\text{Better (SI)} = (A + O)/(A + O + M + I)$$

$$\text{Worse (DSI)} = (-1)(O + M)/(A + O + M + I)$$

The Better coefficient, also known as the satisfaction coefficient, usually has a positive value, which means that user satisfaction will increase if a certain functional attribute is provided. The larger the positive value and the closer to 1, the greater the impact on user satisfaction, and the faster the user satisfaction will increase. The Worse coefficient, also known as the dissatisfaction coefficient, usually has a negative value, representing that user satisfaction decreases if a certain functional attribute is not provided. The more negative the value is and the closer it is to -1, the greater the impact on user dissatisfaction and the faster the decrease in satisfaction. Therefore, based on the value of the better-worse coefficient for each function, a four-quadrant scatter diagram can be drawn to prioritize user requirements and thus clarify the design direction of the handheld head.

3 Handheld Gimbal User Requirements Analysis Based on Kano Model

3.1 User Orientation

According to the data of the 2019 China Handheld Gimbal Industry Research Report by iResearch Consulting, Chinese handheld gimbal consumers are mainly divided into tool-focused attribute professional consumers and hobby enthusiasts who focus on entertainment attributes, accounting for 19.3% and 29.9%, respectively. This paper studies handheld gimbals for mass consumers, and therefore, mainly hobby enthusiasts. There is no occupational or job requirement for the consumption motivation of this group, they like photography, video recording, posting vlogs, etc. Among the interest enthusiasts, consumers aged 26–30 account for 54.5% and consumers aged 31–35 account for 23.4%. Consumers aged 26–35 are the main consumer group. Among them, the female group is more, accounting for 62.5%, they have a higher income level, willing to pay for quality, is the enjoyer who pays attention to life [5].

Therefore, this research targets young people aged 26–35 who love photography, video recording, posting video logs, etc. to understand users' attitudes toward the design needs of handheld gimbals and to provide guidance for designing innovative handheld gimbals that meet users' functional needs and have high satisfaction.

3.2 User Needs Research

User requirement analysis can guide the direction of product design. In this paper, we use the kano model to analyze the information feedback and the user's functional requirement level for handheld gimbals, so as to develop a suitable product design strategy.

Firstly, through the method of desktop research, we collected users' feedback information about handheld gimbals on the Internet, the main channels are industry reports, related literature, forums related to handheld gimbals and major Internet platforms such as Taobao, Jingdong, Zhihu, and Tieba. Then, the information vocabulary with high frequency of functional configuration and guiding effect on design is extracted. Next, we conducted user interviews to investigate the real experience and needs of target users for handheld gimbals, and combined with the previously sorted out information vocabulary. We filtered and extracted 22 functional requirements related to handheld gimbals, and divided them into three categories: styling design, functional design and interaction design, as shown in Table 3.

Table 3. User's functional requirements for the hand-held gimbal

No	Styling design	Functional design	Interaction design
1	Simplicity	Smart beauty	Community exchange
2	Rounded appearance	Multi-mode shooting	Exclusive app
3	Head and camera integration	USB charging	Interactive touch screen
4	Easy to carry	Wireless charging	One click to shoot and upload video
5	Colorful	Long battery life	Quick template shooting
6	Fashionable	Smart composition	Voice control
7	Fine details	Self-supporting device	Body control keys
8		Vertical mode	

3.3 Development and Collection of Kano Questionnaires

In order to understand the user's demand level for the handheld gimbal to determine the design direction, the kano questionnaire was prepared to collect the real feeling and evaluation of the target users for the above distilled functional requirements. The sample of the survey is 26–35 years old young people who love photography, video recording, posting video logs, etc. The questionnaire was mainly distributed through online questionnaire, and 116 valid questionnaires were collected after eliminating the illogical or invalid questionnaires that did not meet the conditions.

3.4 Data Analysis

The data analysis was performed on the valid questionnaire data collected, mainly for functional attribute categorization analysis and Better-worse coefficient analysis.

Functional Attribute Categorization Analysis. Functional attribute categorization analysis. According to the categorization comparison table of kano evaluation results shown in Table 2, we organize the results of the kano questionnaire, and add up the counts of each research user's attitude towards this functional demand corresponding to Table 2. Since there may be user data of this function on all six demand dimensions, the data of the same dimensional demand are added up to get the total number of people in each demand dimension. The demand dimension with the highest number of people is the demand type of that function demand. Taking the demand for simple styling design as an example, after statistical analysis of the data, it was found that the number of people with attractive quality was the highest, so the simple style belongs to the attractive quality, as shown in Table 4.

Table 4. Attribute analysis of simple style Kano requirements

		Without simple style				
		Like	Must-be	Neutral	Live with	Dislike
Simple style	Like	Q:4	A:0	A:24	A:24	O:16
	Must-be	R:4	I:4	I:0	I:16	M:16
	Neutral	R:0	I:0	I:4	I:0	M:0
	Live with	R:0	I:0	I:0	I:4	M:0
	Dislike	R:0	R:0	R:0	R:0	Q:0

$A = 48; O = 16; M = 16; I = 28; R = 4; Q = 4$; Attribute of simple style: Attractive Quality.

Better-Worse Coefficient Analysis. By dividing the number of each user attitude in Table 4 by the total number, the percentage of categorization of functional attributes can be obtained, and the Better-worse coefficient value can be calculated by substituting into the formula. Taking the styling demand of simple style as an example, the coefficient values can be obtained by substituting each data in Table 4 into the Better-worse formula as follows.

$$\text{Better (SI)} = (A + O)/(A + O + M + I) = 0.593$$

$$\text{Worse (DSI)} = (-1)(O + M)/(A + O + M + I) = -0.296$$

The questionnaire data were comprehensively organized according to the above method, and the categorization of each functional demand attribute and satisfaction coefficient of the handheld head were calculated, as shown in Table 5. Finally, according to the absolute value of Better and Worse of each functional requirement, the four-quadrant scatter plot is constructed by using the data visualization tool, and the scatter plot is divided into four quadrants with the average value of Better and Worse, as shown in Fig. 3, to clarify the falling quadrant and requirement priority of each functional requirement.

- Quadrant I: Better > 0.5, |Worse| > 0.5, One-dimensional Quality.
- Quadrant II: Better > 0.5, |Worse| < 0.5, Attractive Quality.
- Quadrant III: Better < 0.5, |Worse| < 0.5, Indifferent Quality.
- Quadrant IV: Better < 0.5, |Worse| > 0.5, Must-be Quality.

Table 5. Classification of functional demand attributes and satisfaction coefficient of hand-held gimbal

Functional requirements	Number of people						Attributes	Better	Worse
	M	O	A	I	R	Q			
Simplicity	16	16	48	28	4	4	A	0.593	−0.296
Rounded appearance	0	0	56	52	0	8	A	0.519	0.000
Head and camera integration	0	16	56	40	4	0	A	0.643	−0.143
Easy to carry	28	56	8	20	4	0	O	0.571	−0.750
Colorful	4	12	36	64	0	0	I	0.414	−0.138
Fashionable	20	24	44	28	0	0	A	0.586	−0.379
Fine details	24	48	24	20	0	0	O	0.621	−0.621
Smart beauty	12	28	32	44	0	0	I	0.517	−0.345
Multi-mode shooting	40	32	16	28	0	0	M	0.414	−0.621
USB charging	20	32	28	36	0	0	I	0.517	−0.448
Wireless charging	0	8	68	40	0	0	A	0.655	−0.069
Long battery life	16	40	32	28	0	0	O	0.621	−0.483

(*continued*)

Table 5. (*continued*)

Functional requirements	Number of people						Attributes	Better	Worse
	M	O	A	I	R	Q			
Smart composition	20	16	60	20	0	0	A	0.655	−0.310
Vertical mode	12	8	36	60	0	0	I	0.379	−0.172
Self-supporting device	8	28	36	44	0	0	I	0.552	−0.310
Exclusive app	8	8	12	88	0	0	I	0.172	−0.138
Community exchange	8	8	20	72	8	0	I	0.259	−0.148
Interactive touch screen	4	16	56	40	0	0	A	0.621	−0.172
One click to shoot and upload video	8	24	36	48	0	0	I	0.517	−0.276
Quick template shooting	0	16	52	44	4	0	A	0.607	−0.143
Voice control	0	8	36	68	4	0	I	0.393	−0.071
Body control keys	60	16	12	24	4	0	M	0.250	−0.679

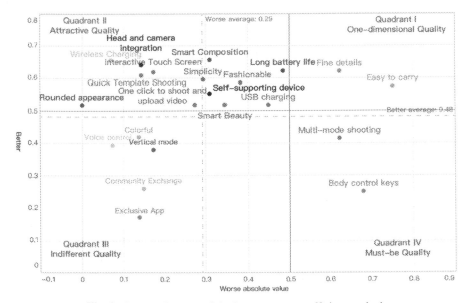

Fig. 3. Scatter diagram of the better-worse coefficient analysis

4   Result

4.1   Functional Design Positioning

The kano model theory usually prioritizes functions in the order of "Must-be Quality > One-dimensional Quality > Attractive Quality > Indifferent Quality". Since indifferent quality are requirements that users do not care much about. Therefore, for cost reasons, it is not necessary to implement the indifferent quality requirements, and the main consideration is to implement the must-be, One-dimensional and attractive quality requirements. The requirements are ranked according to the absolute score of Better-worse coefficient, and the priority ranking of requirements under the same requirement dimension is as follows.

- Must-be Quality: Multi-mode shooting > Body control keys
- One-dimensional Quality: Fine details > Easy to carry
- Attractive Quality: Wireless Charging > Smart Composition > Head and camera integration > Interactive Touch Screen > Quick Template Shooting > Simplicity > Fashionable > Rounded appearance

After getting the priority ranking of requirements under the same requirement dimension, we analyze three aspects of styling design, functional design and interaction design to clearly position the handheld gimbal design. In terms of styling design, fine details > easy to carry > gimbal and camera integration > simple style > fashionable > rounded appearance. In terms of functional design, multi-mode shooting > wireless charging > smart composition. In terms of interactive design, body control keys > interactive touch screen > quick template shooting.

4.2   Design Solutions

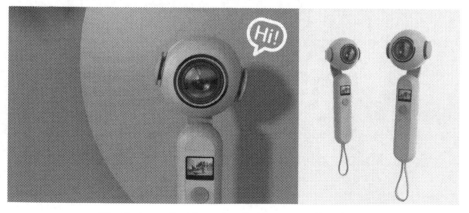

Fig. 4. icamo intelligent handheld camera effect picture

According to the above analysis results, we make innovative design for handheld gimbal. First of all, in terms of styling design, as shown in Fig. 4, the gimbal and camera are integrated, making the overall shape of the handheld gimbal small and convenient to carry out shooting. At the same time, the rounded styling style contrasts with the existing handheld gimbals on the market which are mostly black, hard lines, professional and distance, weakening the professional sense of the handheld gimbal and pulling in the distance between it and the general public consumers. The overall shape is simple and stylish, with a sense of intimacy.

In terms of functional design, the handheld gimbal camera can shoot in multiple modes, quickly switch shooting modes, easy to operate. At the same time, it has smart composition function, double-click the screen, icamo smart handheld gimbal camera will make smart composition according to the shooting scene, content, etc., automatically rotate the lens to adjust to the best angle, friendly to non-professional mass consumers, reduce their learning costs and provide a better user experience. In addition, the handheld gimbal provides wireless charging function, and can still shoot upright when charging (Fig. 5).

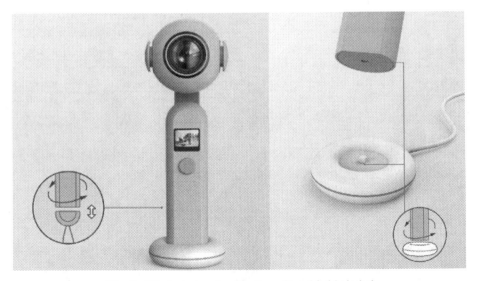

Fig. 5. Wireless charging function of hand-held gimbal

In terms of interaction design, the handheld gimbal simplifies the function buttons in the function area, leaving only the more important and frequently used joystick and mode switch keys, and adding a touch screen for other operation settings (Fig. 6).

Fig. 6. Handheld gimbal functional design details

5   Conclusion

With the rapid development of society, people's needs are more diversified and refined, which promotes the innovation and upgrading of products. Previously, designers focused more on the market and products, but in today's world, more attention should be paid to people and dig out the real needs of users. In this paper, taking handheld gimbal as an example, we use kano model to conduct user research on handheld gimbal products, dig deeper into the functional needs of target users and categorize functional attributes, combine Better-Worse coefficient to rank the importance of user needs, build a visualized four-quadrant scatter diagram, summarize key design elements from three aspects: shape, function and interaction, and guide the program design [6]. This method can precisely meet the priority demand points of target users, avoid functional alignment, improve users' experience and satisfaction when using the product, improve product market competitiveness, and provide reference for related product design development.

References

1. China Handheld Gimbal Industry Research Report (2018). (in Chinese)
2. Wang, J.: Research on the Design of Handheld Gimbal Based on Ergonomics. Hubei University of Technology (2020). (in Chinese)
3. Lin, J., Guo, X.: Intelligent flowerpot product service system design based on KANO model. Design **33**(23), 76–79 (2020). (in Chinese)
4. Senlin, Y., Chen, X.: Research on innovative design of outdoor speakers based on fuzzy Kano model. Packag. Eng. **41**(24), 202–208 (2020). (in Chinese)

5. China Handheld Gimbal Industry Research Report (2019). (in Chinese)
6. Yu, S., Cheng, Q.: Functional improvement design of office desk based on Kano model. Packag. Eng. 1–12 (2021). (in Chinese)

Applying Collaborative Tools for ATM Interface Design in a Remote Context

Arturo Moquillaza$^{(\boxtimes)}$, Fiorella Falconi , Joel Aguirre , and Freddy Paz

Pontificia Universidad Católica del Perú, Av. Universitaria 1801, San Miguel,
Lima 32, Lima, Perú
{amoquillaza,fpaz}@pucp.pe, {ffalconit,aguirre.joel}@pucp.edu.pe

Abstract. In a financial institution in Peru, a framework for ATM (Automated Teller Machine) interface design based on UCD (User-Centered Design) is being implemented and utilized. This framework has defined a set of phases, activities, and tools to carry out a whole process of interface design or redesign. This framework had a highly face-to-face component, but due to the context of the COVID-19 pandemic, where virtualization and remote work became widespread, all activities and tools were updated to support full virtuality. In this way, certain tools were incorporated and, thus, the framework has updated to enable and promote collaboration in a completely remote environment. In this sense, the results of a case study are presented, where the framework was executed in its remote version, for the attention of a design and implementation requirement in ATM. Results were very positive, from the point of view of the evaluation results, and the acceptance of stakeholders. They gave their agreement for the implementation of the proposed design; as well as feedback from the project team members, who consider that the framework has responded adequately to the challenges of remote work.

Keywords: Collaborative tool · Human-computer interaction · Automated Teller Machine · Software design · User-Centered Design · Banking software · Case study

1 Introduction

In the design of user interfaces, several studies evidenced the importance of collaboration and interaction between the team members involved in a project [1, 2]. The focus on the end-user, and their participation throughout the project, has been widely evidenced [3–5].

In this context, in a financial institution in Peru, in collaboration with a local university, a framework for the design of ATM (Automated Teller Machine) interfaces based on UCD (User-Centered Design) was previously implemented and is being used [6, 7]. The framework defined a set of phases, activities, and tools to carry out a whole process of interface design or redesign that had been successfully implemented and utilized in this institution. The framework had a highly face-to-face component, which means

M. M. Soares et al. (Eds.): HCII 2022, LNCS 13323, pp. 213–228, 2022.
https://doi.org/10.1007/978-3-031-05906-3_16

that many of its tools and activities had a high dependency on participants' interaction in meeting rooms to promote collaboration. Due to the COVID-19 pandemic context, virtualization and remote work became widespread [8]; nevertheless, as projects and requirements continued arriving, we tested the framework. All activities and tools had to be updated to support total virtuality. Then, it was necessary to update the framework selecting tools that enable and promote collaboration in a fully remote environment.

In this sense, we present the results of a case study where the framework is executed in its updated remote version to meet a requirement for the design and implementation of part of an ATM withdrawal functionality. The results were positive from the point of view of the Evaluation phase findings. The stakeholders accepted the results and gave their agreement for the implementation of the proposed design. Also, the members of the team considered that the framework had responded adequately to the challenges of remote work.

The rest of the article is divided as follows: In the second section, the most relevant concepts and tools are presented as a context for the present experience. The third section presents the updated framework with the tools and activities that support the virtual environment. In the fourth section, the case study and its results are presented. Finally, the fifth section presents the conclusions and future work of this case study.

2   Background

This section describes the main concepts discussed in this work, as well as the framework that was updated and finally used in the case study.

2.1   Collaborative Multimedia Applications

These are demanding applications that involve two or more users that work together and cooperate to achieve a common goal [9]. Cooperation implies different time and space combinations: different timing and location can define the specific group activities. Timing depends on whether participants act at the same or different times, i.e., synchronous or asynchronous collaboration. The location depends on where the participants are geographical, whether in the same place (co-located collaboration) or at different sites (remote collaboration) [10].

2.2   User-Centered Design

User-centered Design consists of designing and developing applications or products where a team of designers focuses on users' needs in an iterative way [11]. The team members together plan, create, and develop products with the users in mind. While having the user at the center of the process, a user-centered design can be done without any actual participation of real users, who can be virtualized during the whole design/development/evaluation cycle.

2.3 Automated Teller Machines

Automated Teller Machines (ATMs) are self-service devices that allow customers of financial institutions to perform transactions and operations, especially those related to their cash, and usually with the use of a card and a secret code (PIN). These types of devices have now become ubiquitous, and ATM transactions have become part of many people's daily lives. ATMs make it easier for customers to access the financial services that institutions provide, and facilitate and promote the digitalization of customers [7, 12].

2.4 Usability

Usability is nowadays one of the most important quality attributes that companies attempt to guarantee when developing products, systems, or services [13]. There is an interest in ensuring that the interaction between the end-users and the technological products and services that companies provide, is highly satisfactory and pleasant. For this reason, in previous work, we proposed a framework based on UCD to be used by designers and developers in the construction of usable graphical user interfaces for ATMs that allow the achievement of the users' goals with satisfaction [6].

The concept of usability is widely defined in the literature by several specialists and organizations. One of the most accepted proposals has been established by the International Organization for Standardization in the norm ISO 9241–11:1998 [14] which defines usability as the "extent to which a system, product or service can be used by specified users to achieve specified goals with effectiveness, efficiency, and satisfaction in a specified context of use". This definition refers not only to digital products such as software products and interactive systems but also to technological devices and services that companies offer to their customers and consumers. In this concept, it is established that the people use every product and service with a purpose. Therefore, the interaction must allow the achievement of these objectives, and the interfaces should be easy enough to use, understandable and attractive, in a way that generates as an ultimate result, a pleasant experience.

2.5 Related Studies

The process proposed by the ATM Framework consists of three phases: (1) Analysis of the context of use, (2) Requirements specification, and (3) Design and evaluation of interfaces. These phases are aligned with the standard ISO 13047:1999 [13], revised according to the standard ISO 9241–11:1998 [14], and diagrammed in Fig. 1. Depending on the different contexts, the process suggests tools and methods classified as Simple, Fast, and Low-cost.

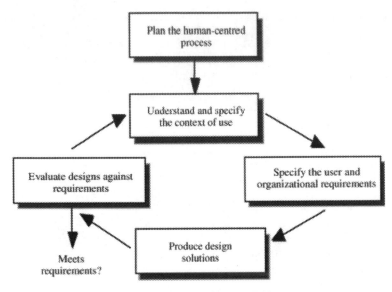

Fig. 1. The UCD process [14].

The teams are free to select the methods that are most suitable for their context. The framework also proposes an Optimal Process that uses methods that are simple and fast to perform but consume little resources. These different sets of methods allowed us to perform different studies on how these processes behave in real projects and various contexts. Figure 2 shows the framework for the design of usable ATM interfaces.

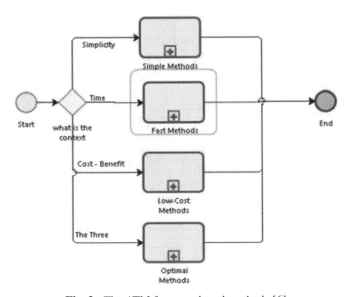

Fig. 2. The ATM framework and methods [6].

The framework has been used successfully in previous studies showing the tools and methods it proposes are suitable for designing usable ATM interfaces in different contexts. In the first attempt to apply this framework, the participants were not familiar with the user-centered approach. For this, they made use of the set of simple methods to redesign the withdrawal interfaces of the ATMs of a financial institution [15].

The framework was used to design new functionality that was required to improve the user experience when withdrawing cash from ATMs. The participants employed the fast methods due to time constraints. The result of this case study was a proposal of QR withdrawal functionality [7]. Other user-centered design approaches were used in related studies; for example, Moquillaza et al. [16] followed a process aligned to Design Thinking to redesign the Main Menu of an ATM.

The different tools and methods were used in previous studies and proposed in different UCD approaches. They were selected depending on the current context of each project. Most of these methods required gatherings (for instance, Focus Groups) and collaboration (i. e. Brainstorming or Software Prototyping). However, it is hard to carry on various activities that require meetings and face-to-face interaction due to the current COVID-19 pandemic context.

3   Framework Update

This section presents the updated framework with the tools and activities identified as necessary to address remote work.

As indicated in the previous section, the framework used for ATM interface design contained a set of methods and tools that supported the process. Table 1 shows the methods and tools proposed by the original framework.

Table 1. Methods and tools proposed by the original ATM framework.

Phase	Method	Description/Tool
Context	Observation	Face-to-face field observation Documentary review, log analysis, or verbatim analysis
	Identify stakeholders	Face-to-face meetings with stakeholders
Requirements	Scenarios of use	MS Word/Google Docs
	User requirements Interview	Face-to-face interviews with users
Design & Evaluation	Brainstorming	Face-to-face sessions
	Software prototyping	Prototyping on paper, prototyping in MS PowerPoint/Google Sheets (individual or in groups)
	Expert judgement	Face-to-face meetings
	Usability testing	Usability Tests in ATM labs

In order to update the framework tools, and with the objective of not affecting the collaboration between the members of the work team, the alternatives that were available for tools that could be used within the organization were reviewed. Given that the organization has access to the Google Suite platform (now Google Workspace), it was found in the literature that this type of platform with multiple SaaS (Software as a Service) applications is widely accepted and favors interaction and collaboration [17, 18], especially in contexts such as this new normality due to the COVID-19 pandemic [19].

Among the incorporated tools are the following [20]:

- Google Drive: Collaborative online files and directories sharing tool.
- Google Docs: Collaborative online word processor.
- Google Sheets: Collaborative online spreadsheet.
- Google Slides: Collaborative online slideshow.
- Google Data Studio: Tool for data analysis and development of management dashboards, with an online and collaborative approach.
- Google Meet: Video Conferencing tool. It is online, does not require local software installation, and allows the sharing of screens, a digital whiteboard, and other options.
- Jamboard: Electronic whiteboard. It allows sharing and working with information with an online and collaborative approach.

Table 2. ATM framework update with methods and tools.

Phase	Method	Description	Tools
Context	Field study	Documentary review, log analysis, or verbatim analysis	Google Drive, Google Docs, Google Sheets, Google Data Studio
	Identify stakeholders	Remote meetings	Google Meet, Google Slides
Requirements	Scenarios of use	Digital elaboration	Google Meet, Google Slides, Draw.io
	User requirements interview	Remote interviews	Google Meet, Google Slides
Design & Evaluation	Brainstorming	Remote meetings	Google Meet, Jamboard
	Software prototyping	Remote meetings	Google Meet, Google Slides, Draw.io, Jamboard
	Expert judgement	Remote meetings, Remote interviews	Google Meet, Google Slides
	Usability testing	Remote usability Testing	Google Meet, Google Slides

- Draw.io: (Now Diagrams.net) Tool that integrates with Google Workspace allows the development of graphics and canvas of various kinds in an online and collaborative way [21].

In that sense, for each phase and method, it was examined which Google suite tool, or connected to it, could support the activity performed. This mapping was satisfactorily completed and validated by an HCI expert, who gave his agreement. The set of tools incorporated can be seen in Table 2.

4 Case Study

This section describes all the phases that we followed to employ the methods proposed in the ATM Framework combined with the collaborative tools under the quarantine's context by the COVID-19. The redesign process focuses on the error message in cases of insufficient balance to make a withdrawal.

4.1 Analyzing the Context of Use

After identifying that the user experience was affected when the user encountered an error due to not having enough balance to carry out their operation, we began to review the problem. When the client was in this error situation, a message was displayed indicating why his operation was denied and the session ended with the expulsion of the card. The message that was displayed can be seen in Fig. 3.

Fig. 3. Error message

Field Study. In a context in which activities are carried out remotely, and social distancing is necessary, it was decided to analyze the activities carried out by users and are recorded in the ATMs. For this purpose, we analyzed data and logs from four different months of the year 2020, in which we were already in a pandemic situation.

For this phase, the Google Workspaces tools were used to create a folder and make the information analyzed, the logs, and the results available to all participants.

The results from the data obtained were the following: Approximately 60,000–70,000 cases of insufficient balance in 1 month. After viewing the error message, customers usually re-enter the card and perform the next operation: 84% try to make a withdrawal again, 9% make a balance inquiry, 2% make a transaction inquiry, and 5% perform other operations.

It was also evidenced that 16% of the customers who after seeing the error tried again to withdraw an amount greater than the balance they had.

Identify Stakeholders. To identify and list the stakeholders, we analyzed the areas involved with the ATM withdrawal functionality. The areas identified were the following: Customers, Commercial Division Team, Development Team, and Channels Operation Team.

Stakeholders belonging to the financial institution were involved in the entire redesign process, and the tools used in each phase were shared with them.

4.2 Specifying the User Requirements

To obtain the necessary requirements for this redesign, we used the scenario of use tool and stakeholder interviews.

Scenario of Use. The case that was subject to redesign was defined with images and descriptions. The images shown in Fig. 4 were made entirely in digital and were uploaded to the Google Slides tool so that all participants can consult them.

The situations reflected in the scenario of use had as input the actions that the logs indicated that the clients carried out when faced with the error message. The information shown in Fig. 5 is what was found in the collected data and then represented.

Stakeholder Interviews. This phase of the redesign process was also conducted 100% remotely, using Google Meet. As they belonged to the same financial institution, all the participants already had google email accounts and were already familiar with the tools, which made the interview run smoothly. At the beginning of the session, an introduc-tion was made to contextualize the specific case analyzed.

User Requirements. After carrying out the two activities, the three main requirements that will later serve to carry out the improved design could be clearly identified.

- Homogenize the screen that is shown in cases of insufficient balance.
- Provide the customer with access to know their balance in the flow.
- Maintain security guidelines.
- Facilitate the flow after the error occurs.

Joel se acerca a un ATM a retirar
100 soles para realizar múltiples
compras.

Ingresa a la opción de retiro y
selecciona la cuenta donde él
cree que tiene dinero suficiente.

Se muestra el mensaje:"No
cuentas con saldo suficiente para
realizar esta operación".

Joel se encuentra confundido
mientras el cajero le devuelve la
tarjeta.

Otra vez tiene que colocar la
tarjeta, ingresar su clave y
empezar de nuevo.

Intenta retirar 80 soles pero otra
vez se muestra el mismo
mensaje y le devuelve la tarjeta.

Joel se desespera porque no
puede retirar y no recuerda cual
es su saldo.

Joel decide hacer una consulta
de saldo, ve que tiene 70 soles y
cuando piensa hacer su
retiro...LE PIDEN QUE RETIRE
LA TARJETA.

Una vez más, Joel pone su
tarjeta en el cajero y por 4ta vez
digital su clave.

Luego de seleccionar otra vez
todos los datos, porfin Joel retira
60 soles

y se retira del cajero viendo como
generó una larga cola.

Fig. 4. Scenario of use

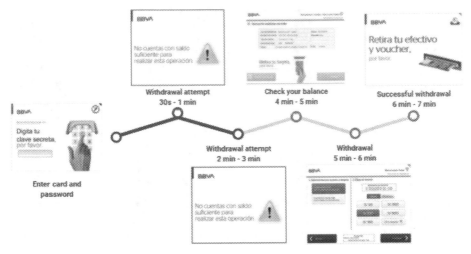

Fig. 5. Timeline of error

4.3 Designing and Evaluating the Interfaces

Brainstorming. Two virtual brainstorming sessions were held with all participants. In order to obtain a collaborative solution, all stakeholders participated in Google Meet sessions. In the sessions, the URL where the dynamics would be performed was provided. The tool used was Jamboard. For the first session, all participants were asked to place a minimum of 3 solutions, explaining that no solution qualified as a wrong solution. In Fig. 6, we show how the first virtual brainstorming session was held.

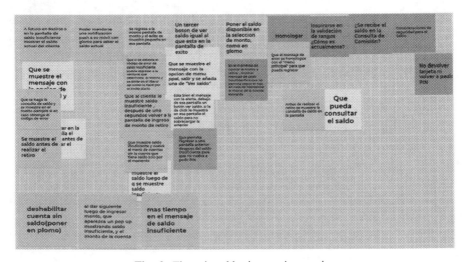

Fig. 6. First virtual brainstorming session

For the second virtual brainstorming session, the same considerations were applied as for the first session. However, this session's objective was to give a score to the different ideas that had arisen in the first session. In Fig. 7, we show how the second virtual brainstorming session was held.

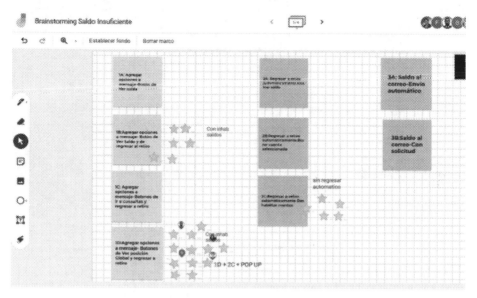

Fig. 7. Second virtual brainstorming session

Software Prototyping. Based on the brainstorming session' input, we proceed to implement prototypes of the three solutions that obtained the highest score. For that purpose, we made the prototypes, and the information was uploaded to Google Slides so that it is accessible to all participants. In these prototypes, it was also shown which screens would be shown in the interactions. Figure 8 shows the first prototype, Fig. 9 shows the second prototype, and Fig. 10 shows the third prototype.

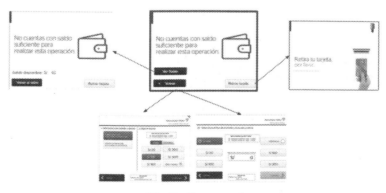

Fig. 8. Prototype 1

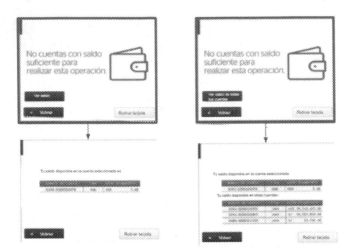

Fig. 9. Prototype 2

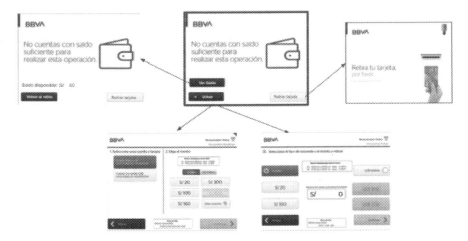

Fig. 10. Prototype 3

Expert Judgement. For this part, the interested parties met through Google meet so that they can express their judgment. Each of them participated in their turn; at the end of all the shifts, they worked collaboratively to land improvements that would be implemented in the final prototype. As shown in Fig. 11, the session had eleven participants and a moderator.

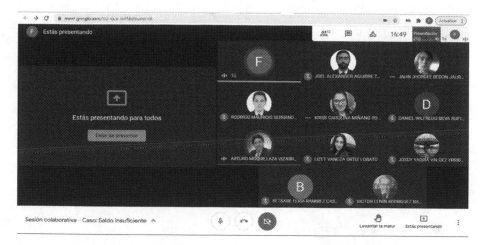

Fig. 11. Expert session on Google meet

4.4 Final Results

After having carried out the last part of the DCU process, remotely and collaboratively, the participants concluded that the best redesign solution would be to implement prototype number two, because it was the prototype that met all the user requirements. In a final session with key stakeholders, the design was approved and sent to be implemented for distribution. It should also be noted that the feedback gathered in this session was positive with respect to the design shown. For this prototype, it was placed as an improvement that the screen is personalized for customers who have only one account and for people who have more than one account. As shown in Fig. 12, this redesign gives the customer three options: the customer can choose to return to make a withdrawal, check the balance or end the operation and withdraw the card. If the customer selects to check the balance, the screen shown in Fig. 13 will be displayed.

It is essential to indicate that this redesign, developed jointly with different financial institution divisions, was developed and implemented for all its clients.

Finally, in the last session with the team, their feedback was requested in a dynamic review, to know their opinions about the framework's application. In this session, it was found that the team members found the tools easy to use and that they did not affect their productivity, interaction, or team collaboration. On the contrary, they promoted it since it was possible to work collaboratively, even in a remote environment. Additionally, even for the elaboration of the report of this experience, using these tools has been maintained, with a very positive result on the part of the authors.

Fig. 12. Prototype for an error message

Fig. 13. Balance option

5 Conclusions and Future Works

The current context due to the COVID-19 pandemic has accelerated digital transformation processes and virtualization of many activities in several areas, among them, in the Engineering divisions of financial companies. However, given that user requirements must be met, mainly so that companies can adapt to new customer needs, current design and development processes must be updated to support virtualization without detracting from the collaboration between the people involved projects and requirements. These updates to the above processes must be applied urgently and improved continuously since this new normality means that many of these activities will be maintained and continued remotely for a long time.

In this sense, a case study has been presented, where an ATM interface design framework has been updated with activities and tools that support remote and collaborative work. This framework has been applied in a requirement of the redesign of functionality related to ATM withdrawals. Evidence of the phases worked together with users and stakeholders, and the final results have been presented.

The results have been positive for the product, given the specialists, users, and stakeholders' feedback, who have approved the design and proceeded to its implementation. For the process, the framework has been shown to have adapted to the remote environment without losing key attributes of these design processes, such as collaboration and teamwork.

Thus, it can be concluded that the updated framework with tools that allow collaboration has yielded positive results, both for the products it generates and for the process it accompanies.

As future work, it is expected to continue with applying this framework in new requirements and projects, with different complexities, and even involving the participation of new profiles.

Likewise, a review of more tools that allow and improve collaboration within the team will be carried out, with which the framework presented can be iterated and improved.

Acknowledgments. We would like to thank the BBVA ATM development team for their participation in this experience. We would also like to thank the HCI-DUXAIT research group for their accompaniment and support throughout this research. HCI-DUXAIT is a research group of the Pontificia Universidad Católica del Perú.

References

1. Ferre, X., Juristo, N., Windl, H., Constantine, L.: Usability basics for software developers. IEEE Softw. **18**(1), 22–29 (2001). https://doi.org/10.1109/52.903160
2. Jones, A., Thoma, V.: Determinants for successful agile collaboration between UX designers and software developers in a complex organisation. Int. J. Hum.-Comput. Interact. **35**(20), 1914–1935 (2019). https://doi.org/10.1080/10447318.2019.1587856
3. Judge, T., Matthews T., Whittaker, S.: Comparing collaboration and individual personas for the design and evaluation of collaboration software. In: Proceedings of the SIGCHI Conference on Human Factors in Computing Systems 1997–2000 (2012).https://doi.org/10.1145/2207676. 2208344
4. Wu, J., Graham, T.C.N., Smith, P.W.: A study of collaboration in software design. In: International Symposium on Empirical Software Engineering, 2003. ISESE 2003. Proceedings., Rome, Italy, 2003, pp. 304–313 (2003). https://doi.org/10.1109/ISESE.2003.1237991
5. Mirri, S., Roccetti, M., Salomoni, P.: Collaborative design of software applications: the role of users. HCIS **8**(1), 1–20 (2018). https://doi.org/10.1186/s13673-018-0129-6
6. Aguirre, J., Moquillaza, A., Paz, F.: A user-centered framework for the design of usable ATM interfaces. In: Marcus, A., Wang, W. (eds.) HCII 2019. LNCS, vol. 11583, pp. 163–178. Springer, Cham (2019). https://doi.org/10.1007/978-3-030-23570-3_13

7. Aguirre, J., Benazar, S., Moquillaza, A.: Applying a UCD framework for ATM interfaces on the design of QR withdrawal: a case study. In: Marcus, A., Rosenzweig, E. (eds.) HCII 2020. LNCS, vol. 12202, pp. 3–19. Springer, Cham (2020). https://doi.org/10.1007/978-3-030-497 57-6_1

8. Gupta, A.: Accelerating Remote Work After COVID-19. Covid Recovery Symposium. The Center of Growth and Opportunity. Utah State University (2020). https://www.thecgo.org/res earch/accelerating-remote-work-after-covid-19/

9. Rhyne, J.R., Wolf, C.G.: Tools for supporting the collaborative process. In: Proceedings of the 5th Annual ACM Symposium on User Interface Software and Technology, pp. 161–170. Association for Computing Machinery, Monteray, California, USA (1992). https://doi.org/10.1145/142621.142645

10. Germani, M., Mengoni, M., Peruzzini, M.: An approach to assessing virtual environments for synchronous and remote collaborative design. Adv. Eng. Inform. **26**(4), 793–813 (2012). ISSN 1474–0346 https://doi.org/10.1016/j.aei.2012.06.003

11. Dopp, A.R., Parisi, K.E., Munson, S.A., Lyon, A.R.: A glossary of user-centered design strategies for implementation experts. Transl. Behav. Med. **9**(6), 1057–1064 (2018). https://doi.org/10.1093/tbm/iby119

12. Chanco, C., Moquillaza, A., Paz, F.: Development and validation of usability heuristics for evaluation of interfaces in ATMs. In: Marcus, A., Wang, W. (eds.) HCII 2019. LNCS, vol. 11586, pp. 3–18. Springer, Cham (2019). https://doi.org/10.1007/978-3-030-23535-2_1

13. International Organization for Standardization: ISO/IEC 13407:1999, Human-centred design processes for interactive systems. Geneva, Switzerland (1999)

14. International Organization for Standardization: ISO/IEC 9241–11:1998, Ergonomic requirements for office work with visual display terminals (VDTs) – Part 11: Guidance on usability. Switzerland, Geneva (1998)

15. Aguirre, J.: Elaboración y validación de un marco de trabajo para el diseño de interfaces para cajeros automáticos. Repositorio de Tesis PUCP. Pontificia Universidad Católica del Perú, Lima, Perú (2020). http://hdl.handle.net/20.500.12404/16055

16. Moquillaza, A., Falconi, F., Paz, F.: Redesigning a main menu ATM interface using a user-centered design approach aligned to design thinking: a case study. In: Marcus, A., Wang, W. (eds.) HCII 2019. LNCS, vol. 11586, pp. 522–532. Springer, Cham (2019). https://doi.org/10.1007/978-3-030-23535-2_38

17. Tan, X., Kim, Y.: User acceptance of SaaS-based collaboration tools: a case of Google Docs. J. Enterp. Inf. Manag. **28**(3), 423–442 (2015). https://doi.org/10.1108/JEIM-04-2014-0039

18. Herrick, D.R.: Google this! using Google apps for collaboration and productivity. In: Proceedings of the 37th annual ACM SIGUCCS fall conference: communication and collaboration (SIGUCCS 2009). Association for Computing Machinery, New York, NY, 55–64 (2009). https://doi.org/10.1145/1629501.1629513

19. Mobo, F.: The impact of google suites amidst the new normal. Int. J. Multi. Appl. Bus. Educ. Res. **2**(2), 179–181 (2021). http://www.ijmaberjournal.org/index.php/ijmaber/article/view/61

20. Google: Trabaje de forma remota con Google Workspace. Google.com (2020). https://workspace.google.com/intl/es-419/working-remotely/

21. Diagrams.net: About Diagrams.net. Diagrams.net (2020). https://www.diagrams.net/about.html

Mojipla Stamp: Interactive Content Using a Stamp Device to Stimulate Programming Thinking Through Word Play

Hiroshi Suzuki[(⊠)] and Sousuke Yagi

Kanagawa Institute of Technology, Shimoogino 1030, Atsugi, Japan
hsuzuki@ic.kanagawa-it.ac.jp, s1823122@cco.kanagawa-it.ac.jp

Abstract. From the year 2020, programming education will become compulsory in all elementary schools in Japan. The aim of programming education is not only to develop programming skills, but also to develop "programming thinking". It is believed that "programmatic thinking" consists of multiple cognitive elements such as "combination," "reasoning," and "decomposition," and educational materials and toys for children that nurture these cognitive elements are being actively developed. In this work, we propose "Mojipla Stamp," an interactive work that uses word play to stimulate the above elements. In this paper, we give an overview of the proposed work and describe the findings obtained through demonstrations of the implemented work.

Keywords: Edutainment · xR contents · UI/UX design · Interaction design · M5stack · ITC system

1 Background

In Japan, programming education has been implemented in elementary schools since 2020. The aim of programming education is not only to acquire "programming skills" but also to foster "programming thinking". According to the Ministry of Education, Culture, Sports, Science and Technology (MEXT), programming thinking is defined as "the ability to think logically about whether a combination of coherent movements is necessary to realize a series of activities that one intends, how to combine symbols corresponding to each movement, and how to approach the intended activity by improving the combination of symbols [1]. This ability is generally considered to consist of multiple cognitive elements such as (1) decomposition, (2) abstraction, (3) generalization, (4) combination, and (5) reasoning [2], and a variety of teaching materials and toys have appeared with the aim of fostering the above elements. For example, the "Tower of Hanoi" [3], in which players move a disk according to rules, and the "Gravity Maze" [4], a three-dimensional maze that creates a path to the goal, are examples of such toys.

For young children, word-based puzzles are generally considered as teaching materials that not only help them learn words, but also foster "combination" and "reasoning". For example, "Mojimoji ZOO" [5], in which words are created by rearranging animals, and "crossword puzzles" [6], in which words are inserted into squares according to clues. Thus, word puzzles are considered to be educational materials that stimulate cognitive elements that also lead to programming thinking. Therefore, in this work, we propose "Mojipla Stamp" as an interactive work that combines word play and real-world interaction for young children.

2   Features of this System

The interactive work proposed by the authors, "Mojipla Stamp", is an interactive puzzle that aims to stimulate children's programming thinking by using real-world stamp elements and digital elements. The feature of this work is that it combines not only GUI interaction but also the user's real-world movements. Specifically, the player takes a stamp-shaped controller and presses a stamp against a two-letter object that appears on the screen and has some meaning. Each stamp has an arbitrary letter, and by adding this letter, the word can be transformed into a word with a different meaning. This work stimulates the elements of programming thinking, such as "combination," "deduction," and "decomposition," through this kind of word play. In addition, we designed it to be familiar to children by incorporating characterized objects into the contents.

3   Related Cases

Examples of interactive word games using digital technology include "Mojipittan," a video game in which players combine blocks to make words, [7] and "Mojipoppun" [8]. Other games using words include "Kotopazura" [9], a game in which words are created by swapping letters, "Mojitan", a game in which words are searched from a table of letters, and "Word Puzzle - a brain training game played by connecting letters" [10], in which words are created by connecting predetermined words. These hiragana-based video games are designed to be played with GUI controls using a touch screen, and there are no video games that combine real-world user actions with word puzzles." Sticky Teams" [11] is also a letter-based puzzle, but its concept is clearly different from this work because it focuses on the visual elements of letters and aims to increase interest in words and letters, rather than on the combination of letter meanings and voice operations. The purpose of this work is to integrate interaction with physical devices and word play. In this paper, we describe the outline of this work, the results of the demonstration experiments conducted to evaluate the concept, and our future prospects.

4   Overview of the Mojipla Stamp

This work is a puzzle in which a new word is created by adding a letter to the beginning, middle, or end of the word. Figure 1 shows a detailed description of the puzzle.

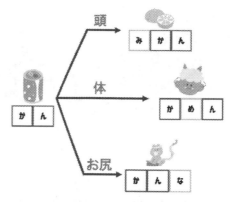

Fig. 1. Explain of the puzzle

For example, there is a word "kan". Add a letter to the beginning, middle and end of the word to create a new word with a different meaning. If you add "mi" to the beginning of the word, you get "mikan"; if you add "na" to the center of the word, you get "kamen"; if you add "na" to the end of the word, you get "kanna". In this work, the act of adding letters is made possible by pressing a stamp-type device on the screen. In this work, the action of adding letters to a two-letter word can be achieved by using a stamp-type device. In Japan, seals are given specific character information, and the act of stamping a seal has the same meaning as writing character information on a piece of paper. In other words, the act of stamping a seal has the same meaning as writing textual information on paper. In this work, the metaphor of the seal is incorporated into the content by implementing the textual information of the seal as a digitally editable device. It has been reported that a controller that satisfies the consistency between the real world and the virtual world improves the immersion of the work [12, 13], and it is expected that the immersion will be improved in this work as well, which will be remembered by the players.

In this work, a theme is set for each stage, and the stage is cleared by converting all objects into objects that match the theme. The GUI of the title screen and play screen of the implemented prototype is shown in Fig. 2. Figure 3 is shown a stamp-type device and a Hiragana characters cards for editing Hiragana characters.

Fig. 2. GUI for title screen and game screen

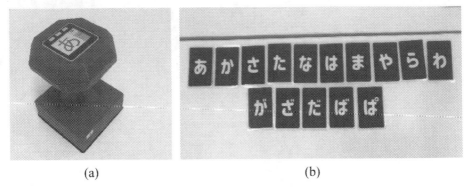

(a)   (b)

(a) Stamp-type device to be held and operated by the child
(b) Hiragana card for changing character information (consonants)

Fig. 3. Implemented stamp-type device and hiragana card

4.1 Overview of the System

The system diagram of this work is shown in Fig. 4. The following five processes are necessary for the requirements of this work.

- Reading of characters to be typed in stamps
- Screen output of characters loaded on the stamp
- Recognition of stamping on an object
- Output of video content
- Playback of audio

The reading of characters and the recognition of stamp presses are performed by RFID. The above is a short-range wireless communication system in which a special tag is read by a reader. In addition to RFID, M5Stack is also used for reading characters. The above is a small color display, which can be assigned to a built-in button. To specify a character, consonants (a, ka, sa) are specified by reading the tag (A, KA, SA…) Vowels (A, I, U…) are specified by pressing a button on the M5Stack.

The video content is output by a projector. A tag is attached to the location of each object, and the tag is read by a reader to recognize the stamp.

4.2 Details of Contents

In this work, we created four stages with the image of "Animal," "Toy," "Food," and "Festival" as the theme of word change. The screen images of this work are shown in Fig. 5. In each stage, a theme is set at the top of the screen, and the stage is cleared by changing all the objects to match the theme. Even if an object does not meet the clearing condition, it can be transformed into another meaningful object. The illustrations used in this work were drawn especially for this work, and we used cute illustrations so that children would feel familiar with them. In addition, the waiting objects move in

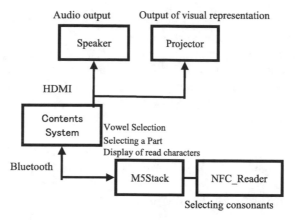

Fig. 4. Overall system diagram and configuration

various ways to keep players and spectators visually entertained while guessing the word combinations.

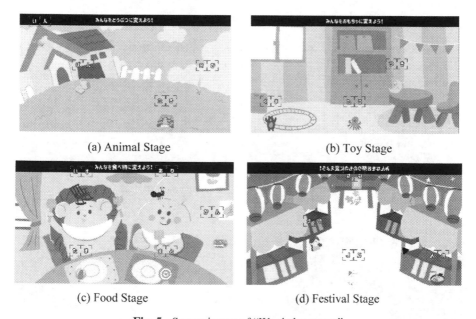

(a) Animal Stage

(b) Toy Stage

(c) Food Stage

(d) Festival Stage

Fig. 5. Screen image of "Word plus stamp"

4.3 Stimulation of Programming Thinking

As a work that stimulates "programmatic thinking," this work contains two major elements: the first is the component of "combination. In this work, new letters are added to the objects on the screen to create new words. To add a letter, the user needs to select the position to add the letter from the beginning, center, or end. The user has to search for a meaningful word among more than 100 possible word combinations.

The other component is "guessing". Through the aforementioned "combination," the player needs to name multiple meaningful words that satisfy the rear conditions of the theme. Reasoning is the ability required for this. In the example of the contents shown in Fig. 5, the theme of the stage is a cafeteria, so all the objects need to be changed to food. The above elements stimulate the programming thinking contained in this work. In this work, we aim to develop children's programming thinking by providing them with a fun way to experience "combination" and "reasoning" through game-like contents.

5   System Evaluation by Exhibition

5.1   Exhibition Outline

This work was exhibited at the Environmental Zone of Fukuoka City Science Museum in Fukuoka City, Fukuoka Prefecture. The period of the exhibition was from December 19, 2021 to January 11, 2022.

Figure 4 shows the Mojipla Stamp experience. Since the work was intended to be operated unattended, the authors did not explain the system to the visitors when they came to the exhibition booth.

We allowed them to freely experience the system and observed their behavior. In order to analyze the behavioral history of the users, the following four play data were obtained.

1. The number of characters that were changed.
2. The part of the character that was changed
3. Time until the change
4. Final score

In this chapter, we will evaluate this system by describing the experience and the play data.

Fig. 6. Exhibition at the Fukuoka city science museum

5.2 Field Research Evaluation

Observation of Play. We observed users' experiences during the exhibition period. We observed users playing the game in groups, such as parents, siblings, and friends. When playing with multiple people, there was cooperation and support, and they were able to inspire new words smoothly. On the other hand, when playing alone, there were some challenges in understanding the rules of the system. Sometimes, some users abandoned the game even though there was still time left, but once they understood the rules, they tended to leave the exhibition zone once and come back a while later to play again and again.

In addition, when the next user came, they started from the middle of the play that the previous user was experiencing, so there was a problem that people who touched the game for the first time did not understand the game content.

Interaction with Stamp-type Devices. Interaction using stamps was very popular and people were seen actively playing the game. However, when a meaningful word was created, the character would change, but when a meaningless word was created, there was no visual change, so the user could not distinguish whether the word was wrong or the device was not responding. In this case, almost all the users judged that the device was not responding and pushed the device in a Roughly manner.

The tutorials prepared by the system were not read by most of the users, and they often understood the rules by actually playing the game. Until they learned the rules. There were some users who stamped the letters instead of the illustrations, some who tried to make words without thinking about the three parts, and some who did not know how to change the letters on the stamp. In each of these errors For each of these errors, there was no interaction that prompted the user to correct the error, which led to the user getting lost.

Hardware Issues. In terms of the device, there were cases in which the pillar of the stamp-type device broke when the stamp device was dropped from the display table because the center of gravity was on the top, and cases in which the LCD of the M5Stack installed on the top of the device was damaged. This could be caused by the weak strength of the joints that connect the device parts, or by the direct impact on the M5Stack when the device was dropped. As a countermeasure, the joints need to be made of metal and the design needs to be such that no direct impact is transmitted to the M5Stack.

The battery was expected to operate for about three hours in the simulation, but in reality, it became difficult to operate normally after about two hours, and the battery needed to be replaced frequently. We found that a program for energy saving on the device side is necessary.

5.3 Trends in Variant Inspiration from Play Data

A graph of the bias in the number of people for each score collected through the exhibit is shown in Fig. 7. In this graph, for each score, the number of experiencers who obtained that score is represented. The sample of scores is 70, and the average score is 6.46 points. Looking at the graph, we can see that most of the participants scored between 0 and 11 points. Most of the participants were able to transform the characters by stamping them, but 5 participants scored 0 points.

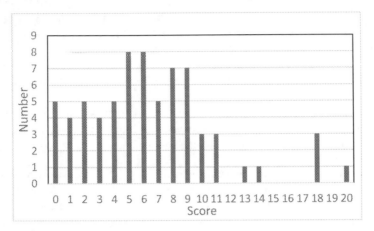

Fig. 7. Exhibition at the Fukuoka city science museum

However, five participants scored zero points, indicating that they did not understand the rules of the game and were not able to transform the characters. Four of the participants scored 18 points or more, which is very high. A graph of the number of transformations for each site for all users within the exhibition period is shown in Fig. 8(a). The graph shows how many transformations were performed on each part of the body from the total play data. The total number of transformations performed within the exhibition period was 452. Figure 8(b) shows the number of transformations prepared for the content, for each part of the body. Comparing these two graphs, it can be seen that most of the words prepared in advance as contents add letters to the head or body, but the number of words prepared in advance as contents does not increase.

(a) (b)

Fig. 8. User's character change history data (a) and number of variants that can change (b)

However, when we look at the history data of the experiencers, we can see that many of them added letters to the head and buttocks. This indicates that words with letters added to the body tend to be less likely to be associated than words with letters added to the beginning or end.

6 Discussion

In this chapter, we discuss the potential of this system based on the exhibition at the Fukuoka City Science Museum and the historical data obtained.

The interaction using the stamp-type device was well received, and it was suggested that the act of using the stamp to make a character mean something else was a fresh and enjoyable experience. There were shouts of joy when more than one person successfully associated a word. In addition, users who had learned the rules completely often played the game again after a while. This is considered to indicate that the experience provided by this system is excellent. On the other hand, in terms of the complexity of the game system, the exhibition revealed many issues. In particular, the linkage between the GUI and the stamp-type device is very important. In order to make the user understand the rules unattended, it is necessary to carefully return detailed feedback on the user's actions one by one. In particular, it is necessary to improve the current system for selecting the stamp status and hiragana cards, and provide a mechanism for intuitive understanding. For example, at present, the selection of each part of the body is transitioned by a button on a single stamp, but it is possible to prepare special stamps such as a head stamp, a body stamp, and a butt stamp, for a total of three stamps for the experience. Also, the hiragana cards could be changed to display the hiragana required by the program by projection and use the displayed hiragana, instead of having the user select from all the current hiragana. In this way, we believe that the system should be improved to present as few elements as possible for users to select through the system, so that they can understand the rules intuitively without stress.

7 Summary

In this research, we created the "Mojipla Stamp" as word play content using the stamp metaphor. It was designed to communicate the game content in an easy-to-understand manner using a tutorial and a stamp-type device. However, from the evaluation of the exhibition, we found that the game was not played in the way we had expected, as the tutorial was not read and the surface of the device was not pressed. At the moment, the exhibition format is designed to be unattended, and we found that the rules of the game are too complicated for children to play alone and understand the rules smoothly. In particular, it was found that the target children, aged 3 to 7, had difficulty in predicting the behavior of the game, and the device was sometimes damaged by pushing the stamps too hard, indicating a lack of stability in terms of operation. For the future, we propose to abolish the tutorials that require the user to read the text and to explain the rules in a hands-on manner, or to place illustrations that explain the rules. In terms of operation, we can consider reducing the impact on the LCD by incorporating metal into the joint of the stamp-type device, or changing the design of the device significantly so that the center of gravity is not unstable, or changing the material of the filament. On the other hand, as for the content, it was highly evaluated as an experience that can stimulate children's word play. We would like to improve the issues revealed in this exhibition and continue development of the system as an exhibition system that can be permanently installed even unattended.

References

1. MEXT, A Guide to Elementary School Programming Education (3rd Edition). https://www.mext.go.jp/content/20200218-mxt_jogai02-100003171_002.pdf. Accessed 10 Feb 2022
2. What is Programming Thinking Explained in Figures | Benesse's Programming Education Information. https://benesse.jp/programming/beneprog/2018/07/13/computationalthinking. Accessed Feb 2022
3. Katsuno: Tower of Hanoi | Hanayama Corporation. https://www.hanayamatoys.co.jp/product/category/puzzle/katsunou/katsunou-hanoi.html. Accessed 10 Feb 2022
4. Gravity Maze | Play and Learn! A programming toy specialty store, hirameki box coporii. https://www.coporii.com/?pid=113705634. Accessed 10 Feb 2022
5. Mojiji ZOO. https://www.eyeup.co.jp/pressrelease/pdf/mojimojizoo.pdf. Accessed 10 Feb 2022
6. How to play, rule and solve crossword puzzles|WEB Nikoli. https://www.nikoli.co.jp/ja/puzles/crossword/. Accessed 10 Feb 2022
7. Word Puzzle Mojipittan Encore | Namco Bandai Entertainment Official Site. https://encore.mojipittan.jp/. Accessed 10 Feb 2022
8. MojiPoppun. http://moji.gungho.jp/. Accessed 10 Feb 2022
9. Word Puzzle - a brain training game played by connecting letters. https://www.zenlifegames.com/. Accessed 10 Feb 2022
10. Koto Pazura | sigtown. http://sigtown.net/. Accessed 10 Feb 2022
11. StickyTerms, https://www.kamibox.de/stickyterms. Accessed 10 Feb 2022
12. Saei, O., Makioka, S.: Interference effect of hand constraint on memory of hand-operated objects: a study of hand location and visibility. Cogn. Sci. **27**(3), pp. 250–261(2020)
13. Pietschmann, D., Valtin, G., Ohler, P.: The Effect of Authentic Input Devices on Computer Game Immersion, pp. 279–292. Computer Games and New Media Cultures, Springer (2012)

A Design Based on Location Game for Children in the Museum

Meilun Tan[✉], Yan Guan, and Wenda Tian

Tsinghua University, Beijing, People's Republic of China
13975383871@163.com, guany@tsinghua.edu.cn

Abstract. As a repository of knowledge, museums have always played an important role in knowledge dissemination. The purpose of this paper is to explore better services for children's learning in the museum environment, and provide a learning service based on positioning games to promote children to discover fun and stimulate interest in learning through interactive experience and positioning games in the museum environment. First, we reviewed the inadequacies and causes of past museum interactive display designs for children in China, and summarized the ideal elements for children to learn in museums. Second, we introduced the positioning game and brought it to the museum exhibit for exploration and experimentation. Third, according to the interactive design concept and using design tools to continuously change the version, we generate a set of positioning games based on the knowledge content of the Prehistoric Biology Hall of the China Geological Museum. Finally, this set of learning services based on positioning games will be implemented in the China Geological Museum.

Keywords: Studying in the museum · Game-based learning · Interactive design · Location game

1 Introduction

With the entry into the era of knowledge economy, the way of learning is diversified, and it is no longer limited to traditional classroom education or training institutions. There are increasing ways for children to acquire knowledge outside the classroom, such as reading books, observing the natural world or visiting museums. In particular, visiting museums is crucial for cultivating children's innovative thinking, satisfying children's interests, stimulating children's curiosity, and guiding children to establish a correct world view and values. Educators Dewey and Piaget advocated paying attention to children's participation, emphasizing that children's participation and experience are particularly important, and put forward the educational concepts of "hands-on learning" and "learning by doing", which are widely used in today's museum education. Therefore, a high degree of interactive participation experience allows children to devote themselves to the immersive learning atmosphere. To increase children's engagement, museums should design diverse and fun interactive installations. In addition, The scholars such as Piaget, Vygotsky and Erickson have also emphasized the importance of play to children. Many research reports have shown that with the development and widespread use of mobile devices, game-based learning services are of great significance for visiting museums. It can strengthen children's ability to understand the contents of museums, tap children's autonomous learning ability, and improve children's understanding of museums. The enthusiasm for learning the content of the exhibition. Therefore, diversified interactive devices and game design based on mobile devices can promote children's learning experience in museums and are an important factor in museum learning. However, most children's museums in China are in their infancy, lacking systematic theoretical foundations and practical standards. Some exhibition forms and educational activities tend to be highly similar, and some children's museums are even confused with children's playgrounds. A lot of problems are being exposed. For example, the traditional way of outputting content is still using groups of "teachers" or "volunteers" to guide children to visit and explain the content in the form of lectures. Additionally, most museums targeting children's content are still using traditional fixed displays. In order to promote children to learn in a lively and enjoyable way in the museum and maximize children's subjective initiative, this paper proposes a learning service practice based on positioning games to help museums. In this practice, the interaction experience and positioning the logic, narrative structure and interface style in the game are important considerations in the design process. Games create a strong connection between the physical world and virtual games by adding geographic locations on top of interesting content. And after some attempts, AR (augmented reality) technology is brought into it to increase the diversity of game presentation methods, which can better bring children an immersive experience.

2 Museum Display Questions and Games

2.1 Museum Exhibits and Game Forms

In China, the presentation format of most of the special exhibitions in museums for children is relatively simple, usually in the form of traditional and primitive oral explanations and rigid pictures and texts, which often emphasize one-way information transmission. In the absence of creative display design, the output content can be accepted and understood by a child audience with an average intelligence level? Can it stimulate children's interest? According to relevant researches, the cognitive development of children is a construction process that continuously develops from low level to high level, and is limited by the influence of age and education level. Therefore, when the museum does not display the content according to the mode of children's thinking, it will cause children to have difficulties in understanding and cannot stimulate children's interest. In addition, the existing museum education practices for children in China rarely take into account the interaction of children with other visitors and museum exhibits. In the CML (Situational Learning Model) model, a recognized guideline for designing learning-focused museum services for diverse visitors in a museum setting, it emphasizes the importance of sociocultural attributes in museum learning. It follows from this that it is necessary to take into account the social interactions between children and other participants when designing exhibition formats for museums.

2.2 The Importance of Play in Child Psychology

A large number of studies have shown that due to the lack of awareness of the characteristics of children's cognitive ability and logical thinking development stage, the exhibition design for children's exhibition halls has the phenomenon that the content lacks in-depth exploration, the theme has no logic, and the communication method is homogeneous. Although in recent years, with the vigorous development of technical means, many interactive devices that can interact, give people an immersive experience, and mobilize the human body's various senses have emerged in the museum, but the difficulty of operating and interpreting the exhibits in the museum will still lead to children in Negative impact on museum learning. In this case, what most designers do is stack some technology in the museum from an adult's perspective. Although the display design of domestic museums is affected by the cognitive limitations of children's groups, the educational theory of children's games has been developing. Children need games, and children can realize many wishes that cannot be satisfied in real life in games. Therefore, play can be seen as a way to help children learn knowledge, acquire skills, stimulate children's innovative ideas, and this way can also be used as a way of presentation for museum exhibitions. It is worth noting that games are also divided into entertainment and puzzle categories. As designers, we should make use of the resource integration ability of design, and through the selection and transformation of different types of games, combined with the corresponding psychological needs of children, to make Good guide.

2.3 The Importance of Games in Sociocultural Theory

According to Dooley and Welch's observation and analysis of children's visiting behavior in museums, in the museum environment, children will acquire knowledge and construct their own learning system in the process of dialogue and interaction with others. Therefore, we need to pay attention to children's socio-cultural development and encourage children to learn through interaction with others, including collaboration, dialogue, competition in museums. Although in recent years, with the development of multimedia and other technologies, more and more interactive services are applied to museums, but game-based learning services are still one of the most popular interactive methods. Because it is fun and interactive and has a variety of forms, it can meet the needs of children for social interaction.

2.4 The Ideal Museum Learning Model

We hope that by building a child-centered interactive game experience, starting from children's own interests, giving children the greatest degree of freedom, and providing children with an interesting and vivid game experience, rather than a monotonous information dissemination mode. We hope that the design of the museum learning model has the following characteristics: 1. Children's autonomy is the center. The more constraints and interventions they receive, the more boring children feel. In a relaxed and free atmosphere, children can imagine and create as much as they want, release Infinite energy. 2. Diverse forms of presentation can mobilize the enthusiasm and creativity of children's participation. Create an immersive and fun learning place for children through technology. Overall, we wanted to provide a flexible and diverse space for children.

3 The Combination of Museum Display and Games

3.1 Location Based Game

Location-based games based on mobile devices and location-sensing capabilities have exploded in recent years, with popular titles such as Pokemon Go and Ingress appearing. This type of game usually uses Map and GPS positioning as technical support to transform the real-world geographical environment into a virtual place in the game, and superimpose animated characters on the real-world image through AR technology to mix the virtual and physical environments, providing players with a Immersive experience space. The gameplay of the game usually requires players to reach a designated geographic location and complete the corresponding game tasks to obtain rewards. 6Relevant research shows that the movement element is an important part of this type of game experience, which requires the player to move widely in various places, and it also increases the player's ability to observe the surrounding environment. In addition, these types of games also have social features, where nearby players can share and discuss in the community. Based on our analysis, we found that we could try to include location games as a practice in the design of museum displays for children.

3.2 Location Relationship and Wayfinding System

LBG (Location Based Game) is a location-based sports game, which is usually developed and designed based on map data such as Google Maps or OpenStreetMap. The game uses the GPS positioning system to confirm the player's location, and changes the game content according to the movement of the player's real geographic location. Players only need to operate a mobile phone with GPS function and complete the tasks corresponding to the real location in the game APP to get rewards. It is worth noting that this type of game realizes the interaction between the real world and the virtual game world by providing the service of geographic location. After analyzing some positioning games on the market, we found that such games have a positive potential for guiding children to learn in museums. We try to introduce the positioning function of such games into the guide system of museum learning, guide children's viewing routes by designing positional relationships, and integrate it into the design to make it one of the service elements of the museum. Specifically, it is to associate the position elements in the positioning game with the positions of each showcase in the museum, in which the important position nodes are strongly associated with the key exhibits in the museum, and each node appears in the form of a game avatar or game level. On this basis, each point is connected into a line with a storyline, and finally an invisible map is formed in the museum. Considering that the museum exhibition hall is smaller than the urban environment, we replace the map data with a Bluetooth module to achieve the positioning function in the museum exhibition hall. The Bluetooth receiver is triggered by children's actions in the museum, and the obtained signal strength can determine the distance from the Bluetooth target, and push relevant game content to the children according to the distance. According to this model, the interaction between children and exhibits is enhanced (Figs. 1 and 2).

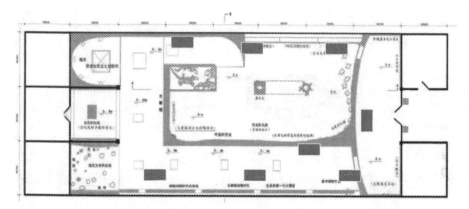

Fig. 1. The location of the Bluetooth receivers distributed in the Prehistoric Biology Hall of the China geological museum

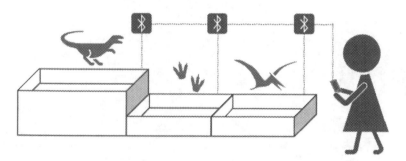

Fig. 2. Interact with exhibits via Bluetooth module

3.3 Game Logic and Presentation

Narrative elements are often invaluable tools for building games, supporting the world-view of the game space and acting throughout the game as a whole. In positioning games, the narrative background is often one of the important factors to attract players. For example, "Pokémon Go" is a treasure hunt game based on the "Pokémon" story setting. It uses the "Pokémon" series as a narrative element. It evoked people's nostalgia, which also played an important role in its success. Based on the above analysis, we anthropomorphic the exhibits in the Prehistoric Biology Hall of the China Geological Museum, and endow the exhibits with anthropomorphic images, sounds and storylines, and finally present them through mobile games. For example, the knowledge point of "Oviraptor" in the museum, first of all, we restore the image of Oviraptor according to its characteristics, and set it as an egg-stealing dinosaur according to its background. Take back the dragon egg. In this process, the egg-stealing dragon will ask a question to embarrass the child. Only when the answer is correct can he win and retrieve the dragon's egg. Otherwise, he will give his food to the egg-stealing dragon to gain freedom. In order to create a child-centered museum learning service, we abandon the monotonous exhibition method, draw on the narrative elements in the positioning game, try to design a display method for children through the form of "storytelling", and integrate it into the game design. Make it one of the elements in the service of the museum. Further, it is to combine many story modules into a large narrative main line. Children can choose the story modules and the levels and avatars they encounter according to the order they like. From the point of view of user experience, this not only guarantees the freedom of children Learning in a relaxed atmosphere also greatly arouses the interest of children (Fig. 3).

ROLE DESIGN	Eggstealer	Chinese dragon bird	Mr.Yunnan headworm	Ms.cupdeer
The role of setting	Age: 8 Hobby: Eat egg, Mischief Character: Naughty, Bad	Age: 32 Hobby: Play sports Character: Smart, Fair	Age: 88 Hobby: Help people Character: poor memory. Kind	Age: 18 Hobby: Jump Character: Vividly, Lovely
Story	The egg thief dragon is a very greedy dragon. It likes to get something for nothing. It specializes in robbery and stealing. Once you encounter him, you must deal with it carefully.	Chinese dragon bird is smart and helpful, he has news about the lost dragon egg, but you have to prove that you are smarter than him	Yunnan Headworm is an old grandmother. She has a bad memory and often forgets her name. She has no clue, but she wants you can help her. if you can help her, she will give a small gift for you!	Mr. Cuphandle Deer was blocked in the puzzle by the bad guys because he knew the important clues. Only by solving it can he get the clues!
Game module	punishment mechanism	Xiaoxiaole	Q&A	Jigsaw puzzle

Fig. 3. Story modules of the exhibits in the Prehistoric Biology Hall of the China geological museum

4   Practical Achievements

4.1   Game Logic Design

Based on the inspiration of location relationship and game logic in positioning games, we designed an egg-hunting mobile game set in the prehistoric era. The game has a strong narrative and requires children's immersive participation in the story. First of all, we designed an avatar of "elf", which plays a role in guiding the development of the story in the game, and will accompany children throughout the game process. To a certain extent, it can alleviate the unfamiliar psychology of children just entering the game.. In addition, according to the different characteristics of the fossils in the showcase, their avatars are designed to promote the development of the story through their dialogues with children. The vivid and real images and the form of dialogue can shorten the psychological distance between children and the exhibits, and effectively promote children's psychological participation. Secondly, in the game, children play the role of a person who accidentally travels to prehistoric times and shoulders the role of helping the dragon mother find dragon eggs. The role-playing in the game can fully mobilize and give play to children's enthusiasm, initiative and creativity, and stimulate children's interest. After logging into the game system, children are required to run and walk in the museum space with their mobile phones, so that the game space can interact with the pre-hidden Bluetooth devices. When children arrive in front of the preset exhibits, the mobile phone interface will pop up the tasks and virtual images corresponding to the exhibits. Each task has its own independent role, knowledge point and background, and also has connections with other tasks, and all tasks are gathered in the same story background. In addition, we tried to integrate AR (augmented reality) technology into it, and designed that when the game starts, the real-time shooting of the camera is turned on synchronously. When interacting with the exhibits set in advance, the virtual image and the real scene appear on the game interface in real time. middle. In the game, we have designed game activities such as you ask me and answer, match with the same class, puzzle, guess the shadow, and find the difference, which correspond to different avatars. For example, the corresponding game of Find Different is the fossil of the basalt turtle. It got separated from the vertebrate team in an accident. Ask the child to help him find his extended family, and then guide the child to help him through the connection method. Answer correctly or If you answer incorrectly, feedback will be given. During this process, the children answered the questions through play, which

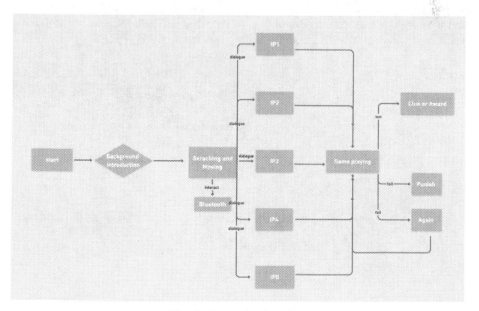

Fig. 4. Interactive flowchart

not only improved the children's interest in observing various fossils, but also learned relevant knowledge in an interesting atmosphere (Fig. 4).

4.2 Image Design

Considering that children have different perceptions of biological images and colors, we try to design the biological fossils in the museum from the perspective of children. Relevant research shows that children are more inclined to abstract and simple, hand-drawn style design elements. Therefore, when designing, we try to subtract the images based on the fossil itself as much as possible, so that it looks easy to understand and at the same time retains the lovely and rounded temperament (Fig. 5).

Fig. 5. Image design of some fossils

As for the avatar corresponding to the game level, the basic elements we use are abstract and simple geometry, and the final image is composed of geometry. Of course, we also tried a round, lovely and realistic image effect. After comparison, we found that the image design based on geometric elements is unique, creative and more sculptural. And we consider making the doll image into a real object, and the geometric splicing can also stimulate children's creativity to the greatest extent (Fig. 6).

Fig. 6. Animal character design in game levels

4.3 Interface Design

This paper finally produces an interactive application based on location movement. The overall interface design is simple and cartoonish, and the overall color is blue-green. Part of the inspiration comes from the colors in the Prehistoric Biology Hall of the China Geological Museum, and the other part comes from the colors of nature. In the design of elements in the interface, we try to image them, such as the clicked buttons, to make them more in line with children's cognition and minimize the obstacles to children during the interaction process. It can be seen that functional components are concentrated in the upper and lower areas of the interface, maintaining the simplicity and order of the interface (Fig. 7).

Fig. 7. Game interface design renderings

5 Discussion

5.1 Practical Significance

The existing museum education activities for children in China are relatively lacking in both theoretical and practical aspects. Although there are many lessons for children to learn in museums abroad, due to different national conditions, we still need to study the characteristics of domestic children's learning and how museums carry out educational practice, and explore how to open up museums for children that are suitable for their physical and mental health. educational space. In this design practice, the development of game technology makes the concept of edutainment possible, it promotes a meaningful learning dialogue exhibition, and allows us to see the infinite possibilities of gamified learning in the future.

5.2 Weaknesses in Research

In the design practice of the museum exhibition hall, we found that there is still a lot of room for improvement. The existing design requires children to interact through mobile devices, which limits children's initiative to a certain extent. How to enhance the immersive experience for children and flexibly apply games to museum learning is worth exploring.

6 Conclusion

In this practice, we provide a location-based game-based learning service for children in a museum setting. Its purpose is to serve as a reference for designers who want to research exhibitions for the Children's Design Museum. Reasonable use of the opportunities brought by technological development, through design, provide children with a variety of education, and realize the era of children's museums in the future.

References

1. Allen, S.: Designs for learning: studying science museum exhibits that do more than entertainment. Sci. Educ. **88**(1), 17–33 (2004)
2. Piscitelli, B., Anderson, D.: Young children's perspectives of museum settings and experiences. Mus. Manag. Curatorship **19**(3), 269–282 (2001)
3. Avouris, N., Yiannoutsou, N.: A review of mobile location-based games for learning across physical and virtual spaces. J. Univ. Comput. Sci. **18**(15), 2120–2142 (2012)
4. Hsu, T.-Y., Liang, H.Y., Chiou, C.-K., Tseng, J.C.: CoboChild: a blended mobile game-based learning service for children in museum contexts. Data Technol. Appl. (2018)
5. Puchner, L., Rapoport, R., Gaskins, S.: Learning in children's museums: is it really happening? Curator Mus. J. **44**(3), 237–259 (2010)
6. Dooley, M.M., Welch, M.M.: Nature of interactions among young children and adult caregivers in a children's museum. Early Child. Educ. J. **42**(2), 125–132 (2014)
7. Zhou, J., Lu, J.: A preliminary study on the educational guidelines for children aged 6, 7–11, and 12 in the museum. China Mus. **32**(1), 33–40 (2015)

MISOhungry: A Platform that Encourages Easy Access to Recipe Search, Management, and Traditional Recipes

Prajakta Thakur[✉] and Swati Chandna

SRH University Heidelberg, Heidelberg, Germany
prajakta.d.thakur@gmail.com, swati.chandna@srh.de

Abstract. Cooking has played an essential role in the growth of culture and civilization for the past 1.8 million years. However, the lockdown in various countries, including Germany, has prompted people to improve their health and well-being due to the coronavirus pandemic. While doing this, searching for recipes becomes one of the popular and essential activities as it allows people worldwide to prepare dishes from various countries. But finding recipes on the internet is like searching in the wild with thousands of recipes available for a single dish. Traditional recipes are essential in a human being's life. However, for students away from home or working young people who have little time to cook, many recipes have been forgotten for a long time. Therefore, MISOhungry gives solutions to both the user groups through this platform. The recipes provided are by scraping data from online food blogs to create recipes complete with ingredients nutritional information. On the same site, youngsters may also access traditional recipes provided by the elderly. Studies show that sharing recipes linked with memories stimulates generative activity in older adults and makes them happy later. The study demonstrates that the platform is accessible to both user groups, young people are interested in receiving traditional recipes, and they would like to use this platform which directly bridges the generation gap in recipe sharing, search, and management. MISOhungry promotes the idea of "Happiness is Homemade" by making cooking more accessible to both user groups.

Keywords: Web scraping · Recipe search and manage · Traditional recipes · Young and elderly people

1 Introduction

Food is necessary for human survival. It not only provides us with energy, but it also shapes our identity and culture. The old saying goes that we are what we eat, and food-related activities like cooking, eating and talking about it occupy a

© The Author(s), under exclusive license to Springer Nature Switzerland AG 2022
M. M. Soares et al. (Eds.): HCII 2022, LNCS 13323, pp. 249–264, 2022.
https://doi.org/10.1007/978-3-031-05906-3_19

significant part of our daily lives. In the internet age, food culture has expanded faster than ever before. As a result, many individuals are altering their lifestyles these days. Due to the increasing number of people interested in culinary, the demand for recipe applications has increased. However, searching for recipes for cooking may be difficult, particularly for novices, since there are hundreds of recipes accessible for each meal. Traditional food knowledge may provide a person with the ability to make healthy, safe, and culturally appropriate meals. Also, there will inevitably be a time when a person must leave the house and will miss the reach to home-cooked feeds with it. Moreover, the lack of trust in the ability to prepare homemade meals might affect the healthy lifestyle of young generations.

The motivation for this research originated from combining the two principles above to create a digital platform for recipe search that could be managed in a short amount of time while also connecting with unique traditional recipes from the elderly. As a result, the elderly may enhance their generative activity by exchanging recipes and sharing memories. Furthermore, the health of younger generations can be improved by encouraging them to prepare homemade meals utilizing an easily accessible digital platform.

With busy lives, cooking seems like a distant luxury for people. However, taking into account the working population and students, the major obstacles to healthy eating are:

- A lack of time owing to studies/offices
- The high cost of nutritious meals purchased outside of the home
- Difficulty for home cooks to discover healthy dishes without having to sift through millions of recipes on the internet in short span of time.
- Lack of familiarity with traditional recipes

While on the other hand, following are the main barriers to healthy eating and recipe sharing for elderly people:

- In old age, due to living alone, one develops a loss of interest in eating and preparing meals.
- Elderly people are unaware of digital platforms and are afraid to utilize interfaces because they find it too overwhelming.
- Not many platforms are available for traditional recipe sharing and recipe memory sharing.

This research seeks to improve the user experience by analyzing the limitations of existing recipe management and search systems and taking a small step toward developing a user interface to bridge the gap between the elderly and the younger generation in recipe sharing. This study addresses the challenges that working people, new home cooks, and students have in balancing a busy schedule while being healthy. The first research study creates a user interface enabling older people to exchange traditional recipes and connected memories. After considering all of the constraints associated with the two user groups, the following research questions were identified:

1. What are some approaches to enhance the user experience while searching for and managing recipes?
2. How a web interface platform can be used to bridge the gap between the elderly and young concerning recipe sharing?
3. How can the double diamond technique be utilized to allow users to exchange recipe memories and learn how younger people respond to recipes given to them by older relatives?

2   Related Work

There exist several platforms related to recipe search and management. However, very few focus on retrieving data in real-time and saving it to the user's account. While researching the concept of recipe search and management, a website that comes up is allrecipes.com [1]. The website allrecipes.com is the most popular recipe website and has been operating since 1997. It provides the user with hundreds of recipes for a single dish. Here comes this particular study into focus where home chefs can discover the best healthy dishes without having to sift through millions of recipes on the internet, thus saving the energy and time of the user. A few more limitations of the existing platform allrecipes.com are listed below .

- **There are no sorting options available.** On this site, there are hundreds of choices for each dish. However, recipes cannot be sorted by rating on the site.
- **Search Results** Similar systems on the market include search capabilities that enable users to search recipes. However, it results in thousands of dishes' recipes; thus, sifting through them to find one becomes difficult. The search functionality can be enhanced by using a search for giving a sorted list of top-most recipes based on ratings, thus improving the search function's accuracy and saving time.
- **Less user experience** The major recipe platforms are built around static ideas, allowing users to browse recipes. User interaction is lacking because interactive features such as saving recipes to the personal account are not promoted on most platforms like allrecipes.com, yummly.com.
- **Poor user interface** The user reviews of the allrecipes.com and advertising banner take up nearly half of the page which makes it almost impossible to read a recipe correctly these days. Any interface with advertisements may be overwhelming for elderly persons.

The authors of [7] explain the idea of allrecipes.com, the primary website for scraping recipes in MISOhungry. allrecipes.com [1] is the most well-known and largest food-related social media platform. Recipes are submitted by members using the website and then copyedited by staff. Members may share recipes and evaluate and rate them and upload pictures of meals they have made using the recipe. The writers also examine the benefits and limits of allrecipes.com. However, unlike other sites, allrecipes.com [1] search function allows for the inclusion and removal of particular components. Users may enter in search keywords to include or exclude from the system, and the system will scan their database for matches. This function, however, is inefficient since users may input whatever terms they like, and the machine will still look for them. All of the findings may be incorporated when designing the MISOhungry platform.

The study below focuses on the interviews and research conducted to bridge the recipe-sharing gap between older and younger generations. It also emphasizes how sharing recipes and memories with them aid the elderly in their development, which indirectly promotes good later life development and intergenerational learning. Again, different blogs and some study is done in this field.

The study [9] examines how older people feel about sharing recipes with younger generations and how that influences their expression of generativity when interacting with younger generations. In study one, 30 older people (age 65+) were interviewed in semi-structured interviews about their experiences with intergenerational recipe sharing. Before and after participating in a simple recipe sharing activity, participants will complete a survey of generative concern. Responses will emphasize emotions of autonomy and aspirations to educate others and leave a legacy by prior research on generative art activities. It is also predicted that as a result of the recipe sharing job, generative worry would rise.

Following preliminary research, Study two looked at how the kind of recipe (special occasion vs. daily), method of sharing (oral vs. written), and identity of the recipe receiver (related vs. stranger) affect generative concern in 792 older people.

Intergenerational learning, well-being, and ego integrity in later life are addressed as implications and future directions. A study has examined the effect of sharing recipes on generativity in the elderly for the first time. The qualitative and quantitative results will offer preliminary proof that recipe sharing enhances emotions of well-being. Individuals who are optimistic about themselves, their life choices, and their contributions to their position in society can feel good about themselves. Intergenerational recipe sharing will help personal development. Families, caregivers, social workers, and politicians interested in promoting good late-life development and intergenerational learning may find the information gathered from this helpful study [9].

The qualitative interview research [11] aimed to find out what it meant to prepare, cook, and serve meals to retired single and cohabiting women. Sixty-three women from two Swedish cities and their surrounding rural areas participated in the study. The results revealed that the most profound meaning was to help others. The act of preparing a meal may be compared to preparing a gift for others. While their power was preserved, cohabiting women continued to cook with the same sense of responsibility and pleasure before retiring. Most studies show that sharing recipes and establishing a network where the elderly may share and interact is a generative activity. Unfortunately, they have a limited number of platforms and equipment to carry out this operation. MISOhungry is trying to address a couple of the needs of this specific user group.

The study by [10] discusses the significance of traditional food knowledge in fostering biocultural diversity and enhancing citizen food production capability is investigated. Food variety is an essential aspect of human nutrition and may indicate a region's biocultural diversity. In addition, traditional culinary knowledge may help individuals connect to the natural environment while expressing their cultural identity. Intergenerational learning and integration with formal knowledge are the goals of this study. The MISOhungry platform tries to address the limitations and better understand how young people respond to traditional recipes by using design thinking approach and usability testing.

3   Proposed System Design

After careful analysis of a problem field and the results of predecessors, it was evident that previous solutions have some limitations concerning recipe search, management, and reach of traditional recipes discussed in Sect. 2. Therefore, after going through the breadth of possibilities and features, the conceptual solution section describes the solution in the form of features for the MISOhungry website answering the problems defined. The proposed system architecture is shown in Fig. 1.

The whole architecture is split into three distinct tiers. The core four categories for basic functionalities and two web and mobile interfaces in the client layer can be observed in version one. The features are primarily aimed at addressing the constraints of earlier research. The next part explains implementing the double diamond technique to include and omit features depending on user groups.

3.1   Design Thinking Process

This section focuses on utilizing the double diamond method [8] to achieve consistently superior design choices as shown in Fig. 2. This involves doing user research to identify and define the design issue and creating solutions tailored to particular target groups. The primary aim was to identify frequent mistakes and develop a robust and user-centered design approach.

When considering features, websites are often designed to cater to specific target groups (in this instance, young generations and the elderly) while disregarding other users (middle-aged user group in this case). Often, this occurs inadvertently as a result of a project's lack of time. This is where the Double Diamond method was helpful in this specific study. The following is split into four stages and comprises two diamond-shaped sections. The first diamond contains two phases and is devoted to the information collection and user research, such as asking, listening, and sorting. The second diamond is divided into two phases, one for information processing and the other for the iterative design process. The primary responsibilities here were to create, test, and design.

Following is brief explanation of the four distinct phases and their outcomes.

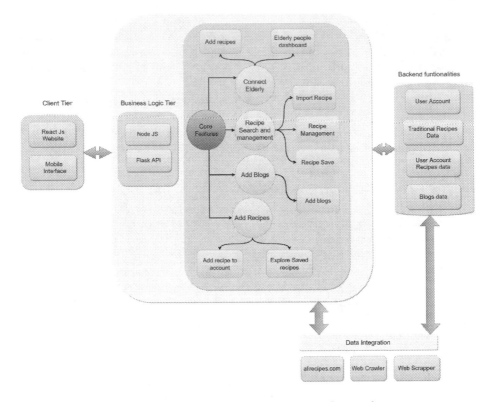

Fig. 1. Architecture for MISOhungry [Author]

User Research - Understanding the Problem. The user was the focus at this phase. The goal was an in-depth understanding of their preferences, motives, and issues. Building online surveys and customer journey maps were chosen from a variety of well-established user research techniques that may be utilized for this purpose. Survey Monkey [6] platform was used to create both the surveys. Both the surveys were distributed among the targeted user groups. A total of nine questions were included in the surveys, including questions from the platforms used before for searching and managing recipes, difficulties faced by users on these particular platforms and, any features they want on such digital platform.

The following are the findings regarding the demand for various platform features by both user groups.

1. **Young Student and Working Population** Participants' different features for such a digital platform include detailed and structured recipes with a description of the time required to prepare, a clean user interface, and good accessibility. However, the most exciting feature mentioned is the specifications or history of the particular recipe, a desire to know about recipes, and some stories to connect with the people sharing them. Some people wanted

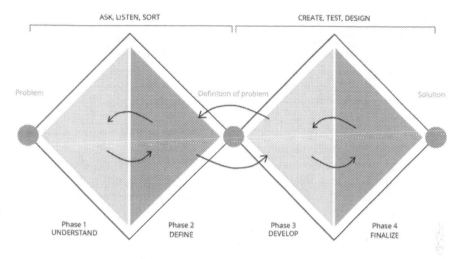

Fig. 2. Double diamond process [8]

them to surprise with some new features related to recipe search in MISO-
hungry platform.

2. **Elderly People** Quick UI, steps to utilize the platform, easy access, and
   ad-free since advertisements are overwhelming for users were some of the
   advantages highlighted for MISOhungry by participants who had accessibility
   issues. For example, one of the eleven participants requested an infinite space
   to explain the recipe instructions. At the same time, the other three wanted a
   separate area where they could share their memories or tips with the readers,
   similar to a blog.

Defining the Problem. The qualitative analysis and interpretation of survey
notes and the quantitative answers from the diary research were included here.
A key finding was drawn from analyzing the data and finding common themes
and trends among users. These were the significant revelations that pushed the
design process forward.

1. It takes a long time for most young users to find a recipe for a meal among
   the wide range of recipes available on the internet.
2. Cooking ideas and methods, as well as recipe sharing, are desired by younger
   generations.
3. The majority of recipes are given orally via phone conversations or face-to-
   face contacts, and most steps are forgotten as a result.
4. Elderly folks are hesitant to use or share recipes on high-tech UI platforms.
5. Cooking with family members promotes emotions of intimacy and connection,
   and sharing recipes ensures that they are passed down to future generations.
6. Users place a high value on sharing recipes, experiences, and culinary advice,
   and it is something they aspire to accomplish themselves.

Defining Personas. Personas were developed to represent each user group based on the data to assist set limits and concentrate on design to meet users requirements. Based on the two user categories indicated below, two personas were developed.

1. **Persona Type: Receiver**
   The Persona created for the young students, and the working population comes under this category. The key points covered in this category of Persona-based on insights were summarized in the form of Motivations, Fears, Problems faced, Needs and Challenges. This Persona was of a young Graduate student who likes homemade food but has limited cooking time. The biggest challenge he has been losing culinary suggestions or recipes provided by his mother while on the phone. It's also challenging to move from one platform to another to search, store, and manage recipes. He needs a platform to search for a few top-ranked recipes for a special dinner and save them for future use. For him, finding traditional recipes on the same platform would be the cherry on the cake.

2. **Persona Type: Sender**
   The Persona created for Elderly comes under this category. The key points covered in this category of Persona-based on insights were summarized in the form of Motivations, Fears, Problems faced, Needs and Challenges. This persona represented an elderly woman who enjoys cooking and sharing recipes, but is unfamiliar with using digital platforms to share traditional recipes. Also, it is overwhelming to use high-tech platforms, being not so tech-savvy.

Developing Possible Solutions. The following step is to start looking for potential solutions after arriving at a clearly defined issue. At initially, quantity will take precedence over quality. Brainstorming, ideation, and workshops with the team (or even with users) helped to create a range of solutions ideas.

Brainstorming: One of the most well-known methods for generating ideas is brainstorming. No specialists are needed to carry out this process since it is accessible and well-known. The quality of the findings is dependent on the proper phrasing of the query at the outset. Brainstorming aimed to generate as many fresh ideas as possible in a group setting. Every participant in theory was actively engaged in the process. Different aspects to all of the problems were conceived from the brainstorming sessions, and card sorting was used to improve the information architecture. The results of card sorting where first all the features where listed followed by sorting the features based on user groups.

Information Architecture: Information architecture (IA) visually depicts the product's infrastructure, features, and hierarchy, similar to a blueprint [2]. The information architecture created, in this case, is based on all available functionalities of the platform MISOhungry shown in Fig. 3.

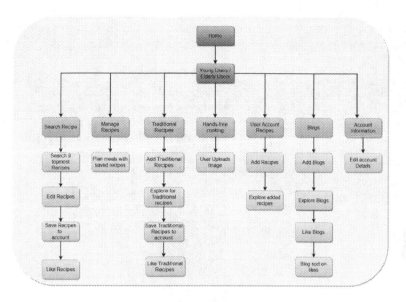

Fig. 3. Information architecture [Author]

3.2 Rapid Prototyping, LoFi Mockups and Guerilla Testing

Simple low-fidelity prototypes or mock-ups were created and presented to the target audience. The three to four alternatives that were created aided in developing a single design with specified information architecture characteristics. The goal was to obtain user input as soon as possible. Which prototype effectively gets to the core of the consumers' issue and solves it? In what areas do consumers still have doubts or a lack of understanding?

The Low-Fidelity setup began with a paper model or sketch, focusing on the location of the website's elements. Next, a basic concept for certain aesthetic aspects of the final website was drawn. With the help of the wireframe application, Figma [3], this drawing was transformed into an interactive wireframe. The purpose of the wireframes was to test the application components interactively and make changes as needed.

Guerilla Testing: Guerrilla testing (also known as hallway usability testing) was used to quickly and casually test concepts to get high-level input and possibly discover user experience issues. The primary objective of Guerrilla testing, in this case, was to get feedback from users on the prototype and the features featured on the whole platform to help narrow things down for the next version. The test was performed in two locations with a small number of people from various user categories. Guerrilla testing was in charge of getting the MISOhungry platform in front of consumers, whether real users or John from down the street, who uses every app imaginable. Users were given a brief overview of the whole idea and a demonstration of the prototypes created. One of the major concerns was completing each test reasonably without being too talkative.

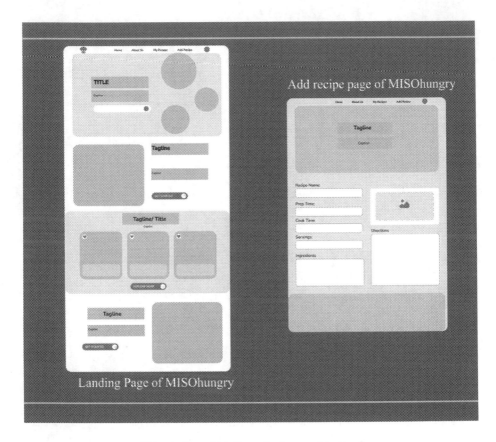

Fig. 4. Low-Fidelity wireframes [Author]

The findings from Guerrilla testing are discussed and implemented in next phase while developing the High Fidelity clickable prototype.

3.3   Development of the Final Features and Solutions

The findings of the guerilla testings helped improve the design, as shown in the High Fidelity Prototype. The high-fidelity prototype is shown in Fig. 5 is build in Figma [3]. The images used on entire platform are from [4,5,12]. It is a detailed and realistic design of MISOhungry used to test it with four different participants from each user group after implementation.

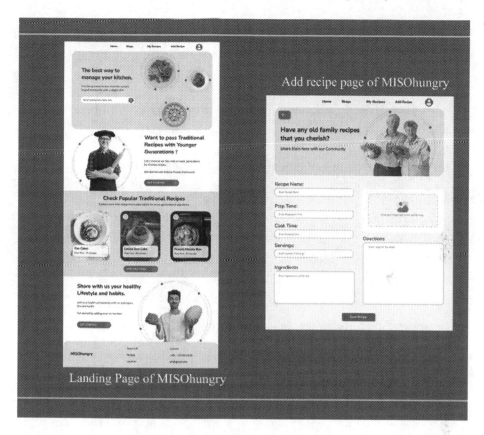

Fig. 5. High fidelity prototype [Author]

4   Remote Usability Testing

To help test the interface and interactions with the website's main elements, a clickable prototype of the design idea was developed. A series of activities was developed to aid in the understanding of user interactions with the system and mental models. The prototype was put through its tests with five users from each group. It was clear from watching users execute their tasks that they grasped the fundamental concept of the platform MISOhungry. The user feedback confirmed the design ideas and offered useful information for enhancing the final designs.

1. **Participants** The prototype was put through its tests with five users from each group. Table 1 and Table 2 shows the data for both user groups.
2. **Apparatus** Due to the fact of COVID-19 situation, the usability testing was conducted through video conference call. Two of the college students served as an observer while the author served as moderator. Two observers were employed for elderly group since they are sensitive to technology. With the participants' consent, the video conference was videotaped in order to delve

Table 1. Participants from user group 1 usability testing [Author]

Name	Age	Gender	Occupation
Aditi Dave	26 Years	Female	Dance instructor
Akshay Shinde	29 Years	Male	IT specialist
Mavis Dsouza	29 Years	Female	Student
Shraddha Pawar	27 Years	Female	Student

Table 2. Participants from user group 2 usability testing [Author]

Name	Age	Gender	Occupation
Manasi Pawar	66 Years	Female	Working - Mother of two daughters
Sophie John	65 Years	Female	Housewife - Mother of two sons
Jayawant Dalvi	60 Years	Male	Retired officer- Father of two sons
Veena Thakur	63 Years	Female	Housewife - Mother of daughter

further into my website. Throughout the testing, a data logger was utilized to record all of the results.

3. **Procedure** The process started with a brief introduction to the usability testing team members. Following that, they were given some basic questions about themselves to assist them in relaxing. Having participated in the usability testing for the first time, a comprehensive explanation of the process followed. Before giving them a demo of the MISOhungry website, they were informed about the Think-Aloud method. Finally, an effort was made to fully explain the method by answering as many questions as feasible. A demonstration of the website followed, and many topics were discussed, as most of them were unfamiliar with website usage like this. Since this group was not technologically aware, being extra patient with them while explaining everything was primary.

4. **Tasks given to Participants** Both groups of users were given the same tasks. The number of tasks given to participants are as followed:
   (a) You are a graduate student away from home who wants to savor the pleasures of traditional cuisine. Could you look for the traditional recipes page and see if any of the dishes appeal to you?
   (b) You are a mother's son who enjoys cooking. You know many traditional recipes because of her, and you want to pass them on to students like you. On this website, where can you upload traditional recipes for younger generations?
   (c) Your are a working mom and wants to save recipes on digital platform to save time for future use. You came across MISOhungry and here can you find an option to add recipes to your personal account?
   (d) You are a chef who enjoys reading food-related tales from a wide range of individuals. Is there a blog dedicated to recipe memories?

(e) You are a student who wants to find the best recipes for a particular meal. Were you able to locate that option on the MISOhungry platform?

5. **Results**

The data logger framework's observer results and video recording findings provided various usability testing results for this specific user group. The findings are linked to the recipe information page's tiny buttons and the lack of back buttons. A few of them suggested an option for picture replacement should be retained since it was previously absent. One of them was perplexed by the difference between adding a recipe to an account and using the usual add option for traditional recipes. The observer outcomes and video recording findings from the data logger framework offered a range of usability testing results for this particular user group. The results are related to the like button that is not displayed on cards and just a handful of the requested help using this website. The prep time and cook time input boxes have to be precise (minutes, secs).

The key findings from usability testing were responsible for final version of user flow and system architecture.

5   System Implementation

The above-stated functionalities of MISOhungry are realized through a final version of the system architecture for easy extensibility. As mentioned before, the MERN stack consists of MongoDB, ExpressJS, ReactJS, and NodeJS, supporting MVC architecture. In addition, the system architecture will enable the creation of a simplified workflow for every tier available. MISOhungry has a four-tier system architecture: client, business logic, functionalities, and database as shown in Fig. 6. Three stages comprised the MISOhungry implementation procedure. First, It was decided to work on the back-end. After then, the front-end development began. Once that, the application was deployed after that integration was completed. For understanding the functionality of the architecture and implementation, the following is the explanation of system architecture in detail.

5.1   Application Logic

All of the tools and packages were installed at the start of the development process. The real coding of the website began after the first setup. "Client" and "Server" are two directories. The client folder contains all front-end files and directories, whereas the server folder includes all back-end files and folders. The primary source code is in the "src" folder. The code's entry point is in the "App.js" file. The functions of each folder will be explained in more detail later.

5.2   Backend and Frontend Development

The application's backend development included the connection of Mongoose, creation of Mongoose models, backend user authentication and authorization,

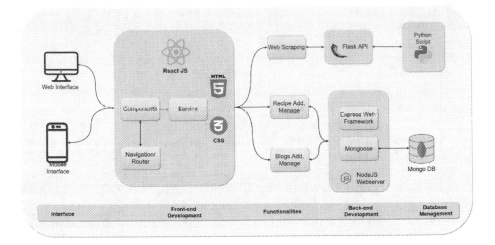

Fig. 6. Architecture of MISOhungry final version [Author]

routing and APIs, WebScraping Logic and API Developement. The frontend development of the program includes frontend user authentication, web scraping integration, and the creation of a variety of distinct pages. The different pages in Frontend development are explained while discussing the core funtionalities part of architecture Fig. 6. The entire Frontend of website is developed based on the designs which were created in Figma after the 5 stage design thinking process.

6   Evaluation

The evaluation of the quality and value of the response to the issues raised in the introduction and exploration for the research questions posed is done in this section. Most users considered that finding topmost recipes for a particular dish is a helpful feature and a novel one to utilize daily when reviewing the methods employed to save time in recipe search and management. MISOhungry's entire platform benefits both users and meets their demands by considering the needs of younger generations and the elderly. According to Usability Testing results, the stated red route tasks were performed to the maximum extent by users of both categories, indicating that the platform is readily accessible for both groups. The majority of the survey findings revealed that young people were delighted to get recipes from the elderly and placed a high value on them, which addresses our fourth study question. This study is just the first practical step towards the idea of cooking with roots, finding long-lost traditional recipes. The study has several areas that may be expanded in the future, which is further discussed in the next section

7   Discussion

MISOhungry provides answers to some of the problems that young people and the elderly encounter. MISOhungry is a platform where the recipe sharing activity of the elderly and the receiving recipes of the young people are proven to be helpful to both groups in some manner. MISOhungry uses the idea of web scraping to find the best nine recipes from the well-known platform allrecipes.com, which has thousands of recipes for every given cuisine. This feature of MISOhungry will assist both categories in meeting their objectives and will save a lot of users time. The platform's whole design is based on a 5-stage design thinking approach to enhancing users' digital experiences. In an age where digital platforms are sweeping the market, a platform like MISOhungry may have a substantial and beneficial impact on the lives of two very different user groups, thereby bridging the gap between them. Furthermore, MISOhungry, as one of the few platforms connecting the young with traditional recipes from the old, encourages the sharing of recipes across generations.

8   Conclusion and Future Scope

Students, new cooks, and the working population find it challenging to find recipes online for a specific dish because there are thousands of recipes available, so finding the ideal one is time-consuming. Also, most people consider it a waste of time watching a whole video of recipes to discover chefs' tiny tips and secrets for a particular dish since they are not mentioned in the video captions. The majority of platforms on the market focus on modern recipes, with just a handful dedicated to traditional recipes. According to this study, most respondents were interested in traditional and contemporary handmade recipes. When it comes to the sharing of traditional recipes, research indicates that very little research has been done in this area, and techniques should be developed to assist older people in sharing recipes. Elderly individuals lose interest in cooking due to loneliness due to loneliness, yet sharing recipes keeps them happy. As this study is one of the few to highlight the need for a platform to bridge the gap between young and older adults concerning recipe sharing, there are a few areas for further research. First, the time required to fetch the scraped recipe results should be reduced. Second, the platform should include a voice-over-interface function for senior users. MISOhungry should also include a connecting platform where young people can connect with individuals who provide these recipes and take courses from them, which will directly assist the elderly in earning money while staying at home during this COVID period. A chef bot may be connected with the platform to ascertain users' actual recipes and supply them with the relevant results. In the same way that food has particular significance, recipes do. Food links us all to our connections, beliefs, history, and futures.

References

1. Allrecipes - https://www.allrecipes.com/
2. The comprehensive guide to information architecture. https://www.toptal.com/designers/ia/guide-to-information-architecture
3. The designing tool - figma. https://www.figma.com/
4. Freepik graphic resources for everyone. https://www.freepik.com
5. Pexels graphic resources for everyone. https://www.pexels.com/
6. Surveymonkey platform. https://www.surveymonkey.com
7. Ann, E., Hao, N., Goh, W.W., Hee, K.: Feast. In: A machine learning image recognition model of recipe and lifestyle applications. MATEC Web of Conferences, vol. 335, p. 04006 (2021). https://doi.org/10.1051/matecconf/202133504006
8. Eissa, C.: How the double diamond process can help you work in a more user-centred way (2019). https://www.testingtime.com/en/blog/double-diamond-process/
9. Kitada, L.R.: Cooking with roots: How older adults strengthen connection with younger generations through recipe sharing (2016)
10. Kwik, J.C.: Traditional food knowledge: Renewing culture and restoring health. Master's thesis, University of Waterloo (2008)
11. Sidenvall, B., Nydahl, M., Fjellström, C.: The meal as a gift-the meaning of cooking among retired women. J. Appl. Gerontol. **19**, 405–423 (2000)
12. Unsplash: Beautiful free images & pictures unsplash. https://unsplash.com/

The Post-pandemic Era Study on the Design of High-speed Railway Seats

Xi Wu and Zhang Zhang[✉]

School of Art Design and Media, East China University of Science and Technology,
NO. 130, Meilong Road, Xuhui District, Shanghai, China
618746761@qq.com

Abstract. The COVID-19 has led to people's increased concern about health issues. In this paper, we investigate the needs of users traveling by high-speed rail in the post-pandemic era and optimize the design of high-speed rail seats, and evaluate the feasibility. Methodology: Using INPD combined with AHP and QFD to guide the design of high-speed railway seats, we use INPD as the main line of research and SET factor analysis to find the product opportunity gaps; using questionnaires and user interviews to research different high-speed railway travelers and derive various needs of users for high-speed railway seats; AHP was used to calculate and prioritize the target user requirements, and then QFD was used to determine the weights of each design requirement point. Conclusion: This paper aims to provide design ideas and future development trends for the design of high-speed railway seats in the post-pandemic era by using INPD, AHP and QFD methods.

Keywords: COVID-19 · High-speed rail seats · DUXU

1 Introduction

Since the reform and opening up, the rapid growth of China's economy has led to the rapid development of China's high-speed rail, which has become one of the main modes of travel for people today, according to the Ministry of Transport. With the continuous development of economy and technology, and combined with the current increase in health concerns triggered by the COVID-19, passengers' needs in high-speed rail travel have increased. Therefore, this study focuses on exploring the needs of users traveling by high-speed rail in the post-pandemic era and evaluates the feasibility of optimizing the design of high-speed rail seats, which are the closest and longest in contact with the human body. The INPD method is used as the main line of research in this paper. The research is based on the SET factor analysis of high-speed railway seats to clarify the opportunity gap of high-speed railway seats; through questionnaire survey and user interview to explore the user needs; followed by the AHP hierarchical analysis to build the corresponding hierarchical index model of user needs and QFD to build the quality house model of user needs and design needs; finally, according to the weight ranking of design needs, the product design concept matrix is created to understand the opportunities and conceptualize the product opportunities. conceptualize and realize the optimized design of the high-speed rail seat.

M. M. Soares et al. (Eds.): HCII 2022, LNCS 13323, pp. 265–278, 2022.
https://doi.org/10.1007/978-3-031-05906-3_20

2   Overview of Research Methodology

2.1   Integrated New Product Development (INPD)

The INPD method is an integrated user-centered approach to new product development that integrates design, business and mechanical engineering. The approach covers four main phases: identifying product opportunity gaps, understanding the opportunities, conceptualizing the product opportunities, and realizing the product opportunities. Compared to the traditional approach to product development, this method integrates various factors such as market trends, user needs and technical requirements in the product development process [1]. Product opportunities are obtained through in-depth analysis of social, economic, and technological aspects, and qualitative and quantitative methods are used to understand and eventually realize product opportunities.

2.2   Analytic Hierarchy Process (AHP)

AHP Hierarchical analysis was proposed by American operations researcher Professor T. L. Saaty in the 1970s to systematize complex problems by establishing a hierarchical structural model of the decision-making process and quantitatively calculating the perceptual factors in the process. The basic steps of AHP hierarchical analysis are as follows: (1) constructing a hierarchical structural model; (2) determining the relative importance among the evaluation indicators, establishing and calculating the judgment matrix; (3) consistency test; (4) calculate the weights of each index and perform the overall ranking [2].

2.3   Quality Function Deployment (QFD)

The QFD method was proposed by Japanese scholars Akao and Mizuno in 1966 as a way to improve the quality of design by transforming user requirements into design requirements in a rational and effective way. The core of QFD is the quality house, which consists of user requirements and weights, product/service characteristics, the relationship matrix of user requirements-quality characteristics, the autocorrelation matrix between quality characteristics, the planning matrix and the design matrix of quality characteristics [3]. By constructing a quality house, user requirements and engineering technology are systematically combined to complete the transformation of user requirements and ensure that user requirements are taken into account in the whole process of product design.

3   High-Speed Railway Seats Design Based on INPD with AHP and QFD Methods

3.1   Identify Product Opportunity Gaps

In the first phase of the INPD approach identification of opportunities, multidisciplinary knowledge needs to be combined with each other to explore a large number of potential product opportunity gaps and then find the most suitable opportunity gaps. In this paper, we use SET factor analysis to find the gap opportunity gaps for high-speed rail seats

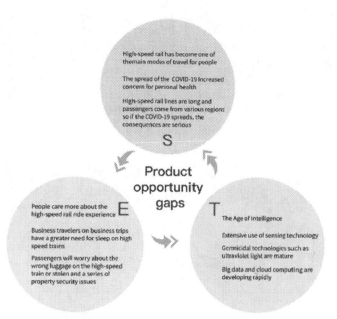

Fig. 1. SET analysis for the design of high-speed rail seats

in the post-epidemic era from three aspects: society (S) and economy (E) as well as technology (T) through desktop research, which is shown in Fig. 1.

Combining the shortcomings of the existing high-speed rail seats, SET analysis shows that, in terms of social aspects, the high-speed rail seats can be designed to be more independent to avoid direct connection between the seats for the protection of the Covid-19. In terms of economic factors, the comfort and privacy of high-speed rail seats should be improved to optimize the passenger experience. In terms of technology, some smart devices and intelligent auxiliary functions can be added to the seats to address passengers' concerns about health, property loss and overstaying.

3.2 Understand the Opportunities

In the second phase of the iNPD approach, qualitative and quantitative research should be conducted to further clarify product opportunity points for the identified product opportunity gaps. In this study, a questionnaire survey was conducted for different travel groups so as to understand the demand for high-speed rail seats among travel passengers in the post-epidemic era, and then product opportunity points were identified in combination with existing high-speed rail seats. The questionnaires were distributed to different travel groups, such as business travelers, tourists, students, middle-aged and elderly people, etc. A total of 120 questionnaires were distributed in this study, and 100 valid results were returned.

Construct User Needs Hierarchy Diagram. Using the Affinity Diagram method, a large number of user demand indicators collected from the questionnaire research were graded and summarized, and then a hierarchical model of user demand progression was constructed. The target level of this structural model is the goal of this study, i.e., the design of high-speed trains seats in the post-epidemic era. Functionality, operability, safety, comfort, and aesthetics of high-speed railway seats are considered as the criterion layer, while the specific needs of each category are considered as the third layer, i.e., the user needs indicator layer. See Fig. 2 for details.

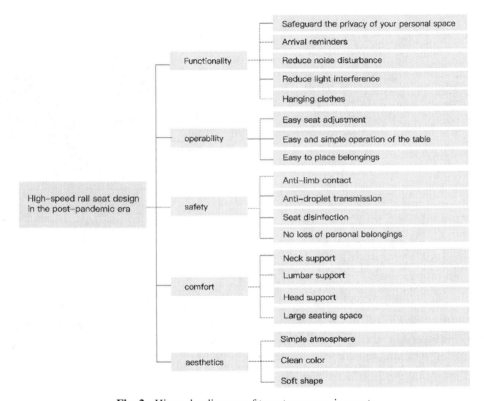

Fig. 2. Hierarchy diagram of target user requirements

Build Judgment Matrix and Calculate User Requirement Index Weights.
In this stage, a judgment matrix needs to be constructed to compare the importance between each demand point at the same level in the user demand hierarchy model in a two-by-two manner and to find out the weight value between each demand point [4].

In this study, 15 experts in related fields and 15 frequent users of high-speed railway seats were selected to form the decision makers. They were asked to apply the 9 importance levels given by Professor Satty to compare and evaluate the demand points of HSR seats in the post-epidemic era on a two-by-two basis and score them. Generally, the 9 importance levels take the values of 1/9, 1/7, 1/5, 1/3, 1, 3, 5, 7, 9, and also the reciprocal and intermediate values of each of these values [4]. The judgment matrix A is constructed as follows.

$$
A = (a_{ij})_{n \times n} = \begin{bmatrix} a_{11} & a_{12} & \cdots & a_{1n} \\ a_{21} & a_{22} & \cdots & a_{2n} \\ \vdots & \vdots & & \vdots \\ a_{n1} & a_{n2} & \cdots & a_{nn} \end{bmatrix} \tag{1}
$$

In this matrix, a_{ij} indicates the importance of indicator i relative to indicator j and $a_{ij} > 0$, $a_{ii} = 1$, $a_{ij} = \frac{1}{a_{ji}}$ (i, j = 1, 2, 3......), the weight value of each demand indicator is calculated by applying the geometric mean method according to the above judgment matrix.

First, the values of the judgment matrix A are normalized,

$$
b_{ij} = \frac{a_{ij}}{\sum_{i=1}^{n} a_{ij}} (i = 1, 2, \ldots, n) \tag{2}
$$

After normalization, the resulting matrix is summed in each row as follows.

$$
\overline{c_i} = \sum_{j=1}^{n} b_{ij} (i = 1, 2, \cdots, n) \tag{3}
$$

The weight of each demand indicator ω_i^1 (i = 1, 2, $\cdots$, n) is calculated accordingly, where the formula for calculating the weight of each demand indicator is as follows.

$$
\omega_i^1 = \frac{\overline{c_i}}{\sum_{j=1}^{n} \overline{c_i}} (i = 1, 2, \cdots, n) \tag{4}
$$

To avoid the influence of subjective factors of decision makers, the resulting matrix and related data need to be tested for consistency, and the test procedure is as follows.

First calculate the consistency index CI.

$$
CI = \frac{\lambda_{max} - n}{n - 1} \tag{5}
$$

The λ_{max} in the formula is the maximum eigenvalue

$$
\lambda_{max} = \frac{1}{n} \sum_{i=1}^{n} \frac{(AW)_i}{\omega_i} \tag{6}
$$

where $(Aw)_i$ is the i-th element of the vector Aw.

Next, the corresponding average random consistency index RI is found, and the consistency test is performed by calculating the consistency ratio CR. When $CR = \frac{CI}{RI} < 0.1$, the judgment matrix satisfies the consistency and the weights are valid. the values of RI are shown in Table 1.

Table 1. RI value table

n	1	2	3	4	5	6	7	8	9	10
RI	0.00	0.00	0.58	0.90	1.12	1.24	1.32	1.41	1.45	1.49

Based on the above process, the second layer in the user requirement hierarchy model, i.e., the criterion layer, is first compared between two, and its judgment matrix and the values of each weight are shown in Table 2, and it is calculated that $CR = 0.0386 < 0.1$, which meets the requirement of consistency test, so the weights are valid.

Table 2. Evaluation index weight under user demand

Total user demand	Functionality	Operability	Safety	Comfort	Aesthetics	Weighting value
Functionality	1	3	1/3	2	3	0.2091
Operability	1/3	1	1/5	1/2	3	0.1005
Safety	3	5	1	5	7	0.5096
Comfort	1/2	2	1/5	1	2	0.1232
Aesthetics	1/3	1/3	1/7	1/2	1	0.0576

Then, the third layer of the structural model, i.e., the demand index layer, was compared by two and two respectively and the corresponding weight values were calculated, and the calculation results are shown in Tables 3, 4, 5, 6 and 7. and the calculated judgment matrices CR were 0.0063, 0.0088, 0.0054, 0.0054, 0.0088, all of which are less than 0.1 and meet the requirements of the consistency test, so the weights are valid.

Table 3. Evaluation index weight under function requirements

Functionality	Safeguard the privacy of personal space	Arrival alerts	Reduce noise disturbance	Reduce light interference	Hanging clothes	Weighting value
Safeguard the privacy of personal space	1	2	3	5	7	0.4436
Arrival alerts	1/2	1	2	3	5	0.2618
Reduce noise disturbance	1/3	1/2	1	2	3	0.1528
Reduce light interference	1/5	1/3	1/2	1	2	0.0892

(continued)

Table 3. (*continued*)

Functionality	Safeguard the privacy of personal space	Arrival alerts	Reduce noise disturbance	Reduce light interference	Hanging clothes	Weighting value
Hanging clothes	1/7	1/5	1/3	1/2	1	0.0526

Table 4. Evaluation index weight under operational requirements

Operability	Easy seats adjustment	Easy to place belongings	Easy and simple operation of the table	Weighting value
Easy seat adjustment	1	1/3	1/2	0.1638
Easy to place belongings	3	1	2	0.539
Easy and simple operation of the table	22	1/2	1	0.2973

Table 5. Evaluation index weight under security requirements

Safety	Anti-limb contact	Anti-droplet transmission	Seat disinfection	No loss of personal belongings	Weighting value
Anti-limb contact	1	1/5	1/3	1/2	0.0883
Anti-droplet transmission	5	1	2	3	0.4824
Seat disinfection	3	1/2	1	2	0.2718
No loss of personal belongings	2	1/3	1/2	1	0.1575

Calculate and Rank the Combined Weight of Each Demand Indicator.

The weight value of each indicator under the total user demand is multiplied with the weight value of its corresponding sub-evaluation indicator to obtain the comprehensive weight value of each sub-evaluation indicator, and the specific weight priority is shown in Fig. 3.

Table 6. Evaluation index weight under comfort needs

Comfort	Neck support	Lumbar support	Head support	Large seating space	Weighting value
Neck support	1	1/2	2	3	0.2718
Lumbar support	2	1	3	5	0.4824
Head support	1/2	1/3	1	2	0.1575
Large seating space	1/3	1/5	1/2	1	0.0883

Table 7. Evaluation index weight under aesthetic needs

Aesthetics	Simple atmosphere	Clean color	Soft shape	Weighting value
Simple atmosphere	1	3	2	0.539
Clean color	1/3	1	1/2	0.1638
Soft shape	1/2	2	1	0.2973

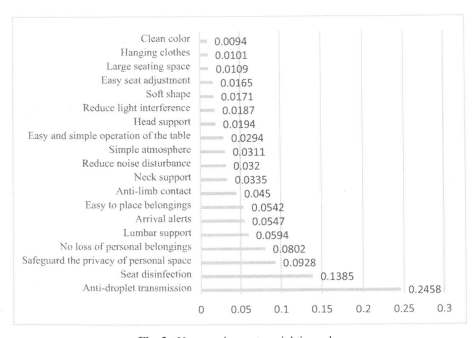

Fig. 3. User requirements weighting value

3.3 QFD-Based Product Design Requirements Analysis

Define Design Requirements. The construction of Quality of House (HOQ) is the core in QFD method, and design requirements are an important part of the quality of house model [5]. The comprehensive weight values of user requirements and the product characteristics of high-speed railway seats were analyzed to obtain the design requirements of high-speed railway seats in the post-pandemic era from D1 functional requirements, D2 operational requirements, D3 human-machine requirements, and D4 aesthetic requirements, and the specific requirements are shown in Table 8.

Table 8. Design requirements for high-speed rail seats

First level design requirements	Secondary design requirements
Functional requirements D1	Health protection d1 Protection of personal privacy d2 Easy placement of items d3
Operational requirements D2	Easy to understand d4 Seats are easy to adjust d5
Human-machine requirements D3	Seating comfort d6 Large space for activities d7
Aesthetic requirements D4	Simple and generous modeling d8 CMF is warm and soft d9

Build a High-speed Rail Seat Design Quality House Model. The above user requirements and weights were input into the QFD quality house to establish the quality house model of user requirements-design requirements of high-speed railway seats in the post-pandemic era, and 15 expert panelists were invited to score the correlation degree between user requirements and design requirements to obtain the corresponding relationship matrix. In the matrix, the symbols ◎, o and △ are used to indicate the relationship between user requirements and design requirements, where ' ◎' indicates strong correlation and takes the value of 5, ' o' indicates medium correlation and takes the value of 3, and ' △' means weak correlation, with a value of 1. The resulting relationship matrix is shown in Table 9.

The table uses F_j to denote the importance of Design Requirement (Design Requirement) DR_j, f_j to denote the relative importance of Design Requirement DR_j, w_i to be the combined weight value of the i-th user requirement, and D_{ij} to be the value of the relationship corresponding to both [6].

$$F_j = \sum_{i=1}^{n} w_i \times D_{ij} (i, j = 1, 2, \ldots, n) \tag{7}$$

$$f_j = \frac{E_j}{\sum_{j=1}^{n} E_j} (j = 1, 2, \ldots, n) \tag{8}$$

Table 9. Quality house model for high-speed rail seats

		D1			D2			D3	D4		User demand weighting
		d1	d2	d3	d4	d5	d6	d7	d8	d9	
Func-tional-ity	privacy	△	◎								0.0928
	Arrival alerts				△						0.0547
	Noise reduction Light						○				0.0320
	reduction						○				0.0187
	Hanging clothes			◎							0.0101
Opera-bility	Easy seat adjustment				◎	◎	○				0.0165
	Easy operation of ta-ble				◎	◎	○				0.0294
	Easy to place belong-ings	△	△	◎	○			△			0.0542
Safety	Anti-limb contact	○						△			0.0450
	Anti-droplet trans-	◎						△			0.2458
	mission	◎									0.1385
	Seat disinfection		○								0.0803
	No loss of belongings										
Com-fort	Neck support						◎				0.0335
	Lumbar support						◎				0.0594
	Head support						◎				0.0194
	Large seating space	△	△	△		○	○	◎ ∘	○		0.0109
Aes-thetics	Simple atmosphere				△			△	◎		0.0311
	Clean color								○	◎	0.0094
	Soft shape								△	○	0.0171
	Design Requirements Im-portance	2.214 0.098		0.584	0.333	0.478	0.265	0.884	0.431	0.234	

The relative importance of each design requirement resulting from the calculation is ranked as shown in Fig. 4.

The design requirements of high-speed railway seats in the post-pandemic era are based on functional requirements of health protection, and the seats should be as comfortable as possible while protecting the privacy of users.

4 Functional Positioning and Design Practice of High-Speed Railway Seats in the Post-pandemic Era

4.1 Product Concept Matrix

The third stage of the INPD method is the product concept design. In this stage, based on the results of the preliminary research and the above study, the design practice of high-speed railway seats in the post-epidemic era is carried out. For the four design requirements, ten design concepts were proposed and filtered by drawing a design concept matrix. The design concept matrix is shown in Fig. 5.

In summary, considering the public use environment of high-speed railway seats in the post-pandemic era, in helping passengers' health protection, the misalignment of

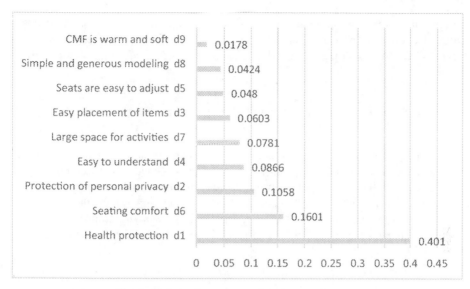

Fig. 4. Relative importance of design requirements

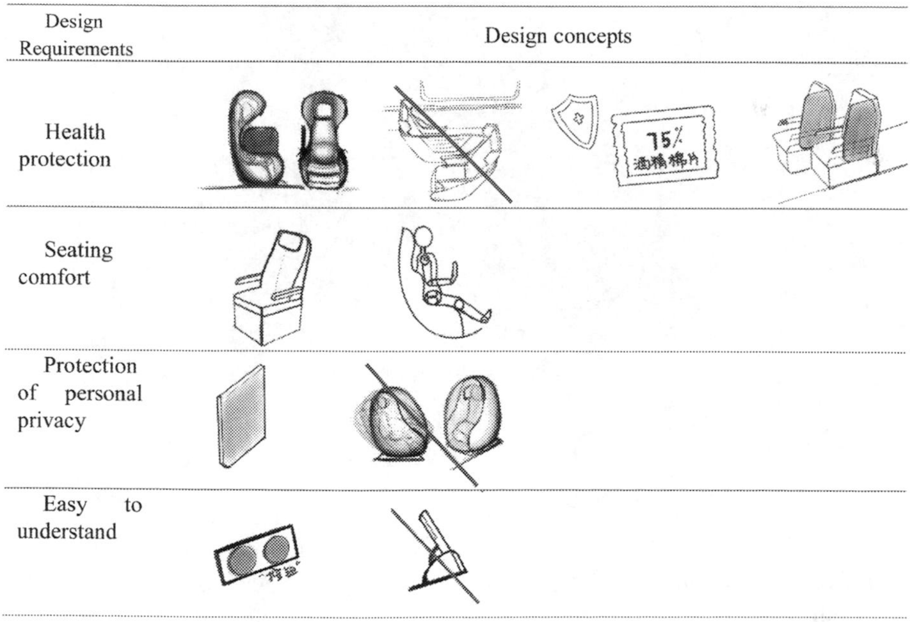

Design Requirements	Design concepts
Health protection	
Seating comfort	
Protection of personal privacy	
Easy to understand	

Fig. 5. Product concept matrix

adjacent seats and the ABS plastic partition integrated with the seats are used to reduce the contact between passengers. The high-speed rail seats backrest provides support for the user at the head and lumbar area, which, together with low user fatigue, improves the comfort of the seat and reduces the user's sedentary fatigue. The seat adjustment button is used instead of the original adjustment method, reducing the user's operational difficulty. The modeling is simple and atmospheric, which greatly improves the user's experience.

4.2 High-Speed Railway Seats Design Solutions in the Post-pandemic Era

The final stage of the INPD approach was to realize the product opportunity. Based on the behavioral and psychological analysis of high-speed rail passengers, the design study of high-speed rail seats in the post-pandemic era was conducted by combining the needs of users and the recommendations of the expert panel. Through discussions with human-machine engineers, the 95th percentile of human sitting height and depth were met, as well as the national standard for passenger seats in moving trains. Through 3D modeling and post-rendering, the final design was derived, see Figs. 6, 7 and 8.

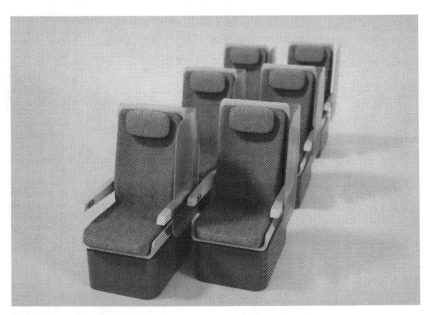

Fig. 6. Effect picture of the high-speed railway seats

The design solution meets the needs of users for health protection when taking high-speed trains in the post-pandemic era through the staggered position of adjacent seats and the ABS plastic partition integrated with the seats, while also maximizing the protection of users' privacy when taking high-speed trains. According to the ergonomics, the seat back provides support for the user in the head and lower back, reducing the user's fatigue of sitting for a long time. The use of seat adjustment buttons instead of the original adjustment method, reducing the user's operational difficulties. The simple and atmospheric shape greatly improves the user's riding experience.

Fig. 7. Effect picture of the high-speed railway seats

Fig. 8. Effect picture of the high-speed railway seats

5   Conclusion

In this study, INPD, AHP and QFD were used as design innovation methods to develop the final design concept for the post-pandemic era high-speed railway seats. The process and conclusion of this study are of high reference value for the future of high-speed railway seats in the post-pandemic era.

Acknowledgments. This research was supported by the project of "Social Innovation and Green Design Research" supported by shanghai summit discipline in design 2022, 2020 Shanghai Pujiang Program (2020PJC026), Special Fund for Research Base of Institute of Art and Design, East China University of Science and Technology, Shanghai Dream Foundation in 2022.

References

1. Cagan, J., Vogel, C.M.: Integrated new product development. In: Clarkson J., Eckert, C. (eds.) Design Process Improvement. Springer, London (2005). https://doi.org/10.1007/978-1-84628-061-0_17
2. Lu, N., Xu, B., Chu, P., Zhi J.Y., Hu, J.: Design evaluation of automatic excretion processor based on fuzzy hierarchical analysis. Packag. Eng. **39**(08), 151–155 (2018). 陆宁, 徐伯初, 支锦亦, 胡杰. 基于模糊层次分析法的自动排泄处理器设计评估. 包装工程, 2018, 39(08):151–155
3. Zhou, S., Zheng, F.: Research on product design methods integrating AHP/QFD/AD. Packag. Eng. **42**(02),150–154+166 (2021). 周生祥, 郑枫. 集成AHP/QFD/AD的产品设计方法研究. 包装工程, 2021, 42(02):150–154+166
4. Chen, N.F., Zhang, Z., Dai, Y.X.: Research on the design of home adapted nursing beds based on INPD and entropy power method [J/OL]. Packag. Eng. 1–14 [2022–02–11]. 陈宁峰, 章彰, 戴宇轩. 基于INPD与熵权法的居家适老护理床设计研究[J/OL]. 包装工程:1–14[2022–02–11]
5. Jianning, S., Wei, J.: Design of rose bud picker based on AHP/QFD/TRIZ. Mach. Des. **37**(08), 121–126 (2020) 苏建宁, 魏晋. 基于AHP/QFD/TRIZ的玫瑰花蕾采摘机设计. 机械设计, 2020, 37(08):121–126
6. Zhou, S., Zheng, F.: Research on product design methods integrating AHP/QFD/AD. Packag. Eng. **42**(02), 150–154+166 (2021). 周生祥, 郑枫. 集成AHP/QFD/AD的产品设计方法研究. 包装工程, 2021, 42(02):150–154+166

Focus Estimation Using Associative Information to Support Understanding of Art

Shota Yamasaki[1]([⊠]) and Takehiro Teraoka[2]

[1] Graduate School of Engineering, Takushoku University, Tokyo, Japan
20m309@st.takushoku-u.ac.jp
[2] Department of Computer Science, Faculty of Engineering, Takushoku University,
815-1 Tatemachi, Hachioji, Tokyo 193-0985, Japan
tteraoka@cs.takushoku-u.ac.jp

Abstract. Research on text reading comprehension support has been conducted mainly through text leveling. Text simplification, for example, is a process of simplifying sentences or rephrasing difficult words into simple ones. However, there are some sentences for which simplification does not support reading comprehension. These include technical texts and texts that explain difficult concepts such as art and design. In this study, we visualize the points of interest that change throughout such texts. By doing so, the meaning of the original text is not lost, and the reader is given the opportunity to learn. Our approach uses time series, association, and word rarity to calculate a weighted average. We treat sentences as period-separated time-series information, and increase the weight of words in sentences that are newly occurring. We also extract the associative distance from an associative concept dictionary and treat the reciprocal as a weight. The rarity of a word is defined as the number of times it appears in Japanese Wikipedia. The higher the number of occurrences, the less rare the word is. Our experiments suggest that visualizing the points of interest in a text can support reading comprehension. In addition, similar concepts that do not appear in the text are output as points of interest, suggesting that they can support learning.

Keywords: Extraction of topics · Learning support · Original text

1 Introduction

With the development of information technology, large-scale data such as images and videos are becoming more widely used than ever. At the same time, text continues to be widely used as well.

For example, text is used to add subtitles to images and videos, and to provide explanations of the content itself. There is sometimes a resolution problem with images: depending on the screen on which an image is displayed, it may be difficult to understand what is depicted. As for movies, they typically have a time limitation, which makes them difficult to view at one's own pace. In addition, depending on the transmission speed and other factors, the resolution may become low or even stop in the middle. Text, on the other hand, is formatted for the specific device being used and is not affected by resolution. Unlike video, we can read text at our own pace, and the amount of information per character is not large. Given this background, it is unlikely that text will disappear from use.

However, reading texts requires training. This is particularly true when reading specialized texts such as art and design descriptions, where it is important to understand the vocabulary and syntax. Such specialized texts typically include many uncommon words, and explanations of the meanings of the objects depicted and the purposes to be achieved by depicting them are often expressed using specialized vocabulary.

Vocabularies consisting of technical terms are often difficult to understand and therefore interfere with reading comprehension. This has led to various research on text simplification to support reading comprehension. The simplification of sentences is often achieved by replacing certain words and phrases with simpler Japanese. For example, Makihara et al. [6] developed a large-scale language resource for lexical simplification consisting of a word difficulty dictionary and a paraphrase dictionary to convert difficult words into easier ones.

Applying word leveling to explanatory text for art and design is not without its problems. By definition, art and design concepts can be difficult to understand, and there are many technical terms used to explain them. However, when these terms are simplified, the original meaning of the technical terms is lost, which may lead to incorrect explanations. Further simplification may result in meaningless sentences such as "good is good".

In this study, we aim to support reading comprehension without changing the original text. Our idea is to arrange sentences as punctuation-separated sentences and then visualize the points of interest in each one. This visualization enables the reader to become aware of the key points and understand the text more comprehensively. In addition, our system is able to output technical terms related to the text, so it not only supports the reading of the text but also promotes the learning of specialized content.

2   Related Work

There are several methods for extracting topics and semantic information from sentences, such as LDA [3], DTM [2], TTM [5], and Word2Vec [7].

Latent Dirichlet Allocation (LDA) is a basic method for topic extraction that automatically obtains topics by unsupervised learning from multiple sentences in advance and then extracts the topics by inputting the sentences for which the topics are to be extracted.

DTM is a method for extracting transitioning topics from time-series data such as newspapers and articles by using a model in which the distribution of words per topic and the ratio of topics evolve with time. Similarly, TTM is a method to visualize the change of interest in users' purchasing behavior. In both methods, sentence updates are treated as time, which means they cannot be applied to each sentence in a text to extract topics.

To support reading comprehension, it is necessary to visualize the concepts represented by each sentence in a text. However, even if the topic "painting" is displayed, it does not support reading comprehension of a text about painting.

In contrast to the above methods, which classify sentences by using topic models, Word2Vec vectorizes words that appear in a corpus. By vectorizing the words that appear in each sentence in a corpus and then performing some kind of calculation the average, we may be able to obtain an effective output for supporting reading comprehension.

Research similar to topic extraction for each sentence has been conducted for topic extraction in dialogue. For example, Georgescul et al. used SVM to perform topic segmentation [4], where they estimated the transition time of a topic in a dialogue. However, while topic segmentation shows that a topic has changed, it does not focus on what the sentence is actually about.

3 Visualization of Points of Interest Using Word2Vec

In this study, we first attempted to visualize points of interest by performing sentence vector estimation using Word2Vec [7]. As an example text, we used the "Construction and Aesthetic Evaluation" entry on the Mona Lisa page [1] of Japanese Wikipedia.

3.1 Extraction of Word Vectors

We extracted the vectors of words in a sentence from wikipedia-jumanpp.model, a model trained by Word2Vec from the full text of Japanese Wikipedia. Words in Japanese text are not separated by spaces, so morphological analysis is essential for preprocessing. In this study, we tokenized Wikipedia with juman++ [8] and used them as a token for training. The resulting model is called wikipedia-jumanpp.model.

3.2 Output Examples of Word2Vec

Examples of the output are shown in Table 1, where we can see many common words such as "draw" and "expression", along with a few incorrect outputs. All outputs were too general to be appropriate for supporting reading comprehension. The reason for such output is that Word2Vec does not take into account the flow of the sentence or the importance of each word that appears. We therefore developed a focus estimation system that uses information such as the flow of the sentence, the importance of each word, and the words associated with each word.

Table 1. Japanese example.

'Japanese sentence' English sentence	Point of interest
'『モナ・リザ』の女性像は、シンプルで安定感のある 三角形の構図で描かれており、重ねられた両手が 三角形の底辺を構成している。' The female figure in the Mona Lisa is depicted as a simple and stable triangular composition, with her overlapping hands forming the base of the triangle.	'構図' Composition
'胸、首、顔、手は光源を同じくする光に照らし出され、 光の効果が丸みを帯びたさまざまな表情を女性に 画面に与えている。' The chest, neck, face, and hands are illuminated by the same light source, and the effect of the light gives the woman a variety of rounded expressions.	'口元' Mouth
'レオナルドは、座する聖母マリアが描かれた、当時の 典型的ともいえる構成で『モナ・リザ』の女性を 描いている。' Leonardo painted the woman in the Mona Lisa in a composition that was typical of the time, with the seated Virgin Mary.	'描く' Painting
'レオナルドがこのような構成で『モナ・リザ』を描いたのは、 この女性像と作品の鑑賞者に距離感を 持たせる効果を意図していた。' Leonardo painted "Mona Lisa" in such a composition to create a sense of distance between the female figure and the viewer.	'表現' Representation
'左腕が乗せられた椅子の肘掛が『モナ・リザ』と鑑賞者とを 隔てる役割を担っている。' The armrest of the chair on which the left arm rests serves to separate "Mona Lisa" from the viewer.	'椅子' Chair
'女性は背筋を伸ばして座り、重ねられた両手は控えめな 立ち振る舞いを意味している。' The woman sits with her back straight, and her hands on top of each other signify her modest behavior.	'両手' Both hands
'視線はまっすぐに鑑賞者に向けられ、この静謐な空間を 共有することを歓迎しているかのように見える。' The woman's gaze is directed straight at the viewer, as if welcoming him or her to share this tranquil space.	'視線' Gaze

4   Visualization of Points of Interest in a Text by Chronology and Association

The vector output from our proposed system is called the focus. The name of the system is the focus estimation system.

4.1   Process Flow of Focus Estimation System

The system flow proceeds in nine steps, as shown in Fig. 1 and described below.

i. The system contains an "occurrence word list" that it manipulates to estimate the focus.

ii. When a sentence is input, it is tokenized. Content words in the sentence are added to the list of occurrences.

iii. The system also adds any words associated with the content words to the list of occurrences.

iv. At this stage, weighting is performed. The weights are calculated using the associativity and specificity of the words.

v. Next, the word vectors of the words in the list are obtained using Word2Vec [7].

vi. The weighted average of the weights of each word and the obtained vector is used as the focus vector.

vii. The word with the highest cosine similarity to the focus vector on wikipedia-jumanpp.model is considered the point of interest.

viii. The system also performs a decay of the weights assigned to the list of occurrences before receiving the next sentence.

ix. Words whose weights are less than zero are removed from the list of occurrences, and the system waits for input.

The word vectors are limited to "nouns", "adjectives", and "verbs". Japanese contains auxiliary verbs that do not have any particular meaning, such as "する" and "みる", which are not simply associated with "do" and "see". We exclude such auxiliary verbs because they have little impact on the focus of the text .

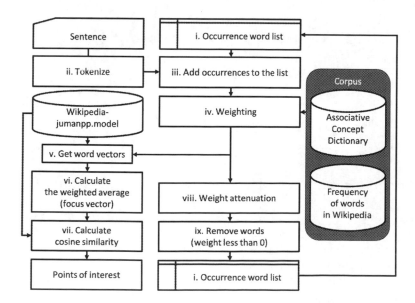

Fig. 1. System flow.

4.2   Interest Value

We define the weight as the interest value. The interest value is calculated for each utterance. Each value is defined as shown in Table 2.

When reading a sentence, a word that appears only once is often forgotten. Words that appear many times, words that are easily associated, and words that are not commonly used are all considered to be close to the focus of the topic. In our system, we use the number of occurrences of a word in a sentence, the association distance between the word and the occurrence, and the number of occurrences of the word in all Japanese Wikipedia sentences to create interest values in the following way. First, the number of occurrences of a word (N) is calculated as $N = 1/\log X$, where X is the number of occurrences in Japanese Wikipedia. If the number of occurrences is less than 10, the word is treated as $X = 10$. This is because the number of occurrences of a word on Japanese Wikipedia, which is several gigabytes in size, is presumed to be sufficiently small if it is less than a certain number. For words that appear in a sentence, N is treated as the interest value. Associative distances are extracted from the associative concept dictionary [9–12]. For words that are associated with a word that appears as a stimulus, the product of N and the reciprocal of the associative distance from the word that appears (N/[associative distance]) is added as the interest value. The N/association distance is set to RN.

The interest value decays after the addition is completed, and words whose interest values are less than 0 are deleted from the list of occurrences. The decay rate of the interest value is SN, where SN is N/M and $M <= N$. For example, if $N = 3$ and $M = 1$, a word that appears once has an effect for three sentence In this work, we set $N = 4$ and $M = 1$.

Table 2. Definition of variables.

Description	Variable
Weight added by occurrence	N
Weight of associated word	RN = N/Association Distance
Weight that decays as conversation progresses	SN = N/M

5   Output Examples of Focus Estimation System

Examples of the output are provided in Table 3. The output includes words such as "allegory" that are not commonly used. Two different outputs, "Description" and "Representation", were obtained by Word2Vec and by the focus estimation system, respectively. In Japanese, "Description" is a word that carries more nuance than "Representation", which makes it more suitable for describing the expression technique of a painting.

6   Experimental

To evaluate our system, we administered a questionnaire to two expert evaluators in art and design. The sentences in the questionnaire were the same as in the output example.

We first asked the evaluators to read through a text we prepared entitled "Construction and Aesthetic Evaluation" of the Mona Lisa [1], which is considered a generally accessible text. The results might be inconsistent depending on

Table 3. Japanese example (focus).

'Japanese sentence' English sentence	Points of interest
'『モナ・リザ』の女性像は、シンプルで安定感のある 三角形の構図で描かれており、重ねられた両手が 三角形の底辺を構成している。' The female figure in the Mona Lisa is depicted as a simple and stable triangular composition, with her overlapping hands forming the base of the triangle.	'構図' Composition
'胸、首、顔、手は光源を同じくする光に照らし出され、 光の効果が丸みを帯びたさまざまな表情を女性に 画面に与えている。' The chest, neck, face, and hands are illuminated by the same light source, and the effect of the light gives the woman a variety of rounded expressions.	'口元' Mouth
'レオナルドは、座する聖母マリアが描かれた、当時の 典型的ともいえる構成で『モナ・リザ』の女性を 描いている。' Leonardo painted the woman in the Mona Lisa in a composition that was typical of the time, with the seated Virgin Mary.	'寓意' Allegory
'レオナルドがこのような構成で『モナ・リザ』を描いたのは、 この女性像と作品の鑑賞者に距離感を 持たせる効果を意図していた。' Leonardo painted "Mona Lisa" in such a composition to create a sense of distance between the female figure and the viewer.	'描写' Description
'左腕が乗せられた椅子の肘掛が『モナ・リザ』と鑑賞者とを 隔てる役割を担っている。' The armrest of the chair on which the left arm rests serves to separate "Mona Lisa" from the viewer.	'椅子' Chair
'女性は背筋を伸ばして座り、重ねられた両手は控えめな 立ち振る舞いを意味している。' The woman sits with her back straight, and her hands on top of each other signify her modest behavior.	'仕草' Gesture
'視線はまっすぐに鑑賞者に向けられ、この静謐な空間を 共有することを歓迎しているかのように見える。' The woman's gaze is directed straight at the viewer, as if welcoming him or her to share this tranquil space.	'視線' Gaze

whether or not the text has been read, so we had the evaluators read through it first. Then, each evaluator was asked to rate each sentence and its corresponding word on a five-point Likert scale ("Excellent", "Good", "Fair", "Poor", and "Very Poor"), starting from the first sentence.

7   Results and Discussion

The results of the questionnaire are shown in Table 4. Focus estimation was the more extreme, with a higher number of "Excellent" and "Very Poor" responses compared to Word2Vec. In Word2Vec, "Fair" was more frequent than in focal estimation.

Table 4. Questionnaire results.

	Excellent	Good	Fair	Poor	Very Poor
Focus estimation system	18	13	3	7	5
Word2Vec	15	16	6	6	3

In addition, the evaluators offered the following comments after the experiment.

Focus Estimation: In the case of description, the system were able to estimate some noteworthy points. However, in the case of criticism, the system often failed to obtain them.

Word2Vec: The general and broadly ambiguous terms "drawing" and "expression" are mentioned several times, and while they don't go far off the mark, they do blur the focus.

7.1   Comparing Word2Vec and the Focus Estimation System

As stated earlier, Word2Vec outputs more words that are relatively common. This is supported by the large number of "Fair" evaluations in the questionnaire results. Although we were able to clarify a lot of the content of the sentence itself, the output of words such as "draw" does not support reading comprehension.

For the focus estimation system, the questionnaire results were mostly "Excellent" and "Very Poor", and the weighting of words by the number of times they appeared in the whole Wikipedia text seems to have had a strong effect. In particular, the word "Allegory" was a special word, since it explains that Mona Lisa was painted in a composition that resembles the Virgin Mary. However, the fact that there were many such unique words caused the text to diverge from its meaning. For example, although not shown in the output example, the output for the sentence "The woman's face is depicted using the sfumato technique, which 'expresses mainly the corners of the mouth and the area around the eyes

(Gombrich)' instead of drawing the contours" was "outlines". This means that the content being denied is the focus of attention. Instead of focusing on that, there are more appropriate points to focus on.

Such a problem can be avoided by improving the method of estimating the point of interest from the focus vector. For example, we currently output the word with the highest cosine similarity. By using the part-of-speech information of the output words and changing the output to only nouns, both Word2Vec and the focus estimation system should be able to produce more appropriate output.

Also, the focus estimation system is able to handle small shifts in topics. However, the text is not a complete time-series data. When there is a sentence where the content of the explanation changes from paragraph to paragraph, the information before the change gets in the way of the focus estimation. Therefore, after estimating the focus of all sentences, we should estimate the change of paragraphs and topics based on the transition of the focus. From the estimated information, the weight of noisy information can be changed to cope with major changes in topic.

8   Summary

In this paper, we proposed system that supports reading comprehension for texts that are difficult to understand, such as explanatory texts on art and design, and for which there are significant disadvantages if we were to make them too simple. We treated the sentences as period-separated time- series data, and visualized the points of interest in each sentence as words. In this way, reading comprehension support can be achieved without overly simplifying the text.

The proposed system is based on the extraction of sentence vectors using Word2Vec and focus estimation using three types of information: time-series information, association information, and word rarity. We found that the output of Word2Vec was not suitable for reading comprehension support because many of the words were extremely common. In contrast, the points of interest output by the focal point estimation were unique words, suggesting that reading comprehension support was possible. However, the words output by the focal estimation tended to be terribly wrong when they were wrong , which is a point we need to improve.

In future work, we will investigate how to weight the words when the content of a sentence changes significantly. We will also use the part-of-speech information to change the words that are output as points of interest. For example, the meaning of a picture changes depending on whether we're talking about "seeing a picture" or "painting a picture". Therefore, we will investigate whether outputting multiple points of interest for each part of speech will help in reading the text.

Acknowledgement. This work was supported by JSPS KAKENHI Grant Numbers JP18K12434 and JP18K11514.

References

1. Mona Lisa - wikipedia. https://ja.wikipedia.org/wiki/⟨processinggraph⟩. (in Japanese)
2. Blei, D.M., Lafferty, J.D.: Dynamic topic models. In: Proceedings of the 23rd International Conference on Machine Learning, pp. 113–120 (2006)
3. Blei, D.M., Ng, A.Y., Jordan, M.I.: Latent Dirichlet allocation. J. Mach. Learn. Res. **3**, 993–1022 (2003)
4. Georgescul, M., Clark, A., Armstrong, S.: Word distributions for thematic segmentation in a support vector machine approach. In: Proceedings of the Tenth Conference on Computational Natural Language Learning (CoNLL-X), pp. 101–108 (2006)
5. Iwata, T., Watanabe, S., Yamada, T., Ueda, N.: Topic tracking model for analyzing consumer purchase behavior. In: Twenty-First International Joint Conference on Artificial Intelligence. Citeseer (2009)
6. Kajiwara, T., Nishihara, D., Kodaira, T., Komachi, M.: Language resources for Japanese lexical simplification. J. Nat. Lang. Process. **27**(4), 801–824 (2020). https://doi.org/10.5715/jnlp.27.801. (in Japanese)
7. Mikolov, T., Sutskever, I., Chen, K., Corrado, G.S., Dean, J.: Distributed representations of words and phrases and their compositionality. In: Burges, C.J.C., Bottou, L., Welling, M., Ghahramani, Z., Weinberger, K.Q. (eds.) Advances in Neural Information Processing Systems 26, pp. 3111–3119. Curran Associates, Inc. (2013). http://papers.nips.cc/paper/5021-distributed-representations-of-words-and-phrases-and-their-compositionality.pdf
8. Morita, H., Kawahara, D., Kurohashi, S.: Morphological analysis for unsegmented languages using recurrent neural network language model. In: Proceedings of the 2015 Conference on Empirical Methods in Natural Language Processing, pp. 2292–2297 (2015)
9. Okamoto, J., Ishizaki, S.: Construction of associative concept dictionary with distance information, and comparison with electronic concept dictionary. J. Nat. Lang. Process. **8**(4), 37–54 (2001). (in Japanese)
10. Teraoka, T., Higashinaka, R., Okamoto, J., Ishizaki, S.: Automatic detection of metonymies using associative relations between words. In: Proceedings of the 34th Annual Conference of the Cognitive Science Society, pp. 2417–2422 (2012)
11. Teraoka, T., Higashinaka, R., Okamoto, J., Ishizaki, S.: Automatic detection of metonymic expressions using associative relation between words. Trans. Jpn. Soc. Artif. Intell. **28**(3), 335–346 (2013). (in Japanese)
12. Teraoka, T., Okamoto, J., Ishizaki, S.: An associative concept dictionary for verbs and its application to elliptical word estimation. In: Proceedings of the 7th International Conference on Language Resources and Evaluation, pp. 3851–3856 (2010)

Design and User Experience
in Emerging Technologies

Exploration of Pixel Digital Visual Design

Xiandong Cheng[1(✉)], Qian Cao[2], and Yushan Jiang[1,2]

[1] Beijing City University, No. 269 Bei Si Huan Zhong Lu, Hai Dian District, Beijing, China
doudesign@126.com
[2] Central Academy of Fine Arts, No. 8 Hua Jia Di Nan St., Chao Yang District, Beijing, China

Abstract. Today is a digital age, new changes have taken place in the tools/performance/presentation/application of visual design, digital image is the development of modern design, both visual content production and information presentation rely on pixels. A pixel is the smallest unit in an image represented by a sequence of numbers. Pixels are also a necessary element in digital visual design, it plays an important role in the process of design, but it is often ignored. This paper is an exploration of pixel visual design method, through the attempt in design teaching, it summarizes the characteristics/forms and methods of pixels in digital vision design. Starting with the basic principle of pixels, combining the relationship between pixels and hardware/pixels and software, the composition of 2D pixels/3D pixels is summarized. Pixels are small but important, pixels largely determine the performance of design services and e-commerce. E-commerce in the digital age is more like a "visual war" of "pixel battle", pixel presentation will make visual design more diverse, and it has better scalability and applicability.

Keywords: Pixel · Digital visual · Design

1 About Pixel

1.1 What Is a Pixel?

Pixels are the basic unit of image display, and they are usually expressed in pixels per inch (PPI) to indicate the size of the image resolution. Resolution and pixels are interchangeable, and pixels are actually the unit of resolution calculation derived from the printing industry. The word pixel is generated from the letters of the words in both picture and element, and it refers to the individual dots that make up an image. Each image contains a number of pixel dots, and the total number of these dots is the size of the resolution, but the term varies depending on the subject and industry involved. When a digital image is enlarged several times, it becomes clear that these continuous tones are actually made up of many small squares of similar color. These little squares are the smallest units that make up the image, and they are the pixels. There is no standard shape for a pixel, except that the smallest unit presented on many electronic display devices is a square. It is commonly understood that a pixel should be a square, but this is not necessarily the case. Pixels can also be rectangular or other shapes, depending on the hardware and electronic file settings.

M. M. Soares et al. (Eds.): HCII 2022, LNCS 13323, pp. 291–299, 2022.
https://doi.org/10.1007/978-3-031-05906-3_22

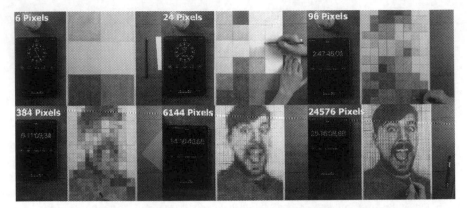

Fig. 1. Video screenshots. (I Draw MrBeast from one pixel to 20.000 pixels)

Form Wikipedia we know pixel as In digital imaging, a pixel, pel, or picture element is a physical point in a raster image, or the smallest addressable element in an all points addressable display device; so it is the smallest controllable element of a picture represented on the screen. A pixel is element with three Light emitting diodes (LED) - Red, Green and Blue. Each of this has controlled brightness[1].

Fig. 2. Reconstructions from pixels (A pixel does not need to be rendered as a small square. This image shows alternative ways of reconstructing an image from a set of pixel values, using dots, lines, or smooth filtering.)

1.2   The Role of Pixels

For both the picture and the camera, the pixel is the smallest imaging unit. The larger the pixel, the larger the resolution of the photo and the larger the printable size, which is the theory. As screen technology continues to advance, other metrics that affect imaging can be upgraded to match. Just the unilateral increase in pixels does not help a lot with the imaging effect. That is to say, the unilateral improvement of the smallest unit (pixel) is not very useful, it needs to be matched with the upgrade as a prerequisite. After the advent of the 5G era, the requirements for imaging have become higher. As screens become

---

[1] https://en.wikipedia.org/wiki/Pixel.

more portable, understanding the pixel principle and development becomes increasingly important for design.

The Number of Pixels and the Size of a Single Pixel are the Art of Balance
The balance and choice of portable screen size is even more of a challenge, for example, for cell phone screens and video cameras. Because the size of the cell phone sensor is currently difficult to see in a short period of time has been significantly improved. And in the case of image sensor size is limited, the number of pixels and unit pixel area of the two will have to make a trade-off. So, the emergence of pixel Quad Bayer Array[2] seems to alleviate this contradiction to a certain extent.

Pixel array of the new sensor
Quad Bayer Array (concetual diagram)

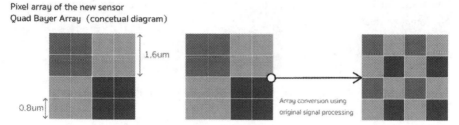

Fig. 3. Pixel array of the new sensor. Quad Bayer Array. (concetual diagram)

2 Pixel and Design

We hear the term "pixel" used quite often—not just in reference to photography, but even in everyday life. As we move further and further into the digital age, "pixel" is becoming somewhat of a household word.

For design, pixels are the key to the final image and the imaging laws that must be followed in the design process. The development of hardware and the update of soft-ware offer the possibility to present a richer pixel representation of the design. The process of hardware development has resulted in a unique pixel style.

2.1 Pixel Development

The history of pixels goes all the way back to 1839, when practical, commercially available photography was born. But, as Van Hemert explains in the video[3], pixels came around much later. When the color television was invented in the 1950s, the world moved much closer to the development of the pixel. In color TVs, electron beams hit an array of triads that created 512 horizontal lines to make up a picture. Those lines were later divided into rectangles. This made digital representation of images possible. Not long after, in 1965, the term "pixel" appeared for the first time.

---

[2] www.gsmarena.com.

[3] History of the Pixel as Fast As Possible. From: www.youtube.com/watch?v=DR2dRWfr7m0.

As technology continues to advance, the number of pixels per unit screen is becoming larger and larger, and the technology that works with it is improving. Image quality has become better and better as a basic requirement for imaging. Various changes in imaging technology have made the role of the pixel more than simply the smallest unit of the screen. For example, in interaction technology, the pixels in the picture become an important part of guiding or performing interaction on smart devices.

Screen Density Variations
High-density screens have more pixels per inch than low-density ones. As a result, UI elements of the same pixel dimensions appear larger on low-density screens. High-density screens have more pixels per inch than low-density ones. As a result, UI elements of the same pixel dimensions appear larger on low-density screens, and smaller on high-density screens.

Calculating Pixel Density
To calculate screen density, you can use this equation:

Screen density = Screen width (or height) in pixels/Screen width (or height) in inches

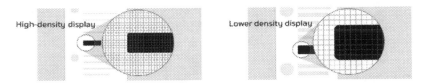

Fig. 4. High-density display & lower density display

Density Independence
Density independence refers to the uniform display of UI elements on screens with different densities.

Density-Independent Pixels
Density-independent pixels, written as dp (pronounced "dips"), are flexible units that scale to have uniform dimensions on any screen. They provide a flexible way to accommodate a design across platforms. Material UIs use density-independent pixels to display elements consistently on screens with different densities.

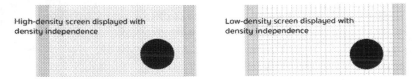

Fig. 5. High-density & low-density screen displayed with density independence

2.2   Pixel and Design Software

What LED of Pixel and Design Software have in Common

The LED has a customisable brightness, and the total levels are 255, so there are 255 different shade of a single led color, from dark (0) to the brightest (255) the color remains the same just the intensity of the light behind that color varies. Can we control this brightness of LED? Of course Yes! Our color system is based on this same thing, When you open color panel in any design software, you will see the values of the RGB as 0 to 255. Each of the shows different color in different combination and thats the level of brightness use put red to 255 you will see the brightest tone of RED, similarly for other colors also. The RGB varying from 0 to 255, holds each and every color inside it.

Pixels Are Good, But Pixel-Perfect Is Much Better

Pixels behave like a very very tiny grid, so we have to design in this grid, it seems to be impossible, but it can be done, but how pixels effect our design?

To find this answer we will do an experiment, I am using Affiniy designer[4] you can use any other design software. Create two similar rectangle, same width, same height and same colors.

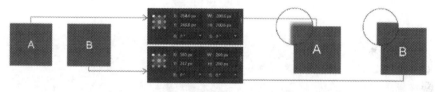

Fig. 6. Experimental process

Let's change the properties of Square A, in transform panel we will keep side of square as 200.6 px, and for Square B we will keep the side as 200 px, now let's export the artboard.

If we zoom the image, we will find the left image (Square A) looks pixelated and Square B looks sharp, this is because for square A we have dimension 200.6 px, so till 200th pixel will have used exact set of 3 LEDs. After for the .6 px, we used just 1 LED of the pixel.

2.3   Pixel Style

The pixel style was born out of the limited storage space and imaging capabilities of early 8-bit/16-bit computers. Sometimes, we call the process of creating pixel style "spriting". The name comes from the computer video game term "sprite" that describes a two-dimensional image that is assembled into a scene.

---

[4] Optimized for the latest tech on Mac, Windows and iPad, Affinity Designer is setting the new industry standard in the world of design. https://affinity.serif.com/en-us/designer/.

Pixel style evolved from the most primitive method of computer graphics representation in the form of a bitmap to a separate style of digital art creation. This style is often referred to as pixel art. Pixel Art does not refer to a single image, but rather emphasizes a style with clear outlines, bright colors, and an unconstrained style. Pixel art first appeared as icons in computer applications (Icon) and in early 8-bit video games. In recent years, it has been widely used in web icons, mini-games in cell phones, and personal pictures in instant messaging software.

The pixel style originated from video games, with early works such as "Pac-Man" (1980), "Space Invaders" (1978), and other well-known games. Early computers and video game consoles did not have the same access to 1080p or 4k as modern computers. So pixel artists found a way around these limitations by creating images from a limited number of pixels. Some people call the pixel style a derivative of the "pointillism" school of painting.

With the development of technology, smooth 2D curves and 3D drawings have become popular. Pixel style has become a retro form of visual expression, and this style at the same time in the culture and video games can not be separated from the relationship, and even become a symbol of game art. This style is still very influential in the eyes of lovers, and recent games are still made in this style. This style is also suitable for web and UI presentation because it consumes less computer resources. The pixel style abstracts the shape to a certain extent, making the graphics more minimalistic.

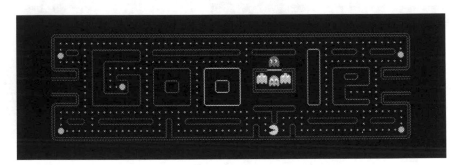

Fig. 7. Game graphics (Pac-Man)

2D Pixels and 3D Pixels
2D pixels are a form of computer graphics that uses the "pixel" as the basic unit. It is characterized by the arrangement of pixels in a distance array to form an image, and when you zoom in to a certain level, you can see the small particles inside, called pixel particles.

This style is similar to the "pointillism" created by the French painter Seurat in the late 19th century. Pointillism is a method of oil painting in which small dots are piled up to create a whole image. The painters of pointillism opposed the method of painting by mixing colors on the panel. They use only the four primary colors to paint, and use dots to build up, just like the principle of television display, taking advantage of the low resolution of the human retina to make people feel a whole image.

Fig. 8. A sunday afternoon on the Island of La Grande Jatte

3D stereoscopic pixel is a three-dimensional sculpture like form that appears in a variety of different materials to achieve two-dimensional or three-dimensional static or dynamic features that can be observed in multiple directions. Strictly speaking, it belongs to the plastic arts and is a visual product presented as a solid. (e.g. MINECRAFT).

Fig. 9. Game graphics (MINECRAFT)

3   Pixelated Visual Design

For the pixel style design approach we conducted a teaching experiment. The main focus is on the study of design methods for 2D pixel graphics and the construction/computation/digital presentation of 3D pixel models, etc.

Main Tools for 2D Pixel Graphics Creation
Pencil: used to set the color of a pixel.
    Eraser: used to clear the drawn pixels.
    Pickup tool (Eyedropper): used to pick up pixels.
    Paint Bucket: Fill an area with a solid color.

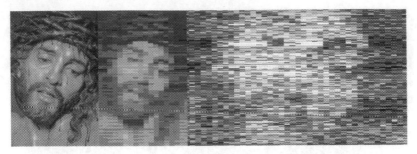

Fig. 10. 2D pixels art. Image by Xiandong Cheng

Fig. 11. AR design (3D Pixels)

This is one of the works in our course. The work uses 3D pixels to present the eaves of traditional Chinese architecture with sacred animals. The final presentation is by AR. (The model was created by MagicalVoxel and the AR was implemented by Unity Vuforia.)

In terms of expression, modern design elements are used to re-express the traditional Chinese image, and in order to better respect the traditional image of the divine beast, Chinese glaze is chosen as the main material. The use of modern interactive means and modern design language to express tradition is what is sought in this design.

4   Summary

The emergence of the pixel came with the electronic display imaging technology. The first processors were relatively low-level, and it did not have a brilliant display effect.

However, pixel graphics had the advantage of taking up less space and running faster, so they were widely used in the earliest days of electronic computers. With the development of graphics technology, pixels have been able to render incredible images. Nowadays, the use and design of pixel graphics is becoming more and more abundant. Pixel imaging must not only meet the visual development, but also take into account more possibilities for digital interaction, such as real-time pixel imaging calculations, etc. We hope that this article will provide more design inspiration and methods.

References

1. Qianbitou, Huihuicai: Designers talk about Pixel Design, 上奇科技出版社, 2004
2. Single-pixel imaging 12 years on: a review [3], https://opg.optica.org/oe/fulltext.cfm?uri=oe-28-19-28190i&id=437999. Accessed 30 Nov 2021
3. How to reconstruct an image if you see only a few pixels [2], https://towardsdatascience.com/how-to-reconstruct-an-image-if-you-see-only-a-few-pixels-e3899d038bf9. Accessed 20 Dec 2021
4. Quad Bayer sensors: what they are and what they are not [1], https://www.gsmarena.com/quad_bayer_sensors_explained-news-37459.php. Accessed 21 Dec 2021
5. Wikipedia, https://en.wikipedia.org/wiki/Pixel. Accessed 24 Dec 2021

Fit Improvement of Facial Interface for Steam Massage Glasses Based on Principal Component Analysis Panel

Yujia Du, Haining Wang$^{(\boxtimes)}$, Meng Qiu, and Yuxin Ju

School of Design, Hunan University, Changsha 410082, China
haining1872@qq.com

Abstract. Steam massage glasses is widely used as a wearable device to relieve eye fatigue. For this emerging product form, the fit of the facial interface and the eye and face region affects the efficacy of the product use and the user's wearing experience directly. This study proposes a virtual fit assessment (VFA)method to verify the fit of the facial interface to the shape of eye and face of Chinese adults. Based on Chinese Headbase (3400 samples), the features of head and facial dimensions were enriched and five representative headforms in different sizes of Chinese adults were conducted through principal component analysis (PCA) panel. This paper improves the facial interface shape of the existing steam massage glasses using the medium size headform by reverse engineering approach. The improved fit effect has been promoted significantly through VFA. The results of the study demonstrate the usability of choosing a medium headform as a reference for "one size fits most" product.

Keywords: Steam massage glasses · 3D anthropometry · Visual fit assessment · Principal component analysis panel

1 Introduction

Eye fatigue caused by long-term use of the eyes has a serious impact on eye health and sleep. Mori et al. [1] reported that a warm ocular environment helps relieve symptoms of dry eye disease (DED). Steam massage glasses relieve visual fatigue by increasing the humidity and temperature around the eyes. Unsuitable facial interface will have a great impact on the wearing experience and the product efficacy. The mismatch between the inner side of the glasses and user's eye and face will lead to excessive local contact pressure and serious skin injury [2].

There are few studies on the fit research of steam massage glasses, but there are many studies on the fit of head worn products. Based on an anthropometric survey of 3997 ventilator users, NIOSH proposed two test panels to construct a representative head to predict ventilator mask fit [3, 4]. Han et al. [5] designed an industrial respiratory mask in three sizes (small, medium, and large) for Korean workers by analyzing anthropometric data. Lee et al. [6] designed four sizes of oxygen masks to fit the facial morphology of

M. M. Soares et al. (Eds.): HCII 2022, LNCS 13323, pp. 300–310, 2022.
https://doi.org/10.1007/978-3-031-05906-3_23

336 Korean Air Forces through virtual fitting method. Ellena et al. [7] developed a new method to calculate the head fit index (HFI) combining 3D scanning technology and the gap distribution between the head and the helmet lining. Wang et al. [8] constructed a representative headform based on the main components of the eye and face to adapt the shape of the VR facial interface. A computerized approach would be a practical solution for the design verification of a large number of virtual individuals [6]. Therefore, it is necessary to explore an effective virtual design verification and design optimization criterion for judging the fit of steam massage glasses.

The purpose of this paper is to virtually fit the facial interface to the representative headforms, and then evaluate the fit of the steam massage glasses and the human eye and face surface according to deviation analysis. Finally, several suggestions were given for the facial interface design of the steam massage glasses.

2 Materials

2.1 Digital Headforms

Representative headforms are often used to verify the morphological design of head worn products. Ball et al. [9] compared the differences between Chinese and Caucasian head shapes using principal component analysis (PCA). Zhuang et al. [10] constructed five different head shapes through PCA panel for American workforce. Wang et al. [11, 12] established the Chinese headbase survey using high-precision 3D scanning technology, and constructed five headform size categories (small, medium, large, long/narrow and short/wide) based on PCA panel [8]. Chinese Headbase [13] was enriched to the size of 3400 in 2020 including 1660 males and 1740 females. Dimension reduction processing was performed using 15 facial characteristics (see Fig. 1) including Head Breadth (M1), Zygofrontale Distance (M2), Frontotemporale Distance (M3), Infraorbitale Distance (M4), Bizygomatic Breadth (M5), Glabella - Infraorbitale Distance (M6), Tragion Distance (M7), Otobasion Superius Distance (M8), Biocular Diameter (M9), Interocular Diameter (M10), Interpupillary Distance (M11), Alare Distance (M12), Nasal Root Breadth (M13), Eye Apex to Ear (Horizontal) (M14) and Eye Apex to Ear (Vertical) (M15). According to ISO/TS 16976-2-2015 [14], all subjects were divided into 8 cells based on PCA scores. The 8 cells in the main component column were divided into five size categories which are "large", "medium", "small", "long/narrow", "short/wide". The subject distribution of the five categories is shown in Table 1.

The medium size headform used in this study is shown in Fig. 2.

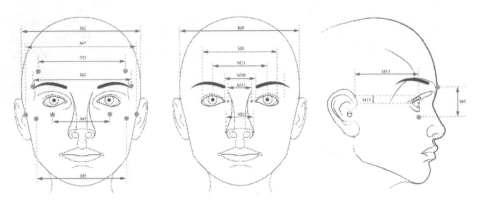

Fig. 1. 15 facial dimensions.

Table 1. Subject distribution by face size category.

Size	Male	Male/%	Female	Female/%	Number	In total/%
Small	25	0.74	347	10.33	372	11.08
Medium	674	20.95	1028	31.96	1702	52.91
Large	367	10.93	17	0.51	384	11.45
Short/Wide	202	6.02	199	5.93	401	11.94
Long/Narrow	282	8.40	76	2.26	358	10.66
In total	1550	46.16	1667	49.64	3217	95.80

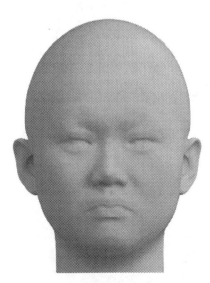

Fig. 2. The medium size headform.

Fig. 3. The steam massage glasses model.

2.2 Steam Glasses Model

Figure 3 shows the first prototype of digital model of steam massage glasses. The more fit the facial interface is to the eye and face region, the better the product use effect. The degree of fit mainly depends on the degree of fit between surface shape of the product and the eye and face region. The original digital model was divided into smaller regions in order to facilitate model analysis. The method of product partitioning adopted in Wang, H et al. [8] and Lee et al. [15] was used in this study. In addition to the overall region, the facial interface was divided into 6 regions, which definition was illustrated in Fig. 4. (1) Forehead (FH) (2) Right Temporal (RT) (3) Left Temporal (LT) (4) Right Zygomatic (RZ) (5) Left Zygomatic (LZ) (6) Nose (NS).

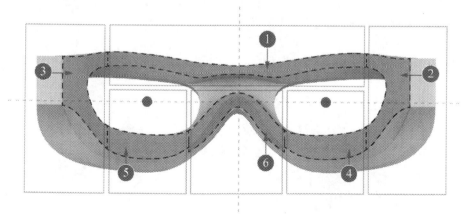

Fig. 4. Six regions of the facial interface.

3 Facial Interface Design

3.1 Wearing Guideline

The original steam massage glasses facial interface doesn't fit Chinese heads properly according to user feedback. After generating a representative headform, the size and shape of the product parts are determined by analyzing the 3D shape variation [16]. Therefore, the adaptability of steam message glasses to Chinese eye and face could be promoted theoretically through improving the interface based on the medium size headform constructed before. A wearing guideline of steam massage glasses was proposed in order to assume the consistency of the facial interface and the medium size headform. The procedures are shown in Fig. 5. The procedures are as follows.

Coordinate System Establishment. (1) Make the Frankfurt plane [17] of the headform horizontal. (2) The line connecting the horizontal midpoints of the inner surface of the sticker is the Z-axis. The parallel line connecting the midpoints of the lenses and intersecting the Z-axis is the Y-axis. The line passing through two intersections and perpendicular to the YOZ plane is the X-axis. Adjust the Z-axis to be vertical.

Coordinate System Plane Alignment. Make the XOZ plane of the steam glasses coincide with the midsagittal plane of the headform [17].

Frame Angle Adjustment. The pantoscopic angle is usually 8° [18] and the frame angle of curvature is generally 6°–10°. We defined 8° as the alignment standard and revolve the glasses frames by 8° around the Y-axis.

Pupil Distance Adjustment. Translate XOY plane to the pupil passing through the head, and move the surface until the interface fits the nose properly.

Alignment Completed.

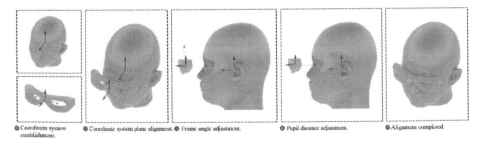

❸ Coordinate system establishment.　❸ Coordinate system plane alignment.　❸ Frame angle adjustment.　❸ Pupil distance adjustment.　❸ Alignment completed.

Fig. 5. The process of glasses-headform alignment.

3.2   Facial Interface Redesign

According to the wearing relationship between the facial interface and the representative headform in the virtual environment, the fit of the steam massage glasses can be improved by modifying the shape of the surface. The improved facial interface of the steam massage glasses is shown in Fig. 6. The design process is as follows.

Edge Line Generation. Copy edge of the bonding surface including the nose bonding surface.

Curvature Adjustment. Adjust the curvature and trend of the edge line according to the eye and face shape of the medium size headform to improve the fitting surface.

Alignment. Align the interface with the representative headform according to wearing guidelines in Sect. 3.1.

Fig. 6. The improved facial interface.

4   Virtual Fit Assessment

Virtual fit assessment (VFA) is a method that uses computer-aided design tools to restore the real wearing relationship between product parts and 3D headforms in a virtual environment, and evaluates the fit of product parts through virtual wearing characteristics. Lee et al. [6] evaluated the horizontal distance between the oxygen mask and the face boundary by virtual fitting to evaluate the suitability of each facial region. Wang, H et al. [19] proposed three conditions of the wearing model between people and products, which include the gap state, interference state and critical fit state.

In this paper, CATIA V5 6R2018 (Dassault Système, Vélizy-Villacoublay, France) was used to analyze the interaction between the glasses and the medium size headform. Fitting properties were evaluated in this study by using deviation analysis to better understand the spatial relative position between products and headform. Gap distance < 0 mm means the existence of interference. Gap distance > 0 mm can be interpreted as gaps. Gap distance = 0 mm means that there is a perfect fit between the two surfaces.

As shown in Fig. 7, the red area indicates that the area is in gap state (>0.6 mm), the blue area indicates interference state (<0.2 mm), and the green area indicates that the area is in critical fit state (−0.2 mm–0.6 mm). According to the deviation analysis data, there are large gaps between RT and LT. And RT, LT, RZ and LZ all have obvious interference. The improved interface has fewer red (gap) and blue (interference) areas, and overall distance distribution is more uniform.

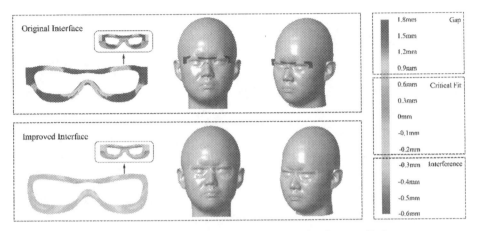

Fig. 7. Deviation analysis texture maps. (Color figure online)

5 Discussion

Three parameters were obtained to describe the VFA in this paper. (1) Gap mean distance (GMD), the average of all positive gap distances. (2) Interference mean distance (IMD), the average of all negative gap distances. (3) Gap Uniformity (GU), the standard deviation of deviation distances [7]. (4) Critical Fit Area (CFA), the ratio of the interface region where is in critical fit state. For steam massage glasses, GMD and IMD indicate the similarity between the shape of the facial interface and the headform. A small GU means a better fit. The larger the critical fit area, the easier it is to relieve the contact pressure generated when user wears [19].

The deviation analysis data is shown in Table 2.

Table 2. The deviation analysis data.

Region	Original			Improved		
	GMD (mm)	IMD (mm)	GU (mm)	GMD (mm)	IMD (mm)	GU (mm)
FH	1.974	0.024	1.147	0.561	0.111	0.305

(continued)

Table 2. (*continued*)

Region	Original			Improved		
	GMD (mm)	IMD (mm)	GU (mm)	GMD (mm)	IMD (mm)	GU (mm)
RT	3.167	2.456	3.088	0.556	0.053	0.297
LT	2.089	3.035	2.662	0.555	0.053	0.297
RZ	0.579	2.420	1.842	0.354	0.104	0.258
LZ	0.468	2.184	1.759	0.353	0.104	0.259
NS	0.728	0.296	0.722	0.447	0.034	0.276
Overall	1.933	1.558	2.294	0.540	0.075	0.311

Table 3. The ratio of different state.

Model	Gap (in %)	Critical fit (in %)	Interference (in %)
Original	51.03	25.79	23.05
Improved	36.03	63.98	0

The IMD results are shown in Fig. 8. The interference before improvement mainly occurs in LT, RT, LZ and RZ. In overall, the IMD was reduced by 95.19%. Interference in RT, LT, RZ and LZ was significantly reduced. The IMD in FH changed from 0.024 mm to 0.111 mm. The small soft tissue thickness in FH indicate that the forehead area is able to withstand bigger contact pressure. After the improvement, there is still some interference in LZ and RZ. Compared with other regions, the cheekbone area has a thicker soft tissue layer, and the facial tissue is more prone to deformation, which can help users withstand a certain degree of interference when actual wearing.

The GMD results are shown in Fig. 9. The GMD was reduced by 72.02% in overall. The major changes were found in RT and LT, which can be explained that the original surface has a slightly valgus shape in LT and RT while the valgus surface was changed when the design was improved. The gap between the steam glasses facial interface and the headform indicates that the user may experience steam leakage when wearing the glasses. It can be seen from the data that the average distribution of the gaps in each region of the improved facial interface is more uniform, which means that when using the steam massage glasses, local high humidity and high temperature will not be caused resulting in liquid water production and thermal discomfort.

The GU before and after improvement is presented in Fig. 10. The improved NS has the lowest GU which indicates the most uniform distance distribution compared to other areas. LT and RT have the highest GU, meaning that these two regions have the worst fit with the medium size headform and were significantly improved after improving. The GU of RT was decreased by 90.39% and the LT was decreased by 88.83% compared with the original design. On the whole, the GU was reduced by 86.42% from 2.29 mm to 0.311 mm. The improved facial interface shows a more uniform distance distribution in all regions.

In Table 3, the CFA was greatly increased to 63.98% from 25.79%. The area in interference state and gap state were both reduced, which means the improved facial interface can better withstand the contact pressure caused by facial tissue deformation.

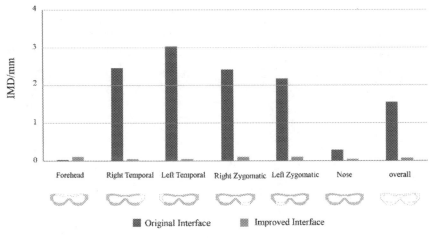

Fig. 8. The statistical results of IMD.

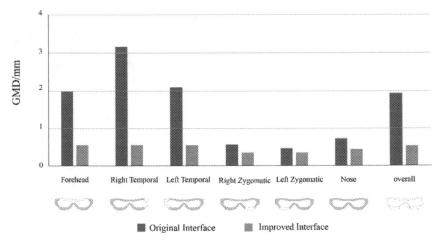

Fig. 9. The statistical results of GMD.

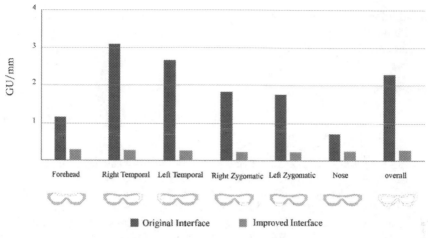

Fig. 10. The statistical results of GU.

6 Conclusion

In order to ensure the comfortable experience of users wearing steam massage glasses and maximize the retention of their product efficacy, this article fit the facial interface of the steam massage glasses to a representative headform. Taking the medium size headform as an example, design suggestions were given based on PCA panel, and a VFA method was conducted to verify the fit index of the improved design. The reduction of the area in interference state can alleviate the excessive local pressure during wearing. The lower the IMD at the same position, the smaller the contact pressure. The reduction of the area in gap state can alleviate the steam leakage problem. The lower the GMD at the same position, the smaller the steam leakage would be. The overall GU is smaller which means the pressure distribution of improved interface is more uniform. The area of critical fit state is larger which means the improved surface fits better to the headform. The VFA of the improved design of the facial interface shows good results. The conclusion of this study demonstrates the usability of choosing a medium size headform as a reference model for "one-size-fits -most" products.

In this paper, five Chinese representative headforms were generated by PCA panel. The facial interface of a steam massage glasses was redesigned by the medium size headform. According to [20], it was verified that there is no significant difference between the subjective evaluation of the improvement of VR facial interface using the medium size headform and using all five headforms, which means the medium size headform selected as "one size fits all" is available. The medium size headform was also adopted as the design reference for steam massage glasses in this paper. Considering the differences among product types and user experience, other headforms will be added into the design procedures in the future research, and subjective experiences will be added to verify that choosing medium size headform as a "one-size-fits-all" [14] model reference for the steam massage glasses is valuable.

In addition, the facial interface of steam massage glasses was regarded as a rigid body with the same material in this study, and the material properties of the face sticker should be taken into account in the future research.

References

1. Mori, A., Shimazaki, J., Shimmura, S., Fujishima, H., Oguchi, Y., Tsubota, K.: Disposable eyelid-warming device for the treatment of meibomian gland dysfunction. Jpn. Dent. Sci. Rev. **47**(6), 578–586 (2003)
2. Dai, J., Yang, J.J., Zhuang, Z.: Sensitivity analysis of important parameters affecting contact pressure between a respirator and a headform. Int. J. Ind. Ergon. **41**(3), 268–279 (2011)
3. Zhuang, Z., Bradtmiller, B., Shaffer, R.E.: New respirator fit test panels representing the current US civilian work force. J. Occup. Environ. Hyg. **4**(9), 647–659 (2007)
4. Zhuang, Z., Bradtmiller, B.: Head-and-face anthropometric survey of US respirator users. J. Occup. Environ. Hyg. **2**(11), 567–576 (2005)
5. Han, D.H., Rhi, J., Lee, J.: Development of prototypes of half-mask facepieces for Koreans using the 3D digitizing design method: a pilot study. Ann. Occup. Hyg. **48**(8), 707–714 (2004)
6. Lee, W., Jung, D., Park, S., Kim, H., You, H.: Development of a virtual fit analysis method for an ergonomic design of pilot oxygen mask. Appl. Sci. **11**(12), 5332 (2021)
7. Ellena, T., Subic, A., Mustafa, H., Pang, T.Y.: The helmet fit index–an intelligent tool for fit assessment and design customisation. Appl. Ergons. **55**, 194–207 (2016)
8. Wang, H., Chi, Z., He, R.: Fit improvement of facial interface for VR headset based on principal component analysis panel. J. Mach. Des. **37**(5), 117–124 (2020)
9. Ball, R., Shu, C., Xi, P., Rioux, M., Luximon, Y., Molenbroek, J.: A comparison between Chinese and Caucasian head shapes. Appl. Ergon. **41**(6), 832–839 (2010)
10. Zhuang, Z., Benson, S., Viscusi, D.: Digital 3-D headforms with facial features representative of the current US workforce. Ergonomics **53**(5), 661–671 (2010)
11. Wang, H., Yu, Y., Chen, W., Yang, W., Ball, R.: Responsive web design for Chinese head and facial database. In: Rau, P.-L.P. (ed.) CCD 2018. LNCS, vol. 10911, pp. 216–231. Springer, Cham (2018). https://doi.org/10.1007/978-3-319-92141-9_17
12. Wang, H., Chen, W., Li, Y., Yu, Y., Yang, W., Ball, R.: A 3D head model fitting method using Chinese head anthropometric data. In: Rau, P.-L. (ed.) CCD 2018. LNCS, vol. 10911, pp. 203–215. Springer, Cham (2018). https://doi.org/10.1007/978-3-319-92141-9_16
13. Wang, H., Yang, W., Yu, Y., Chen, W., Ball, R.: 3D digital anthropometric study on Chinese head and face. In: Proceedings of 3DBODY. TECH 2018–9th Int. Conference and Exhibition on 3D Body Scanning and Processing Technologies, pp. 287–295 (2018)
14. ISO/TS 16976 2: 2015. Respiratory Protective Devices: Human Factors-Part 2.\
15. Lee, W., Yang, X., Jung, D., Park, S., Kim, H., You, H.: Ergonomic evaluation of pilot oxygen mask designs. Appl. Ergon. **67**, 133–141 (2018)
16. Lee, W., et al.: Application of massive 3D head and facial scan datasets in ergonomic head-product design. Int. J. Digit. Hum. **1**(4), 344–360 (2016)
17. Ball, R.: 3-D design tools from the SizeChina project. Ergon. Des. **17**(3), 8–13 (2009)
18. Baboianu, G., Emil, N.I., Comeagă, D.C.: Measurement of anthropometric parameters using opto-mechatronic positioning system. In: 2021 12th International Symposium on Advanced Topics in Electrical Engineering (ATEE), pp. 1–4. IEEE, March 2021
19. Wang, H., Chi, Z.: Fit test method study of wearable products by combining virtuality and reality. Packag. Eng. **42**(12), 84–90 (2021)
20. Chi, Z.: Fit research for the facial interface of virtual reality head mounted display. Unpublished Ph.D. dissertation, Hunan University (2020)

How Well Does the Algorithm Know Me?

A Structured Application of the Levels of Adaptive Sensitive Responses (LASR) on Technical Products

Julia Graefe[1]([⊠]) [iD], Doreen Engelhardt[2], Lena Rittger[2], and Klaus Bengler[1]

[1] Technical University of Munich, Boltzmannstr. 15, 85747 Garching, Germany
{julia.graefe,bengler}@tum.de
[2] Audi AG, Auto-Union-Str. 1, 85057 Ingolstadt, Germany
{doreen.engelhardt,lena.rittger}@audi.de

Abstract. The use of artificial intelligence (AI) in everyday products increases and thereby also the interest on human-AI interaction. Research on user-adaptive systems still lacks uniform terminology and common definitions. To fill this gap, a taxonomy of user-adaptive systems, the *Levels of Adaptive Sensitive Responses (LASR),* has been proposed in previous research. The LASR levels are a first step towards a uniform classification of user-adaptive systems, but still need to be validated in terms of comprehensiveness and accuracy. This paper presents an evaluation of the LASR taxonomy through its application on technical products, to examine whether the taxonomy is complete and applicable in a meaningful way. We used a four steps analysis approach, covering the definition of classification criteria, two research iterations on suitable user-adaptive product features, and the analysis to which degree these features fulfill the classification criteria. As a result, our analysis shows that nine out of eleven analyzed product features can clearly be categorized into one of the five levels of LASR. Two features showed characteristics of two different levels which reveals that the levels are not mutually exclusive but can be combined within one product feature.

Keywords: Human-computer interaction · User-adaptive · Classification

1 Introduction

Within the increasing potentials of artificial intelligence (AI), terms like intelligent, smart, personalized, or adaptive became a selling point for companies [24, 35]. Over the past years, research on the use of AI driven adaptivity to enhance the interaction between humans and technical systems gained a lot of interest in the HCI research community [48]. Adaptive systems change the way how humans interact with machines, as they are able to adjust their properties and behavior automatically, based on trigger events such as user or system states, contextual factors, and current tasks [13, 18]. The benefit of well-designed adaptivity is for example improving the usability of a product through more efficient [2, 32], effective [32], and satisfying interaction [31]. Another reason can be to offer a unique and individual user experience by presenting content in a way that fits the user's needs and interests [3, 5]. Adaptivity also becomes relevant for safety

© The Author(s), under exclusive license to Springer Nature Switzerland AG 2022
M. M. Soares et al. (Eds.): HCII 2022, LNCS 13323, pp. 311–336, 2022.
https://doi.org/10.1007/978-3-031-05906-3_24

aspects in automotive scenarios, as it can reduce the driver's mental workload [30, 46] and help to focus on the most important information or tasks [40, 49]. Although the field of research on user-adaptivity and human-AI interaction is growing, it still lacks uniform terminology and common definitions [26, 48]. Existing taxonomies on adaptive systems classify what kind of properties systems may adapt and which factors can trigger adaptivity [18, 28]. But they do not classify how the system comes to these adaptations, meaning if it's using deterministic if-then conditions or if it is learning about the individual characteristics and needs of a user. However, we believe that this will become relevant for researchers and developers when designing the interaction between humans and adaptive systems. Rittger et al. [42] present the Levels of Adaptive Sensitive Responses (LASR), a taxonomy that classifies adaptive systems regarding their personalization capacities and complexity. The authors propose five levels ranging from LASR 0 (no adaptivity) to LASR 4 (adapt to interpreted user states) and thereby state that adaptive systems can strongly vary regarding their knowledge about actual user needs and preferences. Generally, we see four main advantages for researchers and developers to use the LASR classification: First, LASR provides a uniform basis for researchers and developers to clearly define the capabilities and resulting technical requirements of an adaptive system. Second, using a consistent terminology makes it easier to compare products and communicate technical requirements to all stakeholders. Third, LASR may serve as a framework when evaluating adaptive systems and their HMIs, as the level of adaptivity may result in different requirements and challenges. Fourth, LASR can provide guidance in terms of data privacy as well as technical and legal requirements.

The LASR levels are a first step towards a uniform taxonomy of user-adaptive systems, but still need to be validated in terms of completeness and correctness. Hence, the aim of this paper is to evaluate the LASR taxonomy through its application on adaptive technical products. The goal is to examine whether adaptive features of state-of-the-art products can be categorized distinctly according to the five levels. Based on the findings of these categorizations, we will derive implications for the improvement and optimization of the taxonomy.

2 Background

2.1 Definitions and Terminology

Today's research still lacks an agreed upon definition on the meaning of "intelligent" in the context of human-machine interaction [48]. Terminology in this area varies, as terms like *adaptive, intelligent, personalization, mixed initiative* or *recommender system* are treated interchangeably [28]. Following a dictionary definition, the term *adaptive* is described as "having an ability to change to suit changing conditions" [11]. This is also applicable to adaptive technical systems, as a core characteristic of these systems is the ability to automatically change their content and/or behavior according to trigger elements [13, 18]. Thereby, the adaptations should always serve the needs and goals of individual users or user groups which requires the acquisition and application of a user model [9, 28]. Jameson and Gajos [28] therefore recommend using the term *user-adaptive*. Another term that is often referred to in the context of adaptivity is *intelligent system.* Voelkel et al. [48] conclude based on a literature review that adaptive is a core descriptor for intelligent user interfaces. An intelligent system can be defined as a system that "embodies one or more capabilities that have traditionally been associated more strongly with humans than with computers, such as the abilities to perceive, interpret, learn, use language, reason, plan, and decide" [29].

For consistency purpose in this work, we use the term *user-adaptive system* and thereby refer to technical systems that change their content and/or behavior based on the characteristics and needs of specific users or user groups.

2.2 Taxonomies on the Classification of Adaptive Systems

Literature reveals different approaches to classify user-adaptive systems. The framework by Feigh et al. [18] consists of two taxonomies: Taxonomy of adaptations and taxonomy of triggers. The authors categorize applicational fields of adaptivity into four major categories, namely modification of function allocation, modification of task scheduling, modification of interaction, and modification of content. The goal is to provide developers a guideline to determine the features of a system adaptivity can be applied to. Additionally, the taxonomy of triggers classifies events that may trigger adaptations. Feigh et al. [18] define a trigger for adaptivity as "information which can be sensed, observed, or modeled to create an understanding of context". Following their taxonomy, triggers for adaptations can be categorized into five different types: operator, current or predicted system states, environment, task-based or spatio-temporal based. The authors state that systems will often include adaptations in more than one of the categories and may be triggered by more than one influencing factor.

Another approach for categorizing adaptive systems can be derived from the work by Jameson and Gajos [28] who divide adaptive systems according to their benefit for the users. Therefore, the authors identify two main purposes: supporting system use, e.g., through adaptively offering help, taking over routine tasks, or adapting the interface to individual needs, and supporting information acquisition, e.g., through proactive information presentation, recommendations, or tailoring information.

Both of the above approaches aim to classify adaptive systems according to their functionalities and user benefits. A more technically focused approach is presented by Meyer et al. [34] who propose a multi-dimensional taxonomy, containing three different scales: level of intelligence, location of intelligence, and aggregation level of intelligence. The level of intelligence covers the degree of intelligence in a product which can reach from low to high intelligence. Following the approach by Meyer et al. [34], the lowest requirement for a product to be defined as intelligent the ability of information handling, meaning that the system manages its own information based on external factors. The highest level of intelligence in this taxonomy is defined as decision making, referring to products that can completely manage their own life and every decision relevant to this.

A brought range of taxonomies for technical systems can be found in the field of automation research with various approaches that classify the role of the human and the machine in automation scenarios [17, 38, 41]. Comparing different automation taxonomies reveals that they share basic similarities [47]. Taxonomies of automation focus on who performs a task, ranging from completely manual control, meaning that the human operator controls every action, to completely autonomous system control, without the human's possibility for intervention [38, 47]. In this context, Riley [41] offers an approach for the classification of machine intelligence as part of a framework for automated systems. In this work the author argues that automated systems are framed by two dimensions: the level of autonomy and the level of intelligence. The level of autonomy refers to the degree to which a machine can carry out actions on its own, while the level of intelligence additionally describes how the data is processed in the backend system. Riley's approach contains seven levels of intelligence (Table 1). The lowest level of intelligence does not contain any data processing. According to Riley, the highest level of intelligence is the operator predictive system which is able to predict actions or errors a human operator might make in the future. The levels build upon each other, meaning that higher levels incorporate every characteristic of the lower levels.

Table 1. Seven levels of intelligence by Riley [41]

Level of intelligence	Description
Raw data	No real data processing
Procedural	Act according to predefined procedures
Context responsive	Change behavior based on context
Personalized	Static user model of one particular person's preferences
Inferred intent responsive	Recognize operator intent based on behavior and context
Operator state responsive	Include information on operator's physical state
Operator predictive	Anticipate operator actions

2.3 Levels of Adaptive Sensitive Responses (LASR)

This section gives an overview on the *Levels of Adaptive Sensitive Responses* (LASR) which were developed in earlier work and first presented by Rittger et al. [42]. The framework consists of five mutually exclusive levels that aim to classify the degree of personalized user-adaptivity in technical systems. Even though personalization in LASR levels two and higher is usually achieved using AI and algorithmic decision making, the quality and capacities of the algorithm itself are out of scope of the taxonomy. Out of scope of the taxonomy are also scenarios where AI is not used to achieve user-adaptivity, e.g., image recognition. Originally, LASR was developed in the automotive context but is also applicable in other sectors like smartphone or computer applications.

LASR 0 describes systems that do not offer any kind of permanent personalization, neither manually nor automatically. Actions that are made in these systems will be reset after every use and must be executed again upon restart. LASR 0 does not require user identification and data collection.

LASR 1 systems represent what is called *adaptable systems* by Jameson and Gajos [28]. Users can customize the system's content and/or behavior manually based on their own preferences. These manual adaptations will be saved and applied upon system start.

At this point, user identification is needed to assign saved settings to the corresponding users.

LASR 2 covers the first instance of automated adaptivity, which is based on predefined static rules implemented in the system during development phase. Different to LASR 1, systems on this level do not necessarily need to identify individual users, as the rules are deterministically set for every user or user groups. Instead, systems need observational abilities to identify factors that trigger the predefined adaptations, e.g., user information, system states or environmental factors.

LASR 3 is the first level to incorporate continuous machine learning to realize user-adaptivity based on individual factors. LASR 3 systems can but do not necessarily have to include surrounding factors into the calculation of adaptations, e.g., the context of use and the system state. On this level, user-identification as well as the setup and continuous advancement of an individual user model related to particular users is needed.

LASR 4 includes systems that can detect and learn about internal factors like the user's emotional state or personality. They can transfer their knowledge on inner user states to changes in needs and preferences depending on different states, contexts, and situations. Thereby, the system interprets user needs based on the combination of directly observable (e.g., interaction patterns) and non-directly observable (e.g., emotions) behavior.

3 Classification of User-Adaptive Products

The taxonomy presented in Sect. 2.3 proposes an approach for a uniform understanding of how personalization can be realized in user-adaptive, technical systems. Nevertheless, the five levels need to be validated regarding their applicability and completeness. To achieve this, we have conducted an analysis on currently popular technical products that use adaptivity to enhance the users' interaction. Our goal was to see whether the analyzed product features fit into the LASR classification and thereby reveal if the taxonomy is comprehensive, complete, and applicable in a meaningful way. Even though LASR was developed for the automotive context, we additionally selected technical products from other areas, such as smartphones, web applications, fitness tracker, and smart-home devices, to execute the analysis. This is due to the fact that we believe that LASR is also suitable to other fields of technical products besides the automotive context. The following sections present the procedure of our analysis as well as the outcome of the four analysis steps.

3.1 Step One: Setup of Classification Criteria

To provide an objective way to classify technical products by the LASR levels, we defined criteria that must be fulfilled to achieve a specific level. They are presented in Table 2. Two classification categories are relevant for LASR: the data and the calculation process. Data describes the type of data the system is able to collect and analyze in order to achieve user-adaptivity. Thereby, a system does not necessarily need to consider every data that can play a role in the corresponding level but must fulfill the minimum requirements that are marked in the table below. The data can be differentiated by three sources: User, environment, and system.

User data describes data that is related directly to individual user characteristics and/or behavior. *User identification* refers to any kind of process to identify a person and separate them from others (e.g., user profiles) and includes personal data that is related to the identification, like birthday or gender of a person. *Interaction patterns* describe indirect observations that can be made from the sum of various user inputs within the system and related products, for example whether a certain action is performed several times. *Physiological parameters* are defined as measures made from the human body, e.g., the heart rate or eye movements. *Personal preference settings* are settings included in algorithm-based systems to offer the user the possibility to manually enter additional personal information about themselves to support better adaptivity, e.g., telling the system about vegan nutrition for restaurant recommendations. Last, *inner states* describe human parameters that cannot be measured directly by physical metrics, e.g., emotions or personality.

Environmental data refer to influencing factors from both, the general context of use as well as situational factors and conditions resulting from the surrounding environment. They contain three data types: The *device* that is used to run the system, *spatio-temporal* factors (e.g., location, date, and time) and *environmental conditions* covering all factors influencing the interaction from the outside surrounding.

System data contains *direct manipulation* which refers to any kind of direct inputs made by users, either to trigger a manual adaptation (e.g., change the color of ambient lighting inside a car) or to execute an event which is then linked to an adaptation (e.g., select activating music playlist and automatically get a suitable ambient lighting color). Direct manipulation always refers to one specific self-contained event and not the sum of several different events, what separates it from interaction patterns. *System state* is a status that a system can hold and defines the overall conditions the system is used in from technical point of view. *Meta data* can be understood as information inputs that are given to specific elements of the system from the developer's side (e.g., genre of a movie or company goals that influence adaptivity).

Another influencing factor for the classification according to the LASR taxonomy is the data processing, describing the way how input data is used by the system to achieve user-adaptivity. For the LASR framework, we focus on the basic principles of calculating suitable adaptations and do not go into detail regarding the underlying algorithms. All levels differentiate from each other by how the data is processed and how adaptations are calculated. The following table summarizes the input data and describes the calculation process for each LASR level:

Table 2. Classification criteria for the five LASR levels

LASR	User data	Context data	System data	Data processing
0	—	—	Direct manipulation*	—
1	User identification*	—	Direct manipulation*	Saving and connecting inputs to a specific user*
2	Interaction patterns Physiological parameters	Device Spatio-temporal Environmental conditions	Direct manipulation System state Meta data	Pre-defined adaptations that are similar to every user and do not evolve over time*
3	User identification* Interaction patterns Physiological parameters Personal preference settings	Device Spatio-temporal Environmental conditions	Direct manipulation System state Meta data	Adapting to observations: Live learning based on directly measurable data* User-adaptivity adjusts over time based on continuous learning*
4	User identification* Interaction patterns Physiological parameters Personal preference settings Inner states*	Device Spatio-temporal Environmental conditions	Direct manipulation System state Meta data	Adapting to observations: live learning based on directly measurable data* Adapting to interpretations: learned user-adaptivity is influenced by interpretation of causalities between inner states and resulting situational changes in needs and preferences* User-adaptivity adjusts over time based on continuous learning*

Must apply at this level

3.2   Step Two: Research Iteration One – Products

In a second step, we conducted literature [6, 15] and internet research [24, 39, 44] to find out which technical products are currently popular on the market and in the field of adaptivity. In total, our research revealed twelve categories with one product representing each category. An overview can be found in Table 3. We aimed to cover a wide range of product categories to get an extensive impression on the applicability of LASR in the different fields of use.

Table 3. Product list resulting from first research iteration on user-adaptive products

No.	Product	Category	Description
1	Amazon Shopping	E-commerce	Web
2	Google Maps	Navigation	Smartphone
3	Spotify	Music streaming	Smartphone
4	Fitbit	Activity tracker	Device/Smartphone
5	Instagram	Social network	Smartphone
6	Gmail	Email	Web
7	Siri	Voice assistant	Smartphone
8	Google Search	Web search	Web
9	Netflix	Video streaming	Web
10	Google Pixel 6	Smartphone	Device
11	Nio ES8	Automotive	Device
12	Philips Hue with IFTTT	Smart Home	Device

3.3   Step Three: Research Iteration Two – Features

After we had determined which products should be included into the analysis, our next step was to research specific product features that are suitable to be classified by the LASR taxonomy. We decided to analyze one feature per product to keep the analysis manageable. For this purpose, we carried out an internet research using the predefined keywords "product name + 'AI features'", to get an overview how the products use AI to enhance human interaction and experience with the product. Out of this research, we made up a list of all resulting features for each product from which we then selected one feature each to proceed the analysis (Table 4). We focused on core features of the products that simultaneously have the potential to offer user-adaptive personalization. We excluded AI features that do not refer to user-adaptivity but are used for different purposes, e.g., the camera algorithms from Google Pixel 6 [14], as these features are out of scope for LASR. Additionally, we excluded Apple Siri from further analyses because Siri represents the voice user interface for Apple features rather than a feature on its own. Even though we believe that LASR could be applied to the HMI layer of products as well, the current work focusses on the features themselves. To validate information from the internet research, we double-checked feature descriptions from third party websites with information given on the companies' websites, whenever possible.

Table 4. Feature list resulting from second research iteration

Product	Feature	Description	Reference
Amazon	Amazon personalize	Personalization algorithm to offer individualized real-time product recommendations	[4]
Google Maps	Matches	Indicates the match between a place on Google Maps and the user's individual preferences	[21]
Spotify	Music recommendations	Personalized music recommendations for individual users	[1]
Fitbit	Daily readiness	Calculation of a daily score on the user's fitness to offer recommendations on an appropriate level of physical activities	[19]
Instagram	Intelligent explore page	Presentation of content the user might be interested in based on interaction with similar contents	[33]
Gmail	Smart reply	Suggestions for email replies are tailored to the content of the email and personal interaction style	[25]
Google Search	Personalized advertisement	Presentation of ads that are based on interaction profiles, personal data and current situation	[23]
Netflix	Movie recommendations	Content is promoted to users based on watching history of other users with similar taste	[37]
Google Pixel 6	Material You	The whole UI redesigns based on an input image chosen by the user to match the image's design theme	[22]
Nio ES8	Nomi	Daily routines and travel patterns of a user are used to give routing recommendations and inform about family or business appointments	[16]
Philips Hue with IFTTT	IFTTT applets	Users can define behavior for smart home devices, services and apps based on "if this then that" rules to trigger adaptations	[43]

3.4 Step Four: Feature Analysis

In the last step of the analysis, we matched the information from research iteration two with the previously defined classification criteria. Therefore, we extracted all information on the processed data as well as the calculation process for each feature and listed the results in a table. The input data and calculation process are listed according to the categories from Table 2 and proved by quotes from research references. Using this procedure, we generated a list that offers an overview of the input data as well as the calculation process for every feature. The analysis list can be found in the Appendix of this paper.

4 Results

After analyzing the features, we compared the information from the analysis list with the requirements from Table 2 to make an objective assessment on the features' characteristics and how they can be classified according to the LASR taxonomy. The results are presented in Fig. 1. It shows that every analyzed feature contained at least one element of user-adaptivity, resulting in none of the features being classified as LASR 0. Overall, nine of the eleven features included in the analysis can be classified distinctly as LASR 3 systems. Two features, namely Material You and Philips Hue with IFTTT, showed characteristics of two different levels: LASR 1 and 2. They cannot be categorized clearly into one LASR level.

The analysis results show that the previously defined classification elements of data processing, *adapting to observations* and *adjust adaptivity over time*, apply to eight out of nine features categorized as LASR 3. All nine features are based on a learning system that adapts to individual user needs and preferences through directly measurable data. For eight out of the nine features we also found statements on how the algorithm and thereby the adaptations improve over time. Another classification element that is fulfilled by every feature categorized as LASR 3 is user identification, realized via user profiles or device identification, e.g., IP addresses. As LASR 3 personalization cannot be reached without a minimum of one data source used to calculate adaptations, this is also fulfilled by every feature categorized here as LASR 3. We found that besides environmental conditions, direct manipulation, and system state all types of input data appear at least once within the categorization of LASR 3 and the data sources differ depending on the type of feature. Nevertheless, all features except from *Fitbit daily readiness* analyze interaction patterns as part of their personalization process. Inner states are recognized by none of the analyzed features. As this is a minimum requirement for LASR 4 personalization, none of the analyzed features can be classified as LASR 4.

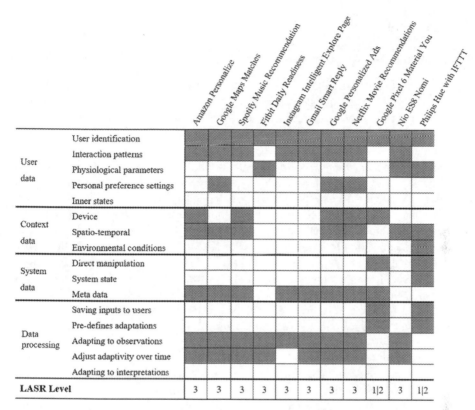

Fig. 1. Classification results

The personalization processes of *Google Material You* and *Philips Hue with IFTTT* did not fit into one distinct level proposed by the LASR taxonomy, as these features showed characteristics from both LASR 1 and LASR 2. Both features require user identification and direct manipulation to allow a manual setup of individualized user-adaptivity by the system. This is included as classification criteria for LASR 1. But in addition, the two features provide automated adaptations to the manually defined parameters once they are set. These adaptations are then fixed either by the users' specifications, as it's the case for *Philips Hue with IFTTT*, or by pre-defined system rules integrated by the developers, e.g., the way colors are extracted from the input image used to customize the *Material You* user interface. Finally, these two features show most of the characteristics related to LASR 2 but also some traits of LASR 1.

5 Discussion

5.1 Evaluation of the LASR Taxonomy

The aim of this paper is to classify state of the art user-adaptive systems according to the five levels of the LASR taxonomy and thereby investigate the taxonomy's applicability, consistency, and comprehensiveness. Our results demonstrate that LASR can be applied sophisticatedly to the features that were subject to this analysis, as nine out of eleven analyzed systems can be assigned explicitly into one of the five levels. For the two remaining features we were not able to classify them clearly to one level, as they showed characteristics of both, LASR 1 and LASR 2 systems. This shows that the individual levels cannot be seen completely independent from each other. Since each level is defined with unique properties that do not built up on each other, they can be combined and thereby complement each other. This is the case specially for the lower levels of personalization in LASR 1 and 2. For LASR 2 we propose to add the option that the pre-defined rules do not necessarily have to be the same to every user but can be individual through manual inputs as practiced for example by *Material You* and *Philips Hue with IFTTT*. A combination of LASR 1 and 2 could also be seen as a step between LASR 2 and LASR 3, as it is more personal than predefined general rules but still needs to be setup manually. Even though we think that this kind of combination is more likely to appear in the lower levels, it is still possible to also appear as a combination between LASR 1 and the higher levels 3 and 4. Therefore, we propose not to add new levels into the taxonomy to represent these kinds of personalization, but to state that it is possible to combine lower and higher levels within one feature. The combination of higher levels with manual control of direct personalization could also be favorable to user-adaptive systems in terms of usability and controllability as it provides a certain amount of control to the users. Nevertheless, our analysis shows that current LASR 3 systems do not offer the option to directly influence the systems personalization but more rely on indirect manipulation of the algorithm's results, e.g., through the option to add additional information on the user's own preferences or implicit and explicit feedback, which is covered by interaction patterns in this analysis.

The results for LASR 3 features demonstrate how these features resemble each other regarding data processing. All features reveal learning from objectively measurable data as well as improvements over time through continuous learning to calculate suitable adaptations. Therefore, the analysis shows that the classification covers the most important points of data processing in LASR 3. Besides user identification, interaction patterns are the most frequently used data type in level 3 features. This shows that interaction patterns currently are the most important kind of data used to achieve individual adaptivity and thereby an important characteristic for LASR level 3. Nevertheless, the example of *Fitbit Daily Readiness* shows that this is not an obligatory property. For further development and a more accurate definition of the LASR levels, interaction patterns may have to be broken down in more detail. Thereby, data like direct and indirect feedback, which is currently classified as interaction patterns, could be listed as separate characteristics for LASR 3 or higher.

Within the analysis, none of the features were classified as LASR 0 or LASR 4 features. For LASR 0, this is due to the research procedure. The research explicitly focused on products that are known for offering personalization and user-adaptivity. Since LASR 0 does not contain any kind of automated or saved personalization, it did not appear within the analysis. Nevertheless, we are still convinced that this level is necessary to form the baseline of the taxonomy. Despite the growing use of AI driven user-adaptivity in everyday products, it will still be important to offer manual standardized features for specific use cases where a high level of consistency is needed, specially within the automotive context. For LASR 4 the analysis shows that this is still not reached by today's user-adaptive products. We believe that this is due to two reasons: First, data collection methods as well as corresponding algorithms may still not be able to reliably identify inner states like emotion or personality. Second, adapting to inner human states in a reasonable way is a challenging task and still needs basic research foundations like for example the work conducted by Braun et al. [7, 8].

Overall, the analysis results prove that the previously defined classification criteria for data collection and processing match currently available user-adaptive products. For the input data, every data type appeared at least once within the analysis. None of the analyzed features used input data that could not be classified into one of the input data categories. The defined calculation processes also proved to be complete and distinctive as proposed by the LASR taxonomy as every product feature fit into one level or a combination of two levels. During the feature analysis we observed that current LASR 3 systems classify users into groups to learn about preferences of these groups and find out more about what similar users are likely to prefer. This basic principle of classifying users into groups is not explicitly mentioned in the LASR taxonomy but can be seen as a basic principle to generate user-adaptivity on LASR levels 3 or higher. The detection of inner states and the resulting interpretation of changes in needs and preferences remains open for verification in the future. This is due to the fact that these procedures are not established within the analyzed user-adaptive products.

In conclusion, the analysis conducted within this work proves that the basic classification approach proposed within the LASR taxonomy can be considered as meaningful and applicable to user-adaptive products. Even though LASR levels 0 and 4 did not appear within the analysis we believe that these levels are important for the completeness of the taxonomy. Within the application process, also the scope and focus of LASR becomes clear. The taxonomy defines how personal and individual user-adaptivity can be realized within technical products. This separates it from existing taxonomies, e.g., by Riley [41] where the focus is more on classifying automation in general and not necessarily in the context of user-adaptivity. Out of scope of the LASR taxonomy is the training of the backend algorithm used to realize the user-adaptivity within levels 2 or higher. Classifications on these factors already exist in form of machine learning classifications as well as AI taxonomies [12] and can be applied in addition to the LASR taxonomy.

5.2 Application of the LASR Taxonomy

To apply the taxonomy to a technical product, the procedure proposed within this work proved to be suitable and applicable. Nevertheless, the application through the classification criteria reveals to be complex and with a high degree regarding the level of detail. This might be too extensive for the everyday use of the taxonomy. Since LASR is meant to offer a fast and straightforward way to classify user-adaptivity, it needs a more practical classification procedure in addition to the one proposed within this paper. This can be realized within the next step of further developing the taxonomy, e.g., by proposing a decision tree to ensure a structured but simple application procedure.

5.3 User-Adaptivity of Today's Everyday Products

In addition to the evaluation of the LASR taxonomy, our analysis reveals an overview on the current state of personalization and user-adaptivity in today's everyday products. The results show that most of the analyzed features allow a high degree of user-adaptivity by fulfilling the criteria of LASR 3 systems. None of the analyzed features uses the detection and interpretation of inner user states. This shows that the highest level of user-adaptivity is still not reached in today's products. Within the LASR 3 features, most of the personalization is reached through the analysis of interaction patterns. None of the analyzed LASR 3 features considers environmental conditions that go beyond spatio-temporal factors. This could be due to the fact that these additional environmental factors, e.g., weather or social environment, are difficult to be detected by the system's sensors and data bases. Nevertheless, we believe that environmental factors offer great possibilities to enhance the advantages of user-adaptivity specially for fast changing usage scenarios, e.g., in the automotive sector.

Within the third analysis step, we excluded Apple's voice interface Siri from the analysis. This is not because Siri does not offer personalization. Digital assistants like Apple Siri or Amazon Alexa mediate the perceived intelligence or empathy of a system or feature. Assistants like any other HMI concept can be adaptive themselves. Hence, in the current work we focused on the adaptivity of products, while LASR could be applied also to the HMI layer of systems.

5.4 Limitations

The presented results are subject to limitations caused by the methodological approach of the analysis. We explicitly focused on user-adaptive product features within our research in analysis steps two and three. This resulted in having no LASR 0 features included in the analysis. The procedure was applied to products currently available on the marked, which excluded future technologies and thereby LASR 4 from the analysis, as this kind of personalization is currently not realized by the analyzed product features. Therefore, we were not able to validate these levels. Additionally, the analysis is based on an external view on the product's personalization strategies. We were only able to rely on information that is published by the companies about their used input data and processing procedures. Detailed information on the realization of user-adaptivity that may not be shared officially by the companies is not covered by the analysis. For companies that do not give insights into their personalization processes, we had to rely on third party information. This was specially the case for Spotify Music Recommendations and Nio ES8 Nomi. This could impact the classification results, as not publicly shared information cannot be covered by the analysis.

6 Conclusion and Future Work

The *Levels of Adaptive Sensitive Responses* by Rittger et al. [42] are a taxonomy that aims to classify personalization and user-adaptivity in technical systems. The taxonomy is meant to offer a first step towards the development of a consistent and standardized understanding on how user-adaptivity can be used to enhance the human-machine interaction. Nevertheless, the five LASR levels are still in an early stage of work and need to be validated regarding comprehensiveness and applicability. The presented work therefore applied a structured application of the LASR taxonomy on currently popular user-adaptive products. Within four analysis steps, a total of eleven user-adaptive features were analyzed regarding data collection and processing procedure and thereby classified into one of the five levels.

The results show that nine out of eleven features can be classified clearly into LASR level 3. Two remaining features showed characteristics from both, LASR 1 and LASR 2, and therefore cannot be categorized distinctly into one level. This validates the five levels to be well defined and suitable to classify user-adaptivity. The defined classification criteria are considered to be comprehensive and meaningful, as they covered all procedures found within the analyzed product features. However, some details on the definition of the different levels remain open. One point that became clear is that the levels cannot be seen as mutually exclusive but may occur combined within one feature. LASR levels 0 and 4 did not occur within the analysis process but are important parts to the taxonomy in terms of completeness. Nevertheless, they could not be validated within this work.

Overall, we believe that LASR offers a well-founded way to classify user-adaptive systems and help developers as well as end users to better understand a systems capacities and limits regarding automated personalization. The work of this paper paves the way to further develop the taxonomy and propose faster and more practical application procedures, e.g., decision trees. In the future, the taxonomy will be optimized and standardized as publicly available standard through the work of an international and interdisciplinary team of the International Organization for Standardization (ISO).

Acknowledgements. The authors would like to thank the AUDI AG for funding this work.

Appendix

Feature	Data	Reference quote	Data processing	Reference quote
Amazon Personalize	**User** Interaction patterns[1] User identification[2]	[1]"User interaction data on the website/ application is captured in the form of events and is sent to Amazon Personalize often via an integration that involves a single line of code. This includes key events such as click, buy, watch, add-to-shopping cart, like, etc." [4] [2]"User profile data including user demographic data such as gender and age. This data is optional." [4]	Live learning of user needs and preferences[1] through observational behavior[2] User-adaptivity adjusts over time based on continuous learning[1]	[1]"Amazon Personalize takes care of machine learning for you. [...] As your data set grows over time from new metadata and the consumption of real-time user event data, your models can be retrained to continuously provide relevant and personalized recommendations. [...] Make your recommendations relevant by responding to the changing intent of your users in real time." [4] [2]See input data
	Context Device[1] Spatio-temporal[1]	[1]"Improve relevance of recommendations by generating them within a context, for instance device type, time of day, and more." [4]		
	System Meta data[1][2]	[1]"This can be any type of catalog including books, videos, news articles or products. This involves item ids and metadata associated with each item. This data is optional." [4] [2]"Consider what's relevant to your users and what is important for your business when generating recommendations. You can define an objective, in addition to relevance, to influence recommendations." [4]		

(continued)

(*continued*)

Feature	Data	Reference quote	Data processing	Reference quote
Google Maps Matches	**User** User identification[1] Interaction patterns[2] Personal preference settings[3]	[1]"To see your matches, you need to sign in to your account" [21] [2]"Whether you've saved, rated, or visited a place or somewhere similar, your interactions with places on Google maps or Google Search" [21] [3]"We use your saved preferences [...] to suggest locations and content you might like" [21]	Live learning of user needs and preferences[1] through observational behavior[2] User-adaptivity adjusts over time based on continuous learning[3]	[2]"As you use Google Maps more often, you'll see matches for various places. These matches show how well a place matches your preferences." [21] [2]See used data [3]"They're unique to you and improve over time." [21]
	Context Spatio-temporal[1]	[1]"Your matches are based on your Google Location History" [21]		
	System Meta data[1]	[1]"The types of cuisine and restaurants you typically visit or avoid" [21]		
Spotify Music recommendations	**User** User Identification[1] Interaction patterns[2]	[1][45] [2]"Brands like Spotify accumulate a mountain of implicit customer data comprised of song preferences, keyword preferences, playlist data, geographic location of listeners, most used devices and more." [1]	Live learning of user needs and preferences based on directly measurable data[1] User-adaptivity adjusts over time based on continuous learning[2]	[1]"On every Monday, each and every users are presented with a customized list of thirty songs. And the recommended playlist comprises tracks – which user might have not heard before" [1] [2]"Machine learning enables the recommendations to improve over a period of time" [1]
	Context Device[1] Spatio-Temporal[1]	[1]"Brands like Spotify accumulate a mountain of implicit customer data comprised of song preferences, keyword preferences, playlist data, geographic location of listeners, most used devices and more." [1]		
	System Meta Data[1]	[1]"Spotify's AI scans a track's metadata as well as blog posts and discussion about specific musicians and news articles about songs or artists on the internet." [1]		

(*continued*)

(continued)

Feature	Data	Reference quote	Data processing	Reference quote
Fitbit daily readiness	**User** User identification[1] Physiological parameters[2]	[1]"Daily Readiness requires a Fitbit Premium membership." [19] [2]"The score compares your recent activity, sleep and heart rate variability (HRV) levels against your personal baseline." [19]	Live learning of user needs and preferences[1] through observational behavior[2] User-adaptivity adjusts over time based on continuous learning[3]	[1]"Before you receive your first daily readiness score, you wear your Fitbit device continuously for 4 days to get your baseline. Your readiness score is then based on how your stats in each category compare to your personal baseline. This data helps you understand how your activity levels, sleep patterns, and stress from the previous days contribute to your energy levels. Wear your device consistently for at least 2 weeks to develop a more accurate personal baseline." [19] [2]See input data [3]"Your daily goals and recommendations adapt with you over time" [19]
	Context —			
	System —			
Instagram Intelligent Explore Page	**User** User identification[1] Interaction Patterns[2]	[1]Instagram requires login to personal profile [2]"[...] we leverage accounts that people have interacted with before (e.g., liked or saved media from an account) on Instagram to identify which other accounts people might be interested in." [33]	Live learning of user needs and preferences[1] through observational behavior[2]	[1]"[...] we leverage accounts that people have interacted with before (e.g., liked or saved media from an account) on Instagram to identify which other accounts people might be interested in." [33] [2]See data
	Context —			

(continued)

(*continued*)

Feature	Data	Reference quote	Data processing	Reference quote
	System Meta data[1]	[1]"The most important signals we look at, in rough order of importance, are: Information about the post. [...] These are signals like how many and how quickly other people are liking, commenting, sharing, and saving a post. [...] we have rules for what we recommend in places like Explore. [...] These include things like avoiding potentially upsetting or sensitive posts, for example, we aim to not show content that promotes tobacco or vaping use in Explore." [36]		
Gmail Smart Reply	**User** User Identification[1] Interaction Patterns[2]	[1]Login to account required [2]"If I'm more of a You're welcome' kind of person, instead of a don't mention it person, over time, it'll suggest the response that better suits me" [25]	Live learning of user needs and preferences[1] through observational behavior[2] User-adaptivity adjusts over time based on continuous learning[3]	[1]"Smart Reply utilizes machine learning to give you better responses the more you use it." [10] [2]See data [3]"Over time, it will suggest the response that better suits me." [25]
	Context —			
	System Meta data1	[1]"The responses suggested by Smart Replay are tailored to the content of the email [...]" [25]		

(*continued*)

(*continued*)

Feature	Data	Reference quote	Data processing	Reference quote
Google Search	**User** User Identification[1][2] Interaction patterns[3] Personal preference settings[4]	[1]"Info in your Google Account, like your age range and gender" [23] [2]"If you're not signed in, your ad settings are saved to your device or browser." [20] [3]"Your current search query, previous search activity, your activity while you were signed in to Google, your previous interactions with ads, types of websites you visit, types of mobile app activity on your device" [23] [4]"Under "How your ads are personalized," select your personal info or interests." [20]	Live learning of user needs and preferences[1] through observational behavior[2] User-adaptivity adjusts over time based on continuous learning[3]	[1]"Google can personalize ads so they're more useful to you." [23] [2]See data [3]"Your previous interactions with ads" [23]
	Context Device[1] Spatio-temporal[2]	[1]"Your activity on another device" [23] [2]"The time of day." [23]		
	System Meta data[1]	[1]"Personalized ads aren't shown or hidden from you based on sensitive categories, like race, religion, sexual orientation, or health." [23]		

(*continued*)

(continued)

Feature	Data	Reference quote	Data processing	Reference quote
Netflix Movie recommendations	**User** User identification[1] Interaction patterns[2] User preference settings[1]	[1]"When you create your Netflix account, or add a new profile in your account, we ask you to choose a few titles that you like. We use these titles to 'jump start' your recommendations." [37] [2]"We estimate the likelihood that you will watch a particular title in our catalog based on a number of factors including: Your interactions with our service (such as your viewing history and how you rated other titles), other members with similar tastes and preferences on our service […]" [37]	Live learning of user needs and preferences[1] based on directly measurable data[2] User-adaptivity adjusts over time based on continuous learning[3]	[1]"Once you start watching titles on the service, this will 'supercede' any initial preferences you provided us, and as you continue to watch over time, the titles you watched more recently will outweigh titles you watched in the past in terms of driving our recommendations system" [37] [2]See data [3]"We take feedback from every visit to the Netflix service and continually re-train our algorithms with those signals to improve the accuracy of their prediction of what you're most likely to watch." [37]
	Context Device[1] Spatio-temporal[1]	[1]"In addition to knowing what you have watched on Netflix, to best personalize the recommendations we also look at things like: the time of day you watch, the devices you are watching Netflix on, and how long you watch" [37]		
	System Meta data[1]	[1]"We estimate the likelihood that you will watch a particular title in our catalog based on a number of factors including: […] information about the titles, such as their genre, categories, actors, release year, etc." [37]		
Google Pixel 6 Material You	**User** User identification[1]	[1]Android Phones require login to Google accounts	Saving and connecting inputs to a specific user[1] Pre-defined adaptations that are similar to every user and do not evolve over time[1]	[1]"When a user chooses a wallpaper, the entire UI and theme update to match." [14]

(continued)

(*continued*)

Feature	Data	Reference quote	Data processing	Reference quote
	Context Device[1]	[1]"The UI reacts to screen changes" [22]		
	System Direct manipulation[1] Meta data[1]	[1]"We built upon this insight to generate unique Material palettes for everyone, derived from a personal signal wallpaper that can be applied to their entire experience" [22]		
Nio ES8 Nomi	**User** User identification[1] Interaction patterns[1] Physiological parameters[2]	[1]"NOMI learns user preferences over time to understand the specific context of the car in relation to its owner. For instance, NOMI can set the personal seating and steering wheel positions whenever it senses a driver approaching the vehicle." [16] [2]"NOMI incorporates artificial intelligence with a charming face-like interface that swivels and blinks its oval "eyes" to address each vehicle occupant directly, depending on their location in the digital cockpit." [16]	Live learning of user needs and preferences[1] based on directly measurable data[2] User-adaptivity adjusts over time based on continuous learning[1]	[1]"NOMI learns user preferences over time to understand the specific context of the car in relation to its owner." [16] [2]See data
	Context Spatio-temporal[1]	[1]"NOMI further engages with users by understanding their daily routines and travel patterns, giving suggestions about the best real-time transit routes, providing notices about family or business appointments" [16]		
	System —			

(*continued*)

(*continued*)

Feature	Data	Reference quote	Data processing	Reference quote
Philips Hue with IFTTT	**User** User identification[1] Physiological parameters[2]	[1] IFTTT requires a Log in to use their applets [2] "Connect your wearables to Philips Hue through IFTTT and it will automatically turn on your lights in the morning when you have reached your sleep goal." [43]	Saving and connecting inputs to a specific user[1] Pre-defined adaptations that are similar to every user and do not evolve over time[2]	[1] "You can create your own Applets or enable published Applets by clicking on them." [27] [2] "IIFTTT, also known as "if this then that," gives you creative control over the products and apps you love. IFTTT Applets are simple connections between products and apps. When something happens in one application, an IFTTT Applet can update it in another." [43]
	Context Spatio-temporal[1] Environmental conditions[2]	[1] "Automatically turn on your Philips Hue lights when you arrive home. You can also create an Applet to turn off your lights when you leave." [43] [2] "Get a rainy weather update and the IFTTT Applet will turn your lights blue so you remember to take an umbrella with you to work." [43]		
	System Direct manipulation[1] System state[2]	[1] "This makes a widget you can add to the home screen on your phone. Then you can press the button to make your Hue lights dance as they do a color loop of rainbow colors." [43] [2] "When something happens, you'll be the first one to know by connecting IFTTT with Philips Hue. No matter if it's a phone call, e-mail or weather update." [43]		

References

1. AI TechPark: How does AI help Spotify in Picking up your Next Tune? (2021). https://ai-techpark.com/how-does-ai-help-spotify-in-picking-up-your-next-tune/. Accessed 10 Feb 2022
2. Aizenberg, E., van den Hoven, J.: Designing for human rights in AI. Big Data Soc. **7**(2) (2020). https://doi.org/10.1177/2053951720949566
3. Alvarez-Cortes, V., Zárate, V.H., Uresti, J.A.R., Zayas, B.E.: Current challenges and applications for adaptive user interfaces. In: Maurtua, I. (ed.) Human-Computer Interaction. InTech (2009)

4. Amazon Web Services: Amazon Personalize - create real-time personalized user experiences faster at scale. https://aws.amazon.com/personalize/?nc1=h_ls. Accessed 10 Feb 2022
5. Amditis, A., Andreone, L., Polychronopoulos, A., Engström, J.: Design and development of an adaptive integrated driver-vehicle interface: overview of the aide project. In: IFAC Proceedings Volumes, vol. 38, no. 1, pp. 103–108 (2005). https://doi.org/10.3182/20050703-6-CZ-1902.01196
6. Amershi, S., et al.: Guidelines for human-AI interaction. In: Brewster, S., Fitzpatrick, G., Cox, A., Kostakos, V. (eds.) Proceedings of the 2019 CHI Conference on Human Factors in Computing Systems. CHI 2019: CHI Conference on Human Factors in Computing Systems, Glasgow, Scotland, UK, pp. 1–13. ACM, New York (2019). https://doi.org/10.1145/3290605.3300233
7. Braun, M., Li, J., Weber, F., Pfleging, B., Butz, A., Alt, F.: What if your car would care? Exploring use cases for affective automotive user interfaces. In: 22nd International Conference on Human-Computer Interaction with Mobile Devices and Services. MobileHCI 2020: 22nd International Conference on Human-Computer Interaction with Mobile Devices and Services, Oldenburg, Germany, pp. 1–12. ACM, New York (2020). https://doi.org/10.1145/3379503.3403530
8. Braun, M., Weber, F., Alt, F.: Affective automotive user interfaces-reviewing the state of driver affect research and emotion regulation in the car. ACM Comput. Surv. 54(7), 1–26 (2021). https://doi.org/10.1145/3460938
9. Brusilovsky, P., Maybury, M.T.: From adaptive hypermedia to the adaptive web. Commun. ACM 45(5), 30–33 (2002). https://doi.org/10.1145/506218.506239
10. Bullock, G.: Save time with smart reply in gmail (2017). https://blog.google/products/gmail/save-time-with-smart-reply-in-gmail/. Accessed 11 Feb 2022
11. Cambridge University Press: Meaning of adaptive in English. https://dictionary.cambridge.org/dictionary/english/adaptive. Accessed 10 Feb 2022
12. Corea, F.: AI Knowledge Map: how to classify AI technologies (2018). https://francesco-ai.medium.com/ai-knowledge-map-how-to-classify-ai-technologies-6c073b969020. Accessed 10 Feb 2022
13. Dorneich, M.C., McGrath, K.A., Dudley, R.F., Morris, M.D.: Analysis of the characteristics of adaptive systems. In: 2013 IEEE International Conference on Systems, Man and Cybernetics (SMC 2013), Manchester, pp. 888–893. IEEE (2013). https://doi.org/10.1109/SMC.2013.156
14. Dotson, K.: Google Pixel 6 and Pixel 6 Pro deliver powerful AI features (2021). https://silico nangle.com/2021/10/19/google-pixel-6-pixel-6-pro-deliver-powerful-ai-features/. Accessed 11 Feb 2022
15. Eiband, M., Völkel, S.T., Buschek, D., Cook, S., Hussmann, H.: When people and algorithms meet. In: Fu, W.-T., Pan, S., Brdiczka, O., Chau, P., Calvary, G. (eds.) Proceedings of the 24th International Conference on Intelligent User Interfaces. IUI 2019: 24th International Conference on Intelligent User Interfaces, Marina del Ray, California, pp. 96–106. ACM, New York (2019). https://doi.org/10.1145/3301275.3302262
16. Electric Vehicle News: NIO's NOMI - World's First In-Vehicle Artificial Intelligence. https://www.electricvehiclesnews.com/TopNews/articles/nio-nomi-02122020.html. Accessed 11 Feb 2022
17. Endsley, M.R.: Designing for Situation Awareness. CRC Press, Boca Raton (2016)
18. Feigh, K.M., Dorneich, M.C., Hayes, C.C.: Toward a characterization of adaptive systems: a framework for researchers and system designers. Hum. Factors 54(6), 1008–1024 (2012). https://doi.org/10.1177/0018720812443983
19. Fitbit International Limited: Daily Readiness Score with Fitbit Premium. https://www.fitbit.com/global/us/technology/daily-readiness-score. Accessed 10 Feb 2022
20. Google: Control the ads you see. https://support.google.com/accounts/answer/2662856?hl=en&ref_topic=7188671. Accessed 11 Feb 2022

21. Google: Find places you'll like. https://support.google.com/maps/answer/7677966?hl=en& co=GENIE.Platform%3DAndroid#zippy=%2Chow-matches-are-created%2Chow-ratings-affect-your-matchest. Accessed 10 Feb 2022
22. Google: Unveiling Material You (2021). https://material.io/blog/announcing-material-you. Accessed 11 Feb 2022
23. Google: Why you're seeing an ad (2022). https://support.google.com/accounts/answer/163 4057?p=adssettings_gapnac&hl=en&visit_id=637790012644866590-302290455&rd=1. Accessed 11 Feb 2022
24. Google Ireland Limited: Pixel 6: Completely reimagined, inside and out (2021). https://store. google.com/us/product/pixel_6?hl=en-US. Accessed 11 Feb 2022
25. Google Workspace: Smart Reply for Gmail (2017). https://www.youtube.com/watch?v= CqHK-HzKbJo. Accessed 11 Feb 2022
26. Graefe, J., Engelhardt, D., Bengler, K.: What does well-designed adaptivity mean for drivers? A research approach to develop recommendations for adaptive in-vehicle user interfaces that are understandable, transparent and controllable. In: 13th International Conference on Automotive User Interfaces and Interactive Vehicular Applications. AutomotiveUI 2021: 13th International Conference on Automotive User Interfaces and Interactive Vehicular Applications, Leeds, United Kingdom, pp. 43–46. ACM, New York (2021). https://doi.org/10.1145/3473682.3480261
27. IFTTT: WTF is IFTTT?https://ifttt.com/explore/new_to_ifttt. Accessed 11 Feb 2022
28. Jameson, A., Gajos, K.Z.: Systems that adapt to their users. In: Jacko, J.A. (ed.) The Human-Computer Interaction Handbook. Fundamentals, Evolving Technologies, and Emerging Applications. Human Factors and Ergonomics, 3rd edn, pp. 431–455. Taylor & Francis, Boca Raton (2012)
29. Jameson, A., Riedl, J.: Introduction to the transactions on interactive intelligent systems. ACM Trans. Interact. Intell. Syst. (1), 1–6 (2011). https://doi.org/10.1145/2030365.2030366
30. Köhler, L.M.: AdaptivesInformationskonzept für beanspruchende urbane Fahrsituationen. Ph.D. thesis, Technical University of Munich (2018)
31. Kussmann, H., et al.: Requirements for AIDE HMI and safety functions (2004). http://www. aide-eu.org/res_sp3.html. Accessed 10 Feb 2022
32. Maybury, M.: Intelligent user interfaces. In: Maybury, M., Szekely, P., Thomas, C.G. (eds.) Proceedings of the 4th International Conference on Intelligent User Interfaces - IUI 1999, Los Angeles, California, United States, pp. 3–4. ACM Press, New York (1999). https://doi. org/10.1145/291080.291081
33. Meta: Powered by AI: Instagram's Explore recommender system (2019). https://ai.facebook. com/blog/powered-by-ai-instagrams-explore-recommender-system/. Accessed 11 Feb 2022
34. Meyer, G.G., Främling, K., Holmström, J.: Intelligent products: a survey. Comput. Ind. (3), 137–148 (2009). https://doi.org/10.1016/j.compind.2008.12.005
35. Microsoft Corporation: Everyday AI in Microsoft 365 (2019). https://www.microsoft.com/ en-us/ai/intelligent-apps. Accessed 18 June 2021
36. Mosseri, A.: Shedding more light on how instagram works (2021). https://about.instagram. com/blog/announcements/shedding-more-light-on-how-instagram-works. Accessed 11 Feb 2022
37. Netflix International B.V.: How Netflix's Recommendations System Works. https://help.net flix.com/en/node/100639. Accessed 11 Feb 2022
38. Parasuraman, R., Sheridan, T.B., Wickens, C.D.: A model for types and levels of human interaction with automation. IEEE Trans. Syst. Man Cybern. Part A Syst. Hum. Public. IEEE Syst. Man Cybern. Soc. **30**(3), 286–297 (2000). https://doi.org/10.1109/3468.844354
39. Pino, N., Skinner, C.-A.: Best smart home devices 2022: automate your home with these gadgets (2022). https://www.techradar.com/news/smart-home-devices. Accessed 11 Feb 2022

40. Reinmüller, K.N.C.: Towards the adaptation of warning driver assistance: behavioral effects and implications. Ph.D. thesis, Katholischen Universität Eichstätt-Ingolstadt (2019)
41. Riley, V.: A general model of mixed-initiative human-machine systems. In: Proceedings of the Human Factors Society Annual Meeting, vol. 33, no. 2, pp. 124–128 (1989). https://doi.org/10.1177/154193128903300227
42. Rittger, L., Engelhardt, D., Stauch, O., Muth, I.: Adaptive User Experience und empathische HMI-Konzepte. ATZ - Automobiltechnische Zeitschrift (11) (2020)
43. Signify Holding: Philips hue works with IFTTT.https://www.philips-hue.com/en-us/explore-hue/works-with/smart-home/ifttt. Accessed 11 Feb 2022
44. Similar Web: Top Apps Ranking (2021). https://www.similarweb.com/apps/top/google/app-index/us/all/top-free/. Accessed 10 Dec 2021
45. Spotify AB: GDPR Article 15 Information (2022). https://support.spotify.com/us/article/gdpr-article-15-information/. Accessed 10 Feb 2022
46. Tchankue, P., Wesson, J., Vogts, D.: The impact of an adaptive user interface on reducing driver distraction. In: Tscheligi, M. (ed.) Proceedings of the 3rd International Conference on Automotive User Interfaces and Interactive Vehicular Applications - AutomotiveUI 2011, Salzburg, Austria, p. 87. ACM Press, New York (2011). https://doi.org/10.1145/2381416.2381430
47. Vagia, M., Transeth, A.A., Fjerdingen, S.A.: A literature review on the levels of automation during the years. What are the different taxonomies that have been proposed? Appl. Ergon. 190–202 (2016). https://doi.org/10.1016/j.apergo.2015.09.013
48. Völkel, S.T., Schneegass, C., Eiband, M., Buschek, D.: What is "intelligent" in intelligent user interfaces? In: Paternò, F., Oliver, N., Conati, C., Spano, L.D., Tintarev, N. (eds.) Proceedings of the 25th International Conference on Intelligent User Interfaces. IUI 2020: 25th International Conference on Intelligent User Interfaces, Cagliari, Italy, 17–20 March 2020, pp. 477–487. ACM, New York (2020). https://doi.org/10.1145/3377325.3377500
49. Walter, N.: Personalization and context-sensitive user interaction of in-vehicle infotainment systems. Ph.D. thesis, Technische Universität München (2018)

Analysis of the Development Trend of Artificial Intelligence Technology Application in the Field of Sports-Based on Patent Measurement

Ti Hu(✉) ⓘ, Jianghao Guoⓘ, Tao Zhangⓘ, Juncheng Liuⓘ, Xuezhang Sunⓘ, and Zhaohe Changⓘ

College of Physical Education and Sports, Beijing Normal University, No. 19, Xinjiekouwai Street, Haidian District, Beijing 100875, People's Republic of China
huti777@126.com

Abstract. The patents related to the application of AI technology in sports from 1963 to 2021 included in the Derwent patent database were used as the data source. With the help of the ISS platform and CiteSpace visual analysis software, the patent data were analyzed in terms of annual application volume, geographical distribution, major patent owners, and hot technologies. The study found that: after 2015, the number of patent applications proliferated. The patents are mainly distributed in the United States, China, Japan, and South Korea, with the number of patents in China and South Korea growing the most. The primary patent owners are multinational giants such as Tencent, Microsoft, and IBM. The main technology areas of patents are distributed in database application technology, computer processing of video games, gaming, sports, and training equipment, and software products. The frontier hot technology areas are concentrated in developing emerging sports and leisure projects, sports e-learning equipment development, and deep learning algorithms.

Keywords: Artificial intelligence · Sports · Patent bibliometrics · Knowledge map

1 Introduction

Artificial intelligence has developed into a synonym for cutting-edge science and technology, leading the way in all walks of life, and has received significant attention from governments experts and scholars worldwide. The United States released "Preparing for the Future of Artificial Intelligence" and "National Artificial Intelligence Research and Development Strategic Plan" in 2016. Japan and South Korea have also released a series of policy documents such as the Next Generation Artificial Intelligence Promotion Strategy and the Mid- and Long-Term Master Plan - Preparing for an Intelligent Information Society [1]. The country also attaches great importance to the development of AI technology, issuing the Development Plan for the Next Generation of Artificial Intelligence in 2017. 2018 also saw the official release of the White Paper on Artificial Intelligence Standardization to promote the healthy and rapid development of China's

© The Author(s), under exclusive license to Springer Nature Switzerland AG 2022
M. M. Soares et al. (Eds.): HCII 2022, LNCS 13323, pp. 337–354, 2022.
https://doi.org/10.1007/978-3-031-05906-3_25

AI industry [2]. In 2021, the 14th Five-Year Plan of National Economic and Social Development of the People's Republic of China and the Outline of Visionary Goals for 2035 listed the "new generation of artificial intelligence" as one of the seven major areas of scientific and technological frontier research. This shows that the development of the world's technology has become a global race of artificial intelligence technology. Since the artificial intelligence player AlphaGo defeated the human world Go champion Lee Sedol in 2016, a wave of research on artificial intelligence technology has been launched in sports academia at home and abroad.

Several researchers have already analyzed the development trend of AI technology applications in sports. For example, Claudino[3] et al. searched articles on group projects using AI techniques or methods through PubMed, Scopus, and WoS databases and found that soccer, basketball, handball, and volleyball are the group projects with more applications of AI techniques and AI techniques show good prospects for application in group projects. Calabuig-Moreno, F et al. [4] conducted a bibliometric analysis of articles published in Web of Science on augmented or virtual reality technology in physical education and concluded that the specific research on the use of this technology in the application of physical education is still in its infancy. Lai-Bing Lu et al. [5, 6] used the literature retrieved from the Web of Science database as a data source and used the CiteSpaceV software to map the knowledge map of the development of artificial intelligence in sports. Gong Lijing et al. [7] analyzed global exercise prescription research hotspots and development trends through bibliometric and visual analysis and summarized the benefits of artificial intelligence technology for prescribing accurate exercise prescriptions. However, most of these studies are based on the perspective of academic papers, and domestic and foreign scholars have not yet studied the development trend of AI technology application in sports from the perspective of patent literature. As a special kind of scientific literature, patents contain more than 90% of the world's technical, economic, and legal intelligence information in various aspects [8]. The mining of patent literature can better identify and grasp technological development's historical, present, and future. Because of this, this study uses an econometric approach to analyze relevant patent data to reveal the current status and technological hotspots of AI technology application development in the field of sports.

2 Data Sources and Research Methods

2.1 Data Source

Derwent Patent Database (referred to as DII) integrates Derwent World Patents Index and Derwent Patents Citation Index, providing patent information from more than 40 patent offices worldwide, and is the most authoritative patent information and science and technology information database in the world [9]. Therefore, the Derwent patent database was chosen as the data source for this study, providing comprehensive and accurate data for this study.

The search strategy was based on the leading AI technologies listed in the "2020 AI Development Report" jointly published by Tsinghua University and the Chinese Academy of Engineering and the classification number represented by "sports" in the IPC classification system. 2021 In April, Tsinghua University and the Chinese Academy of Engineering jointly published the "2020 AI Development Report" (the Report). Artificial Intelligence Development Report" (the Report). The Report divided AI technologies into 7 AI key technologies and 13 AI epitopes based on the independent characteristics of the technologies. Through the analysis of the Report and the summary of the research on the application of AI technologies in sports, machine learning, deep learning, computer vision, human-computer interaction, database, and Internet of Things technologies, which are more closely integrated with the sports field, were selected for critical analysis. Therefore, we add "Machine Learning," "Deep Learning," "Computer Vision," "Human-Computer Interaction," and "Computer Vision." "Human-Computer Interaction," "Database," and "Internet of Things The terms "Artificial Intelligence" and "AI" were used as common subject search terms in addition to "Deep Learning," "Computer Vision," "Human-Computer Interaction," "Database" and "Internet of Things." Based on this, the results were restricted using patent classification numbers to obtain the research data for this Report. The search period was from 1963 to 2021, and 6,926 patents were searched on July 9, 2021 (see Table 1).

Table 1. Research data sources.

Listed items	Content
Data source	Derwent Innovations Index (DII)
Search format	TS = ("Artificial Intelligence" or "AI" or "Machine learning" or "Deep learning" or "Computer vision" or "Human–Computer Interaction" or "Database" or "Internet of Things") and IP = "A63*"
Time span	1963–2021
Search results	6926 patent data

2.2 Research Methodology

This study adopts patent metrics and applies the Intelligent Support System (ISS) for strategic consulting jointly launched by Tsinghua University and the Chinese Academy of Engineering, as well as the CiteSpace visualization and analysis software developed by Prof. Chaomei Chen et al. to draw the knowledge map of patents related to the application of AI technologies in the field of sports. The two analysis software was used to understand the annual application characteristics, geographical distribution, primary patent owners, and technical field distribution of patents related to AI technology application in sports. In order to achieve a more efficient and intuitive metrological analysis of patent documents. By analyzing and processing a large amount of fragmented information in patent information and using various mathematical methods and tools to compare, abstract, summarize and generalize, patent metrology can reveal the quantitative characteristics and intrinsic laws of relevant technology fields and predict the technological development trend of the field [10]. Knowledge mapping is a kind of network diagram that uses information technology and means to present the development trend and structural relationship of scientific knowledge in related fields in a visual form [11], and patent measurement analysis with the help of knowledge mapping can help improve the efficiency and effectiveness of analysis.

3 Overview of the Application Development of Artificial Intelligence Technology in the Field of Sports

3.1 Application Year Analysis

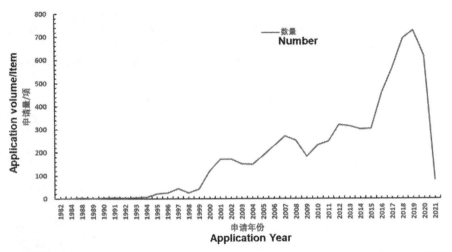

Fig. 1. Trends in patent applications related to artificial intelligence technology in sports (1982–2021).

The annual trend of application volume was plotted based on the patents related to the application of AI technology in sports collected from the DII database (Fig. 1). As can be seen from Fig. 1, although the patent data retrieval started in 1963, the patent applications of AI technologies applied in sports started in 1982. Therefore, the next part of this paper will explore the patents related to the application of AI technology in sports during the period of 1982–2021.

According to international practice, patent applications are published when they reach 18 months [12], thus resulting in some incomplete data for 2020 and 2021. However, the foresight of their application trends can be referred to the previous two years. From the trend of patent applications, the patent applications related to AI technology in sports have roughly gone through three stages.

1. The newborn stage (1982–1999): During this period, patent applications related to the application of artificial intelligence in the field of sports appeared sporadically, with a total of 182 applications, but there were also technological watersheds such as the victory of the artificial intelligence "Deep Blue" developed by IBM over the chess champion Kasparov in 1997. Weak computing power and insufficient intelligence

are the limitations of AI technology in this period, and AI technology in this period is a "weak artificial intelligence."

2. Initial development stage (2000–2014): Entering the 21st century, the number of patent applications for AI technology worldwide ushered in a period of rapid growth. Compared with the period before 2000, the patent applications related to AI technology in the field of sports in the new century ushered in a small peak of development, which is reflected in the continuous growth of the number of patents. The number of patent applications has increased from 120 in 2000 to 210 in 2012. After 2012, the number of patent applications declined slightly. However, it was generally stable, indicating that the inventions and patent applications in artificial intelligence technology in sports became active during this period but did not produce substantial breakthroughs and progress.

3. Rapid development phase (2015–2021): AI technology has made breakthroughs after 2011, and the prosperity of technologies such as deep learning, Internet of Things, and big data has driven the research of AI technology to another climax, and the number of patent outputs has been increasing [13]. The number of patent applications related to AI technologies in sports has climbed rapidly, increasing from 302 in 2014 to a high of 727 patent applications in 2019 and is expected to remain high for the next two years.

3.2 Geographical Distribution

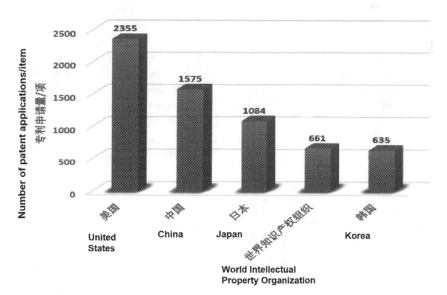

Fig. 2. Top 5 countries/regions in terms of patent applications.

Usually, countries/regions with many patent applications have relatively strong innovation abilities or considerable technological advantages. The top five countries/regions regarding the number of patent applications were obtained through statistical analysis of the number of patent applications (Fig. 2). The United States has the most in-depth research on the application of AI technology in sports, with 2,355 patents, which is the leading position in the world. In second place is China, with 1,575 patents. The third to fifth places are Japan, the World Intellectual Property Organization, and South Korea, with 1084, 661, and 635 patents.

The two-dimensional bubble chart of application time-application country can show the relationship between application time and application volume in each country more clearly, which helps to understand the trend of application volume in each country [14]. Therefore, this study further draws a bubble chart (Fig. 3) to analyze the number of applications in each country. From Fig. 3, it can be seen that the United States has an early development of research on AI applications in sports, which started before the 21st century and showed an increasing trend year by year. The United States pursues a "patent first" strategy, and its patent applications are usually strategically located in multiple countries and regions. Chinese patent applications related to AI in sports started in 2001, which is later than that of the US, and the number of applications in the early stage has been growing slowly. However, since 2015, Chinese patent applications have been proliferating, with the growth rate significantly exceeding that of other countries, and the annual number of applications surpassed that of the United States starting in 2017. Japan also actively applies AI technology in sports and has made relevant patent applications early. Japan's AI technology in sports patent layout started second only to the United States. In the early 21st century, related patent applications occupied the world's leading position. However, Japan, after the Internet era "fallen behind," its AI technology in the field of sports applications may also be affected by its own AI technology development bottleneck [15] related to the bottleneck. However, after Japan fell behind in the Internet era, the application of AI technology in sports may have been affected by the bottleneck of its own AI technology development [15], and the number of related patent applications has decreased instead of increased. The growth rate of related patent applications in Korea in recent years has been developing as fast as that in China, which is related to the strategic shift of Korea's technology giants such as Samsung and

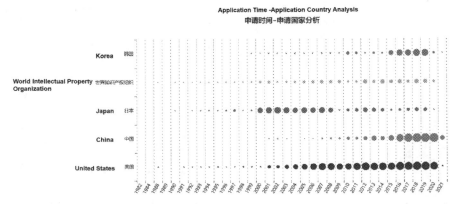

Fig. 3. Two-dimensional analysis of the time of application and the country of application.

LG to develop in the field of AI technology and the high priority given to AI technology by the Korean government.

3.3 Distribution of Patent Owners

The analysis of the leading patent owners within a technology field helps to understand the core R&D team in the field, facilitating the cooperation and communication among subsequent researchers and thus promoting the further development of the technology [16]. From the top 10 key patent owners of patent applications related to AI technology in sports in Table 2, it can be seen that the United States occupies four, China two, Japan three, and South Korea one.

Table 2. Distribution of major patentees.

Patentee	Country of affiliation	Number of patent applications/item
Tencent Technology Shenzhen Co Ltd	CHINA	188
Netease Hangzhou Network Co Ltd	CHINA	74
International Game Technology	USA	66
Bally Gaming Inc	USA	62
Konami Digital Entertainment Kk	JAPAN	59
Microsoft Corp	USA	55
Sankyo Co Ltd	JAPAN	53
Nhn Corp	KOREA	51
Omron Kk	JAPAN	48
Int Business Machines Corp	USA	46

Tencent and NetEase are the organizations with the most significant number of patents related to the application of AI technology in sports, with 188 and 74 patients, respectively. As two leading Internet technology companies in China, Tencent and Netease have business content covering various fields such as social, entertainment, information, and platform, especially in the field of video games, which occupy a considerable market share in China. The survey by Yang Yue [17] shows that domestic young people spend an average of 33% of their leisure time on e-sports and other online game activities, and some of them even reach more than 90%. Even if some people do not directly participate in video games, they choose to consume their leisure time by watching live online games, which shows that domestic video games and the video game industry have a broad development prospect. Through further analysis of the relevant patents applied for by the two companies, it can be seen that the relevant patent technologies of these two companies were applied for after the rise of the AI boom in recent years. Many applications were focused on the protection of technology at the level of commercial applications in the field of electronic games, while the key technologies (chips, platform frameworks, etc.) involving the application of AI technology in the field of sports are still weak.

International Game Technology, Paragon Entertainment, Microsoft, and IBM are the four U.S. patent holders in Table 2 with patents related to the application of artificial intelligence technology in sports. International Game Technology and Paragon Entertainment's primary business is the technical support and development of sports betting, providing platform technology, high-performance hardware, etc., to sports betting operators. Microsoft is an American multinational technology company that produces computer software, consumer electronics, personal computers, and related services. Since 2014, Microsoft has scaled back its hardware business to focus on cloud computing service support. Its patent applications related to artificial intelligence technology in sports are mainly related to video games, human motion recognition, and information push. IBM manufactures and sells computer hardware, middleware, and software and provides hosting and consulting services in the computer field. IBM is also a major research institution, holding the record for the most U.S. patents granted to companies for 28 consecutive years (as of 2020) [18]. IBM is widely involved in computer technology and holds 46 patents related to the application of artificial intelligence technology in sports, mainly covering intelligent platform systems and Internet of Things technology.

Japan's Konami Digital Entertainment is dedicated to providing highly original entertainment products and services to users. The patents it applied for related to the application of artificial intelligence technology in sports are mainly related to database platforms for video games, game character control, etc. Sankyo Corporation specializes in the manufacture of pachinko machines, and most of the relevant patents it applied for are related to pachinko machines. OMRON Corporation, whose primary business is manufacturing and selling automation components, equipment, and systems, has applied for relevant patents related to human body composition analysis, blood pressure monitoring, etc.

NHN is currently the largest Internet service company in Korea and the only Korean IT company in the top 10 in terms of the number of patent applications related to artificial intelligence technology in sports. The patents applied for by NHN are mainly related to artificial intelligence in games, control methods, user demand analysis, etc.

It is clear from the above analysis. The main patentees of domestic and foreign patents related to AI technology in sports are primarily multinational IT companies, especially those whose primary business is electronic games. It shows that video games have become the most extensive testing ground and the most direct application carrier of human frontier technology such as AI technology.

4   Patent Layout of Artificial Intelligence Technology Application in Sports

4.1   IPC Distribution of Artificial Intelligence Technology Applications in Sports

The International Patent Classification (IPC) is an internationally accepted patent classification method. The technical composition of patents in this field and the current technical focus of major innovation institutions can be found through IPC analysis. Generally speaking, an IPC with a high number of public patent applications is relatively more active in innovation in that branch of technology. In contrast, an IPC with a relatively low number of public patent applications has an applicant who is relatively less active in innovation in that branch of technology.

Table 3. Patents' IPC distribution of AI in sports.

IPC classification no.	Meaning of IPC classification number	Quantity/items
A63F-13/00	Video games, i.e. games using two-dimensional or multi-dimensional electronic displays	3389
A63F-09/00	Games not included in other categories	1334
A63B-71/00	Games or sports equipment not included in groups A63B-01/00 to A63B-69/00	945
G06F-17/00	Digital computing devices or data processing devices or data processing methods for specific functions	917
A63B-24/00	A63B-01/00 to A63B-23/00 Electrical or electronic controller for each group of training equipment	653
G06Q-50/00	Systems or methods specifically adapted to specific business sectors	577
A63B-69/00	Training supplies or equipment for special sports	564
G06F-03/00	Input device for transforming the data to be processed into a form that the computer can process	506
G07F-17/32	Coin-operated equipment for rental items; coin-operated apparatus or facilities	502
G06F-19/00	Equipment or methods of digital computing or data processing specifically suited to a particular application	429

Table 3 lists the top 10 IPC distributions of domestic and foreign patents related to the application of AI technology in sports. From the IPC distributions, we can understand the specific application of AI technology in patent applications in sports and can also reflect the accumulation of AI technology's technical capabilities in sports at home and abroad. Analysis of Table 3 reveals that the hot technologies of AI technology patents in the field of sports are mainly concentrated in A63F-13/00 (video games, i.e., games using two-dimensional or multi-dimensional electronic displays), A63F-09/00 (games not included in other categories), A63B-71/00 (games not included in groups A63B-1/00 to A63B-69/00 or sports equipment), which have the highest number of IPC classification numbers in patents, with 3389, 1334 and 945 respectively, a result consistent with that obtained from the analysis of significant patent owners above. Other IPC classifications with a high frequency of occurrence include G06F-17/00 (digital computing devices or data processing devices or data processing methods for specific functions), A63B-24/00 (electrical or electronic controllers for training apparatus of groups A63B-01/00 to A63B-23/00), etc.

From the time-IPC distribution of patent applications related to AI technology in sports (Fig. 4), A63F-13/00 (video games, i.e., games using two-dimensional or multi-dimensional electronic displays) has always been the hot spot for patent applications related to AI technology in sports since the new century. Further analysis of Fig. 4 shows that the early patents on AI technology in sports mainly relate to technical areas such as A63F-09/00 (games not included in other classes) and A63B-69/00 (training supplies or apparatus for particular sports). In recent years A63B-71/00 (games or sports equipment not included in groups A63B-01/00 to A63B-69/00) and A63B-24/00 (electrical or electronic controllers for apparatus in groups A63B-01/00 to A63B-23/00) have seen the most growth. As a representative of the most advanced technology of the same generation, every application of artificial intelligence technology in sports is an innovation. Because the IPC classification itself is continuously updated and improved, there are inevitably cases where the detailed classification is not yet divided. However, new patents have already appeared, so these patented technologies are often classified as "not covered by other categories." Artificial intelligence technology also has its specificity to meet specific needs that cannot be met by other technologies, demonstrating its unique role in adaptive sports, as demonstrated by Kang, S et al., who demonstrated the effectiveness of using VR technology as a sports experience and rehabilitation exercise content for people with disabilities. In addition, in recent years, countries have filed fewer patent applications in some IPC classification areas, which may be because the technology area has been relatively mature and the technology development potential is not high. However, with the further development of AI technology, the application of new technologies may bring colossal development space for these static fields, and enterprises should give sufficient attention to these technology fields and plan their future development strategies.

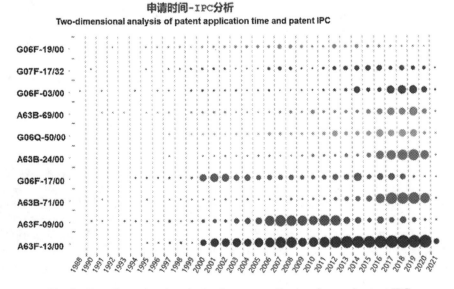

Fig. 4. Two-dimensional analysis of patent application time and patent IPC.

4.2 DMC Distribution of Artificial Intelligence Technology Applications in Sports

Derwent Manual Code (DMC)The DMC is a manual number given to each patent by Derwent indexing experts to indicate the classification of the new technology invented and its application. Compared with the IPC classification system, DMC can better reflect the specific characteristics of patents. Therefore, to further show the characteristics of the patent distribution of AI technology applications in sports, this paper continues to study the relevant patents from the perspective of DMC.

Table 4. 15 high frequency and high centrality technology categories in DMC co-occurrence network.

No.	Frequency	Centrality	DMC	Meaning
1	2870	0.96	T01-J05B4P	Database application technology
2	2400	0.60	W04-X02C	Video games
3	1429	1.47	T01-N01B1	Gambling
4	1355	0.00	T01-S03	Software products
5	898	0.88	T01-J30D	Computer processing of sports and training equipment
6	774	0.12	T01-N02A3C	Servers
7	742	0.39	T05-H05E	Entertainment and recreation systems
8	574	0.32	T01-N01D3	Data transfer (from a remote site or servers)
9	533	0.04	T01-J30B	Computer games animation
10	491	0.04	W04-X01A	Training equipment
11	461	0.00	T01-J05B4M	Database administration
12	438	0.20	W01-C01D3C	Mobile phones
13	396	0.04	W04-X02	Game
14	387	0.53	T05-H08C1	External device controls
15	343	0.12	W04-X01C1	Counting, timing, measuring, scoring, testing

CiteSpace software was used to map the DMC co-occurrence network of patents related to the application of AI technology in sports (Fig. 5) and list the top 15 DMC distributions (Table 4). CiteSpace is an information visualization software developed using Java language. It is mainly based on co-citation analysis theory (Co-citation) and pathfinder network algorithm (Pathfinder), etc., to measure the domain-specific literature (collection). It explores the critical paths of the evolution of the subject area and its knowledge inflection points. Moreover, a series of visual mapping forms an analysis of the potential dynamic mechanisms of disciplinary evolution and the detection of the frontiers of disciplinary development [21]. The year (Year) for mapping the DMC co-occurrence network is selected as 1982–2021, and the time slice (Years Per Slice) is set as 7. Node Types is set as Category. The threshold value is set to Top5%. The Pathfinder algorithm was chosen. The DMC co-occurrence network of patents related to artificial intelligence technology in sports from 1982-to 2021 was obtained (Fig. 5).

In the DMC co-occurrence network, the more frequently the patented technology category appears, the more it indicates that the technology category is receiving more extensive research attention. In addition, some nodes are on the shortest paths of linkages between other different nodes, and these nodes are called intermediary nodes for other nodes. The more nodes these nodes link to, the higher the node's centrality. Centrality is mainly used to discover and measure the importance of keywords in the literature and is another indicator to measure the importance of a node in the whole network [22, 23]. Therefore, in a DMC co-occurrence network characterizing technology categories, the technology categories with the high frequency of occurrence and high centrality generally represent the main technology distribution in the field. As shown in Table 4 and Fig. 5, most of these high-frequency, high-centricity technology categories belong to T01 (digital computers) and W04 (sports equipment), and they form the skeleton of the entire DMC co-occurrence network, linking the whole network in series and forming seven clusters.

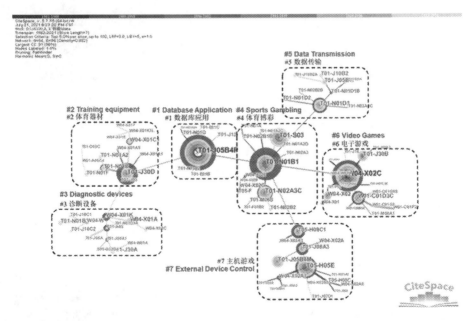

Fig. 5. DMC co-occurrence network of patent about AI applied in sports.

Cluster 1 is centered on database application technologies, and the leading technologies include data selection and comparison, information processing systems, project management, human-computer interaction, search engines, and other technologies. Database application technology is the basic technology of artificial intelligence, and the development of artificial intelligence technology relies on a large scale and variety of database systems and has strict requirements for the data in the database. In sports, extensive data analysis database application technology plays an important role. Since the publication of "Penalties to Gold: The Art of How to Win Unfair Games," written by Michael Lewis in 2003, sports extensive data analysis has attracted significant attention from major professional sports leagues, primary tournament organizers, professional clubs, and so on in the field of sports, and all these organizations and institutions have established These organizations and institutions have established their databases to collect and analyze athlete-related data on a large scale [24]. In addition, with the improvement of sports information collection techniques, big data analytics in sports has been more widely applied to various fields such as school sports.

Cluster 2 centers on computer processing technologies for sports and training equipment, with key technologies including performance testing, information collection, fitness equipment, recreation, Internet of Things, timing, counting, and sports arenas. With the further development of artificial intelligence technology, a variety of intelligent sports equipment and intelligent sports venues have emerged, and the detection and information collection of human functions in sports have also developed in the direction of multi-dimensional, multimodal, remote detection and collection and analysis, and the further development of computer vision, deep learning, data analysis, and data mining technologies have also greatly improved the intelligence level of various sports equipment and sports venues [25].

Cluster 3 is centered on diagnostic devices types of sports or leisure activities, and the leading technologies include neural networks, knowledge processing, medical information systems, treatment planning systems, and online educational technologies. The application of artificial intelligence technology to sports medicine has been a hot research topic in recent years, especially in intelligent diagnosis. Lia Rigamonti et al. confirmed the high accuracy of artificial intelligence in diagnosing patients' injuries and pathologies through five fictitious cases [26]. As an effective deep learning algorithm, applying neural networks to intelligent diagnosis can help further improve the accuracy of intelligent diagnosis results in the future. The artificial intelligence online diagnosis and treatment system can also provide personalized prescription management, intelligent medical consultation, diet planning, and intelligent exercise guidance.

Cluster 4 is centered on gambling, and the leading technologies include software products, servers, forecasting, and monitoring. The sports lottery phenomenon originated in Europe and has undergone various twists and turns in its development over the centuries and has become an indispensable industry in all countries [27]. As an essential part of the sports industry, the sports lottery industry contributes significantly to the healthy development of the sports industry. It also stimulates the enthusiasm and vitality of the masses to pay attention to sports and participate in sports. Artificial intelligence technology in sports betting mainly involves odds prediction and real-time analysis of match data, with the help of related software products and servers to support sports betting services.

Cluster 5 is centered on data transmission technologies, and the leading technologies include file transmission, video transmission, image analysis, network communication, and applications. Computer data is multimedia in nature, combining various media information such as text, graphics, images, animation, audio, and video. The basis of artificial intelligence technology lies in database application technology, and data is the core of the database, so data has become an essential part of the development of artificial intelligence technology. In sports, the collection of human movement data mainly relies on wearable devices, computer vision, etc. These data provide a reference and basis for developing athletes' training programs, individual exercise prescriptions, and conducting health-related fitness tests and clinical exercise tests [28].

Cluster 6 is centered on video games, computer games, and smartphones, and the leading technologies include entertainment systems, personal digital assistants, and games. Video games are one of the teenagers' most popular entertainment items, which initially started with joystick games and arcade games. With the advancement of technology, the increase of personal computer users has made video games shift to computer clients, and the rapid popularity of smartphones in recent years has led to the creation of a large number of mobile video games. The video game industry has developed an enormous scale, and according to intelligence data from Sensor Tower, the world's leading handheld game intelligence platform, Tencent's "Honor of Kings" has generated more than $264 million in the global App Store and Google Play revenue in May 2021 alone [29].

Cluster 7 centers on external device control, entertainment, and amusement systems, with key technologies including database management, gaming devices, etc. This cluster represents console gaming. Although PC and mobile video games continue to be hot and continue to impact the market share of console games, console games continue to maintain their stable development. Ampere Analysis released data showing that the 2020 console game market created a total revenue of about $53.9 billion [30], an increase of 19% compared to 2019, in which host game manufacturers Sony and Microsoft launched game consoles PlayStation, Xbox series sales have reached a million volume, Nintendo's Switch game console sales are more than 10 million units.

4.3 Frontier Hotspot Distribution of Artificial Intelligence Technology Applications in Sports

Kleinberg argues that information flow is characterized by themes that themes increase or decrease over time and that similar phenomena can be seen in the published literature of a particular research area. Accordingly, Kleinberg proposes an algorithm for emergent word detection based on a queueing theory model [31]. Unlike the high-frequency word algorithm, the emergent word detection focuses more on the critical nodes with the most potential and higher activity in the research field, and the detection of emergent words can grasp and predict the development trend of the discipline from a more macroscopic perspective. Burst term function with DMC co-occurrence network is more conducive to the analysis of technology hotspots and the evolution of hotspots; therefore, in this study, based on the DMC co-occurrence network of hot patent technologies of AI technology in sports in Fig. 5, the Burstness function of CiteSpace visual analysis software was used to generate the top ten technology categories of AI technology in sports from 2011–2021. technology categories with high emergence in the field of sports, and listed the top ten technology categories with high emergence among them (Table 5), the year of software setting was chosen 2011–2021, the time slice was set to 1, and other settings were as above.

Table 5. Top 10 High degree of emergence patent of artificial intelligence in sports.

DMC		Burst intensity	Start-ing time	Ending time	burst times diagram
W04-X02	Games	27.24	2011	2012	
W01-C01P2	tablet computers	40.76	2012	2014	
W01-C01G8	Mobile Phones	34.82	2012	2014	
T01-N01A2D	Social Media	29.82	2012	2013	
W01-C01G8S	Smartphones	24.93	2016	2018	
W04-X01K	Sports & Leisure Type	90.22	2019	2021	
W04-W	sports e-learning equipment	65.45	2019	2021	
T01-J16C2	Deep Learning	47.07	2019	2021	
T01-J16C1	Neural Networks	35.12	2019	2021	
T01-J10B2	Image Analysis	33.85	2019	2021	

From Table 5, it can be seen that W04-X01K (sports and leisure type) has the most considerable Burst value of 90.22. This technology category emerged starting in 2019 and continues until 2021. W04-W (sports education equipment) is also a hot technology at the forefront of the application of artificial intelligence in sports. With the development of technology, intelligent sports equipment, whether for competitive sports, mass sports, or school sports, has demonstrated its increasingly broad application prospects.

T01-J16C2 (deep learning), T01-J16C1 (neural networks), and T01-J10B2 (image analysis) are also cutting-edge hot technologies in recent years in the application of artificial intelligence techniques to sports. Deep learning has overcome some of the intractable problems in AI in the past, and with the dramatic increase in chip processing power and training data sets, it has achieved remarkable results in areas such as computer vision and natural language processing. As the main form of deep learning, neural network adopts a widely interconnected structure with an effective learning mechanism to simulate the process of human brain information processing. Deep learning applications can be divided into three major categories by algorithm, namely, convolutional neural network (CNN), recurrent neural network (RNN), and generative adversarial network (GAN). In sports, CNN is most commonly used for human action analysis, while RNN is more often applied for user requirement analysis, and GAN is commonly used for data generation or unsupervised learning. Image analysis is a primary research direction in computer vision, which has broad application prospects in many disciplines such as biology and medicine. Image analysis is commonly used in sports to assist sports medicine diagnosis, action analysis, etc.

5 Conclusion

1. Regarding the number of patents, the number of patent applications related to AI technology in sports has been proliferating worldwide in recent years, and its development momentum is good. The related patent applications mainly come from China, the United States, Japan, and South Korea, which are also the countries with the fastest development of AI technology, indicating that the innovation ability of AI technology plays a vital role in promoting its application in the field of sports. China's related patent applications started late, but the growth rate is fast, and after

2017 has become the fastest-growing country in terms of the number of annual patent applications, and the total number of patents has come to second place.

2. From the perspective of patent owners, among the top 10 major patent owners in terms of the number of patent applications related to AI technology in sports, four companies belong to the United States, three companies belong to Japan, and two companies belong to China. The United States and Japan artificial intelligence technology in sports application research started earlier, the underlying technology accumulated deep. Although the number of relevant domestic patent applications is superior, most of them are oriented to direct commercial applications in recent years, and only a small number of patents involve the core technology of AI technology application in the field of sports, thus leading to the problem of uneven development of the current domestic structure of intelligent sports. In addition, the failure of domestic traditional sports enterprises to be among the significant patents shows that there is still a need to further play the role of artificial intelligence technology in the process of transformation and upgrading of the traditional sports industry and to strengthen the partnership between traditional sports enterprises and Internet companies, both of which are in urgent need of improvement in the future.

3. From the patent application distribution, the patents related to the application of AI technology in sports form seven technical themes: database application, sports equipment, diagnostic equipment, sports betting, data transmission, electronic games, and host games. The core of artificial intelligence lies in data support, and data is also an essential basis for the role of artificial intelligence technology in sports. The number of Internet users in China is the largest globally, and the massive amount of user data provides a constant source of information resources for the development of AI technology applications in the field of sports in China. Relevant research institutions should focus on using the advantages of domestic data to promote the development of intelligent sports. In addition, China's eSports industry is developing rapidly, with the overall market size approaching 150 billion yuan in 2020 [35]. E-sports are developing to be more sports-oriented, popular, and technological. Although the domestic e-sports industry is prosperous, the peripherals of games, game consoles, and other hardware products are firmly occupied by foreign countries, and domestic enterprises lack the right to speak in the game hardware market. In the future, domestic enterprises should use artificial intelligence technology to enhance the intelligent manufacturing level of sports technology products.

4. From the perspective of the patent application development trend, the development of emerging sports and leisure projects, sports e-learning equipment development, and deep learning algorithms are the development trend of AI technology application in sports in recent years. With the continuous progress of AI technology, new technologies are also being applied in sports and are developing in a more in-depth and refined direction.

Social Science Foundation Projects. 1. 2018 Ministry of Education Humanities and Social Sciences Research General Project "Research on the Construction and Application of 'MOOC + Flipped' Classroom Physical Education Teaching Model", Project Approval No.: 18YJC890008.

2. Research on the construction of physical education curriculum to promote the development of core literacy of college students in the context of modernization of higher education, National Social Science Foundation of China 2020, Project Approval No.: 20BTY059.

References

1. Yuan, Y., Wu, C., Li, Q.: Analysis of the international competitive situation of the core technology of artificial intelligence industry. J. China Acad. Electron. Inf. Technol. **15**(11), 1128–1138 (2020)
2. Zang, W., Zhang, W.: A quantitative study of China's artificial intelligence policy texts - current policy status and frontier trends. Sci. Technol. Progr. Policy 1–10 (2021). http://kns.cnki.net/kcms/detail/42.1224.g3.20210517.1710.012.html
3. Claudino, J.G., Capanema, D.D., et al.: Current approaches to the use of artificial intelligence for injury risk assessment and performance prediction in Tealm sports: a systematic review. Sports Med.-Open **5**(1), 28–37 (2019)
4. Calabuig-Moreno, F., Gonzalez-Serrano, M.H., et al.: The emergence of technology in physical education: a general bibliometric analysis with a focus on virtual and augmented reality. Sustainability **12**(7), 2728–2761 (2020)
5. Lu, L., Wang, Y., Ma, Y., Xu, J.: Research analysis of artificial intelligence in sports based on knowledge graph. J. Capital Univ. Phys. Educ. Sports **33**(01), 6–18+66 (2021)
6. Lu, L., Li, X.: Clustering and evolution of artificial intelligence technologies in international sports. J. Shandong Inst. Phys. Educ. Sports **36**(03), 21–32 (2020)
7. Gong, L., Gao, D., Chen, X., Wang, X.: Global exercise prescription research hotspots, trends and insights: an analysis based on CiteSpace V. J. Beijing Sport Univ. **44**(05), 21–33 (2021)
8. Wan, Y., Zhang, Y.: International sports equipment patent technology competitive intelligence study. J. Xi'an Phys. Educ. Univ. **35**(05), 521–531 (2018)
9. Luan, C.: Patent Measurement and Patent Strategy, p. 85. Dalian University of Technology Press, Dalian (2012)
10. Ge, H., Pan, X., Lu, Q., Lu, Q.: A study of technology foresight model integrating scientometric and knowledge visualization methods. J. China Soc. Sci. Tech. Inf. **34**(06), 56–60 (2014)
11. Pan, D.H., Xu, K.: Research on technical knowledge mapping method based on patent document classification code. J. China Soc. Sci. Tech. Inf. **34**(08), 866–874 (2015)
12. Yin, X.: Chinese Patent Law Explained, p. 26. Intellectual Property Publishing House, Beijing (2012)
13. Gao, N., Fu, J., Zhao, Y.: Global patent layout and competition trends of artificial intelligence technology. Sci. Technol. Manag. Res. **40**(08), 176–184 (2020)
14. Chen, X., Li, G., Cui, Y., Xia, Q, Wang, M.: Analysis of the development trend of global artificial intelligence technology application in healthcare based on patent measurement. Sci. Technol. Manag. Res. **41**(03), 139–147 (2021)
15. Wang, H., Gu, L.: Research on the development status of artificial intelligence based on patent measurement and analysis of key technologies. Sci. Technol. Manag. Res. **40**(21), 202–210 (2020)
16. Wang, Y., Luo, J., Zhou, X.: The general pattern of AI research, technology hotspots and future trends based on patent maps. Forum Sci. Technol. China (10), 80–89+127 (2019)
17. Yang, Y.: Research on e-sports and e-sports industry in the new era. China Sport Science **38**(04), 8–21 (2018)
18. Top-patent-holders-of-2020[EB/OL], 29 Jan 2021. https://www.nasdaq.com/articles/top-patent-holders-of-2020-2021-01-29

19. Kang, S., Kang, S.: The study on the application of virtual reality in adapted physical education. Cluster Comput. J. Netw. Softw. Tools Appl. **2**(1), 2351–2355 (2019)
20. Che, R., Li, X., Lu, Y.: Research on patent intelligence of strategic emerging industries from social network perspective. Inf. Sci. **33**(07), 138–144 (2015)
21. Chen, Y., Chen, C., Liu, Z., Hu, Z., Wang, X.: Methodological functions of CiteSpace knowledge graph. Stud. Sci. Sci. **33**(02), 242–253 (2015)
22. Li, L., Wang, H.: 10 years of public sports service research in China (2007–2016): hotspots, trends and prospects - a visual analysis based on CiteSpace III. J. Shenyang Sport Univ. **36**(03), 39–47 (2017)
23. Zhang, Z., Huang, J., Chen, Y.: Frontier identification and trend analysis of artificial intelligence technology based on patent measurement. Sci. Technol. Manag. Res. **38**(05), 36–42 (2018)
24. Hu, X., Xu, W.: A study on the protection of athletes' personal data in sports analytics. Sports Sci. **42**(02), 89–93+120 (2021)
25. Chen, Q., et al.: Analysis of the current demand for R&D in the field of sports engineering in China. China Sport Sci. Technol. **57**(04), 3–23 ()2021
26. Rigamonti, L.I.A., et al.: Use of artificial intelligence in sports medicine: a report of 5 fictional cases. BMC Sports Sci. Med. Rehabil. **13**(1), 1–7 (2021)
27. Xue, J.: Research on the current situation and future development of China's recreational sports lottery industry. J. Guangzhou Sport Univ. **40**(06), 50–52 (2020)
28. Bunn, J.A., Navalta, J.W., Fountaine, C.J., et al.: Current state of commercial wearable technology in physical activity monitoring 2015–2017. Int. J. Exerc. Sci. **11**(7), 503–515 (2018)
29. Sensor Tower: Top 10 global popular mobile game revenue in May 2021 [EB/OL] (2021–0619). https://www.afenxi.com/94634.html
30. Battle of the Big Three, Sony wins in 2020 [EB/OL] (2021–0315). http://www.gamelook.com.cn/2021/03/434432
31. Kleinberg, J.: Bursty and hierarchical structure in streams. Data Min. Knowl. Disc. **7**(4), 373–397 (2003)
32. Zhou, F., Jin, F., Dong, J.: Review of convolutional neural network research Chin. J. Comput. **40**(06), 1229–1251 (2017)
33. Jiao, L., Yang, S., Liu, F., Wang, S., Feng, Z.: Seventy years of neural networks: a review and outlook. Chin. J. Comput. **39**(08), 1697–1716 (2016)
34. Lu, H., Zhang, Q.: A review of research on the application of deep convolutional neural networks in computer vision. J. Data Acquisition Process. **31**(01), 1–17 (2016)
35. 2021 China e-sports industry research report [EB/OL] (2021–04–30). http://report.iresearch.cn/report/202104/3770.shtml

Research on the Application of Coding Art
in Creative Products

Ziyang Li[✉] and HaoYue Sun

Beijing City University, No. 269 Bei si huan Zhong lu, Haidian District, Beijing, China
li.ziyang@bcu.edu.cn

Abstract. The field of coding art has been experiencing a fast growth in recent years and has become a noticeable worldwide phenomenon that is directly connected with the popularization of mobile Internet. This modern form of art has been affecting designers' creative methods as well as the preferences of users that are now increasing the demand for personalized products. This study analyzes the expression techniques of coding art and users' perceptions of this creative form according to four key study cases. A discussion on the development prospects of coding art as a new art form is proposed, also considering the means to combine the standardization of tools, the popularization of applications and the personalization of art into the creative products that result from this programming style.

Keywords: Generative art · Coding art · Digitalmedia marketing · Creative products application

1 Introduction

In recent years, the author has engaged in different interactive art projects and has also been devoted to the teaching research and practical applications of code art. In the global digital-media art show containing code art works are more or less absorbed some experience and some views on future artistic expression. This paper explores the possible research applications of code art in creative products and also discussed the reasonable methods users adopt involving a combination of standardized tools, popular applications, and personalized art for creative products in the digital era.

2 Code Art

Code art is also known as generative art and is considered a better form in the development of digital art. Its principle, quite simple, is to create random values and generate artworks with random beauty by combining computer language and hash function. Some elements and forms in code art are often used, for instance, Fractal. Fractal is a concept commonly used in geometry but not easy to be expressed in traditional paintings. In code art, fractal and iteration can be combined to generate unique art graphics. As creative coding becomes a more popular field, artists are no longer bound by existing software when creating programmed arts. Related programs and software have become a medium, and programmed artworks are no longer just the result of running the software but an extension of the program itself [1].

Tracing the history of code art, Zhao Hongwei pointed out that Ben Laposky, an American mathematician and artist, is a pioneer in electronic art (see Fig. 1), especially in analog aptitude art. He is the one who created the world's first electronic graphic artwork using a cathode-ray oscilloscope in 1950 [2].

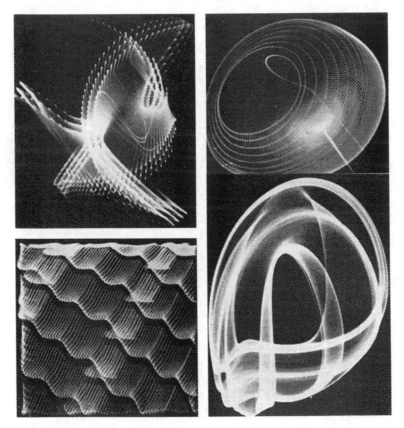

Fig. 1. Electronic Abstraction Number 4, 27, 29, 34 [3]

Professor Philip Galanter of the New York University School of Art once claimed: "An artist applies computer programs, or a set of natural language rules, or a machine, or some other inventions, to produce a process with a certain degree of self-control, the direct or indirect result of which is a complete artwork" [4].

In the study of art and design of educational issues, Stephanie Hoebeke believes that programming is linked creative coding, and classifies it as a new creative material whose purpose is to create something expressive rather than functional [5].

In 2001, artists Casey Reas and Ben Fry were members of M.I.T's Media Lab's Aesthetics and Computation Group founded in 1996. This group was under the leadership of the renowned computer artist John Maeda, who developed the Design By Numbers language and has been working on the perfect combination of computer programming and artistic expression. In the past, C++ and Java were commonly used programming languages, but they most of artists outgrew these technologies, especially the ones who had never been exposed to programming, for it was exceedingly hard for them to write these two types of codes. Reas and Fry were aware of this issue and, influenced by the Design By Numbers language, they developed a new coding language. What they called processing language enabled designers, artists, and other non-programmers to program with computers easily (see Fig. 2). With processing language, professionals can better express their ideas and users can concentrate on the images and the interactive mode in place, free of the complexities of an archaic coding system. In the past few years, processing language has been widely used in many fields like art, humanities, data visualization, and computer science. Tan Liang, an instructor of Guangzhou Academy of Fine Arts, said, "The birth of Processing is a revolution in the creation of code art. As a forward-looking emerging computer language mainly for computer programmers and digital artists, it is an extension of the Java language but much simpler in syntax and more user-friendly in design. People can create breathtaking visual expression and interactive artworks without advanced programming skills needed." [6].

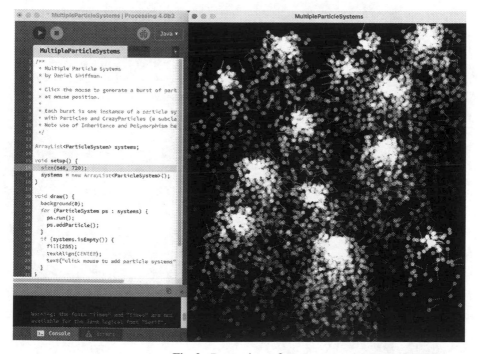

Fig. 2. Processing software

In 2015, Ben Fry and Casey Reas contacted Lauren McCarthy to discuss and envision the possibility of processing being rendered on the Internet. This idea combined with the original intention that Processing is made for artists and designers, they have created p5.js, a JavaScript library to promote the creation of interactive art on the Internet and exude the considerable charm of online creative programming on the Internet (see Fig. 3).

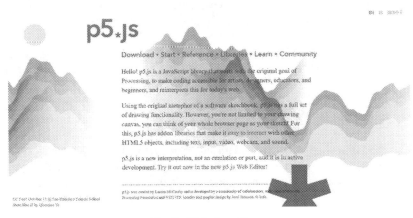

Fig. 3. Website: p5js.org

p5.js can be used to produce web-based images, animations, and interactive works. The code for a line of drawn dots is entered and a pixel point will display on the screen. If the user varies the drawing code slightly, the pixel dot may become an ellipse. If a few more lines of codes are written, the ellipse will move after the mouse does. After the addition of some code statements depicting color, the ellipse will change tones when the mouse is clicked (see Fig. 4). It can be a fun process to write and modify the code to draw graphics and interact step by step.

Fig. 4. Drawing ellipse by mouse

Fig. 5. Website: openprcessing.org. user shared their codes and artwork

The first beta version of p5.js was released in August 2014, and since then it has been widely used by designers and artists around the world. Its success is ascribable to the efforts of a group of different artists and programmers from many different places. They are the ones who have patched vulnerabilities of its core functions, written demonstrations and examples, and shared their codes selflessly (see Fig. 5).

Fig. 6. P5.js tutorial online

p5.js inherits the concept of processing language and continues to be used by creators all over the world, exposing more people to code art, making it more popular, and enabling them to learn to create interactive artworks using code (see Fig. 6), while making code art, a new art form, popular on the Internet.

3   Cases

3.1   Generative Artist Okazz

The Japanese generative artist Okazz is a fairly active artist in the code art community. Most of his works are based on circles, curves and rectangles as basic elements and he makes use of simple geometric shapes with random positions and colors to build graphic images (see Fig. 7). His works perform well on websites such as openprcessing and

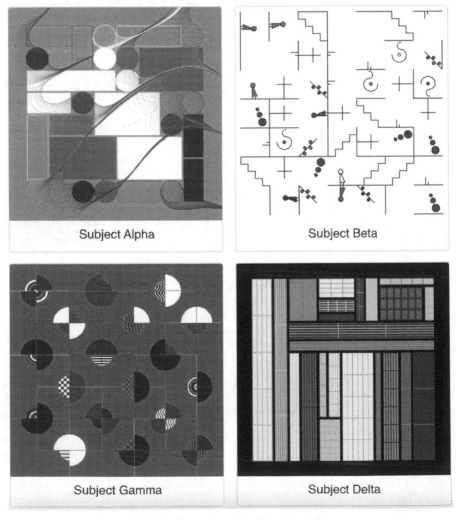

Fig. 7. Generative artist Okazz's works

fxhaash. By analyzing his creations, it can be seen that his pieces created with coding are random, yet creative. The same basic form added with Hash random parameters can present ever-changing graphics, which is an unprecedented creative experience for artists, especially visual ones.

3.2   Realtime Light Painting

The author has recently created a real-time light painting is a project that had very interesting results. Users waves an illuminant in a dark room so that the camera can capture the pixel points presented by the light movement and then record them to form the pattern through the code (see Fig. 8). The idea is that the process is similar to drawing with a light pen.

Fig. 8. Real-time light painting

This project had interesting outcomes during the pre-test stage, but its subsequent demonstration on the spot did not bring about the expected results (see Fig. 9). Furthermore, there were also some issues during the communication with users.

First of all, painting with light in a dark room actually requires some basic drawing skills. The author hired art-learning students to test the prototype, so some interesting graphics could be obtained. However, most of the practitioners were diversified in age and work. They lack drawing abilities and don't feel confident making movements in a dark room. The author interviewed several users and most of the feedback focused on the difficulty of operation. Although many participants felt insecure about potential patterns, most expressed a wish to create unique graphics with different styles.

Fig. 9. Testing code and effect

3.3 Digital Revolution Show

As a well-known digital media show in recent years, Digital Revolution at the Barbican Art Center exhibited all the extremely famed digital media artworks in the past 30 years, which are representative to some extent (see Fig. 10). During the show, the author prepared the age and occupation statistics on the viewers and found that they were not

Fig. 10. The Treachery of Sanctuary, Chris Milk

all the art practitioners or learners, but were from all walks of life. On interacting with them, the author observed that digital-media interactive art really caught their attention, whether video games or other types of creative interactive artworks. In terms of their final creations, they basically do not involve any complex interaction processes and special knowledge background as prerequisites.

3.4 NFT and Fxhash, the Generative Art Site

Being the trending GenerativeTokens platform of late 2021, Fxhash.xyz is set on the Tezos blockchain and created by the French generative artist Baptiste Crespy. Fxhash's philosophy of is quite simple: provide tools so that generative artists can have a space in which they can mint their pieces [7]. There's no curation and the platform is opened to everyone. Compared with Artblocks [8], a more mature blockchain generative-art platform, fxhash is more applicable to most generative artists and ordinary users, and is closer to the decentralized purpose of the blockchain (see Fig. 11). The service was created with the purpose to encourage everyone to create, is living up to its official slogan: "Art is evolving and we were born to witness it!".

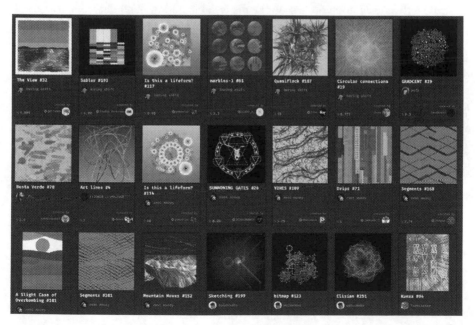

Fig. 11. Website: Fxhash.xyz

4 Application of Code Art in Creative Products

From the above-mentioned examples, it can be concluded that the mainstream general public, who are now bombarded by the Internet and mobile social media, have not yet lost their ability to create. Instead, they may like to come up with creations with the help of some artistic expression tools that can be used in micro-creations, so they can later share and expose what has been done. These groups of people have a distaste for those stereotypical forms of expression and are inclined to go deeper into some issues. They also like the possibility to add a little bit of their touch and thoughts to their creation, that's why opensea and Tiktok are so popular.

The author is working on some technical solutions to design a platform where the public can use processing to create micro-art graphics, which has both the graphic sharing concept of openprocessing.org and the properties of Artblocks, fxhhash blockchain, and copyright. The idea is that this novel software is not just a code-sharing platform but a service that allows users to create parametric art graphics by combining some unique effects and tools. These creations can be given value as derivatives.

5   Conclusion

One of the practical setbacks for the development of digital media art is how to organically combine standardization of tools, popularization of applications, and personalization of art. Evidently, the solution of these problems is subject to in-depth theoretical research and exploration, and the application of such means to innovate the creation mechanism, software selection, and program design can be a good starting point. Therefore, many universities that offer programming courses in digital media art, and many digital artists, designers, and programmers nowadays are co-creating through online platforms. Perhaps strengthening the role of programming in art creation is an effective way to promote code art and related creative products.

References

1. Maeda, J.: Creative Code: Aesthetics+Computation. Thames & Hudson, London (2004)
2. 赵宏伟，　从电子抽象到代码改造——程序艺术的编码方法.《北京电影学院学报》, 19–23 (2019)
3. Laposky, B.F.: Electronic abstracts-art for the space age. In: Proceedings of the Iowa Academy of Science, vol. 65, no. 1, pp. 340–347 (1958)
4. Galanter, P.: What is generative art? Complexity theory as a context for art theory. In: Proceedings of GA2003, Milan, p. 4 (2003)
5. Hoebeke, S., Strand, I., Haakonsen, P.: Programming as a new creative material in art and design education. Techne Ser. – Res. Sloyd Educ. Craft Sci. A **28**(2), 233–240 (2021)
6. 谭亮.: Processing 互动编程艺术. 电子工业出版社, 北京(2001)
7. Fxhash about page. https://www.fxhash.xyz/articles/about-fxhash. Accessed 11 Jan 2022
8. Artblocks Homepage. https://www.artblocks.io. Accessed 11 Jan 2022

Study on the Application of Intelligent Calligraphy Teaching in the Context of Digital Media

Hong Liu[✉], Yuxin Wang, Jingwen Ma, Junya Yu, and Yifan Ma

Beijing City University, No. 269 Bei si Huan Zhong Lu, Hai Dian District, Beijing, China
lhlh312@126.com

Abstract. At the National Educational Work Conference 2020, the Ministry of Education proposed that aesthetic education be incorporated into the supervisory evaluation and assessment system, from a "soft task" to a "hard indicator". This study is the design of a Chinese calligraphy brush that provides timely feedback to the teacher on students' practice by monitoring their grip posture and ink usage in real time by the smart sensor, thus reducing the difficulty in calligraphy teaching. This study conducts data analysis and research on calligraphy teachers' experience and degree of satisfaction through methods such as survey, questionnaire,, uses the empathy map in service design method to dig into user demand, and make user service map. On that basis, this study optimizes the design of the calligraphy teaching methodology, comes up with the final design and blueprint, effectively tackle the difficulty of step-by-step presentations in the calligraphy teaching process by combining digital media technology and product design. In this study, students are the basic users. The smart brush is equipped with nine-axis sensors, pressure sensors, and humidity sensors to monitor students' practice in real time. Furthermore, the backend effectively integrates students' error-prone points in their practice, feeds back to the teacher in order to make corrections in a timely manner, and assists students in refining and deepening their learning of the art of calligraphy.

This study provides new ideas and methods for modern calligraphy teaching by combining modern technology and calligraphy teaching. Compared to traditional calligraphy teaching, that in the context of digital media has the advantages of high efficiency, ease of use, high degree of mutual help, and strong expansion. The accurate teaching assisted by data algorithms can thoroughly collect and analyze students' easy and difficult points in calligraphy practice, summarize and feed back to the teacher to improve the efficiency of calligraphy teaching in class and facilitate learning effect on both the aesthetic of calligraphy art and the learning of writing techniques, which is also of positive significance to modern calligraphy learning. Facilitate learning effect on both the aesthetic of calligraphy art and the learning of writing techniques, which is also of positive significance to modern calligraphy learning.

Keywords: Digital media · Calligraphy teaching · Smart feedback

M. M. Soares et al. (Eds.): HCII 2022, LNCS 13323, pp. 365–383, 2022.
https://doi.org/10.1007/978-3-031-05906-3_27

1 Background and Industrial Analysis of the Application of Intelligent Calligraphy Teaching

1.1 Background

Calligraphy is an external manifestation in Chinese traditional culture that can showcase the beauty of Hanzi (Chinese characters). As information technology has been widely and intensively used in education, changes are taking place in ways of reading and writing with pens (brushes in the past) and paper that has been popular for a long time. Writing with keyboards and reading on screens are increasingly prevalent while paper and brushes, the previous necessary media of writing teaching, are replaced by a variety of electronic devices. The capability of writing and using Hanzi of primary and secondary school students in China is on the wane and some scholars even believe that we are in face of a severe "Hanzi Crisis". Since many people have developed "the Agraphia in the Digital Age", it has become a worrisome social and cultural phenomenon that one forgets how to write when he or she picks up a pen. In response to the phenomenon, the all-round integration of excellent traditional culture into education, the standardization of Hanzi writing, the enhancement of Hanzi using, and the promotion of fine traditional Chinese culture are strongly advocated in the 2017 New Curriculum Standard.

Education is gradually moving from offline to online amid the development of the Internet, especially mobile Internet. And since the outbreak of Covid-19, e-education has developed significantly and the users' needs have vastly changed. Therefore, teachers are required, in the context of booming Internet teaching, to make good use of modern technology platforms, upgrade teaching methods of calligraphy, design effective "AI + calligraphy" teaching models that meet the actual needs of students, and improve the effectiveness of calligraphy teaching in primary schools and provide an experiment of teaching through the shareability of online resources of calligraphy and the diversified presentations from the perspective of AI.

1.2 Industrial Analysis

Generally speaking, there are three categories of Hanzi writing systems. The first is the stroke-oriented Hanzi learning system. In such systems, the order of strokes and "copying" are highlighted, rather than students' original handwriting, so handwriting practice cannot be realized. The second is the touchscreen-based teaching system, which uses digital interactive touchscreens, visual handwriting screens, and other hardware to reproduce the handwriting and the process of writing, and can be adapted to the daily teaching of Chinese calligraphy. And the third is the Hanzi teaching system retaining the writing with paper and brushes, which uses handwriting extraction and Hanzi recognition technologies to digitise the writing process without disturbing or changing the traditional brush-and-paper writing. Specifically, handwriting extraction technology includes image recognition and point recognition, which can analyze and monitor problems emerging in the writing of students as well as remind and answer them. In addition, such technology conducts systematic diagnosis during and after the writing. In this category of systems, the writing habit with paper and brushes is naturally maintained and students' writing habits are subtly affected during the writing, so this category is the most effective.

However, in reality, all of the three categories cannot enable teachers to have adequate follow-ups and assessments of students in calligraphy classes. As a result, many students have misunderstandings of the patterns of strokes, the inter-stroke relationships, character structure, and the origins of Hanzi.

2 SWOT Analysis of the Market of Intelligent Calligraphy Teaching

2.1 Analysis of Existing Problems of Calligraphy Teaching

Calligraphy, as a pivotal part of all-round education, is gradually going into the public eye and growing vigorously. A SWOT analysis has been conducted to find the breakthrough point of calligraphy teaching in schools.

Table 1. SWOT analysis.

Models of Calligraphy Teaching / Environments of Calligraphy Teaching	Advantages	Disadvantages
	1. Promote the traditional culture of calligraphy 2. Cultivate patience and improve quality 3. Online calligraphy education has low cost and is not restricted by time and location 4. Unlimited playback is now available for online calligraphy courses within the validity period, facilitating the relearning	1. Not interesting enough 2. The effect of calligraphy learning is slow to appear and difficult to quantify 3. Calligraphy teaching has not yet formed scientific and complete research and teaching systems 4. Calligraphy classes account for a small proportion in schools 5. Online teaching tests students' self-discipline
Opportunities 1. Calligraphy education is supported in Opinions of the Ministry of Education on the Development of Calligraphy Education in Primary and Secondary Schools issued in 2015 2. Standard for Compulsory Education School Management issued in 2020 proposed to offer calligraphy classes 3. The Ministry of Education advocates that schools set up special calligraphy classrooms 4. The Ministry of Education calls for exploring and promoting new modes of online and offline education and teaching 5. The calligraphy teaching team in society is growing 6.Related calligraphy APP products have a certain product basis	1. The increasing number of students graduating from the calligraphy major drive the development of the industry 2. There is great room for the calligraphy industry to grow with support from national policies and the Ministry of Education. 3. The calligraphy teaching in school is subtly combined with that in society 4. The Ministry of Education calls for promoting the new mode of integrating online and offline teaching	1. The digitised teaching makes calligraphy learning more interesting 2. Complete research and teaching systems are established via technology 3. The lack of teachers can be eliminated by professional systems or products and teaching can be made more efficient 4. The standardised teaching of online education leads to clearer teaching objectives
Threats 1. Schools now devote little time to calligraphy teaching 2. Parents do not attach enough importance to calligraphy teaching 3. It is difficult to move online (because calligraphy teaching is professional and practical that requires one-to-one instruction in many cases)	1. The country needs to publicise and support calligraphy teaching and schools need to pay more attention to it 2. The existing problems of calligraphy teaching should be resolved to eliminate parents' doubts and confusion 3. The teaching modes should be upgraded to make it easier for calligraphy to get into campuses and families	1. Prevent students from losing interest in calligraphy 2. Neglect of both the families and the schools are not conducive to students' calligraphy learning 3. Focus on technology and product innovation based on calligraphy tools 4. Consider the integration of online and offline when moving online is difficult

According to Table 1, Opinions of the Ministry of Education on the Development of Calligraphy Education in Primary and Secondary Schools issued in 2015 proposed the policy that calligraphy teaching should be conducted at the compulsory education level in accordance with the curriculum standard and one class hour of calligraphy class per week should be arranged for grades 3 to 6. In the Standard for Compulsory Education School Management issued by the Ministry of Education in 2020, it was specified that education on fine Chinese traditional culture should be actively carried out, music and art classes should be sufficiently offered and calligraphy classes should be set up in accordance with national requirements. This shows that there is great room for the calligraphy industry to grow with the support from national policies and the Ministry of Education. As more calligraphy majors graduate year on year, an increasing number of professionals will work in this industry, thus promoting its development and providing more possibilities for calligraphy teaching. The SWOT analysis shows that calligraphy teaching mainly involves two groups of people, students and teachers. Therefore, surveys and research have been conducted on the two groups in order to better explore user needs.

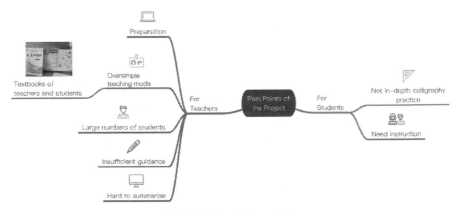

Fig. 1. Pain points analysis

According to the user research on calligraphy teachers in Shunyi District, there are four major pain points: oversimple teaching mode, large numbers of students, limited instruction, and lack of summary. (Fig. 1) The oversimple teaching mode is largely manifested in the following aspects. Firstly, it is clarified in Guidance on Calligraphy Practice – Teacher's Book that it is imperative to intensify writing practice. But the teaching is mainly based on video explanation, which is not attractive enough for students. Secondly, in a class of about 42 students, one teacher is not enough for calligraphy teaching. Thirdly, the syllabus proposes that a class should be divided into 10–15 min of "guidance on techniques" and 25–30 min of "guidance on practice". The guidance on techniques includes the cultural background of Hanzi, how to hold the brush, how to wield the brush, etc. Guidance on practice refers to students' sufficient calligraphy practice and specific guidance by teachers. However, due to the limited time and large numbers of students, teachers are not able to guide and comment on every student, leading to the fact that some students cannot spot and correct their mistakes in time for calligraphy practice and develop wrong writing habits (Fig. 2). On account of the aforementioned problem, teachers cannot have the feedback from every student in time, thus failing to have a comprehensive summary of students' mistake-prone points and optimize the teaching modes (Fig. 3), which influences, to some extent, the experiences of calligraphy for both teachers and students.

Observations of students show that there are two types of students, proactive and industrious. Proactive students are concentrated in class, give feedback actively during calligraphy practice, and take the initiative to solve the problems of character structure, radicals, etc. Teachers pay more attention to these students. Industrious students listen carefully to the key points in class and tend to practice silently, who may not choose to raise hands and resort to teachers for help. Thus, for these students, teachers are required to identify their problems and provide guidance accordingly (Fig. 4).

Fig. 2. Practice

Fig. 3. Practice

Fig. 4. Studying

2.2 User Journey Map

Thorough research has been conducted at the early stage to make a user journey map, which can help us analyze users' needs and find better solutions. The figure presents the problems and satisfying aspects during use, enabling us to extract places for improvement and opportunities. The following rules are used to analyze the real needs of users (Fig. 5).

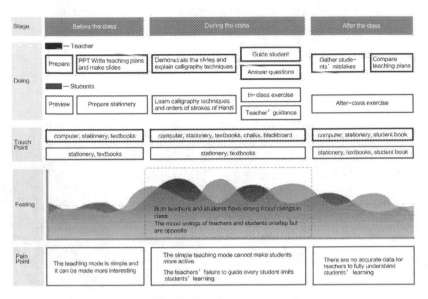

Fig. 5. User journey map

It can be seen from Fig. 5 that teachers initiate the evaluations of teaching and students reflect the quality of teaching.

It has been found that some students make mistakes in holding the brush and even the structure of Hanzi while others are too introverted to ask help from teachers thus making their calligraphy learning neglected. In addition, students are more likely to miss the key points and mistake-prone points if teachers' demonstrations go too fast. Meanwhile, teachers cannot sufficiently instruct each student in class due to the number of students, so the calligraphy teaching is somewhat one-sided.

The research shows that teachers, when in face of problems, need an educational system that can comprehensively record students' practice and summarize mistake-prone points, enabling them to have an overall understanding of the students' performance in class and during practice, so they can spare most of their energy to instruct the students, improve their teaching, and promote efficiency.

2.3 Research on Competitors in Calligraphy Teaching

It has been suggested in the SWOT analysis that there are calligraphy-related Apps and products in the market and corresponding in-depth research has been conducted. The Wisdom digital calligraphy system developed by Huawen Zhonghe, a system based on teaching and learning, is designed to resolve problems of calligraphy teaching. It advocates using real brushes, ink, and paper to write and avoiding the adverse effects induced by experiences such as electronic simulation, water writing paper, etc. Meanwhile, it helps students to have a deeper understanding of calligraphy culture by combining lectures of modern calligraphy masters. Qihua Education Technology Co., LTD in Shandong Province has also launched products and systems related to calligraphy education, whose school edition is Hanhe 9th (Hanhe Wisdom Calligraphy Standard Classroom 9.0). The standalone version, as an intelligent calligraphy teaching software system, adopts a special imitation screen applicable to various occasions. It can realize multiple functions and meet varied teaching and learning needs, which is currently the most capable collection of software systems in the industry. In addition, traditional educational institutions of calligraphy such as Hanzi Institute, Renren Writing, Xingche Hard-tipped Pen Calligraphy Class, and Good Calligraphy have gradually moved online. Supported by digital technology, calligraphy education is embracing new possibilities of development.

There are many calligraphy learning Apps on the market, such as Yiguan Calligraphy, Buyan Calligraphy, Imitation Master, Fingertip Calligraphy, etc., all including a large number of high-resolution copybooks and books of rubbings, along with explanations and notes. Furthermore, multiple functions are available, such as inscription and copybook selection, character enlargement, handwriting practice, imitation and comparison, and various changes and handling of pictures. However, there exist some shortcomings. The definition of some copybooks needs to be improved. The function of character collection is not convenient enough. The function of imitation is oversimple. The operation interfaces are not well-designed and functions are complicated though comprehensive. Despite the convenience and low cost of Apps, they cannot replace paper copybooks for different reasons. Firstly, it is difficult for Apps to imitate the original sizes of characters, thus the practice is less effective. Secondly, if a beginner is accustomed to using an App to look up and practice at the beginning, he or she is less likely to develop good calligraphy habits. Moreover, some Apps are not professional and make mistakes sometimes, which affects the effects of calligraphy learning. In a nutshell, there are problems to be resolved in the R & D of calligraphy-related products and Apps (Figs. 6 and 7).

Fig. 6. Competitor analysis

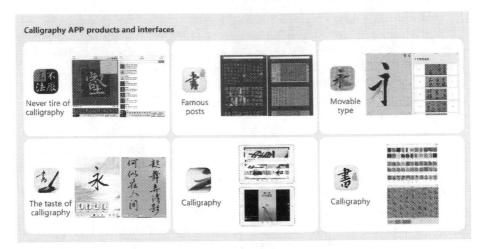

Fig. 7. Competitor analysis

3   Design Strategy of the Functions of Intelligent Calligraphy Teaching

3.1   Traditional Calligraphy Techniques and Digital Restoration

This project, based on the current situation of calligraphy teaching in primary and secondary schools in China, with Guidelines on Calligraphy Education for Primary and Secondary Schools (Draft for Comments) as the specific guidance, develops an intelligent calligraphy teaching system in the context of digital media, through scientific and reasonable practice and research activities related to calligraphy teaching and the summary of advantages and disadvantages of traditional Chinese calligraphy teaching. This platform system, built on the innovative concept of digital calligraphy teaching, combines the interactive methods of digital media with intelligent products, from the perspectives of scientificity, efficiency, convenience, and enjoyment, which preserves not only the traditional ways of writing but also the texture of brushes and ink, enables students to feel the charm of calligraphy, and makes them more interested in traditional calligraphy.

This teaching system, combined with smart brushes, simulates the key points of brush writing, lifting, pressing, turning, and folding. The simulation on the electronic device is realized with sensing technology and the teaching is completed with the calligraphy teaching software for primary school students. The system is divided into different levels according to the general requirements and goals of calligraphy education for primary and secondary schools, which enables students to have correct, standardized, and neat handwriting after practice. In addition, this system helps students to lay a solid foundation of calligraphy, improve their abilities to imitate masters' works, have a brief understanding and realization of the history of Chinese calligraphy and the origins of Hanzi, and foster their interest in Chinese calligraphy and love for traditional culture, thus reaching the goal of improving cultural taste and overall quality.

3.2 Real-Time Observation of Intelligent Calligraphy Class

Intelligent teaching platforms make the real-time data interaction between teachers and students possible, realizing the synchronous transmission and display of graphic data between the two. Reciprocal Teaching, proposed by American educational psychologists A.L. Brown and A.S. Palincsar, focuses on fostering students' specific strategies to promote understanding, advocates equal communication and independent interaction between teaching and learning centered on specific topics, realizes the exchange of information among learners and underscores the development of students' techniques and knowledge. In addition, it is advisable that teaching and learning revolve around concrete issues in a macro teaching situation, allowing teachers and students to interact with each other in a targeted manner, which is reflected in the context of intelligent calligraphy teaching modes that teachers can observe each student's practice in real time to get a comprehensive understanding of the current situation in class. The real-time exchange of data between the teacher side and student side ensures the visibility and practicality of the teaching and learning process. The intelligent calligraphy teaching system, with a distributed network pattern, uses convenient digital auxiliary means of teaching, conducts transregional assisted teaching calligraphy design, and breaks through the limitations of traditional teaching space.

3.3 Real-Time Feedback of Intelligent Calligraphy Class

This platform, based on the key points of brush writing, lifting, pressing, turning, folding, etc., establishes a digital model and a backend database to make it more convenient for teachers to check every student's learning and provide guidance. At the same time, the backend provides feedback on the mistake-prone points to help teachers improve their teaching plans. Sensing technology is applied to the design of smart brushes to detect problems with the students' brush holding and movement, and to provide feedback to teachers. Since calligraphy is a practical subject, its writing techniques need to be consolidated in time. Teachers can mark students' assignments through the platform and provide real-time feedback to students, breaking the barriers of time and realizing timely correction. Students, on the other hand, can select appropriate tasks and content through the resources provided by the platform to learn and practice. In a word, the intelligent calligraphy teaching system breaks through the limitations of calligraphy teaching in traditional classrooms and changes the traditional teaching method of "imitation". Therefore, it promotes a spirit of exploration and maintains students' interest in calligraphy.

4   Product Design of Intelligent Calligraphy Teaching

This calligraphy teaching product has been designed based on extensive research, including the product end and the computer end. The former records the process and results of students using the brush and the latter is used by teachers, which enables teachers to replay the recordings and check the difficulties and mistake-prone points that students encounter during practice.

4.1 The Application of the Intelligent Module

The brush, including the shaft and the head (the brush tip), is a manifestation of the functions of the product. Several modules are placed inside the shaft: communication module, core module, power module, pressure sensor, nine-axis sensor, etc.

Specifically, the power module supplies power for the core module. Two types of pressure sensors are used to collect the pressure of the brush tip to the paper and that of students' holding the shaft respectively. The communication module is used to connect the brush and the teacher-side device and record data of writing. The nine-axis module records the state of writing, including the moving trajectory of the tip, the speed, and the accelerated speed of the movement, which can give realistic feedback on the movement of the traditional brush and then analyzes the problems that students tend to have when writing by combining the feedback data from the tip. The product realizes smart assessment of writing by the smart brush and data analysis, meeting the needs of calligraphy fans to learn and improve their handwriting skills (Figs. 8, 9, 10, 11 and 12).

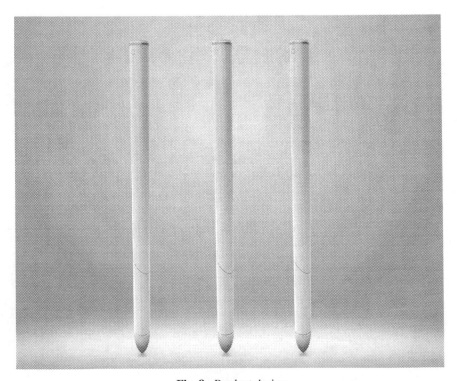

Fig. 8. Product design

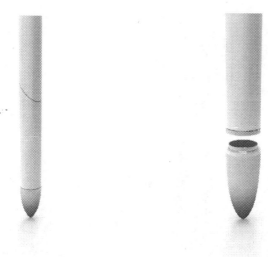

Fig. 9. Pressure sensor   **Fig. 10.** Brush tip with interchangeable sizes

Fig. 11. Magnetic charging

Fig. 12. Magnetic charging

4.2 Function Design of the Online Platform

The Teacher's Platform. There are four pages on the teachers' platform, home, correction, preparation, and class, with white as the base colour and blue and green as the complementary colours. White is used to alleviate the pressure on the teachers' eyes while blue and green do not offend the eyes and can highlight the key points. A low saturation colour is used at the bottom of each icon, to make the icon stand out, on the

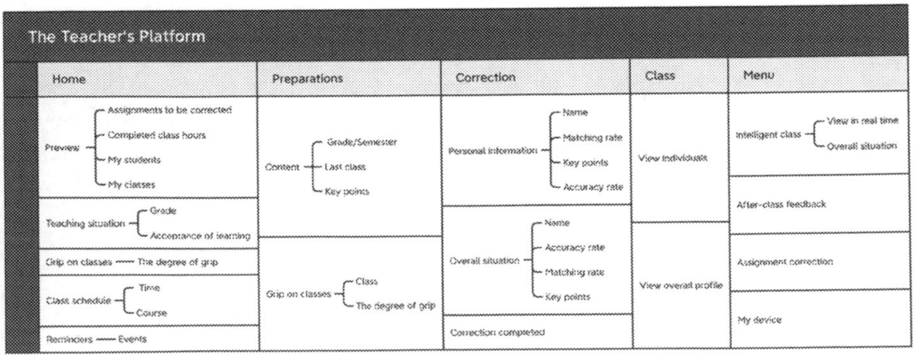

The Teacher's Platform				
Home	**Preparations**	**Correction**	**Class**	**Menu**
Preview ┬ Assignments to be corrected / Completed class hours / My students / My classes	Content ┬ Grade/Semester / Last class / Key points	Personal information ┬ Name / Matching rate / Key points / Accuracy rate	View individuals	Intelligent class ┬ View in real time / Overall situation
Teaching situation ┬ Grade / Acceptance of learning		Overall situation ┬ Name / Accuracy rate / Matching rate / Key points	View overall profile	After-class feedback
Grip on classes ─── The degree of grip				Assignment correction
Class schedule ┬ Time / Course	Grip on classes ┬ Class / The degree of grip			My device
Reminders ─── Events		Correction completed		

Fig. 13. The function framework of the teacher's platform

one hand, and to match the overall design of the page and create a sense of beauty, on the other hand (Fig. 13).

The homepage, as a guide page, contains the overview of teaching and the class schedule and time that teachers are most concerned about. The menu bar on the left-hand side includes the following functions, teaching & preparation, intelligent class, feedback, assignment correction, course replay, data statistics, and students' devices. And on the right-hand side lie the key reminders for teachers (Fig. 14).

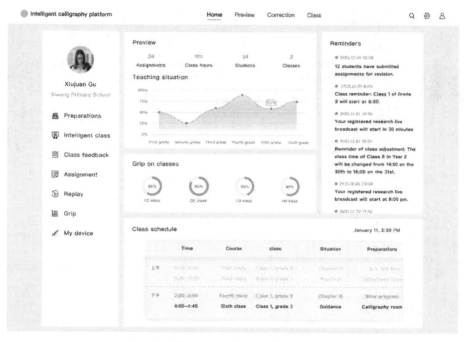

Fig. 14. Homepage of the teacher's platform

The correction page shows the process of assignment correction, the content of each class, and the correction of each student's assignment. Meanwhile, teachers can check each student's mistake-prone points in class and correct them timely in class (Fig. 15).

Fig. 15. The correction page of the teacher's platform

The preparation page presents teachers' preparations for different grades and classes. The previous assignments and problems emerging in students' practice are available on this page to help teachers make better preparations (Fig. 16).

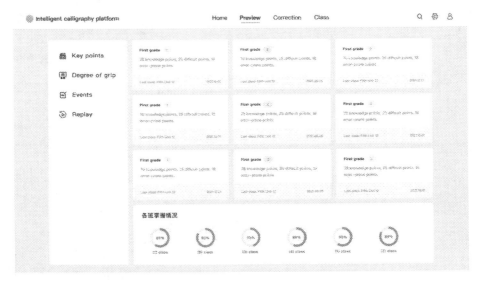

Fig. 16. The preparation page of the teacher's platform

The last page shows the class in real time, on which teachers can have a comprehensive grip of the whole class, and conduct a systematic analysis of each character or radical or personalized analysis of students, in order to help students to remedy their weaknesses as soon as possible (Fig. 17).

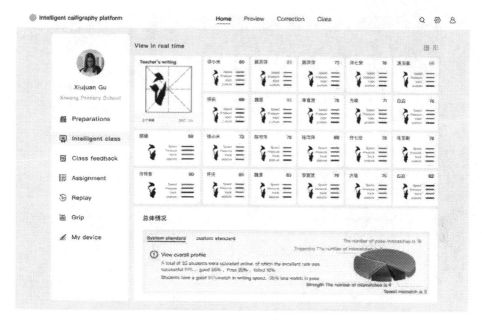

Fig. 17. The real-time class page of the teacher's platform

The Student's Platform. There are three main pages on the student's platform, home, assignment, and class. The style is consistent with the teacher's platform, with green as the dominant hue to relieve students' eye strain (Fig. 18).

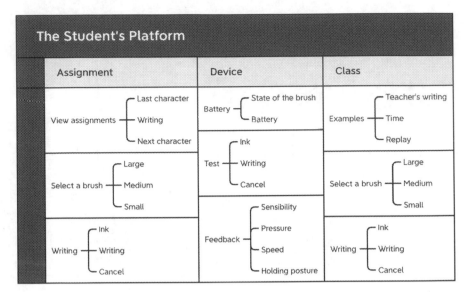

Fig. 18. The function framework of the student's platform

The class page, as the main page of the student's platform, contains viewing teachers' writing, selecting a brush, ink, and writing Hanzi in the grid. The homework page, largely similar to the class page, does not have teachers' writing and shows the content that the student is about to write in the top left corner. In addition, students can repeatedly practice before submitting by clicking the cancel button in the top right corner (Fig. 19).

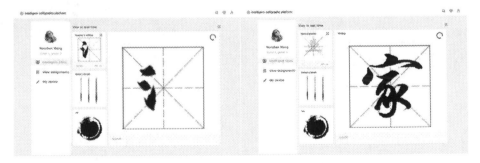

Fig. 19. The assignment page of the student's platform

Both the teacher's platform and the student's platform have the page of device management and test. To match the supporting products and test the performance of the smart brush, this page contains multiple tests including sensitivity of the brush, holding pressure, speed, holding posture, etc., which facilitates more convenient and efficient use of the smart brush (Fig. 20).

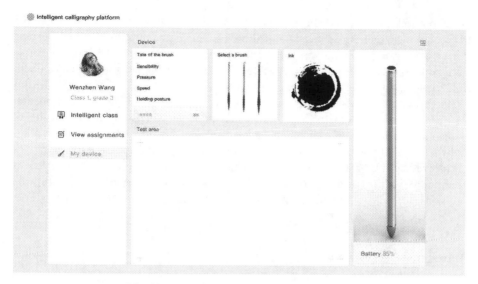

Fig. 20. The test page of the student's platform

5   The Application Value and Meaning of Intelligent Calligraphy Teaching

5.1   The Application Value of Intelligent Calligraphy Teaching

When teachers write with intelligent calligraphy products, students can feel the process of each stroke of Hanzi. They can truly understand the rules of calligraphy and appreciate the unique charm of calligraphy by imitation, thus the calligraphy classes are more effective. During the class, intelligent calligraphy products monitor students' holding postures, writing trajectories, writing speed and strength in real time and feedback to the teachers' smart terminal, where the sensors record students' practice to make calligraphy easier and boost students' interest.

These resources are conducive to creating a relaxing environment of practice and help students to grasp knowledge about calligraphy more easily. Meanwhile, explanations and demonstrations of calligraphy teaching are made more efficient and online education and calligraphy class are perfectly integrated to improve the traditional teaching mode. Particularly, the combination and application of paper & brush, modern technology, and information-based education greatly facilitate the innovation of teaching mode. The simple and flexible digital paper & brush is in line with the value orientation of information-based education featuring putting people first, efficient education, and smart education.

5.2   The Meaning of Designing Intelligent Calligraphy Teaching

As the country attaches greater importance to the traditional culture of handwriting, calligraphy education is playing an increasingly significant role in schools, especially in junior grades, where learning calligraphy is a combination of literacy and writing. Intelligent calligraphy teaching is aimed at enhancing students' literacy and writing skills, rather than replacing paper and pens. In turn, it is intended to boost students' calligraphy skills via information technology, which is a teaching method uniting modern technology and traditional calligraphy teaching.

In this era of big data, digital media, as a new product of high-tech information storage and output, gradually fit into our study and life. This study integrates digital media into calligraphy teaching in school and combines modern technology with calligraphy teaching. It manages to, from the perspectives of learning and teaching, improves the utilization of educational resources, enhances the efficiency and effectiveness of calligraphy teaching, and in turn promotes the dissemination and development of the traditional Chinese art of calligraphy, while also providing new ideas and methods for modern calligraphy teaching.

References

1. L Botao 2014 The Influence of Calligraphy Space Teaching on Children's Intelligence and Emotional Development East China Normal University China
2. Cai, Z.: Some thoughts on combining multimedia in calligraphy teaching in primary schools. Comic Mont. (Z2), 68–69 (2022)
3. Zhao, J.: Using information technology to improve the effectiveness of primary school calligraphy classroom. Inf. Technol. Educ. Prim. Second. Sch. (S1), 36–38 (2021)
4. Chang, Y.: The practice and research of calligraphy classroom teaching in primary and secondary schools from the perspective of digital calligraphy. New Curric. (51), 1 (2021)
5. Zheng, C.: "Xing" in the wrist, "interest" in the pen - talking about cultivating children's interest in calligraphy. Educ. Arts (12), 81–82 (2021)
6. Chen, P.: Research on teaching strategies for cultivating interest in calligraphy. Cult. Ind. (35), 160–162 (2021)
7. Q Linna 2020 Research on Calligraphy Teaching Practice in Primary Schools Guangxi Normal University China
8. X Mei 2019 Research on Problems and Countermeasures of School-Based Curriculum Development of Primary School Calligraphy Hebei Normal University China
9. Mi, W.: Calligraphy education in primary and secondary schools in the context of "Internet+". Res. Electron. Educ. 39(09), 109–113+128 (2018)
10. L Ting 2016 Practical Research on Teaching Methods in Primary School Calligraphy Education Chongqing Normal University China
11. C Yaruo 2015 Confucius Institute Calligraphy Teaching Survey and Calligraphy Experience Course Teaching Design Shandong University China
12. D Chao 2015 Research on the Current Situation of Calligraphy Education in Primary and Secondary Schools Southwest University China
13. Zhou, B., Li, R.: Preliminary ideas on "calligraphy education curriculum standards". Calligr. Apprec. (2) (2009)
14. Huang, L.: On the development of calligraphy in the era of "Internet+". Chin. Calligr. (24) (2016)
15. Liu, G., Li, J., Liang, H.: Thinking and countermeasures of teaching innovation in colleges and universities in the "Internet+" era. China High. Educ. Res. (2) (2017)
16. C Xiaojuan 2017 Investigation and Research on the Current Situation of Calligraphy Education in Primary Schools Yangzhou University China

17. Tian, Z.: Analysis of the current situation of calligraphy education in primary schools and solutions. Art Educ. Res. (06), 116–117 (2016)
18. Y Suixian L Xing K Hui L Qing 2019 Interaction design and experience under the background of Internet + intelligent design Packag. Eng. 40 16 1 13
19. Y Jiumin L Li L Xiaoli Z Fangfang G Shurui P Zhongling 2018 Analysis of interaction design in online open courses and its application status Res. Electron. Educ. 39 11 61 68
20. Qin, J.: Big interaction design in the era of big data. Packag. Eng. 36(08), 1–5+161 (2015)

Development the Cockpit of the Autonomous Cars

Diana Reis[1(✉)] and Ernesto Filgueiras[1,2]

[1] University of Beira Interior, Convento de Sto. António, 6201-001 Covilhã, Portugal
dianaareis@outlook.pt, evf@ubi.pt
[2] CIAUD - Research Centre for Architecture, Urbanism and Design, University of Beira Interior, Convento de Sto. António, Covilhã, Portugal

Abstract. The evolution of cars has been notorious over the years, since the first four-wheeled car, that emerged in mid-1891 up to the present day, where it's already possible to see semi-autonomous cars.

Currently, and with the constant automotive evolution, the cars practically drive themselves, without the need for users go with maximum attention in several situations. It was around 1980 that the first autonomous cars appeared, such as the NavLab which became a big innovation, evolving also the automotive industry and thus beginning the season of studies on autonomous cars. Nowadays Tesla is the great brand that innovated the auto-motive future, being that, is not completely autonomous, but in many situations the driver also becomes the passenger. It's important to refer that Tesla until to these days only makes semi-autonomous cars, being which, several other tests are being conducted, not only by Tesla, but also by other big brands, like the Google, which is developing a totally autonomous car. Fully autonomous cars are still a big innovation, both for design, like for engineering, as it's essential to gather the conditions so that these can be placed on the market, without any hindrance and protecting the Human from any dangers that may raise, and for that very reason, it's necessary understand and study this new "era". Throughout this dissertation several important aspects for the realization and creation of a cockpit for the completely autonomous car will be analyzed, by analyzing users, the cars, but also the legislation and ongoing tests about the subject. To deal with this new "era" in which cars can be shared, and drive themselves, it's essential to understand how this can be possible, what steps are needed for implementation, and what the design and engineering of the fully autonomous cars might look like. The aspects of these vehicles will be analyzed as well as the users. Ultimately, virtual reality tests will be performed, to understand what the interior of the car will be like and understand how users behave inside an autonomous car.

Keywords: Car · Passengers · Autonomous cars · Design and engineering · Cockpit

1 Introduction

Currently, to satisfy his desires, man easily creates or extinguishes instruments and objects. The act of acquiring any object provides the feeling of comfort, well-being, power, abundance, and even status, and for many this means achieving happiness. (Baudrillard 1995). Nowadays happiness is still seen in the same way, more and more society evolve in search of something better, as an example of this we have the constant evolution of automobiles. Over the years, the automotive industry has had a significant growth in people's daily lives. Today we can move from one place to another without much effort; we have planes, trains, boats, motorcycles, but the most common form of transportation is still the automobile.

The automotive industry, especially in Europe, is a very important industry as it accounts for 14% of total production and capital investment. Fully Autonomous cars has been studied since the 1920s, with the first autonomous cars appearing in the 1980s, such as NavLab, an autonomous van that appeared in 1984, and the EUREKA Prometheus project of Mercedes Benz at Bundeswehr University Munich in 1987 (Ondruša, et al. 2020 apud Kalašová et al. 2018). Companies such as Toyota, Audi, Hyundai Motor Company, Tesla, and others have been developing research and prototypes of the autonomous vehicles. In the year 2010 to the present day, Google has been developing an autonomous vehicle, in 2013 Vislab presented a vehicle that moved autonomously the BRAiVE, it was also in this year that the UK approved the testing of autonomous vehicles on private property. As of 2014, Tesla Motors is constantly evolving to install full autonomy in its cars, starting with Autopilot, already known worldwide.

According to Joshi (2021), although the concept of autonomous cars has evolved a lot, they are not yet a reality for most people. The idea of autonomous cars, although it was utopian, is increasingly coming closer to reality in today's world. In the future the advancement of automotive systems and technologies such as artificial intelligence and the Internet of things will allow autonomous cars to become more mainstream among people. There are still many advances that need to be made, as the autonomous car has several flaws that need to be seen and evaluated for proper functioning on the road, as it will start to become more usual to see them among us. The idea of autonomous cars, although it was utopian, is increasingly coming closer to reality in today's world. In the future the advancement of automotive systems and technologies such as artificial intelligence and the Internet of things will allow autonomous cars to become more mainstream among people. There are still many advances that need to be made, as the autonomous car has several flaws that need to be seen and evaluated for proper functioning on the road, as it will start to become more usual to see them among us.

It's therefore important for the realization of this work to experiment in virtual reality, thus getting a sense of what the autonomous car will be like, and how people feel inside it.

1.1 Autonomous Cars and Their Features

The evolution of technology, especially the autonomous cars technology, is already at an advanced level, yet the idea of self-driving cars on the road is still a little scary for people (Henrique 2017).

According to Nakata Automotiva (2019), cars with some degree of autonomy, such as cars that have driver assistance, are considered semi-autonomous cars, because they need the human interface to drive. Cars that do not require a human interface to drive are considered autonomous vehicles. Autonomous cars were envisioned to reduce four common problems on urban roads and highways such as accidents, pollution and noise pollution, and traffic jams, with the goal of making the future better. One of the features of autonomous cars is that they will have sensors scattered throughout the vehicle, thus allowing it to be guided without the need for human interaction, just artificial intelligence. The sensors will be responsible for identifying pedestrians, or any other kind of obstacle that may appear on the road, including other vehicles. Artificial intelligence will be key in tire pressure analysis, putting an end to "blind spots"[1], and act quickly and effectively in possible dangerous situations, respecting the speed limits, and identifying lane changes, among other tasks. (Mapfre 2021).

1.2   Autonomous and Semiautonomous Cars that are Already on the Road

According to Piper (2020), Google is currently developing the autonomous car, Waymo, and has been in testing phase since 2017. Waymo can be considered an autonomous car that is already on the road, refuting that it's just drives around the company with someone always watching in case something unexpected happens. The Uber also had autonomous cabs running on the road, but in 2018 de- after an accident the company decided to sell its research on the autonomous cars to the company Aurora Innovation. These days it can be considered that there are still no fully autonomous cars and so we can conclude that Tesla is the company that so far has its semi-autonomous cars driving on the road most accurately. Although these cars are not yet completely self-driving, because they need the driver to be always alert on country roads, and on the highway the brand's cars are viable requiring the driver to be attentive on the road but leaving him/her more at ease to perform other tasks.

1.3   Study Problem

In these days, with the increasing evolution in the automotive industry, the evolution of self-driving cars has started to be a question asked by manufacturers and users. It was promised that in 2020 we would have the first autonomous car on the road, and to this day we only have prototypes of fully autonomous cars (level 5). The most advanced level we have in 2021 are level 4 cars, like as an example the Google's car, Waymo.

The study problem of this dissertation is the autonomous car, it's necessary to research and investigate how the design of the car can be, to understand what the obstacles are for the colocation of the car in the market, as well as to analyze and investigate what the users most look for and need in the car. That said, all the elements of the internal environment of a current car, that's a non-piloted car, will be analyzed, and analyze how can the autonomous car environment be, testing different environments in virtual reality, to contain results that will guide us into this new era in the future.

The dissertation aims to develop the cockpit of a fully autonomous, level 5 car and analyze what its design, the type of drivers, passengers and activities that can be done in the car might look like, and furthermore to create a viable cockpit for the future.

---

[1] Blind spots are the area around the vehicle that cannot be seen directly, or through the rear-view mirrors, while driving (Paulo 2015).

This article aims to introduce all the important and essential research that has been done over time, focusing not on showing the result, but rather the beginning of a study, which will later be posted the results with all the tests performed and with the cockpit fully developed and tested by people.

2 Literature Review

The first cars appeared around the XVIII century, and the cars ran on steam and electricity, both of which were already used to move trains. William Morrison built the first electric car in the United States. In 1898 Ferdinand Porsche created the first hybrid vehicle, which was powered by gas and electricity. In 1885 Karl Benz invented the first gas-powered car, which had had three wheels and room for two people, in 1891 came the first cars with four wheels. The first cars were very different from what we know today. They had no windshields, no round steering wheel, no doors, and no blinkers. The production of modern vehicles was driven by Karl Benz's gasoline-powered cars, and many companies tried to follow in his footsteps, but it was with the Henry Ford's Model T in 1908 that automobiles began to resemble what we know today, thanks to Ford's invention of the assembly line, the Model T went into mass production. When oil was discovered in Texas, gasoline became cheap, and sales of gasoline-powered vehicles began to increase. Today, with the high cost of gasoline and concerns about environmental pollution, electric vehicles are on the rising. With the evolution of mass production came new features that were missing in the old cars such as seat belts, windshields, and rear-view mirrors. In the early 1990s keyless entry systems keyless entry systems, electric windows and among other things. Today's modern cars already have Bluetooth, advanced security systems, GPS, and Wi-Fi. The automobile has undergone several changes over the years and has gone through several phases of invention (Drive Safety 2020). Cars are increasingly connected to people's reality, and the future lies in connecting cars to cities and to the world that surrounds them.

2.1 Driving Levels

To understand the evolution of automobiles, it is necessary to understand the levels of driving. There are six levels, from 0 to 5, and each level will be analyzed below. According to Vitor (2018), the level zero (0), has no automation, but this is the level where "it all started", the driver performs all operational tasks, such as braking, accelerating, etc., all driving information must be analyzed by the driver himself, including the reaction to dangers. This level came about with the creation of the automobile (Fig. 1). Level one (1) is driver assistance and at this first level some automation can already be considered. This is the most common level on today's roads, the car helps in some functions, but these are shared with the driver, and both share control of the vehicle, as an example of this level we have the parking assistance to the driver, in which the driver oversees the car's speed, while the car parks itself alone (Hall 2020). According to Vitor (2021), this level one technology began to be implemented in 2007 and started what are now called "modern vehicles". It is important to note that this technology prevails to this day. Level two (2) is partial automation, at this level the cars have internal systems that take care of all aspects of driving, such as acceleration and braking, allowing the driver to abstract from some of his tasks. This level is known as "hands-off". (Hall 2020). According to Vítor (2021) it's important to mention that the driver must always be ready to take control of the car, as an example of this level we have the Tesla, because it's able to keep drivers in the right lane of the road and at a safe distance from the car in front. Level three (3) is conditional automation, according to Hall (2020) these cars can already be considered "autonomous", because at this level the driver can relax while the car drives itself, even so, the driver must always be alerted to intervene. Level four (4) is autonomous driving, cars at this level are known as "mind-off" because the driver does not need to intervene, and if he wants, he can even sleep. At this level there are still some restrictions because the fully autonomous driving mode can only be "activated" in certain areas or traffic jams. If the vehicle is not in the specified area, it must be able to take over in case of emergencies if the driver is unable to do so (Hall 2020). In concordance with Vitor (2021), In this automation phase the vehicles are already expected to have a high level of connectivity between them, such as vehicle-to-vehicle (V2V) and vehicle-to-infrastructure (V2I) communication. As an example of level 4 we have Google's Waymo car, which drives without a driver, but always has a person on the lookout in case something goes wrong so that he can intervene. Level five (5) cars are the full automation cars, and according to Hall (2020), these cars no longer require any human interaction, they are fully autonomous. According to Vitor (2021), at this level there is no longer a need for drivers to know how to drive, since the vehicle is in full control of the car itself. It's important to mention that there is still no legislation for this level, and this will be the level that will be deepened in order to obtain results for virtual reality tests, at the end of these tests we will have the results to create a cockpit with the features that users most prioritize in a car.

Fig. 1. Oldsmobile Curver Dash, zero level of automation (Source: Felipe 2018)

2.2 Advantages and Disadvantages of Autonomous Cars

The advance of technologies in vehicles has been significant and evolutionary, but associated with these advances there are also challenges or drawbacks that arise over time and that must be analyzed in order for this evolution to be possible and happen.

According to Mitti (2020) and Henrique (2017), the advantages of autonomous cars are:

- Reduction of traffic accidents caused by human factors, since the car will be able to drive itself.
- People with disabilities (motor or visual disabilities) will be able to use the car without the need for assistance.
- The driver will have the opportunity to perform other tasks, such as catching up on work, or reading a book, and therefore will not need to waste time on driving, increasing the user's productivity.
- Increased traffic, with reduced distances between vehicles.
- Autonomous cars compared to humans will decrease the occurrence of accidents and human failures (remembering that the car has to be well programmed).
- Autonomous vehicles compared to humans offer more safety, as a well-programmed machine avoids human failures and consequently the occurrence of accidents.
- The comfort that the autonomous cars offer because the person would not need to own a vehicle, just a car sharing service would suffice, and it would take the person to the desired destination.

According to Mitti (2020) and Henrique (2017), the disadvantages of autonomous cars are:

- Legal liabilities for events caused by the automobile must be defined.
- Need to regulate traffic laws for autonomous vehicles.
- Develop sensors.
- All machines are subject to failure, just like human beings, and one of the biggest problems is the decisions that the vehicle can make, especially when it comes to human lives.

2.3 Passenger's Classes

In city cars there are three classes of passengers, the driver, who is the person driving the car, the passenger, who is next to the driver, and the passengers, who are the people in the back seats of the car, but the analysis of the autonomous car should be based not only on cars, but also on airplanes. It's important to mention that in the autonomous car everyone ends up being a passenger, so if we analyze the viewpoint from the cockpit of an airplane, passengers are distinguished by class.

According to Yamany (2019), there are three classes of service on a flight, first class, business class, and economy class, each class has different prices and has its own characteristics, both in terms of price and in terms of passenger comfort and comfort. First class is the best seats on the plane, it has all the advantages of business class, with the privilege of being in the first seats on the plane. Executive class is designed for comfort, and is very similar to first class, the only difference being in the seats. Economy class is the most basic class, and has the services needed for a minimally comfortable flight. In the dissertation the autonomous vehicle can also be differentiated by its classes, just like the airplane since, as mentioned before, everyone who is going to use the car is a passenger. The autonomy of the car and the engineering would not be questioned, all vehicles would be autonomous, what could differentiate the vehicles was their class (their interior design, and their comfort level).

2.4   Autonomous Cars in Portugal

According to Aguiar (2021), at the Portugal Mobi Summit 2021 it was realized that Portugal is on the right path to decarbonization and to the advancement of technology in vehicles, making the automotive sector a service provider and not only an equipment seller. Cars are used very little, and 90% of the time they are stationary. Aira de Mello, Director of Consumer Experience at Volvo Cars Portugal said that autonomous driving will be the best option, where via app it will be possible to book a vehicle to take consumers from point A to point B, in a safe way, where the consumer can take advantage of the car and only worry about their daily chores, arriving at the destination the car can be "rented" by another person, when the user no longer needs it. Currently the electric cars have a higher demand, and in Volvo's case there are already fuel cars that are being discontinued. In Portugal, autonomous cars are estimated to appear around 2025, but it is important to refute those laws do not yet allow the use of autonomous cars on public roads. According to Lusa (2021), the head of the "Bosch Car Multimedia" project says that in 2050 Portugal will reach its peak in the use of autonomous cars, but fifth generation infrastructures, the 5G, must be in place. In Portugal 5G started to emerge around this year (2021) and it is estimated that by 2023 70% of the Portuguese area will have 5G coverage, and by 2025 90% of that area will have 5G coverage.

3   Study Objective and Methodology

The goal of this study is to understand how the interior elements of an autonomous vehicle act on passenger perception and behavior, thus developing a final cockpit that connects all the elements and creates a welcoming space that is less like the traditional car. Testing in virtual reality the behavior of passengers inside an autonomous car is also a goal, because only with these tests will we be able to reach the largest number of people, and only then can we create something with foundation.

The methodology used to elaborate this work is a methodology with a theoretical and practical approach, the research and data collection will be analyzed using the bibliographical study, through scientific articles and papers, books, reliable websites, also analyzing other studies that are being developed. The practical part, will be carried out with people who will test the interior of the vehicle in virtual reality, thus getting the opinion of users, and study each opinion that was provided in order to create a cockpit for the autonomous car in rendering, studying all the answers provided by users, in order to obtain reliable and viable results for future research.

Below is the flow chart with all the development phases of the study (Fig. 2):

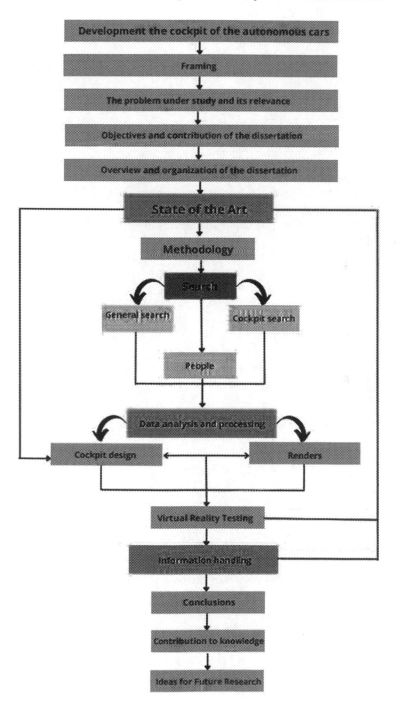

Fig. 2. Phase organization chart (by Diana Reis)

4   Class Definition for Autonomous Cars' Interior

Autonomous vehicles are still evolving, over the years companies have been creating prototypes of vehicles to be implemented, and several ideas have emerged of how would be these cars that are the innovation of the future. Companies like Google and Volvo among others, have very different concepts of what in their vision will be the car of the future, but ideas that can be implemented and executed by companies with the right technology. Autonomous cars are innovating the idea of driving, so driving will no longer be used, to give way to different activities inside the vehicle. Autonomous vehicles have numerous features that differentiate them from each other, with some having more technology and others being just like the more common cars currently on the market. To better understand how autonomous cars can be very different in their cockpit and design, three classes have been identified, mentioned below, to better understand the difference between them.

These classes were created throughout the literature review, with the research conducted it was noticeable that autonomous cars were resembling airplanes, trains, or even ships, because although they all have a driver most of the time these types of transport drive themselves, most of the time everyone is a passenger. Thus, concluding that all these means of transportation are good examples and studies that should and have been analyzed, to reach these conclusions that will be described below.

Throughout the research, three different "Habitats" or classes were created, with many aspects in common, thinking of all the characteristics of the means of transportation mentioned above, and also thinking of their advantages and disadvantages.

4.1   Habitat Class 1 - Traditional Model

The class one (1) was defined as the traditional model, the most usual class for the cockpit of the car. The cockpit is identical to the cars that are driven today, it is a more traditional model in that there is still a steering wheel, and the seats are in the forward position (all passengers face the car).

Passengers will be able to enjoy a fully autonomous car, and re-drive other activities in the car, such as reading a book. For those who like to drive, the traditional model of the autonomous car is the most suitable. The driver becomes the passenger but can always want to take control of the car and drive it.

We can see in the pictures below how the cockpits of the most usual cars will look like.

In Figs. 3, 4 and 5 we can see that the environment of the car is identical to what we currently know, the seats are in the front position, it is a robust environment where you can perform some activities, thus stating that this is the typical traditional car that we know today, with the particularity of being fully autonomous.

It is in this class that those who like to drive can still do it, because this is the ideal car for those who have passion for driving.

Fig. 3. Samsung digital cockpit (Pplware 2021)

Fig. 4. Concept i, Toyota's proposed autonomous vehicle (Universo Lambda 2017)

4.2 Habitat Class 2 - Completely Disconnected Autonomous

Class two (2), defined as completely disconnected autonomous car, is the intermediate class of autonomous cars. These vehicles may or may not have a steering wheel, that's the steering wheel may be removable, or the user may simply keep it hidden, the passenger is driver only when he or she wishes. The car looks like a living room, as the seats face

Fig. 5. Nissan Xmotion interior, autonomous car (Nissan 2018)

each other, thus allowing you to talk, play, and do various activities inside the car. The space in this car is compact, but cozy, thus making it a completely shared car.

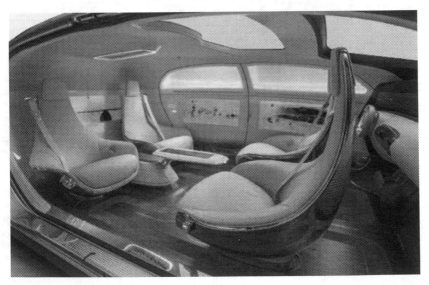

Fig. 6. Concept F015 da Mercedes-Benz inside, autonomous vehicle (Allthecars 2015)

In Figs. 6, 7 and 8 we can see that the car has now become a comfort zone, where people can go and talk facing each other, have more space inside the car to do various activities, it even looks like a living room.

Fig. 7. Panasonic's autonomous cockpit concept (Motor1.com 2017)

Fig. 8. Concept car SEDRIC, Volksvagen, inside (Volksvagen 2017)

4.3 Habitat Class 3 - Autonomous Fully Convertible Car

Class three (3) was named as "Fully convertible autonomous car". It is in this class that some differences emerge that in the above classes it is not possible to identify. This is also the most versatile class. Like the classes described above, class three may or may not have a steering wheel, because the steering wheel can be hidden or even non-existent, everything depends on the driver's choice. The car becomes a comfort zone, and we can see this car as being like a "Hotel" or a living room, the seats become beds, containing compartments to put essential things for long trips. In the Level 3 autonomous car, everyone is a passenger. You can do the most varied tasks, from watching movies, reading, playing a game, getting food and dinner in the car, etc.

In Figs. 9 and 10, the car has become a walking house "like the snail with the house on its back", but in this case we can say that the car becomes even more comfortable

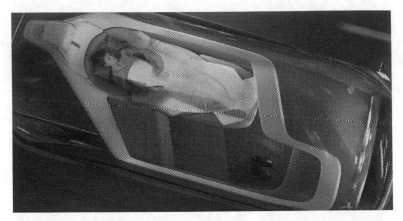

Fig. 9. Volvo 360c, inside (Volvo 2021)

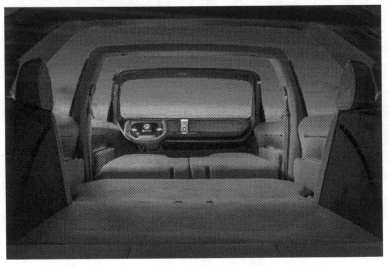

Fig. 10. Concept car LIFE, Volksvagen, inside (Volksvagen 2021).

than an airplane, we can perform several activities in the same way as in other cars, but the particularity is that for long trips it becomes a complete room, of course in this initial stage we can't take many people inside the car yet, but it is an innovation for those who want to travel without wasting time in airport lines, for example.

Above were described the three types of autonomous vehicles that may exist in the future, their characteristics are identical, but their interior can be a real home in some cars. Automotive innovation is something that has been talked about over the years, and sooner or later, cars were going to start driving themselves and one day may even fly.

Currently several features are being tested to get these cars on the road as soon as possible, but in the meantime, we can create, innovate, and figure out what will meet the consumer. After this intensive research, the cockpit design will be made and rendered in Blender, and later will be placed in Unity in order to place cameras inside, in order to test in virtual reality all the cockpits created for this dissertation. The tests in virtual reality will be made with people from the university in order to understand which of the three cockpits is ideal for the majority, thus being able to make a study and create the final cockpit with all the ideas taken from the virtual experiment.

5   Expected Results

Currently the evolution of the automotive industry is constantly growing, although autonomous vehicles are nothing new to the industry, to outsiders it is still a very distant reality. People see the automobile as reliable, safe, and able to transport them from one place to another in most situations.

During the work, I was questioning people about what they thought the autonomous car would be, and they all answered that it will never exist, because for them the industry is not yet prepared for such a big evolution and "these things only exist in movies". The truth is that the industry is increasingly able to create new things and innovate in various aspects, and of course, the automotive industry is always in constant evolution to make not only their cars safer, but also to ensure the advancement of cars.

In the course of this research, it was possible to understand more about the cars and their future, thus being able to draw conclusions for future cars to further the research, and to create a viable cockpit for the passengers.

Throughout the research several important aspects were mentioned for the development of the topic, for the creation of the three completely different autonomous car cockpits.

The expected results of this research are to create three different cockpits for the three "Habitats" developed, gathering as much information as possible with people, using renders that will be developed and tested in virtual reality in order to understand which cockpit users like best. The goal is also to start developing research for other future research, letting other people know of new ideas for both design and engineering. The renders are still under development to later be tested by real people. Once the renders are finished, the final conclusions of this still ongoing research will be drawn and the results of the cockpit of the autonomous car that best fits today's lifestyle will be presented.

Soon we will publish the results of the evaluation with users in test with virtual reality, which should serve to guide designers in the creation of more efficient autonomous vehicle habitat.

Acknowledgements. This work is financed by national funds through FCT - Fundação para a Ciência e a Tecnologia, I.P., under the Strategic Project with the reference UIDB/04008/2020.

References

Aguiar, C.: A new era will bring electric and autonomous vehicle through NA app. Portugal MOBI summit (2021). https://portugalms.com/en/a-new-era-will-bring-electric-and-autonomous-veh icles-through-an-app/. Accessed 11 Oct 2021

Alecrim, E.: Primeiro protótipo funcional do carro autónomo do Google está pronto. Tecnoblog. https://tecnoblog.net/171745/prototipo-carro-autonomo-google/. Accessed 15 Oct 2021

Allthecars: Mercedes presents autonomous car prototype. All the Cars (2015). https://allthecars. wordpress.com/2015/01/07/mercedes-apresenta-prototipo-de-carro-autonomo/

Baudrillard, J.: The consumer society (1995). BAUDRILLARD_1995_A_sociedade_de_consumo.pdf. Accessed 15 Oct 2021

Bellis, M.: History of the automobile ThoughtCo (2019). https.//www.thoughtco.com/automobile-history-1991458?terms=History+Of+The+Automobile. Accessed 21 Nov 2021

Bruce, C.: Panasonic autonomous car. Motor1 (2017). https://www.motor1.com/news/132914/pan asonic-autonomous-cabin-concept-ces/

Drive Safety: Evolution of the Automobile (2020). https://www.idrivesafely.com/defensive-dri ving/trending/evolution-automobile. Accessed 22 Nov 2021

Felipe, C.: What are the 5 levels of autonomous cars and what do they mean. Connected World (2018). https://mundoconectado.com.br/artigos/v/5004/quais-sao-os-5-niveis-de-carros-autonomos-e-o-que-significam

Hall, C.: Autonomous cars: levels of autonomous driving explained. Pocket-lint (2020). https://www.pocket-lint.com/pt-br/carros/noticias/143955-sao-explicados-os-niveis-de-direcao-aut onoma. Accessed 22 Nov 2021

Henrique, M.: Autonomous cars: one solution or one more problem? Blastingnews (2017).https://br.blastingnews.com/tecnologia/2017/01/carros-autonomos-uma-solucao-ou-mais-um-pro blema-001398121.html. Accessed 02 Dec 2021

Joshi, N.: How virtual reality can improve autonomous vehicles. BBNTIMES. How Virtual Reality Can Improve Autonomous Vehicles (2021). http://bbntimes.com

Lusa: Autonomous cars should only arrive in Portugal in 2025. TSF Rádio de Notícias (2021). https://www.tsf.pt/futuro/carros-autonomos-so-devem-chegar-a-portugal-em-2025-13390062.html. Accessed 02 Dec 2021

Mapfre: What is an autonomous car. https://www.mapfre.com.br/para-voce/seguro-auto/artigos/o-que-e-um-carro-autonomo/. Accessed 03 Dec 2021

Mitti: The advantages and challenges of autonomous cars (2020). http://www.mitti.com.br/as-van tagens-e-desafios-dos-carros-autonomos/

Nakata Automotiva: Autonomous cars: complete guide to understand everything about the subject (2019). https://blog.nakata.com.br/carros-autonomos-guia-completo-para-entender-tudo-sobre-o-assunto/. Accessed 03 Dec 2021

Nissan: The Nissan X motion, Nissan (2018). https://www.nissanusa.com/vehicles/future-concept/xmotion-autonomous-suv.html

Ondruša, J., et al.: How do autonomous cars work? ScienceDirect (2020). https://www.sciencedi rect.com/science/article/pii/S2352146520300995. Accessed 06 Dec 2021

Piper, K.: It's 2020. Where are our self-driving cars? Vox, 28 de fevereiro 2020. https://www.vox.com/future-perfect/2020/2/14/21063487/self-driving-cars-autonomous-vehicles-waymo-cruise-uber. Accessed 14 Dec 2021

PPLWARE: Samsung shows off its digital cockpit for autonomous electric cars (2021). PPLWARE: https://pplware.sapo.pt/motores/samsung-mostra-o-seu-cockpit-digital-para-carros-eletricos-autonomos/

Universo Lambda: Cars: vision of the future (2017). UL: https://universolambda.com.br/carros visao-de-futuro/

Vitor, M.: Autonomous cars - discover the 5 driving levels (2018). PPLWARE: https://pplware. sapo.pt/motores/carros-autonomos-conheca-os-5-niveis-de-conducao/, Accessed 16 Dec 2021

Volksvagen: SEDRIC- Generous interior with lounge atmosphere despite compact dimensions (2017). VW: https://www.volkswagen-newsroom.com/en/sedric-concept-car-3552

Volksvagen: Volksvagen ID. LIFE, concept car (2021). VW: https://www.volkswagen-newsroom.com/en/the-id-life-world-premiere-7469

Volvo: A new way to travel. Volvo (2021). https://www.volvocars.com/intl/cars/concepts/360c

Yamany, P.: Economy class, business class and first class: understand the differences (2019). Skyscanner: https://www.skyscanner.com.br/noticias/dicas/classe-economica-classe-executiva-e-primeira-classe-entenda-as-diferencas

Possibilities of the Wearables: Teaching Method for Digital Jewelry Design of the Future

Yi Song, Zhilu Cheng[⊠], and Chi Zhang

Beijing Institute of Fashion Technology, Beijing 100029, China
zhilucheng@qq.com

Abstract. Considering that digital technology comprehensively promotes the transformation of traditional industries, this paper aims to discuss the new framework by putting jewelry teaching into the future scene and construct a set of future-oriented digital jewelry design teaching methods. The teaching framework of Future, Tool, Scenario, Body, and Technology are proposed and connected into elastic micro-cycle teaching module and implicit teaching closed-loop to deepen and extend the content and requirements of teaching. Based on the teaching framework, the evaluation and verification model are established, and then the validity of the teaching theory and method is verified through teaching practice and achievements. Under the guidance of this teaching method, students can jump out of the traditional jewelry making logic to stand in the future perspective. Consequently, their future-oriented creativity and imagination can be stimulated, providing new teaching methods for the integration of design and technology innovation.

Keywords: Future scenario · Jewelry design · Digital technology · Teaching method

1 Introduction

Jewelry is a unique carrier reflecting the social-historical process, human spirit, and lifestyle. As an essential issue of wearables, jewelry integrates several factors such as culture, economy, science and technology, and design, with the characteristics of interdisciplinary research and practice. Under the background of design, the jewelry research dimension has gradually expanded from formal aesthetics to comprehensive and forward-looking connotations. In the information age, digital technology, as a technical element with intensive cross-innovation and extensive penetration, influences the process, behavior, and method of design innovation, contributing to driving the social process, discipline, and industrial development. "No longer dictating or restricting the creativity of the making process, computer software, digital technologies, and the tools of a large scale of manufacturing are instead being applied in unconventional ways to enhance and assist it." [1] Digital technology has become the key driving force for the diversified development of jewelry, and increasing jewelry design colleges and universities have included digital technology in the teaching category. However, most digital jewelry teaching tends to start from a single technical software or digital manufacturing

M. M. Soares et al. (Eds.): HCII 2022, LNCS 13323, pp. 400–413, 2022.
https://doi.org/10.1007/978-3-031-05906-3_30

process and set the course tasks in a combination of the brainstorming method. Thus, the innovation of design results and students' imagination and creativity are limited. If indeed, the contemporary phenomena of "digital thinking" are different from traditional models, resulting in emerging pressure to pioneer new teaching paradigms. "Theories and methods of digital design can no longer be conceptualized as the merging of computational tools with conventional formulations of design thinking." [2] The design itself is a future-oriented creative behavior. Students can better adapt to the rapid change of the technological environment and make full preparations for the future in advance by taking the future as the theme of teaching and training in the context of various forms of digital technology changing with each passing day. Given the above problems, this paper tries to discuss the new framework and teaching ideas with thematic teaching tasks by putting digital jewelry teaching into the future scene and then construct a set of future-oriented digital jewelry teaching methods. "Increasingly, future-oriented practices are influencing the design disciplines of today." [3] Future scenarios are adopted as an effective means to stimulate students' imagination. Therefore, they obtain new thinking by exploring potential future scenarios. Meanwhile, the diversified forms of digital technologies are integrated to construct future scenes, assist body artifacts, and enhance the comprehensive ability of display and communication, so as to respond to new demands in future scenes and rethink the new relationship between design and technology.

The challenge of this study is to take jewelry as a research medium to constantly broaden the definition and boundaries of jewelry through future-oriented instructional design, so as to break students' traditional thinking and aesthetic rules. From the future perspective, a new design path is constructed to guide students to output their design imagination using the uncertainty of the future and then generate design creativity with future thinking. The future-oriented teaching process goes beyond skill training and jumps out of business logic, allowing the design to explore issues in a more innovative, inspiring, and forward-looking way.

2 Teaching Framework

Based on the characteristics of jewelry design education and future-oriented teaching vision, the elastic teaching framework of Future, Tool, Scenario, Body, and Technology are proposed in this paper (see Fig. 1). In the teaching framework of future jewelry digital design, the classification and positioning of the future are first presented. The scope of the Future faced by the course is positioned by classifying fuzzy, abstract, and uncertain futures. Second, the exploration and deduction of Tool are performed with independently developed exploration tools to deduce scenes in a specific scope of the future. Third, the fiction and imagination of the new Scenario are conducted. Specifically, it invents and imagines the future scenarios triggered by the current trend or hot events. Fourth, body and dress guide students to expand their body cognition and motivate body wears and props in future scenarios. The fifth step is Technology. The design scheme is realized by integrating comprehensive digital technologies at the design end, manufacturing end, and display end. Then, body wearables are put into the constructed future scenarios. The above five steps constitute the basic path of future jewelry digital design teaching.

Besides, the contents and requirements of deepening and extending curriculum teaching are elaborated in this paper by connecting the above elements into elastic

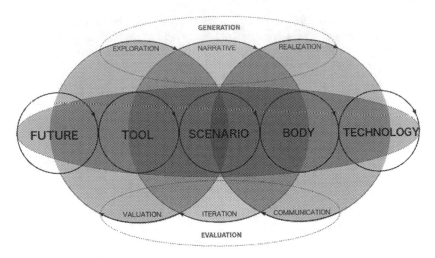

Fig. 1. Teaching framework of future jewelry design

micro-circulation teaching content modules and recessive teaching closed-loop. Firstly, Future, Tool, and Scenario are intersected to con-struct a teaching content module with "Exploration" and "Valuation" as the target. Secondly, Tool, Scenario, and Body are intersected to construct a teaching content module with "Narrative" and "Iteration" as the target. Furthermore, Scenario, Body, and Technology are intersected to construct a teaching content module with "Realization" and "Communication" as the target. The three modules are interwoven and superimposed to form the "Generation" clue with Exploration, Narrative, and Realization as the target, as well as the "Valuation" clue with Communication, Iteration, and Valuation as the target, so as to achieve a complete teaching closed-loop. Finally, an assessment and evaluation model are established based on this teaching framework. The effectiveness of the teaching theory and method is verified through teaching practice and teaching results. Under the guidance of this teaching method, students can jump out of traditional jewelry creation logic and guide the comprehensive application of the technology through conceptual creativity.

2.1   Cycle Module 1: From Exploration to Value

The purpose of cycle module I is to guide students to recognize various future types, conduct exploratory investigations within the scope of the future encouraged by the course, and complete the target positioning of design value output. "It is conceivable that more effective methods and tools can be developed to support conceptual design if one understands how cognitive processes are stimulated to generate design ideas." [4] Therefore, the main task of this module is to encourage students to reflect on the single cognition of the real world in the macro time clue, break through the "present", and generate a new starting point for design with future classification and scene positioning tool diagrams.

According to the complex characteristics of Future, abstract summary, induction, and classification, then used as recognition tools to help students complete exploratory research. As illustrated in Fig. 2, the potential Future rooted in past and present social, economic, and technological conditions is one of the people's expectations for the current situation. Therefore, the past, present, and future are set on the timeline simultaneously to demonstrate the evolution relationship between the three time points. Meanwhile, the special attributes of Future can be compared more clearly. Based on the history and present, Future can be reasonably imagined and judged through analysis, prediction, and deduction. In this paper, the category of Future is further subdivided to make the future focused on by the course clearer. The first category is the "reasonable" future, which is a linear continuation of what already exists, easy to imagine, create, and acquire. Since this kind of future is more certain, it limits the imagination by being too close to the present reality. The second category is the "expected" future, which is a reasonable imagination of what may happen in the future. This is not only consistent with common sense but also full of unknown and uncertainty. The third category is the "unexpected" future, which is close to imaginary imagination and cannot be predicted regarding whether it can happen. The three futures mentioned above have different characteristics, and students should be encouraged to pay attention to the second category in teaching. The scenario imagination in this category of Future is the most enlightening and transforms uncertainty into creativity with reasonable deduction, contributing to the formation of a fundamental difference from traditional courses.

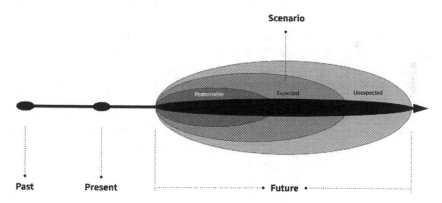

Fig. 2. Future classification and scene positioning tool diagram

Based on classification cognition and focus orientation, extensive information investigation and knowledge exploration are conducted in the corresponding category of Future to clarify the value attribute of design influence. Mass information is identified with positioning tools and then is learned, analyzed, and deduced. The investigation contents are mainly composed of introspective cultural phenomena, hot social events, discussion topics triggered by technological updates, tendency judgment, and insight into regulations. Through the observation, research, and deep thinking of the above investigation content, students can form reasonable speculation and moderate imagination about the fuzziness of Future. The methods of exploratory research majorly involve browsing hot news, literature reading, new knowledge investigation, and expert interview. The breadth and depth are combined, and then the integration analysis is conducted to reveal the enlightening "potential stimulus" and stimulate the subsequent design actions. Hence, the ambiguous future begins to clear.

2.2 Cycle Module 2: From Narrative to Iteration

The future indicates that it has not yet been experienced and happened. Different from the present situation, it has certain uncertainties and unknowns. The key to teaching in cycle module 2 lies in building concrete future scenarios with tools and transforming uncertainty and unpredictability into the creativity of design. In the future scene, the creative imagination with the body as the media is generated, and the possibility of the future body is imagined with the design scheme continuously iterated and optimized. "Scenes provide systems of identification and connection while simultaneously inviting acts of novelty, invention, and innovation." [5] Emphasizing the importance of the scene in the design process can shift the focus of the design from single to systematic, from static to moving, and from objects to relationships. However, the scenes with future attributes are relatively reasonable imaginations of the future following experience or current clues. The construction of future scenes is not only based on critical reflection of the present and an accurate preview of future possibilities but also exhibits the vision and the comprehensive ability to construct a nonlinear space-time system. "Scenarios are not meant to be predictions of the future, while their art means is to predict possible future circumstances, to reflect on these an inform action to be taken." [6] The behavior of constructing future scenes can activate people's willingness to actively participate in the future scenes they describe to a large extent, providing the initiative of the design.

The future scene in this module adopts narration to present a series of microscopic sets of people, relationships, behaviors, and environments in a specific time and space. To better produce narrative imagination, the course developed a future scene canvas tool to achieve the above effect and thus stimulated students to produce design ideas under hypothetical conditions. As suggested in Fig. 3, the canvas tool consists of deductive imagination of people, relationships, behaviors, and environments according to potential stimulus conditions, narration, and presentation in the form of keywords, text, or images. Then, the described scene is continuously expanded outward in detail, and the key role of the body in the scene is imagined, to invent and transform the "body prop" that can stimulate the narrative, namely, the specific design scheme of jewelry. The content of the design scheme involves the form, structure, color, and function of the jewelry. Then, it is drawn in the form of a sketch. In this way, jewelry is a key "prop" produced naturally by the body after the intervention rather than an abrupt and stiff existence. Apart from stimulating specific design schemes with scene narration, iteration is also a crucial work link. In other words, it is constantly restored to the scene for reflection, evaluation, and continuous optimization modification in the process of producing the scheme, guaranteeing that the future scenarios described are logical and desirable. This tool is a critical part of this teaching strategy that cannot be obtained and is also understood as teaching support. This is in that it triggers, standardizes, and constrains design behaviors through visual and written forms, and proposes clear requirements for subsequent design implementation and technical application.

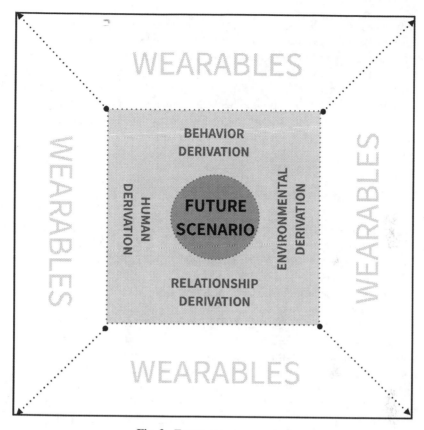

Fig. 3. Future scene canvas tool

2.3 Cycle Module 3: From Implementation to Communication

The teaching task of cycle module 3 aims to complete the modeling and digital manufacturing of the jewelry design scheme and then use multi-media narrative means to visualize future scenes, complete the presentation of concepts and schemes, and communicate and exchange with the public. Creative design concepts and program requirements are produced with the promotion of the first two cycle modules. The teaching goal of Cycle Module 3 is to use various digital technologies to respond to pre-order needs. The existing digital technology forms are integrated from the design, the manufacturing, and the dissemination. For example, 2D and 3D software tools on the design side are applied to complete visual modeling and rendering, simulate and verify the structure, or generate shapes with the help of parametric. The personalized 3D printing technology and CNC-milling technology at the manufacturing are employed to complete the auxiliary manufacturing of physical samples. The communication and presentation of the design are completed with the simulation animation technology, web technology, virtual reality technology, and augmented reality technology at the dissemination. "Innovative Software, 3D scanners, manipulation of new materials, and contamination between skills shape new product scenarios and completely subvert the old way of designing. This is the landscape in which a series of pilot experiments highlight a renewed relationship between design, jewelry, and technology." [7] With diversified digital technologies, fictional future scenes can be presented more effectively. Thus, students can be encouraged to rethink the innovative relationship between design creativity and technology application and then perceive the "positive role" played by technologies in developing future-oriented innovation. The comprehensive application of multiple digital technological methods tests students' ability to quickly master new technologies. This can be effectively supported by third-party tool platforms, small service providers, and mature technical interfaces.

3   Teaching Implementation Effect

The teaching implementation results are applied to verify the practical effect of future jewelry design teaching model applications. "Jewelers need to understand the kinds of work that are available to them, given the set of attributes they possess. The specific balance of knowledge, experience, technical ability, and temperament that is unique to each of students will lend themselves to different kinds of outcomes." [8] According to the real teaching process and students' practice, the teaching method and theory are validated, and then the teaching effect is demonstrated. The course is guided by future scenarios and supported by jewelry digitization knowledge. Afterward, the teaching tasks are completed by group collaboration, and the teaching processes such as positioning the future, tool integration, narrative deduction, wearable design, and technology realization are finished. A total of 15 juniors participated in this course practice and were divided into three groups (5 in each group) to perform the teaching practice for three weeks. The following three groups of cases are students' design projects under the guidance of future jewelry design teaching methods.

3.1   Case 1: Plant Healing Jewelry

As exhibited in Fig. 4, the jewelry with healing function in the future context is actively explored with "Plant Healing" as the clue. The narrative scene is set as a "Plant Healing Center", which adopts portable and wearable plants to help people overcome physical and mental obstacles, improve physical, mental, and spiritual states, and comfort the inner world of wearers through the interaction between people and plants as well as the five-sense (sight, hearing, touch, smell, and taste) experience. This case makes the living plant jewelry become a slow release "healing medicament" by combining with people's emotional states. Finally, 3D modeling, elastic resin 3D printing, and virtual reality display are taken to conduct design implementation and communication, and the future jewelry system of human healing through plants is established, so as to present a series of valuable "wearable plant jewelry" to the audience.

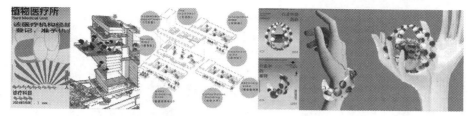

Fig. 4. Design process of plant healing jewelry

3.2   Case 2: Body Stamp Jewelry

As presented in Fig. 5, this case reflects on traditional body decoration ways starting from hot social events. It sets the narrative scene as a body stamping clinic through the future scene canvas tool and then explores the design of portable jewelry stamping tools. Using the simulating surgery, the gemstone pattern is imprinted with the body. In this case, a series of gemstone seals with the attributes of surgical tools are manufactured to visually exhibit the medical scene and rethink the "inset" relationship between gemstones and the body. The design scheme is generated by exploring the new "inset" relationship between body and gem in future scenarios. Finally, the design implementation and display are performed through 3D modeling, 3D printing combined with CNC-milling technology, and interactive digital images. Consequently, the method of stimulating creative thinking is widened using tools to produce a body-centered narrative.

Fig. 5. Design process of body stamp jewelry

3.3   Case 3: Scent Memory Jewelry

As suggested in Fig. 6, this case sets the future scene as a virtual experience museum that can carry odor memory, explores jewelry with odor retention through design, and supports users to interact through the virtual exhibition hall. Users can upload their stories online and customize jewelry with their memories. Meanwhile, memory stories about food smell are selected from the story files generated by the system, and then special materials that can retain the smell are generated with a special way of preparation. Moreover, jewelry is used as a wearable carrier to carry the smell, as displayed in the store section of the website platform. This case generates the design through users' unique smell memory experience and finally realizes the interactive communication mechanism from the online experience to offline realization through 3D modeling, 3D printing technology, WEB, and simulation animation technology, contributing to stimulating multiple possibilities of design.

Fig. 6. Design process of scent memory jewelry

The above practical cases are all based on the teaching model of future jewelry design, as illustrated in Fig. 7. The valuable future context is deduced with the "Exploration-Value" module. Narrative and iterative design schemes are positioned through the "Narration - Iteration" module. Meanwhile, design, production, and presentation are finally performed through the "Realization-Communication" module. Besides, the three modules are interwoven to produce "Generative Clues" and "Evaluation Clues". Among them, the feasibility and effectiveness of the design scheme are evaluated and selected through the evaluation clue "Communication - Iteration - Value", after the effective design scheme is stimulated by the generation clue "Exploration - Narrative - Realization". Finally, a circular teaching process is formed.

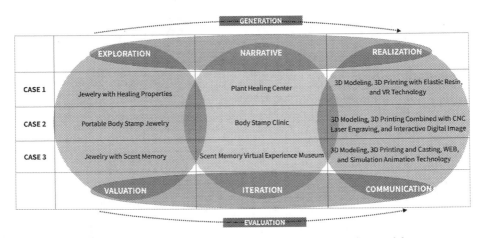

Fig. 7. Three cases based on future jewelry design teaching model

4   Evaluation and Verification

4.1   Progress Implementation

When the teaching process ends, 6 professional tutors aged 28–60 engaged in jewelry design teaching are invited to participate in the evaluation of the design results of students to verify the implementation effect of the teaching method. Among them, 2 lecturers, 2 associate professors, and 2 professors are included, with 2 males and 4 females. The above tutors are committed to different jewelry design research directions and undertake different professional courses, involving jewelry making technology, cultural research, material innovation, design methods, as well as commercial jewelry product development. They have rich experience in jewelry design practice and research. The six tutors participate in the assessment of three groups of students (15 in total), including the design process demonstration, observation of physical works, and participation in interactive display experience. After the assessment, the tutors score the students' design results from the perspective of experts. This evaluation can reflect tutors' attitudes and opinions on the creative performance of each group of students while verifying whether this teaching method can achieve good teaching effects.

4.2 Evaluation and Validation Model

By combining with the particularity of teaching objectives and corresponding to the three cyclic modules in the teaching framework, the evaluation and verification model including value, ability, and effect is proposed (Fig. 8). Cycle module 1 corresponds to the evaluation at the value level, with three evaluation indexes of novelty, inspiration, and prospectiveness. Cycle module 2 corresponds to the evaluation of the ability level, with three evaluation indexes of divergence ability, derivation ability, and analysis ability. Cycle module 3 corresponds to the evaluation of the effect level of technology use, with three evaluation indexes of design effect, manufacturing effect, and display effect. Each assessment point has five evaluation levels: worse, poor, general, good, and excellent. Each group is scored according to the evaluation points in the evaluation model, in which 0–1, 1–2, 2–3, 3–4, and 4–5 indicate worse, poor, general, good, and excellent, respectively. The specific indicators in the model are explained as follows. In the value level, novelty suggests the degree of differentiation of results compared with most other designs; inspiration refers to the ability to provide new ideas and methodological reference and stimulation for other designs; prospectiveness reflects breakthrough meaning, which can provide direct guidance for other designs. In the ability level divergent ability refers to the ability to actively trigger multiple design associations following certain information; deduction ability implies the ability to logically deduce new design cognition based on existing information; analytical ability designates the ability to disassemble and discern key information that drives designs. In the effect level, design effect indicates the comprehensive visual effect of the design in terms of shape, color, structure, and function; manufacturing effect demonstrates the quality of the process and the degree of fineness of the design; display effect means to present the design result through comprehensive means, making the concept and idea behind the design be perceived by the public. Under the instruction of the evaluation and verification model, students develop a clear understanding of creative performance at different levels and realize the key role of different assessment points in the learning process. The evaluation model is not only an assessment tool for students' work achievements but also presents the advantages and characteristics of the teaching method, providing ideas and references for the validity verification of the teaching method.

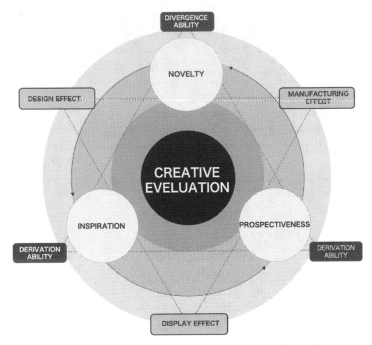

Fig. 8. Evaluation and verification model of teaching effects

4.3   Verification Analysis

After finishing the scoring, the scores of all teachers were sorted out and analyzed. In Fig. 9, the average comprehensive score of Cases 1–3 is 3.62, 3.78, and 3.68, respectively. Figure 10 reveals that the comprehensive performance of Case 2 is the best, followed by Case 3 and Case 1. However, the average comprehensive score of the three groups of cases is greater than 3.5, demonstrating that the overall evaluation effect reaches a good level. The teachers have a high evaluation of the students' overall design creativity, implying that the implementation of this teaching method achieves a good effect.

NAME	N	AVERAGE SCORE	MINIMUM SCORE	MAXIMUN SCORE
CASE 1	6	3.62	3.37	4.20
CASE 2	6	3.78	3.60	4.12
CASE 3	6	3.68	3.33	4.14

Fig. 9. Average comprehensive score of works of three cases of students

Overall Average Score

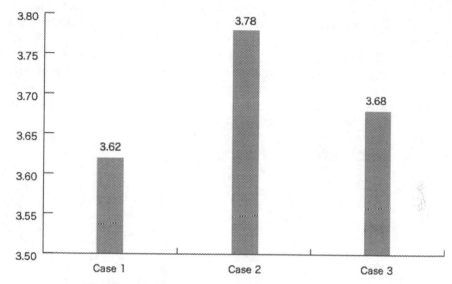

Fig. 10. Visual bar chart of scores of 3 cases of students

INDEX	MINIMUM SCORE	MAXIMUN SCORE	MEAN	STANDARD DEVIATION
NOVELTY	2.8	4.8	3.78	0.56
INSPIRATION	3.0	4.5	3.77	0.53
PROSPECTIVENESS	2.5	4.8	3.37	0.65
DIVERGENCE ABILITY	2.8	4.8	3.63	0.67
DERIVATION ABILITY	2.8	4.8	3.66	0.52
ANALYSIS ABILITY	2.6	4.2	3.47	0.49
DESIGN EFFECT	2.2	4.6	3.49	0.63
MANUFACTURING EFFECT	2.8	4.8	3.75	0.59
DISPLAY EFFECT	3.5	4.8	4.32	0.44

Fig. 11. Scores of the three groups of students at each index point

Based on the whole analysis, the performance of three groups of students in each evaluation index point is emphasized. As illustrated in Fig. 11, the standard deviation value indicates that teachers have relatively consistent opinions on the evaluation of each index point.

In Fig. 12, the performance of the three cases on the evaluation index points is ranked visually and is excellent in display effect and novelty but an average performance in analytical ability and prospectiveness compared with other indexes. However, the comprehensive scores of all the index points are above 3, reaching a good level. This verifies that the effect of students' homework can reflect the characteristics of this teaching method. Therefore, it is necessary to strengthen the cultivation of analytical ability and foresight in the future.

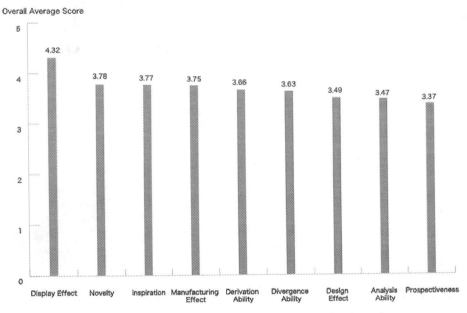

Fig. 12. Scores of the three groups of students at each index point

5   Conclusions

Future-oriented thinking, with the end as the starting point, is a positive attitude to manage changes, a strong sense of shaping the unknown, and the comprehensive ability to obtain the opportunities. Thus, it can effectively drive students' forward-looking thinking. Based on the future-oriented teaching framework model, this paper guides students to construct a new relationship among human beings, objects, and the environment in a specific future scenario and expands the design boundary of body artifacts in the digital environment. Therefore, students can identify, analyze, and predict future trends through active research. Tools are used to create new future scenarios to stimulate narrative and design concepts following critical thinking and logical deduction. Afterward, the design work is conducted and deepened from the perspective of future strategy with the digital prototype. Finally, the design scheme and the wearables are displayed through high-quality visual output. By verifying the teaching process, the above teaching methods are employed to compare and analyze students' design process in each key section and achieve innovation effects, validating the effectiveness of the method. Hopefully, the teaching process can be continuously iterated and optimized based on the existing experience in the future. From the perspective of the teaching framework, the future is regarded as the pre-complement of the design process. Hence, it is still necessary to continue the challenge of integrating the critical thinking into each step. Furthermore, new technological forms will be incubated and invented for potential future scenarios, allowing scene innovation to guide the way of technological progress. In a word, future-oriented digital jewelry design teaching form breaks through the possibility of exploring design from the perspective of form aesthetics, shape, material, technology, and other traditional factors, providing inspiration and motivation for the present action. It can stimulate creativity and imagination. Therefore, it not only responds to diversified jewelry research topics but also enlightens the integration innovation of jewelry design.

References

1. Lucy, J.: Digital Handmade: Craftsmanship and The New Industrial Revolution, 1st edn. Thames & Hudson, London (2015)
2. Rivka, O.: Re-thinking digital design. WIT Trans. Built. Environ. **90**, 239–247 (2006). https://doi.org/10.2495/DARC060241
3. Zoë, P., Santini, B.: Futures thinking: a mind-set, not a method. Touchpoint **10**(2) (2021). https://medium.com/touchpoint/futures-thinking-a-mind-set-not-a-method-64c9b5f9da37. Accessed 21 Dec 2021
4. Yan, J., Oren, B.: Creative patterns and stimulation in conceptual design. Artif. Intell. Eng. Des. Anal. Manuf. **24**(2), 191–209 (2010). https://doi.org/10.1017/S0890060410000053
5. Benjamin, W., Jamie, R., Stuart, R.P.: Scene thinking. Cult. Stud. **29**(3), 285–297 (2015). https://doi.org/10.1080/09502386.2014.937950
6. Anne, M.W.: Designing back from the future. Des. Philos. Papers **12**(2), 151–160 (2015). https://doi.org/10.2752/144871314X14159818597595
7. Jie, S., Elizabeth, F.: Spirit of Luxury and Design: A Perspective from Contemporary Fashion and Jewellery, 1st edn. Tongji University Press and ORO Editions, Shanghai (2021)
8. Peter, D.: Contemporary Jewellery in Context: a Handshake Blueprint, 1st edn. Arnoldsche Art Publishers, Stuttgart (2017)

Dynamic Motion Graphic Innovation in Mid-digital Era

Mengyao Wang[1](✉) and Jingyu Wang[2]

[1] School of Sino-British Digital Media (Digital Media) Art, Luxun Academy of Fine Arts, Dalian 116650, Liaoning Province, China
wangmengyao@lumei.edu.cn
[2] Institute Of Textile and Fashion Design, Luxun Academy of Fine Arts, Shenyang 110004, Liaoning, China

Abstract. During the mid-digital era as we are in, computer science and Internet technology are developing rapidly, we can see the fusion of numerous academic subjects and forms of art, and the collusion of digital media art and graphic visual design to form a temporal dynamic expression of art with its unique advantages. And its all-rounded development which has its own diversification goes in many different phases. Dynamic Image Design in this era not only enriched the expression of traditional information, but it also brings out the information in a much more vivid way by improving its expressiveness. This new method has changed human's definition of the word "beautiful". Dynamic Image Design requires creating a system that merges graphic language and Dynamic Image language, focuses much more on the diversification of expressiveness and propagation of its content as well as enhances the visual impact on the viewers, in order to diversify the development of the Dynamic Image. This article will take a deeper look on its development, discuss the innovational expression through Dynamic Image Design and the possibility of what mid-digital era can bring during this very special era.

Keywords: Digital media · Dynamic graphics · Graphic design

1 The Basic Concept of Dynamic Motion Graphic Design

The word "dynamic" in Dynamic Image Design indicated the fact that the image itself will be characterized by constant change of its content, while focusing on its movements. Comparing to graphic design, the expression becomes much more vivid to the viewers to catch the eyes of the viewers, to draw them closer.

Dynamic is not only the production of development of digital media, but optimized both visually and auditorily. By using dynamic elements while being presented, it organically blends in many different fields of art. Also, in any form of visual arts, because Dynamic Image can be designed into however you like, its content can be tweaked into the versions that are more welcomed by the viewers. Along with the development of technology, Dynamic Image is seen more often in our life.

Dynamic Image Design originated from the word "Motion Graphic Design", "MG" in short. Literally, it means "the graphic that moves". The first recorded use of this was

M. M. Soares et al. (Eds.): HCII 2022, LNCS 13323, pp. 414–427, 2022.
https://doi.org/10.1007/978-3-031-05906-3_31

back in 1960, when an American graphic designer John Whitney founded a company called "Motion Graphic". From then, this specific term has been widely used. We can see them in opening and credit scene of a movie, or just simply shown as a 3D spinning Logo on the left or the right corner on your TV screen and may other places. The US artist Matt Frantz "motion graphic" as "a visual graphic design that changes with the passing of time without the story telling and the embodying, it differentiates from traditional motion graphic and even comics. It emphasizes the changes of the graphic through time, also, it is the very first method to express the view of the designer as well as the definition of Motion Graphic Design from a more visualized stand point." In a narrow sense, Dynamic Motion Graphic specifically represents arts that based on graphic design that doesn't mainly focus on story telling but states its own idea by utilizing motion pictures and video editing. Besides that, it also involves with lots of designs which are related to time and motion. According to the researchers and professionals, by studying the history of Motion Graphic Design and its relation to the traditional graphic design, cartoon and movies. I will be able say it confidently that any design that are widely used which also uses text, shape and graphic as its basic design elements and makes it change throughout time without mainly focusing on story telling for recreational purpose can be categorized in Dynamic Motion Graphic. And along with the development of this, Dynamic Motion Graphic grows.

2 The Visual Styles of Dynamic Motion Graphic

2.1 Displaying Characters in Motion

Through the constant changes of forms and shapes, motion characters become much more dynamic and impactful. Texts and characters themselves start playing important roles in graphic design, and clever typography accelerates the effectiveness of the characters, in order to drastically change the viewers viewing experiences. The great visual impact under Dynamic Motion Graphic brings infinite possibility to traditional characters. During the mid-digital era, by implementing motions into the characters and typography, the results are enhanced which has given life to the characters that weren't supposed to be moving. Just like the work showing below from Ting an He, a Taiwanese designer. From redesigning the model of the character, he infused the original meaning of the character into the text. In his Dynamic Motion Graphic designs, he not only used a brand-new design which involves his own research if the characters, graphic design, motion designs, but he designed based on the original meaning and shapes of characters, which totally differentiated the western designs. Among his design inventory, he returns the meaning back to the word itself and expanded his characteristic of the characters to explore the possibilities the potential change of the Han characters.

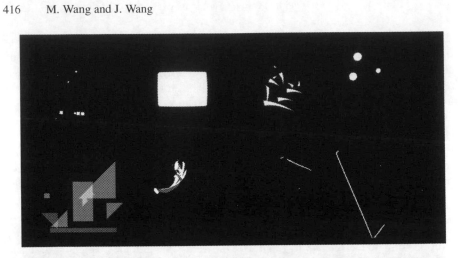

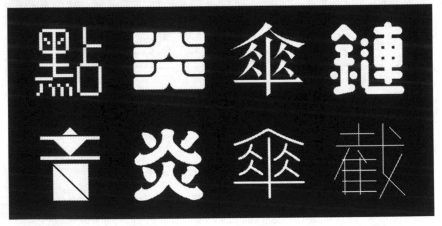

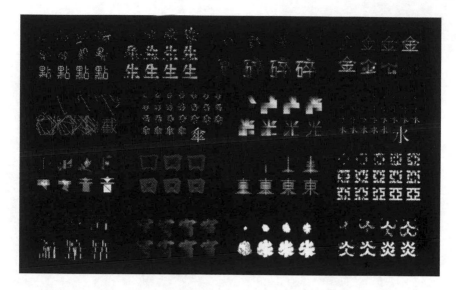

2.2 Displaying Graphics in Motion

Graphics are the foundation of visual design. We all know, by mimicking and expressing the objects in our daily life, it will make the object itself show more of its true color. Same with graphics, when being put in motion, graphic elements move and change with the change of space and time. Graphic shown through digital media tends to be more expressive than the traditional media like newspaper. These days, fewer and fewer people acquire their graphic information from newspaper, instead, cell-phone is the go-to. Adding motion into traditional graphics rides the tide of the digital evolution. Acil & Pierre Art Studio designed a set of dynamic motion graphic images for Galerie Kero. These graphics' idea was generated from their own art works, capturing a part of the features and emphasized some of the key elements. While exaggerated the idea of the original picture, the shape and rhythm of the original copy were preserved. Within its motion changes, there are perspective shape change, and geometrical reshapes, stretch and rotation. Motion and art itself go hand-in-hand, endows extra meaning to the art work itself. Something is worth mentioning, the pace change of the motion movements was on point, it brings way better visual experience while seeking expressiveness.

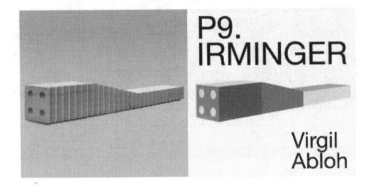

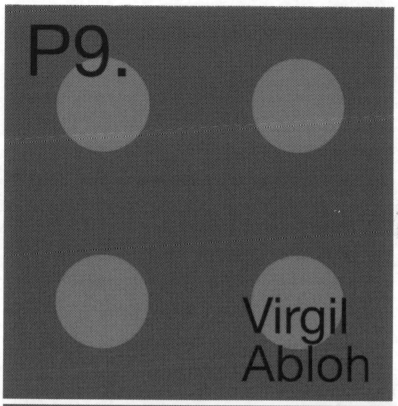

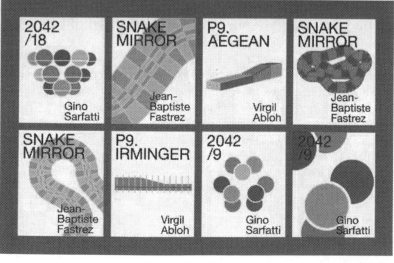

3   The Innovation of Dynamic Motion Graphic's Manifestation in This Era

Dynamic Motion Graphic makes you think more and leaves you an open-ended topic. It has a lot to do with constructing multi-dimension of space. In traditional graphic design, the entire is boxed in frame, what remains outside of the box is unseen. As concept of the world is changing, the open composition appeared. The art itself starts connecting with the "outer world", and creates a much larger space for our mind. Traditional non-motion graphics are presented mostly in two-dimension space. The form of these types of art and media is restricted and only carry limited information. Dynamic Motion Graphic not only transform a 2D art work in to 3D, it also introduces the 4th dimension, which is time. This type of multi-dimension concept expresses the idea of the designer in much more precise way, bringing a more influential and interactive viewing experience while leaving a impactful memory other viewers, creating an aftertaste to leave the viewer to memorize and think about.

Dynamic Motion Graphic puts more information than the traditional graphics, it simply narrates better. Compares to its predecessor which its manifestation isn't really diverse, and can be buried in tons of other information. Dynamic Motion Graphic combines graphics, videos, static and dynamic information. It shows the transformation from a static state to a dynamic state. And within the spectacular transformation, it lashes out the vitality and rhythm of the graphic, creating a resonance in and in-between the viewers. By relying on space and time, the viewers usually receive the information more precisely under the effect of graphic and information change. Therefore, Dynamic Motion Graphic stands out in this digital era.

4   Applying Dynamic Motion Graphic in Mid-digital Era

In mid-digital era, in order to adapt different types of digital media, Dynamic Motion Graphic can be found in many different form and shapes. As one of the major dissemination mediums, digital screens pave and widen the way visual expression, accelerate the development of Dynamic Motion Graphic, letting Dynamic Motion Graphic have more ways be manifested. Such as Dynamic Motion Graphic effects that use timeline and After Effect plugins, After Effect motion posters, GIFs in our forums and chat apps, C4D rendered dynamic or static scenes and other creative digital media works, not to mention virtual reality that everyone seems to be talking about. Also, most of the film companies' logo were designed in Dynamic Motion Graphic rendered in C4D. To be more specific, A virtual entertainment company called WAVE build a 3D virtual stage for Justin Bieber's Meta Verse concert during the pandemic. The development of technology provides infinite possibility to the dissemination of virtual information. In 2019, the logo of the Top 30 hottest hits for Golden Melody Awards in China used Lissajous curve as its basic concept, and can be seen in Logo Bumpers, stage designs and the introduction videos of the nominees. With the change of the curves synchronized with the music and the texts, and the help of the function, coding software, and visual design tools, the producers combined geometrical concept and dynamic motion graphic together and pushed the quality of the visual effect to another level with the help of technology.

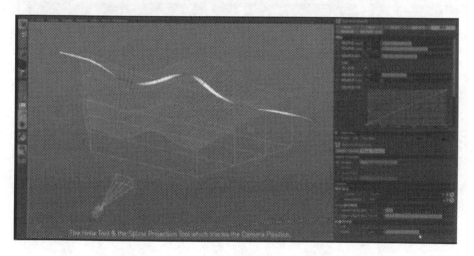

Everywhere we go, we can see video walls, rear projection screen, curved LEC screen and other digital media equipment, they display enormous Dynamic Motion Graphic in public space in almost every major city and also uses animation, interactive, lighting and auditorial technology to connect physical and virtual dimension, in order to provide the viewers a much more immersive experience. Infinity Room is an immersive vision project started by Refik Anadol, a Turkish multi-media art designer, it also researches on visual and auditorial equipment. Infinity Room projects Dynamic Motion Graphic in a limited space, it became a subversive experience for all compares to the traditional graphic design. During the art show, it destructed the structure of the space that already there by projecting simple geometrical line and shapes' motion graphic, along with arranged audio, lighting, perspective space. And eventually, with the help of the motion of lines, it turned graphics into 3D, so it can be viewed prospectively like a 3D model. The project use light as its main element to explore the inner features of virtual reality and what its visual graphic brings to us. Dynamic Motion Graphic naturally brings a more immersed experience to the viewers and makes you fall into the 0gravity and levitation world.

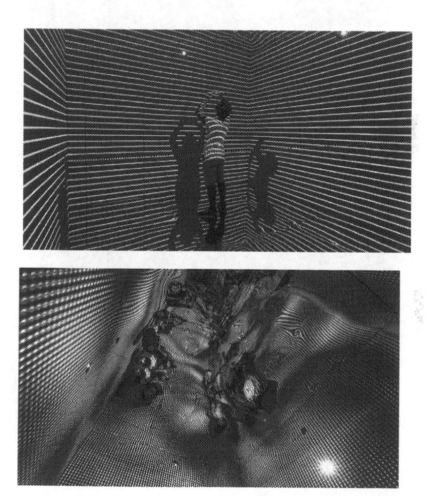

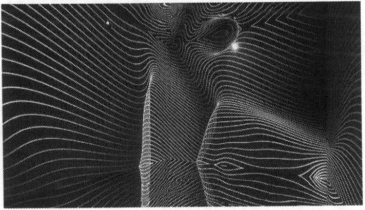

By using many kinds of detecting equipment to monitor viewers motion, sound and emotion, analyzing the statistics, and process the collected data, Infinity Room makes change with real time to stimulate the viewer to interact more. It communicates with viewers through Motion Graphic, music and lights back and forth. In an enhanced virtual space environment, it achieved interactive motion graphic design via computer simulation. The viewers can enter another reality by rotating, sliding and flipping pages on the screen. Infinity Room performs motion changes according to the viewers motion change, pace, location, and movement tracks as well as different interactive models in order to trigger a difference experience for the viewers. In digital era, the users switch sides from the receiving information passively to acquiring information themselves or even take part in creating information. Such as Sony's T series projectors, a series of interactive projectors. T is a conceptional prototype to create an interactive space on a surface. In this space, the displayed content immerses in the object that has been projected on. Through changing the object's placement, moving the projector or even giving a hand gesture within the space, the users can experiment on the virtual object that has been projected. The projector also comes with a story book. When we open the book, the project can recognize the image and the text. Within just seconds, the projector visualizes the image and the content of the book, and turned the readable text into a set of virtual reality scene. The users can simply wave their hand to highlight a passage or put characters within the book on the surface. When you make a move within the projector's range, the environment changes accordingly.

5 Conclusion

Today, with the rapid development of computer, digital and multimedia technology, our surroundings are also changing, which brings the possibility to us to dig deeper into Dynamic Motion Graphic. At the same time, the change of the multimedia platform and methods of dissemination also pave the way for its development. In virtual reality that build by computers, interacted through cell-phone, these two methods are the corner stones of improving viewers' experience and are making huge impact on people's life. In this digital era, Dynamic Motion Graphic enters many different domains thanks to its dissemination effectiveness, rich creatable content and wide coverage. In Dynamic Motion Graphic design, information can be display by using motion as its core, visual signal as its foundation, through integrating space and time to blend in graphics. Also, with the change of characters and virtual scenes, it can be turn into one powerful art work which not only with pack full of information, but it's also displayed in much more vivid way. As Dynamic Motion Graphic develops, it will be valued more in the field that involves tons of interaction. Along with that, the concept of acquiring information has been changed, again. Most people will not only be receiving information anymore through traditional graphics, instead they can be a part of them which I have to say, who doesn't want that? And from a production companies' stand point, they value the users experience more as the days go by. Dynamic Motion Graphic that contains information not only have effect on our viewing experience and even motion, it's also an easier display of concepts and message that hide behind the visual information. It allows the viewers to enter a virtuous circle of visual information and experience sensation, to create a much better virtual environment for us to enjoy.

References

1. Rozendaal, R.: If no yes (2013). http://www.ifnoyes.com/. Accessed 1 May 2016
2. Schaps, D.M.: The invention of coinage and the monetization of ancient Greece. Univ. of Michigan Press, Ann Arbor, Mich (2004)
3. Terranova, T.: Free labor. Producing culture for the digital economy. Social Text **63**(2), 33–58 (2000)
4. Williams, R.: The Animator's Survival Kit. A Manual of Methods, Principles and Formulas for Classical, Computer, Games, Stop Motion and Internet Animators. Grâ-Bretanha: Faber & Faber UK (2002)
5. Turvey, M.: The Filming of Modern Life: European Avant-Garde Film of the 1920s. The MIT Press, Cambridge (2011)
6. Turvey, M.: The Filming of Modern Life: European Avant-Garde Film of the 1920s. The MIT Press, Cambridge (2011)
7. Machado, A.: Pré-cinemas & pós-cinemas. Papirus, São Paulo (2014)
8. Martin, M.: A linguagem cinematografica. Dina livro, Lisboa (2005)

Evaluation of the Difference in the Reality of the Bow Device with and Without Arrows

Masasuke Yasumoto(✉)

Faculty of Information Technology, Kanagawa Institute of Technology, 1030 Shimo-ogino, Atsugi 243-0292, Kanagawa, Japan
yasumoto@ic.kanagawa-it.ac.jp

Abstract. This research is related to physical e-sports, which emphasize physicality, progress by training the body, and are played using abilities equivalent to those of reality. In physical e-sports, devices that resemble real-life tools such as bows and guns are used as an interface, and the ability to operate them is the same as in reality. In particular, I focused on the bow. The bow device that I am currently using shoots in the air without using arrows for safety reasons. Therefore, to what extent is there a difference in the experience of using a bow with or without an arrow? Verification of the safety of not using arrows. The experiment was conducted to see how the experience would change when a device that uses arrows but does not fire them is installed. In order to obtain objective data, I made a bow-launching device, and measured the values of the acceleration sensor and strain gauge attached to the bow for evaluation. Based on these results, I will investigate the optimal form of bow device for physical e-sports.

Keywords: Archery · Physical eSports · Arrows

1 Introduction

The purpose of this research is to realize physical e-sports, which is a new sport that emphasizes physicality, improves by training the body, moves the body with all its might, and can be played using the same abilities as in reality, and to create new fun by incorporating various xR technologies into it. The interface devices with a bow motif that have been proven so far are the Electric Bow Interface [1] based on the Japanese bow shown in Fig. 1, the Electric Bow 3D [2] based on archery with all the electronics built into the bow, and the VAIR Bow [3] that has 6DOF of freedom and can be played by many players simultaneously using the htc Vive Tracker. This research is based on the VAIR Bow used in the physical e-sports competition VAIR Field [3], and is to clarify the relationship between the interface and the body in order to realize an experience close to reality.

I have produced three bow-shaped devices so far, and one thing they all have in common is that they shoot without using arrows. Although this is a prohibited and dangerous activity, I have taken safety measures by making the bow stronger and taking measures against shock, and no accidents have occurred so far. However, even though visual information is generated at the right time to provide a good shooting experience, there is no fundamental act of holding the arrow, so the experience will be different to some extent. In addition, when shooting without using arrows, even though countermeasures were taken, the bow itself was subjected to a large impact, which often caused the sensor to output abnormal values.

Fig. 1. Bow-shaped devices produced, from left to right: the Electric Bow Interface, the Electric Bow 3D, VAIR Bow.

Therefore, this study will evaluate the differences between shooting with and without arrows based on objective data, as well as examine the safety of shooting without arrows and how the use of devices that use arrows but do not fire them affects the experience.

There has been a study that evaluated the bow-type interface device based on objective numerical data [4]. This study clarified the relationship between the amount of string pull and strain gauge in a recurve bow, which is significant for the production of accurate and reproducible bow devices. However, no evaluation of the bow interface device with or without arrows has been done, nor has the safety of shooting in the air by not using arrows been verified. Studies on bow devices that use arrows but inhibit the firing of arrows [5, 6] have not examined the difference in experience of installing the device.

2 Experimental Equipment

In this study, I will clarify the difference in the bow when shooting with and without arrows. In addition, it has been pointed out that shooting without arrows is dangerous, but no damage to the bow has been confirmed so far with the VAIR Bow or the Electric Bow Interface based on the recurve bow. However, in the absence of objective data, it is necessary to objectively demonstrate the safety of the bow.

The measurement is done by accelerometer and strain gauge attached to the bow, and also by high-speed shooting at 960 fps. The shooting device shown in Fig. 2 was constructed for this experiment. The bow is bolted to the experimental apparatus, which is made of aluminum frame, and a target to stop the arrow is placed in front. On the floor, I used weights to prevent slippage and to fix the device, thus improving its strength and stability. The string is set at 50 cm, which is the limit of what can be pulled with this bow, and the amount of string pull can be measured with a scale fixed to the device. A special trigger type releaser is used as shown in Fig. 4, and a mechanism is made at the position where the string is pulled as shown in Fig. 3. This was done to minimize the difference between each shot. In this experiment, the bow was an international standard recurve bow, and the limbs strength was 18 lb.

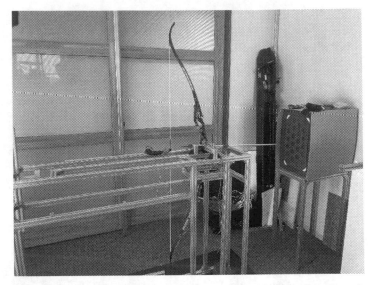

Fig. 2. Equipment for shooting experiments, arrow catcher in front for safety

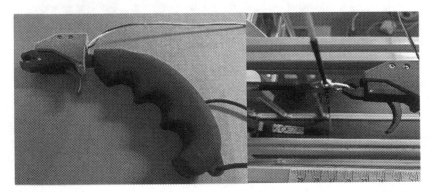

Fig. 3. Trigger-type releaser for plucking strings with built-in electrical switch

This releaser has a switch embedded in it, and at the moment the trigger is pulled and the string is released, an electrical signal is sent to the microcomputer shown in Fig. 4 attached to the bow, which automatically records the strain and acceleration, and after the recording is finished, the information is sent to the PC. The microcomputer is an M5 Stick, which is capable of high-speed processing and wireless communication. The microcomputer is fixed in a special 3D printed case, which is screwed to the bow body and reinforced with plastic tape to prevent it from shifting due to the impact of shooting. Inside the case are two HX711 modules, each processing the signals from the strain gauges above and below the grip. The measurement signals are sent to a PC wired via USB to ensure stability.

As shown in Fig. 5, four strain gages are attached to the front and back of the limbs mounting area of the bow grip in two places, upper and lower, as a set. By mounting

Fig. 4. M5 Stick attached to the top of the grip

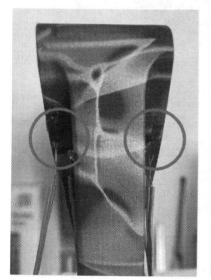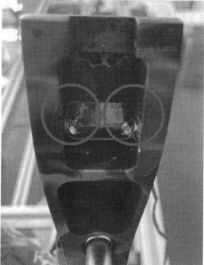

Fig. 5. Attach strain gauges to the red circles at the limbs attachment points on the top and bottom of the bow grip.

them directly under the limbs, it is planned to obtain a large strain value, and a hole is drilled for the strain gauge. The holes are small enough that there is no major problem with the strength of the bow. When measuring, the value is automatically corrected for each shot, and adjustments are made based on the current load so that the current strain value is near zero.

The high-speed camera (DSC-RX100M7) was fixed on a tripod at the side of the device as shown in Fig. 6. Since the camera and microcomputer are not synchronized, I

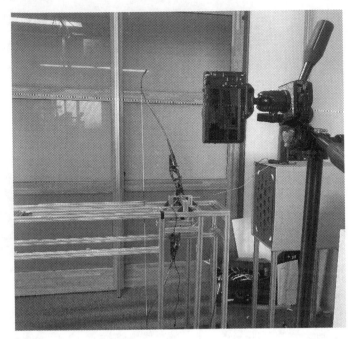

Fig. 6. High-speed camera attached to the bow to capture its behavior.

took pictures with a little room before and after the camera, and analyzed the recorded images with After Effects. I considered using an optical motion capture device (Optitrack V120 Duo) that can automatically acquire positional information, but the frame rate was low at 120 fps and it was difficult to attach a retroreflective marker to the tip of the bow limbs, so I did not use it for this measurement.

3   Comparison with and Without Arrows

Using this device, I performed shooting with and without arrows, and compared the results. The data were compared by analyzing high-speed video, accelerometers attached to the bow grip, and strain gauges attached to the top and bottom of the limbs attachment.

3.1   Video Analysis

The 960 fps high-speed video was automatically stretched to 60 fps by 16 times, and the image quality was rough and noisy. 2 locations in the video were tracked by After Effects as shown in Fig. 7. The first one is the upper string on the limbs and the second one is the arrow on the string at the bottom of the figure. The first one is the upper string on the limbs, and the second one is the arrow on the string at the bottom of the figure. The first part of the second one is not visible, so it was tracked after it appeared in the screen.

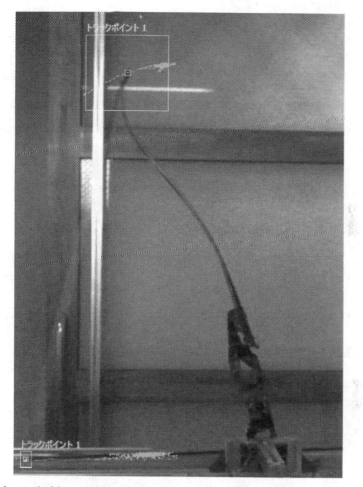

Fig. 7. High-speed video, tracking the intersection of the upper string and the limbs, and the intersection of the lower string and the arrow.

Figure 8 shows the movement of the string and limbs when an arrow is used. The movement of the limbs appears to be irregular in the graph, but it is greatly affected by noise and tracking accuracy. The movement of the string appears to be relatively regular, and its movement is clear when limited to the X-axis direction, and since this is a graph of up to 12 s at 60 fps, it is clear that the movements converge in less than 0.75 s in real time. The movement of the limbs converges faster than the movement of the string.

Figure 9 shows the movement of the string and limbs when shooting without arrows. Compared to the case with arrows, the X-axis movement of the string is irregular and the X-axis movement of the limbs is violent. It was also found that the movements themselves converged earlier than when arrows were used.

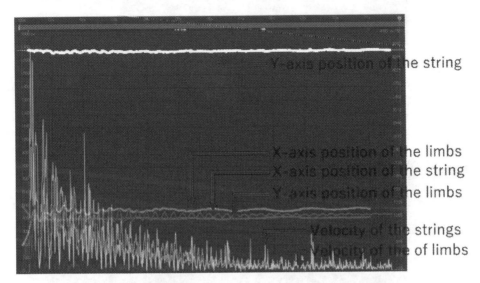

Fig. 8. Tracking results when arrows are used.

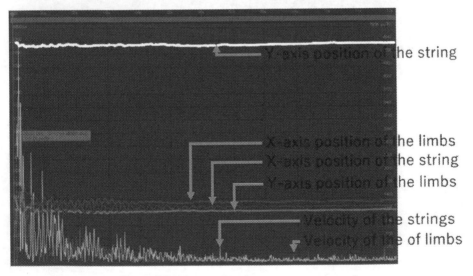

Fig. 9. Tracking results when no arrows are used.

From these results, it was found that the string vibration became irregular and the limbs fluctuation increased when no arrow was used, but the speed of string movement was slow and convergence was relatively fast.

3.2 Acceleration and Strain Analysis

I compared the 3-axis acceleration and vertical strain values acquired by the microcontroller. 200 values were acquired in one trial, requiring an average of 2338 ms. The HX711 module was changed from 10 Hz to 80 Hz (Fig. 10).

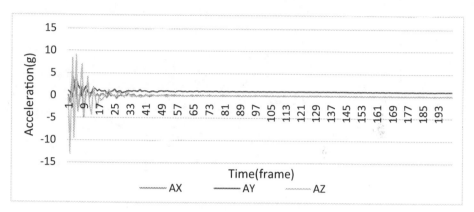

Fig. 10. Acceleration when using arrows

Figure 11 shows a graph of the change in acceleration applied to the grip when an arrow is used. This is a graph of only one trial out of 10 trials, but in common, the change in acceleration in the Z-axis direction, that is, the direction of the arrow, is the largest. All of them converged within 0.5 s.

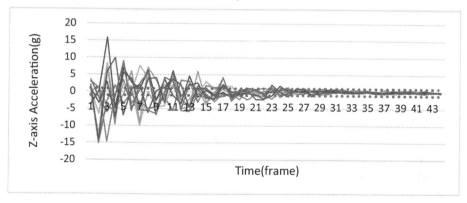

Fig. 11. Z-axis acceleration values for 10 trials when using arrows, red dotted line is ±1 g

Figure 12 shows the acceleration of the Z axis for the first 44 frames of the 10 trials, and after 30 frames, all the accelerations were less than ±1 g, and none of them exceeded the measurement limit of ±16 g. It can be observed that the value swings greatly in the direction of arrow shooting at first, and then the vibration converges.

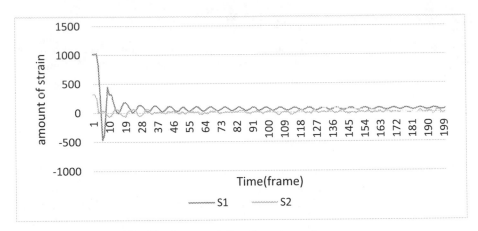

Fig. 12. Amount of distortion when using arrows

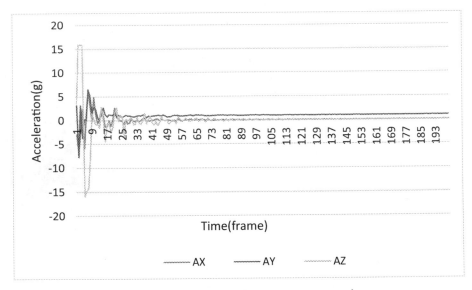

Fig. 13. Acceleration when no arrows are used

Figure 13 shows the changes in the values of the strain gauges when arrows are used, where S1 is the upper strain gauge and S2 is the lower strain gauge, and the tendency for S1 to swing significantly in the negative direction was observed in all trials. After that, they both converge, but a certain amount of noise is always generated, and looking at the amount of change, they converge at around 30 frames, which tends to be slightly faster than the convergence of acceleration.

Figure 14 is a graph of the change in acceleration values when shooting without arrows, where the change in the Z-axis direction is the largest, and the wavelength and amplitude are larger and longer than when using arrows. The convergence time is less than 1 s, but it also tends to be longer than when using arrows.

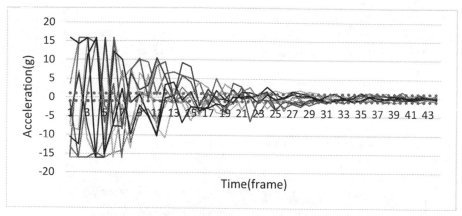

Fig. 14. Z-axis acceleration values for 10 trials when no arrows are used, red dotted line is ±1 g

Figure 15 shows the acceleration of the Z axis for the first 44 frames of the 10 trials, and after 44 frames, the acceleration is less than ±1 g. Some of the accelerations were reversed from the first frame, probably because the resolution of the measurement was less than the speed of the bow vibration. This is because the resolution of the measurement is less than the speed of the bow vibration.

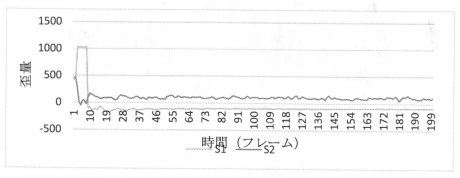

Fig. 15. Amount of strain when arrows are not used

Figure 16 shows the change in the values of the strain gauges. S1 is the upper strain gauge and S2 is the lower strain gauge, and the values of S1 tend to increase abnormally at first, but then stabilize. On the other hand, the initial change in S2 is calm, but after that, a lot of noise can be seen. The same tendency was observed for all trials, and it is thought that this is a problem with the position and condition of the strain gage. Looking at the amount of change in the value, it seems to converge in about 30 frames, which is faster than the acceleration.

From these results, it was found that by not using arrows, the impact on the grip became larger, the movement of the string became unstable, and the value of the strain gauge also measured abnormal values. Furthermore, the bow was shot about 1,000 times without using arrows, but the bow was not damaged and the string did not come off.

From these results, it can be said that even without arrows, the bow was not damaged by the limbs of at least 18 lb strength, and the safety of the bow was confirmed. However, because of the different force applied to the grip, the difference in shooting feel was felt to the fullest.

4 Consideration of an Arrow Launch Prevention Device

Next, I used arrows, and I designed and made a place to stop the arrows to verify this effect.

Fig. 16. Broken arrow launch prevention device

Figure 16 shows the bow device with this device attached and fixed to the experimental apparatus. The A6063 aluminum alloy pipe, which is fixed with a shock absorber material at the tip using the mounting holes of the sight and clicker on the bow grip, is held by an iron clamp, and it is held by the PA12 material 3D printed by the high-strength MJF method. In addition, a stabilizer mounting hole was used to attach a guide to stabilize the pipe. However, as shown in the figure, the 3D printed parts were damaged after one test shot as a preliminary experiment.

Figure 17 shows the clamp and pipe attachment parts made of machined aluminum alloy A7075 to increase the strength. The end of the aluminum pipe is threaded, and a larger aluminum pipe is screwed to prevent the aluminum pipe from moving before the fixed part. However, this device also broke after three attempts and the threaded part broke. This shows that even an 18-pound bow needs a lot of strength to stop an arrow, and to make it stronger, it would need to be completely welded or made of stronger stainless steel. However, even at present, the arrow stopper is large and bulky, and any further increase in weight is undesirable (Fig. 18).

Fig. 17. Changed the aluminum pipe holding part to aluminum alloy.

Fig. 18. Aluminum pipe side is damaged.

Of the data that could be measured without damage, acceleration is shown in Fig. 19 and strain in Fig. 20. As for the acceleration, I can see that, unlike the previous two, a large force is also applied in the X-axis direction. The force applied to the Z-axis is less than when the arrow is not used, and is about the same as when the arrow is used. However, since the number of data obtained is small, this is only a guess. No significant difference was observed in the amount of distortion.

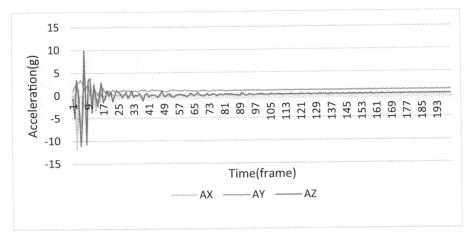

Fig. 19. Acceleration when using arrow launch prevention device

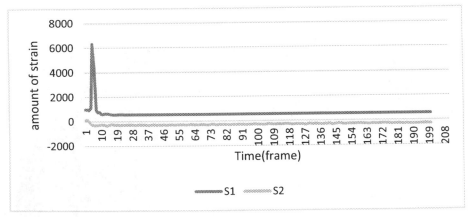

Fig. 20. Amount of strain when using arrow launch prevention device

By using international standard archery, the aim was to improve the handling and reality of limbs replacement. However, even with the weakest 18-pound limbs available for international standard bows, the power of the arrow was quite large due to the size of the bow, and it took a lot of force to pull out an arrow stuck in the target. Therefore, even if an arrow launch prevention device could be made without any strength problems, its safety would be questionable. At the very least, it should not be used on people, and should be limited to training for one person only. It is suitable for comparison experiments with real objects, but from this point of view, it is not suitable as equipment for physical e-sports.

5 Discussion and Future Tasks

From this study, it was first confirmed that an 18-pound limbs of an international standard recurve bow would not be damaged when shot without an arrow. Therefore, it was found that it is safe and possible to use the bow in a simulated manner by shooting without arrows on a weaker limbs.

Next, it was found that extra force was applied to the grip when not using an arrow compared to when using an arrow. Therefore, the hand of the person holding the bow is subjected to a different impact when shooting than usual. However, the direction of the force applied does not change, so it is not likely to be that uncomfortable. As for the distortion, it may cause a large amount of noise, which may lead to false detection of shooting. Therefore, the placement of the strain gauge needs to be considered.

Finally, the mechanism for stopping the firing of arrows did not give good results. First of all, it takes a lot of force to stop a fired arrow, and it is not suitable for use with people because of the risk of damage and the risk of the arrow being fired. A stronger, smaller bow or a weaker limbs would reduce the possibility of breakage, but it would be fundamentally dangerous. In addition, the device that stops the arrow from firing would itself be heavier, changing the balance of weight, which would defeat the purpose of making it more realistic. Furthermore, when the arrow stopping device is attached to the bow, the force is applied in a direction that does not occur in normal shooting or shooting without arrows, so the feel of shooting the bow will be very different and uncomfortable. From this perspective, a device that uses arrows but does not fire them is inappropriate for improving the reality of the experience.

In the future, I would like to use these findings to create a bow device that is closer to a real shooting experience.

References

1. Yasumoto, M., Ohta, T.: The electric bow interface. In: Shumaker, R. (ed.) VAMR 2013. LNCS, vol. 8022, pp. 436–442. Springer, Heidelberg (2013). https://doi.org/10.1007/978-3-642-39420-1_46
2. Yasumoto, M., Teraoka, T.: Electric bow interface 3D. In: SIGGRAPH Asia 2015, Emerging Technologies (SA 2015), pp. 11:1–11:2 (2015)
3. Yasumoto, M., Teraoka, T.: Physical e-Sports in VAIR field system. In: SIGGRAPH Asia 2019 XR (SA 2019), pp. 31–33. ACM, New York (2019)
4. Yasumoto, M., Shida, K., Teraoka, T.: Possibility of using high-quality bow interface in VAIR field. In: Marcus, Aaron, Rosenzweig, Elizabeth (eds.) HCII 2020. LNCS, vol. 12201, pp. 605–619. Springer, Cham (2020). https://doi.org/10.1007/978-3-030-49760-6_43
5. The Fist Virtual Reality Archery. https://infinityleap.com/the-first-virtual-reality-archery/
6. Drochtert, D., Owetschkin, K., Meyer, L., Geiger, C.: Demonstration of mobile virtual archery. In: SIGGRAPH Asia 2013 Symposium on Mobile Graphics and Interactive Applications (SA 2013), pp. 62:1–62:1. ACM, New York (2013)

Research on the Interactive Relationship of Immersive Art

Wenjing Yin[1,2(✉)] and Jiangbo Jin[2]

[1] South China University of Technology, Guangzhou 510006, China
yinwj@scut.edu.cn
[2] Shanghai Academy of Fine Arts of Shanghai University, Shanghai 200040, China

Abstract. The theoretical discussion on immersive art is still in its infancy. With the rapid development of science and technology and the continuous progress of the times, immersive art is a contemporary form of "full sense art" that emphasizes participation, interaction, integration and penetration. This paper will discuss and interpret the concept definition, external supporting elements, internal characteristics, value connotation and sustainable development of immersive art by means of case study, field research and literature research. This paper holds that in the context of contemporary media integration, immersive art is characterized by interactivity, technicality and experience, and gradually constructs the structural relationship of technical interaction, environmental interaction and interpersonal interaction. In the dimension of time and space, immersive art gradually immerses the virtual into reality through technological upgrading, brings the most extreme sensory experience to the public, and realizes the economic goals in the consumer society. On the other hand, it quietly returns to the concern of "humanity", showing the artistic spiritual ideal of reshaping the realistic environment and regenerating the humanistic spirit.

Keywords: Immersive art · Interactive relationship · Value construction · Sustainable development

1 Introduction

1.1 About Immersion

Immersion, which represents a psychological state, is "a whole experience that people feel when they fully participate in activities" [1]. In the 1960s, American psychologist Mihaly Csikszentmihalyi shifted the focus of research from the functions and benefits of games to the pleasure brought by games, and extended this research on pleasure to other activities that have different forms, internal mobility and goals, such as artistic activities. In 1975, he put forward the Flow Theory for the first time from the psychological point of view, which was mostly translated into immersion theory in China. In 1990, Csikszentmihalyi published the book "Flow: The Psychology of Optimal Experience", which systematically introduced the theory of immersion. He believed that immersion was a kind of experience that can make a person deeply immersed in it and make people

M. M. Soares et al. (Eds.): HCII 2022, LNCS 13323, pp. 442–453, 2022.
https://doi.org/10.1007/978-3-031-05906-3_33

forget the passage of time and be unaware of their existence, and put forward nine psychological characteristics of immersion. That is, challenge and skill balance, clear goals, feedback, fusion of behavior and awareness, concentration, perceptual control, loss of self-awareness, temporal distortion, and purposefulness of the experience itself. Therefore, the development of immersion theory has entered a relatively perfect stage, which explains a subjective state that people are fully engaged in certain daily activity situations and focus their attention on the current activity. This subjective state is usually accompanied by a positive, pleasant, and exciting emotional experience, thereby ignoring the individual cost.

Immersion means the state of high participation and the best experience. Immersion experience is the core concept in FLOW theory. Immersion is closely related to experience, and can generate a series of cognitive, emotional, psychological, physiological, and behavioral responses related to experience. We believe that "immersion" is from the perspective of the object, and it studies how the objects build a place that can provide rich perceptual opportunities, and how to immerse people; while "experience" is from the perspective of the subject, emphasizing people's perception of object and place environment. They are inseparable and interdependent. In Experiential Psychology, Ф·Е·Василюк said that people's sense of experience comes from a special activity when people are in a difficult situation. With the development of experiential psychology, many scholars believe that "experience" is a psychological phenomenon expressed through the five senses of human beings, and it is a common effect between emotions under the comprehensive action. Immersion experience usually uses technical installations, lighting engineering and exhibition activities and other rich forms to open people's comprehensive sensory experience and cognitive experience. By creating, highlighting and strengthening the field atmosphere, participants can consciously or unconsciously integrate into the specific time and space. It is often accompanied by a sense of time and space travel, novelty, adventure, uncertainty and other characteristics, which make people have strong substitution emotions. People can devote themselves to it, just like wandering in a dream, losing self-control without knowing it and being completely controlled by the current scene, forgetting the existence of time and space for a while. The immersive scene builds an experience space where virtual and reality coexist, bringing people a brand-new memory.

1.2 About Immersive Art

The purpose of immersive art is to create opportunities and scenes for people to experience "immersion". With the rapid development of science and technology and the continuous progress of the times, immersive art can be described as a contemporary form of "full sense art" that emphasizes participation, interaction, integration and penetration. The reason why it is included in the category of contemporary art is that in the contemporary era, the media limitation of art has already been completely broken through. When we talk about art, we have turned from the viewing mode to the experience mode, which fully activates people's full sensory system. In such a media-integrated "full-sense art era", the value noumenon of immersive art does not lie in the artists or the works, but in the multi-level participation, interaction, observation and perception of the public.

Immersive art usually shows that the artists use multi-media to create an perceptual scene that is both real and fantasy for the audience. The design intention is to eliminate all the interference of the established cognition as much as possible, so that the participants can highly concentrate on completing the expected behavior, and interact with the art in multiple dimensions. In the immersive art experience, many narrative clues unfold at the same time, which in turn triggers emotional resonance between individuals and artworks, exchange of ideas, and even reshaping of individual concepts. The artistic emotion accumulated by the public during the immersion experience is as important as the artwork itself, and it promotes the regeneration of new meanings. In the dimension of time and space, immersive art gradually immerses the virtual into reality through technological upgrading, brings the most extreme sensory experience to the public, and realizes the economic goals in the consumer society. On the other hand, it quietly returns to the concern of "humanity", showing the spiritual ideal of art reshaping the realistic environment and regenerating the humanistic spirit.

Nowadays, we live in a complete "image world". Immersive art that can make people "immersive" is the aesthetic medium to create public relations in the consumption era. It makes "image world become a challenging space for experience and interpretation, which is a result of creative mind and imagination [2]. To some extent, it is a living organism. It can constantly update the public's aesthetic cognition, connect the public's aesthetic feelings, and expand the public's imagination and understanding of art. By deconstructing the real experience world to counter the monotonous and formatted daily life, it can lead to group reflection and judgment. This aesthetic view enables human beings to observe the past, think about the present and imagine the future more freely from a new perspective.

2   External Supporting Factors of Immersive Art

2.1   Spatial Scene Elements

Psychologist James J Gibson believed that the body is based on space, and the rest of the perception is derived from people's curiosity about space. Human cognition of external environment space is as important as all kinds of perceptual experience. The space mentioned here not only refers to the scene environment of physical space, but also can be further interpreted as a multi-complex relationship network. As Robert Scoble said, the Context is "the sum of the relationships between people and the surrounding scenery"[3] . Immersive art is inseparable from the setting of the scene environment, and even more inseparable from the cognition of the relationships among people, events, objects, nature, universe and so on. Only in this way can we practice the fundamental purpose of art, that is, "to make the external and heteronomous social norms more naturally internalized into the demands of individual self-discipline, so that the connection between society and individuals will have the most fundamental fit" [4]. Contemporary art is inherently reflective, and so is immersive art. It emphasizes the characteristics of public participation and interactive experience. In the established open real space environment, it reshapes new time and space and scenes, so that virtual and reality are linked to expand people's broader cognitive horizons and shape multi-dimensional complex relationship. It enables people to re-understand themselves, nature, society and history while producing an immersive experience, thus generating "meaning".

Immersive art has various types of real space scenes, which are not only presented in places such as museums and art galleries, but also often appear in commercial spaces and leisure spaces that meet the needs of mass consumption, and meet the emotional demands of consumers in terms of interaction, socialization and pleasure. It can be said that immersive art is quietly immersed in the daily life of the public, blurring the boundary between art and life. It can reawaken the public's memory identity and emotional identity by means of virtual dynamic images, scene reappearance and reconstruction, light design and other design means. It connects the past with the present in a unique way of art, and leads life to a better future through personal experience, review, perception and reflection. It can rekindle the glory of the past, tell the story of the development of people and cities, highlight the inheritance of ancient civilization and show the brand-new features of the times. It not only shapes the physical scene space, but also cultivates people's spiritual field. Just as "Art activities related to the spirit are an indispensable form of life for human beings", [2] immersive art reflects more attention to the needs of the public, is committed to the sharing and co-creation of the public, and restores the essence of art to human spirit.

Jiaxing Red Boat "Guanghe" Architectural Space Light Sculpture Show (2021) is an immersive artistic presentation engraved with the imprint of the times and the spirit of the city. It was staged shockingly in the old factory building space along the ancient canal in Jiaxing. It used 3D holographic projection technology to carry out image light sculpture on the facade of historical buildings, breaking the boundary of real physical space. The illusion and change of visual light and shadow vividly interpret the "spatial butterfly change" of narrative fusion. It is not so much a performance, but rather an art installation engraved with time, the regional imprint of the canal, and Jiangnan style. It presents the renewal and imagination of Jiaxing city. When the memory travels through time and space and is reappeared in front of the public in an artistic way, the cocoon library, which has experienced the years, has achieved a magnificent turn in the space art carrier of the light sculpture show. The public perceives the ancient canal civilization with an all-round immersive experience. The rendering of environment, the creation of scenes and the construction of relationships are the creative embodiment of immersive art and the manifestation of artistic spirit.

2.2 Science and Technology Integration Elements

The combination of art and science and technology has a long history, but it has never been as direct and close as immersive art, with unique foresight. Baudrillard said that images can no longer make people imagine reality, because it is reality. Images can no longer make people fantasize about real things, because it is their virtual reality. The newest and most subtle world of regeneration is the world of artificial synthesis. All this depends on the support of technology. In addition to being used by Benjamin to describe the new ways of art and feeling in the age of mechanical reproduction, Paul Valery's statement is still applicable to the age of digital creation, that is, "all arts have physical parts, but they can no longer be treated as usual, nor can they be influenced by the operation of modern power and knowledge........ We should expect such an important new situation to transform all art and technology, thereby promoting invention and even subtly changing the concept of art itself." The high technology is an important tool for the innovation of immersive art works. Just as paint brushstrokes can express the presence of traditional art, digital technology and contemporary art forms nourish each other, penetrate close and maintain a distance, constructing a brand-new "aura" of art in the new era.

In the era of digital creation, digital reconstructs the public life, and the concept of the interconnection of everything further derives that everything can be immersed, which makes art constantly improve its dimension across borders. With the impetus of science and technology, the level of human sensory experience has been deepened to the greatest extent, and it tends to the extreme "flow" experience. This is the dividend of the times brought by cutting-edge technology. A large number of technological means such as internet technology, 3D holographic projection technology, chip sensing technology, VR(Virtual Reality) /AR (Augmented Reality)/MR (Mixed Reality) /XR(Extended Reality) and other virtual reality technologies, AI artificial intelligence, big data blockchain are integrated for combined application. The new technology constantly breaks the boundaries of physical space, creating a completely virtual "reality", showing new spaces and new scenes from the virtual to the reality, and constantly extending to the surroundings, which makes the public indulge in the construction of ideal situations of virtual reality, or the future utopia supported by science and technology.

Technology has promoted the creation of many new experiences. According to the VR gyro "VR/AR Industry 2020 Industry Report", in terms of hardware, AR glasses have begun to iterate, ultra-short focus products have been listed centrally, mainstream VR heads are in the form of all-in-one machine and have entered the stage of partial immersion, and the chip research and development is competitive. In terms of software, system interaction and platform intercommunication have been constantly improved and optimized. In terms of content, 5G promotes cloud VR and continuously activates user activity. High-tech has become the most important support of immersive art experience, and it will inevitably become a necessary cost of for immersive art construction. The MSG Sphere, which is still under construction, is currently the largest spherical theater in the world, with a center stage and 17,500 seats, which can accommodate 21,500 people. The project was developed and designed by Populous Company, and its purpose is to build the world's most advanced technology and entertainment immersive place. The structure of the sphere is 112 m high and 157 m wide. The entire facade is equipped with a 54,000-square-meter programmable LED screen, and the interior is equipped with the world's largest high-definition display screen with a resolution of 19000×13500 pixels, surrounding the upper and rear of the stage. In order to upgrade the technology and entertainment experience, MSG has upgraded the system design for people's vision, hearing, touch, smell and other senses, and strives to create an all-round and full-sensory immersion. Technology integration is an important means and technical guarantee for the realization of immersive art, and it is also a cutting-edge experimental position in line with the development trend of art and technology integration.

2.3 Industrial Economic Elements

With the help of high-tech and creative design, immersive art undoubtedly provides a high-quality experience for the public, thus developing into a high-attraction, high-value and high-investment consumption form in the consumer society. In the era of consumption, the increasingly severe market competition has prompted enterprise distributors and brands to constantly look for the differential advantages of new products or services. Immersion industry has become the focus of attention of all parties in recent years, and the industrialization development of immersion art will surely bring real benefits to all parties. According to the data of "2020 White Paper on the Development of China's Immersion Industry", the related search volume for new consumption formats of immersion experience has increased by 3,800% in 2017, and the total output value of China's immersion industry in 2019 was 4.82 billion. So far, the immersion experience is moving towards full-sensory personality experience, and the immersion industry is developing rapidly. Although the industrial development of immersive art is still in the initial stage, it is undoubtedly in line with the essence and progressive trend of economic value. "In the context of cultural industry, 'immersive experience' defines the value obtained from interactive cultural and creative works or projects, ... creating a sense of intimacy and connection in virtual or real space with limited boundaries" [5]. It can be seen that providing consumers with an immersive experience has become the core value of the new economy, and a complete set of formulas has been formed, namely, situational narrative (story)-technology integration (means)-immersion experience (scene)-spiritual worship (belief)-commodity transformation (industry)-consumption realization (economic purpose). The cultural and industrial economy is the sustained support strength and inevitable path for the development of immersive art, which conforms to the characteristics of the consumption era, and is also the material guarantee for the ultimate ideal of practical art.

2.4 Media Elements

Benjamin said that, at each important historical stage, the way people feel and receive is changing with the development of the times. Digital technology means bringing together a new experience, the power of technological innovation and the power of human imagination for the future into the power of communication. Looking back on the development history of communication media, we have already entered the "third media era". With the in-depth development of interactive communication to immersion communication, mass communication to general public communication, artistic medium has gradually expanded from the dimension of material space to the dimension of time and virtual space, which are presented in the imaginary reality of the fusion of virtual and reality. Its form is no longer simply limited to the form of real object, nor is it merely a virtual object existing in the form of digital image, video and information, but is complex, pluralistic and interpenetrating. The dissemination of immersive art presents an open pattern of fusion of virtual and reality, using everything as a medium and breaking all boundaries. "When the media 'as a means of communication' becomes the world itself, the so-called media is no longer just a medium, no longer just a bridge to the other side, but also the other side itself" [6]. Communication media and technological evolution complement each other and become the source of power for immersive art to move forward infinitely. People's immersive experience and cognition of their own living environment have also been deepened.

3   Intrinsic Features of Immersive Art

3.1   Technology Integration Realizes the Convergence of Time and Space

Immanuel Kant once pointed out that time and space are the basis for human existence, the basis for human cognition of the world, and the absolute prerequisite for the existence of human perceptual, intellectual and rational forms. With the revolutionary development of digital technology and virtual reality technology, "the boundary of human existence space-time is disappearing constantly, and the absoluteness of space-time is also being dissolved constantly, which is dissolved in a virtual space-time jointly created by 3D holographic virtual images and the physical world" [6]. All space and time are interpenetrated in one space-time world where we live, and people's psychology and perception determine "at this moment" and "presence". Through the integration of high technology, we can even experience the future through the construction of space-time and experience the coexistence of organisms in multi-dimensional space and time.

On October 30th, 2021, the first opening exhibition of AI Factory Artificial Intelligence Art Center in China was opened in Shanghai, presenting the imaginary world created by artificial intelligence and virtual reality technology to the public. People can observe and even adopt virtual butterflies that have evolved beyond reality; can understand the biological information of artificial life as digital natives in the meta-universe constructed by AR; can read the poems randomly written by the computer, and even get the novel experience of writing poems with the machines; and can also experience the amazing learning ability and creativity of artificial intelligence in the most intuitive way. The digital world is closely intertwined with the physical world, showing the public both the real and the fantasy of the new media era.

3.2   Full Sense of Personality Experience Expands Aesthetic Dimension

Dewey said that the flourishing of art is the final measure of cultural nature. A work of art always has an aesthetic meaning, which can convey a certain idea or achieve a certain function. Art naturally invites people to experience it aesthetically. Philosopher Cassirer pointed out, "our aesthetic perception is more diverse than our common sensory perception and belongs to a more complex level… It breeds infinite possibilities that can never be realized in ordinary sensory experience" [7]. Immersive art can realize full perceptive design presentation through technology, which can quickly shorten the relationship between individuals and space, trigger the public's desire for spiritual echo and communication and sharing, and bring people a new interconnected experience. These individual experiences generate their own unique meanings, and ultimately condense into a cultural experience, expanding people's aesthetic cognition dimension in the social community. Immersive art has a "representation of the infinite meaning of transcendence", as Susanne Langer refers to "the 'otherness' away from reality", which enables the public to cognize people, society, nature, history and culture sensibly and profoundly with their unique experience of art, thereby opening up new meaning connections and realizing the reshaping of the integrity of life.

As the first immersive live-action opera performance in China, the garden version of Kunqu opera "Six Records of A Floating Life" is a fitting example. It is an innovative combination of Canglang Pavilion, a world cultural heritage, and Kunqu Opera, a world intangible cultural heritage. It is also a high-quality cultural output with the unique cultural meaning of Jiangnan in China. It integrates nature, architecture and humanities, and shows the classical Jiangnan cultural aesthetics in a panoramic way. The whole Canglang Pavilion garden has become a stage for Kunqu Opera performance, with crisscrossing spaces and fantastic scenes. The audience and actors are inseparable, completely replicating the ancient Kunqu Opera performance in a private house. The most primitive life style of Gusu City is gradually revealed. The audience and the actors are immersed in the true and touching love story of Shen Fu and Yun Niang.

3.3 Creative Narrative Builds Deep Interaction

From a historical point of view, once a work of art is determined in the form of material or immaterial media, it begins to enter the process of interaction with the viewer, whether it is the interaction of form or the interaction of content. The creative narrative of immersive art has planned multiple clues for interactive experience and brought the immersive experience directly to the public. "This immersive experience aims to seek a deeper connection with the audience" [8]. French philosopher Nicolas Bourriaud believes that the consumer society makes the relationship between people more alienated in the representation of "landscape". However, immersive art seems to open up a different space. In this specific space, the deep interaction between the past and the future, the individual and the other, the reality and the imagination is constructed.

On the one hand, it temporarily frees the public from the spiritual shackles brought by reality with a pleasant perceptual experience, connects the public's emotional memory, relieves mental pressure, brings people an "escape experience", and becomes an emotional bond for establishing relationships, with the function of emotional healing. On the other hand, it is a contemporary cultural form integrating entertainment, communication and dialogue. Through creative narrative, it conveys an attitude concept, a complex emotion, a virtual and real image, and an unfinished story. Immersive experience connect individuals into a cultural community with interaction, mutual penetration, and deepen the participation of the subjects, and form the connection of shared experiences. "The ideal artistic reception is not only an external 'knowing about the world', but also the echo and resonance inside. Here, the recipient and the artist become one in the sense of experience" [2].

The new and highly anticipated New York drama "TAMMANY HALL" is an immersive drama with few political themes and certain requirements for participants. The overall idea is a mayoral campaign story conceived based on the real historical events in 1929. Therefore, participants are required to have the corresponding background and historical knowledge reserves.The form of the play builds a multi-level layout structure, which brings people a strong sense of reality and relevance. The creative narrative that integrates the real and the virtual is palpable, fully activating the public's subject consciousness and participation, and the rich historical content and content. The setting of characters makes the public maintain a lasting desire for exploration and active interaction.

3.4 Interconnection of Everything Brings Self-discovery

Immersive art can open up a wider cognitive world to us, "as if we were led into a world outside the real world, which is nothing but a deeper reality of the world in which we live through our daily experience. We are taken out of ourselves to discover ourselves" [9]. It defines nature with the cultural connotation and spiritual orientation of art, and expands the whole world that people can perceive. With the development of science and technology, art has the nature of interconnection of everything, which further shows us a virtual nature that is opposite to the real world and derived from human civilization.

For the memories of the past, the expectations of the future and the observation of reality, immersive art brings the diversity of the interconnection of all things directly to the public with a unique way of full perception. This diversity is a kind of future of mankind. It is guaranteed that we can see, hear, touch, smell, coexist with the body, and mobilize the body to feel and respond to it. Immersive art not only satisfies the functions of some physiological experiences, but also these rich and diverse sensory experiences make us return to reality after a brief separation from true life. The soul and thoughts of the people, build the inner communication and dialogue with the self, and finally become the symbol of the spirit, which promotes the reshaping of the common humanistic spirit and value. The silence of art is indeed far better than a thousand words of statement.

4   Sustainability of Immersive Art

4.1   Symbiosis of Art and Technology

Herbert Marcuse mentioned in his book "One-dimensional Man", "Technological civilization has created a special relationship between art and technology…The rationality of art, the energy it projects on real life, the ability to define the possibility that has not yet been realized can be squared up from now on. It has played and is playing an active and effective role in the world scientific and technological revolution, and is no longer the handmaiden of the existing industrial machinery, no longer used to beautify business transactions and comfort its unfortunate maid" [10]. In the digital age, with the continuous progress of technology, art presents a more forward-looking exploration appearance. And technology is also catalyzed by art.It is no longer rational and cold, but more romantic and interesting. From public spaces, commercial spaces and leisure spaces in urban and rural areas, to cultural venues such as museums, art galleries and libraries, to outdoor fields, forests and vast land, immersive art appears more and more frequently in public daily life, and gradually becomes an important part of future lifestyle. The proposition of "combining art and technology" has maintained lasting and vigorous vitality, shouldering our infinite reverie about the future.

But what needs to be kept vigilant is that immersive art must not blindly emphasize the dazzling application of high-tech, and simply turn art into a tool for mass entertainment consumption and pure sensory stimulation in the landscape society, to turn the public into a "one-dimensional person" in Marcuse's article. It cannot lose the inherent leadership, criticality and transcendence of art, and lose the core value of art. Immersive art should maintain sensitivity to the surrounding environment with an open creative system, export internal cultural concepts and humanistic spirit, and pay attention to the aesthetic infiltration of the public. If we say that we are already in a landscape society, the boundary between reality and image disappears completely, and reality and virtuality are confused as one, then the immersive art still needs to be separated from the "real" illusion created by itself, to reflect on reality and keep thinking, so as to build a new meaning of development. Immersive art based on technology, while embracing technology, maintains criticism of technology, restores the original spiritual connotation and cultural value of art, and restores it to the reshaping of "people".

4.2 Balance Between Art and Entertainment

Philosopher Cassirer said, "No one can deny that artworks give us the highest pleasure, perhaps the most lasting and intense pleasure that human nature can have" [7]. In order to meet the current personalized consumption needs, immersive art is widely used in entertainment consumption scenes in the consumption era, enabling consumers to get more scene-based experiences, providing social themes for interactive communication, and constantly creating a dream-making space for consumption upgrades and experience upgrades for the public. The new lifestyle experience space has gradually become a key advantage in market competition. However, there are often problems such as weakened orientation, lack of culture and poor aesthetics. Art disguised as a packaging coat for entertainment consumption has become superficial and utilitarian. How to balance the curiosity of commercial entertainment and the introspection of artistic depth, how to prevent immersive art becoming a purely hedonic consumption experience, and how to avoid "immersion" stay on the surface, are issues that we need to think about further.

To avoid the trap of superficial art and pure sensory enjoyment, it is particularly important to construct the creative content and cultural connotation of immersive art. The experience needs to form new memory and meaning. The "immersive" commercial space created by SKP-S (Beijing) provides us with a perfect example by using art and technology to interact with people. The theme idea of "Digital-Analog-Future" tells a complete story about "immigration to Mars" one hundred years later. The whole space has completed a whole set of creative narrations from theme planning, scene construction and installation design, creating a sense of time and space and a sense of cutting-edge technology. Feeling the space, all the senses are greatly satisfied, and the daily behavior of individual shopping has become an immersive exploration experience shared by people. At the same time, behind the immersive art works it displays, there are many reflections on reality, such as the replica sheep and mechanical sheep in the future farm, the sculpture works precisely made by the robot arms and so on. "SKP-S Art Experiment Space" is the starting point of its whole spatial layout, and it also carries the reflective appeal to explore the original nature. For example, deep thinking about environmental protection, ecology and sustainable development. And how to find a new balance between natural reality and precise fiction when the technology tries to connect the emotion in the physical world.

4.3 Co-construction of Art, Social Culture and Industrial Economy

Art sociologist Hauser Arnold once put forward the famous "interaction theory" between art and society. He believed that art and society are interactive, and this interaction is a complex and dynamic process that affects and refers to each other. In this dynamic interaction, the meaning of art is generated. Immersive art has attracted much attention because of its imaginative and rendering effect and immersive experience of all senses. It is a civilized product and an important part of the progress of humanistic society. The development of social culture is unified and mutually reinforcing, and it has become the latest medium for social culture to spread and display, reflecting, participating in and promoting the change and development of social culture. All the material and spiritual achievements of society have also become the source of inspiration, creative resources and in-depth content of immersive art. Originally, art is the reproduction of social and cultural sublimation. The richer the cultural relationship and realistic relationship it can reflect, the richer the spiritual content of the emotional experience it presents. Hegel pointed out in the first volume of "Aesthetics" that the sense of "special aesthetic emotion" is not an innate blind instinct, which alone can't distinguish beauty. Therefore, it needs the infiltration and nourishment of "cultural accomplishment" and "complete rationality and solid and lively mind" [11]. The integration and interaction of artistic trends and cultural genes make immersive art contain unique connotation and build deep value significance.

In addition, from the perspective of industrial economy, the immersion industry is still in the field of innovation, and the industrialization of immersion art has a large room for growth and development potential. First of all, the industrial chain of immersive art needs to be systematically constructed, which is not limited to a single work itself, but should be constructed with a branded image, connected with upstream and downstream service facilities, and based on the integration with the city and life. Secondly, the art industry space featuring immersive art experience needs to strengthen its agglomeration and generate a synergy effect. Combine the city's geographical advantages, economic advantages, and resource advantages to maintain the sustainability of the industrial ecology and stimulate its potential in a three-dimensional and all-round way. At the same time, it is necessary to expand the industrial model of innovative immersive art, focus on derivative development, and effectively implant the concept of immersive art into the context of other fields to achieve cross-border upgrading and industrial win-win. For the sustainable development of immersive art, it is necessary to grasp its intrinsic value generation, create an immersive artistic life style, and realize the effective cultivation and output of immersive artistic concepts. Finally, the industrial ecosystem will present a trend of compound development, high-level development and mutual promotion.

References

1. Csikszentmihalyi, M.F.: Play and intrinsic rewards. J. Humanist. Psychol. **15**(3), 41–63 (1975)
2. Ding Ning, T.: Image Silence-Interpreting the Meaning of Art, 1st edn. Encyclopedia of China Publishing House, Beijing (2019)

3. Robert Scoble, F., Shel Israel, S.T.: Age of Context: Mobile, Sensors, Data and the Future of Privacy, Trans. Qianqun Zhao, Baoyao Zhou, 1st edn. Beijing United Publishing Co., Ltd., Beijing (2014)
4. Zehou Li, F., Jigang Liu, S.T.: History of Chinese Aesthetics, 1st edn. Anhui Literature and Art Publishing House, Hefei (1999)
5. Fan Wu, F.: Focusing on immersive experience and building industrial chain value: a study on the development strategy and countermeasures of China's immersive industry. J. Nanjing Univ. Arts (Art Des.) (4), 88–93 (2021)
6. Qin Li, T.: Being Media: The Theory and Practice of Immersive Communication, 1st edn. China Renmin University Press, Beijing (2019)
7. Ernst Cassirer, T.: An Essay on Man: An Introduction to a Philosophy of Human Culture, Trans. Yang Gan, 1st edn. Shanghai Translation Publishing House, Shanghai (2013)
8. B. Joseph Pine II, F., James, H., Gilmore, S.T.: The Experience Economy, Trans. Chongyi Bi, China Machine Press, Beijing (2016)
9. John Dewey, T.: Art as Experience, Trans. Jianping Gao, 1st edn. The Commercial Press, Beijing (2010)
10. Herbert Marcuse, T.: One-Dimensional Man, Trans. Ji Liu, 11th edn. Shanghai Translation Publishing House, Shanghai (2014)
11. Hegel, G.W.F., T.: Aesthetics, Trans. Guangqian Zhu, 2nd edn. The Commercial Press, Beijing (1997)

Envisioning the Future Trends of Smart Assistive Devices to Support Activities of Daily Living for Older Adults with Disabilities

Di Zhu, Ruonan Huang, Zhejun Zhang, Fan Yang, Ruikang Wang, Bojuan Ren, and Wei Liu[✉]

Beijing Normal University, Beijing 100875, People's Republic of China
{di.zhu,wei.liu}@bnu.edu.cn, {ruonan.huang,zhejun.zhang,
202128061059,202128061050,202128061041}@mail.bnu.edu.cn

Abstract. The elderly care industry will face significant pressure, especially the disabled older adults will be the crucial object of service and support. Older adults with a disability who have lost the ability to live independently due to congenital or disease will prioritize living at home. Subsequently, many manufacturers and institutions have developed a kind of home-based assistive device for older adults with disabilities, such as portable toilets, turn-over nursing devices, and so on. Most products aim to support activities of daily living (ADL). The others concentrate on caring support. However, such products do not consider the user experience of the elderly themselves and caregivers and even harm the elderly's self-efficacy and emotion. Therefore, based on interviews and product analysis, this study proposes four core needs of older adults with disability, including self-care ability enhancement, information transmission, reception, daily activities support, and comfort improvement. The study guides designers and developers who design smart assistive devices in the future.

Keywords: User eXperience · Smart assistive devices · Older adults with disability · Qualitive study · Trends analysis

1 Introduction

Older adults with disabilities refer to the elderly who have lost the ability to take care of themselves. The cause of disability may be old age, disease complications, or disability [1]. Older adults with disabilities are a prominent vulnerable group in society. Their physical and mental functions are damaged, resulting in the inability to take care of themselves in daily life and the need for accompanying long-term care. Moreover, because of the high cost of the care centers and hospitals, family care is still the primary way of care. Most older adults with disability rely on family caregivers, which brings tremendous pressure to the family children [2]. To support older adults with disability, they are encouraged to take rehabilitations or purchase assistive devices, such as wheelchairs cane. However, at this stage, old age with many diseases is a significant characteristic of older adults with disabilities, and they are in the cross-process of disease growth and

M. M. Soares et al. (Eds.): HCII 2022, LNCS 13323, pp. 454–466, 2022.
https://doi.org/10.1007/978-3-031-05906-3_34

weakening of self-care. Therefore, a single aspect of care has been challenging to meet their needs [3]. The assistive devices should satisfy more requirements instead of support activities of daily living. Further, assistive devices are more powerful than traditional devices combined with technologies.

Assistive devices have two types: ordinary products and intelligent products. Typical products are mainly special assistive devices, which can be fixedly installed in the family environment or used with existing assistive devices, such as navigable wheelchairs [4], or non-fixedly installed products, such as sit-to-stand systems [5]. Or clothing based on new materials [6]. In addition to general intelligent products, such as watches, bracelets, mobile phones, smart speakers, and smart TVs, there are few unique intelligent products, such as SmartCane [7]. Available wearable devices mainly focus on some functions, such as anti-fall detection bracelets. However, the technology could support older adults with disability better. Home furnishing Internet plus technology has brought higher possibilities for smart homes with technology development. However, less research aimed to help older adults with disabilities as a particular population. We understand better how to design a better wheelchair than creating a smart assistive device. Therefore, this study aims to identify the requirements and envision the future of smart assistive devices for older adults with disabilities.

2   Related Work

"Disability" refers to the loss of self-life ability. According to the internationally accepted standards of activities of daily life (ADL), there are six indicators, including eating, dressing, getting in and out of bed, going to the toilet, walking indoors, and bathing. Among them, one or two "unable" elderly is "slightly older adults with disabilities," Three to four items of "can't do" are defined as "moderately older adults with disabilities." Five to six items of "can't do" are defined as "severely older adults with disabilities" [1]. This section reviews smart assistive devices for older adults with a disability on basic and instrumental activities of daily living.

2.1   Daily Diet Support

Dietary aids are essential tools to help older adults with disabilities compensate for their eating function, improve their current eating disorders, develop their potential and handle life skills [8]. Among the current domestic products suitable for aging, mobility aids, such as wheelchairs and walking aids, have the highest usage rate. There are a few types of diet support aids and single functions. They mainly include anti-spill teacups, anti-shake chopsticks, spoons, easy-to-grip handles, and tableware for rehabilitation training. At the same time, the acceptance of dietary aids among the elderly is relatively low. Studies have shown that more than half of older adults with disabilities need help in eating, but the unsatisfied rate exceeds 40%. According to the survey of some elderly care institutions in Shanghai, almost no dietary aids to support older adults with disabilities in eating [9].

There are two main reasons for the current status of dietary aids: one is the improper configuration of the aids, which cannot meet the needs of the elderly. There are few scientific research talents in the Chinese assistive device industry dedicated to developing assistive devices. The lack of technical skills directly leads to the availability and ease of use of elderly assistive devices that do not meet the needs of the elderly. The impaired use of inappropriate tableware by older adults with disabilities fails to improve their dysfunction and affects the older adults with disabilities' sense of self-identity. The second is the cognition of the elderly on diet aids. Eating is one of the spontaneous human activities. With the increase of age, older adults with disabilities often show that the coordination of hands decreases, and eating-related disorders appear. However, many elderlies are unwilling to try diet aids because of their self-esteem and lack of correct cognition. Comfort improvement. Comfort is one of the crucial characteristics of intelligent assistive devices for the elderly. At present, there are some gaps of products as following aspects:

From the perspective of material analysis, the assistive devices of daily necessities for the elderly generally use softer and skin-friendly materials. Research studies the ease of cleaning the cloth for safety monitoring hardware products. Some smart assistive devices require regular charging. Plugin the charging material to improve the ease of use of the product. In addition, due to the decline in exercise performance of the elderly, they are prone to falling when they are indoors. Therefore, in selecting innovative assistive materials, non-slip, fall prevention, and product stability are crucial factors that need to be considered [10]. From the analysis of the impact on the family, most older adults with disabilities cannot realize self-care and need the care of their children. Therefore, most older adults with disabilities live with their children. Especially for the elderly in China, they psychologically hope to reduce the disturbance to their children as much as possible. Therefore, in terms of improving the product's comfort, reducing the impact on the family is very important for the elderly. The current intelligent assistive devices on the market mainly achieve the ease of installation of the product and the reduction of interference during operation. The elderly smart auxiliary products generally use voice control to facilitate the elderly to start and install independently. At the same time, it is necessary to reduce the interference of background noise to others.

2.2 Dress Support

In the context of today's aging society, the state advocates more attention to the elderly group, which is now receiving more and more attention from all walks of life, and more and more people are beginning to care and understand them [11]. The elderly group has more and more urgent needs for social security. The study found that the elderly group wants clothing to have good comfort and fabrics with warmth and structural design to cope with incontinence. Moreover, the dress should be easy to put on and take off, reducing zippers and buttons and other design aspects. In addition, they require a variety of clothing, with clothing that can be suitable for various occasions in daily life.

In most cases, beautiful, functional clothing or suitable textiles could improve the quality of life of older adults with disability. Older people generally have special needs for clothing or other fabrics, such as wheelchair users or bedridden people, where the warmth of clothing is essential because of their low heat production. Skin perspiration is also a problematic issue, and in many cases, the durability of materials in certain parts of the garment also needs to be considered. Scholars have also carried out designing garments for wheelchair users. In terms of structural design, ergonomic optimization makes it easy to put on and take off. The cloth meets the elderly sitting and to lie for a long time, and easy to put on and take off the performance of the clothing also facilitate toileting. The combination of different fiber fabrics gives the dress softness [12], warmth, breathability, and antibacterial properties to wear durable clothing. With the progress of technology in society, clothing design links to technology. Japanese researchers have invented high-tech clothing called robot suits. They can easily lift heavy objects and help the dressed elderly climb the stairs, playing a single clothing piece impossible to complete.

2.3 Toileting Support

Perhaps the easiest and cheapest way for older adults is to use non-technical methods, such as taking notes or having a close relative or caregiver assist. However, this is ineffective, especially for people with short-term memory loss [13]. Most of the current toilet assistance products for the elderly are redesigned toilets. There are four main categories of products on the market in this area of toilet booster devices for the elderly.

The first type of toilet booster is mainly through the motor to push the cylinder to lift the elderly from the toilet slowly. The advantage is that the engine provides power for sitting and getting up the elderly without self-power, stable operation. The disadvantage is the high price, the need for a wet external power supply in the bathroom, easy to cause damage, cannot stop in the middle, the fixed structure of the washer affects the regular use of the toilet, etc. The second type of toilet booster is mainly a bracket structure. The older adults need to force themselves after the toilet and rely on the support of the bracket to get up. Its form especially has a handrail and booster bracket. Its advantages are low price, simple structure, easy to move, and not prevent others from using the toilet typically; the disadvantage is that the elderly need to force themselves to finish sitting down and getting up. It does not play a protective role in the knees. The third category is a wearable device with non-invasive sensors connected to the body and monitored 24/7 using ultrasound technology. The data collected from the sensors will be analyzed to predict when a bathroom break is needed, and then notifications will be sent to a phone or tablet to let seniors know it's time to go to the bathroom. The fourth type of toilet booster product can be installed to mount on any toilet, whose sensors determine who the user is. The toilet is then scanned to determine the excrement's size, color, consistency, frequency, and shape. This information is provided to senior life managers to monitor the user's health status.

2.4 Indoor Sports Support

The elderly is more likely to have health problems than other age groups. Through effective monitoring and alarm system, the adverse effects of unpredictable events such as sudden diseases and falls can be improved to a certain extent [14]. Aging has produced a series of problems, such as falls, sarcopenia, osteoporosis, etc. The incidence of falls among the urban elderly in China is about 15%. In the current environment, the outdoor activities of the elderly have brought significant restrictions and inconvenience due to environmental pollution, epidemic, and other reasons. And under the influence of the current external air environment and epidemic situation, it brings some restrictions to the outdoor sports of the elderly. Especially for the older adults with disabilities, the reduction of their outdoor activities is more affected. Therefore, more and more attention is paid to indoor sports for older adults with disabilities. At present, most of the indoor sports products for older adults with disabilities prevent them from falling or assist them in taking objects and getting on and off the bed. And some studies have explored the application of virtual reality in indoor activities for the elderly. The virtual interactive environment can affect posture control and fall events by stimulating sensory cues to maintain balance and direction. At the same time, ensure the benefits of indoor exercise for the elderly [15]. Exercise plays an indispensable role in the mental and physical health of the elderly, especially the older adults with disabilities. They lose their motor function to a certain extent, and long-term static posture will make them feel irritable and helpless. Moreover, most of the current products to assist older adults with disabilities in the natural movement are to help move their position, which cannot make them move.

2.5 Nursing Support

Nursing support products can meet the various needs of the elderly. The corresponding product targets are not only the elderly but also their family members and caregivers. Because in most cases, the elderly obtains information about assistive devices accidentally, and they rarely actively seek relevant information about the equipment. Information often comes from formal or informal caregivers [16]. In the past, nursing equipment focused on the experience of the elderly, and the use of relevant caregivers in the process was equally important. There are also many types of care products for the disabled. Classified according to different functions, including portable electronic devices, such as vital tech smartwatches, while having fall detection, it is waterproof sweat-proof. It can even be charged directly on the wrist. Wearable devices, such as Neuro Rehab VR, use VR technology to provide a virtual reality experience for elderly patients undergoing physical therapy or suffering from neurodegenerative diseases after stroke, brain injury, or spinal cord injury. Remote caregiver equipment. Relatives and caregivers of the elderly can remotely monitor and care for the status of the elderly through the equipment. At the same time, the elderly can use the equipment to alarm for help remotely. The equipment is combined with fixed and portable equipment to facilitate the use and communication of various users. Today's nursing technology and equipment reject because of their complex use and high cost. Users believe that they have the problems of high learning cost and insufficient applicability [17], which should be paid attention to and considered in the design of nursing equipment in the future.

3 Material and Methods

Investigate the market and research for assistive devices suitable for older persons with impairments and caregivers [18], examine their benefits and drawbacks, and describe design issues and product characteristics. This paper covers existing product design methodologies for older persons with disabilities, including ageing design and inclusive design for older adults with disabilities [19], by consulting relevant literature. The older persons with disabilities and their caregivers were recruited based on the present product characteristics to undertake semi-structured interviews to better understand their product use process and user needs. The development direction and characteristics of intelligent aids are then refined and incorporated utilizing open code [20], in combination with the user needs collected during the user interview and the existing product characteristics.

4   Future Trends

This section summarizes the future trends of design future smart assistive devices trends for older adults with disabilities. Each trend has sub-trends and user requirements.

4.1   Overview of Future Trends

The disability state of the elderly is a gradual process. In the face of the elderly with different degrees of disability and different challenging situations in their life, it is necessary to design auxiliary devices with other functions. In general, in the design of assistive devices for older adults with disabilities, it is essential to have good use of comfort and give the elderly a good user experience. At the same time, it is necessary to monitor the daily life of the elderly and analyze the relevant data, analyze the obtained data and give a good solution, and pass the solution to the elderly and appropriate nursing staff effectively. It should notice that studies have shown that the use of auxiliary equipment also makes the elderly more dependent on caregivers, thus increasing the pressure on caregivers [21]. Therefore, it is necessary to improve the elderly's self-care ability while solving the problems to reduce the workload on relevant caregivers and family members. Following sections describe themes of smart assistive devices trends for older adults with disabilities (Table 1).

Table 1. Themes of smart assistive devices trends for older adults with disabilities.

Trends	Sub-trends	User requirement
Self-care ability enhancement	Body posture maintenance	Easy assistance with turning over
		One-piece to adjust the height of the lift chair
		Change body posture to inhibit muscle atrophy
		Assists in sitting up and down
		Adjusts the range of lifting pillars according to body size
		Self-performing sit-to-stand transfer
		Assisted transfer from wheelchair to other surfaces

(continued)

Table 1. (*continued*)

Trends	Sub-trends	User requirement
		It helps users get in and out of bed
	Save energy	Retractable gripper
		Voice Control
	Barrier-free facilities	Accessibility rating access
		Find an accessible location near you
		Accessibility ratings and reviews
		User Profile Location Favorites
		With rest angle for easy wheelchair use
		Lighting
Information delivery and reception	Emergency alarm	Emergency call
		Helping the elderly to seek help in time
	Information input and notification	Receive notifications on mobile devices at any time
		The device supports multiple input methods
		Radio
		Voice control
Daily testing activities and enhancements	Emergency alarm	Automatic fall alerts
		Manual audible and visual alarms
		Flashing light warning
	Scheduled reminders	Meal plan reminders
	Monitoring analysis	Non-invasive sensors monitor organs throughout the day
		Data analysis to predict organ needs
		Detects hand tremors
		Measure weight body load
		Daily activity detection
		Blood glucose monitoring
	Cognitive development	Color recognition exercises
		Active hands to keep busy
Comfortable to use to enhance	Material	Soft and skin-friendly material

(*continued*)

Table 1. (*continued*)

Trends	Sub-trends	User requirement
		Plug-and-charge attachment is easy to clean
		Anti-slip to prevent falls
		Stable
	Impact on family	Insensitive to voice capability or background noise, low interference
		Easy to install

4.2 Self-care Ability Enhancement

Traditionally, self-care has been defined as activities related to health promotion. It represents a set of behaviors that individuals engage in to promote or restore their health [22]. Improving the living condition of the elderly with disabilities, encouraging self-reliance and self-care ability, and improving their quality of life has become key concern of society. The products on the market for enhancing the self-care ability of the elderly with disabilities are promoted in terms of helping to maintain body posture, labor-saving, accessibility, and other aspects. The demand for maintaining body posture of the older adults with disabilities manifests itself in easy assistance in turning over, changing body posture to inhibit muscle atrophy, assisting in getting up and sitting, helping to get in and out of bed, etc. The function of maintaining body posture is to adjust the height of the lift chair, change the range of lift pillars according to the body size, execute sit-to-stand transfer independently, and assist in transferring from wheelchair to other surfaces with assistive devices. The demand for labor-saving for older adults with disabilities is mainly manifested in the ability to control by voice, etc. The labor-saving products are specialized from the function of the retractable gripper assistive device. The needs of the elderly with disabilities for accessibility are mainly expressed in accessibility rating access, finding accessible locations nearby, accessibility rating, and reviews. The accessibility facilities on the market are primarily realized from user profile location favorites, easy-to-use wheelchair, lighting, and other assistive features.

4.3 Information Transmission and Reception

Under the background of the post epidemic era, the epidemic has brought great inconvenience to the life of the elderly. The elderly usually like to go out and communicate face-to-face with others. The epidemic has dramatically reduced the opportunities for the elderly to go out and socialize, so their way of information transmission and acceptance is gradually turning indoor and online. However, the elderly will also encounter various problems indoors, such as slipping, sudden diseases, and the inability to use smart devices. Moreover, the older adults with disabilities group cannot independently use some equipment to meet their activity needs to a certain extent. Especially when they are in danger, their lives will be endangered if they do not get timely alarm treatment. Therefore, assistive devices could pay more attention to similar alarm functions such as emergency alarm, emergency call, and helping the elderly seek help to allow the elderly to seek help immediately in case of danger and get out of the dangerous situation. At present, there is a lot of research on wearable devices to prevent or detect falls of the elderly. Most of the study is to let subjects wear specific sensors to carry out fall alarm tests in a simulated environment, and the technology will become more and more mature. And the elderly believe that the use of remote monitoring gives them a greater sense of security [23].

Nowadays, the smart assistive devices for information transmission and reception for the elderly also pays attention to their equipment's information reception mode. Because the learning ability of the elderly is significantly reduced compared with that of the young. Some operation designs for ordinary users may be challenging to be accepted by the elderly. Therefore, there are some design characteristics of information operation for the elderly, such as the equipment supporting a variety of input modes, Voice control, and receiving notification at any time. For example, smart home speakers can control other home devices through voice interaction. Others include integrating some alarm functions and radio functions into one device (such as intelligent crutches), which can meet the operation needs of the elderly to quickly and easily complete information transmission and reception.

4.4 Daily Activities Support

Among the intelligent assistive devices currently on the market, there is a class of assistive devices that focus on monitoring the physiological indicators and daily activities of the elderly and will be based on alerts when abnormalities occur, which we categorize as daily activity detection assistive devices. Daily activity detection assistive devices can be broadly divided into three categories: emergency alerts, regular reminders, and monitoring and analysis [24–26]. Falls are one of the most critical factors affecting the health of the elderly, so many assistive devices come with automatic alarm functions for falls, which may be alerted by sound signals or by flashing lights. In addition, there are also assistive devices that can regularly remind the elderly to drink water toilets, and there are even reminders for the elderly to provide meal plans regularly. Finally, many assistive devices on the market analyze the health status of the elderly. Non-invasive sensors, for example, can monitor organs around the clock, and they can predict organ needs through data analysis. Some aids, such as electronic chopsticks, can monitor the hand tremors that distinguish the elderly. In addition, there are assistive devices that monitor the elderly's blood sugar and blood pressure indicators and assistive devices that measure the weight and body load of the elderly. All of these aids aim to help the elderly find a better way of life, as well as to detect abnormal indicators, eliminate dangers and protect their health.

4.5 Comfort Improvement

Comfort is one of the crucial characteristics of intelligent assistive devices for the elderly. At present, the comfort of products is mainly improved through the following aspects:

From the perspective of material analysis, the assistive devices of daily necessities for the elderly generally use softer and skin-friendly materials. For safety monitoring hardware products, the ease of cleaning the cloth is considered. Some smart assistive devices that require regular charging are generally used. Plugin the charging material to improve the ease of use of the product. In addition, due to the decline in exercise performance of the elderly, they are prone to falling when they are indoors. Therefore, in selecting innovative assistive materials, non-slip, fall prevention, and product stability are crucial factors that need to be considered.

From the analysis of the impact on the family, most older adults with disabilities cannot realize self-care and need the care of their children. Therefore, most of the older adults with disabilities live with their children. Especially for the elderly in China, they psychologically hope to reduce the disturbance to their children as much as possible. Therefore, in terms of improving the product's comfort, reducing the impact on the family is very important for the elderly. The current intelligent assistive devices on the market are mainly realized from the ease of installation of the product and the reduction of interference during operation. The elderly intelligent auxiliary products generally use voice control to facilitate the elderly to start and install independently. At the same time, it is necessary to reduce the interference of background noise to others.

5   Discussion

Technologies could support the daily living of older adults in many contexts. Currently, technology acceptance of older adults could be divided into aspects and be measured. Many attributes will affect the final acceptance, such as health anxiety, service quality, privacy security, operation difficulty [6]. However, we know how older adults with a disability will accept smart assistive devices and which factors affect them the most. Moreover, there is still a lack of relevant research based on the technology acceptance model. While interactive prototype could be tested by target users [27]. Therefore, we will design functioning prototypes that older adults with a disability could use in future studies. It will provide further evidence about these requirements and collect more detailed feedback. The results will show the key factors that affect the acceptance of smart assistive devices, which could guide future product design. Moreover, older adults may have various disabilities and different severity, such as dementia, stroke, in low vision, and aphasia. Older adults with severe dementia may have trouble using smart devices [28], monitoring and safety consideration will priority. Therefore, one product could not serve all older adults with disability at the same time. We should fully understand the required structure of older adults with a different type of disabilities and realize the matching of supply and required structure of intelligent care. There are many possibilities combined with assistive devices and technologies, especially for special groups. For instance, an assistive technology enables older adults with aphasia to convey daily experiences through the use of digital images [29], a running guide used vibrotactile feedback to assist visually impaired people in marathon [30], an interactive lamp to support emotion regulation for pregnant women [31]. Hence, these innovations could inspire more useful assistive devices for older adults with disabilities.

6 Conclusion

Traditional assistive devices have many limitations, with the help of the technology, older adults with disability will improve their self-management, such as transport, self-monitoring. This study identifies requirements of smart assistive devices form literature review, product analysis and interviews. There are four core trends of older adults with disabilities. The future smart assistive devices should consider features to enhance self-care ability, transfer, and receive critical information, especially health-related information. Furthermore, the devices should support daily activities and feel the product's comfortable. The results show older adults with disabilities have more concern about self-management support, safety issues, and comfort. We should satisfy these requirements firstly. In addition, the government should put more effort into developing smart assistive devices and services at the same time because the devices assist the caring service.

Acknowledgment. We would like to thank our participants and China Institute of Education and Social Development 2021 Grant, Beijing Normal University (ID: Wa2021025).

References

1. Feng, Q., Zhen, Z., Gu, D., Wu, B., Duncan, P.W., Purser, J.L.: Trends in ADL and IADL disability in community-dwelling older adults in Shanghai, China, 1998–2008. J. Gerontol. B Psychol. Sci. Soc. Sci. **68**(3), 476–485 (2013)
2. Andrea, J., Darzi, A.: Officer, Ola.Stakeholders' perceptions of rehabilitation services for individuals living with disability: a survey study. Health Qual. Life Outcomes **14**(1) (2016)
3. Brandt, Å., Jensen, M.P., Søberg, M.S., Andersen, S.D., Sund, T.: Information and communication technology-based assistive technology to compensate for impaired cognition in everyday life: a systematic review. Disabil. Rehabil. Assist. Technol. **15**(7), 810–824 (2020)
4. Dalsaniya, A.K., Gawali, D.H.: Smart phone based wheelchair navigation and home automation for disabled. In: 2016 10th International Conference on Intelligent Systems and Control (ISCO). IEEE (2016)
5. Kim, I., Cho, W., Yuk, G., Yang, H., Jo, B. R., Min, B.H.: Kinematic analysis of sit-to-stand assistive device for the elderly and disabled. In: 2011 IEEE International Conference on Rehabilitation Robotics. IEEE (2011)
6. Shore, L., et al.: Exoscore: a design tool to evaluate factors associated with technology acceptance of soft lower limb exosuits by older adults. Hum. Factors **62**(3), 391–410 (2020)
7. Wu, W.H., et al.: The SmartCane system: an assistive device for geriatrics. In: BodyNets. Citeseer (2008)
8. Grønning, K., et al.: Psychological distress in elderly people is associated with diet, wellbeing, health status, social support and physical functioning-a HUNT3 study. BMC Geriatr. **18**(1), 1–8 (2018)
9. Feng, Z., et al.: Risk factors and protective factors associated with incident or increase of frailty among community-dwelling older adults: a systematic review of longitudinal studies. PLoS ONE **12**(6), e0178383 (2017)
10. Lee, L.N., Kim, M.J.: A critical review of smart residential environments for older adults with a focus on pleasurable experience. Front. Psychol. 3080 (2020)

11. Bangor, A., Kortum, P., Miller, J.: Determining what individual SUS scores mean: adding an adjective rating scale. J. Usability Stud. **4**(3), 114–123 (2009)
12. Finstad, K.: The usability metric for user experience. Interact. Comput. **22**(5), 323–327 (2010)
13. Mohammed, H.B.M., Ibrahim, D., Cavus, N.: Mobile device based smart medication reminder for older people with disabilities. Qual. Quant. **52**(2), 1329–1342 (2018). https://doi.org/10. 1007/s11135-018-0707-8
14. Wang, Z., Yang, Z., Dong, T.: A review of wearable technologies for elderly care that can accurately track indoor position, recognize physical activities and monitor vital signs in real time. Sensors **17**(2), 341 (2017)
15. de Bruin, E.D., Schoene, D., Pichierri, G., Smith, S.T.: Use of virtual reality technique for the training of motor control in the elderly. Z. Gerontol. Geriatr. **43**(4), 229–234 (2010)
16. Gramstad, A., Storli, S.L., Hamran, T.: "Do I need it? Do I really need it?" Elderly peoples experiences of unmet assistive technology device needs. Disabil. Rehabil. Assist. Technol. **8**(4), 287–293 (2013)
17. Makowka, J., Lau, T., Kachnowski, S.: Caregivers & technology: what they want and need: a guide for innovators—research from a nationally representative sample of America's 40 million family caregivers. Telehealth Med. Today (2017)
18. De Rouck, S., Jacobs, A., Leys, M.: A methodology for shifting the focus of e-health support design onto user needs: a case in the homecare field. Int. J. Med. Inform. **77**(9), 589–601 (2008)
19. Zhu, D., et al.: Social inclusion in an aging world: envisioning elderly-friendly digital interfaces. In: Ahram, T., Taiar, R. (eds.) IHIET 2021. LNNS, vol. 319, pp. 1082–1087. Springer, Cham (2022). https://doi.org/10.1007/978-3-030-85540-6_139
20. Irazoki, E., et al.: A qualitative study of the cognitive rehabilitation program GRADIOR for people with cognitive impairment: outcomes of the focus group methodology. J. Clin. Med. **10**(4) (2021)
21. Sriram, V., Jenkinson, C., Peters, M.: Informal carers' experience of assistive technology use in dementia care at home: a systematic review. BMC Geriatr. **19**(1), 1–25 (2019)
22. Nicholas, P.K.: Hardiness, self-care practices and perceived health status in older adults. J. Adv. Nurs. **18**(7), 1085–1094 (1993)
23. Chaudhuri, S., Thompson, H., Demiris, G.: Fall detection devices and their use with older adults: a systematic review. J. Geriatr. Phys. Therapy (2001) **37**(4), 178 (2014)
24. Bosley, J.J.: Creating a short usability metric for user experience (UMUX) scale. Interact. Comput. **25**(4), 317–319 (2013)
25. Wu, D.W., Wang, Y.Y., Li, J.: Design of functional daily wear for wheelchair users. In: Advanced Materials Research. Trans Tech Publ. (2011)
26. Meinander, H., Varheenmaa, M.: Clothing and textiles for disabled and elderly people. VTT TIEDOTTEITA (2002)
27. Zhu, Y., et al.: Wellbeing and healthcare: exploring ways of interactive prototyping with mental process. In: Markopoulos, E., Goonetilleke, R.S., Ho, A.G., Luximon, Y. (eds.) AHFE 2021. LNNS, vol. 276, pp. 123–127. Springer, Cham (2021). https://doi.org/10.1007/978-3-030-80094-9_15
28. Emery, V.O.: Alzheimer disease: are we intervening too late? Pro. J. Neural Transm. (Vienna) **118**(9), 1361–1378 (2011)
29. Mahmud, A.A., Limpens, Y., Martens, J.B.: Expressing through digital photographs: an assistive tool for persons with aphasia. Univ. Access Inf. Soc. **12**(3), 309–326 (2013)
30. Zhu, Y., Wang, C., Liu, W., Lv, Y.: Running guide: design of a marathon navigation system for visually impaired people. In: Proceedings of the Seventh International Symposium of Chinese. CHI 2019, pp. 7–15. Association for Computing Machinery, Xiamen (2019)

31. Zhu, D., Liu, W., Zhu, Y.: NuanNuan: an interactive lamp for pregnant women to regulate emotions. In: Shoji, H., et al. (eds.) KEER 2020. AISC, vol. 1256, pp. 274–283. Springer, Singapore (2020). https://doi.org/10.1007/978-981-15-7801-4_29

Simultaneously Monitoring System Design for Infants' Temperature: A Human-Centred Design (HCD) in Fashion Practice

Yushan Zou[1,2(✉)] ⓘ and Fanke Peng[2,3] ⓘ

[1] Southwest University, No. 2 Tiansheng Road, Beibei District, Chongqing City 400715, China
yushan.zou@canberra.edu.au
[2] University of Canberra, 11 Kirinari Street, Bruce, ACT 2617, Australia
[3] University of South Australia, 101 Currie Street, Adelaide, SA 5001, Australia

Abstract. Finding a convenient way to simultaneously monitor an infant's temperature is a major concern in the domain of childcare [26]. This study proposes a novel system for simultaneously monitoring the skin temperature of infants using a thermochromic textile in a modified garment design. Thermochromic materials use pigment activation to provide an easy to comprehend visual indication of an infant's temperature change. They can detect signs of infants' skin temperature change, making it possible to monitor a fever by simply watching garments and accessories change color. This paper presents a human-centered methodological approach towards thermochromic textile design for use with infants. It details the approaches taken to explore problems and find solutions, including in-depth semi-structured interviews, laboratory experiments and experimental prototyping. This interdisciplinary project seeks to achieve low-cost and convenient real-time monitoring of infants' skin surface temperature via a smart textile design. The feedback collected after the textile experiments and design prototyping demonstrated positive potential when applying thermochromic textiles to manage infant health.

Keywords: Thermochromic textile · Infants' skin temperature · Human-centered design · Design for health · Temperature monitor

1 Introduction

The word "infants" is usually understood to be children from birth to 1 year old. Monitoring a fever can be an important aspect of managing the health of an infant. Temperatures can change rapidly throughout the day and night, so it is highly recommended to regularly check infants' temperature to determine whether they are too hot or too cold, especially when they are suffering from a fever [18]. Although caregivers try their best to take good care of their infants, when they have a fever or catch a cold, it is not always possible to be aware of their body temperature all the time. Moreover, infants can have a fever but not realize it. It is suggested that caregivers should continue to monitor themselves to ensure they feel comfortable and remain pain-free until the fever has resolved [23].

© The Author(s), under exclusive license to Springer Nature Switzerland AG 2022
M. M. Soares et al. (Eds.): HCII 2022, LNCS 13323, pp. 467–481, 2022.
https://doi.org/10.1007/978-3-031-05906-3_35

The thermal sensation and thermoregulatory responses of infants and toddlers differ from those of adults. According to Garcia-Souto and Dabnichki [6], the human body temperature in the first three years is typically lower than in other periods, especially in the regions of the forehead, upper arm, upper chest, hands, abdomen and shins (as demonstrated in Fig. 1). Infants' thermal comfort and skin temperature are also distinct from those of adults. Thus, if parents choose to monitor their child by assessing their 'warmth' or 'coldness' by sensation, health problems can remain undetected. Parents typically cater to their children based on their own experience; however, caregivers need to ensure that the external environment and clothing are safe and comfortable for their infant throughout the day and night.

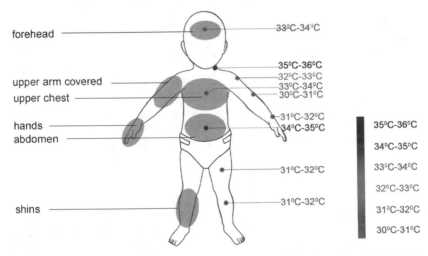

Fig. 1. The key areas where infants' skin temperature differs from that of adults [7]

Furthermore, infants' thermoregulatory system is relatively weak compared to that of adults. These thermoregulatory functions may vary at different ages [21]. Neonates' thermosensitivity is active, but both heat production and heat loss effector mechanisms are swiftly exhausted. Febrile or hypothermic responses to infection may develop and result in confusion ages [21]. In terms of the above considerations, it is essential to ensure that infants are neither too hot nor too cold.

1.1 Thermochromic Material

Thermochromic textiles are materials that reveal a change in color with changes in temperature [19]. Thermochromism is defined as a reversible change in the color of a compound in response to temperature. This thermochromic colour change is easily noted, often dramatic and occurs over a small temperature interval [4]. The range of non-textile applications already incorporating thermochromic materials are diverse and include thermometers and temperature indicators. Due to some limitations, the thermochromic materials used in the textile sector are not properly exploited and experience a responsiveness lag [4]. Thermochromic materials occupy a unique place in research, as they are exciting materials, not yet fully explored in the context of textiles, as there are problems associated with its application on textile substrates [4]. Research shows that developing thermochromic intelligent textiles has much practical significance [11]. The reversible thermochromic fibres are sensitive to temperature change and return to their initial state in a short time frame [27]. The physical proximity and surface area of textiles provide what is required to sense human's physiological signals, body positions, and activities. Social ubiquity is bringing these measurement techniques out of the hospital, clinic, or laboratory to extend their benefits [5]. Microcapsules contain leuco dyes, capable of changing their chemical structure to alter the dye molecule's absorbance, providing a visual tool to indicate skin temperature [17].

In preventative care, thermochromic materials/textiles are an area with immense benefits to the cost of health care and to the well-being of patients; the wearer's comfort is paramount and must be preserved in the design of any monitoring technology [5]. Thermochromic materials have excellent potential for remarkable visual expression on pattern, colour and appearance. Benefiting from the utilisation of thermochromic materials, textile fabrics were endowed with thermochromic properties [28]. In terms of their potential in new creative designs, thermochromic materials are generating intense interest among the artists and designers, due to their interactions, responsiveness, and ultimate functionality [4]. Research into the application of the fabrication of thermochromic fibre/yarn on textiles has gathered pace significantly, increasing the opportunity to unlock commercially significant nascent high-tech applications for the simultaneous and continuous monitoring of skin temperature.

1.2 "Watch the Temperature" Project

The research project "Watch the temperature" aims to address how best to monitor infants' temperature utilising a textile from a fashion design perspective. This research presents a collection of fashion and product designs for a thermochromic pigment specifically targeting infant temperature monitoring. Temperature and heat alert garments and accessories were designed to simultaneously monitor real-time temperature. The "Watch the temperature" project provides easy options, to allow the carers of infants to monitor their temperature through garments and accessories, without using an additional tool, such as a thermometer.

Miettinen [13] emphasised the importance of interactions between human beings and products during the design process. He also mentioned that such interaction helps refine the outcomes reported by stakeholders [13]. The stakeholders engaged in a human centred design process can be anyone who might interact with products, and who may contribute ideas to the design process. The stakeholders involved in this project include infants, their parents, grandparents, care givers and nurses. Notably, the designers need to gather data not only related to the project, but also to further refine their design output [22].

Based on these considerations, the research design phase of this project contains five steps, beginning with the experimental research. This step aims to explore and develop understanding of the chemistry of thermo change. It is then followed by interviews and analysis relating to the current state. By conducting in-depth interviews to understand the requirements of infant's temperature monitoring, the third step is to develop design performance outcomes called design prototypes. The fourth step is feedback and testing, which focuses on examining thermochromic design solutions. The final step involves rethinking the designs and evaluating the entire process.

2   Methods and Methodology

To explore the specific preconceptions or anxieties about materials that arise in specific settings, we need an interdisciplinary approach that includes scientific studies and ethnographic methods [24]. There are various design methods available for designers to consider when developing a conceptual product [13], including the user-centred design approach, qualitative and quantitative research methods, data analysis, illustration and model-making. The research methodology combines a practice-based, and human-centred participatory design. Empathy is the first step in the design process. Designers must not only be committed to research and theoretical thinking, but also to acknowledging that the field of design as crucial to our understanding of contemporary materials and experiences of visual worlds [22].

Designers are increasingly becoming engaged in influencing the development of materials in the laboratory [24]. This experiment was defined as a series of tests designed to input the variables of the process so that researchers can observe the responses outputted [15]. This research tested thermochromic materials using different designs and applications of pigment-based thermochromic materials to attain first-hand sources. Colour change behaviour, the character of reversible thermochromic materials and the character of reversible thermal yarn response were tested in the research. Through laboratory experiments, the core research team gained a clearer understanding of the materials to encourage them to explore materials in different forms.

Human-Centred Design (HCD) describes the creative exploration of human needs, knowledge and experience, which aims to extend human capabilities and improve quality of life [7]. The HCD approach involves developing solutions to problems, advocating a more intuitive, easier to learn environment, freer of performance errors [16]. HCD involves techniques which include communicating, interacting with, empathising with and stimulating the people involved, to obtain an understanding of their needs, desires and experiences, to an extent that often transcends that which the people themselves previously knew and realised [14]. HCD, which involves the end user throughout the product development and testing phase, is crucial in ensuring that designs meet the needs and capabilities of users, particularly in terms of safety and user experience [7]. It has been broadly acknowledged that HCD is required so as to develop feasible textile solutions that address complex healthcare problems. In this research, infant babies, parents and caregivers are the key stakeholders interacted with. Due to the difficulties communicating with infants, this research mainly conducted interview with parents, grandparents, caregivers and nurses. Moreover, the evaluation phase highlights the fact that approaches to participatory research are changing the landscape of design practice, creating new domains of collective creativity. It is anticipated that this evaluation will support a future shift towards more sustainable ways of living.

2.1 Semi-structured Interviews

In the early stages of this research project, the core design team aimed to explore and understand parents' and carers' experiences, needs and concerns about monitoring infants' temperature through semi-structured interviews. The difference between an ordinary conversation and interview is that the aim of an interview is to gain further information relating to the specific ongoing study [3]. The researcher chose the semi-structured interview method because it can be used to narrow down certain aspects that are closely related to the research questions. By conducting semi-structured interviews, it is possible to discover previously unknown issues, and address complex questions using probes and clarification, ensuring that particular points are covered by each participant. It also allows participants and interviewers to raise additional concerns and questions, while providing a redirection mechanism for conversations that digress too far from the main topic [25]. Rigorous development of a qualitative semi-structured interview guide maximises the objectivity and trustworthiness of studies and makes the results more credible [7]. They also provide a degree of flexibility to interviewers, while still enabling broad comparisons to be made across interviews [25].

Online interviews are convenient to both parties involved and make it possible to interview informants that would otherwise be difficult to contact [12]. For this research, 20 interviews were conducted either face-to-face or virtually via the social media (WeChat). The participants were infant sitters, nurses, parents, and grandparents of infants to ensure access to primary carers. The majority of the interviewees were Chinese. Purposive sampling was employed to select infants' parents (n = 12), grandparents (n = 4), clinical nurse (n = 2), and caregivers (n = 2) (see Table 1), due to their key role in infants' daily care. Qualified nurses were interviewed to acquire a clear perspective on professional care and knowledge.

Table 1. The different types of interview participants.

Participant type	Participant code	Total: 20
Infants' parents	P1, 2, 3, 4, 5, 6, 7, 8, 9, 10, 11, 12	12
Infants' grandparents	GP 1, 2, 3, 4	4
Infants' caregivers	C 1, 2	2
Nurses	N 1, 2,	2

Questions consisted of a combination of Yes/No queries and open-ended questions. The questions included:

- Do you think monitoring infants' temperature is important?
- Are you satisfied with the current temperature monitoring products for infants?
- What are the most important considerations when buying a temperature monitor for infants, and why?
- When do you use temperature real-time monitors for your babies/infants?
- What is your attitude towards using smart textile/thermochromic textiles for infants?

By analysing the transcripts of the interviews, several insights can be derived. Following this approach, designers can immerse themselves in the target group and identify challenges from stakeholders' perspectives [9].

2.2 Laboratory Experiments

By testing the chemistry and mechanism involved, the application of textiles and evaluation procedure for performance, the core design team can attain a better understanding of materials and tailor them to meet the requirements of this project. The materials (as shown in Table 2) presented in the experiments include: boric acid, bisphenol A, and tetradecyl alcohol, combined with bromocresol green ($C21H14Br4O5S$), bromocresol purple ($C21H16Br2O5S$) and bromocresol blue ($C19H10Br4O5S$), respectively. These materials can be used for testing thermochromic pigment characterisation during the discovery stage. The thermochromic materials available to the current market measure a wide range of temperature between 10 °C and 65 °C, while the default temperature options for the textile market are 22 °C, 31 °C and 45 °C. Considering the skin temperature of infants mostly ranges from 30–35 °C [6], the activation temperature of the thermochromic yarn used in the heat sensitive test and prototypes for this research is approximately 31 °C. The fabric used in the test is a white knitted fabric. The reason for selecting this cloth is because the color change effect from a white background is most obvious, and the surface of the stitching in the stretch fabric is flat. The polypropylene fiber is dyed in thermochromic powder after microcapsule processing. These microcapsules contain leuco dyes, which change chemical structures to allow dye molecule absorbance. The researcher designed several tests, for example, temperature sensitivity testing, color change rate-testing and real-time temperature testing using a point-thermometer. To assist in the easy and visual determination of physical exhaustion, thermochromic pigments were applied to spandex fabric using the pigment activation temperature as an indication for exhaustion. Both materials were chosen to activate at a pre-determined physiological skin temperature range of between 23 °C and 32 °C.

2.3 Experimental Prototyping

The prototyping journey is a useful resource during the innovation process, and can convert intangible, abstract and yet to be imagined concepts into concrete and meaningful solutions and outcomes [8]. Experimental prototyping in this project involved three types of thermochromic sampling: printing, stitching, and knitting. The prototypes can then be used to explore, evaluate, and communicate design ideas and concepts. The materials for prototyping (as seen in Table 2) include thermochromic yarn and heat sensitive thermochromic liquid red ink. The raw materials are polypropylene fiber.

3 Results and Discussion

3.1 The Semi-structured Interview

To investigate the users' requirements for infants' skin temperature monitoring, five questions were designed to query the interviewee's attitudes towards temperature monitoring when caring for infants. 20 people including infants' relatives, carers and nurses

Table 2. Principal materials used in laboratory experiments and prototyping

Stages	Materials	Visualisation
Laboratory experiential	Boric acid, bisphenol A, tetradecyl alcohol, bromocresol green ($C_{21}H_{14}Br_4O_5S$), bromocresol purple ($C_{21}H_{16}Br_2O_5S$) and bromocresol blue ($C_{19}H_{10}Br_4O_5S$)	
Heat-sensitive test & Application process-stitching and knitting	Thermochromic yarn (150D/2, 100g) made with polypropylene PP yarn	
Application process-printing	Heat sensitive thermochromic liquid ink.	

were interviewed. Based on the 20 in-depth interviews with infants' relatives, caregivers and nurses, the current study set out to investigate the key characteristics of temperature indicators. Based on innate needs, the value framework provides guidance for the design of thermochromic products. The interviews revealed the following three key findings:

The Importance of Monitoring Infants' Temperature. There was some dispute over the importance of monitoring an infant's temperature. "I think monitoring temperature is not always important, when my son looks good, or shows active performance, I would not be concerned about his health" (P2). Another interviewee (P6) argued that "checking the temperature of infants is important, as abnormal temperature always relates to some disease, so I think daily checking infants' temperature is important, I check small babies' temperature from birth to 1 month on a daily basis. This helps me learn more about the condition of their health. If the temperature shows an unusual figure, we should pay more attention on their daily performance". N2 works in a confinement center, and said she suggests that parents regularly check and record their baby's temperature after leaving the confinement center. In addition, most of the interviewees mentioned that infants' parents and their grandparents often falsely think that an infants' temperature should be the same as an adult.

Monitoring During a Fever. Almost all of the interviewees agreed that monitoring temperature during a fever is essential. Caregivers are often mentally stressed and physically tired when they have to wake up to check an infants' temperature repeatedly during the night. If the infant's fever persists for several days and caretakers are also stressed by work during the day, they are often exhausted by anxiety. This situation needs to be improved [10]. P1 emphasised: "I think for our daily life, the need for real-time monitoring is not that important. When my daughter gets a fever, I would check her temperature from time to time… Maybe because our environment is getting worse, nowadays infants are more and more frequently getting colds or fevers, so I think monitoring an infant's temperature is very important. Besides, unlike adults, when infants get a fever, it is hard to see the effect of their illness on performance, they are energetic and still engage in daily activities. Therefore, monitoring temperature during a fever was considered to have high applicability."

Accuracy of Monitoring Products. The ratings from the interviews revealed highly significant agreement pertaining to the importance of accurate temperature monitoring products. The interview data revealed high agreement that most daily measurements of an infant's temperature are subjective; GP 3 who takes care of her grandson on a daily basis stated that if my grandson feels sick, I always check his temperature by touching his forehead." "Sometimes elderly people excessively protect their grandchildren" (P4). A father who has a 3-year-old child insist accuracy is the priority of purchasing a temperature monitoring product: "Accuracy, if I buy something that has some function, I hope it can be an accurate monitor of temperature. Or if it is of limited usefulness, I won't buy it", P 7 said.

3.2 Laboratory Experiments

Color Change Behavior Testing for Reversible Thermochromic Materials. The thermochromism experiments in this research are described below in Fig. 2. The raw materials are boric acid, tetradecyl alcohol with bromocresol green, ($C21H14Br4O5S$) bromocresol purple ($C21H16Br2O5S$), or bromocresol blue ($C19H10Br4O5S$) respectively. The fabrication rate in this experiment is 5:40:1. Three sets of materials were placed into three glass beakers and heated in the water tank. After heating, the compound turned into a light liquid. After cooling to the indoor temperature (17 °C), it became a dark solid. Of the three mixtures, the bromocresol green showed the most obvious response in terms of color change.

The thermochromic organic colourant mixtures cannot be used directly for coloration, as they do not have any affinity for textiles. Both require microencapsulation. Microcapsules have been defined as (spherical) particles, comprised of an excipient polymer matrix (or wall/coating), referred to as a shell and an incipient active component, known as a core material. The typical particle sizes of microcapsules are in the range 50 nm to approximately 2 mm [4].

Temperature Sensitivity Testing. The color reaction shows a significant change between 32 °C to an indoor temperature (approximately 22 °C). The fiber changes

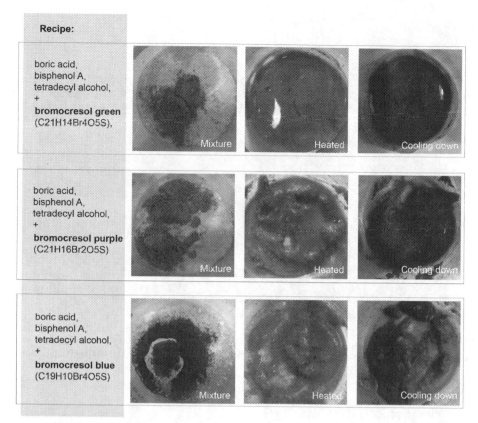

Fig. 2. Color change behavior testing of thermochromic material heated and after cooling (Color figure online)

from dark to white when the temperature changes from 22 °C, reaching approximately 32 °C. This phenomenon indicates the activation temperature for this specific type of thermochromic fiber around 31 °C. Once the external heat input is cut, the color of the fiber reverts to the dark color (as shown in Fig. 3) at room temperature (22 °C). While the color changed slightly from 22 °C to 25 °C, it can be easily seen that the temperature range for obvious color change is between 25 °C and 32 °C.

The reverse thermal response of thermochromic yarn was tested. Knowledge of the temperature sensitivity of thermochromic materials is key to structural design and advanced research. Temperature-sensitive testing demonstrates that the sample thermochromic yarn changed colour and had a quick thermal response in this experiment. Figure 3 (b) shows the colour change when temperature fell every six seconds in an indoor environment. Based on this experiment, it shows great potential for application as a real-time temperature monitor due to its quick response.

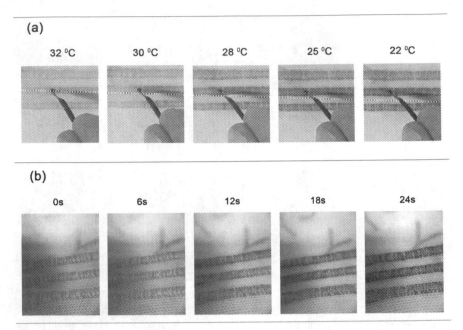

Fig. 3. (a). Real-time temperature testing by point-thermometer (b). Color-change experiment for heat-sensitive sample test (from left to right: temperature decreasing every six seconds) (Color figure online)

3.3 Prototyping

Prototyping enables design team members, users and clients to gain first-hand appreciation of existing or future conditions through engaging actively with prototypes. Research demonstrates that the value of such prototypes can be reflected in three critical design activities: understanding existing experiences, exploring design ideas and communicating design concepts for commercial design projects [2]. Since inter-disciplinary study relies heavily on approaches to co-creation, many people need to be able to take part, evaluate, and understand the design process. To ensure freedom of inclusion and in terms of approaches, designers need to evaluate the ramifications of the decisions they make on projects. The techniques they decide to use and approaches to the expertise and knowledge possessed by other stakeholders will affect the outcomes and satisfaction of services [1].

Below there are three experimental prototypes that reveal different design concepts and techniques: printing, stitching and knitting fabric. The proposed novel system (as seen in Table 3) includes three interconnected parts, using thermochromic materials in various forms and textures. From top to bottom, they are: 1. printing a fever pad with thermochromic ink; 2. stitching thermochromic thread onto a white fabric and 3. knitting fabric with thermochromic fiber. The three prototypes offer strong supporting evidence of my approach to highlighting problems and unpacking the qualities of thermochromic displays representing skin conductance. The existing rationale informing the designs is that dominant color will disappear when an infant's body temperature rises above their normal skin temperature or color will appear when it falls below the normal level. This color-change process is fully reversible.

Table 3. Novel solutions for thermochromic textiles

Solutions	Sketch and Prototype	Brief description
Printing		Left-pigment printing solution and application on a fever pad. Right-improved solutions after feedback.
Stitching		Stitched thermochromic fibre on the edge of hat. The application of stitching can be used on different areas of clothing.
Knitting		The application of knitted thermochromic fabric in garment pattern design and accessories design.

Novel Solution 1 – Printing: Thermochromic Materials Used on Fever Pad.

The first novel solution is a fever pad with thermochromic ink on it. Table 3 - printing shows the outlook and application of the design, and thermochromic ink as part of the pattern was designed and printed on the fever pad. Printing thermochromic pigments on the fever pad can raises an intelligent alarm, alerting carers to changes in body temperature. The pigment chosen for printing is non-toxic and thermochromic. The product might be expected to be useful for medical application and real-time monitoring. Color change in the pigment prototype was well recognizable and reversible. However, the overall appearance of the color on the fabric was dark to transparent. As infants' high temperature can last for days if they have a fever, with proper medication, all caretakers need to do is to monitor the infants' body temperatures and take remedial steps where possible. When using the thermochromic fever pad, caregivers can lie beside infants to take care of them more easily and see the temperature more clearly through the color change.

Novel Solution 2 – Stitching Thermochromic Fibers. Thermochromic fibers can be stitched into baby accessories, such as wristbands, hats and socks. A thermochromic stitching sample (Table 3 – stitching) can be used to demonstrate the feasibility of the color change and temperature display. The corresponding temperature is displayed in the stitching area. If the infant's body temperature is normal, the textile shows a specified color. If the infant's body temperature is above normal, the color disappears. Inclusion of thermochromic stitching in the band is flexible, and it can be used on the wrist, ankle, neck, etc. For example, it is suggested that almost every new-born baby should wear a hat to protect their fontanel from catching a chill [20]. As visualized in Table 3, stitching thermochromic fibers on the edge of the hat is one way to monitor forehead temperature. This novel concept can also be applied to the infant's wrist and neck. One of the advantages of this product design is that the function can be embedded into infants clothing to monitor their temperature.

Novel Solution 3 – Textile: Garment Pattern Design and Accessories Design.
Thermochromic pigments can be applied (knitted) to cotton or spandex fabric, to create a series of garments and accessories for infants and toddlers [28]. The third solution is intended to use knitted fabric made of cotton, wool or polyester (Table 3 – knitting fabric). Knitted textiles are designed for use on the cuff, waistband and turnup. The knitted textile also can be designed for use in accessories like socks. The color on the cloth is sensitive to temperature change, and it is suitable for application on infants' clothing, as temperature change is obvious in this case. The color of the thermochromic pigment-based interlock fabrics changed from color to non-color in the temperature range 23 °C to 33 °C.

The core design team attempted user testing after prototyping, mainly focusing on feedback related to different novel solutions. After designing novel solutions, the stakeholders were asked to select their favorite one from three design solutions and explain their choice (Fig. 4). Most of the stakeholders believed the printing solution to be the best of the three. "I like this solution because I think it offers a fantastic combination of fever pad and thermochromic material, and I doubt I will need to monitor temperature all the time" (P 5). "This design would help me a lot in the right scenario" (P 8). They also give some suggestions on this design: "The graphic patterns on the fever pad could be improved, it can be more interesting and fun, as this is for an infant" (P4, P8 & P12). The feedback for the stitching varied. Some of the interviewees like the design is because of the flexible application. The thermochromic stitching could be added anywhere, like hats, bracelets, or cloth. The embroidery pattern design can be flexible as well. They considered that this design could be applied widely but expressed concern about the textile resistance of the stitched products. N2 argued that placing stitching on the hat was not sensible, because if the infant overheats, it is suggested that any hat be removed to expose the skin to the air for heat dissipation. Therefore, this design would only be used during winter. Besides, they mentioned the third design solution is fun, and they would like to buy it for entertainment. When they interacted with the thermochromic socks prototype, they were surprised by the color change, and agreed that if there is a visual reference color, then caretakers could easily check for an unusual temperature with thermochromic textiles.

Overall, the interviewees who selected the thermochromic printing as their preferred choice opined that the design is of great value when monitoring temperature during a fever. The majority claim that they would buy if it were available in the market. However, there were also a few concerns and recommendations expressed regarding these products:

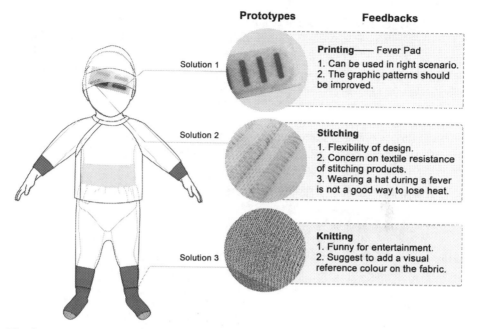

Fig. 4. A novel system for simultaneously monitoring the body skin temperature of infants using a thermochromic textile and garment design. A pilot study to test the system was conducted.

1. Concerns about using chemical products on infants' skin. Potuck [17] also indicated that the application of thermochromic materials has health risks, which is a limitation when employing innovative science and technology options.
2. The stakeholders were also concerned about the textile's resistance and the accuracy of the design. As N1 mentioned, she considers the most accurate way to check a temperature is by using a thermometer.

4 Conclusion

This article described an interdisciplinary research project "watch the temperature", which proposes a novel system for simultaneously monitoring the body skin temperature of infants using a thermochromic textile and garment design, including stitching, printing, and a garment pattern design. The core design team developed and tested the prototype designs (low-cost printed fever pad, visual-aid stitched textiles and knitted socks). The research project aims to establish a novel system for simultaneously monitoring the body skin temperature of infants using a thermochromic textile and garment design to avoid physical exhaustion due to heat in infants under various environmental conditions. The design, including both a cloth and reversible thermochromic pigment-based design, can continuously take the wearers' body temperature. As a relatively low-tech solution, this novel system could be applied relatively universally. When the infant's skin temperature is lower than the default value, it shows colour, indicating that the infant has no fever. If the infant's skin temperature goes over 37.5 °C, the colouration of the wristband disappears. This monitoring function can help reduce caregivers' stress over monitoring infant health. The theoretical contribution of this research is to human-centred design in the interdisciplinary textile and fashion research. Although the obstacles to realising the potential of "smart" clothing are complex and interrelated [5], this project investigated the interface affecting infant health, design, and chemical engineering, as it relates to newly emerging technologies and scientific platforms and their application in the domains of health and well-being. The potential impact would be to demonstrably contribute to advancing fashion design practices and infant wellbeing.

5   Limitations and Future Research

There is a great potential to turn this novel system into an Internet of Things (IoT) project. The data collected could then be sent to the parents and carers' smart phones. Further research would include testing the application of pigment to varying fibre types, to establish how specific items of infant apparel might respond to stress on the textile, at the surface of the textile, and in the seams. Future research is also required to improve the construction and longevity of the thermochromic garment, as well as its maintainability, durability, usability and functionality through abrasion resilience, colourfastness, and colour activation verification, using skin temperature modelling to meet the requirements of infants' skin-to-skin garments. Furthermore, based on the solutions and feedback, many details including colour choice and graphic/pattern design should be further explored. Thus, any future study would ideally focus on the development of these three aspects in detail.

Acknowledgments. This work was supported by the Fundamental Research Fund for Central Universities in China under Grant XDJK2015C083.

References

1. Blomkvist, J., Holmlid, S.: Service designers on including stakeholders in service prototyping. In: Proceedings of INCLUDE (2011)
2. Buchenau, M., Suri, J.F.: Experience prototyping. In: Proceedings of the 3rd Conference on Designing Interactive Systems: Processes, Practices, Methods, and Techniques, pp. 424–433 (2000)
3. Castillo-Montoya, M.: Preparing for interview research: the interview protocol refinement framework. Qual. Rep. **21**(5), 811–831 (2016)
4. Chowdhury, M.A., Joshi, M., Butola, B.S.: Photochromic and thermochromic colorants in textile applications. J. Eng. Fibers Fabr. **9**(1), 107–123 (2014)
5. Dunne, L.: Smart clothing in practice: key design barriers to commercialization. Fash. Pract. **2**(1), 41–65 (2010)
6. Garcia-Souto, M.D.P., Dabnichki, P.: Core and local skin temperature: 3–24 months old toddlers and comparison to adults. Build. Environ. **104**, 286–295 (2016)
7. Harte, R., et al.: A human-centered design methodology to enhance the usability, human factors, and user experience of connected health systems: a three-phase methodology. JMIR Hum. Factors **4**(1), e8 (2017)

8. Kocsis, A.: Prototyping: the journey and the ripple effect of knowledgeability. Fusion J. (18), 60 (2020)
9. Lam, Y.Y., Suen, B.Y.S.: Experiencing empathy in design education through community engagement. Int. J. Continuing Educ. Lifelong Learn. 7(2), 53–69 (2015)
10. Li, B., Fan, H.T., Zang, S.Q., Li, H.Y., Wang, L.Y.: Metal-containing crystalline luminescent thermochromic materials. Coord. Chem. Rev. 377, 307–329 (2018)
11. Ma, X., Zhao, S., Wang, L., Zhou, H.: Research on the behaviors of extending thermochromic colors for a new thermochromic microcapsule. J. Text. Inst. 111(8), 1097–1105 (2020)
12. Mann, S.: The Research Interviews. Reflective Practice and Reflexivity in Research Processes (2016)
13. Miettinen, S.: Who are These Service Designers in This is Service Design Thinking: Basics-Tools-Cases (Ed. by, Stickdorn, M., Schneider, J.), pp. 168–227. BIS Publishers, Amsterdam (2012)
14. Mohedas, I.: Characterizing the application of design ethnography techniques to improve novice human-centered design processes (2016)
15. Montgomery, D.C.: Design and Analysis of Experiments. Wiley, Hoboken (2017)
16. Oviatt, S.: Human-centered design meets cognitive load theory: designing interfaces that help people think. In: Proceedings of the 14th ACM International Conference on Multimedia, pp. 871–880 (2006)
17. Potuck, A., et al.: Development of thermochromic pigment-based sportswear for detection of physical exhaustion. Fash. Pract. 8(2), 279–295 (2016)
18. Ramakrishnan, S., Wang, X., Sanjayan, J., Wilson, J.: Thermal performance of buildings integrated with phase change materials to reduce heat stress risks during extreme heatwave events. Appl. Energy 194, 410–421 (2017)
19. Ramlow, H., Andrade, K.L., Immich, A.P.S.: Smart textiles: an overview of recent progress on chromic textiles. J. Text. Inst. 1–20 (2020)
20. Sacks, E., Moss, W.J., Winch, P.J., Thuma, P., van Dijk, J.H., Mullany, L.C.: Skin, thermal and umbilical cord care practices for neonates in southern, rural Zambia: a qualitative study. BMC Pregnancy Childbirth 15(1), 149 (2015)
21. Székely, M., Garai, J.: Thermoregulation and age. In: Handbook of Clinical Neurology, vol. 156, pp. 377–395. Elsevier, Amsterdam (2018)
22. Ventura, J., Bichard, J.A.: Design anthropology or anthropological design? Towards 'social design.' Int. J. Des. Creativity Innov. 5(3–4), 222–234 (2017)
23. Walsh, A., Edwards, H., Fraser, J.: Parents' childhood fever management: community survey and instrument development. J. Adv. Nurs. 63(4), 376–388 (2008)
24. Wilkes, S., Wongsriruksa, S., Howes, P., et al.: Design tools for interdisciplinary translation of material experiences. Mater. Des. 90, 1228–1237 (2016)
25. Wilson, C.: Interview Techniques for UX Practitioners: A User-Centered Design Method. Newnes, London (2013)
26. Zakaria, N.A., Saleh, F.N.B.M., Razak, M.A.A.: IoT (internet of things) based infant body temperature monitoring. In: 2nd International Conference on BioSignal Analysis, Processing and Systems (ICBAPS), pp. 148–153. IEEE, New York (2018)
27. Zhang, Y., Hu, Z., Xiang, H., Zhai, G., Zhu, M.: Fabrication of visual textile temperature indicators based on reversible thermochromic fibers. Dyes Pigm. 162, 705–711 (2019)
28. Zhang, Y., Li, Q., Li, Z.: Application of thermochromic materials in textile pattern design. J. Text. Res. 4 (2016)

Author Index